Exceptions in International Law

Exceptions in International Law

Edited by

LORAND BARTELS
FEDERICA PADDEU

OXFORD
UNIVERSITY PRESS

OXFORD
UNIVERSITY PRESS

Great Clarendon Street, Oxford, OX2 6DP,
United Kingdom

Oxford University Press is a department of the University of Oxford.
It furthers the University's objective of excellence in research, scholarship,
and education by publishing worldwide. Oxford is a registered trade mark of
Oxford University Press in the UK and in certain other countries

First Edition published in 2020
Impression: 1

Published in the United States of America by Oxford University Press
198 Madison Avenue, New York, NY 10016, United States of America

British Library Cataloguing in Publication Data
Data available

Library of Congress Control Number: 2019951118

ISBN 978–0–19–878932–1

Printed and bound by
CPI Group (UK) Ltd, Croydon, CR0 4YY

Table of Contents

List of Contributors

Kai Ambos. Chair of Criminal Law, Criminal Procedure, Comparative Law and International Criminal Law at the Georg-August-University Göttingen.

Gustavo Arosemena. Teacher of International and European Law, Faculty of Law, Maastricht University.

Lorand Bartels. Reader in International Law and Fellow of Trinity Hall, University of Cambridge.

Luís Duarte d'Almeida. Professor of Jurisprudence, Edinburgh Law School, University of Edinburgh.

Andrea Dolcetti. Junior Research Fellow, Trinity College, University of Oxford.

Malgosia Fitzmaurice. Chair of Public International Law, Department of Law, Queen Mary University of London.

Jaap Hage. Professor of Foundations and Methods of Law, Faculty of Law, Maastricht University.

James Harrison. Professor of Environmental Law, Edinburgh Law School, University of Edinburgh.

Caroline Henckels. Senior Lecturer, Faculty of Law, Monash University.

André de Hoogh. Associate Professor in International Law, University of Groningen.

Valentin Jeutner. Postdoctoral Fellow, Department of Law, Lund University.

Robert Kolb. Professor of Public International Law, Faculty of Law, University of Geneva.

Ulf Linderfalk. Professor at the Department of Law, Lund University.

Eleni Methymaki. DPhil Candidate, Faculty of Law, University of Oxford.

Federica Paddeu. John Tiley Fellow in Law, Queens' College, University of Cambridge.

Joost Pauwelyn. Professor of International Law, Graduate Institute of International and Development Studies and Murase Visiting Professor of Law, Georgetown University Law Center.

Giovanni Battista Ratti. Associate Professor of Legal Philosophy, Tarello Institute for Legal Philosophy, Department of Law, University of Genoa.

Giovanni Sartor. Professor of Legal Informatics and Legal Theory, European University Institute of Florence, and Professore di informatica giuridica, University of Bologna.

Frederick Schauer. David and Mary Harrison Distinguished Professor of Law at the University of Virginia.

Iain Scobbie. Professor of Public International Law, University of Manchester.

Oisin Suttle. Assistant Professor of Law, Maynooth University.

Kimberley Trapp. Professor of Public International Law, Faculty of Laws, University College London.

Antonios Tzanakopoulos. Associate Professor of Public International Law, University of Oxford.

Jorge Viñuales. Harold Samuel Chair of Law and Environmental Policy, University of Cambridge.

Antonia Waltermann. Assistant Professor in Foundations and Methods of Law, Faculty of Law, Maastricht University.

1
Introduction

Lorand Bartels and Federica Paddeu

In international law, as in every legal system, rules are invariably subject to exceptions. Our intention in producing this book was to investigate this phenomenon from both a theoretical and a doctrinal perspective. To this end, we invited scholars from legal theory and from international law to engage in a process of cross-fertilization of insights and experience. This introduction summarizes these results, and draws out common themes addressed in the different chapters of the book.

1 Rules and Exceptions

The book begins with several chapters identifying a conceptual understanding of the notion of a 'rule' to which an exception can apply. In its simplest form, a rule is a norm that, when its preconditions[1] and internal conditions are satisfied,[2] generates a specified outcome.[3] Such outcomes can be of several types, and there can be more than one outcome for each rule. One basic outcome of applying a rule will be definitional. To the extent that the antecedent element of a rule is applied to a particular fact, it generates a legal conclusion about that fact. Thus, a rule might set out the criteria for a certain type of fact to be an 'island', a 'state', or even 'wrongful', and when applied to any given fact (or 'case') it generates a conclusion that that particular fact is (or, of course, is not) an 'island', 'state', or 'wrongful'.

Some rules do no more than this, but that does not make them redundant, as anyone who has ever looked at the definitions in a legal instrument will appreciate. That is because the legal conclusions generated by these definitional rules are frequently used as a factual basis for the application of other rules (sometimes even in a different legal system). But most rules are more sophisticated, and to the antecedent also add a consequential element, which establishes more concrete consequences that follow when the conditions of the antecedent are satisfied.[4] Rules regulating conduct, for example, typically state that when a given event occurs (the antecedent), a given legal person must (obligation) or may (a right) engage in a certain type of conduct (the consequent).[5]

[1] These preconditions are based on the application of relevant meta-norms that are themselves applicable to the rule. Examples are rules on the validity of the rule at issue, rules on its interpretation, and, as discussed below, rules on the existence of a subject to which a rule is addressed.

[2] Schauer distinguishes between general rules that apply to a class of facts and prescriptions that apply to a single fact.

[3] Sartor puts this in the terms of information theory: a rule is a mechanism that triggers an output when it receives a given input.

[4] Hage, Waltermann, and Arosemena distinguish between 'counts as' rules, which are constitutive, 'fact-to-fact' rules, which attach new facts to other facts which exist simultaneously (e.g. a person gains a duty), and dynamic rules, which attach legal consequences to the occurrence of an event.

[5] At this level of analysis, it makes no difference whether the event specified in the antecedent is a bare event or whether it is conduct, and if conduct, whether it is conduct of the same legal person, or of another legal person. These criteria are important to distinctions between 'primary' and 'secondary' rules, and between 'procedural'

Lorand Bartels and Federica Paddeu, *Introduction* In: *Exceptions in International Law*. Edited by: Lorand Bartels and Federica Paddeu, Oxford University Press (2020). © Lorand Bartels and Federica Paddeu.
DOI: 10.1093/oso/9780198789321.003.0001

No matter their type, these rules have one feature in common: there can be reasons why they are not applied, even when their preconditions and internal conditions are satisfied. Importantly, this is as true for definitional rules (for example, the status of territory acquired or statehood established as a result of an illegal use of force) as it is for rules specifying a normative outcome (e.g. a use of force that is not prohibited when it is exercised in self-defence). And, as Hage, Waltermann, and Arosemena say in their opening chapter, it is in these cases, when there is a reason for not applying a rule, that one can speak of an 'exception' being made to that rule.

It is possible to systematize, at a general level, the reasons that a rule should not be applied in a given case. The first is when a rule should not be applied when its application would not serve its proper purpose. The second is when a rule should not be applied when its application would conflict with another rule within the same legal system (which is given priority).[6] And the third is when a rule should not be applied when its application would conflict with a value (or 'principle') within the same legal system or even (at least until incorporated) outside of that legal system. For ease of reference, we will speak of 'exceptions' in this introduction to refer to these sets of reasons for not applying a rule—for making an exception to that rule.

2 Confining Exceptions

At least the first two of these reasons for not applying a rule—that it is not being applied for its purpose, and that it conflicts with another rule—can be codified, although they can also exist in unwritten (customary) form. Thus, Article 26 of the Vienna Convention on the Law of Treaties requires treaties to be performed in good faith, meaning that their rules are not to be applied contrary to their purpose, while Article 51 of the UN Charter states that '[n]othing in the present Charter shall impair the inherent right of individual or collective self-defence' when certain conditions are met. Scobbie illustrates the third reason for not applying a rule—that its application must not conflict with a principle—by reference to the way the law of armed conflict was affected in the colonial context by the newly developed principle of self-determination.

The decentralized nature of international law involves some risks in the making of exceptions, whether these are written or unwritten. Schauer points to the psychological phenomenon of self-interested 'motivated reasoning', according to which actors relying on exceptions tend to exaggerate their scope. He quotes Carl Schmitt: 'sovereign is he who decides on the exception'. One can see this in practice in the expansive interpretations that are given to the right to use force in self-defence, a point discussed by Scobbie. Some international law regimes attempt to tame the reliance on exceptions by providing for some degree of scrutiny over their invocation. Trapp, speaking of the international human rights regime, Harrison, speaking of the international environmental law regime, and Suttle, speaking of the WTO, all show how these regimes provide for ongoing multilateral scrutiny of invocations of at least some exceptions to their rules. In some areas, however, one sees the opposite phenomenon,

and 'substantive' rules. As several contributors note, these distinctions are often used in different ways, not always sensibly.

[6] Alternatively, such a situation might be conceptualized as one in which a precondition to the application of the rule, namely, that it is not disapplied in cases of conflict, is not met.

with legal regimes endorsing motivated reasoning in the form of light standards of review, sometimes by giving states a 'margin of appreciation' in determining how to implement their obligations.

Unwritten exceptions are frequently more contested than written exceptions, and the development of international law has therefore, in part, taken the form of codifying previously accepted unwritten exceptions, in some cases taking the opportunity also to narrow their scope. Probably the most striking and best known example of this concerns the use of force, once 'seen as natural, noble, and necessary', in Scobbie's words, which was reduced last century to a conditional 'right' of self-defence, unless specifically authorized by the UN Security Council. There are also other examples, some continuing today. Thus, Kolb shows how the international legal system absorbed, and reduced, the *rebus sic stantibus* doctrine, Fitzmaurice how treaty law has effectively abandoned the *exceptio inadimplenti* doctrine, and Henckels how modern international investment treaties are coming to codify previously unwritten rights to regulate in express exceptions provisions.

Schauer's reference to Schmitt is even more pertinent to the third category of reasons mentioned earlier—that a rule may not apply because it conflicts with a value or principle within or even outside the legal order—because in these cases the possibility of an exception has not been contemplated or foreseen by the drafters of the rule. The risk of motivated reasoning is particularly high in a decentralized legal system without a guaranteed arbiter, and, where this is the case, Schauer posits that international law might therefore be better served by seeing its rules as, in principle, not being subject to exception in unforeseen circumstances.

4 Identifying Exceptions

In the examples mentioned above, it may be clear what the rule is, and what the exception to that rule is. But this is not always the case. Thus, Methymaki and Tzanakopoulos examine the relationship between the rule that states can exercise jurisdiction over their territory, and the opposing rule that other states are immune from such jurisdiction (which is itself subject to exceptions). As they say, there is simply no way to say which of these is the rule, and which the exception, and this is because both are immediately derived from the basis of international law, namely state sovereignty.

In other cases, looking at a legal concept in terms of a rule-exception dyad can help to understand where that concept fits into a broader legal structure. Thus, writing elsewhere, Shany has shown how the doctrine of admissibility (or inadmissibility) can be seen as an exception to the rule that a tribunal with jurisdiction must exercise that jurisdiction.[7] In this volume, Linderfalk shows, in a similarly clarifying way, that the duty to act in good faith is not a stand-alone obligation, but rather an exception to a right to act for a particular purpose. As such, a state cannot violate that duty; at most, the state cannot exercise its right. Similarly, Dolcetti and Ratti critique the ICJ's ruling in *Jurisdictional Immunities* that the doctrine of state immunity is not affected by *jus cogens* norms. For the ICJ, this was because the rule on state immunity is procedural, whereas *jus cogens* is 'substantive', and so they do not conflict.[8] For Dolcetti and Ratti, however, the implication of the case is that

[7] Yuval Shany, *Questions of Jurisdiction and Admissibility before International Courts* (Cambridge University Press 2016).

[8] *Jurisdictional Immunities of the State (Germany v Italy, Greece intervening)* (Judgment) [2012] ICJ Rep 99, para 93 (3 February 2012).

state immunity does, in fact, operate as an exception even to *jus cogens* norms. As they say, 'the distinction between procedural and substantive norms seems to be simply a smoke-screen to identify an implicit exception that may lead one to derogate from a substantive *jus cogens* norm'.

In these examples, concepts sometimes seen as stand-alone are properly categorized as exceptions to rules. Sometimes there is more untangling to be done. This is the case with Article 2 of the International Law Commission's Articles on State Responsibility, which states that '[t]here is an internationally wrongful act of a State when conduct consisting of an action or omission: . . . (b) constitutes a breach of an international obligation of the State'. The problem, as discussed in detail by Duarte d'Almeida and Paddeu, is that Chapter V of the same Articles lists six 'circumstances' (consent, self-defence, countermeasures, *force majeure*, distress, and necessity) that 'preclude [the] wrongfulness' of the very same conduct. How, then, can conduct be both wrongful and, in certain circumstances, not wrongful? Duarte d'Almeida and Paddeu answer this conundrum by identifying a category of conduct that is incompatible with an obligation (when a rule applies) but that is still not wrongful (because one of the circumstances precluding wrongfulness applies).

5 Exceptions and Scope Limitations

Even when an 'exception', in the broad sense, can be identified, it can exist in a variety of different forms, which are explored by Viñuales, in particular. Nonetheless, as Sartor shows, these differences essentially resolve into two main types: conditions limiting the scope of application of a rule (scope limitations), and conditions deeming a rule not to apply for independent reasons (exceptions provisions). In turn, scope limitations can be positive ('do not kill a person' necessarily excludes mosquitos) or negative ('do not kill animals except insects'), and they can also be internal or external ('the rule on killing animals does not apply to insects')—this can be called a carve-out. In principle, as several authors note, the same result can be achieved by any of these means. And yet, there are secondary complications, making it frequently important to determine whether a given norm is a scope limitation or an exception. What, then, are the differences?

Sartor emphasizes that the rationales for scope limitations tend to be based on the rationale for the obligation, whereas rationales for exceptions tend to be different. However, other factors are also important. One is normative: as several contributors put it, citing a famous phrase, there is a difference between the lawfulness of killing a mosquito, and killing a person in self-defence.[9] Similarly, Henckels says, with reference to the replacement of scope limitations with exceptions clauses in investment treaties,

> [e]ven though a finding that a state has engaged in prohibited conduct is only made as a step in the reasoning process (and therefore defeasible), it is nevertheless symbolically significant from the point of view of the responding state, who might consider it more politically palatable for certain conduct to be outside the scope of the obligations than to be perceived to have acted inconsistently with those obligations in in the first place.

[9] Hans Welzel, 'Die Regelung von Vorsatz und Irrtum im Strafrecht als legislatorisches Problem' (1955) 67 Zeitschrift für die gesamte Strafrechtswissenschaft 196, 211.

This normative hierarchy between rule and exception persists in other ways. One is the interpretation of conditions in exceptions in light of the rules to which they are exceptions. An example concerns the right to adopt 'necessary' measures, which is interpreted in many areas of international law to mean measures that achieve the stated objective which are also the least restrictive of the value reflected in the obligation (or regime) at issue. Thus, in the General Agreement on Tariffs and Trade (GATT), necessary measures are those that are least restrictive of trade, while in international criminal law, a 'necessary' measure is one that is least restrictive of the rights of the suspect or accused.[10] It is the same for necessity tests in other areas of law, such as human rights. But there are limits. As several contributors note, the notion that exceptions are ipso facto to be interpreted narrowly is one that seems to have passed its expiry date.

A normative priority for rules may underlie the way that tribunals approach their task analytically. As Pauwelyn and Viñuales say, tribunals have a tendency to analyse rules before exceptions and, within rules, to consider scope limitations before dealing with the obligation itself. Frequently, this is justified on the grounds of logic: there is no reason to consider an exception to a rule unless there has been a breach. But of course, there is also no need to analyse an obligation to which an exception applies, and this order of analysis has also been adopted, for example in *Continental Casualty v Argentina*,[11] *Russia—Traffic in Transit*,[12] and in *Oil Platforms*.[13] The point is that there is no necessary logic to the order of analysis. What underpins the order of analysis is the possibility of stating that conduct still contradicts an important value, even if it is, all things considered, justified by a countervailing value. It functions as a type of caution.

Alongside normative signalling, and its interpretive implications, there are also practical differences between scope limitations (whether internal or external) and exceptions. One important difference, which for Duarte d'Almeida is the defining difference, is the allocation of the burden of proof. Pauwelyn deals in forensic detail with the different burdens applicable to raising an issue, producing evidence, and persuading an arbiter, along with standards of proof and standards of review, and shows how these elements can be combined in different ways within rules and exceptions. The allocation of these burdens can be to tag conduct with a given normative value, but it can also be based on reasons of fairness, or convenience. Thus, for example, a respondent in WTO proceedings has to show that a measure is 'necessary' because there is no less restrictive alternative measure reasonably available that achieves the same objective, but, as the respondent cannot be asked to prove the 'universe' of all possible alternative measures, it is up to the complainant to identify potential alternative measures which are subjected to this test.[14]

There is also at least one other situation in which it is substantively important to distinguish between a scope limitation and an exception, which is when a metanorm determines that a rule cannot have any exceptions. This can occur at an institutional level. Thus, for example, the WTO Appellate Body will not decline to apply WTO law for any reasons that are not based on WTO law. But the most prominent example of such rules in international

[10] Judgment on the Prosecutor's appeal against the decision of Pre-Trial Chamber I entitled 'Decision Establishing General Principles Governing Applications to Restrict Disclosure pursuant to Rule 81 (2) and (4) of the Rules of Procedure and Evidence' *Prosecutor v Lubanga Dyilo*, ICC-01/04-01/06-568 (13 October 2006) para 37.

[11] *Continental Casualty Company v Argentine Republic*, ICSID Case ARB/ 03/ 9, Award (5 September 2008) para 161.

[12] WTO Panel Report, *Russia—Traffic in Transit*, WT/DS512/R (adopted 26 April 2019) para 7.108.

[13] *Case Concerning Oil Platforms (Iran v US)* (Merits) [2003] ICJ Rep 161, para 34.

[14] WTO Appellate Body Report, *US—Gambling*, WT/DS285/AB/R (adopted 20 April 2005) para 309.

law, of course, is the concept of *jus cogens* norms, which are stated to be non-derogable.[15] As such, *jus cogens* norms cannot be subject to exceptions, but at most to scope limitations. This presents something of a conundrum for *jus cogens* norms that are subject to conditions that, in other contexts, look rather like exceptions than scope limitations, such as the prohibition on the use of force, which is only illegal if it is non-consensual and not in self-defence. De Hoogh tackles this conundrum from the perspective of theory and doctrinal practice, and after considering various options concludes that the *jus cogens* element of the prohibition must be limited to cases of aggression, which excludes cases of self-defence and consent, rather than the use of force more generally.

In sum, one can distinguish several differences between scope limitations, whether internal or external to the rule, and exceptions. Sometimes the mere categorization of a norm as a scope limitation or as an exception can be significant as a matter of signalling the acceptability of conduct (moreover, as Paddeu and Ambos show, by reference to general international law and international criminal law respectively, even different types of exceptions can have different normative implications: thus, justifications, which preclude a finding of breach of the relevant obligation, involve permissions of the legal order, whereas excuses, which preclude responsibility or blameworthiness, do not). And this normative signal can have tangible consequences, by, for example, affecting the interpretation of the norm at issue, or leading to findings of (prima facie) breach which are later justified or to findings of breach for which the actor excused. Other effects include the allocation of the various burdens of raising and proving that the conditions of the norm are satisfied. In many cases, however, as Duarte d'Almeida argues in particular, it is not these consequences that determine whether a condition is scope limitation or an exception; rather, those are the designations that are given to provisions in order to generate these consequences. The GATT drafters knew that by calling Article XX of the GATT 'General Exceptions' they would impose the burden of proving that its conditions were met on the respondent, and the same is true of decisions by tribunals, even if it is often less transparent.

6 Rule Preconditions

Finally, we note a different type of 'exception'. It will be recalled that we have been speaking so far of rules that are applicable, because their preconditions and internal conditions are satisfied, but for one reason or another they are not applied. But, as will be recalled, such rules are only applicable in the first place when their *preconditions* are also met. The main precondition for the application for any rule is its validity.[16] However, there are also others; indeed, following Dolcetti and Ratti, there will be an absent precondition whenever a meta-norm authorizing the application of a subordinate norm is itself disapplied. This can have extremely disruptive effects on the underlying legal system. Thus, Kolb explains that the doctrine *rebus sic stantibus* was at one point seen (at least by some) as an expression of the notion that the principle *pacta sunt servanda* 'does not extend at all to inapplicable treaties (i.e. the ones contrary to the independence and vital interests of the State)'.

[15] Article 53 of the Vienna Convention on the Law of Treaties states that '[f]or the purposes of the present Convention, a peremptory norm of general international law is a norm accepted and recognized by the international community of States as a whole as a norm from which no derogation is permitted and which can be modified only by a subsequent norm of general international law having the same character.'

[16] Note, however, that not all tribunals are empowered to determine the validity of rules under which they are established. This is true in particular, of constitutional courts, on which see Simeon McIntosh, *Kelsen in the 'Grenada Court': Essays on Revolutionary Legality* (Ian Randle 2008) 151–56.

This understanding of *rebus sic stantibus* is of course no longer current. But another remains, namely, a precondition that the addressee of the rule continues to exist, or, rather, would not exist if it did not act in a certain way. Schauer sets up the problem with a domestic example: a promise to make dinner is cancelled by the death of the promisor.[17] Jeutner then extends this by reference to the ICJ's suggestion in *Nuclear Weapons* that the threat or use of nuclear weapons might not be illegal if the very survival of a state were at stake.[18] Of course, the parallel is not exact, because in Jeutner's case the state continues to exist at the time that the obligation vests. But insofar as the state would *not* exist if it did not use nuclear weapons, the hypothetical is still the relevant counter-factual. For Jeutner, the answer is that, in such a situation, there would be a 'legal dilemma' insofar as the threat or use of nuclear weapons would be lawful, but would still be subject to the consequences of unlawfulness.[19] Others, of course, following Schauer, might simply say that the obligation is cancelled.

7 Conclusion

We conclude, then, similarly to where we began, with a structural approach to rules and exceptions. And this is appropriate, because what has emerged from this project is a firm conviction that legal concepts are best understood in terms of their formal position in an overall framework. If it is possible to represent the relationship between rules and exceptions in the form of flow charts, as does Sartor, then this must underpin any interpretation of what those rules and exceptions mean. Of course, law is more than simply logic—and, as our contributors show, in a detailed manner, whether a given norm is a rule or an exception (or even exceptions of different types) comes with political, moral, and practical implications. What we hope also to have shown in this book, however, is that such issues have their own dynamic, and drive the characterization of norms as rules or exceptions, rather than this being the other way around. That, we hope, is a satisfying outcome.

[17] This is not a reason for not enforcing the promise, such as *force majeure*, which presupposes the continuing existence of the duty bearer. See Article 23 of the Articles on State Responsibility; cf the slightly narrower art 61 of the Vienna Convention on the Law of Treaties.

[18] *Nuclear Weapons* [1996] ICJ Rep 226, para 105(2)(E).

[19] Something like Jeutner's proposal exists in the institution of non-violation nullification and impairment claims in WTO law, where certain acts that are lawful are still subject to the same 'rebalancing' as if they were unlawful.

PART I
THEMES

2
Exceptions in International Law

*Jaap Hage, Antonia Waltermann, and Gustavo Arosemena**

1 Introduction

'The exception proves the rule' is a commonplace statement in everyday language. Logically speaking, matters are more complicated than that, however: if a universal statement such as 'All owls can fly' has an 'exception', this means that the statement is false because it turns out that not *all* owls can fly after all. In legal theory, meanwhile, rules attach consequences to factual situations, and they typically do so when their conditions are satisfied by a factual situation (a 'case'). Sometimes, however, they do not attach consequences to a case, even though the case satisfies the rule conditions: despite being applicable, the rule is not applied to the case. Then we speak of an exception to the rule. Such an exception, as long as it is exceptional, does not make the rule false or—better—invalid. The rule remains valid, but if there is an exception to it, the rule is not applied.

1.1 Exceptions in international law

Rules take a central place in law, and accordingly, rule exceptions play an important role. This is particularly the case in international law, because international law has many features that make conflicts of rules frequent and recalcitrant, and rule conflicts are a major reason for exceptions. There are several reasons why international law is ripe for rule conflict. First, international law is 'fragmented': it is not clear whether it constitutes a single legal system or an archipelago of mutually interacting international legal regimes. This, together with the growing interaction between international, domestic, and regional legal orders, implies that any discussion of rule conflicts in international law will have to account for conflicts across different legal orders.[1]

Secondly, the importance of the formal sources of international law has decreased: the list of formal sources has little power to control what counts as law and what does not. In fact, many academics suggest that having a clear view of international law requires us to bypass the doctrine of sources and identify as law those rules that have real world effectiveness and/or political legitimacy.[2] The resulting obscurity regarding what counts as international law is also a potential cause of rule conflicts. Thirdly, and related to the second point, international law operates without a central legislator. Treaties and customs are generated through the

* The authors thank Lorand Bartels and the other participants in the Cambridge seminar on Exceptions in International Law for useful comments on earlier versions of this contribution.

[1] See Martti Koskenniemi and Päivi Leino, 'Fragmentation of International Law? Postmodern Anxieties' (2002) 15 Leiden Journal of International Law 553.

[2] See Thomas M Franck, *The Power of Legitimacy among Nations* (Oxford University Press 1990) and Anthony C Arend, *Legal Rules and International Society* (Oxford University Press 1999).

Jaap Hage, Antonia Waltermann, and Gustavo Arosemena, *Exceptions in International Law* In: *Exceptions in International Law*. Edited by: Lorand Bartels and Federica Paddeu, Oxford University Press (2020). © Lorand Bartels and Federica Paddeu.
DOI: 10.1093/oso/9780198789321.003.0002

agency of more or less uncoordinated actors, which means that no central authority can attempt to minimize rule conflicts or prevent them from arising.

Apart from these three reasons which apply especially to international law, there is also the wish of the rule creator—for example, the parties to a treaty—to divide the burden of proof, which can underlie the existence of rules with exceptions (see sections 6 and 9.1). In short, international lawyers as well as academics will inevitably be confronted with exceptions in international law, whether these exceptions have their grounds in international, domestic, or other (possibly non-legal) sources.

1.2 Aim

Because exceptions play a crucial role in (international) law, a thorough understanding of what goes on when we make exceptions to rules is an essential precondition for international legal science. Our purpose in this contribution is to provide clarity with regard to the nature of exceptions to rules, in particular as concerns international law, by creating a precise conceptual framework in which important notions are interconnected. As will become clear from our argument, this conceptual framework must account for exceptions, rules, their applicability, and application, and shifts in the burden of proof which, as we will argue, differentiate exceptions to rules from 'mere' negative rule conditions.

Two caveats are in place here. The first one is that a conceptual framework is—and should be—neutral with regard to the content of the law. Conceptual jurisprudence, the theory according to which the content of the law is to some extent determined by the concepts used in creating and describing that content, has rightly attracted much criticism.[3] The inverse of this neutrality is that readers should not expect that the conceptual framework that is developed here can provide them with the solutions for specific legal controversies. Clear concepts can contribute to clear thinking, but it is the substantive law itself, and not the concepts by means of which law is created or described, that provides cases with their solutions.

The second caveat is that, in their standard usage, the concepts and the terms used to express them are not always very clear and a theory which aims to provide clear concepts and precisely defined terms cannot and should not be in complete accordance with actual usage. A copy of how words are used in actual legal discourse would also copy all the ambiguities and vagueness of this discourse. The conceptual and terminological proposals of this contribution should therefore be judged on their usefulness for the production of legal science, and not—at least, not in the first place—on their conformity with the actual practice. Our aim is to improve, not to describe.

1.3 Roadmap

As mentioned, the purpose of this contribution is to provide clarity with regard to the nature of exceptions to rules, in particular as concerns international law, by creating a precise conceptual framework in which important notions are interconnected. In order to do so, we will consider the notions of rules and reasons in sections 3 and 4, respectively. However,

[3] See Michael Marx, 'Systeme des 19 Jahrhunderts' in Arthur Kaufman and Winfried Hassemer (eds), *Einführung in Rechtsphilosophie und Rechtstheorie der Gegenwart* (Müller 1977).

before doing so, we will present in section 2 two examples that will often be referred to in our argument.

Section 5 will consider the applicability and application of rules, two notions that are highly relevant to our definition of an exception. Section 6 takes a closer look at the grounds for making exceptions to rules. One of the main grounds for making exceptions is that rules conflict with each other. Section 7 distinguishes two ways in which rules can conflict, and section 8 discusses a number of ways in which rule conflicts can be avoided, thereby taking away the need for exceptions to rules.

In section 9, we take a closer look at the shape in which exceptions to rules can occur. Sections 10 and 11 are devoted to the alleged necessity of allowing exceptions to rules. Section 10 discusses a technique to make exceptions superfluous, while section 11 argues that exceptions are unavoidable if one wants to maintain the possibility to divide the burden of proof in legal argumentation.

The argument of this contribution is summarized in section 12.

2 Recurring Examples

We will use two examples repeatedly in the arguments that follow. In this section, we will briefly introduce these recurring examples and the provisions on which they rest.

2.1 Prohibition of force

The first example concerns the use of force in international law. Article 2(4) of the UN Charter prohibits the use of force: 'All Members shall refrain in their international relations from the threat or use of force against the territorial integrity or political independence of any State, or in any other manner inconsistent with the Purposes of the United Nations.'
An exception to this general prohibition of force can be based on Article 42 of the Charter:

> Should the Security Council consider that measures provided for in Article 41 would be inadequate or have proved to be inadequate, it may take such action by air, sea, or land forces as may be necessary to maintain or restore international peace and security. Such action may include demonstrations, blockade, and other operations by air, sea, or land forces of Members of the United Nations.

2.2 State responsibility

The second example concerns the responsibility of states to make full reparation for injury caused by an internationally wrongful act. This topic is dealt with by the Articles on Responsibility of States for Internationally Wrongful Acts (ARSIWA).

Article 1 states: 'Every internationally wrongful act of a State entails the international responsibility of that State.'

Article 2 provides the main rule defining what counts as an internationally wrongful act: 'There is an internationally wrongful act of a State when conduct consisting of an action or omission: (a) is attributable to the State under international law; and (b) constitutes a breach of an international obligation of the State.'

Exceptional circumstances may make that the breach of an international obligation nevertheless does not count as an internationally wrongful act. One of those is when a state has acted out of self-defence. Article 21 of the ARSIWA reads: 'The wrongfulness of an act of a State is precluded if the act constitutes a lawful measure of self-defence taken in conformity with the Charter of the United Nations.'

Lastly, Article 31 of the ARSIWA defines what the state responsibility brings about. It states that:

1. The responsible State is under an obligation to make full reparation for the injury caused by the internationally wrongful act.
2. Injury includes any damage, whether material or moral, caused by the internationally wrongful act of a State.

3 Rules

Before we turn to exceptions to rules, we need to have a solid understanding of what rules are in the first place. However, rules—or, as some prefer, norms—are hard to characterize.[4] They may be seen as social artefacts which mandate, prohibit, or permit certain forms of conduct. Following Hart's distinction of primary and secondary rules,[5] the behaviour in question can be the conduct of human affairs generally, or conduct dealing with the creation, modification, application, and extinction of rules. Even this distinction is unsatisfactorily narrow, however, because some rules, rather than governing behaviour, constitute states of affairs. In this contribution, we will be using the following circumscription of rules: that rules are a kind of thing which attach new facts to already existing ones. These new facts exist purely because they are the result of rule application, and they are constituted by the rule.[6]

3.1 Kinds of rules

Different kinds of rules can be distinguished, such as:

- 'Counts-as' rules, which make some things also count as (be) other things. For example, the king of the Belgians also counts as (is) the commander-in-chief of the Belgian army. These rules include legal definitions, such as 'Vehicles in the sense of the Traffic Law are cars, motorcycles, and bicycles.'
- 'Fact-to-fact rules', which attach new facts to other facts which exist simultaneously. Examples are that the government of a state has the power to conclude treaties on behalf of that state, and that car drivers have the duty to carry a driver's licence.
- Dynamic rules, which attach legal consequences to the occurrence of an event. For instance, if a state commits an internationally unlawful act, and thereby causes damage

[4] For a more extensive analysis than can be provided here see Jaap Hage, *Studies in Legal Logic* (Springer 2005) 159–202.

[5] See Herbert Lionel Adolphus Hart, *The Concept of Law* (Oxford University Press 2012) 91–99.

[6] See Jaap Hage, 'Separating Rules from Normativity' in Michal Araszkiewicz, Pawel Banaś, Tomasz Gizbert-Studnicki, and Krzystof Pleszka (eds), *Problems of Normativity, Rules and Rule-Following* (Springer 2015) 13–30.

to another state, the former state incurs at that moment the liability to compensate the latter state for the damage it suffered.

Mandatory norms, which prescribe behaviour, are either fact-to-fact rules, as when a state has the duty to respect the human rights it has recognized through conclusion and ratification of a human rights treaty,[7] or dynamic rules, as when a state is assigned the obligation to compensate the damage it has unlawfully caused to another state.

3.2 Rules and language

It is important to distinguish between, on the one hand, rules as entities which are to a large extent language-independent[8] and, on the other hand, rule formulations and the sources through which rules are created—treaties, legislation, and judicial decisions—which are both necessarily language-dependent. A rule, as we use the concept here, is the connection between kinds of facts. For instance, the rule that the king of the Belgians counts as the commander-in-chief of the Belgian army connects the fact that somebody is the king of the Belgians to the fact that this particular person is commander-in-chief of the Belgian army. The rule is defined by its content, which consists of the kinds of facts the rule connects. The rule about the Belgian king is defined by the fact that it connects facts of the kind 'being the king of the Belgians' to facts of the kind 'being the commander-in-chief of the Belgian army'. This connecting rule may be formulated in any of the three official languages of Belgium—Dutch, French, and German—but they are all formulations of the same rule. Therefore, all formulations of the rule must mention the same rule conditions and the same rule conclusion, be it not necessarily in the same language. We also see that the rule itself is independent from the rule formulation when considering that the prohibition of slavery can be expressed in many different languages, such as 'la esclavitud está prohibida' or 'slavernij is verboden'.

Equally, we see the difference between rule and rule source when considering that the prohibition of slavery is, at once, brought about by Article 4 of the European Convention on Human Rights (ECHR) and Article 8 of the International Covenant on Civil and Political Rights, and is also part of customary international law, and of *jus cogens*.[9]

Furthermore, the formulation of a rule is not identical to the official text by means of which the rule was created: the formulation mentions only the conditions and the conclusion of the rule. One-on-one correspondence is not required, as the example of Article 330 of the Treaty on the Functioning of the European Union (TFEU) shows. This article, which is not subdivided into sections, is arguably the source of four different rules:

a. All members of the Council can (have the competence to) participate in its deliberations.

[7] Notice that the rule imposing the duty to respect a particular human right came about as the result of a dynamic rule, namely a rule of change in the Hartian sense, but that the rule itself is a fact-to-fact rule, which attaches the fact that a state has a duty to respect the human right to the fact that the state in question is party to the treaty. On rules of change see Hart, *The Concept of Law* (n 5) 95–96.

[8] Rules are only 'to a large extent' language-independent, because every rule needs to have a formulation, and this formulation requires a language to formulate the rule in. This means that the conditions and the conclusion of a rule, although not linguistic entities themselves, must be expressible in some language.

[9] We assume here, for the sake of argument, that these sources all underlie the same rule. Of course, this may be disputed, as it may be disputed for any concrete example. However, disputing the example amounts to recognition of the point we want to make, namely that there may be more than one source for the same rule.

b. Only members of the Council representing the Member States participating in enhanced cooperation can (have the competence to) take part in the vote.
c. Only the votes of the representatives of the participating Member States are relevant for the determination of whether unanimity exists.
d. A qualified majority is established in accordance with Article 238(3).

The conditions and conclusions of these rules can be formulated in different ways, and in different languages, but to the extent that they all convey the same conditions and conclusion, they are all formulations of the same rules. Moreover, none of the rule formulations actually coincides with Article 330 of the TFEU.

We emphasize this distinction between rule formulations and the sources by means of which rules are created, because interpretation is the step from a rule source to a rule formulation. Sometimes, interpretation is a means to avoid rule conflicts or exceptions to rules and, if it is, it can fulfil this function because it leads to a different rule (formulation) on the basis of the same source. This is something we elaborate on in section 8.3. On this terminology, only sources for rules are interpreted, but rules themselves never are.[10] This also means that, when we speak of exceptions, we mean exceptions to rules, rather than something which takes place at the level of rule formulations.

4 Reasons

Another basic notion that plays a central role in our theory about rule exceptions is the notion of a reason. Perhaps even more than rules, reasons are the topic of an overwhelming amount of literature, both in legal[11] and in ethical theory.[12] Apodictically brief, reasons might be circumscribed as facts that are relevant for some conclusion. So there are two aspects to each reason:

a. the reason is a fact
b. this fact is relevant for some conclusion.

4.1 Classification of reasons

Reasons can plead for or against different kinds of conclusions. For example, the fact that a witness declared that Alice stole perfume from the shop is a reason—not necessarily a decisive one—to *believe* that Alice is a thief. In this case, the reason is a *reason to believe* and the conclusion is that somebody is justified in believing something.

[10] The determination whether a particular fact situation falls under a rule depends on the conditions of the actual rule—e.g. was this act internationally unlawful?—but this step in the application of a rule is better labelled as classification of the facts than as interpretation of the rule. See Jaap Hage, *Reasoning with Rules* (Kluwer 1997) 95–97.

[11] See e.g. Joseph Raz, *Practical Reason and Norms* (OUP 1999); and María Cristina Redondo, *Reasons for Action and the Law* (Springer 2013).

[12] See e.g. Thomas M Scanlon, *Being Realistic about Reasons* (OUP 2014) and Maria Alvarez, 'Reasons for Action: Justification, Motivation, Explanation' in Edward N Zalta (ed), *The Stanford Encyclopedia of Philosophy* (Winter 2017 edn) https://plato.stanford.edu/archives/win2017/entries/reasons-just-vs-expl/.

The fact that the United Nations Security Council (UNSC) has authorized intervention in Libya is the reason why (it was the case that) foreign troops were allowed to intervene in the Libyan civil war. This reason is a reason why something is the case, a *constitutive reason*.

And, finally, the fact that a state is liable to repair injury caused to another state, is a reason for the International Court of Justice (ICJ) to order the former state to pay damages. The last example illustrates a *reason for action*, a reason for or against doing something.

4.2 Universalizability of reasons

Reasons are concrete facts, such as the fact that a witness declared that Alice stole perfume from the shop. Concrete facts can only be reasons for particular conclusions if similar facts are also reasons for similar conclusions. Authorization by the UNSC can only be a reason why armed intervention is permissible in a particular case if authorization by the UNSC tends to be a reason that allows armed interventions in general. This move from particular cases to more general statements can be expressed by saying that reasons are universalizable, or—which boils down to the same thing—by saying that underlying every concrete reason for a particular conclusion is a rule (or principle[13]) which makes facts of that kind into reasons for that kind of conclusion.[14]

Every reason has an underlying rule, and that is important because the rules underlying reasons are amenable to exceptions. If there is such an exception, a fact which normally would be a reason exceptionally does not count as a reason anymore. For instance, the rule that thieves are punishable makes the fact that somebody is a thief into a legal reason why this person is punishable. However, if there is an exception to the rule, for instance because the person in question is only three years old, the fact is not a legal reason for punishment. As we will see later (in section 9), this 'exclusion' of a reason[15] should be distinguished from the situation that the reason is outweighed by some colliding reason.

The reasons discussed above are contributory reasons. This means that they plead for (pro-reasons) or against (con-reasons) a particular conclusion, but are not necessarily decisive by themselves. If there are contributory reasons both for and against a particular conclusion, these reasons need to be 'weighed', or 'balanced'. In this connection, weighing and balancing are mere metaphors; what really goes on is that some decision is made which set of reasons wins against the other set. Such a decision, which can itself be based on one or more reasons, can be laid down as a premise of an argument.

An example may illustrate this. The fact that the publication of a photograph is an exercise of the freedom of the press is a reason against prohibiting the publication. The fact that this publication would violate the privacy of the person in the photo is a reason for prohibiting its publication. The fact that the publication of the photograph does not serve a public interest is a reason why the contributory reason based on privacy outweighs the contributory reason

[13] At this place we do not distinguish between rules and principles. A distinction between the two can well be made, however. For instance, while rules can have exceptions, it does not make sense to speak of exceptions to principles. More about the difference between rules and principles in Hage, *Reasoning with Rules* (n 10) 110–13.

[14] The universalizability of reasons is discussed more extensively in Jaap Hage, 'The Justification of Value Judgments: Theoretical Foundations for Arguments about the Best Level to Regulate European Private Law' in Bram Akkermans, Jaap Hage, Nicole Kornet, and Jan Smits (eds), *Who Does What? On the Allocation of Regulatory Competences in European Private Law* (Intersentia 2015) 15–56, with references to earlier literature.

[15] See Raz, *Practical Reason and Norms* (n 11) 35–48.

based on the freedom of the press. Therefore, the former reason outweighs the latter reason, and the court should prohibit the publication of the photograph in question.[16]

If the sets of reasons are in balance, which includes the situation that there are neither pro- nor con-reasons, nothing follows, unless the burden of proof decides the issue. We will consider this in section 11.

5 Applicability and Application

We define an exception to a rule as the situation where a rule is applicable to a case, but is nevertheless not applied to it. In this connection, 'applicability' and 'application' are technical terms with a precise meaning that we will explore in this section.

If a rule is applied to a case, it attaches its consequence to the case. So, if the rule which makes a state responsible for internationally wrongful acts is applied to the case that Outopia breached an international obligation, it makes Outopia responsible for that breach.

Applicability of a rule to a case is determined by three factors:

1. the rule must exist
2. the case must fall within the—territorial, temporal, and personal—scope of the rule and
3. the case must satisfy the ordinary conditions of the rule.

Let us talk about each of these factors, starting first with the requirement that a rule must exist. It may seem obvious that a rule needs to exist in order to be applied, yet the existence of rules becomes the subject of legal debate at times. In a legal dispute, one party may argue that a rule invoked by the other party does not exist. This is usually formulated as a claim that the rule is not valid, as a rule that lacks validity cannot be applied to any case. This is different for exceptions, which only make that the rule is not applied to this particular case. There is a further difference between the two arguments that has to do with the burden of proof; we will consider this in section 11.

Secondly, a case must fall within the scope of the rule in order for it to be applicable. Typically, rules have certain scope conditions: the rule applies only on a particular territory, during a particular time frame, or to particular persons. We will talk about scope conditions in more depth in section 8.2.

Thirdly, the case must satisfy the ordinary conditions of the rule for it to be applicable. These conditions are given with the rule formulation. For example, if it were binding, Article 36 of the ARSIWA would create a rule that defines a state's liability for particular damage. It mentions four conditions for this liability:

1. there must have been an internationally wrongful act,
2. a state must have been responsible for this act,
3. the damage was caused by this act, and
4. the damage was not (yet) made good by restitution.

[16] See European Court of Human Rights (ECtHR) *Von Hannover v Germany* App no 59320/00 (24 September 2004).

These four factors determine the applicability of the rule. At times, it happens that a rule is not applicable to a case but is nevertheless applied to it. This is most often a case of rule application by analogy. We will not pay attention to this possibility here.[17]

If a rule is applicable to a case, this is a contributory reason for applying the rule to that case. Since applicability is only a contributory reason for application of the rule, this reason may have to be balanced against reasons against application. Because we define an exception to a rule as non-application of an applicable rule, reasons against the application of an applicable rule are ipso facto reasons for making an exception to the rule.

6 Grounds for Exceptions

Before continuing our argument it is useful to take a step back and look at the grounds for making an exception to a rule. We have defined an exception as the situation in which a rule is applicable to a case, but is nevertheless not applied to this case. There are several reasons for making an exception to a rule.

First, the rule-exception structure can be used in order to create a division in the burden of proof. For instance, Article 2 of the ARSIWA defines what counts as an internationally wrongful act, while Article 21 says that this wrongfulness is precluded if, amongst others, the act constitutes a lawful measure of self-defence taken in conformity with the Charter of the United Nations. Article 21 is meant to make an exception to Article 2, and by using this rule-exception construction, the maker of these rules has created a division in the burden of proof. The state that wants its damage to be compensated bears this burden for the conditions of the rule defining international wrongfulness, while the state that wants to avoid being held responsible has the burden of proof for the exception. We will return to the relation between exceptions and the burden of proof in section 11.

Secondly, it may be deemed undesirable that the legal consequences of the rule come into being for a particular case, although the rule is applicable to this case. There are three variants of this possibility:

a. Application of the rule in this case would violate the purpose of the rule. We return to this possibility in section 9.
b. Application of the rule would lead to legal consequences that are incompatible with the consequences of some other rule that is also applicable to the case. These so-called 'rule conflicts' will be discussed in the sections 7, 8, and 9.2.
c. Application of the rule in this case would harm values or goals that were not, or insufficiently, taken into account when the rule was created. When the application of a rule to a particular case has bad consequences, this seems at first sight to be a reason against applying the rule, and therefore for making an exception to the rule. This may be different if these bad consequences were sufficiently taken into account when drafting the rule, because then, apparently, the bad consequences were deemed to be outweighed by the advantages of the rule. This reason against applying an applicable rule is also discussed in section 9.2.

[17] The interested reader may consult Hage, *Reasoning with Rules* (n 10) 118–21.

7 Rule Conflicts

As we mentioned in the previous section, rule conflicts, when they arise, are a frequent cause of exceptions to rules. As such, exceptions are a tool to deal with, rather than to avoid, rule conflicts. There are at least two different types of rule conflicts, namely conflicts of imposition and conflicts of compliance. The former are conflicts whereby the conflicting rules impose incompatible states of affairs upon the world,[18] which cannot coexist. The latter are conflicts whereby the conflicting rules prescribe incompatible forms of behaviour.

7.1 Conflicts of imposition

Consider, by way of example, the situation of Latin America in the early 19th century, where *uti possidetis facto* and *uti possidetis juris* developed as separate principles. According to *uti possidetis juris*, Spanish legal documents were decisive for locating borders; according to *uti possidetis facto*, the land actually held by a state at independence would determine its borders.[19] Suppose that a certain territory is under the factual possession of Province A, while legal documents state that it belongs to Province B. Province A becomes State A upon independence, and the territory remains in State A's factual possession. Province B becomes State B upon independence. According to the principle of *uti possidetis facto*, the territory falls within the borders of State A. According to the principle of *uti possidetis juris*, the territory falls within the borders of State B. Owing to the nature of territory, it cannot belong to both State A and State B at the same time, and so the effects of the rules are incompatible.

It is important here to note that the incompatibility of the consequences of these rules, and therefore also the rule conflict in this case, depends on the existence of other rules, namely those of how territory works and that territory cannot belong to two or more states at the same time. Generally speaking, whether rules conflict can depend on a presupposed background, which means that some facts cannot go together and that some states of affairs are incompatible with one another.[20]

Another example of a conflict of imposition is the following: the UN Charter prohibits the use of force, but military action with authorization by the UNSC is permitted.[21] One rule prohibits an armed intervention into another sovereign state, while the other permits precisely this behaviour. The state of affairs that armed intervention is prohibited and the state of affairs that it is permitted are incompatible, and therefore these rules are in conflict. Note that the focus here is on the states of affairs imposed on the world: given that a permission is not a duty to intervene, there is no conflict of compliance in this case.[22]

[18] We use the expression 'state of affairs' to denote a possible fact. A fact is then a state of affairs that actually obtains. Cf Ludwig Wittgenstein, *Tractatus Logico Philosophicus* (1921, Suhrkamp 1984) Thesis 2; and Mark Textor, 'States of Affairs' in Edward N Zalta (ed), *The Stanford Encyclopedia of Philosophy* (Winter 2016 edn) https://plato.stanford.edu/archives/win2016/entries/states-of-affairs/.

[19] Cf Steven R Ratner, 'Drawing a Better Line: Uti Possidetis and the Borders of New States' (1996) 90(40 American Journal of International Law 594

[20] Jaap Hage, 'Rule Consistency' (2000) 19 Law and Philosophy 369 and Hage, *Studies in Legal Logic* (n 4) 135–57 explore the theme of how rules themselves can be part of the background that causes rule conflicts.

[21] Confusingly, this permission to intervene is sometimes called a 'right' to intervene.

[22] The conflict may seem to some to be a conflict of compliance, because the conflicting norms deal with actions. However a conflict between a prohibition and a permission is not one of compliance. It is possible to comply with both norms by abstaining from the prohibited behaviour, since such abstinence does not violate the permission. (Permissions cannot be violated at all.) However, there is a conflict of imposition, since the states of affairs that some kind of action is prohibited and permitted are not compatible.

7.2 Conflicts of compliance

Consider a state which is obliged, on the basis of two human rights treaties it has signed and ratified, to invest money in both education and health care, while the state has only sufficient money and resources to invest in one of them. Alternatively, think of the example of the journalist who is obliged to reveal her sources for a controversial publication, while she promised her informant not to reveal his identity. In both cases, a conflict arises because the agent in question cannot comply with both obligations.

Conflicts of compliance can arise because the obligations themselves are in conflict (such as a prescription and a prohibition of the same behaviour[23]), or because factual circumstances make compliance impossible, as was the case for the state with too limited resources. These kinds of conflicts can only exist between mandatory rules (prescription and prohibitions) and should be avoided. When they occur, they force the obligated agent to choose which obligation to violate. Conflicts of imposition, meanwhile, can exist between all kinds of rules, including those that assign statuses (e.g. the status of a piece of land as belonging to one or the other state).

8 Making Exceptions Superfluous

Exceptions are, amongst others, a way to deal with rule conflicts when they arise. In this section, we will consider a number of tools and techniques that can keep such conflicts from coming into existence in the first place, thereby taking away the need to make an exception at all. The list of tools and techniques in the following is not meant to be exhaustive.

8.1 Subscripting

Rule conflicts can arise between rules of one system, or between rules of different normative systems. Think again of the example of a journalist who promised not to reveal her source. This example illustrates a conflict between a legal requirement to reveal, and a moral obligation not to do so. The distinction between normative systems becomes visible in the necessity to add subscripts ('legally' and 'morally', or 'according to German law' and according to French law') to legal judgments. Take, for instance, the question of whether State A may use military force to intervene in State B to prevent gross human rights violations. If normative systems are distinct, the judgment must be that, legally, State A is prohibited from intervening (in the absence of UNSC authorization), but morally, it should. In this example, the subscripts distinguish between the legal and the moral point of view. However, it is also possible to distinguish between different legal points of view. For instance, according to European Union law, certain forms of positive discrimination are not permissible, whereas according to the Committee on the Elimination of Discrimination against Women, they are required.[24]

[23] If the same *kind* of behaviour is both mandatory and prohibited because of two conflicting rules, there is a conflict of imposition, because the states of affairs that some kind of behaviour is prohibited and mandatory are incompatible. If a kind of action is a sub-kind of two different more general kinds of action, and one of these more general kinds is mandatory while the other kind is prohibited, the conflict is one of compliance.

[24] See Lisa Waddington and Laura Visser, 'Temporary Special Measures under the Women's Convention and Positive Action under EU Law: Mutually Compatible or Irreconcilable?' in Ingrid Westendorp (ed), *The Women's Convention Turned 30: Achievements, Setbacks, and Prospects* (Intersentia 2012). This example presupposes that

If the legal and other judgments are subscripted, seemingly conflicting judgments are rendered logically consistent because we see that, for a legal decision, the moral rules are simply not applicable. A legal permission is consistent with a moral prohibition, and a competence that exists according to the law of one country may be absent according to the law of another country. Nevertheless, an agent who is confronted with mandatory rules from different legal systems that both demand obedience but the rules of which cannot both be complied with, is still burdened with a conflict of compliance.

8.2 The scope of rules

One of the factors determining the applicability of a rule is its scope. Most legal rules identify by means of their conditions to what kind of cases and to which persons they are applicable. This can be everybody, as in Article 2 of the ECHR, or sets of agents such as the judges in the European Court of Human Rights, as in Article 21 of the same Convention. However, there are also limitations on the cases and persons to which a rule applies that are not mentioned in the ordinary conditions of the rule. These are scope conditions, which combine with the ordinary rule conditions to determine to which cases or persons rules are applicable.[25]

There can be personal, spatial (territorial), and temporal scope conditions. Personal scope limitations occur when a rule only applies to a certain class of persons, even though this is not necessarily mentioned in the rule conditions. So, for instance, WTO law applies to members of the WTO, but not to non-WTO members. Spatial or territorial scope limitations, meanwhile, refer to a distinction depending on the place where certain events take place. So, for instance, the penal laws of states typically apply to events that take place in their own territory, but not in the territory of another state. Temporal scope limitations postulate that the rules apply in different time periods. For example, the customary rules of treaty interpretation and the rules found in the Vienna Convention on the Law of Treaties 1969 are different and thus they seem bound to conflict, but the conflict can be avoided by postulating that the rules of the Vienna Convention apply only to treaties that entered into force after 1980, as in fact stated in the Convention itself.

By limiting the applicability of rules, scope conditions prevent rule conflicts, because two rules can only conflict if they are both applicable to the same case.

8.3 Interpretation

Another technique to avoid conflicts is to interpret a legal source in such a way that the resulting rule is not applicable to the case in question. The following example[26] illustrates this.

different legal regimes created by different legal instruments, such as the human rights regimes of the European Union and of the Convention on the Elimination of All Forms of Discrimination against Women, constitute different legal systems. Whether and to what extent this is the case is a difficult question, which cannot be dealt with in the present contribution.

[25] The recognition of scope conditions which are not mentioned in the rule and which are therefore not rule conditions is important because it makes clear that rule conflicts may not exist, even where the explicit rule conditions suggest their presence.

[26] The example was inspired by, but is not identical to, the circumstances of the case *Avena and Other Mexican Nationals*. See International Court of Justice Avena and Other Mexican Nationals *(Mexico v United States of America)* (Judgment) [2004] ICJ Rep 12.

Assume that the constitution of a federal state prescribes that the state respect the constraints of federalism, while international law prescribes that the federal state stop one of its constituent states from certain forms of behaviour. These actions cannot both be performed. The rule conflict seems clear, and a breach of either an international or domestic duty seems unavoidable. Given this impasse, it may be possible to interpret an obligation of a specific type—for example, stop damage-causing behaviour—as an obligation of a more general type—for example, avoid causing lasting damage. It is possible to comply with this latter obligation without violating the former obligation, for instance by compensating the damage that results from the behaviour. If this is done, the demands of both legal systems are deemed to be satisfied, and the conflict is avoided.

A related technique is that a new type of action is created, which can solve the impasse between two colliding norms for an important range of cases. On a straightforward interpretation, the UN Charter rules out all acts of aggression that are non-defensive and not authorized by the UNSC. It has been argued that there is a developing rule of international law that suggests that states have a duty to intervene in cases of genocide, war crimes, and crimes against humanity to defend the civilian population, and this duty exists irrespective of whether UNSC authorization has been given or not. If a case of genocide breaks out, and the UNSC does not authorize action, the two rules will conflict. One way to ease the conflict is to devise new action types such as 'peacekeeping' or 'humanitarian intervention' that do not fall within the concept of aggression that is prohibited by the UN Charter.

8.4 Derogation

At times, rules conflict with factual necessity, or with rules made to cope with factual circumstances such as in states of emergency. Human rights on privacy might, for instance, conflict with measures taken to prevent terrorist attacks or to investigate them. One tool to prevent such conflicts from arising is derogation. Derogation allows a state to take measures derogating from its obligations under a treaty, to the extent necessary to handle certain situations (see e.g. Article 15 of the ECHR). Logically speaking, there is no conflict in cases of derogation between the rule of the treaty and the rule on the basis of which the measures are taken, because derogation means that the treaty rule is inapplicable for the duration of the derogation. In short, derogation involves the temporary suspension of applicability of a potentially conflicting rule, thereby avoiding the conflict.[27]

8.5 Incorporation and reference

The easiest way to avoid the dilemma of inter-systemic rule conflicts is to ensure that such conflicts do not occur. We have seen that interpretation and derogation, but also scope limitations, can fulfil this function, in that, for example, the national law of one state is limited in its application to the territory of that state only. With regard to international law in particular, however, scope limitations do not manage to avoid all conflicts. Methods such as incorporation and reference can prevent inter-systemic conflicts from arising as well.

[27] It may also be argued that derogation is making a temporary exception to the derogated rule. On this interpretation the derogated rule is still applicable, but should temporarily not be applied. Derogation would then not be a way to avoid rule conflicts, but a way to deal with them.

Rules of a foreign system can be used in a legal system through a technique which may be called 'reference'. The foreign rules are not incorporated in the legal system, but their existence and content is considered by the system as facts that are legally relevant from the point of view of the legal system. Reference avoids conflicts between the rules of the referring system and the rules of the system to which reference is made, because the content of the referring system is adapted to the content of the referred system. Private international law provides many examples of this, because it contains meta-rules that determine which national legal system provides the applicable rules. For example, the judgment whether a couple has divorced is given in country A on the basis of the rules of country B, the validity of which is from the perspective of country A, a matter of fact. These rules are not incorporated in some international set of object-level rules, and neither is there an independent international system. Sometimes there are treaties dealing with conflicts of rules of different national systems, but the rules of these treaties are applied because they become part of the national systems of the parties to the treaties. As a consequence, the rules of the national systems determine the outcomes of cases, without a potential conflict with rules of another national system. In this way, rule conflicts can be avoided.

In cases of reference, the content of a foreign system is treated by the own legal system as a matter of fact that co-determines the application of the domestic law. In case of *incorporation*, meanwhile, foreign law becomes part of domestic law. The typical example of this phenomenon is the incorporation of international law in a national legal system in so-called 'monist' legal systems. The Dutch legal system nicely illustrates incorporation. Provisions from international treaties ratified by the Netherlands and rules created by international organizations in which the Netherlands participates (in particular the European Union) automatically become part of the Dutch legal system (Article 93 of the *Grondwet*). The foreign rules are not foreign anymore, except in the sense that they were not created by native Dutch legislative bodies. They are part of the Dutch legal system to the same extent as home-made rules.

Strictly speaking, incorporation is not a technique to deal with conflicts between rules of different systems, but a way to ensure that only one legal system is relevant.[28] If European Union (EU) regulations become automatically part of Dutch national law, there is no need any more to pay attention to EU law as such, because the relevant rules are already part of Dutch national law. In the case of the EU one may even ask whether there exists such a thing as the EU legal system which contains rules that are directly applicable in the Member States. For those directly applicable rules arguably it holds that the EU only provides organs which can create (uniform) law that becomes part of the national legal systems of the Member States. If all counties would have similar monist systems with regard to the relation between laws of domestic and laws of non-domestic origin, the same might be said about the provisions of human rights treaties that are directly applicable.[29] These treaties would then create uniform human rights in different legal systems and it might be argued then that there is no separate international human rights system. However, theoretically it is imaginable that some legal system incorporates part of a foreign legal system, while that foreign system has

[28] This holds at least from the perspective of the incorporating system. However, the mere incorporation of rules of international law into a national legal system does not make any statement about the place of the incorporated rules in the hierarchy of norms of that legal system. International law will hold itself to be above the constitution, while national law might give the incorporated rules a different status. This brings us back to the issue of subscripting, whereby the national legal system holds that it is the only relevant system because it has incorporated rules of international law, while international law might nevertheless claim relevance.

[29] Since not all countries use a monist system, this exercise is theoretical. However, it is useful to see what the effects of incorporation might be.

independent existence. The situation is then comparable to one country that uses the national currency of some other country.

If 'foreign' rules are incorporated in a national legal system they are not foreign rules anymore but merely rules with a foreign origin. Such rules may still conflict with rules of a national origin, or with other rules of foreign origin. However, because of the incorporation, such conflicts are not conflicts between legal systems anymore. What is avoided by incorporation is not a conflict of rules, but a conflict of legal systems.[30] If there is still a conflict of rules, the techniques used within a single legal system to deal with conflicts, such as making exceptions, can be used to deal with possible conflicts between rules from national and international sources.

8.6 Limitation of rule-creating powers

A common way to avoid inconsistencies within a single legal system is to avoid rule conflicts by preventing conflicting rules from entering into existence at all. A national legislator, for instance, might make an exception to the general right of free speech for cases of hate speech. This will disempower a local legislator to make an exception to this exception for hate speech against people of a particular origin, such as French speaking people from Wallonia. If a local legislator nevertheless attempted to do so, its rules would simply not be recognized as valid law: the local legislator does not have the power to make rules that conflict with the 'higher' rules of the national legislator. This limitation of power avoids conflicting rules by impacting the first of the three factors determinative of applicability.

With regard to international law, however, limitations of the powers of states occur less frequently.[31] This is because such limitations suggest an overarching organization of the distribution of rule creating power that can divest certain actors of their ability to create rules. Such organization is absent on the international plane. As mentioned in the introduction, rule creation in international law is decentralized and tends towards anarchy as even the doctrine of the sources of law has only relative weight. Instead of limitation of state power, international law usually creates prohibitions, which can be violated. The typical sanction is not invalidity, but the need to make full reparation, which may range from monetary compensation, to restitution, to guarantees of non-repetition.

9 Classification of Exceptions

In the previous section, we considered tools to prevent rule conflicts. Given that rule conflicts are a frequent cause of exceptions, these tools can negate the need for exceptions. However, not all rule conflicts can be avoided, and we saw in section 6 that there are other grounds for exceptions as well. In short, exceptions cannot always be avoided. In this section, we will have a closer look at exceptions and how to classify them.

An exception is made to a rule if the rule is not applied to a case, although it is applicable to that case. If a rule is applicable to a case, this is normally a contributory reason for applying

[30] As a matter of fact, incorporation makes more rule conflicts possible, because rules from different systems can, because of subscripting (see section 8.1), only lead to conflicts of compliance, while rules that belong to the same system can also lead to conflicts of imposition.

[31] The powers of international organizations are often limited.

the rule to that case. Barring additional contributory reasons against application, this means that the rule should be applied to the case.

This last clause indicates how exceptions to a rule may come into play.[32] First, it may be the case that, because of exceptional circumstances, the applicability of the rule does not count as a contributory reason to apply the rule. This possibility is studied in section 9.1. Secondly, it may be the case that, although the applicability of the rule counts as a contributory reason for application, this reason is outweighed by one or more reasons against application. This possibility will be explored in section 9.2.

9.1 Exceptions in the shape of undercutting

So far, we have said that the applicability of a rule to a case is a contributory reason for its application to that case. Sometimes, however, it turns out that this reason for applying the rule is exceptionally not a reason at all. Why, however, should we make such an exception to the general rule that applicability is a contributory reason for application?

In section 6, we identified one possible reason to do so, namely that a rule-exception construction was used by the maker of the rule in order to create a division in the burden of proof. The party in a dispute which wants the rule to be applied has the burden of proving that the rule conditions are satisfied; the party which does not want the rule to apply has the burden of proving that the exception-creating rule applies. When the maker of the rules has chosen this mechanism for distributing the burden of proof, and if it has been proven that the exception-generating rule applies, there is no need any more to balance the applicability of the main rule against the ground for the exception. This balance was already made by the creator of the rules and normally this decision should be respected.

Another possibility is that the application of the rule would be against the rule's purpose in this case. An example by Fuller[33] illustrates this point: there is a rule that forbids sleeping in railway stations, which has as its purpose to keep tramps from occupying the station as a place to spend the night. An old lady who wants to meet a friend at the station dozes off when the evening train turns out to be delayed. If the prohibition were applied to this old lady, this would arguably not be encompassed by the purpose of the rule. One might argue that because the case of the old lady is not caught by the purpose of the rule, the fact that the rule is technically applicable to her case is irrelevant and therefore loses its function as a contributory reason for application. If this argument is made, we are not weighing reasons for applying the rule (applicability) against reasons against applying the rule. Instead, we are saying that there is no reason to apply the rule at all.[34]

When we have a reason or reasons why a fact, such as the applicability of a rule, that would normally count as a reason should exceptionally not count as a reason after all, we speak of 'undercutting defeaters' in epistemology[35] or of 'exclusionary reasons' in cases of reasons for action.[36] It is important to note, however, that undercutting defeaters are not only relevant in

[32] In legal practice, exceptions to rules are often avoided by interpreting the need for an exception away. Sections 10 and 11 discuss this technique and its limitations.

[33] Lon L Fuller, 'Positivism and Fidelity to Law: A Reply to Professor Hart' (1958) 71 Harvard Law Review 630.

[34] We will see in the following section, however, that the same example can be construed differently.

[35] See John L Pollock and Joseph Cruz, *Contemporary Theories of Knowledge* (Rowman & Littlefield 1999) 196 ff. These undercutting defeaters are also discussed in Henry Prakken, *Logical Tools for Modelling Legal Argument. A Study of Defeasible Reasoning in Law* (Kluwer 1997) 102–103; and Giovanni Sartor, *Legal Reasoning. A Treatise of Legal Philosophy and General Jurisprudence* (Springer 2005) 682–85.

[36] Raz, *Practical Reason and Norms* (n 11) 35–48.

connection with reasons to believe (Pollock and Cruz) or reasons for action (Raz); they are relevant for all reasons.

9.2 Exceptions in the shape of rebuttal

As we have mentioned, if a rule is applicable to a case, this is usually a contributory reason to apply the rule to this case. However, a contributory reason is not as such decisive. If there are contributory reasons against applying the rule as well, then the reasons for and against application must be balanced. If the balance favours the con-reasons, the rule does not apply. Since the rule was, *ex hypothesi*, applicable, the result would be non-application of an applicable rule and therefore an exception to the rule.

Because application of a rule leads to the facts that the rule attaches to the case to which it is applied, reasons against applying a rule are usually reasons why the attached facts are undesirable. They may be undesirable for reasons which have nothing to do with law, as when, because of exceptional circumstances, the application of a rule about free trade leads to a decrease rather than an increase of welfare. They may also be undesirable because the consequences of one applicable rule conflict with the consequences of another rule which is applicable too, as we saw in section 7. And, finally, they may be undesirable because the actual consequences would violate the rule's purpose.[37]

This brings us back to the example of the old lady who falls asleep at the train station. While the argument can be made, as we did in the previous section, that the irrelevance of the rule's purpose negates the function of applicability as a contributory reason for application, a different interpretation is equally possible.[38] On an alternate account, we can still consider applicability of the rule a contributory reason for its application to the case of the old lady, while we consider the irrelevance or even violation of purpose a reason against application. If, in balancing the two, the reason against application wins out, we make an exception to the rule in the case of the old lady.

If application of a rule to a particular case leads to undesirable consequences, this is a reason against the application of the rule to that case. This reason still needs to be balanced against the applicability of the rule as reason for application. Usually, the balancing of these reasons is conceptualized as the determination of which rule prevails over the other rule. The reason based on the prevailing rule outweighs the reason based on the other rule. Several contributory reasons can be—and in fact are—recognized in this connection:[39] one option is that the rule that better fits in the overall legal system prevails over the less fitting rule (*coherence*). Another option is that the rule that was made by the 'higher' authority prevails over the rule made by the 'lower' authority (*lex superior*). Equally, the more specific rule could prevail over the more general rule (*lex specialis*), or the more recent rule over the older one (*lex posterior*).[40]

[37] This distinction between three categories, which harkens back to section 4, does not claim that the three categories are mutually exclusive.

[38] This also shows that logic and legal theory can be of great help in classifying possibilities, but that it depends on substantive arguments or reasons which choices should be made. We briefly talk about the role of legal theory in this context in section 11.

[39] The following is a non-exhaustive list.

[40] Taking the *lex posterior* rule even one step further is the tool of implied repeal, whereby it is presumed that if the later rule conflicts with the earlier rule, the later rule not only prevails, but the earlier rule is in fact repealed. However, if one of the 'conflicting' rules counts as repealed, there is no real conflict, since the repealed rule does not exist anymore and can for that reason not be applicable.

There is much more to be said about what should become the outcome of this operation of balancing competing rules, and in particular about the authority of law in this connection,[41] but this is not the place to go into the details of these substantive reasons. We will confine ourselves to the logical aspects of these so-called 'rebutting defeaters'.[42] They are as follows. If a rule applies to a case, its consequences are attached to the case. If these consequences are for some reason undesirable, the same reason is also a reason why the rule should not be applied. This reason must be balanced against the applicability of the rule as reason for application, and depending on the outcome of this balancing, it may be the case that the rule should not be applied. If the rule does not apply, even though it is applicable, there is an exception to the rule.

Let us use the example of the old lady in the railway station (in its second construal) again to clarify this. Since the old lady was not allowed to sleep in the station, a rule prescribes the manager of the station to send her away. If it is not desirable that the old lady will be sent away, it is also not desirable that the rule, which prescribes to send her away, is applied. This undesirability is a reason not to apply the rule, and this reason should be balanced against the applicability of the rule as a reason for application. If the result of this balancing operation is that the rule should not be applied, an exception is made to the rule.

9.3 Two observations concerning exceptions

We would like to make two observations in connection with exceptions to rules. The first concerns the difference between exceptions based on undercutting defeaters and exceptions based on rebutting defeaters. In the former situation, there are no reasons for applying the rule, because applicability exceptionally does not count as a reason for application. In the latter situation, there is at least one reason for applying the rule, the rule's applicability, but this reason is outweighed by reasons against application, typically reasons involving the undesirability of the rule conclusion.

The second observation concerns the role of exceptions in relation to the non-application of a rule. That there is an exception to a rule is, in the terminology proposed here, not a reason against the application of the rule, but a conclusion based on the premise that the rule is applicable and that the rule does not apply. There must be a reason why the rule does not apply, and this can be an undercutting defeater or a rebutting defeater. However, neither one kind of defeater *is* the exception to the rule. It is at best what brings about the exception to the rule. So we would not call the fact that causes an exception to a rule an exception, and neither would we call the rule which makes this fact into a defeater an exception. In our terminology, an exception to a rule is never itself a rule.

An example may clarify this point. (See Table 2.1.)

In this example, the rule of Article 2 does not apply even though it is applicable, which means that there is an exception to that rule. This exception was brought about by the self-defence of the state, which in turn derived its legal relevance from the rule of Article 21. However, neither the self-defence nor the rule of Article 21 *is* the exception to the rule of Article 2. They both contributed in their own way to that exception, but neither one of them

[41] See e.g. Frederick Schauer, *Playing by the Rules: A Philosophical Examination of Rule-Based Decision-Making in Law and in Life* (Clarendon Press 1991) 38–111.

[42] Pollock and Cruz, *Contemporary Theories of Knowledge* (n 35) 196.

Table 2.1 Exceptions and the Burden of Proof

<table>
<tr><th>Substance</th><th>Effect</th></tr>
<tr><td>According to Article 2 ARSIWA, there is an internationally wrongful act if the act constitutes the breach of an international obligation.</td><td rowspan="2">Article 2 ARSIWA is applicable.</td></tr>
<tr><td>In case X, State A acted in a way that breached an international obligation.</td></tr>
<tr><td>According to Article 21 ARSIWA, the wrongfulness of an act of a state is precluded if the act constitutes a lawful measure of self-defence taken in conformity with the UN Charter.</td><td rowspan="2">Article 21 ARSIWA is applicable.</td></tr>
<tr><td>State A acted in self-defence.</td></tr>
<tr><td rowspan="3">State A's act is not internationally wrongful.</td><td>Due to Article 21, the applicability of Article 2 does not count as a reason for application of that rule (undercutting defeater).</td></tr>
<tr><td>Article 2 is not applied despite its applicability.</td></tr>
<tr><td>The facts that Article 2 is applicable, but nevertheless not applied, together mean that an exception is made to (the rule of) this article.</td></tr>
</table>

should be identified with it. The exception is the combination of the facts that the rule is applicable and nevertheless not applied.

10 Derived Rules

If an exception to a rule is made—be it for reasons undercutting the application of the rule or for reasons rebutting it—some cases or persons are excluded from the application of the rule. The same effect can be brought about by means of scope conditions or 'negative' rule conditions. The ordinary conditions of Article 10 of the ECHR (freedom of expression), for instance, contain such 'negative conditions', since they explicitly exclude amongst others the licensing of broadcasting from the protection of this article. It is also possible to 'read' such negative rule conditions into the rule by means of interpretation, as we will see later in the discussion of Article 2(4) of the UN Charter.

When we ask which cases are governed by rules of international law, there are at least three kinds of reasons why some cases are not governed by particular rules, and they are negative rule conditions, scope conditions, and exceptions. How can exceptions be distinguished from ordinary negative rule conditions?[43] The answer is provided in this and the following section, and the burden of proof plays a central role in it.

The idea that legal rules are open to exceptions is somewhat controversial. This has to do with a certain ambiguity in the notion of a legal rule. In section 3.1, we talked about the

[43] To withhold this contribution from becoming too lengthy, we ignore scope conditions from here on.

distinction between rules and rule formulations. A legal rule may be seen as something that can be found in a legal source, such as a treaty, legislation, international custom, or case law. It may also be seen as a general connection between operative legal facts and legal consequences. The latter is the understanding of 'legal rules' with which we operate here. A simple example may again illustrate that these two understandings are not identical.

According to Article 2(4) of the UN Charter, the use of force is prohibited. Article 42 of the Charter holds that the UNSC may authorize military intervention, in which case it is deemed to be permitted. These two rules seem to conflict, and since the second rule is a *lex specialis* with regard to the rule that the use of force is prohibited, it would normally prevail over it. Application of the second rule then makes an exception to the first.

However, it comes naturally to state that there is just one rule, namely that the use of force is prohibited unless authorized by the UNSC. We can arrive at this rule by 'interpreting' Articles 2(4) and 42 in combination. We will call this a 'derived rule'. For this derived rule, there is no need to make an exception. In fact, it has the absence of the exceptional circumstance as one of its conditions, and hence the prohibition would not be applicable if the UNSC has authorized the use of force. Since exceptions are made when an applicable rule is not applied, no exception would be necessary—or even possible—in case of authorized use of force.

Let us have a closer look at this phenomenon of derived rules.[44] If a rule is applicable to a case this normally means that the rule is applied to that case and attaches its legal consequences to it. This is so normal that the logic of rule application seems to be nothing else than an ordinary syllogistic argument.[45] The facts of a case are subsumed under a general rule, and the conclusion that describes the legal consequences of the case follows deductively. This deductive application of rules seems so natural that it requires explanation that exceptions to rules are possible. If a rule seemingly has an exception, why not say that the rule was not formulated properly, and that it actually has an additional condition namely that the exceptional circumstances are absent?

The insight that rules can have exceptions can be reconciled with the impression that rules can be applied in deductive arguments by means of so-called 'case-legal consequence pairs' (CLCPs).[46] CLCPs describe the effects of rules such as the prohibition of the use of force and the permission of military action when authorized by the UNSC. The two inconsistent rules are combined into a single 'rule' that leads to a single consistent result. We use quotation marks here to indicate that this 'rule' differs from the two rules that were used to construct it. Both the rule prohibiting the use of force and the rule permitting it in cases of UNSC authorization are based on an official legal source, in this case the UN Charter. The derived 'rule', however, cannot be traced back directly to such a source, but is the result of combining the two original rules in light of their apparent purposes, thereby creating a CLCP.

It is possible to characterize a legal system as defined by an exhaustive set of such CLCPs: for every kind of case that has legal consequences, there exists a CLCP that gives the characteristics of the kind of case and the legal consequences attached to it. These CLCPs are

[44] The question whether it is possible to derive rules (or 'norms', which is the more frequently used term) from other rules is highly debated. For an overview see Pablo E Navarro and Jorge L Rodriguez, *Deontic Logic and Legal Systems* (Cambridge University Press 2014) ch 2.

[45] Robert Alexy, *Theorie der juristischen Argumentation. Die Theorie des rationalen Diskurses als Theorie der juristischen Begründung* (Suhrkamp 1983) 273–83; Neil MacCormick, *Legal Reasoning and Legal Theory* (Clarendon Press 1994) 19–53

[46] Hage, *Studies in Legal Logic* (n 4) 27. This idea of CLCPs was inspired by the theory of Alchourrón and Bulygin about the Universe of Cases. See Carlos Alchourrón and Eugenio Bulygin, *Normative Systems* (Springer 1971) 24–30.

the outcome of the original rules (including rights and legal principles or incorporated or referred rules) of the system, interpretation and solutions of potential rule conflicts by means of prevalence (such as *lex superior*), or any other technique the system in question employs to resolve rule conflicts.

The CLCPs are constructed in such a way that no particular case can fall under two different generic cases to which incompatible consequences are attached. For example, there will be a case for 'military action without Security Council authorization' and one for 'military action with Security Council authorization', but not one for military action in general, because the latter might give different legal consequences in concrete cases of military actions with and without UNSC authorization. Understanding a legal system as an exhaustive set of CLCPs, it is not possible that a case has inconsistent legal consequences. Imminent inconsistencies are filtered out in the step from the original (conflicting!) rules to the CLCP. Moreover, there are no exceptions to CLCPs. If there seems to be an exception, this means that the CLCP was formulated too broadly: there should be two different CLCPs, one for the normal cases and one for the exceptional cases.

If a legal system is interpreted as an exhaustive set of CLCPs, exceptions to rules only play a role in this step from the original rules based on legal sources to the derived 'rules'—the CLCPs—that define the outcome of all the interacting original rules. It is this step that cannot be handled well by means of deductive logic. When we discuss exceptions to rules, we are not necessarily talking about the immediate application of rules to cases; we may also be talking about the construction of CLCPs which can in turn be used for legal justification is a deductively valid manner. The derivation of the legal consequences of a case by applying the relevant CLCP to that case can be purely deductive, because all exceptions have already been filtered out in constructing the CLCP.[47]

11 Burden of Proof

As we have seen in section 10, it is theoretically possible to maintain the syllogistic form of legal argument and to remove exceptions entirely from a legal system by viewing a legal system as an exhaustive set of CLCPs. However, in this section we argue that, while theoretically possible, this view neglects an important function of exceptions, which is connected to the burden of proof.

In order to understand this function, we must replace our understanding of legal arguments as ordinary syllogisms with a view of the legal system as a dialogic practice.[48] Imagine a dialogue between two parties: the one party, the proponent, wants to establish a particular legal consequence for a case and to do so it invokes a legal rule and wants it to apply. The other party, the opponent, does not want that consequence and therefore does not want the rule to be applied. Both proponent and opponent can adduce reasons: the proponent reasons why the rule should be applied, the opponent reasons why the rule should not be applied. For instance, the proponent should adduce that the rule conditions are satisfied by the case to which he wants the rule to apply. The opponent might adduce reasons why the rule

[47] Notice that we merely discuss logic here. In practice it is not possible to construct a complete set of CLCPs for a legal domain, or even a complete legal system.

[48] An overview of this 'dialogical' approach to logic can be found in Else M Barth and Erik C Krabbe, *From Axiom to Dialogue: A Philosophical Study of Logics and Argumentation* (Walter de Gruyter 1982). See also Hage, *Studies in Legal Logic* (n 4) 227–64.

should nevertheless not be applied and which would lead to an exception if they outweigh the reasons adduced by the proponent.

If all reasons for and against application of the rule have been adduced, there are three possibilities:

1. the reasons for application outweigh the reasons against application;
2. the reasons against application outweigh the reasons for application;
3. the reasons are, at least for the purpose of decision making, in balance; there is a draw.

In the first case, the rule should be applied and its consequences are attached to the case as the proponent would want. In the second case, the rule should not be applied and its consequences are not attached to the case as the opponent would want. But what to do with the third case, when the reasons are in balance? Here is where the burden of proof comes in. The third case should either lead to an outcome that favours the proponent, or to an outcome that favours the opponent. In the former case we say that the burden of proof lies with the opponent, because if the opponent does not want the rule to apply, he must make sure that the balance of reasons does not end in a draw. In the latter case we say that the burden of proof lies with the proponent, because then the proponent has an interest in avoiding a draw in the balance of reasons.

The burden of proof translates into the burden of production, with which the burden of proof is easily confused.[49] If the balance of the reasons that have been adopted at a certain moment during a legal dialogue would lead for an outcome that favours the proponent, it is up to the opponent to produce more reasons.[50] At that moment, the opponent has the burden of production. It is possible that the opponent succeeds in doing so, and then the burden of production shifts to the proponent. The process of the production of more reasons, with a shift in the burden of production as result, may continue for some time, and the burden of production may shift several times during a dialogue. However, it is the situation at the end of the dialogue, and in particular which side in the dialogue benefits from a draw, which determines who has the burden of proof. The burden of proof never shifts, but it determines, together with the state of the dialogue, which party has at a certain moment the burden of production.

This connection between exceptions and the burden of production (and ultimately of proof) cannot be accounted for if we abolish exceptions by viewing the legal system as an exhaustive set of CLCPs. To illustrate further the view of a legal system as dialogic and to show how dialogues can be used to model legal reasoning and the operation of exceptions, we will consider an example. Our example will feature State O and State V. State O breaches an international obligation, and State V, which suffered damage as result, wants reparations from State O.

[49] We took the distinction between the burden of proof and the burden of production from the contribution of Joost Pauwelyn to this volume.

[50] Actually, there are more possibilities to make the burden of production shift, including showing that the seeming reasons adduced by the other party cannot withstand criticism. However, this is not the place to discuss these possibilities.

11.1 Step 1: straightforward rule application

A party who wants a rule to apply must prove that the normal conditions of the rule are satisfied.[51] Given the rule of Article 31 of the ARSIWA, State V must prove that State O committed an internationally wrongful act.[52] Given the rule of Article 2 of the ARSIWA, State V must therefore prove that State O conducted itself in a way that was either an act or omission, conduct that can be attributed to State O, and that breached an international obligation of State O. We ignore the attribution aspect, to find that, according to the rule of Article 12 of the ARSIWA, concerning breach of obligations, State V has to prove that the act of State O was not in conformity with an international obligation of State O.

We see a chain of rules, where the conclusion of the one rule means that some condition of another rule is satisfied, and the chain ends with an obligation to repair for State O. State V must prove that the conditions of all these rules are satisfied, and can sometimes fulfil this burden by justifying the application of another rule in the chain.

11.2 Step 2: preclusion

Suppose that State V in Example 1 has proven that State O breached an international obligation and that this can be attributed to State O. Normally, this means that the rule of Article 2 of the ARSIWA is applicable and that would be a reason to apply that rule with the consequence that the conduct of State O counts as a wrongful act. However, State O can block the step from the applicability of the rule to its application by invoking the rule of Article 21 of the ARSIWA. To do so it must prove that it acted in self-defence, that therefore the rule of Article 21 of the ARSIWA is applicable, that therefore this rule applies, and that that the wrongfulness of what State O did is precluded. If State O succeeds in doing so, the rule of Article 2 is applicable, but does not apply, and there is an exception to this rule.

Note that State V has the burden of proof with regard to the question of whether State O must repair the damage, but that State O has the burden of proof for the presence of self-defence. If State V would have had the burden of proving that there was no self-defence, the absence of self-defence would have been a negative condition of the rule of Article 2. Apparently, the burden of proof is relative to the issue at stake. State V bears the burden of proof regarding the obligation to make reparations, while State O bears the burden of proof regarding self-defence.

Because there are two burdens of proof, for two issues, there is no shift in the burden of proof. However, there is a shift in the burden of production, because State O does not have to do anything until State V proves that State O breached an international obligation. Only when State V succeeds does the burden of production shift to State O, which must prove self-defence.

[51] In these examples we will ignore the possibility of analogous rule application, and also the role of scope conditions.

[52] We will assume, for the sake of exposition, that the validity of the rule does not have to be proven, because the court knows the law (*ius curia novit*). Strictly speaking this introduces a third party (the court) into the dialogue, but, again for the sake of exposition, we ignore this complication.

11.3 The role of legal theory

Whether the applicability of Article 21 of the ARSIWA makes for an exception, with a shift in the burden of production, or whether this article combines with Article 2 (and some other articles) as sources for a complicated rule that has some negative conditions, is something that must be established by interpretation of the ARSIWA. There is no simple test for it, and the difference between negative rule conditions and exceptions is therefore a matter of interpretation too. The only thing that legal theory has to offer in this connection is that, if there is no shift in the burden of production, we have reason to regard the relevant article as a negative rule condition, and that if there is such a shift, we have reason to regard it as an exception.[53]

12 Conclusion

Exceptions to rules play an important role in law, and in particular in international law. A proper understanding of exceptions is therefore of crucial importance for legal practice, legal doctrine, and legal theory. The aim of this chapter is to contribute to this understanding; it is not to describe the law or the present usage with regard to rules and exceptions.

As background for the development of a theory about exceptions to rules, sections 3 and 4 have gone into some detail concerning rules, rule formulations, legal sources, reasons, and their logic. In section 5, the distinction between the applicability and the application of a rule was elaborated. A rule is applicable to a case if the rule is valid, and if its ordinary and scope conditions are satisfied by the case. If a rule is applied to a case, the rule attaches its legal consequences to the facts of the case. Normally the applicability of a rule to a case is a contributory reason why the rule should be applied to the case. An exception to a rule in a case is defined as the situation in which a rule is applicable to, but nevertheless not applied to the case.

In section 6, two main grounds for making an exception to a rule were identified. First, the maker of the rule may use the rule-exception construction to create a division in the burden of proof. As argued in section 9, this leads to a so-called undercutting defeater. Secondly, there may be reasons why the legal consequences of the rule in the case are undesirable. This leads to a reason against applying the rule, which needs to be balanced to the applicability of the rule as reason for application. In this situation we speak of rebutting defeaters (see section 9.2).

An important reason why it is undesirable to apply a rule to a case is that application would generate a conflict with another applicable rule. Section 8 discussed a number of tools and techniques that can be used to avoid rule conflicts and which would in that way make exceptions superfluous.

Finally, the question may be raised of whether legal rules really have exceptions. Is it not the case that if a rule is well-formulated, it mentions all 'exceptions' as negative rule conditions? Such a well-formulated 'derived' rule can then be applied deductively to cases that satisfy the rule conditions. In sections 10 and 11, we discussed this possibility and showed that this use of derived rules blocks the possibility of modelling the division of burden of proof which is implicitly given with the rule exception model.

53 Again, we ignore possible third ways, such as scope conditions.

3

Rules and Exceptions, in Law and Elsewhere

Giovanni Sartor

> Every law has a presumption, and applies in any given case, unless it is proved that some impediment or contradiction has emerged, which would generate an exception extracted from another law. But in that case the burden of proof is transferred to the person who adduces the exception.[1]

1 Introduction: Systems of Rules

The computer scientist and theorist of complexity John Holland, who was a pioneer in what became known as evolutionary algorithms, argued that complex systems should be characterized 'in terms of a set of signal-processing rules called *classifier rules*'.[2] Each of such rules represents a mechanism which 'accepts certain signals as inputs (specified by the *condition* part of the rule) and then processes the signals to produce outgoing signals (the *action* part of the rule)'. A rule's outcome may be directed outside of the system or may rather have an impact on the activation of other rules of the system, for example, provide inputs than can trigger their activation, or that could block such activation.

This perspective can be applied at different levels of abstraction, in different domains. For instance, rule mechanisms at the cellular level define chemical interactions between proteins, as induced by catalytic mechanisms or inhibited by anti-catalytic ones. At the DNA-RNA level, rule mechanisms are provided by genes (and parts of them), which accept bases meeting the gene's receptors and deliver corresponding proteins. A gene may be regulated by other genes, which send signals that repress (turn off) or induce (turn on) the functioning of the gene rules at issue. Similarly, the working of the human brain at the neurone level can be viewed as a rule mechanism: each neurone receives electric signals through its input filaments (dendrites), which may be excitatory or inhibitory. When the neurone's threshold is reached, an electric signal is sent out through the neurone's outcome filament (axon), to stimulate or repress linked neurones in the nervous system, or to activate other cells (e.g. muscles) outside this system. The behaviour of all animals is largely governed by a system of reflex rules, namely, reactions to input stimuli that include the feeling of heat or cold, the sight, smell, or taste of food, the perception of incoming dangers, etc. Such reflexes can be innate or learned through experience, that is, through conditioning and reinforcement. In some animals, reflexes are integrated with deliberative processes and means-end reasoning, but still reflexes explain a large part of animal behaviour.

[1] GottfriedW Leibniz, 'De legum interpretatione, rationibus, applicatione, systemate' in *Sämtliche Briefe und Werke: Reihe VI, Philosophische Schriften, Band 4* (Akademie-Verlag 1999) 2782–91 (my translation).
[2] John Holland, *Signals and Boundaries Building Blocks for Complex Adaptive Systems* (MIT 2012) 28.

Giovanni Sartor, *Rules and Exceptions, in Law and Elsewhere* In: *Exceptions in International Law*. Edited by: Lorand Bartels and Federica Paddeu, Oxford University Press (2020). © Lorand Bartels and Federica Paddeu.
DOI: 10.1093/oso/9780198789321.003.0003

In computer systems, rules-based architectures are ubiquitous. Procedural programming languages consist of sequences of conditional imperatives, instructing the computer on what it should do under various circumstances. Logic programs consist also of rules specifying inference patterns. The rule-like structure of human brains is replicated in artificial neural network, made up of nodes which are activated by input signals, through weighed connections, and deliver corresponding output signals. In cellular automata, rules determine how the cells in the automaton are going to change over time: given a certain configuration of a cell and the neighbouring cells (e.g. which ones are full or empty), the subsequent state of that cell is determined (e.g. a rule may establish that if a cell is full and three of its neighbouring cells are full, then in the following step the cell will be empty). In classifier systems, sets of rules compete and evolve to determine the system's behaviour. In systems of business rules, the interaction of rules provides for models of, and constraints over, the functioning of organizations, etc.

I will argue that social and legal rules can also be viewed as conditioned triggers, meant to provide certain output signals when their input conditions are met. By analysing the structure, or topology, of sets of such triggers, and the triggering patterns that govern them, we will be able to understand the functioning of rule-systems in the law. In particular, we will be able to understand the aspects of such systems that pertain to the interaction of rules and exceptions.

In the following sections, I shall consider different patterns of rules, presenting an increasingly complex structure, and corresponding algorithms to apply such rules, namely to determine what outcomes they provide given certain sets of input signals. I shall distinguish different patterns for exceptions: inhibitory links in a rule, preventing the derivation of the rule's conclusion; inhibitory rules, blocking the application of a separate rule; prevailing contrary rules, preventing incompatible outcomes of weaker rules.

2 Monolayered and Monovalent Rule Systems

The simplest topology of rule systems is the monolayered and monovalent type: the rule system consists of one level of rules, each rule linking one output node to one or more excitatory bundles of input nodes.

Each rule, denoted by a small square containing the rule name (r1, …, rn), links one or more sets of input bundles, each denoted by a small circle, to one or more output node, denoted by a rectangle. We assume that input and output nodes are disjoint. Each bundle performs an excitatory function, namely it may induce the rule to trigger, as indicated by the + sign. Each bundle collects one of more input nodes, each denoted by rounded rectangles. Such nodes are linked to corresponding nodes in the input stream, namely the information from the outside world that is accessible to the system (e.g. the input provided by perception in humans, by incoming molecules in biological systems, by the evidence provided by the party in the legal case, etc).

Let us now consider the functioning of the rule system. Each node in the system can be in one of two positions, namely, IN (active) or OUT (non-active). In the graphs, IN nodes, rules and bundles have a thick continuous border, while OUT nodes, rules and bundles have a dashed thin border. For instance, in Figure 3.1 nodes I1 and I2 are IN, while node I3 is OUT.

The nodes that are IN perform their function, namely to contribute to triggering a rule. When all input nodes to an input bundle to a rule are IN, the input bundle is also in IN. Consequently, the rule is IN and so is its output node. For instance, in Figure 3.1, since node

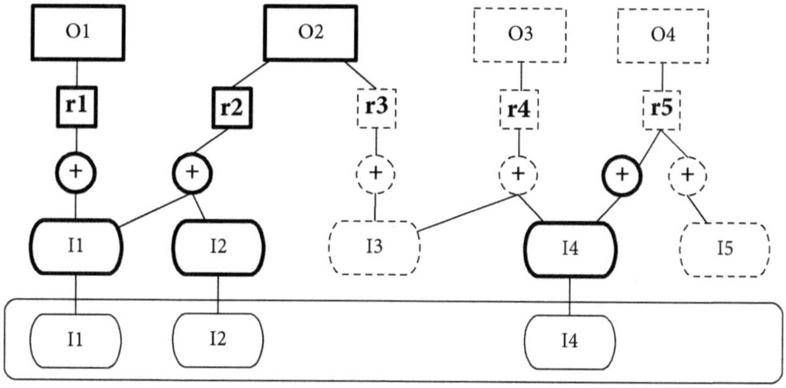

Figure 3.1 Flat and excitatory rules

I1 is IN, rule r1 is also IN, and so is its output O1. Similarly, since I1 and I2 are IN, so is rule r2, with its outcome O2. On the contrary, input node I3 is OUT, and consequently, rule r3 is also OUT, and so is its output O3. Also, input I5 is OUT and consequently rule r4 and output O4 are OUT.

Thus, the criteria for evaluating nodes can be summarized according to the following definition:

Definition 1a. Labelling algorithm (for monovalent rules)

1. A node *n* is IN if
   a. *n* is in the input stream; or
   b. *n* is the output of a rule which is IN.
2. An input bundle is IN if all its input nodes are IN.
3. A rule is IN if it has an input bundle which is IN.
4. When a node, rule, or input bundle is not IN, according to propositions 1, 2 and 3, it is OUT.

We can construct systems of legal norms having this simple topology: they consist only of rules linking normative effects—obligations, permissions, liabilities, sanctions, or other qualifications—to certain antecedent conditions. Examples of such rules can be found typically in criminal codes. Here is a rule on theft extracted from the Italian Criminal Code (Article 624), reformulated in an explicit if-then structure: 'If a person takes possession of a movable object of another, and the person has the aim of gaining profits from the object, then the person is subject to punishment of a term of imprisonment of up to three years.'

A similar pattern may be extracted from Article 31 of the 2001 Articles on Responsibility of States for Internationally Wrongful Acts (in the following Articles on Responsibility of States): 'If a State is responsible for an internationally wrongful act, and the acts causes injury, then the State is under an obligation to make full reparation for that injury.' In Figure 3.2, one can see a graphical representation of the latter norm. Note that in representing the elements (effects and antecedents) of general rules, we use variables whose name express informally the type of the entities to be covered by that variable. For instance, we abbreviate '*x* is a state, *y* is a wrongful act and *x* is responsible for *y*' into 'STATE1 is

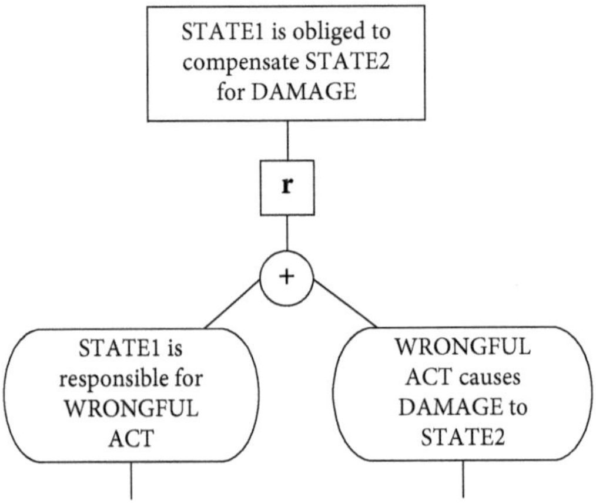

Figure 3.2 Example of an excitatory rule

responsible for WRONGFUL ACT' and treat such typed variables accordingly (variables are in upper case).[3]

A general rule fires when its condition matches specific input facts, which are 'subsumed' under the rule. In our representation, this is indicated by substituting the variables in the rule with the name referring to a specific object, event, or individual, which is assumed to match the type of the variable. We use the expression *v*=*C* to denote the substitution of variable *v* with constant name *C*.

For example, let us consider the famous 1985 case concerning the ship *Rainbow Warrior*. The ship was a Greenpeace vessel which was protesting against French nuclear testing in the Moruroa Atoll. When moored in Auckland, it was bombed by French agents. New Zealand sought compensation for the costs incurred in clearing the port of Auckland, the police investigation, and subsequent criminal trial of the French agents, as well as for the violation of its sovereignty. Compensation was awarded on this basis by the Secretary-General of the United Nations who, acting as binding mediator, issued a ruling in 1986.

In Figure 3.3, we represent the rule on state liability, as applied to this case, by using appropriate abbreviations. For instance, the statement 'STATE1=FR is responsible for WRONGFUL ACT: SinkingRW' asserts that France is responsible for sinking of the *Rainbow Warrior*. Similarly, the statement WRONGFUL ACT= SinkingRW causes DAMAGE= CostsRW to STATE2=NZ is an abbreviation for the statement that the wrongful act consisting in the sinking of the *Rainbow Warrior* caused the damage consisting in the costs incurred by the State of New Zealand in connection with the sinking (for our purposes it is not necessary to examine the controversial issue of the nature of these costs, or whether moral damages were also included).

Figure 3.3 shows an application of the rule above to this case. Since both antecedent conditions are in the input stream, both are satisfied. This leads to triggering the conclusion of the rule, namely France's obligation to compensate New Zealand for the damage.

[3] Various logical models are available for typed variables, such as description logic or discourse representation theory. See e.g. Daniele Nardi and Ronald J Bratman, 'An Introduction to Description Logics' in Franz Baader, Diego Calvanese, Deborah McGuinness, Daniele Nardi, and Peter Patel-Schneider (eds), *Description Logic Handbook* (2nd edn, Cambridge University Press 2007) 1–43; Hans Kamp, *From Discourse to Logic* (Kluwer 1993).

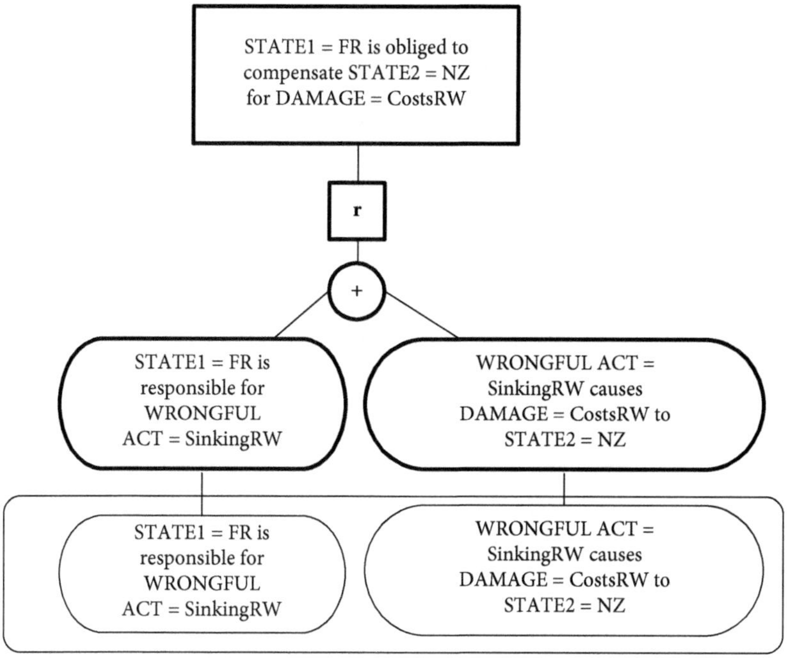

Figure 3.3 Application of an excitatory rule

3 Multilayered Monovalent Rule System

In a multilayered rule system, besides rules directly sending a message outside of the rules system, we have rules sending internal messages, namely messages that are meant to trigger other rules. This situation is represented in Figure 3.4, which illustrates different triggering patterns. For instance, while input I1 directly triggers, via rule r1, the top outcome O1, input I2 triggers outcome 05 indirectly: I2 triggers via rule r2 the intermediate outcome O2, which triggers via r6 the top outcome O5.

The algorithm for labelling the nodes in a multilayered but monovalent rule system is the same as in a flat system: a node is IN if it is the input stream or it is the output of a rule which is IN, having an input bundle which is IN, all the bundle's input nodes being IN. For example, node O1 is IN, since it is the output of rule r1, whose input bundle, including only node I1 is satisfied, I1being in the input stream. Similarly, node O5 is IN since it is the output of rule r6, whose input bundle, including only node O2 is satisfied.

Systems of legal rules usually have a multilayered structure: non-legal facts trigger legal properties or statuses, which in turn trigger obligations, permissions, and sanctions.[4] As a simple example, consider the rules in a citizenship statute that establish under what conditions one acquires citizenship. The legal status ascribed by these rules, namely citizenship, triggers further legal outcomes, namely the obligations and rights that are possessed by citizens.

As an example in international law, consider Articles 1 and 2 of the 2001 Articles on Responsibility of States, expressed in the if-then form. Article 2 states that if a conduct, that

[4] On intermediate legal concepts see the classical contribution of Alf Ross, 'Tû-Tû' (1957) 1 Scandinavian Studies in Law 139. On the logic of such concepts see also Lars Lindahl and Jan Odelstad, 'Stratification of normative systems with intermediaries' (2011) Journal of Applied Logic 113; Jaap C Hage and Dietmar von der Pfordten (eds), *Concepts in Law* (Hart Publishing 2008); and Giovanni Sartor, 'Legal concepts as inferential nodes and ontological categories' (2009) 17 Artificial Intelligence and Law 217–51.

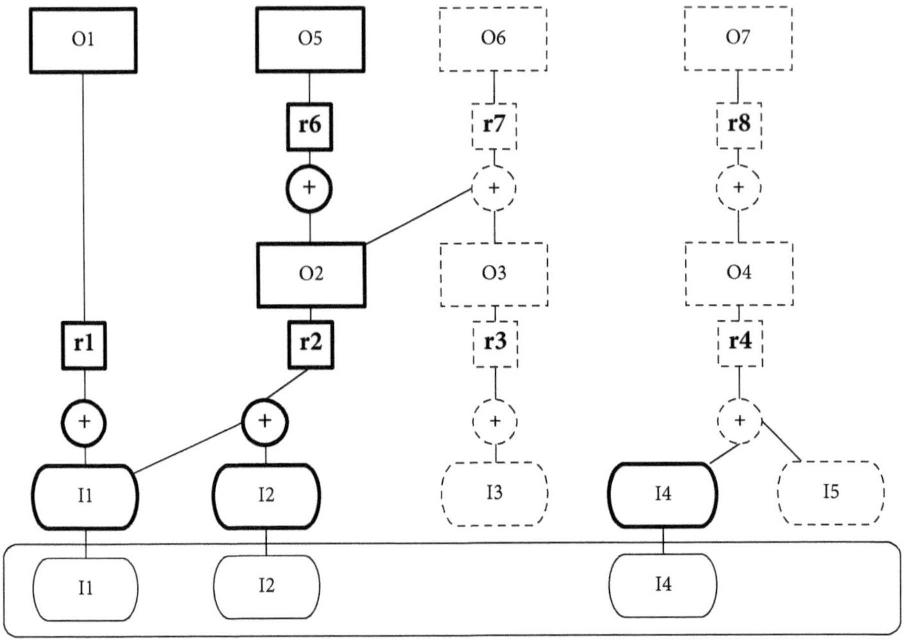

Figure 3.4 Multi-layered excitatory rules

is, an action or omission, (a) is attributable to a state, and (b) constitutes a breach of an international obligation of that state, then this conduct is an internationally wrongful act of the state. Article 1, states that if a state commits an internationally wrongful act, then that state is internationally responsible for that act. This logical structure is represented in graphical form in Figure 3.5, where the application of these rules to the *Rainbow Warrior* case is depicted.

4 Bivalent Rule Systems: Inhibitory Links

While monovalent rules systems only include excitatory links, bivalent rule systems also include inhibitory links. This is shown in Figure 3.6, where, for instance input I1 plays an excitatory function relatively to rule r1, and an inhibitory function relatively to r2.

The logic of bivalent rule systems is different from the logic of monovalent rule systems: the requirement for a rule to be IN includes both a positive condition (at least one excitatory input bundle must be IN), and a negative one (no inhibitory input bundle must be IN). Therefore, we need to change our previous Definition 1a into the following Definition 1b. (The modification concerns point 2.)

Definition 1b. Labelling algorithm (for bivalent rules)

1. A node *n* is IN if
   a. *n* is in the input stream; or
   b. *n* is the output of a rule which is IN.
2. A rule is IN if
   a. an excitatory input bundle to *r* is IN and
   b. no inhibitory input bundle to *r* is IN
3. An input bundle is IN if all its input nodes are IN.

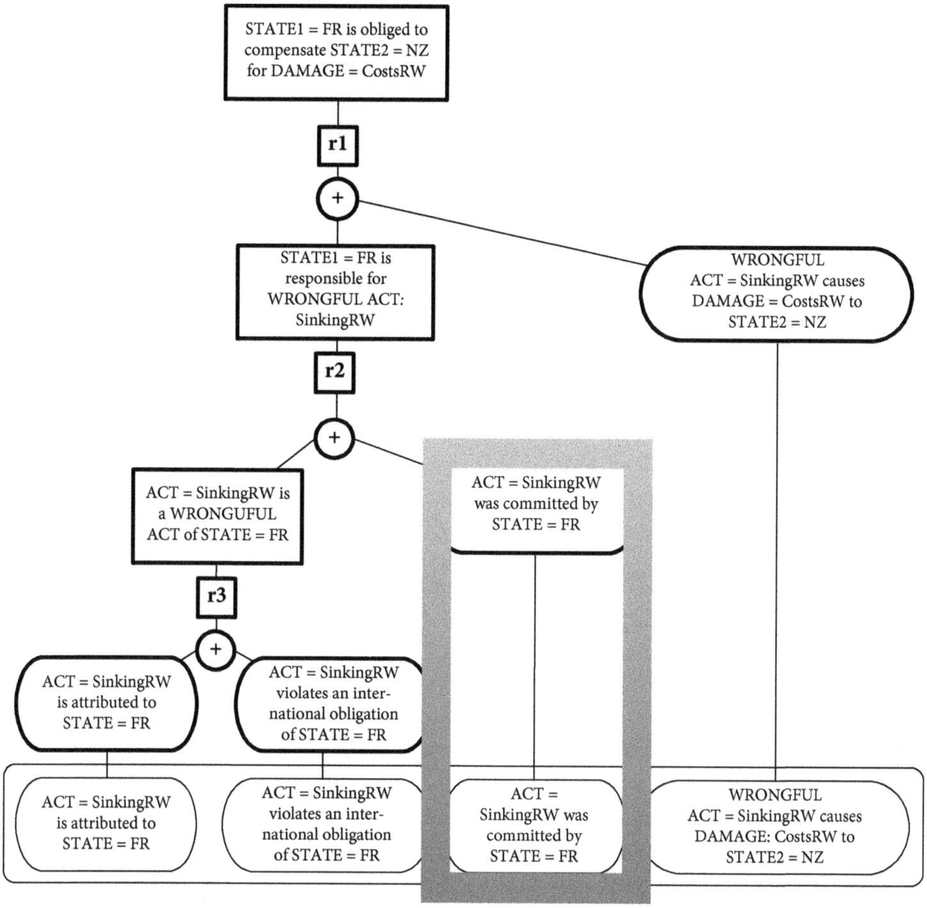

Figure 3.5 The application of a multi-layered mono-valued rule system

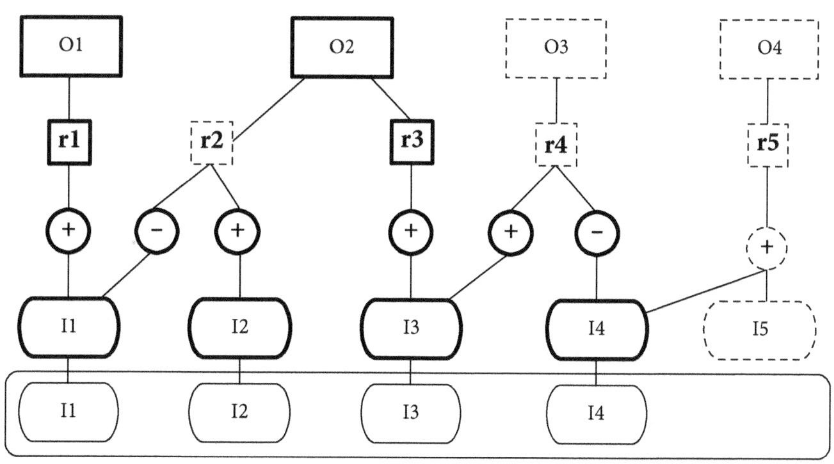

Figure 3.6 Bivalent rules

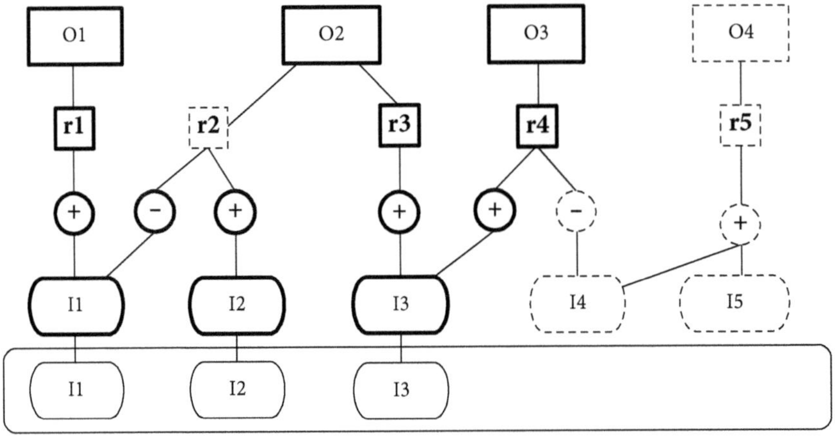

Figure 3.7 Defeasibility with bivalent rules: outcome expansion by removing an input node

For instance, in Figure 3.6 the top nodes O1 and O2 are IN. Node O2 is the outcome of rule r2, which has a positive input bundle that is satisfied, namely the bundle consisting of I2, which is IN. However, rule r2 is unable to deliver its outcome, namely, O2, since it has also a negative input bundle that is satisfied, namely the negative bundle consisting of I1. However, O2 is IN, since it is the output also of rule r3, whose input bundle is IN. On the other hand, rule r4 cannot fire, even though it has a positive input bundle (I3) which is satisfied, since it has a negative bundle that is also satisfied, namely, the bundle consisting of I4.

Bivalent rule systems provide for non-monotonicity. A rule system is monotonic when no output of the system is lost when the input is expanded. So, assume that a system *S* responds to input set Is with output set Os. If S is monotonic, when provided with an input set Is' that is larger than Is (Is ⊂ Is'), S will always respond with an output set Os' that includes Os (Os ⊆ Os'). On the contrary, if S is non-monotonic, it may possibly respond with an output set Os' that does not include all of the input set Os (it is possible that Os ⊈ Os'). In other words, by adding nodes to the input stream of a non-monotonic system, we may lose some of the outcomes that could be triggered by the smaller input stream. For instance, Figure 3.7 shows that, if we remove I4 from the input stream of Figure 3.6, we gain output O3. The reason is that, by removing I4 from the input stream, node I4 is no longer IN. Consequently, the negative input bundle to r4 is no longer satisfied, and therefore the positive input bundle (I3) can make r4 fire and deliver its output O3.

Note that inhibitory nodes play a role that is different from the role of negative excitatory nodes. Figure 3.6 shows two rules both having output O, but under different conditions. The first is triggered by I1 and is inhibited by I2; the second is triggered by the combination of I1 with the falsity of I2, denoted as ¬I2.

Let us consider eight possible input streams to the rules in Figure 3.8: {}, {I1}, {I2}, {¬ I1}, {¬ I2}, {I1, I2}, {I1, ¬I2}, {¬ I1, I2}, {¬ I1, ¬ I2}. Rule r1 is triggered by two input streams, {I1} and {I1, ¬I2}, while r2 is triggered only by {I1, ¬I2}. In other terms, I1 alone is sufficient to trigger r1 (although r1 can be inhibited by I2), while I1 alone cannot trigger r2, since ¬I2 is also needed. When neither I2 nor ¬I2 is in the input stream (the information available includes neither of them), r1 delivers O1, while r2 is silent so that O2 remains OUT. Consider also that for the working of rule r1 only detectors of positive inputs are needed. For the

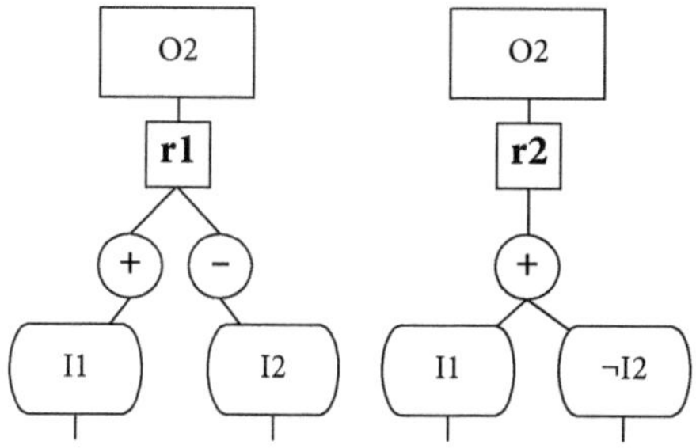

Figure 3.8 Inhibitory links versus negative rule-conditions

working of r2, detectors of negative inputs are also needed. This raises the issue of how negative inputs can be detected. Usually, detecting a negative node ¬I requires detecting a positive input that is incompatible with I.

In the language of legal sources, inhibitory links are usually expressed by the use of the locutions 'unless' or 'except that'. Here are two examples from Italian civil law. Article 1481 (Danger of revendication) states that '[t]he buyer can suspend payment of the price when he has reason to fear that the thing or part of it could be reclaimed by a third party, unless the seller provides suitable guarantees.' On the basis of this norm, the seller, by showing that he has provided suitable guarantees, may inhibit the derivation of the buyers' right to suspend payment. Similarly, Article 2051 (Damage caused by things in custody) affirms that '[a] person is liable for damage caused by things in his custody except where he shows evidence of a fortuitous case.' Here, by showing that a fortuitous case has happened, the custodian may inhibit the damage from triggering his liability.

Within international law, an example of an 'unless' can be found in Article 25 of the Articles on Responsibility:

> Necessity may not be invoked by a State as a ground for precluding the wrongfulness of an act not in conformity with an international obligation of that State unless the act: (a) is the only way for the State to safeguard an essential interest against a grave and imminent peril; and (b) does not seriously impair an essential interest of the State or States towards which the obligation exists, or of the international community as a whole.

According to this article, two alternative conditions may inhibit necessity from precluding wrongfulness: either (a) the act is not 'the only way for the State to safeguard an essential interest against a grave and imminent peril' (i.e. there are other ways to safeguard the essential interest at stake); or (b) the act does 'seriously impair an essential interest of the State or States towards which the obligation exists, or of the international community as a whole'.

An example of a rule of international law including an inhibitory link is also given by Article 3(1) of the 1980 United Nations Convention on the International Sale of Goods (CISG):[5] 'Contracts for the supply of goods to be manufactured or produced are to be considered sales unless the party who orders the goods undertakes to supply a substantial part

[5] United Nations Convention on the International Sale of Goods (CISG) (signed on 11 April 1980, entered into force on 1 January 1988) (1980) 1489 UNTS 3.

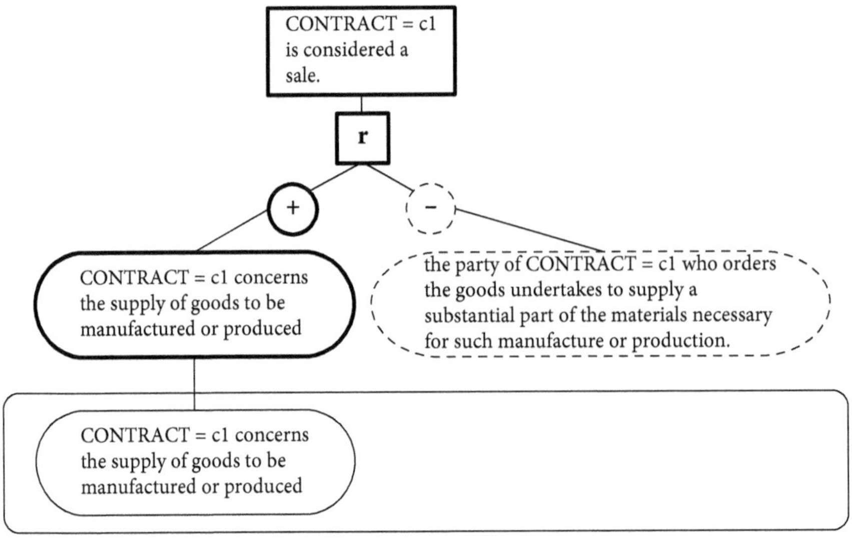

Figure 3.9 An inhibitory link in contract law

of the materials necessary for such manufacture or production.' Here is the graphical representation of the rule corresponding to this provision, as applied to a contract c1, where the input stream contains the information that the contract concerned the supply of goods to be manufactured or produced, but it contains no information on the supply of the material by the buyer. Under such conditions, as the diagram in Figure 3.9 shows, rule r delivers the conclusion that c1 is considered a sale contract.

Assume that the input stream is expanded, so that it also includes the information that the buyer has provided the materials. Under such conditions, as shown in Figure 3.10, the contract is no longer considered a sale.

In this paragraph, we have seen a first kind of exception structure, namely inhibitory links to rules. This exception structure enables exception conditions, namely the conditions that activate inhibitory links to block the linked rules from triggering. In the example of Figure 3.10, an inhibitory link connects the supply of the material to rule r. Correspondingly, the fact that in contract c1 the materials were indeed supplied is an exception condition blocking rule r.

We may also say that inhibitory bundles are defeaters of the rules to which they are attached, since whenever they are IN, they deprive the rule concerned of the ability to deliver its output. In particular, we may call them undercutters,[6] considering that they cut the link between the excitatory bundle in the rule and the rule's conclusion. In law and ethics, they are usually called exclusionary reasons,[7] meaning that they exclude the relevance of the conditions included in the excitatory bundle.

As the above examples show, negative facts, consisting in the non-realization of certain circumstances, usually do not play an excitatory role. On the contrary, their complements inhibit the derivation of the corresponding conclusion. This means that the conclusion (e.g.

[6] John L Pollock, *Cognitive Carpentry: A Blueprint for How to Build a Person* (MIT 1995) 41.

[7] Joseph Raz, *Practical Reason and Norms* (Hutchinson 1975). The distinction between contributory and exclusionary reasons is addressed in the chapter by Jaap Hage, Antonia Waltermann, and Gustavo Arosemena in this volume.

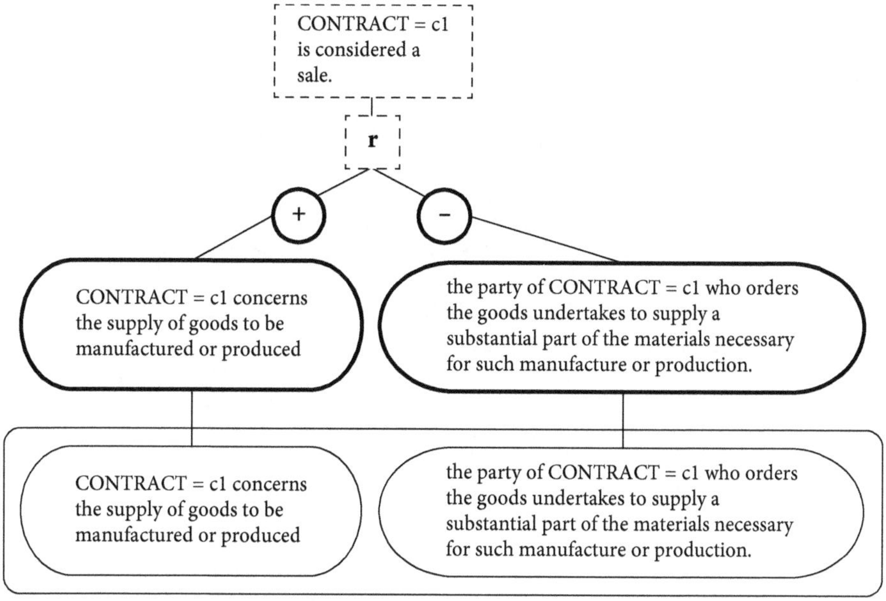

Figure 3.10 Defeat through an inhibitory link in contract law

the possibility of invoking the necessity of an act, in the example from Article 25) that is dependent on the negative fact (e.g. the absence of alternative ways to safeguard an essential interest) can be established also in the absence of evidence for that fact, as long as no evidence is provided for its complement (the availability of an alternative way to safeguard the interest). This is expressed by the traditional maxim *negativa non sunt probanda* (negative facts are not to be proved). However, there are rules whose conclusion is only triggered if negative facts are established. As an example, consider Article 23(1), according to which for an 'irresistible force' or an 'unforeseen event' to count as *force majeure*, the force or event must be 'beyond the control of the State'. To invoke *force majeure* effectively, the acting state must establish the negative fact that it had no possibility of controlling the force or event at issue.

5 Inhibitory Rules

While inhibitory links block the triggering of the rule in which they are included, inhibitory rules issue messages that are meant to block the triggering of other rules. Figure 3.11 provides an example of inhibitory rules, namely r1 and r3, which can inhibit r2 and r4, respectively. Inhibitory rules, when their input conditions are satisfied, send out the message, denoted by a triangle including a minus (−) sign, that the rule linked to the point of the triangle is not applicable.

In Figure 3.11, rule r2 is not inhibited by r1 (whose input bundle is not satisfied), while r4 is inhibited by r3. This rule pattern also exhibits non-monotonicity: should we add input I1, r1 would be triggered, and this would inhibit r2, so that also output O1 would not be produced.

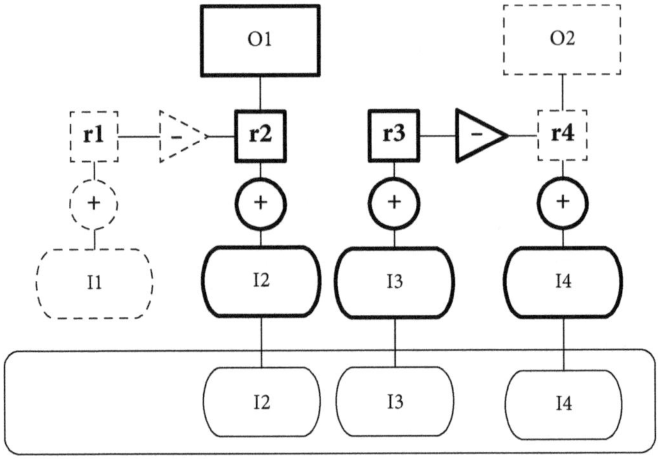

Figure 3.11 Inhibitory rules

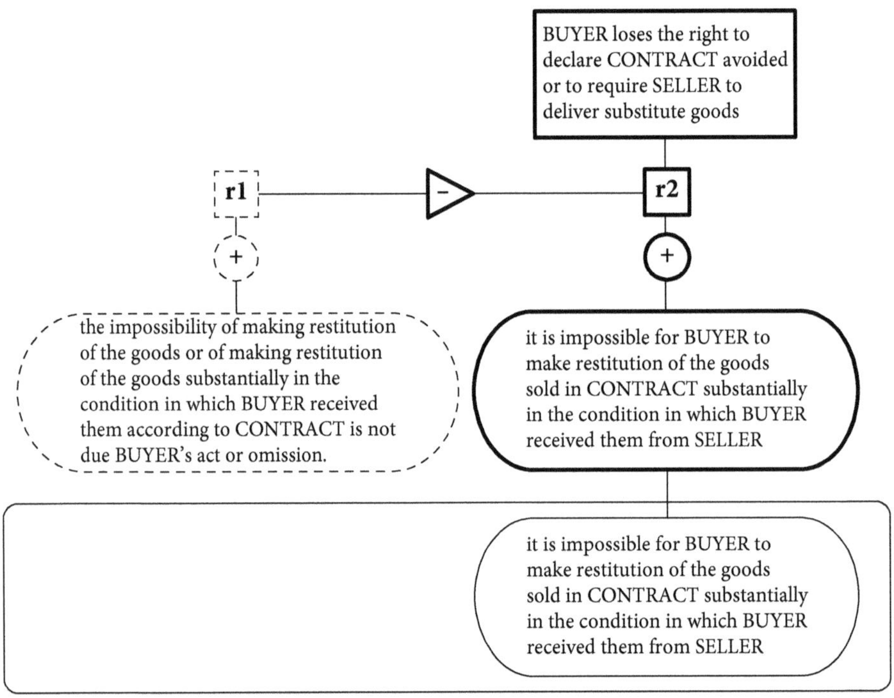

Figure 3.12 Inhibitory rule: impossibility in contract law

For addressing inhibitory rules, we need to change again point 2 in the definition of the labelling algorithm presented in section 3.2.

Definition 1c. Labelling algorithm (for bivalent and inhibitory rules)

1. A node *n* is IN if
   c. *n* is in the input stream; or
   d. *n* is the output of a rule which is IN.

2. An input bundle is IN if all its input nodes are IN.
3. A rule is IN if
   a. an excitatory input bundle to ***r*** is IN and
   b. no inhibitory input bundle to ***r*** is IN
   c. no rule inhibiting ***r*** is IN.

A legal example of explicitly inhibitory rules is provided by Article 82 of the CISG:

> (1) The buyer loses the right to declare the contract avoided or to require the seller to deliver substitute goods if it is impossible for him to make restitution of the goods substantially in the condition in which he received them.
> (2) The preceding paragraph does not apply: (a) if the impossibility of making restitution of the goods or of making restitution of the goods substantially in the condition in which the buyer received them is not due to his act or omission.

In Figure 3.12 is the graphical representation of this combination of these rules:

Note that in case the input stream also contains the information that the impossibility is not attributable to the buyer's act or omission, then the conclusion that the buyer loses its right does not hold, as shown in Figure 3.13.

Another example of explicitly inhibitory (and inhibited) rules, let us consider Article 23(2) of the Articles on Responsibility of States, according to Article 23(1), precluding wrongfulness in case of *force majeure*, which does not apply when the state invoking a situation of *force majeure* caused that situation or assumed the risk of it.

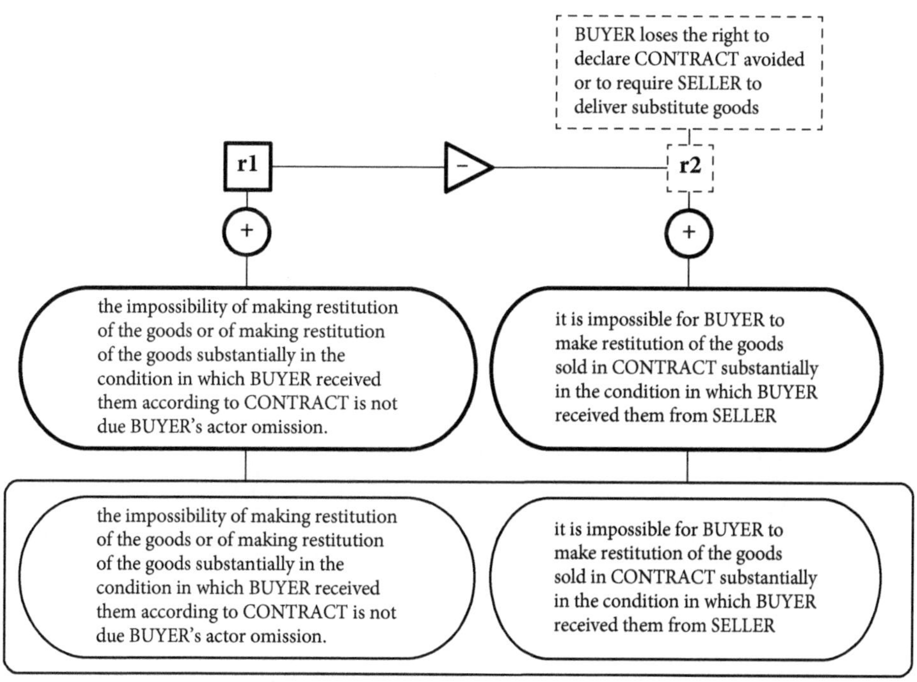

Figure 3.13 Defeat though an inhibitory rule: impossibility in contract law

Inhibitory rules also defeat the rule they attack, and they also instantiate the idea of undercutting. They cut the link between the rule's input bundles and the rule's output, in the sense that when an inhibitory rule is IN, the inhibited rule cannot deliver its output, even though appropriate input conditions are satisfied.

6 Prevailing Contrary Rules

A rule system may also include rules delivering incompatible messages, namely messages that cannot coexist in the given system. Three different situations can be distinguished: (1) only one of the conflicting rules is triggered; (2) both rules are triggered and one prevails; (3) both rules are triggered and none prevails.

All these situations are represented in Figure 3.14, where joined arrows connecting two rules indicate a conflict between two rules, that is, that they have incompatible outcomes (such outcomes cannot coexist in the system). Let us consider first the relation between r1 and r3. Let us first observe that r1 prevails over r3, according to r2. Therefore, if there were a live conflict between the output of r1 and the output of r2, r1's output, namely O1 would prevail. This would mean that O1 rather than ¬O1 should be IN. However, in the situation represented in Figure 3.14, r1's input bundle is not satisfied, while, r3's is. Therefore, there is no live conflict, only r3 is triggered, so that ¬O1 can be IN.

Figure 3.14 also shows a live conflict between r4 and r6. The two rules have incompatible outcomes, namely O2 and ¬O2, and both rules have input bundles which are satisfied, namely I4 and I6 respectively. Given that the two outputs are incompatible, they cannot be jointly delivered; the system must make a choice. The criterion for the choice is provided by rule r5, which states that r4 prevails over r6. This means that r4 successfully attacks r6, preventing it to be IN, while r6 is unable successfully to attack r4, so that r4 is IN, regardless of the incompatibility.

Let us now consider r7 and r8. These rules also provide for incompatible conclusions. However, in this case no rule provides for a priority between them. Therefore, their

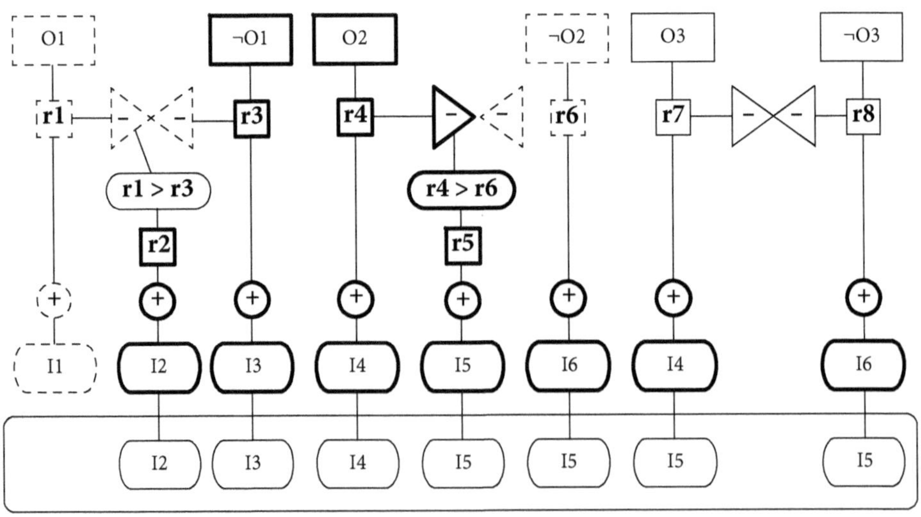

Figure 3.14 Prioritized conflicting rules

conclusions rebut each other, and none of them is IN. However, these conclusions are not fully OUT: they remain uncertain. We can say that they are both plausible, or defensible, although not justified.[8] This is indicated by a thin continuous border in our graph.

To cover these situations, we may use the notion of rebutting: a rule *r'* rebuts a rule *r* if *r'* delivers an outcome which is incompatible with the outcome of *r*, under the proviso that and *r'* is non-weaker *r*. If a *r* was, according to the rule system, stronger than *r'*, it would be able to deliver its outcome, regardless of the conflict. More exactly, we can define rebutting as follows:

Definition 2, Rebutting.
A rule *r'*, is a rebutter of rule *r* if

1. the output of *r'* is incompatible with the output of *r*, and
2. no IN-node states that *r* is stronger than *r'*.

For instance, in Figure 3.14, node ¬O1 is a rebutter of node O1, O2 is a rebutter of ¬O2, while O3 and ¬O3 are rebutters of each other. If a rebutter is IN, or it would be IN unless for the conflict at issue, then the node it attacks cannot be IN. Conflicting rules, over which a preference relation is defined, allow for rebuttals and thus for defeasibility. Assume, for instance, that the input stream of Figure 3.14 were extended so that it would also contain I1, the antecedent of rule r1. Then the input bundle of r1 would be satisfied, and its outcome O1 would be able to rebut, given the priority (for r1 over r3) established by r2, the outcome ¬O1 of r3, which would lose its IN status.

The algorithm for rule systems including conflicting prioritized rules may be defined as follows:

Definition 1d. Labelling algorithm (for bivalent, inhibitory, and conflicting rules)

1. A node *n* is IN if
   a. *n* is in the input stream; or
   b. *n* is the output of a rule which is IN.
2. An input bundle is IN if all its input nodes are IN.
3. A rule is IN if
   a. an excitatory input bundle to ***r*** is IN and
   b. no inhibitory input bundle to ***r*** is IN
   c. no rule inhibiting ***r*** is IN
   d. no rebutter of ***r*** is IN
4. When a node, rule, or input bundle is not IN, according to propositions 1, 2 and 3, it is OUT.

This definition needs to be expanded, if we admit the possibility that there are undecided conflicts between incompatible rules. To address such cases, we need to introduce the notion of a node being a *certain* or *justified* outcome, that is, being IN according to every possible assignment of IN or OUT values to the nodes in the rule system (respecting the constraints established in Definition 1d, and a node being a *possible* or *defensible* outcome when it is IN,

[8] The concept of defensible conclusions was introduced in Henry Prakken and G Sartor, 'Argument-based extended logic programming with defeasible priorities' (1997) 7 Journal of Applied Non-Classical Logics 25. In artificial intelligence, the term 'credulous' is also used to denote what is supported by reasons that are balanced, but not outweighed by reasons to the contrary.

according to some (although not necessarily all) assignments of IN and OUT to all nodes in the system. Alternatively, we can introduce the concept of a node being defensible (supported by the input, an IN node or a defensible node, and not attacked by an IN node), and characterize an IN node as one having no defensible attacker.[9]

Rule systems with prioritized conflicting outcomes can be found in several natural and artificial systems. For instance, John Holland argued that evolution tends to develop hierarchies of conflicting rules and exceptions, as a flexible approach to deal with complex situations.[10] He also argued that mental models (in humans and animals) can be based on prioritized conflicting rules:[11]

> The rules that constitute a category do not provide a definition of the category. Instead they provide a set of expectations that are taken to be true only so long as they are not contradicted by more specific information. In the absence of additional information these 'default' expectations provide the best available sketch of the current situation. Rules and rule clusters can be organized into default hierarchies, that is, hierarchies ordered by default expectations based on subordinate/superordinate relations among concepts. For example, knowing that something is a bird produces certain default expectations about it, but these can be overridden by more specific expectations produced by evidence that the animal is a penguin.

In legal systems, priorities are introduced in multiple ways. They may correspond to certain general meta-rules, such as the principles of the priority for special laws over the (more) general one (*lex specialis derogat legi generali*), for later laws over earlier ones (*lex posterior derogat legi priori*), or for laws being issues by higher authorities over those issued by inferior ones (*lex superior derogat legi inferiori*). In some cases, priorities may also be conveyed by various linguistic clues, or implicitly by the function of the dispositions at issue.

Consider the connection between two rules in the Articles on Responsibility of States:

> Article 2 (Elements of an internationally wrongful act of a State)
>
> There is an internationally wrongful act of a State when conduct consisting of an act or omission:
>
> (a) is attributable to the State under international law; and
> (b) conduct constitutes a breach of an international obligation of the State.

> Article 21. Self-defence
>
> The wrongfulness of an act of a State is precluded if the act constitutes a lawful measure of self-defence taken in conformity with the Charter of the United Nations.

[9] The assessment may be applied to arguments, rather than to rules and outcomes, according to the perspective developed, among others, by PhanMinh Dung, 'On the acceptability of arguments and its fundamental role in nonmonotonic reasoning, logic programming, and n–person games' (1995) 77 Artificial Intelligence 321; Prakken and Sartor, 'Argument-based extended logic programming with defeasible priorities' (n 8); Henry Prakken, 'An abstract framework for argumentation with structured arguments' (2010) 1 Argument and Computation 93.

[10] John Holland, 'Genetic Algorithms' (1992) 267 Scientific American 66.

[11] John Holland, Keith J Holyoak, Richard E Nisbett, and Paul R Thagard, *Induction. Processes of Inference, Learning and Discovery* (MIT 1989) 38.

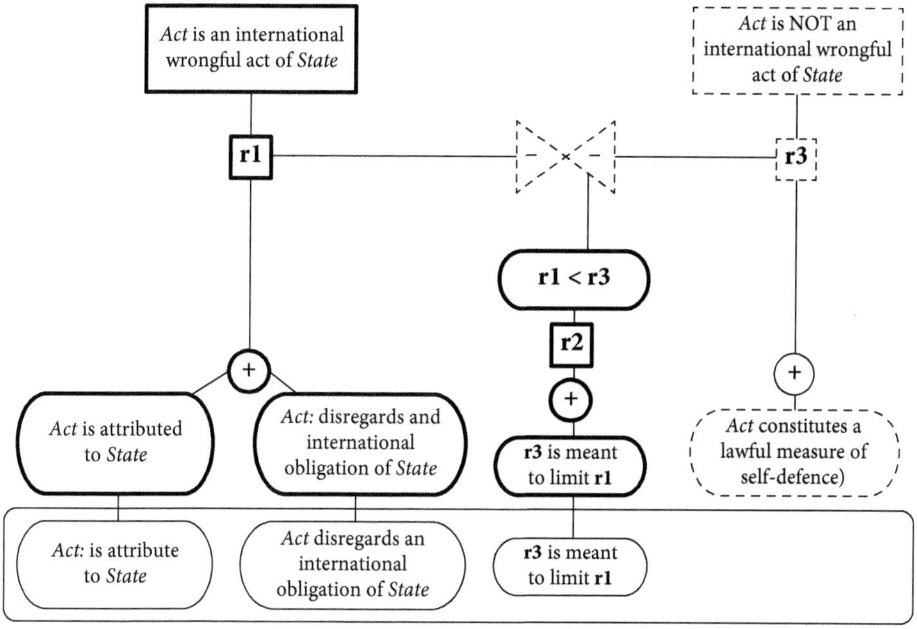

Figure 3.15 Self-defence in international law

These rules lead to incompatible outcomes when a state is attributed a conduct constituting a breach of an international obligation and this conduct is a lawful measure of self-defence. However, the indication resulting from the wording of the rule, and by the very function of self-defence in legal systems, is that the self-defence rule prevails, so that the act would not be wrongful in case self-defence was established (or at least if elements supporting it could be provided).

This representation in Figure 3.15 is meant to capture a situation where the input stream does not contain the information that the act at issue constitutes a lawful measure of self-defence. Should this information be added then the outcome would be different; namely, there would no longer be a wrongful act, as shown in Figure 3.16.

As shown in Figure 3.16, when the input stream includes the fact that the act at issue constitutes a measure of self-defence, the output is that the act is not an international wrongful act (even though it is attributed to a state, and it disregards an international obligation of that state).

This situation—that is, the fact that in case of a conflict of rules, one of the two rules prevails—follows in a broad range of cases from the principle of *lex specialis*. As a simple example for *lex specialis*, we can consider the relation between the general principle of state immunity under international law, and exceptions to that principle, which arise from international law, and have recently been codified in the United Nations Convention on Jurisdictional Immunities of States of 2004.[12] As stated in Article 5, '[a] State enjoys immunity, in respect of itself and its property, from the jurisdiction of the courts of another State.' This general principle is limited by several exceptions, concerning the situations when

[12] United Nations Convention on Jurisdictional Immunities of States and Their Property (signed on 2 December 2004, not yet in force). On state immunities see the chapter by Antonios Tzanakopoulos and Eleni Methymaki in this volume.

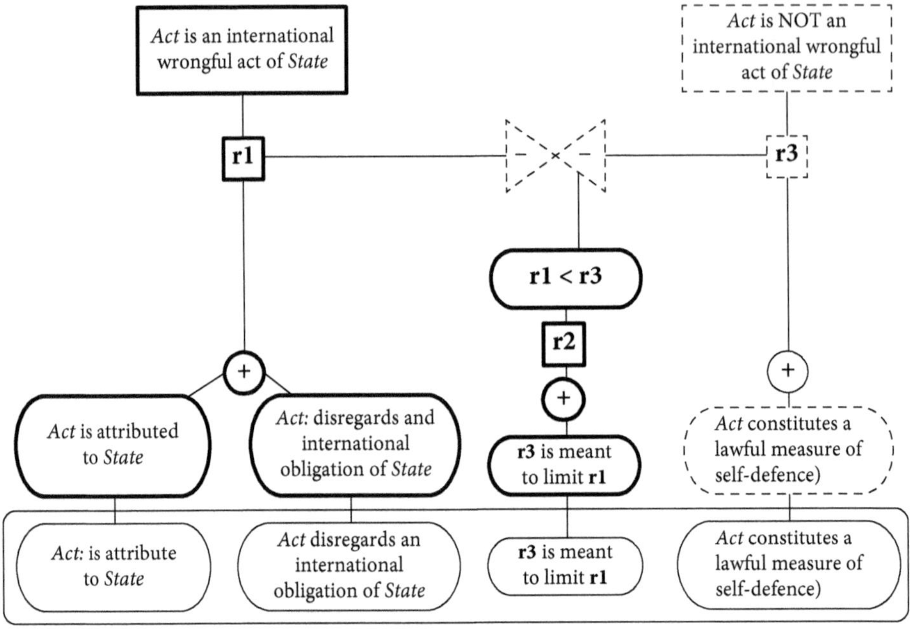

Figure 3.16 Defeat through self-defence

a state has 'consented to the exercise of jurisdiction' (Article 7), or when the 'State engages in a commercial transaction with a foreign natural or juridical person', or when the proceeding at issue concerns 'pecuniary compensation for death or injury to the person, or damage to or loss of tangible property' (Article 12).

The last exception—immunity should not apply to proceedings concerning pecuniary compensation for death or injury—was at issue in a recent case[13] opposing Germany and Italy before the International Court of Justice, as shown in Figure 3.17. The case was brought by Germany after various decisions by Italian courts to ignore the state immunity of Germany when confronted with claims for compensation by victims of Nazi-era war crimes.

Unfortunately for Italy, the judges adopted the view represented in Figure 3.18, advanced by Germany, namely the first level exception to immunity invoked by Italy (there is no immunity for acts causing death or injury) was inhibited by a second level exception (the immunity exception for death or injury does not apply to military activity).

Italy advanced a third level exception, in that it claimed that the second level exception concerning military activity did not apply in the case at hand, since this case involved a serious violation of human rights, that is, reprisals against innocent civilians. This exception would indeed block that immunity rule concerning military activity (and enable a liability conclusion) not only in this but also in other cases involving such reprisals. The Court, however, did not endorse the exception proposed by Italy, and ruled for Germany.

[13] *Jurisdictional Immunities of the State (Germany v Italy: Greece intervening)* (Judgment) [2012] ICJ Rep 99.

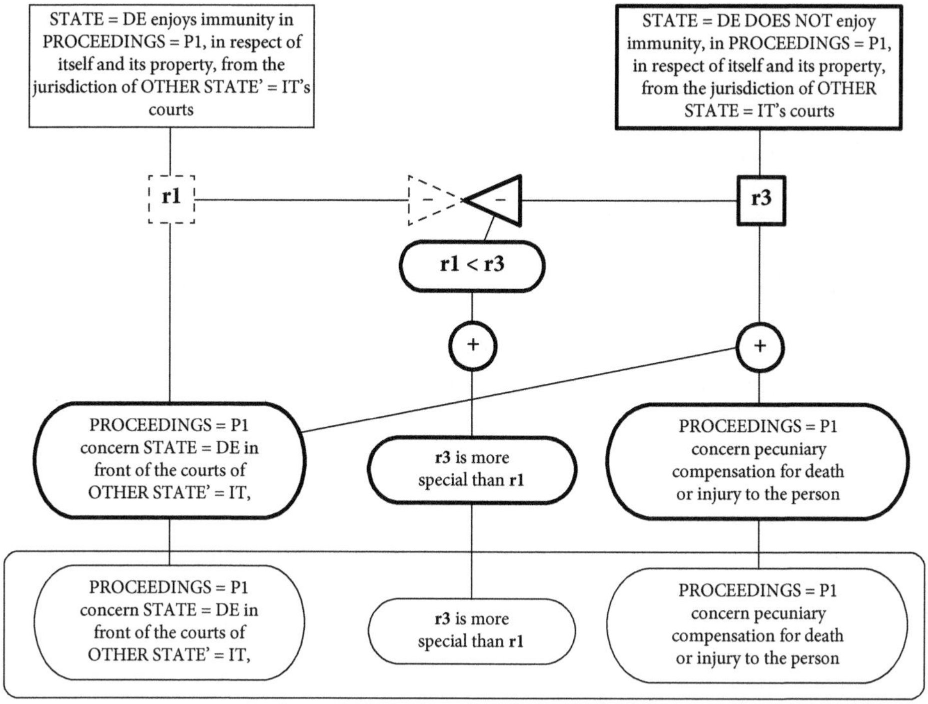

Figure 3.17 The case of immunity: exception for compensation for death or injury

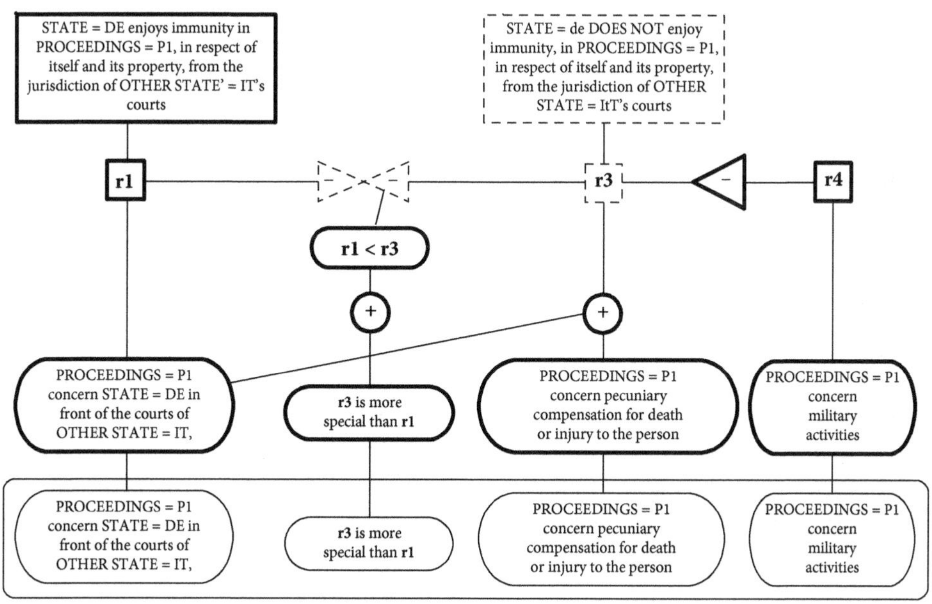

Figure 3.18 The case of immunity: exception (to exception) for military activities

7 Conclusion

We have presented three different exception structures in law:

- inhibitory links
- inhibitory rules
- prevailing contrary rules.

We have seen that a rule system including such structures may exhibit defeasibility or non-monotonicity, that is, it may no longer provide certain outputs when its input set is extended. Note that this notion of defeasibility or non-monotonicity assumes that the rule system is not changed: it only addresses additions to the input stream.

In legal theory, a different idea is often also associated with the term defeasibility, namely the idea that some outputs of a rule system R may be lost when the system is modified into a different system R1, by rewriting some rules of the system.[14] Different changes are possible. One change may consist in restricting a rule, that is, by adding some additional input conditions to the rule or specifying such conditions (e.g. a rule having universal applicability is substituted with a rule only applying to citizens). Another change may also consist in broadening a rule, that is, in deleting some input conditions of it or substituting more general input conditions for more specific ones (e.g. a rule only concerning citizens is transformed into a rule concerning everybody). A change in the rule system may also consist in introducing one of the exceptions structures we have identified, namely in adding an inhibitory bundle to a rule, or an inhibitory rule, or a preferred rule (e.g. a more special one).[15] For instance, had the Court accepted the exception proposed by Italy to limit the immunity of states in cases involving serious violations of human rights, the rule system of state immunities (including also the case law of the Court) would have been modified with the addition of this rule.

Used in this broad way, the concept of defeasibility merges with the concept of the revisability of a rule system, namely of the extent to which, and the conditions under which, a norm system is susceptible to being changed, by modifying, deleting, or adding some of its rules.[16] In a very broad sense, we may indeed say that these processes of rule change consist in making exceptions: when a rule stating 'if I1, then O1' is transformed into the rule 'if I1 and I2, then O1', then some cases (those where I1 is satisfied, but I2 is not) are in a sense excepted from the rule, that is, they no longer trigger its output.

I think that this expansion of the idea of defeasibility/exception, to cover also revisions of normative systems, should be resisted, for the sake of conceptual and analytical clarity. The dialectic of rule and exceptions within an unmodified rule system, which is the issue I have addressed in this chapter, is a distinct phenomenon, having its own logical structure. This does not exclude the possibility that logical models of the law can be constructed which use defeasible inference both to change the rules in a system, through interpretation or analogical construction (e.g. by broadening or restricting such rules) and to apply the rules so obtained.

[14] For various approaches to defeasibility in the law, see Jordi Ferrer Beltran and Giovanni B Ratti (eds), *The Logic of Legal Requirements: Essays on Defeasibility* (Oxford University Press 2012).

[15] On the dynamic that takes place in a case law system through distinctions (new *rationes decidendi* introducing exceptions) see Henry Prakken and Giovanni Sartor, 'Modelling Reasoning with Precedents in a Formal Dialogue Game' (1998) 6 Artificial Intelligence and Law 231; John F Horty, 'Rules and reasons in the theory of precedent' (2011) 10 Legal Theory 1.

[16] A logical approach to the issue of the revision of normative systems was proposed by CE Alchourrón and David Makinson, 'Hierarchies of Regulations and Their Logic' in R Hilpinen (ed), *New Studies on Deontic Logic* (Reidel 1981) 123–48. This triggered a whole line of research on knowledge and belief revision: see CE Alchourrón, P Gärdenfors, and David Makinson, 'On the logic of theory change: Partial meet contraction and revision functions' (1985) 50 Journal of Symbolic Logic 510.

4
Rules, Defeasibility, and the Psychology of Exceptions

*Frederick Schauer**

Rules purport to tell people what to do. Sometimes the rules speak directly to their subjects, and announce prescriptions (prohibitions, mandates, commands, permissions, etc) of primary conduct. And sometimes rules are directed to judges and enforcers,[1] providing them with decision rules instructing them on how to assess the primary conduct they are empowered to enforce and adjudicate. But whether the rules are conduct rules or decision rules,[2] it remains the case that rules, or at least regulative rules,[3] are prescriptive, applying some deontic operator to some course of conduct, and typically indicating as well the consequences of engaging (or not engaging) in that course of conduct.[4]

What makes a rule a rule, and what distinguishes rules from other sorts of prescriptions, is that rules are general.[5] Parents may often tell their children to go to bed 'now!' and police officers may sometimes instruct a particular person at a particular time to 'get back', but such particular prescriptions are different from rules, which cover multiple instances of conduct at multiple times, typically for multiple subjects. 'Go to bed now' is a particular prescription, but 'you will go to bed at nine o'clock every night' is a rule, just as 'Speed Limit 110 kph' is a

* David and Mary Harrison Distinguished Professor of Law, University of Virginia. This chapter was prepared for the Symposium on Exceptions and Defences in International Law, held at Queens' College, Cambridge University (31 March–1 April 2016). The current version has benefited greatly from the comments and questions of the other participants on that occasion.

[1] I note but put aside the perspective of Hans Kelsen, for whom all law was reducible to authorizations to judges or equivalent legal decision-makers. See Hans Kelsen, *The Pure Theory of Law* (Max Knight (trans), University of California Press 1967); Stanley L Paulson, 'Material and Formal Authorisation in Kelsen's Pure Theory', (1980) 39 Cambridge Law Journal 172–93.

[2] On the distinction between conduct rules and decision rules, a distinction originally suggested by Jeremy Bentham see especially Meir Dan-Cohen, 'Decision Rules and Conduct Rules: On Acoustic Separation in Criminal Law' (1984) 97 Harvard Law Review 625.

[3] For purposes of this chapter, I accept John Searle's distinction between constitutive rules and regulative rules, and here focus principally on the latter. See John R Searle, *Speech Acts: An Essay in the Philosophy of Language* (Cambridge University Press 1969) 33–42. The distinction is not without its detractors. See especially Joseph Raz, *Practical Reason and Norms* (1975, Princeton University Press 1990) 108–11.

[4] John Austin, *The Province of Jurisprudence Determined* (1832, Wilfred E Rumble (ed), Cambridge University Press 1985) notwithstanding, rules, and even legal rules, need not contain or authorize sanctions in order to qualify as rules, a point made most prominently in HLA Hart, *The Concept of Law* (1961, 3rd edn, Oxford University Press 2012). That legal rules need not and sometimes do not contain or authorize sanctions, however, should not be understood as minimizing the ubiquity and importance of sanctions, sanctioning, and other forms of coercion in modern legal systems. See Frederick Schauer, *The Force of Law* (Harvard University Press 2015).

[5] What follows is a highly abbreviated version of an analysis of rules initially presented in Frederick Schauer, *Playing By the Rules: A Philosophical Examination of Rule-Based Decision-Making in Law and in Life* (Clarendon Press 1991). See also Frederick Schauer, *Thinking Like a Lawyer: A New Introduction to Legal Reasoning* (Harvard University Press 2009) ch 2.

Frederick Schauer, *Rules, Defeasibility, and the Psychology of Exceptions* In: *Exceptions in International Law*. Edited by: Lorand Bartels and Federica Paddeu, Oxford University Press (2020). © Lorand Bartels and Federica Paddeu.
DOI: 10.1093/oso/9780198789321.003.0004

rule in a way that 'Slow down!' is not. In the army, 'Take that hill!' or 'At ease!' are particular prescriptions, but 'All enlisted personnel shall salute all officers' is a rule.[6]

Because rules are general, the possibility always exists that a rule will produce a wrong or suboptimal outcome when applied on a particular occasion to particular facts, with wrongness or suboptimality being measured by reference to the background purpose or purposes a rule is designed to serve[7] or by reference to even larger considerations of morality and public policy. The purpose (or justification) lying behind the rule in the military requiring enlisted personnel to salute officers, for example, is that saluting demonstrates respect and reinforces hierarchical authority, but such goals are not served by requiring the private with a broken arm nevertheless to offer a salute to a captain. Similarly, speed limits are typically designed to achieve highway safety, but safety and larger moral considerations may be impeded rather than fostered by enforcing the speed limit against someone rushing an injured person to the hospital. And there are often good reasons on particular occasions for why requiring a child to go to bed at the rule-prescribed hour would be suboptimal in light of the various health and other reasons that might justify the rule.

Although the kind of suboptimality—or wrongness—represented by the examples in the previous paragraph is measured by reference to the result that would be generated by direct application of a particular rule's background purpose or justification, suboptimality may also occur when application of a rule is consistent with the rule's background justification, but nevertheless produces a suboptimal or wrong result under a more global conception of suboptimality or wrongness. In H.L.A. Hart's classic example of a rule prohibiting vehicles in the park,[8] we might suppose that the purpose behind the rule was the prevention of noise or danger. If the rule were then applied to the fire brigade's fire engine entering the park to extinguish a fire in a wooden structure within the park, it is likely that both noise and danger would be increased, but still to some overall benefit. In that sense, strict application of the rule would be optimal vis-à-vis the purpose lying immediately behind the rule, but suboptimal under a broader and all-things-considered understanding of either purpose or optimality.

Rules because of their generality will thus sometimes (or often, depending on the nature of the rule and the nature of the domain that it regulates) produce what Willard Quine in a related but different context referred to as 'recalcitrant experiences'.[9] Here, a recalcitrant experience is not a misapplication of a rule, but rather arises when a faithful[10] interpretation or

[6] The distinction between particular directives and general rules is discussed by Austin, *The Province of Jurisprudence Determined* (n 4) 25–29, who distinguished 'laws or rules' from 'occasional or particular commands'. See also Hart, *The Concept of Law* (n 4) 8–10, 20–22.

[7] I say 'always' to acknowledge the phenomenon of *open texture*, using that term in the precise way in which Friedrich Waismann, who coined the term, used it. Friedrich Waismann, 'Verifiability' in AGN Flew (ed), *Logic and Language* (Basil Blackwell 1951) 117–44. Waismann insisted that open texture was different from vagueness, with open texture not being extant vagueness, but rather the ineliminable *possibility* of vagueness in even the most precise of terms or concepts. Waismann's claim was thus that that *all* terms and all concepts are open textured. As a result, all rules, which are understood in language, are open textured as well, and are thus potentially vague or otherwise indeterminate, no matter how much we may think at the time of drafting or adoption that the rules have anticipated every possible application or non-application of the rule. On the relationship between the open texture of language and the open texture of law see Frederick Schauer, 'On the Open Texture of Law' (2013) 87 *Grazer Philosophische Studien* 195; Frederick Schauer, 'On the Supposed Defeasibility of Legal Rules' (1998) 51(1) Current Legal Problems 223.

[8] HLA Hart, 'Positivism and the Separation of Law and Morals' (1958) 71 Harvard Law Review 593, 606–15. For a tediously long analysis of the example see Frederick Schauer, 'A Critical Guide to Vehicles in the Park' (2008) 83 New York University Law Review 1109.

[9] Willard Van Orman Quine, 'Two Dogmas of Empiricism' in Willard Van Orman Quine (ed), *From a Logical Point of View* (Harvard University Press 1980) 20–46, at 43.

[10] What it is to interpret a rule 'faithfully' implicates the entire domain of legal interpretation. For some, a faithful interpretation is one that interprets a rule according to the plain (at times ordinary and at times technical) meaning

application of the rule might produce a result that is in some way wrong or suboptimal from a perspective larger than the rule itself. Famously, Aristotle recognized the phenomenon in his argument for the power of equitable correction of law, describing equity as 'a rectification of law in so far as law is defective on account of its generality'.[11] And, even earlier, Plato has offered a similar analysis in the *Statesman*, where the Eleatic Stranger observes that to legislate for 'the herd' is inevitably to run the risk that the legislation will produce poor outcomes in particular instances.[12]

'Defeasibility' is the common covering term embracing a number of different ways in which rules might be understood as dealing with the occurrence of the recalcitrance experience. More precisely, a rule can be considered defeasible insofar as the rule is subject to correction (or nullification) in the face of a recalcitrant experience, a correction designed to produce the 'correct' rule-independent result. Of course it might be the case in some decision-making environment the rules would not be defeasible at all, and that recalcitrant experiences would simply be accepted as such, despite their wrongness or suboptimality,[13] as the price to be paid for the virtues of clear guidance, coordination among multiple rule-subjects, constraint on interpreter or enforcer discretion, and the production of stability as an independent good. But in those domains in which rules are considered defeasible, there exist multiple ways in which the occasions for defeat might arise.

Sometimes rules might be understood as subject to defeat when the outcome produced by faithful application of the rule differs from what the creators of the rule (perhaps drafters and perhaps other adopters) actually intended or would have intended when faced with the reality of the recalcitrant experience.[14] Alternatively, rules might be defeated when the conditions for application of the rule do not exist. A rule of chess that does not explicitly limit its application to games of chess might be thought by someone to apply outside of that domain, and thus we might suppose that a rule is or should be defeasible insofar as there is a failure of the initial conditions for its application. To use an example provided by Walter Sinnott-Armstrong, my promise to cook you dinner is *cancelled* by your death.[15] It is not that your

of the rule's terms. For others, a faithful interpretation is an interpretation that adheres to the original intentions of the rule's adopters. And for still others, a faithful interpretation tracks the original public meaning (but not the original intentions, as mental states) of the rule's terms. There is no need here to delve into these issues, for the point is only that under any understanding of what a rule means, there is always the possibility of divergence between what a rule means and what the best all-things-considered outcome would be, and also of divergence between what a rule means and what the deeper justification lying behind the rule is understood to be.

[11] Aristotle, *Nicomachean Ethics* (JAK Thomson (trans), Penguin 1977) 1137b. For more extensive commentary along the lines I mention here see Frederick Schauer, *Profiles, Probabilities, and Stereotypes* (Harvard University Press 2003) 41–48. See also Georgios Anagnostopoulos, *Aristotle on the Goals and Exactness of Ethics* (University of California Press 1994) 363–82; Bernard Yack, *The Problems of the Political Animal: Community, Justice, and Conflict in Aristotelian Political Thought* (University of California Press 1993) 193–94; Roger Shiner, 'Aristotle's Theory of Equity' (1987) 27 Loyola of Los Angeles Law Review 1245.

[12] Plato, *Statesman*, 294a–b, as translated in JB Skemp, *Plato's Statesman: A Translation of the Politicus of Plato with Introductory Essays and Footnotes* (Bristol Classical Press 1952). For commentary see Charles H Kahn, 'The Place of *Statesman* in Plato's Later Work' in Christopher J Rowe (ed), *Reading the Statesman* (Academia Verlag 1995) 51 ff.

[13] See John Manning, 'The Absurdity Doctrine' (2003) 116 Harvard Law Review 2387; Frederick Schauer, 'Is Defeasibility an Essential Property of Law?' in Jordi Ferrer Beltran and Giovanni Battista Ratti (eds), *The Logic of Legal Requirements: Essays on Defeasibility* (Oxford University Press 2012) 77–88; Frederick Schauer, 'Formalism' (1988) 97 Yale Law Journal 509.

[14] 'Actually intended' and 'would have intended' are in fact quite different. The former is more or less straightforwardly factual, but the latter, in practice, typically uses the device of hypothetical intent as a way of importing the interpreter's conception of reasonableness or justice or purpose into the determination that the rule should be defeated on some occasion.

[15] Walter Sinnott-Armstrong, *Moral Dilemmas* (Basil Blackwell 1988) 41–42.

death overrides my promise, but that my promise is conditional on a certain state of affairs, and when that state of affairs does not obtain the obligation is cancelled, or is simply inapplicable at the outset.

Similarly, but not identically, we might suppose that a rule could be or should be defeated when the purpose for having it is not present, even though the rule itself appears to cover some form of behaviour. Relatively recently, for example, the Supreme Court of the United States was required to decide a case called *Yates v United States*,[16] which arose from an application of the Sarbanes-Oxley Act, a 2002 statute enacted in the wake of the collapse of the Enron Corporation and which was designed, in relevant part, to deal with the shredding and related destruction of financial records of companies in financial difficulties. The statute prohibited the 'destruction, alteration, falsification, or concealment of any record, document, or tangible object', where the destruction etc was designed to 'impede an investigation'.[17] But when the federal authorities attempted to apply the statute against a fisherman who had thrown undersized fish back into the sea to prevent a prosecution for taking undersized fish, the authorities argued that Yates's conduct was literally prohibited by the law because a fish was a 'tangible object' and because Yates's conduct was unarguably intended to prevent prosecution. Yates, in response, argued that the purpose behind the law, to prevent the destruction of financial records that might be used in a fraud prosecution, was in no way applicable here, and thus that the statute should not be applied. And although Yates prevailed by a bare majority in the Supreme Court, the question is not whether this particular decision was correct or incorrect. Rather, and independent of the soundness of the outcome, *Yates* presents a typical example of a rule that might be thought to be defeated by virtue of the inapplicability of its purpose.[18] And along with the rule that might be defeated by the inapplicability of the conditions for its relevance, we could categorize these types of defeasibility as forms of *internal defeat*.

By contrast, rules might be subject to what we can label *external defeat*. Often discussed under the heading of 'overridability',[19] a rule is subject to external defeat when its prescriptions are set aside not by something about the failure of the rule itself, but instead by more exigent considerations coming from elsewhere, where the 'elsewhere' might come from other parts of the law, or might, and more commonly, come from extra-legal considerations. Consider, for example, the widely discussed case of *Riggs v Palmer*,[20] made famous in contemporary jurisprudential circles by Ronald Dworkin,[21] but extensively discussed even earlier in the writings of Roscoe Pound,[22] Benjamin Cardozo,[23] in the Legal Process teaching

[16] 135 S Ct 1074 (2015).

[17] 116 Stat 745 (2002), 18 USC §1519.

[18] *Yates* is merely the latest of a long line of examples in which literal application of a rule is inconsistent with the rule's purpose, of which one of the oldest is Pufendorf's example, repeated by Blackstone in the *Commentaries* (bk 1, p 60) of a surgeon in Bologna who was prosecuted (or who was thought by some to be prosecutable) under a statute prohibiting letting blood in the streets for performing what we would now describe as emergency surgery. Presumably, the purpose of the statute was to prevent public duelling and other forms of fighting, but at least according to the example (possibly real and possibly apocryphal), there was a clear conflict between what the statute said and what it was intended to do. For a comprehensive discussion of the 'interplay between purpose and text' see Caleb Nelson, *Statutory Interpretation* (Foundation Press 2011) 1–80.

[19] See Sinnott-Armstrong (n 15) 15–22. See also Robert Nozick, 'Moral Complications and Moral Structures' (1968) 13 Natural Law Forum 1; Frederick Schauer, 'A Comment on the Structure of Rights' (1993) 27 Georgia Law Review 415; Judith Thomson, 'Some Ruminations on Rights' (1977) 19 Arizona Law Review 45.

[20] 22 NE 188 (1889). A thorough exploration of the history of the case and its surrounding legal doctrine is contained in Nelson (n 18) 7–27.

[21] Ronald Dworkin, *Taking Rights Seriously* (Duckworth 1977); Ronald Dworkin, *Law's Empire* (Harvard University Press 1986).

[22] Roscoe Pound, 'Spurious Interpretation' (1907) 7 Columbia Law Review 379.

[23] Benjamin N Cardozo, *The Nature of the Judicial Process* (Yale University Press 1921) 4041.

materials of Henry Hart and Albert Sacks,[24] and in various contemporaneous commentaries on developments in the law of wills and related topics.[25] Elmer Palmer was duly named in the will of his grandfather Francis Palmer as the principal beneficiary of Francis' estate, but Elmer came to be in a position to inherit because he had poisoned his grandfather, partly to prevent his grandfather, the testator, from changing his will, and partly simply to accelerate his own inheritance.

The most immediately applicable rule in *Riggs v Palmer* was the New York Statute of Wills, the provisions of which would have allowed the inheritance to go to Elmer, notwithstanding Elmer's crime and notwithstanding Elmer's murder of the testator.[26] Nevertheless, the New York Court of Appeals found in favour of the alternative beneficiaries, relying on the 'no person may profit from his own wrong' principle to set aside the result that was prescribed by the most immediately applicable rule.

For Dworkin, *Riggs* is a case demonstrating that the notion of 'the law' is capacious, including both rules and principles and, more importantly, including within the law a host of moral considerations that under a standard positivist account would be considered extra-legal.[27] But from a more conventional (some would say positivist, but that is beside the point) perspective, *Riggs* is a case demonstrating that the indications of a rule might be overridden by more pressing concerns of justice. Other cases might arise in which more pressing concerns of policy might serve the same function, and in countless additional instances we recognize that rules need not be absolute, and thus that their indications might have to give way to more important considerations coming from outside the rule. Thus, the rule requiring that I keep my promises might be overridden when my promise to meet you for lunch conflicts with an intervening family emergency, and the speed limit rule might be treated as subject to override in cases of medical emergency or natural disaster necessitating evacuation.

It is important to recognize that defeasibility is not a property of rules themselves, nor is it a necessary feature of rule systems of legal systems.[28] Some systems through their secondary rules might choose to treat their rules as defeasible, but others might choose differently.[29] For our purposes here, the essential point is that defeasibility is a device of institutional design, and thus the choice to treat the rules within a system as defeasible is the product of a congeries of moral, political, policy, and efficiency concerns that might well vary from system to system, and from rule culture to rule culture.

On occasion, the issue of defeasibility arises with respect to rules that list the exceptions to those rules. Article 10 of the European Convention on Human Rights, for example, guarantees the right to freedom of expression, but then includes within that article a list of

[24] Henry M Hart Jr and Albert M Sacks, *The Legal Process: Basic Problems in the Making and Application of Law* (1957, Foundation Press 1994) 68–102.

[25] 'Wills—Murder of the Testator by Legatee' (1889) 3 Harvard Law Review 234.

[26] Elmer was in fact a fourteen-year old juvenile when he committed the crime, for which he was duly tried and convicted (of murder in the second degree). As a result, his sentence in a juvenile facility was shorter than had he been an adult, and he had been released from confinement by the time the case was finally adjudicated.

[27] I put aside here the contemporary debates between so-called inclusive and exclusive positivists, recognizing that for the former group, moral principles can be part of the law as long as some society, as a contingent social fact, chooses to treat them as part of the law. Inclusive positivists distinguish themselves from the traditional natural law position by virtue of insisting that including the moral within the legal is a contingent social fact about some legal systems, and not part of the very nature of law. Whether inclusive legal positivism differs from the Dworkinian account of law is a matter of some controversy, with Dworkin maintaining that there is little difference except the label. See Ronald Dworkin, 'Thirty Years On' (2002) 115 Harvard Law Review 1655.

[28] See Schauer, 'On the Supposed Defeasibility of Legal Rules' (n 7).

[29] ibid.

the various exceptions—defamation, invasion of privacy, national security, public order, protection of health, and morals, etc—to the primary guarantee. Similarly, the Canadian Charter of Rights and Freedoms and the Constitution of South Africa include more comprehensive (i.e. not attached to specific articles) limiting clauses, providing that any of the rights protected may be limited when necessary in a democratic society. But whether the exceptions are all-encompassing, as in Canada and South Africa, or more particular, as in Article 10 of the European Convention, the basic point remains that sometimes defeasibility is manifested by the process of explicitly listing the possible exceptions to some general prescription.

When exceptions are explicitly stated in this way, it might be thought that there is little difference between an exception designated as such and an exception that is incorporated within the primary prohibition. As a matter of logic, it may seem that there is little difference between the protection of freedom of expression subject to override or defeat in cases of defamation and the protection of non-defamatory expression.[30] But as Claire Finkelstein,[31] Carlos Alchourrón,[32] Jorge Rodriguez,[33] and, most recently and most extensively, Luis Duarte d'Almeida[34] have demonstrated, a rule incorporating an exception into the primary prohibition typically (or necessarily) places the burden of showing the inapplicability of the exception on the rule-applier, but a rule whose exceptions are separately stated typically places the burden on the subject to show that the exception applies. Burdens of proof are important, in life as well as in law, and thus it is important to recognize that the decision to incorporate an exception into a primary prohibition or instead to treat the exception as an independently stated grounds for defeat may have considerable practical as well as theoretical consequences.

Although the complications regarding rules with a listed catalogue (whether vague or precise) of possible exceptions are interesting and important, most of the contemporary literature on defeasibility, and most of the problems that surround the question of defeasibility, are about the occasions and consequences of uncatalogued and unacknowledged exceptions—the occurrence of an event that was not considered when the rule was drafted or adopted, but which now presents the rule-interpreter or rule-applier (or rule-subject, for that matter) with a quandary precisely because a totally unanticipated and thus unprovided-for event has now taken place. As J.L. Austin put it, following on Friedrich Waismann's highly influential idea of open texture[35] and applying it to our seeing what we thought was a goldfinch but which then proceeds to explode or quote Virginia Woolf, 'we don't know what to say'.[36]

For most contemporary commentators, the central problem of defeasibility arises in just such circumstances, when the genuinely unexpected event causes a failure in what had previously been thought to be the guidance of some rule. It is at this point that some would say that it is in the nature of rules or the nature of law that an exception should be added at the

[30] See Frederick Schauer, 'Exceptions' (1991) 58 University of Chicago Law Review 871.

[31] Claire O Finkelstein, 'When the Rule Swallows the Exception' in Linda Meyer (ed), *Rules and Reasoning: Essays in Honour of Fred Schauer* (Hart Publishing 1999) 145–75.

[32] Ronald P Loui, 'Alchourron and von Wright on Conflict among Norms' in Donald Nute (ed), *Defeasible Deontic Logic* (Springer 1997) 345–52.

[33] Jorge J Rodriguez, 'Against Defeasibility of Legal Rules' in Jordi Ferrer Beltran and Giovanni Battista Ratti (eds), *The Logic of Legal Requirements: Essays on Defeasibility* (Oxford University Press 2012) 89–107.

[34] Luis Duarte d'Almeida, *Accounting for Exceptions: A Theory of Defences and Defeasibility in Law* (Oxford University Press 2015).

[35] Friedrich Waismann, 'Verifiability' in AGN Flew (ed), *Logic and Language* (Basil Blackwell 1952) 117–144.

[36] JL Austin, 'Other Minds' in JO Urmson and GJ Warnock (eds), *Philosophical Papers* (3rd edn, Oxford University Press 1979) 79–116, at 88.

moment of application,[37] while others, including this author, would argue that doing so is a contingent feature of some legal or rule systems, but that enduring the consequences of the newly-arising poor fit between the rule and the world is a plausible choice with law and within many other rule-governed environments.

These questions are interesting and important, but they often ignore the question of just who it is who should be doing the defeating when rules are treated as defeasible in this way. Assume for the moment that in *Riggs v Palmer* none of the rule-of-recognition-recognized sources that the New York Court of Appeals relied on to find an exception that denied Elmer Palmer his inheritance had existed.[38] Even were that so, it still might have been the case that New York treated all of its legal rules as defeasible, such that not only the Statute of Wills but also all of the other rules that comprised New York law were treated as subject to defeat or modification or exception, added at the moment of application when application of the rule to an unanticipated event would produce an injustice. If this were the case, then it would have been up to the judge to determine whether the circumstances justified making an exception at the moment of application.

That the judge was the decision-maker charged with determining whether to create an exception in this instance seems obvious, and to most people seems obviously correct. But suppose, counterfactually, that the decision about whether to create an exception was to be made by the residuary beneficiaries. Under these circumstances, we would be rightly suspicious, fearing that the residuary beneficiaries, for reasons of self-interest, would be especially inclined to find an exception. And if the decision about whether to create an exception was to be left to Elmer Palmer, we would be equally suspicious, worrying that Elmer would be as disinclined to find an exception as the residuary beneficiaries would be inclined to find one. In the context of law and adjudication, neither of these possibilities would present themselves, because we almost take for granted that a disinterested judge will make the decision, and that the disinterested judge is the appropriate agent to transcend the obvious biases of the parties themselves.

Rules and possible exceptions exist, however, in many domains other than that of formal adjudication. Consider the rules we make for ourselves. Suppose in order to lose weight I make a rule for myself that I will exercise every morning and that I will eat no bread.[39] If asked at the time of making the rule, I would acknowledge that I will make exceptions at the moment of application for serious illness, for major injury, and for circumstances of genuine catastrophe-induced starvation. But then suppose I have an important meeting later in the day, and believe I need the time that missing exercise will produce, and need the energy that additional carbohydrates will provide. Like many other people, I believe I would say that the circumstances justify an exception on just this one occasion, and I promise myself that I will return to my rule-based regimen the next day.

But now it is a week later, and something else comes up. I have been invited to lunch by a friend, and he suggests a sandwich shop. Wishing to be accommodating, I agree, and I then proceed to have a sandwich (with bread, of course) at lunch, for fear of implicitly being taken to have criticized my friend's choice of locations for lunch. So once again I make an exception, promising myself I will do so only rarely. And so it goes, the next time, and the next time, and the time after that.

[37] See e.g. Richard Posner, 'The Jurisprudence of Skepticism' (1988) 86 Michigan Law Review 827; Richard Tur, 'Defeasibilism' (2001) 21 Oxford Journal of Legal Studies 355.

[38] In fact, the court drew heavily on decisions from other jurisdictions, on classic legal secondary sources, and on other plainly legal materials, arguably making the case a poor example of Dworkin's point.

[39] Put aside whether this is a good way to lose weight, a subject about which I claim no expertise.

I take it that this scenario, whether for the purpose of dieting or stopping smoking or learning French or anything else, is familiar to most of us.[40] And the lesson, of course, is the same as it was when we think about the possibility that the residuary beneficiaries in *Riggs v Palmer* might be the ones to decide whether an exception should be made on this occasion under these specific circumstances—the power to make an exception is scarcely to be entrusted to those who might benefit from the exception. To give the phenomenon a label, this is an example of what in the psychological literature is called *motivated reasoning*[41]—the tendency to see facts, plans, and much else in light of our preferred outcome. Whether a goal in football has been scored is a factual question—did the ball cross the line or not?—but a familiar phenomenon is for spectators to align their answer to this factual question to their preferences for an outcome—to give or see the answer that will be consistent with their desired outcome. Supporters of one side see it as a goal, and supporters of the opposing side see it as no goal, even though the matter at issue is simply one of fact and not of value.

This all may seem obvious and banal, but the conclusion about the likely outcome when people are empowered to decide whether an exception to a restrictive rule should be made for their case or on this occasion is supported by an additional array of psychological insights. Thus, in addition to knowing that people often engage in motivated reasoning, we know that there is often excess inflation of the comparative importance of immediate events and excess discounting of that which is to occur in the future. If making an exception on this occasion presents some risk of encouraging future and less justified exceptions, people will exaggerate the importance of this exception and minimize the likelihood of downstream or future effects.[42] When I break my dieting or exercise rule, I will overemphasize the value of doing so now, and underestimate the likelihood that making an exception on this occasion will produce other exceptions in the future.

The lesson of all of this is that the question of defeasibility cannot be (or at least should not be) separated from the question of who is to decide when the defeating conditions obtain, and thus the question of exceptions cannot, as Carl Schmitt memorably discussed, be separated from the question of who has the power to decide that an exception is warranted on some occasion.[43]

In the normal operation of domestic law, these questions are often far in the background, because the question of whether a rule applies and the question of whether an exception to that rule should be made are typically made by a judge or other seemingly (or at least theoretically) disinterested adjudicator. And although judges may well have their own biases and engage in motivated reasoning themselves—or at least so the legal realists supposed[44]—the

[40] See Thomas Schelling, 'Enforcing Rules on Oneself' (1985) 1 Journal of Law, Economics & Organization 357.

[41] See Roy F Baumeister and Leonard S Newman, 'Self-Regulation of Cognitive Inference and Decision Processes' (1994) 20 Journal of Personality and Social Psychology Bulletin 3; Ziva Kunda, 'Motivated Inference: Self-Serving Generation and Evaluation of Causal Theories' (1987) 53 Journal of Personality and Social Psychology 636; Ziva Kunda, 'The Case for Motivated Reasoning' (1990) 108 Psychological Bulletin 480.

[42] The effect of immediacy is but one application of the larger phenomenon of *availability*—that which is closest, whether in time or in distance, is more cognitively available, and people tend to exaggerate the prevalence, probability, and importance of that which is more cognitively available. Amos Tversy and Daniel Kahneman, 'Availability: A Heuristic for Judging Frequency and Probability' (1973) 5 Cognitive Psychology 207.

[43] 'Sovereign is he who decides on the exception.' See Carl Schmitt, *Political Theology: Four Chapters on the Concept of Sovereignty* (George Schwab (trans), University of Chicago Press 2005) 5. See also Giorgio Agamben, *State of Exception* (University of Chicago Press 2005); Bruno Gullì, 'The Sovereign Exception: Notes on Schmitt's Word that Sovereign is He Who Decides on the Exception' (2009) 1 Glossator 23 www.glossator.org.

[44] At least that facet of Legal Realism most commonly associated with Jerome Frank, *Law and the Modern Mind* (Brentano's 1930), and more recently associated with so-called *attitudinalists* in the political science of judicial behaviour. See e.g. Jeffrey Segal and Harold Spaeth, *The Supreme Court and the Attitudinal Model Revisited*

problems and complications seem quantitatively less in the case of the theoretically disinterested adjudicator than they do when we are making rules for ourselves, enforcing rules on ourselves, and deciding on whether an exception should be made in our own case.

The implications of this for international law should be apparent. Although John Austin in the nineteenth century and many sceptics now doubt the status of international law as law because of its frequent lack of enforcement or sanctioning ability,[45] it has been widely understood since H.L.A. Hart[46] that international law can be law whenever some relevant group internalizes its primary and secondary rules, as is undoubtedly the case today. But when we deal with the actual operation of the rules of international law, the frequent lack of credible adjudicators and credible sanctions may come back into the picture. Although Article 19 of the International Covenant on Political and Civil Rights, for example, protects freedom of expression, it also provides that there are relevant exceptions, and seems also implicitly to assume that the protection is defeasible under previously unforeseen and possible unforeseeable circumstances. But if the conditions for defeat are to be determined by the same state whose activities are constrained by the legal rule, the problems with treating the rules as defeasible rise to the surface.

The likelihood of the phenomenon is supported by yet another set of psychological findings. Following Joseph Raz,[47] we can understand much of law as imposing second-order constraints on first-order moral or policy preferences. But we know as an empirical matter that, when sanctions are removed from the equation, people will rarely set aside their own first-order policy or moral preferences in the service of these second-order procedural, constitutional, or more broadly legal values. In a number of experiments, researchers provided to their subjects scenarios in which the subjects' policy preferences diverged from what was required by the law, and here not only lay people but also law students and lawyers tended strongly to choose the preferred policy outcome over the legally required one, at least when sanctions, broadly defined, were removed from the equation.[48]

Thus, although sanction-free international law is, or at least can be, law, it is a different question whether that law is effective in having a causal influence on the actual behaviour of international actors. There does exist research that has suggested such an influence,[49] but much of it is plagued by a failure to differentiate behaviour that is consistent with the law from behaviour that is caused by the law. Just as my refusal to engage in murder, burglary, and rape is consistent with the law but in no way caused by it—my behaviour on these topics would not change if the legal prohibitions were removed—so too in the context of international law is a great deal of state practice consistent with international law but not caused by, and possibly not much influenced by, that international law.

(Cambridge University Press 2002). And see also Duncan Kennedy, 'Freedom and Constraint in Adjudication: A Critical Phenomenology' (1986) 36 Journal of Legal Education 518.

[45] See n 5 above.

[46] Hart, *The Concept of Law* (n 4) 213–237.

[47] Joseph Raz, *The Authority of Law: Essays on Law and Morality* (Clarendon Press 1979); Joseph Raz, *Practical Reason and Norms* (1975, 2nd edn, Princeton University Press 1990).

[48] See e.g. Joshua P Furgeson, Linda Babcock, and Peter M Shane, 'Do a Law's Policy Implications Affect Beliefs about Its Constitutionality? An Experimental Test' (2008) 32 Law and Human Behavior 219; Joshua P Furgeson, Linda Babcock, and Peter M. Shane, 'Behind the Mask of Method: Political Orientation and Constitutional Interpretive Preferences' (2008) 32 Law and Human Behavior.

[49] See e.g. Abram Chayes and Antonia Handler Chayes, 'On Compliance' (1993) 47 International Organization 175.

If it turns out, therefore, that state policy preferences typically prevail over international law when the two diverge, then there may be little grounds for confidence that international actors can be trusted to decide when an exception to a stated rule of international law is applicable, or when in the face of unforeseen circumstances the rule should be treated as defeasible and thus set aside. And if that is the case, then there may be good reason, as a matter of institutional design, to treat the rules of international law as non-defeasible, believing that, whatever the force of a rule unsupported by sanctions, that force is likely to be greater when the temptation of the exception is removed.

5

Seven Ways of Escaping a Rule

Of Exceptions and Their Avatars in International Law

*Jorge E. Viñuales**

1 Introduction

There are two types of exceptions to a rule: those than can be anticipated, and the true ones.

By definition, I can only address the first category. In this context, the purpose of this chapter is (1) to identify seven legal techniques through which certain situations that could otherwise fall within the scope of a rule or a set of rules are excluded from it and (2) to clarify the implications (technical and practical) of using such techniques and the terminology that comes with them. Indeed, using the term 'exception' rather than other terms such as 'carve-out' or 'exemption' may have significant legal implications as regards matters such as (i) the burden of proof, (ii) the interpretative approach, (iii) the degree of deference accorded to a respondent under a provision, or (iv) the interplay with certain referral clauses.

It would be all too easy for the legal academic or practitioner to state that each provision is to be analysed on its own, without the need for rigid characterizations subsuming it under this or that category. On its face, this statement is certainly accurate. Yet, on closer inspection, arguments about the operation of such provisions will necessarily touch upon their legal implications and, at that stage, whether explicitly or implicitly, their characterization will come into play to lend more (or less) support to arguments about their implications. And it would be difficult to question that a provision considered to embody an 'exception' to a rule is likely to attract a different type of scrutiny, with the attendant practical, if not legal implications. Thus, calling a provision an 'exception', without further reflection, may amount to conceding much to the opponent carelessly. Even beyond a litigation context, the potential characterization of a provision when drafting an instrument will be likely to influence its operation. To state this point concisely, conceptual elaboration is not without interest for practice, and practice always relies (explicitly or implicitly) on some form of conceptual elaboration in addressing ways of escaping a rule.

The structure of the chapter follows its purpose. I first address the techniques themselves, by reference to concrete examples and, when possible, also to illustrations of their operation in a litigation context. Secondly, I discuss some transversal implications both from a technical standpoint and from the more prosaic, yet obscure, perspective of their practical or 'clinical' use.

* Harold Samuel Professor, University of Cambridge. The views expressed in this chapter are in my strict academic capacity.

Jorge E. Viñuales, *Seven Ways of Escaping a Rule* In: *Exceptions in International Law*. Edited by: Lorand Bartels and Federica Paddeu, Oxford University Press (2020). © Lorand Bartels and Federica Paddeu. DOI: 10.1093/oso/9780198789321.003.0005

2 Seven Ways of Escaping a Rule

The term 'exception' is used in international legal discourse to refer to a wide variety of techniques that provide special legal treatment to certain situations otherwise governed by a general rule. As such, they seek to bring the broad legal ontology established by rules closer to the topography of the realities being regulated. In this section, I explore the specific features of seven such techniques, organized from the less to the more exceptional: delimitation of the scope of a norm or set of norms (section 2.1); specific carve-outs (section 2.2); flexibilities (section 2.3); derogations (section 2.4); exceptions *stricto sensu* (section 2.5); excuses (section 2.6), and circumstances precluding wrongfulness (section2.7).

The scale from less to more exceptional is intuitive, yet it calls for some further clarification. It relies on a distinction between norms defining conduct or obligations (often called primary norms) and other norms that define the latter's scope and modalities of application or their effects (a set that only partly overlaps with the classical conception of 'secondary norms' introduced by R. Ago in the context of the codification of the law of state responsibility). Norms defining the spatial, temporal, personal, or substantive scope of application of a treaty or a norm (discussed in section 2.1) will exclude vast parcels of reality from the application of norms of conduct or obligations contained in a treaty or a norm. Such exclusions condition the application of a norm in the first place. Other techniques (discussed in sections 2.2 to 2.4) intervene only when these preliminary conditions have been met and they aim at excluding specific parcels of reality from the operation of an otherwise relevant norm or treaty or at introducing modalities for the operation of the norm or, still, at suspending such operation under specific circumstances. The remaining techniques (discussed in sections 2.5 to 2.7) take as a starting point the existence of a breach of a primary norm and their operation aims at justifying, or excusing or even precluding the wrongfulness of the breach. As such, they introduce modalities to the effects of a breach. Even when their operation is to make an unlawful act lawful, they assume initial illegality.

Of course, a scale could also be built on the basis of other criteria such as the substantive scope of the exception (some exceptions operating only in respect of a narrow rule and others for most international obligations). One could also attempt to organize techniques using criteria such as those that I have called implications (burden of proof; interpretation; deference; interaction with referral norms). But these and other legally-relevant analytical categories[1] would all converge in the purpose pursued by this section, namely to capture how international law has addressed the need to introduce nuance into the application of rules or, in a more imaged language, how it has tried to add colour to the black and white picture of rules and exceptions.

2.1 Delimitation of the scope of a norm or set of norms

The application of any norm or set of norms is generally defined, whether explicitly or implicitly, by reference to its four dimensions: substantive (*ratione materiae*), personal (*ratione personae*), temporal (*ratione temporis*), and spatial (*ratione loci*). These dimensions, elaborated to define the sphere of competence of states or state organs (e.g. tribunals), cannot

[1] On the analytical framework underpinning the use of these categories see Jorge E Viñuales, 'On Legal Inquiry' in Denis Alland and others (eds), *Unity and Diversity of International Law. Essays in Honour of Professor Pierre-Marie Dupuy* (Martinus Nijhoff 2014) 45–75.

be seen as such as techniques to escape a norm because they intervene initially to define the scope of the norm or of a set of norms. In other words, they define the rule, not the exception. What may instead be of interest to the present inquiry are the techniques through which such scope is defined. One can distinguish in this regard explicit and implicit ways of delimitating the overall scope of a norm or set of norms. The first category is obvious enough not to call for much comment. Most norms and treaties define their scope of application in various explicit ways, typically at the beginning of the treaty text. More interesting are the techniques through which some parts of this scope left unaddressed are delimitated by resort to a combination of interpretative and other (e.g. *lex specialis* or non-retroactivity) techniques.

An example will help to illustrate this point. In its *Advisory Opinion on the Construction of a Wall in Occupied Palestine Territory*,[2] the International Court of Justice (ICJ) had to address, among others, the substantive and spatial scopes of application of certain human rights treaties. In a previous advisory opinion,[3] the Court had already asserted that, from the standpoint of their substance, human rights treaties (specifically, the International Covenant on Civil and Political Rights (ICCPR)[4]) continued to apply during armed conflict or, in other words, that deprivation of life during armed conflict was not excluded from the scope of the ICCPR. The principle of *lex specialis*, which could have served as the basis for such an exclusion, was instead used as an articulation device whereby certain terms in the ICCPR (the term 'arbitrarily' in Article 6) were to be interpreted in the light of what the *lex specialis*, that is, *jus in bello*, dictated.[5] In the *Wall Opinion*, the Court went a step further and asserted that the spatial scope of application of the ICCPR, as defined in Article 2(1), had to be construed as extending to individuals beyond the territory of a state (Israel) but under its jurisdiction (as a result of occupation).[6] Importantly, in both advisory opinions, the Court noted that the protection offered by the ICCPR could cease (or, more specifically, be suspended) by the operation of a peculiar type of provision (Article 4) that authorizes derogations from some provisions if certain conditions are met. I will discuss this technique later in this chapter but, for present purposes, it suffices to emphasize the distinction between the definition of a scope of a treaty (which *in casu* extends to deprivation of life during armed conflict even beyond the territory of a contracting party) and the potential suspension of the protection offered by an otherwise applicable treaty.

2.2 Specific carve-outs or exemptions

Some provisions target measures, persons or objects that would normally be covered by the scope of the norm or set of norms, as defined by parameters discussed in the previous section, but that for a specific reason are excluded from the scope of one or more provisions. Such 'carve-outs' can be characterized by three main features. First, they normally respond to a specific reason, such as the protection of a specific interest considered as being of overriding importance as compared to the goals pursued by the norm or set of norms. Secondly, they rely on specific wording or on an explicit formulation. Thirdly, depending

[2] *Legal Consequences of the Construction of a Wall in the Occupied Palestinian Territory* (Advisory Opinion) [2004] ICJ Rep 136.
[3] *Legality of the Threat or Use of Nuclear Weapons* (Advisory Opinion) [1996] ICJ Rep 226.
[4] International Covenant on Civil and Political Rights (ICCPR) (16 December 1966) 999 UNTS 171.
[5] *Legality of the Threat or Use of Nuclear Weapons* (n 3) para 25.
[6] *Wall Opinion* (n 2) paras 108–109.

on their formulation, their operation is not to exclude a measure, person, or object from the entire scope of a treaty but only from that of one or several specific provisions or from a section. Their use is very frequent in treaty practice and because of the potential conflation with other techniques of a more 'exceptional' and restrictive nature, it is important to provide some examples from different areas of international law.

The first example concerns foreign investment disputes and is derived from the decision of an ad hoc committee organized under ICSID Arbitration Rules to review an application for annulment against the arbitral award rendered in *CMS v Argentina*.[7] The initial tribunal had interpreted a specific carve-out (Article XI) excluding measures in pursuance of essential security interests from the scope of the US–Argentina Bilateral Investment Treaty (BIT) in the light of the conditions governing the availability of the necessity defence under customary international law. Although it did not annul the award on this point, the Committee severely criticized the approach followed by the tribunal as an error of law. Specifically, it noted the legal impossibility for the necessity defence to operate at the same stage as Article XI because, if the measures fell indeed under the latter provision, there could be no breach that necessity could excuse.[8] In stating this important difference, the Committee emphasized the distinction between carve-outs and more exceptional forms of escaping a norm (*in casu* excuses). The carve-out in question excluded certain measures from the applicable primary norms whereas the necessity defence took both the application and the breach of such primary norms as a starting-point for its potential operation.

The operation of specific carve-outs, sometimes also called exemptions or derogations (in the trade context), is increasingly well understood in international dispute settlement. Continuing with the example of foreign investment disputes, in a case decided in 2016 in *Mesa v Canada*,[9] an arbitral tribunal expressly characterized a treaty provision (Article 1108(7)(a) of the North American Free Trade Agreement (NAFTA)) as a carve-out,[10] concluding that the measure challenged fell under the remit of this provision and, therefore, there could be no breach of the primary norm. Specifically, the investor had claimed among others that Canada had treated it in a discriminatory manner in the process of awarding contracts under a feed-in-tariff scheme. Article 1108(7)(a) states that the most-favoured-nation (MFN) and national treatment (NT) clauses of the NAFTA do not apply to 'Procurement by a Party or State enterprise'. The investor argued that the term 'procurement' had to be interpreted restrictively because Article 1108(7)(a) was an 'exception'.[11] The tribunal rejected the argument, considering that the mere characterization of a provision as an 'exception' did not necessarily call for a restrictive interpretation and that the term 'procurement' had to be elucidated in the light of the normal principles of treaty interpretation.[12] This passage illustrates the way in which conceptual distinctions among ways of escaping a norm may be mobilized in support of certain effects, although in this case the allegation was unsuccessful. Indeed, the tribunal reasoned that the measures at stake constituted procurement by the Government of Ontario and, therefore, they were not covered by the MFN and NT clauses.[13]

[7] *CMS Gas Transmission Company v Argentine Republic*, ICSID Case No ARB/01/08 Decision on Annulment (25 September 2007) (*CMS Annulment*). This decision reviewed the award rendered in 2005: *CMS Gas Transmission Company v Argentine Republic*, ICSID Case No ARB/01/8, Award (12 May 2005) (CMS Award).

[8] *CMS Annulment* (n 7) para 132.

[9] *Mesa Power Group, LLC v Government of Canada*, UNCITRAL, PCA Case No. 2012-17, Award (24 March 2016).

[10] ibid para 427.

[11] ibid para 405.

[12] ibid paras 405–406.

[13] ibid paras 460, 465.

This case is of interest because it provides an illustration of a broader body of practice in the area of international economic law.[14]

But specific carve-outs or exemptions have also been recognized in other areas. Of note is the decision of the ICJ in *Whaling in the Antarctic*,[15] where the Court clarified the operation of a specific provision (Article VIII(1)) of the 1946 Whaling Convention.[16] The case was brought by Australia against Japan, with New Zealand intervening, in connection with the whaling activities of Japan allegedly for scientific, rather than commercial purposes. In the 1980s, the Schedule of the Whaling Convention had been amended to ban (in paragraph 10(e)) whaling for commercial purposes. Article VIII(1) of the Convention provides, however, that a party may grant special permits for the taking of whales 'for purposes of scientific research', which Japan did through its Japanese Whale Research Programmes under Special Permit in the Antarctic (JARPA and JARPA II). As could be expected, Australia argued that Article VIII(1), read in the light of the other provisions of the Convention, had to be treated as a 'limited exception' and therefore was to be interpreted restrictively.[17] Conversely, Japan argued that the provision was an 'exemption' to be interpreted in the light of the freedom enjoyed by states under international law to engage in whaling.[18] Again, the positions of the parties illustrate the way in which conceptual distinctions are used in practice to seek certain effects. The Court rejected the claim that either a restrictive or an expansive interpretation was required and simply interpreted Article VIII(1) in the light of the object and purpose of the Convention.[19] It noted, however, that this provision gave discretion to Japan to grant special permits or set the conditions for them to be granted, although such discretion was not without limits.[20] *In casu*, after analysing in detail the operation of JARPA II, the Court concluded that the design and implementation of this programme was not reasonable in relation to the achievement of its stated objectives.[21] As a result, the measures were not excluded by the operation of Article VIII(1) from the scope of the Convention and therefore were in breach of the moratorium on commercial whaling in paragraph 10(e) of the Schedule.

From the three cases reviewed, one can derive two main conclusions. First, the operation of a specific carve-out or exemption, if available, is to exclude a given measure from the scope

[14] For other illustrations of the characterization of a provision as a 'carve-out' or an exemption see e.g. *Canada—Certain Measures Affecting the Renewable Energy Generation Sector—Canada—Measures Relating to the Feed-In Tariff Program*, WT/DS412/AB/R, WT/DS426/AB/R (6 May 2013) para 5.56 (characterizing art III:8(a) of the GATT as a 'derogation' excluding the application of art III in its entirety); *Argentina—Measures Affecting the Importation of Goods*, WT/DS438/AB/R, WT/DS444/AB/R, and WT/DS445/AB/R (15 January 2015) para 5.219 (discussing the operation of art XI:2 of the GATT). In some cases, the carve-out operates less automatically in that it only provides guidance to a tribunal on how to interpret certain investment protection standards as regards certain types of measures, e.g. regulations for a public purpose. See e.g. *Adel A Hamadi Al Tamimi v Sultanate of Oman*, ICSID Case No ARB/11/33, Award (3 November 2015) paras 387–90 (discussing the interpretation of the international minimum standard of treatment in the light of a treaty provision—art 10.10 of the US–Oman Free Trade Agreement—shielding environmental protection measures). Similar considerations would apply to the analysis of concepts such as the police powers doctrine or the margin of appreciation doctrines as applied in a foreign investment law context. See e.g. *Chemtura Corporation v Government of Canada*, UNCITRAL Rules, Award (2 August 2010) para 266 (discussing the application of the police powers doctrine to justify a targeted measure); *Philip Morris Brands Sàrl, Philip Morris Products SA and Abal Hermanos SA v Oriental Republic of Uruguay*, ICSID Case No ARB/10/7, Award (8 July 2016) para 399 (endorsing the existence of a margin of appreciation of States in the exercise of their regulatory powers).

[15] *Whaling in the Antarctic (Australia v Japan: New Zealand intervening) (Judgment)* [2014] ICJ Rep 226.

[16] International Convention for the Regulation of Whaling with Schedule of Whaling Regulations (2 December 1946) 161 UNTS 361.

[17] *Whaling in the Antarctic* (n 15) paras 53 and 57.

[18] ibid paras 52 and 57.

[19] ibid para 58.

[20] ibid para 61.

[21] ibid para 224.

of one or more primary norms. This is to be distinguished from a situation where the primary norm applies to the measure but the tribunal, after assessing the facts, concludes that there is no breach. Secondly, the parties referred—whether successfully or not—to conceptual distinctions between exemptions and exceptions in order to derive consequences as to certain effects (e.g. type of interpretation, degree of deference) of the provision. I will discuss later the potential implications of different characterizations, but the need for a conceptual basis to make the argument seems well established.

2.3 Flexibilities

The term flexibilities refers here to a diverse array of techniques which, although broadly similar to carve-outs and exemptions, present some distinctive features. A first feature is the absence of a generally agreed reason to exempt certain regulated objects from the treaty regime. Rather than exempting certain objects for emergency, health, environmental, or other reasons, the rationale underpinning the granting of flexibility is the need for wider state participation in the regime, even if states have very different situations and interests. Secondly, the lack of overriding reasons, other than the aim to achieve wide participation, sets the bounds within which flexibility is granted. These bounds are derived from the fundamental object and purpose pursued by the treaty. Flexibilities are carefully crafted so as not to jeopardize such purposes. Thirdly, flexibilities often carry a temporal dimension, whether because they are provisional in nature or because time is offered as a modality to accommodate specific interests. These three features are shared by at least four types of flexibilities.

One technique is to provide for *time-barred specific exemptions* allowing countries to adjust gradually to the requirements of a treaty or to maintain some narrow allowances under some conditions. By way of illustration, the Stockholm Convention on Persistent Organic Pollutants (POP Convention)[22] provides for certain types 'specific exemptions' in connection with the production and use of the substances in Annexes A and B. To benefit from one of the available types of exemptions, a state must specifically register with the Secretariat, which keeps a register. Once registered, a state can use the exemption for a period of five years, unless an extension is granted.[23] If at any point in time, a type of exemption has no registered states, it is removed and no state may benefit from it in the future. Such was the case of the use of hexachlorobenzene as a 'close system site-limited intermediate', which was removed on 17 May 2009.[24] Time-barred exemptions were also used in trade law by the Agreement on Subsidies and Countervailing Measures (SCM Agreement)[25] for so-called 'non-actionable subsidies' but this category of subsidies applied provisionally for five years and expired, in the absence of consensus to extend it, on 31 December 1999.

A slightly different technique consists of introducing *exemptions that are generally available* but only for as long as a technical entity considers them justifiable. In such a case, although in theory the exemption is not time-barred, in practice it is, as the entity entitled to influence the scope of the exemption may close it altogether. By way of illustration, the POP Convention provides that an otherwise banned substance, Dichlorodiphenyltrichloroethane

[22] Stockholm Convention on Persistent Organic Pollutants (22 May 2001) 40 ILM 532.
[23] ibid art 4(7).
[24] ibid Annex A, n 1.
[25] Agreement on Subsidies and Countervailing Measures (15 April 1994) 1867 UNTS 14 art 8 (Non-actionable subsidies), which elapsed after five years (art 31).

(DDT), can be produced and used for the specific purpose of '[d]isease vector control ... in accordance with Part II of [Annex B]'.[26] Part II in turn provides that: 'Each Party that produces and/or uses DDT shall restrict such production and/or use for disease vector control in accordance with the World Health Organization recommendations and guidelines on the use of DDT and when locally safe, effective and affordable alternatives are not available to the Party in question.'

Any state can avail itself of this exemption without the need for registration but only under the stated conditions. The WHO recommends use of DDT as disease vector control (against malaria-spreading mosquitoes) only for 'indoor residual spraying' and 'until locally appropriate and cost-effective alternatives are available for a sustainable transition from DDT'.[27] The scope is narrowly circumscribed, thus highlighting the exceptionality of the allowance, and in both texts there is explicit reference to the temporary character of DDT production and use.

The time dimension is also an important consideration in another approach for the granting of flexibility in view of increasing state participation, namely *differentiation* techniques. The subject is vast and could easily fill a volume but, for present purposes, it will suffice to illustrate it by reference to the Montreal Protocol on Substances that Deplete the Ozone Layer.[28] The Protocol requires all states to phase down and/or out their production and consumption of certain substances, but developing states benefit from two types of flexibilities, namely a different time schedule (allowing for an additional decade)[29] and assistance, both financial and technological.[30] The latter element was specifically introduced shortly after the Protocol's adoption (through the London amendment) to cover the incremental costs of converting certain facilities and hence to persuade China and India, among others, to join the Protocol.[31] This approach to differentiation has been essentially maintained in the important Kigali Amendment adopted in late 2016 to bring certain powerful climate forcers (hydrofluorocarbons (HFCs)) under the Protocol, although more timeframes (two for developed countries and two for developing countries) are envisioned and a high ambient temperature (HAT) exemption has also been introduced.[32]

The fourth and final technique that can be considered as a form of flexibility is the regulation of the ability of states to make *reservations* to certain provisions of a treaty. The use of reservations to promote participation to certain treaties was recognized very early in the case law of the ICJ, in its *Advisory Opinion on Reservations to the Genocide Convention*,[33] by reference to the earlier Latin-American practice. The Court also recognized the downside of such an approach, namely the potential undermining of the 'object and purpose' of the treaty. In order to strike a balance between participation and effectiveness, many treaties regulate the ability of states to make reservations. Among the numerous examples one could give, it may be useful to refer to Article 298 of the UNCLOS. Compulsory dispute settlement was part of the package deal of the UNCLOS in that a state that wished to become a party had to

[26] Stockholm Convention (n 22) Annex B, Pt I.

[27] World Health Organization, *The Use of DDT in Malaria Vector Control. WHO Position Statement* (WHO 2011).

[28] Montreal Protocol on Substances that Deplete the Ozone Layer (16 September 1987) 1522 UNTS 29.

[29] ibid art 5.

[30] ibid arts 10 and 10A.

[31] Richard E Benedick, *Ozone Diplomacy: New Directions in Safeguarding the Planet* (Harvard University Press 1998) 187–88.

[32] See Decision XXVIII/1 'Further Amendment of the Montreal Protocol' (14 October 2016) UNEP/OzL.Pro.28/CRP/10; and Decision XXVIII/2 'Decision related to the amendment phasing down hydrofluorocarbons' (14 October 2016) UNEP/OzL.Pro.28/CRP/11 (together the 'Kigali Amendment').

[33] *Reservations to the Convention on Genocide* (Advisory Opinion), [1951] ICJ Rep 15.

accept compulsory dispute settlement. However, in order to add some flexibility on sensitive issues,[34] the treaty allowed for some carve-outs (e.g. Article 297 paragraphs (2)(a)(i)–(ii) and (3)(a), which are submitted to conciliation),[35] as well as for the possibility of making some specific types of reservations to the dispute settlement mechanisms. Indeed, Article 298, entitled 'Optional exceptions to applicability of section 2', allows in its paragraph (1) states parties to exclude from compulsory dispute settlement (of Part XV of the UNCLOS) certain types of disputes, such as questions of maritime delimitation or involving historic bays or titles (which remain subject to conciliation except when they necessarily entail the settlement of a dispute over land or insular territory), disputes relating to military and law enforcement activities, and disputes that are being addressed by the UN Security Council. In order to avail itself of such exclusions, a state has to make a specific written declaration at the time of joining the convention or at any time thereafter, before the dispute arises. The declaration may be withdrawn at any time and, even if maintained, it does not prevent a declarant state from agreeing to dispute settlement in respect of an excluded dispute. Although such declarations introduce potentially permanent exclusions, the great ease with which they can be withdrawn (or reintroduced) and, above all, the fact that they can only concern a specific category of disputes, is a way of regulating the power to make reservations so as to strike a balance between participation and effectiveness.

As discussed next, there are other techniques that rely on a circumscribed set of options, a time dimension and some stringent conditions, regularly used in the context of human rights instruments.

2.4 Derogations

Several human rights treaties specifically address the possibility for states to suspend the effect of certain human rights provisions in case of public emergency.[36] The operation of such clauses is complex and would require detailed commentary.[37] However, for present purposes it suffices to characterize the technique as such and distinguish it from other techniques, particularly carve-outs and flexibilities. Despite some variation in the wording used by different clauses, derogations are generally subject to both substantive (existence of a public emergency of sufficient gravity, identification of non-derogable rights, proportionality,

[34] *In the matter of the Chagos Marine Protected Area Arbitration before an Arbitral Tribunal constituted under Annex VII of the United Nations Convention on the Law of the Sea (Mauritius v UK)* Award (18 March 2015) paras 216–19 (discussing the reasons underpinning the carve-outs and flexibilities provided for in arts 297 and 298).

[35] ibid para 216 (using specifically the term 'carve-out').

[36] See ICCPR (n 4) art 4; Convention for the Protection of Human Rights and Fundamental Freedoms (4 November 1950) 213 UNTS 221 art 15; American Convention on Human Rights (ACHR) (22 November 1969) 1144 UNTS 123 art 27. There is no equivalent provision in the African context. See African Charter on Human and Peoples' Rights (27 June 1981) 21 ILM 58 (1982) and *Commission nationale des droits de l'Homme et des libertés v Chad* African Commission Communication no 74/92 (October 1995) para 21.

[37] For a detailed commentary of what is perhaps the most emblematic provision see Human Rights Committee, *General Comment 29, States of Emergency (art 4)* UN Doc CCPR/C/21/Rev.1/Add.11 (2001). For a concise comparative analysis see David Kretzmer, 'State of Emergency' in *Max Planck Encyclopedia of Public International Law* (February 2008) http://opil.ouplaw.com (accessed 10 December 2016), referring to some applications of derogation clauses in different regional contexts: *The Greek Case* App nos 3321/67, 3322/67, 3323/67, and 3344/67 (ECommHR Report of the Sub-Commission vol I(1) 5 November 1969) paras 112–25; *Case of Brannigan and McBride v the United Kingdom* App nos 14553/89 and 14554/89 (ECtHR 25 May 1993) paras 40–74 (assessing a derogation from art 5). For a recent study see Evan J Criddle (ed), *Human Rights in Emergencies* (Cambridge University Press 2016).

temporality, and non-discriminatory character of derogation measures) and procedural conditions (official proclamation and international notification).

Unlike carve-outs, derogations are inherently temporary in their application, which follows the very concept of a state of emergency. The Human Rights Committee has expressed concern in the past regarding the prolonged states of emergency prevailing in countries such as Israel, Egypt, or Syria.[38] Derogations are thus distinct from the limitations or restrictions to human rights expressly envisioned in the wording of certain provisions. By way of illustration, the enjoyment of the freedom of thought, conscience, and religion, which is non-derogable under the ICCPR and the American Convention on Human Rights (ACHR), may nevertheless be subject to limitations 'as are prescribed by law and are necessary to protect public safety, order, health, or morals or the fundamental rights and freedoms of others' (Article 18(3)).[39] Moreover, derogations require specific procedural action from the state, which in order to avail itself from a derogation needs to declare the situation of public emergency, notify its existence, and specify the rights it intends to derogate from.

Moreover, unlike flexibilities and carve-outs, derogations do not redefine the specific scope of a primary norm as it applies to a state but only modulate their application. Rather than suspending the operation of the relevant human rights, the effect of derogations is to suspend their 'full and effective exercise'.[40] The extent to which such exercise is suspended is circumscribed by the 'exigencies of the situation' and the proportionality reasoning used to assess this question is applicable both to the derogation (the measure declaring or embodying the derogation) and to specific instances where the derogation is effectively used. That means that even a right from which a state has validly derogated remains applicable and in operation to all the extent that the derogation is not strictly required by the emergency situation.

However, where a measure and its specific implementation fall under a valid derogation, there is technically no breach of the human right in question. In this regard, derogations operate like carve-outs and flexibilities. As discussed next, there are other techniques, which take as a starting point the existence of breach in order to come into play.

2.5 Exceptions *stricto sensu*

A well-known and influential exception clause is Article XX of the General Agreement on Tariffs and Trade (GATT).[41] The general import of this clause is to allow World Trade Organization (WTO) members to adopt certain measures for non-trade purposes, even if such measures are inconsistent with other provisions of the GATT or of some related agreements.

Conceptually, this clause can be characterized as an exception *stricto sensu* in that its operation assumes a prior finding of inconsistency with a primary norm. The distinction between the two inquiries, one relating to the breach of primary norm (which would be excluded if a carve-out in the primary norm were available) and the other focusing on whether the breach can be justified, has been consistently emphasized by the WTO Appellate Body.[42]

[38] Kretzmer (n 37) para 21.

[39] ibid para 24.

[40] *Habeas Corpus in Emergency Situations (Arts. 27(2) and 7(6) of the American Convention on Human Rights)*, ICtHR, Advisory Opinion OC-8/87 (30 January 1987) para 18. See also General Comment 29 (n 37) para 4.

[41] See General Agreement on Tariffs and Trade (15 April 1994) 1867 UNTS 187 art XX.

[42] See *United States—Standards for Reformulated and Conventional Gasoline*, WT/DS2/AB/R (29 April 1996) 23; *European Communities—Measures Affecting Asbestos and Asbestos-Containing Products*, WT/DS135/AB/R (12

The remarks of the Appellate Body in *Thailand—Cigarettes (Philippines)* are particularly apposite:

> [I]n examining a specific measure, a panel may be called upon to analyze a substantive obligation and an affirmative defence, and to apply both to that measure. It is also true that such an exercise will require a panel to find and apply a 'line of equilibrium' between a substantive obligation and an exception. Yet this does not render that panel's analyses of the obligation and the exception a single and integrated one. *On the contrary, an analysis of whether a measure infringes an obligation necessarily precedes, and is distinct from, the 'further and separate' assessment of whether such measure is otherwise justified.*[43]

The nature of the clause has implications for its operation, particularly as regards inter alia the burden of proving the 'exception' or 'affirmative defence'[44] and the stringent and still quite unclear[45] conditions for its operation. Such operation has, in turn, important implications for certain policy issues, including for the room for legitimate differentiation between goods the processes and production methods of which have widely different environmental footprints. At present, such differentiation is essentially unavailable at the level of the primary norm (e.g. as a carve-out to or a flexibility in a non-discrimination standard), and it therefore remains confined within the narrow bounds of a stringent exception.[46] This illustration emphasizes the practical relevance of conceptually distinguishing among different techniques to escape a rule.

2.6 Excuses (preclusion of responsibility)

International lawyers are familiar with the six 'circumstances precluding wrongfulness' envisioned in Part One, Chapter V of the ILC Articles on State Responsibility.[47] Those who have followed the many decades of codification efforts[48] will be aware of the debate over the scope and characterization of such circumstances. Whether some of these clauses are more appropriately characterized as a primary norm in their own right, or as an excuse (precluding responsibility), or, still, as a genuine circumstance precluding wrongfulness, the six clauses share the fact that their operation does not affect the underlying primary norm, which continues to exist (Article 27(a)). They have this feature in common with derogations and exceptions *stricto sensu*. They also share with the latter category the fact that they suppose a form of inconsistency (here, a 'breach') with a primary norm.[49] However, unlike derogations

March 2001) para 115; *Thailand—Customs and Fiscal Measures on Cigarettes from the Philippines*, WT/DS371/AB/R (17 June 2011) para 173.

[43] *Thailand—Cigarettes (Philippines)* (n 42) para 173 (italics added).

[44] ibid para 176.

[45] On the ambiguities affecting the understanding of the chapeau of art XX see Lorand Bartels, 'The Chapeau of the General Exceptions in the WTO GATT and GATS Agreements: A Reconstruction' (2015) 109 American Journal of International Law 95.

[46] See Pierre-Marie Dupuy, Jorge E Viñuales, *International Environmental Law* (Cambridge University Press 2015) 400–403.

[47] Responsibility of States for Internationally Wrongful Acts, GA Res 56/83, UN Doc A/RES/56/83 (12 December 2001) (ILC Articles).

[48] See generally James Crawford, *State Responsibility. The General Part* (Cambridge University Press 2013) 28–44, 274–321.

[49] *CMS Annulment* (n 7) para 132.

and exceptions *stricto sensu*, the clauses in Chapter V are all of general application[50] in that their operation is not limited to a given norm, treaty, or set of legally linked treaties. This is an important feature distinguishing these clauses from the exception clauses identified in the previous section. Other specificities depend upon the specific characterization of each of the clauses in Chapter V.

Leaving aside the question of whether a circumstance such as self-defence is a primary norm in its own right, there are two recognizable sets of clauses in Chapter V, namely 'excuses' and circumstances genuinely excluding wrongfulness. Excuses, such as the necessity defence (Article 25) and perhaps also distress (Article 24) and *force majeure* (Article 23),[51] are more appropriately characterized as techniques excluding not the wrongfulness of the conduct but the responsibility triggered by the breach.[52] Stating that a breach of a primary norm is temporarily excused (hence precluding responsibility) is intuitively distinct from the utter absence of a breach (preclusion of wrongfulness) owing, for example, to consent of the injured state (Article 20). It is indeed not the same for an act to be 'wrongful but excused' or simply 'not wrongful'. This subtle difference is reflected legally in a number of ways, including the stringent requirements set to the availability of excuses, their effects, and their normative implications.

Regarding, first, the requirements conditioning excuses, the clearest example is provided by necessity. Out of the six circumstances envisioned in Chapter V, necessity is the only one that has been deliberately formulated in negative language ('[n]ecessity may not be invoked …'). This wording is intended to highlight the exceptional nature of this excuse.[53] Moreover, as noted by the ICJ in the case concerning the *Gabčíkovo-Nagymaros Project*, the exceptional nature of a plea of necessity is further emphasized by the fact that it 'can only be invoked under certain strictly defined conditions which must be cumulatively satisfied; and the State concerned is not the sole judge of whether those conditions have been met'.[54] Furthermore, necessity (like *force majeure*[55] and distress[56]) is not available when the state that seeks to excuse its conduct has itself contributed to the situation of necessity.[57] There is, in such a case, no sufficient excuse for the wrongful conduct. Significantly, this 'legitimacy' condition seems to be specific to excuses and is not present in circumstances precluding wrongfulness.

The distinction between the implications of excuses and circumstances precluding wrongfulness is also implicit in Article 27 of the ILC Articles, which leaves enough room to accommodate the effects of different circumstances. Excuses are more likely to call for compensation in broad terms, that is, for 'making good' any loss suffered by the injured state as

[50] ILC Articles (n 47) Commentary and ch V, para 2.

[51] The ILC Articles, commentary and art 25 notes, at para 2, that, unlike the other circumstances, necessity, distress and *force majeure* are not dependent upon prior conduct of the injured state. There are of course differences among arts 23, 24, and 25, which the commentary also emphasizes, but their shared basis is further reflected in the types of conditions set for their availability.

[52] The distinction between preclusion of wrongfulness ('not wrongful') and preclusion of responsibility ('wrongful but excused') is emphasized by Vaughan Lowe, 'Precluding Wrongfulness or Responsibility: A Plea for Excuses' (1999) 10 European Journal of International Law 405. See also Théodore Christakis, 'Les "circonstances excluant l'illicéité": une illusion optique?' in Nicolas Angelet (ed), *Droit du pouvoir, Pouvoir du droit—Mélanges offerts à Jean Salmon* (Bruylant 2007) 223–70, 244. More generally, the distinction was outlined by the ICJ in the *Case concerning United States Diplomatic and Consular Staff in Tehran* (Judgment) [1980] ICJ Rep 3, para 89. For a comprehensive treatment see Federica Paddeu, *Justification and Excuse in International Law: Concept and Theory of General Defences* (Cambridge University Press, 2018), chapters 1 to 3 as well as the contributions of Paddeu (at section 2.2) and d'Almeida (at section 2.1) in this volume.

[53] ILC Articles (n 47) commentary and art 25, para 14.

[54] *Gabčíkovo-Nagymaros Project (Hungary v Slovakia)* (Judgment) [1997] ICJ Rep 7, para 51.

[55] ILC Articles (n 47) art 23(2)(a).

[56] ibid art 24(2)(a).

[57] ibid art 25(2)(b).

a result of the excused conduct.[58] Such payments would not intervene, technically, as a form of reparation under the ILC Articles because the secondary norms governing reparation are not triggered.[59]

Thirdly, the distinction between the two techniques is also relevant from a policy perspective to the extent that treating an act as 'wrong but excused' rather than as 'not wrong' may be desirable to heighten the normative pull of a primary norm, particularly if one takes into account that other states (beyond the injured state) may have an interest in the consolidation of the authority of the relevant primary norm.[60]

2.7 Circumstances precluding wrongfulness

Circumstances precluding the wrongfulness of certain conduct do more than excuse wrongdoing; they turn a conduct which is apparently incompatible with a primary norm into 'justified' conduct or, in other words, they make the conduct entirely lawful. Circumstances precluding wrongfulness constitute permissions to act in a certain way, which would otherwise be prohibited by another norm of the legal order.[61] These rules thus combine features of both primary and secondary norms: they guide the conduct of states (primary norm), but are relevant to the determination of responsibility (secondary norm).[62] It was said above that this category of rules supposes that the conduct is inconsistent with the primary norm. This should not be equated, in respect of circumstances precluding wrongfulness, with the existence of a 'breach' of the primary norm in question, as has often been stated in the literature and the case law.[63] Whether a breach of a primary norm exists is the conclusion of the reasoning, and the consideration of whether a circumstance precluding wrongfulness applies *is* a step in that reasoning. At most, one can speak of a 'prima facie' breach as a step in the reasoning, namely the step prior to the consideration of whether a circumstance precluding wrongfulness applies. Indeed, the whole point of raising a justification is precisely to establish that no breach has occurred.[64]

There has been significant debate as to the inclusion of some specific circumstances (e.g. consent and self-defence) in the ILC Articles, but such discussions are less important for present purposes than the characterization of these circumstances as a technique to escape a rule. Importantly, the effect of these circumstances is wide-ranging not only because they are of general application to all suitable primary norms, but also because, unlike excuses, their presence does more than excuse conduct; indeed, it normalizes it.

Their operation can be illustrated by reference to the *DRC v Uganda* case before the ICJ.[65] The case concerned the military activities of Uganda in the eastern part of the Democratic Republic of the Congo. Uganda argued that its military presence was justified by the consent

[58] *Gabčíkovo-Nagymaros* (n 54) para 48. See also Crawford (n 48) 279 (referring to the position of several states that, unlike situations of *force majeure*, distress, and necessity, in case of consent, self-defence, and countermeasures, the state is 'under no duty to pay compensation').

[59] See ILC Articles (n 47) Commentary and art 27, paras 4–6.

[60] See Lowe (n 52); Paddeu, *Justification and Excuse* (n 52) 94–7 (with examples from investment arbitration practice).

[61] See Paddeu, *Justification and Excuse* (n 52) 102–106.

[62] ibid 57–61.

[63] See the contribution of F Paddeu (at section 1) in the present volume.

[64] See Paddeu, *Justification and Excuse* (n 52) 106–10.

[65] *Armed Activities on the Territory of the Congo (Democratic Republic of the Congo v Uganda)* (Judgment) [2005] ICJ Rep 168.

of the DRC and by self-defence. The Court distinguished two main periods, namely before August 1998, when this presence was consented by the DRC, and after this date, once the DRC had withdrawn such consent. The analysis of the issue of consent in each period sheds light on how this circumstance precluding wrongfulness operates in practice. When discussing the early military operations of Uganda against anti-Uganda rebels, the Court noted that, until August 1998, the DRC had not objected to Ugandan military presence.[66] The Court characterized the formalities of 'consent' by reference to the legal source of such consent. Whereas Uganda argued that a Protocol signed by both parties provided consent, the Court derived consent from the practice without objection both prior and subsequent to the signing of the Protocol.[67] Hence, it was the implicit authorization that founded consent and such consent did not require any formalities to be withdrawn. The Court further noted that the consent thus given was not open-ended and unconditional. It concerned the fight against the rebels on the border and remained geographically restricted.[68] The Court concluded that in all events such consent had been withdrawn by early August 1998. Beyond this time period, Uganda sought to justify its subsequent action by reference to certain agreements, including a calendar for the withdrawal of Ugandan troops.[69] The Court rejected this argument stating that, although the agreements, particularly the withdrawal calendars and disengagement plans, acknowledged the presence of Ugandan troops for certain periods defined by reference to specific events, those terms only amounted to acknowledging a situation on the ground and a *modus operandi* to carry out the withdrawal. They could not be understood as general consent from the DRC to the presence of Ugandan troops, except for one specific authorization (in the Luanda Agreement) to station troops in Mount Ruwenzori, if necessary, after the withdrawal had been completed, and this because both parties acknowledged Uganda's security interest in the area concerned.[70] Thus, the agreements could not be considered to 'validat[e] that [military] presence in law'.[71] The reference to validation is significant because it conveys that the apparent illegality (a potential breach of sovereignty and territorial integrity) could be justified or 'validated', and as such be rendered lawful, rather than 'excused'.

Uganda also claimed that its conduct was an exercise of its right to self-defence.[72] The Court conducted a detailed analysis of the facts and referred to Article 51 of the UN Charter to assess whether the conditions of self-defence were met. Of note is the fact that some military incursions for which the consent defence had been excluded (the taking of certain towns and airports) could also, potentially, fall under the self-defence justification. The Court concluded, however, that the conditions were not met. Uganda had not reported to the UN Security Council its action of early September 1998 and it could not establish that it had suffered an 'armed attack' from the Congolese army, as the military action against Uganda came from rebel groups whose acts were not attributable to the DRC.[73] Moreover, the Court

[66] ibid para 45.
[67] ibid paras 46–47.
[68] ibid paras 51–3. The Court further emphasized this point later in the decision, in connection with Uganda's taking of certain towns and airports in the border region, and it noted that '[t]he issue of when any consent may have terminated is irrelevant when the actions concerned are so clearly beyond co-operation "in order to ensure peace and security along the common border", as had been confirmed in the Protocol of 27 April 1998': ibid para 111.
[69] ibid para 92.
[70] ibid paras 104–105.
[71] ibid para 105 *in fine*.
[72] ibid paras 118 ff.
[73] ibid para 146.

added as an *obiter dictum* that the action of Uganda could have hardly met the further conditions of proportionality and necessity.[74]

Having reached the conclusion that Uganda had neither acted with the DRC's consent nor in self-defence, the Court characterized the action of Uganda as violations of the prohibition of the use of force,[75] the principle of non-intervention,[76] and the sovereignty and territorial integrity of the DRC.[77] However, the specific contours of the two circumstances in connection with these norms were not clearly spelt out by the Court. Whereas there is no doubt that action in self-defence is not constitutive of a breach of the prohibition on the use of force, the Court suggested that some military intervention, which could also constitute such a breach, could be justified by consent. Such justification power seems beyond the reach of excuses. Moreover, despite the reference to 'validation' in respect of consent, which implies (but only on the facts of the case) a sequential element between the breach and the justification, the operation of these circumstances seems to place the challenged conduct under a safe harbour and thus make it legal *ab initio*, as long as it remains within the bounds of this safe harbour. In that respect, circumstances precluding wrongfulness can be compared to some techniques discussed earlier in this chapter, particularly the definition of the scope of a norm, carve-outs, and, perhaps, derogations. They remain different, however, in at least three respects. First, circumstances precluding wrongfulness are of general application. Secondly, unlike scope limitations and carve-outs, the scope of the primary norm in question makes it clearly applicable to the situation, in a way comparable to the continued operation of human rights norms despite derogation, which only affects their full enjoyment. Perhaps a third distinction lies in the type of primary norms that are subject to the reach of circumstances precluding wrongfulness, which include not only more norms (because of their general application) but arguably also some more important norms, such as the prohibition of the use of force (under self-defence). In fairness, the third difference is not of a technical but only of a descriptive nature, and it would require finer-grained (norm-by-norm) analysis to be established. But it provides some perspective on otherwise comparable and sometimes amalgamated concepts. However, as discussed next, it is important not to conflate these many ways of escaping a rule, because the arguments that can be made by reference to one or the other category and the actual effects of their operation differ significantly.

3 Implications of Different Techniques

3.1 Types of implications

Using or applying each of these types of techniques may carry different legal implications. Some of these implications have been identified when characterizing each type of technique. By way of illustration, some techniques are of general application, whereas others only concern specific primary norms. Also, in some cases the exceptional treatment is permanently organized (through a permanent exclusion), whereas in others it is only of a temporal nature. Still another implication concerns the applicability of a primary norm, which in some cases is simply excluded (the scope of the norm is defined or carved in a certain way), whereas in

[74] ibid para 147.
[75] ibid para 153.
[76] ibid para 163.
[77] ibid para 165.

some others it remains applicable to all the extent not derogated from, excused, or justified. In this section, my purpose is to concentrate on four other types of implications of significant practical importance, namely those regarding (3.2) the burden of proof, (3.3) the interpretative approach, (3.4) the degree of deference afforded under a clause, and (3.5) the interaction of different techniques with referral clauses.

But before analysing these types of implications, it is necessary to recall how they may come into play. Two levels can be distinguished. A first level concerns the legal effects of characterizing, technically, a given clause as a certain type of exception. For example, characterizing a clause as an exemption or a carve-out will refer to the manner in which the clause operates (excluding the application of the primary norm to the situation in question), which is different from the characterization as a derogation from human rights provisions (which would carry certain procedural requirements) or as an exception or an excuse (a circumstance precluding responsibility such as necessity), which suppose a prior breach of a primary norm. In practice, of course, some doubt is permitted as to whether it is the characterization of the clause as a certain type of technique or the clause itself (e.g. Article XX of the GATT or the necessity defence codified in Article 25 of the ILC Articles), which carries such effects. The cautious—and simple—answer is that each clause is to be specifically interpreted before any effects are attached to its operation.

However, on closer inspection, the very reasoning through which a given clause is argued to deploy certain effects or operate in a certain manner relies upon conceptual categories that often remain inchoate in the pleadings of the parties, the decisions of courts and tribunals, or the writings of scholars about the operation of certain clauses. At this second and deeper level, the seven techniques identified are used, explicitly or implicitly, to shape legal reasoning and implementation. They are hence more than merely descriptive patterns of how to organize special treatment of certain situations; they are normative patterns in that (i) they are mobilized in order to support certain legal effects and, in some cases, (ii) these effects are successfully established and become the new normal (e.g. it is now widely recognized as a fallback legal position that the burden of proving an exception lies with the party invoking it). Thus, what is understood to be the law is largely driven by less explicit and deeper shared understandings regarding the relations between the conceptual understanding of exceptions and the expected legal implications. There is, of course, much variation from one clause or tribunal to another and over time. But, as I will endeavour to show, there are also some discernible trends.

My purpose in the following sections is to discuss, for each of the four types of implications identified above, these two levels by reference to examples derived from the case law of international courts and tribunals.

3.2 Burden of proof

The connection between the level of exceptionality of a clause and the allocation of the burden of proof is frequently argued in practice, although it is not always explicitly addressed in decisions. It is not my purpose here to conduct a study of the allocation of the burden of proof for a specific clause (e.g. Article XX of the GATT) or sub-clause (e.g. letter (b) in Article XX of the GATT), or even certain elements of a clause (e.g. the burden of proving 'clean hands' or no contribution under the customary necessity defence). Nor is it my purpose to conduct a study of the burden of proof as regards a given 'type' of exception (e.g. carve-outs, derogations, exceptions, excuses, etc) across their different embodiments in specific clauses or applications by different tribunals or over time. The analytical unit for a proper and cautious legal analysis would be likely to be a specific clause or a type of exception in a given context (e.g. exemptions and exceptions in the WTO system, or excuses and justifications in the context of Part One, Chapter V of the ILC Articles) and, more importantly, it would have to rely on a comprehensive survey of the relevant case law. My purpose is to analyse the role of the conceptual characterization of a clause (by reference to certain models or 'types' of exceptions) in the reasoning intended to effect (whether it succeeds or not) a certain allocation of the burden of proof.

References to the level of exceptionality of a clause are frequently mobilized to place the burden of proof on the party benefiting from the applicability of the clause. By way of illustration, in *Brannigan and McBride v UK*, the applicants admitted as a general matter the existence of a public emergency in the meaning of Article 15 of the European Convention on Human Rights (ECHR), but they argued that the burden of proving that there was actually and specifically a situation of public emergency threatening the life of the nation at the relevant times lay with the respondent.[78] Of note is the broader position underpinning this claim, namely that the margin of appreciation of states in this regard had to be more strictly construed when the derogation targets rights that are essential for safeguarding non-derogable rights and, particularly, when the emergency has become a permanent state of affairs.[79] A similar argumentation can be found in the *CMS Award*, with respect to a different type of clause, namely the customary necessity defence and the emergency clauses in the Argentina–US BIT.[80] The claimant sought to characterize Article XI (later found, by the ad hoc committee reviewing the award, to be a carve-out[81]) as 'very narrow and specific exceptions to liability'.[82] Yet another illustration is provided by the position of Mauritius in the *Chagos Arbitration*. The specific context was the understanding of Articles 297 and 298 of the UNCLOS. Mauritius argued that 'the United Kingdom bears the burden of establishing that an express exception of the Tribunal's jurisdiction, such as those set out in Articles 297 and 298, is applicable'.[83] The tribunal conducted a detailed analysis of the relevant provisions and admitted the objections to jurisdiction for three out of four submissions made by Mauritius. But that conclusion reached by the tribunal in this and other cases[84] is less important than the more general point that can be derived from them.

[78] *Brannigan v UK* (n 37) paras 44 and 45. The Court concluded that the existence of such an emergency at the relevant times was established (para 47). Although it did not explicitly address the burden of proof, it referred in support of its reasoning to an earlier case, *Lawless v Ireland*, where it had stated that Ireland had 'reasonably deduced' the existence of such an emergency from 'a combination of several factors'. See *Lawless v Ireland* App no 332/57 (ECtHR 1 July 1961) para 28. In the *Greek Case* (n 37) the ECommHR clearly stated at para 114 that: 'the burden lies upon the respondent government to show that the conditions justifying measures of derogation under Article 15 have been and continue to be met, due regard being had to the "margin of appreciation" which, according to the constant jurisprudence of the Commission, the Government has in judging the situation in Greece as from the moment it assumed power on the 21st April 1967.'

[79] *Brannigan v UK* (n 37) paras 41–42.

[80] *CMS Award* (n 7) paras 313, 336.

[81] *CMS Annulment* (n 7) para 129.

[82] *CMS Award* (n 7) 336.

[83] *Chagos Arbitration* (n 34) para 161.

[84] For cases accepting the link between, on the one hand, derogations to human rights or exceptions *stricto sensu* or circumstances precluding wrongfulness and, on the other hand, regarding the burden of proof see e.g. the *Greek Case* (n 37) para 114; *Thailand—Cigarettes* (n 42) para 176; *DRC v Uganda* (n 65) para 127. In other cases, the burden of proving the facts underpinning the availability of a clause explicitly characterized as a 'carve-out' (rather than an exception) has been placed on the party invoking it but, importantly, the burden of proving that a referral clause (relied upon to exclude the operation of the carve-out as a mere exception) applies lies with the claimant, e.g. *Mesa v Canada* (n 9) 237, 401 (the assumption in the latter paragraph is that the claimant must establish that the treaty indeed applies to the measure challenged). However, in some other cases, the existence of a link has been left open. See e.g. *Canada—Renewables* (n 14) para 5.56.

Indeed, despite the differences among the clauses at stake in these cases, there is a clear attempt at emphasizing or downplaying their level of exceptionality, often explicitly seeking a characterization of an otherwise uncharacterized clause, in order to seek a specific allocation of the burden of proof. As discussed next, a similar trend is apparent in connection with other implications, such as the proper interpretation approach or the level of deference entailed by each clause or, still, their interaction with referral clauses.

3.3 Interpretation approach

The backdrop of any discussion regarding interpretation is that treaties are to be interpreted in accordance with the rules of interpretation codified in Articles 31 and 32 of the Vienna Convention on the Law of Treaties (VCLT),[85] which reflect customary law on this question. However comfortable as a starting-point, this observation is of limited interest for the understanding of the operation of the techniques discussed in this chapter. Indeed, 'beyond' or 'within' the usual rules, one finds other interpretation techniques, including the teleological interpretation applied to constituent instruments (treaties or otherwise) of international organizations, the progressive interpretation applied in the context of human rights law, the interpretation of treaties in the light of contemporary environmental norms, the rules on inter-temporal law, the maxim according to which restrictions to sovereignty are not to be presumed, the reference to other contemporary treaties (e.g. those signed by a given state in a specific area) to ascertain the intention of the parties to a treaty (a similar type of treaty with a third state), the techniques of authentic interpretation not included in Articles 31(3)(a)–(b), the so-called *ejusdem generis* maxim, and many others. Whether these approaches are considered to be part of the interpretation rules in the VCLT, arise from a *lex specialis* or from general international law or, still, operate as mere maxims, they all reflect more specific approaches to the interpretation of certain clauses. This is also the case of the interpretation approach associated with different clauses according to their level of exceptionality. As with the burden of proof, what matters for present purposes is the conceptual frames underpinning the way in which certain effects are sought.

A useful illustration in this regard is provided by the *Whaling* case before the ICJ. The case concerned the applicability of the Whaling Convention to certain programmes conducted by Japan which entailed the killing of whales. Whaling for commercial purposes is prohibited under paragraph 10(e) of the Convention's Schedule but Japan argued that it could do so for purposes of scientific research under Article VIII(1). In an attempt to shield its action, Japan argued first that Article VIII(1) was a scope provision that entirely excluded scientific programmes from the Convention and, as a 'free-standing' clause, it was to be read 'in isolation from the other provisions of the Convention'.[86] It subsequently admitted that the clause was not free-standing, but it argued that it was an 'exemption' to be understood in the light of 'sustainable exploitation' as the object and purpose of the Convention and the 'freedom to engage in whaling enjoyed by states under customary international law'.[87] By contrast, Australia and New Zealand sought to characterize the clause as an 'exception to the general rules of the Convention' calling for 'restrictive interpretation'.[88] The Court reasoned that the

[85] Vienna Convention on the Law of Treaties (23 May 1969) 1155 UNTS 331.
[86] *Whaling in the Antarctic* (n 15) para 52.
[87] ibid paras 52 and 57.
[88] ibid para 57.

preamble and the provisions of the Convention did not call for either an expansive or a restrictive interpretation, but it dealt with the clause as a carve-out or exemption, as discussed earlier in this chapter. The Court's approach may reflect some reluctance in recent years to take unnecessary principled positions. However, when the level of exceptionality is not in doubt, the Court has not hesitated to take principled stances, such as the assertion in the *Gabčíkovo-Nagymaros* case that the customary necessity defence must only be exceptionally admitted, subject to strict cumulative conditions, of which the state invoking the excuse is not the sole judge. Other tribunals subsequently followed the same approach and even extended it—incorrectly—to the assessment of carve-outs.[89]

This approach can be contrasted with the broader interpretation of clauses defining the scope of application of a treaty or a specific provision. By way of illustration, the extraterritorial scope of human rights obligations has been largely grounded on an extended conception of the term 'jurisdiction' encompassing situations beyond a state's territory or even in the territory of other states. Initially, the European Court of Human Rights (ECtHR) was reluctant to extend the interpretation of the term 'jurisdiction' in the ECHR in such a way, as illustrated by the *Bankovic* case.[90] But this reluctance gave way subsequently to a broader understanding of the term 'jurisdiction' in the provisions defining the scope of application of the ECHR,[91] more in line with the jurisprudence of other human rights bodies. This extension is now widely recognized both for treaties that define their scope by reference to the 'territory' and 'jurisdiction' of states parties[92] and for treaties that do not contain an explicit clause in this regard.[93] Beyond provisions defining the scope of a treaty, a comparable trend can be discerned in connection with the interpretation of some carve-outs or exemptions. In a number of trade and investment cases, including *ADF v United States*,[94] *UPS v Canada*,[95] *Canada—Renewables*,[96] and *Mesa v Canada*,[97] the term 'procurement' in a carve-out clause has been broadly interpreted, thus excluding procurement measures from the scope of one or more primary norms. Of note is the fact that, in the latter case, the claimant specifically sought to characterize the clause as an 'exception' that must be restrictively interpreted

[89] See e.g. *CMS Award* (n 7) para 317.

[90] *Bankovic and Others v Belgium and Others* App no 52207/99 (ECtHR Decision on Admissibility) (12 December 2001) para 75.

[91] See *Al Skeini and Others v United Kingdom* App no 55721/07 (ECtHR 7 July 2011) paras 130–40 (particularly 136) and the case law following this jurisprudential shift.

[92] In the global context see ICCPR (n 4) art 2(1) ('territory and subject to its jurisdiction') and the following interpretations: *Wall Opinion* (n 2) paras 108–12; *Delia Saldias de Lopez v Uruguay*, HRC Comm No 52/1979 (29 July 1981) paras 12.1 and 12.3; General Comment No 31, *Nature of the General Legal Obligation Imposed on States Parties to the Covenant*, CCPR/C/21/Rev.1/Add.13 (26 May 2004) para 10. In the American context see ACHR (n 36) art 1(1) ('persons subject to their jurisdiction') and the following interpretations: Case 11.589 *Alejandre and Others v Cuba* (1999) IACommHR Report no 86/99 paras 23–25; Inter-State Petition IP-02 *Ecuador v Colombia*,(2010) IACommHR Report no 112/10 para 91.

[93] At the global level see International Covenant on Economic, Social and Cultural Rights (ICESCR) (1966) 993 UNTS 3 and the following interpretation: Committee on Economic, Social and Cultural Rights, *General Comment 8: The Relationship between Economic Sanctions and Respect for Economic, Social and Cultural Rights* UN Doc E/C.12/1997/8 (12 December 1997) paras 9–14. At the African level see African Charter (n 36) and the following interpretation: *Association pour la sauvegarde de la paix au Burundi v Tanzania, Kenya, Uganda, Rwanda, Zaire and Zambia* Comm no 157/96 (African Commission 29 May 2003) para 75.

[94] *ADF Group Inc. v United States*, ICSID Case No ARB (AF)/00/1) Award (9 January 2003) paras 160–74.

[95] *United Parcel Service of America Inc v Government of Canada*, UNCITRAL Rules, Award on the Merits (24 May 2007) paras 121–36.

[96] *Canada—Renewables* (n 14) 5.59.

[97] *Mesa v Canada* (n 9) paras 407–39.

and the tribunal rejected this interpretation stating, among others, that the clause was a carve-out.[98]

These examples suggest that international courts and tribunals, while applying the usual rules of treaty interpretation, do take into account the way in which some situations are placed beyond the scope of a treaty or a norm. Clauses defining the scope of a treaty or that of a norm leave more space for a broad interpretation than more exceptional clauses such as necessity. More importantly, as with the burden of proof, the conceptual frames mobilized by the parties to argue for a certain type of interpretation, whether on a principled basis (e.g. 'expansive' or 'restrictive' interpretation) or a more pragmatic one (e.g. 'jurisdiction' encompasses extraterritorial situations or a broad definition of 'procurement'), aim to emphasize or downplay the level of exceptionality of the clause.

3.4 Degree of deference

The analysis of deference to state authorities in international law can adopt three main angles. First, deference can be ingrained in the rules governing the scope of the review of an adjudicatory or quasi-adjudicatory body. Such limitations are commonplace in domestic law, where the judicial and administrative authorities are vertically organized and the types of recourses are well defined. However, such limitations only reflect considerations of deference when some degree of administrative or political discretion is exercised and the recourse aims to preserve that space. In international law, there are also some examples of rules specifically restraining the scope for judicial or quasi-judicial review of a matter (e.g. the rules governing annulment of awards under ICSID, the statutes of certain compliance committees that can only review certain matters, etc). But they are rare and, quite often, they do not reflect considerations of deference but rather other matters such as efficiency or, simply, lack of consent from the state to submit certain matters to judicial settlement. In lieu of such explicit rules, some tribunals have developed judicial practices, such as the margin of appreciation doctrine, which must be understood as an exercise of judicial self-restraint in the interpretation and application of the law. The second approach consists of ingraining deference in the primary norm or rule of conduct of the state. Many international norms entail some measure of discretion or policy space for states, which are implicit in the very interpretation of the norm. By way of illustration, human rights, investment standards, and trade disciplines are often interpreted in a manner that introduces reasonable restrictions of the scope of a provision to allow for legitimate governmental action. The third approach is the use of the techniques discussed in this chapter, with their many variations. Although these approaches are often combined or conflated in the jurisprudence, in this section I follow essentially the third perspective, taking into account when necessary the interpretive concepts developed by tribunals under the first perspective. I will endeavour to show by reference to

[98] See e.g. ibid para 405. The tribunal noted in this regard that it did 'not consider that the mere characterization of a treaty term as an "exception" requires an interpretation different from other treaty terms. Indeed, whatever their characterization, all terms of a treaty are subject to the ordinary rules of treaty interpretation' (para 405). This statement is to be understood by reference to the title of art 1108 of the NAFTA (Reservations and Exceptions). In fact, the tribunal provided a broad interpretation in line with previous cases and, as I have already noted earlier in this chapter, it characterized the clause as a 'carve-out'. See paras 407–21 (characterizing the term 'procurement') and paras 422–39 (where the tribunal rejected the claimant's interpretation, inter alia by characterizing the relevant clause as a 'carve-out').

some examples that the level of exceptionality also plays a role in the scope for deference left by different techniques.

Some of the cases discussed earlier provide suitable illustrations. In the *Whaling* case, Japan argued that it enjoyed discretion under Article VIII(1) of the Whaling Convention to issue permits for scientific research and, as a result, the Court could only review the extent to which Japan's use of the discretion provided that the exemption had been '"arbitrary or capricious", "manifestly unreasonable" or made in bad faith'.[99] Australia and New Zealand argued, on the contrary, that the standard arising from Article VIII(1), which they characterized as an 'exception', was of an objective nature and therefore 'the Court's power of review should not be limited to scrutiny for good faith, with a strong presumption in favour of the authorizing state, as this would render the multilateral regime for the collective management of a common resource established by the ICRW ineffective'.[100] The Court followed a combination of both approaches and stated that:

> Article VIII gives discretion to a State party to the ICRW to reject the request for a special permit or to specify the conditions under which a permit will be granted. However, whether the killing, taking and treating of whales pursuant to a requested special permit is for purposes of scientific research cannot depend simply on that State's perception.[101]

It then set an objective standard in paragraph 67, which left significant space to Japan's discretion but, applied to the facts, led to the conclusion that Article VIII(1) was not available.

Similar arguments relating to the characterization of a clause in order to derive consequences as to the degree of deference afforded by it are found in other contexts. In the *CMS Award*, the parties extensively debated whether Article XI was a 'self-judging' provision or, in other words, the extent to which Argentina had discretion to adopt measures under this clause. As noted earlier, the tribunal confused carve-outs with exceptions and excuses, and it tended to place the entire inquiry under the approach called for by the latter. Although the ad hoc committee corrected the amalgamation made by the tribunal, reference to the discussion in the award remains useful to illustrate the conceptual frames used in arguing for different degrees of deference. After discussing the positions of the parties and their experts, the tribunal identified three main positions, namely that of the claimant and its expert (i.e. that the clause was not self-judging and the tribunal was entitled to determine whether and the extent to which the 'essential interests' envisioned in the clause were at stake), that of the respondent (i.e. that the clause was self-judging and therefore the tribunal could not second-guess the discretionary determination made by the respondent), and that of the respondent's expert (i.e. review was possible but limited to good faith).[102] The tribunal followed the approach suggested by the claimant, which is in line with the characterization of the clause as an exception and its conflation with the customary necessity defence. The ad hoc committee questioned the sufficiency of the tribunal's reasoning on this point but it did not annul the award in this regard.[103]

A third illustration of the link between exceptionality and deference is provided by the practice of regional human rights courts in connection with derogations from human rights

[99] *Whaling in the Antarctic* (n 15) para 65.
[100] ibid para 63.
[101] ibid para 61.
[102] *CMS Award* (n 7) para 367.
[103] *CMS Annulment* (n 7) paras 122–27.

provisions. In *Brannigan and McBride v UK* the parties debated the extent of the margin of appreciation afforded to states in connection with derogations. The applicants and some non-governmental organizations argued in favour of a narrow margin of appreciation as a result of the 'quasi-permanent nature' of the emergency in Northern Ireland and the importance of procedural guarantees (which the state had derogated from) for the enjoyment of non-derogable rights.[104] The ECtHR restated the reasons why states enjoy, in connection with derogations, a 'wide margin of appreciation', namely the fact that:

> [b]y reason of their direct and continuous contact with the pressing needs of the moment, the national authorities are in principle in a better position than the international judge to decide both on the presence of such an emergency and on the nature and scope of derogations necessary to avert it.[105]

But it then circumscribed the margin of appreciation left to states by reference to the supervisory role of the Court in assessing whether states have gone 'beyond the "extent strictly required by the exigencies" of the crisis', particularly in the light of 'the nature of the rights affected by the derogation, the circumstances leading to, and the duration of, the emergency situation'.[106] Significantly, in so doing, the Court recognized that the level of exceptionality of a situation may play an ambiguous role to the extent that, the more exceptional the situation, the broader discretion states would enjoy, but, at the same time, the more certain rights would deserve protection, as argued by Amnesty International during the proceedings.

3.5 Interaction with referral clauses

In discussing the operation of different techniques, I have referred to the distinction made by certain adjudicatory bodies between carve-outs or exemptions and 'exceptions' *stricto sensu*. In the context of investment disputes, the clearest statement of this distinction appears in *CMS Annulment*, where the ad hoc committee noted that: 'Article XI is a threshold requirement: if it applies, the substantive obligations under the Treaty do not apply. By contrast, Article 25 is an excuse which is only relevant once it has been decided that there has otherwise been a breach of those substantive obligations.'[107]

Similarly, in the trade context, the WTO Appellate Body cautioned in its 1996 ruling in the *US—Gasoline* case against confusing: 'the question of whether inconsistency with a substantive rule existed [*in casu* Article III:4 of the GATT], with the further and separate question arising under the chapeau of Article XX as to whether that inconsistency was nevertheless justified'.[108]

The distinction between the two types of clauses is not only important for the stage at which each type of clause operates or the other implications discussed in previous sections; it may also have decisive effects as regards the interplay with a variety of clauses that, for present purposes, can be called 'referral clauses'. Referral clauses (e.g. MFN clauses, linking clauses, etc) are often used to import from other treaties or sections of a treaty certain contents. As

[104] *Brannigan v UK* (n 37) paras 41–42.
[105] ibid para 43.
[106] ibid para 43.
[107] *CMS Annulment* (n 7) para 129.
[108] *US—Gasoline* (n 42) 23.

I will discuss next by reference to two cases, the distinction between 'carve-outs' and 'exceptions' has implications for the operation of referral clauses.

The first illustration is provided by *Mesa v Canada*. In this case, the claimant sought to exclude the operation of a clause (Article 1108 of the NAFTA) by reference to a referral clause (the MFN clause in Article 1103 of the NAFTA). According to the claimant, Article 1108, which allowed for differential treatment of investors in the context of public procurement, was to be considered as an 'exception' to the non-discrimination standards of the NAFTA and, therefore, it was not available if a non-discrimination standard imported from another treaty did not contain the procurement exception. *In casu*, argued the claimant, this standard could be imported by the operation of the MFN clause in Article 1103 of the NAFTA.[109] The respondent challenged this position, stating that Article 1108 was not an exception but a carve-out and, therefore, it excluded the operation of Article 1103 altogether for procurement measures (whether for non-discrimination purposes or for the purpose of importing a standard from another treaty).[110] In this specific context, one can clearly see the importance of the conceptual distinction between a carve-out and an exception. If the procurement clause is indeed an exception *stricto sensu*, then it could not operate to exclude the importing power of the MFN clause in Article 1103, but only—exceptionally—the non-discrimination standard in this provision. Conversely, if the procurement clause is a carve-out, then it means that whenever a measure falls within its scope, Article 1103 is simply not applicable for any purposes, whether as a non-discrimination standard or as a referral clause. This was the solution retained by the tribunal. Interestingly, the burden of proving that the referral clause was indeed applicable lay with the claimant, not the respondent.[111]

Another illustration discussing the operation of a different type of referral clause is offered by *Canada—Renewables*. In this case, the EU argued that trade-related investment measures identified in certain referral clauses (Article 2.2 and the Illustrative List of the Agreement on Trade-related Investment Measures (TRIMs)[112]) were by definition inconsistent with the national treatment obligation in Article III:4 of the GATT.[113] Article 2.2 of the TRIMs refers indeed to '[a]n illustrative list of TRIMs that are inconsistent with the obligation of national treatment provided for in paragraph 4 of Article III of GATT 1994'. However, Article III:8(a) of the GATT states that the article 'shall not apply' to procurement measures. As in *Mesa v Canada*, the question that arose was whether Article III:8(a) defeated the linkage between, on the one hand, Article 2.2 and the list of the TRIMs and, on the other hand, the non-discrimination standard in Article III:4 of the GATT. The Appellate Body reasoned that Article III:8(a) was a carve-out (the term used was 'derogation') excluding certain measures from Article III as a whole. Therefore, when a measure falls within the scope of Article III:8(a), it cannot be inconsistent with Article III.[114] Thus, Article III would simply not apply to such measures, which is technically different from a situation where Article III:4 would indeed apply (and would hence be breached by virtue of the linkage with Article 2.2 and the list of the TRIMs) but the breach could be justified by reference to the 'exception' in Article III:8(a).

These cases offer two suitable illustrations of some potential implications of the conceptual distinctions explored in this chapter. They also show that these distinctions, although

[109] *Mesa v Canada* (n 9) paras 385, 386, and 400.
[110] ibid para 380.
[111] ibid para 401–402.
[112] Agreement on Trade-related Investment Measures (15 April 1994) 1868 UNTS 186.
[113] *Canada—Renewables* (n 14) para 5.21.
[114] ibid para 5.26.

present to some extent in the argumentation of the parties and the reasoning of tribunals, often remain conceptually inchoate. They nevertheless operate as reference frames, even implicitly, that could become relevant in this or some other connection resulting in specific legal effects. It is therefore useful to keep them in mind, not only for merely descriptive purposes, but in order to understand the normative reasons underpinning the effects potentially attached to different clauses.

4 Concluding Observations

The use of the term 'exception' in legal discourse is comfortable, but it hides a range of specific techniques with very different features and legal implications. In this chapter, I have reviewed seven such techniques and a number of technique-specific implications, as well as some transversal implications related to the level of exceptionality of the technique. In highlighting the features and implications of each technique, my goal has been to show that there is much more texture in the fabric of international law than that which the binary distinction between rules and exceptions may convey. Perhaps more fundamentally, the conceptual distinctions identified have significant practical relevance, whether they are consciously and expressly used or, as is more often the case, when they operate as conceptual reference frames and remain inchoate in the legal reasoning that relies upon them.

Sufficient knowledge of the range of techniques may be useful for treaty design in order to safeguard general (public) or specific (industry or country) interests or to facilitate participation in a multilateral regime. Such knowledge is also important not merely for the sake of argumentation in a litigation context but also for adjudicatory and quasi-adjudicatory bodies to realize fully the space (or lack thereof) they afford to special situations in interpreting and applying such techniques. A certain understanding of a given clause, as a scope provision, a carve-out, an exception *stricto sensu*, or an excuse, may set important bounds to the subsequent development of an entire body of jurisprudence. I referred in this regard to the extension of the scope of human rights obligations to extraterritorial situations or the space carved-out for public procurement measures in trade and investment cases. A similar reasoning could apply to the narrow space left by the current understanding of both primary norms (e.g. the term 'likeness') and general exceptions in the context of the trade and environment debate. Indeed, the current legal frontier in the differentiation of goods based on the environmental footprint of their processes and production methods depends upon this—still narrow—understanding upheld by the WTO Appellate Body. The same point could be made in connection with the regulatory space left to states by the investment jurisprudence, which partly depends on the understanding of clauses reserving the right of states to regulate for the public good.

The responsibility for identifying the conceptual distinctions and spelling out their implications rests, perhaps above all, on the shoulders of academics writing about different provisions and training future generations of lawyers. It is my hope that this chapter, as well as the other contributions to this edited collection, will serve this purpose. Law is in many ways a technology and, as such, its understanding and operation must be constantly refined and improved.

6
Defences and the Burden of Proof in International Law

*Joost Pauwelyn**

1 Introduction

Modern treaties include an increasingly complex set of rules, carve-outs, and exceptions, ensuring, for example, the policy space of states.[1] Their impact may be tempered also by outside instruments or custom. International law disputes, in turn, are increasingly fact-intensive, addressing, for example, complex scientific, environmental, or economic questions. This double evolution enhances the role, in international litigation, of defences and the importance of who carries the burden of proof for them.

Some international tribunals may spend more time than necessary on questions of the burden of proof and different types of claims in defence (dispute settlement at the World Trade Organization (WTO) comes to mind); most, however, tend to underestimate the issue and do not devote enough attention to it (for example, the International Court of Justice (ICJ)).

The burden of proving a defence is said to be on the party invoking it. As trite as this proposition may sound, in international law it hides a far more complex litigation reality. Distinctions must be made both in terms of (i) *types of claims* in defence, and (ii) *types of burdens* this may impose (or not) on the respondent.

First, the exact burden on respondents may depend on the precise *type of claim* a respondent makes 'in its defence'. In this respect, it is important to distinguish between:

(i) Preliminary objections and whether such objections relate to the jurisdiction of the tribunal[2] or the admissibility[3] of a specific claim.
(ii) Treaty reservations, rule exemptions (carve-outs or alternative rules[4]), or other claims in defence which result in the treaty or rule allegedly violated

* The author would like to thank Marta Bo, Antonio Coco, and Sanja Dragic for helpful research assistance, as well as participants at the Conference on *Exceptions and Defences in International Law* held in Cambridge on 31 March–1 April 2016 and the editors of this volume for extremely helpful comments on earlier drafts of this chapter. The cut-off date for this contribution is 11 July 2017.

[1] See Viñuales, ch 5 in this volume.

[2] Commonly referred to examples of jurisdictional objections are: absence of consent to arbitration or lack of a protected investment or investor in investor–state dispute settlement; lack of temporal jurisdiction of a tribunal.

[3] Commonly referred to examples of admissibility objections are: exhaustion of domestic remedies; invocation of a forum exclusion or fork in the road clause for a specific claim; expiry of time limits to file a claim; defence of *res judicata* (in support: *Question of the Delimitation of the Continental Shelf between Nicaragua and Colombia beyond 200 Nautical Miles from the Nicaraguan Coast (Nicaragua v Colombia)* (Preliminary Objections, Judgment) [2016] ICJ Rep 100, para 48).

[4] Examples of alternative rules or autonomous rights (to be distinguished from exceptions or affirmative defences) are art 3.3 of the WTO Agreement on Sanitary and Phytosanitary Measures (SPS Agreement) and art 2.4 of the WTO Agreement on Technical Barriers to Trade (TBT Agreement) allowing WTO members to deviate from international standards under certain conditions.

Joost Pauwelyn, *Defences and the Burden of Proof in International Law* In: *Exceptions in International Law*. Edited by: Lorand Bartels and Federica Paddeu, Oxford University Press (2020).
DOI: 10.1093/oso/9780198789321.003.0006

not to apply in the first place[5] (e.g. as a result of a *lex specialis, lex posterior*, or *lex superior*[6]).

(iii) Respondent claims that, although the rule applies, the constituent elements for breach are not met.

(iv) Exceptions to a rule in primary international law (be it in the treaty examined or in another treaty or norm) which, notwithstanding application and prima facie breach of such rule, lead to the conclusion that there is no rule breach.

(v) Defences under secondary rules of international law that avoid wrongfulness or responsibility for breach,[7] be it all responsibility or some elements only (e.g. the act in breach is excused but damages for harm caused must still be paid[8]).

Secondly, where any of the above claims 'in defence' may be relevant, a distinction must be made between the various *types of burden* this may impose on the respondent, claimant, or tribunal:

(i) Must the respondent raise or assert the claim, must the tribunal address it at its own initiative, or is it up to the claimant to raise the issue? (hereafter: the *burden of raising*).

(ii) The burden of producing arguments and evidence be it to substantiate or oppose a claim (hereafter: the *burden of production*) as opposed to the ultimate burden of proving or disproving a claim (hereafter: the *burden of persuasion* or the *real burden of proof*).

(iii) The amount, level, or quantum of proof that the party having the burden of proof must provide to prevail on its claim (hereafter: *standard of proof*), not to be confused with the degree of deference or scrutiny that the tribunal must use when examining a certain measure or conduct (hereafter: *standard of review*) or the question of whether the tribunal must adopt a broad or restrictive approach to treaty *interpretation*.

[5] Jaap Hage, Antonia Waltermann, and Gustavo Arosemena, ch 2 in this volume, refer in this respect to 'applicability of rules', to be distinguished from 'application of rules'.

[6] These can be referred to as 'priority rules' or mere 'conflicts in the applicable law': the conflicting rules (say, a *lex generalis* and a *lex specialis*) are both valid and legal and continue both to exist but in the situation only one of them (the priority rule, here *lex specialis*) is applied. See Joost Pauwelyn, *Conflict of Norms in Public International Law* (CUP 2003) 327.

[7] See *CMS v Argentine Republic*, ICSID Case No ARB/01/8, Decision on Annulment (25 September 2007) para 134, identifying art XI of the US–Argentina BIT on essential security as an exception under the treaty (primary law; going to the question of breach) and necessity under customary international law (art 25 of the International Law Commission (ILC)'s Articles on State Responsibility) as a defence under secondary law (going to the question of responsibility): 'If, on the contrary, state of necessity in customary international law goes to the issue of responsibility, it would be a secondary rule of international law—and this was the position taken by the ILC. In this case, the Tribunal would have been under an obligation to consider first whether there had been any breach of the BIT and whether such a breach was excluded by Article XI. Only if it concluded that there was conduct not in conformity with the Treaty would it have had to consider whether Argentina's responsibility could be precluded in whole or in part under customary international law.'

[8] See *EDF v Argentine Republic*, ICSID Case No ARB/03/23, Award (11 June 2012) para 1178, finding that even if Argentina could rely on ILC art 25 necessity 'at some reasonable point in time, Respondent should have compensated Claimants for injury suffered as a result of measures enacted during any arguable period of necessity in late December 2001'. See also ILC art 27(b): 'The invocation of a circumstance precluding wrongfulness in accordance with this chapter [which includes necessity under art 25] is without prejudice to ... the question of compensation for any material loss caused by the act in question'.

Table 6.1 Types of Claims in Defence and Types of Burdens on the Parties/Tribunal

CLAIMS IN DEFENCE	Burden of Raising	Burden of Persuasion	Burden of Production	Standard of Proof	Standard of Review
Preliminary objection to - Jurisdiction - Admissibility	Tribunal Respondent	Claimant Respondent	Both parties may shift after prima facie case	Preponderance of the evidence Sometimes: lower prima facie evidence or higher 'fully conclusive' or 'beyond reasonable doubt' standard	De novo v. Objective review v. Reasonable Assessment v. Self-judging
Claim that the rule does not apply (exemption, alternative rule)	Respondent/ tribunal	Claimant			
Claim that the rule is not breached	Respondent/ Tribunal	Claimant			
Exception to the rule	Respondent	Respondent			
Defence under secondary rule	Respondent	Respondent			

Table 6.1 links the types of claims in defence to the respective burdens they conventionally impose on the parties or tribunal, as further discussed below (exceptions to the general rule are not included in Table 6.1 but are discussed in the text or footnotes).

Complexity in this area of international law has increased owing to three factors: (i) the creation of more international tribunals with compulsory jurisdiction and a higher case load in specific sub-fields such as World Trade Organization (WTO) or investor–state dispute settlement (ISDS); (ii) disputes that are increasingly fact-intensive, including in technical areas such as environmental or health protection (increasingly submitted also to the ICJ) or highly sensitive, case-specific matters such as use of force or economic emergencies; (iii) increasingly complex, lengthy, and carefully negotiated treaties with, as one commentator phrased it in the wake of the 2,700 page Trans-Pacific Partnership (TPP), 'exceptions to general principle, exceptions to exceptions, explicit exclusions, implicit exclusions, grandfathering, optional undertakings, clarifications, caveats, limiting rules of application, and, of course, carve-outs'.[9]

2 The Burden of *Raising* a Claim in Defence

The burden of raising, pleading, or invoking a claim in defence is generally on the respondent. In the event of silence, it is not for the tribunal, let alone the claimant, to make the respondent's defence. More specifically, if the respondent does not invoke an exception (under primary rules) or a defence (under secondary rules), the tribunal itself cannot invoke or apply it (*non ultra petita*).

Three potential exceptions come to mind. First, jurisdictional objections, although often raised by the respondent, must be raised and examined by the tribunal on its own initiative,

[9] Thomas J Bollyky, 'TPP Tobacco Exception Proves the New Rule in Trade' Expert Brief, Council on Foreign Relations (4 February 2016) http://www.cfr.org/trade/tpp-tobacco-exception-proves-new-rule-trade/p37509.

even where the respondent failed to do so, or did so only belatedly.[10] In contrast, objections to admissibility must generally be raised by the respondent.[11] Secondly, even if the respondent does not raise a claim that a constituent element of rule breach is absent, the tribunal must objectively examine whether these elements are present in order to decide whether the claimant has discharged its burden of proving breach. In most cases, however, the respondent itself will submit such claims in its defence (this is why the relevant box in Table 6.1 above states 'Respondent/Tribunal').

Thirdly, and more difficult, is the question of whether treaty carve-outs, reservations, exemptions, or alternative rules (e.g. *lex specialis*) must be invoked or decided upon at the tribunal's own initiative: if such exemption or alternative rule applies, the rule claimed to be breached is not applicable in the first place. This places at least some burden on the tribunal to make sure that the rule applies, as part of its task to check whether the claimant has discharged its burden of proving breach.[12] At the same time, there may be multiple exemptions, carve-outs, or alternative rules (including outside the specific treaty invoked) making it difficult for the tribunal to go through each one of them at its own initiative. In practice, tribunals will only examine exemptions or alternative rules invoked by the respondent or obviously relevant or applicable (in which case the tribunal can raise the issue in questions to the parties, and the respondent can always invoke the exemption or alternative rule as its own claim in defence). This is also why this box in Table 6.1 above states 'Respondent/Tribunal'. However, where the tribunal concludes that the exemption (not the general rule) does apply and this exemption amounts to an alternative rule or *lex specialis*—think of Article 3.3 of the Agreement on the Application of Sanitary and Phytosanitary Measures (SPS Agreement), which, as an alternative rule, not as an exception, allows WTO members to deviate from international standards when certain conditions are met—it is *for the claimant* to claim breach of this alternative rule or *lex specialis* (if not, the tribunal would simply find that the general rule under Article 3.1 of the SPS Agreement does not apply and dismiss the case).[13]

[10] See *Case of Blečić v Croatia* App no 59532/00 [2004] ECHR 397, (2005) 41 EHRR 185 (8 March 2006) in respect of a jurisdictional objection *ratione temporis* that the respondent invoked late, the Court 'has to satisfy itself that it has jurisdiction in any case brought before it, and is therefore obliged to examine the question of its jurisdiction at every stage of the proceedings' (para 67); 'despite the Government's failure to raise the relevant objection earlier . . . the Chamber examined its competence *ratione temporis* of its own motion'.

[11] See *Ahmadou Sadio Diallo (Republic of Guinea v Democratic Republic of the Congo)* (Preliminary Objections) [2007] ICJ Rep 582, para 45: the DRC did not raise exhaustion of domestic remedies in relation to the arrest or detention of Diallo (only in respect of his expulsion); as a result, the ICJ decided not to address the issue. For an exception see admissibility before the International Criminal Court. Article 19.1 of the Rome Statute provides: 'The Court may, on its own motion, determine the admissibility of a case in accordance with article 17 [on complementarity between the ICC and national proceedings].' See also *Walker v United Kingdom* (dec), no 34979/97, ECHR 2000-I, in respect of the six months admissibility rule within which claims must be filed; the Court will apply this six-month rule even if the respondent state did not make a preliminary objection to that effect, on the ground that the rule serves the interests not only of the respondent government but also of legal certainty as a value in itself.

[12] See *Case Relating to the Territorial Jurisdiction of the International Commission of the River Oder* (1929) PCIJ Series A No 23, Series C No 17-11, 18–19, where the PCIJ dismissed the objection of the parties to the dispute that Poland invoked belatedly that it had not ratified the Barcelona Convention (a claim in defence that leads to the rule invoked not applying in the first place). The Court pointed out that this was a matter of law to be examined by the Court *ex officio*: 'The fact that Poland has not ratified the Barcelona Convention not being contested, it is evident that the matter is purely one of law such as the Court could and should examine ex *officio.* It may further be observed that neither the Polish Case nor the Counter-Case contains anything from which it may definitely be concluded that they intended to abandon the argument based on non-ratification.'

[13] A Dissent on the Panel on *EC—Tariff Preferences* (Panel Report, *European Communities—Conditions for the Granting of Tariff Preferences to Developing Countries*, WT/DS246/R (adopted 20 April 2004) DSR 2004:III, 1009 at paras 9.2 ff) found, for example, that the enabling clause was an autonomous right (not an exception) and that since the claimant (India) had not claimed breach of it, the case should have been dismissed. See also the Appellate Body position in *India—Additional and Extra-Additional Duties on Imports from the United States*, WT/DS360/AB/R (adopted 17 November 2008) DSR 2008:XX, 8223, putting some burden on the defendant to assert that the

Somewhat surprisingly, perhaps, there may also be instances where it is for the *claimant* to raise claims in defence of its opponent. In *EC—Tariff Preferences*, for example, the WTO Appellate Body found that, although the enabling clause (which allows for tariff preferences to be granted exclusively to developing countries) is an *exception* to the Article I of the General Agreement on Trade and Tariffs (GATT) most-favoured nation obligation—under which the respondent bears the burden of proof—it was, mainly for due process considerations, up to the *claimant* (India) to *raise* the enabling clause in its panel request in the first place.[14]

3 The Burden of *Persuasion* or Real Burden of Proof

3.1 Exceptions and defences versus exemptions and breach

Once a claim in defence has been raised or is before the tribunal, is it always the respondent who bears the burden of proof? This is the case in many situations but not all. The respondent has the burden of proving (i) *exceptions* such as Article XX of the GATT health measures[15] or Article XI essential security in the US–Argentina bilateral investment treaty (BIT) and (ii) *defences* under secondary rules, such as necessity under Article 25 of the ILC Articles on States Responsibility.[16] In contrast, it is generally for the claimant to prove (i) that an *exemption* is *not* applicable and that the rule allegedly breached *is*[17] and (ii) that all the constituent elements of breach *are* present.[18]

challenged duties are justified under the exemption in GATT art II:2(a) but, in the circumstances, placing most of the burden, as well as the real of burden of proof, on the United States to establish that the exemption in GATT art II:2(a) is *not* met. See n 18 below.

[14] Appellate Body Report, *European Communities—Conditions for the Granting of Tariff Preferences to Developing Countries*, WT/DS246/AB/R (adopted 20 April 2004) DSR 2004:III, 925, para 113.

[15] Other provisions qualified in WTO jurisprudence as exceptions are: GATT art XV, TRIPS exceptions arts 13, 17, and 30, and the fifth sentence of footnote 59 in the SCM Agreement. GATT art XI:2 has also traditionally been defined as an exception to the prohibition on quantitative restrictions in art XI:1. However, in a recent case, the Appellate Body used language indicating that it may instead be an exemption. See Appellate Body Report, *Argentina—Measures Affecting the Importation of Goods*, WT/DS438/AB/R / WT/DS444/AB/R/WT/DS445/AB/R (adopted 26 January 2015) para 5.219: 'Article XI:2 of the GATT 1994 further restricts the scope of application of Article XI:1 by providing that the provisions of Article XI:1 shall not extend to the areas listed in Article XI:2.'

[16] Other examples are: consent, self-defence, countermeasures, *force majeure*, distress in ILC arts 20–24.

[17] Examples of exemptions or autonomous rights in WTO jurisprudence (burden of proof on claimant) are: ATC art 6, SPS art 3.3, TBT art 2.4, SCM Agreement art 27.2(b), Agreement on Agriculture art 13, SPS art 5.7 and GATT art II:2. In *India—Additional Duties* (n 13), the Appellate Body confirmed that GATT art II:2(a)—allowing for certain charges on imports that are equivalent to internal taxes—is an exemption from art II:1(b) on customs duties and other charges for which the burden of proof is on the claimant (here, the United States). In other words, 'in order to establish a *prima facie* case of a violation of Article II:1(b), the United States was also required to present arguments and evidence that the [Indian duties] are not justified under Article II:2(a)' (para 190). At the same time, a claimant making a claim of violation under art II:1(b) must not *in all cases* prove also that the challenged charge is not justified under art II:2: only 'if, due to the characteristics of the measures at issue or the arguments presented by the responding party, there is a reasonable basis to understand that the challenged measure may not result in a violation of Article II:1(b) because it satisfies the requirements of Article II:2(a), then the complaining party bears some burden in establishing that the conditions of Article II:2(a) are not met' (para 192). However, 'once a responding party asserts and supports a defence under Article II:2(a), "the ultimate burden would rest with the complaining party to rebut and ultimately disprove that evidence and argument"' (para 191). This is why when the Appellate Body concluded it did not have the facts available to conclude the analysis under Article II:2(a), the United States lost the case as the burden of proof was on the United States to demonstrate that the Indian duties were *not* justified under art II:2(a).

[18] See e.g. *Oil Platforms (Islamic Republic of Iran v United States of America)* (Preliminary Objection, Judgment) [1996] ICJ Rep 803, para 119, in respect of the claim of violation of the United States that Iran violated art X of the Treaty of Amity on freedom of commerce and navigation ('The United States bears the burden of proof that the

Tribunals do not always consistently apply the above principles on burden of proof. One oft-litigated example of a defence under secondary rules is the claim of necessity under customary international law (Article 25 ILC).[19] The burden of proving this demanding defence—which requires, inter alia, that the act adopted was 'the only way' to safeguard the state's essential interest and that the state did not 'contribute' to the state of necessity—rests on the respondent invoking the defence.[20] Yet, at times, tribunals or dissenting arbitrators seem to have wrongly put the burden of proof on claimants, for example, for the claimant to prove that the host state *did* contribute to the state of necessity.[21] This 'mistake' may be explained by the intuition that a party should not be required to prove an infinite negative. For example, Argentina should not have to prove that *no* other alternative was available or that *nothing* in its policies contributed to the necessity. If taken seriously, this would require Argentina to go through each and every one of its policies and each and every possible alternative response. However, this problem may be solved by shifting the burden of *production* rather than shifting the real burden of proof. For example, once Argentina has established a prima facie case of necessity, it may be for the investor–claimant to point at alternative measures Argentina could have adopted or at Argentine policies that contributed to the crisis, after which it is again for Argentina to show that the alternative was *not* available or that the policy referred to did *not* contribute. If, at the end of this back and forth, the tribunal remains in doubt, since the real burden of proof (burden of persuasion) remains on Argentina throughout, the claimant wins (the defence must be rejected and breach confirmed).

Whereas some tribunals may devote excessive attention to the burden of proof (think of WTO jurisprudence), others hardly mention it. In the recent *Whaling* dispute before the ICJ, for example, the core substantive and highly fact-intensive issue was whether Japan could rely on Article VIII of the International Whaling Convention on whaling for purposes of scientific research. Yet, the Court did not once mention the burden of proof. Similarly, in the *Oil Platforms* case one of main questions was whether the United States could rely on the essential security provision in Article XX of the Iran–US Treaty of Amity. There, as well, the Court never formally allocated the burden of proof under Article XX. It did find, however, that since the United States claimed self-defence the burden of proof of the existence of an armed attack by Iran on the United States was on the United States.[22] The Court ultimately

vessels which were attacked were engaged in commerce or navigation between the territories of the United States and Iran').

[19] See *Gabčíkovo-Nagymaros Project (Hungary v Slovakia)* (Judgment) [1997] ICJ Rep 7 and *Pulp Mills on the River Uruguay (Argentina v Uruguay)* (Judgment) [2010] ICJ Rep 18.

[20] See e.g. *Impregilo v Argentine Republic*, ICSID Case No ARB/07/17, Award (21 June 2011) para 345: 'As the Party pleading the defence, Argentina must meet the significant burden of proving that it should be allowed to justify its failure to perform its valid international obligations under the BIT on grounds of necessity' and *EDF v Argentine Republic*, ICSID Case No ARB/03/23, Decision on Annulment (5 February 2016) paras 326, 331.

[21] *Impregilo v Argentine Republic* (n 20) para 358 ('the Arbitral Tribunal has been persuaded by substantial evidence proffered by Impregilo that Argentina's own economic policies over several years prior to the crisis rendered the economy of the country vulnerable to exogenous shocks and pressures, and impacted adversely the sustainability of its economic model on the national and local levels') and, especially, the dissent by Arbitrator Stern in para 360 of the Award ('the State's contribution to a situation of economic crisis should not be lightly assumed and, on the concrete level, [Arbitrator Stern] is not convinced that a substantial contribution of the Argentine authorities to the crisis has been satisfactorily proven by strong and convincing evidence'). See also *LG&E v Argentine Republic*, ICSID Case No ARB/02/1, Decision on Liability (3 October 2006) para 257 ('The Tribunal considers that, in the first place, Claimants have not proved that Argentina has contributed to cause the severe crisis faced by the country').

[22] *Oil Platforms (Islamic Republic of Iran v United States of America)* (Judgment) [2003] ICJ Rep 161,para 57: 'For present purposes, the Court has simply to determine whether the United States has demonstrated that it was the victim of an "armed attack" by Iran such as to justify it using armed force in self-defence; and the burden of proof of the facts showing the existence of such an attack rests on the United States . . . if at the end of the day the evidence

found that the United States had not discharged this burden and could, therefore, not rely on self-defence nor on Article XX of the Treaty of Amity.[23]

3.2 Preliminary objections: jurisdiction versus admissibility

Somewhat less straightforward is who carries the burden of persuasion under preliminary objections. Regarding objections to *jurisdiction*, as discussed in section 2, it is for the tribunal *ex officio* to double-check and establish its own jurisdiction. Since, in the words of Judge Higgins, there is no 'jurisdictional presumption in favour of the plaintiff',[24] this would seem to imply that, in the face of an objection to jurisdiction, the real burden of proof is and consistently remains with the claimant to prove that all jurisdictional requirements *are* met[25] (even if, as discussed below, during the evaluation of whether claimant has discharged this burden, the burden of *production* may shift to the respondent). In *Marshall Islands v UK*, for example, the UK claimed in its defence that there was no 'dispute' between the parties so that the ICJ had no jurisdiction. The ICJ ruled that '[w]hile it is a legal matter for the Court to determine whether it has jurisdiction, it remains for the Applicant to demonstrate the facts underlying its case that a dispute exists'.[26] In other words, for jurisdictional objections, the burden remains on the claimant to demonstrate that the ICJ *has* jurisdiction.[27]

Another approach is to state that claimant must only make a prima facie case of jurisdiction (e.g. to show that its investment falls prima facie under the protection of the BIT), after which the burden of proving a precise jurisdictional objection shifts to the respondent (to demonstrate, for example, that the investment was made in violation of host state law).[28] It

available is insufficient to establish that the missile was fired by Iran, then the necessary burden of proof has not been discharged by the United States.'

[23] ibid paras 59 ('In considering whether the United States has discharged the burden of proof that Iranian forces fired the missile that struck the *Sea Isle City*, the Court must take note of this deficiency in the evidence available'), para 61 ('the evidence indicative of Iranian responsibility for the attack on the *Sea Isle City* is not sufficient to support the contentions of the United States'), para 64 ('no persuasive evidence has been supplied to support this allegation'), para 71 ('This evidence is highly suggestive, but not conclusive') and paras 78–79 (ultimately declining application of art XX).

[24] *Oil Platforms (Islamic Republic of Iran v United States of America)* (Separate Opinion of Judge Higgins) [2003] ICJ Rep 225, para 35.

[25] In support: *Salini v Jordan*, ICSID Case No ARB/02/13, Decision on Jurisdiction (9 November 2004) para 151 ('In conformity with [substantial] jurisprudence, the Tribunal will accordingly seek to determine whether the facts alleged by the Claimant in this case, if established, are capable of coming within those provisions of the BIT which have been invoked'); *Perenco v Ecuador*, ICSID Case No ARB/08/6, Decision on Jurisdiction (30 June 2011), in respect of an objection that the claimant was not a French national (the claimant invoked, however, French control over the investment), para 98: 'The burden of proof to establish the facts supporting its claim to standing lies with the Claimant.'

[26] *Obligations Concerning Negotiations Relating to Cessation of the Nuclear Arms Race and to Nuclear Disarmament (Marshall Islands v United Kingdom)* (Preliminary Objections) [2016] ICJ Rep 833, para 44 (referring in support to *Border and Transborder Armed Actions (Nicaragua v Honduras)* (Judgment) [1988] ICJ Rep 69, 75, para 16).

[27] In support, but in respect of counterclaims raised by respondent: *Spyridon Roussalis v Romania*, ICSID Case No ARB/06/1, Award (7 December 2011) para 860: 'Being the party asserting that the Tribunal has jurisdiction to hear and determine the counterclaims which it seeks to bring before the Tribunal, the Respondent carries the burden of establishing that jurisdiction exists.'

[28] See e.g. *Teinver v Argentine Republic*, ICSID Case No ARB/09/1, Decision on Jurisdiction (12 December 2012) para 324: 'Respondent has failed to demonstrate that Claimants, as a factual matter, committed illegalities in the process of *acquiring* their investment in the Argentine Airlines. In this respect, the onus is on Respondent. While Claimants must make a prima facie showing that their investment comes within the protections of the Treaty Respondent has not, with this objection, raised any issue of fact to counter Claimants' showing.' A number of tribunals have held that a respondent bears the burden of proof with respect to the facts alleged in its jurisdictional objections. See e.g. *Rompetrol Group N.V. v Romania*, ICSID Case No ARB/06/3, Decision on Jurisdiction

may be more accurate, in those scenarios, to speak of a shifting burden of *production*, while the real burden of proof or burden of persuasion stays with the claimant so that, in the end, when all the evidence has been submitted by both parties but it remains in equipoise on the question of *jurisdiction*, the claimant loses (and the case must be dismissed).[29]

In contrast, a preliminary objection to *admissibility* must normally not only be raised by the respondent (see the discussion in section 2) it must generally also be proven by the respondent. In other words, once jurisdiction of the tribunal is established, the claim is presumed to be admissible unless the respondent claims and proves otherwise. An investor may, for example, qualify within the jurisdiction *ratione personae* of an ISDS tribunal. Yet, the respondent state may subsequently invoke a 'denial of benefits' clause arguing that the claim is not admissible (e.g. because the investor is owned by an enterprise with nationality of a third-country with which the respondent state does not maintain diplomatic relations). The burden of proof is then on the respondent state to prove that the conditions for such 'denial of benefits' are met (e.g. the investor is, in fact, controlled by a third-country national).[30] Here as well, a ping-pong game of shifting burdens may sometimes be prescribed. Exhaustion of domestic remedies offers a good example. It is generally qualified as a matter of admissibility. Hence, it should be for the respondent to prove that domestic remedies have *not* been exhausted. However, this burden is often said to be split or shifting. The ICJ in *Diallo v DRC*, for example, found that, first, it is for the respondent (the DRC) to identify 'available and effective remedies' (paragraph 48; the DRC failed to do so and the ICJ rejected the objection); secondly, if remedies have been identified, it is for the claimant to show it exhausted them or there are exceptional circumstances.[31] Here, as well, it may be more accurate to speak of a shifting burden of *production*, while the real burden of proof or burden of persuasion stays with the respondent so that, in the end, when all the evidence has been submitted by both parties but it remains in equipoise on the question of exhaustion of domestic remedies, the respondent loses (the objection is dismissed and the case goes to the merits).

(18 April 2008) para 75 ('It will be seen that the jurisdictional objection entails issues of fact (whether the investments were and are under Mr. Patriciu's dominant control; whether the origin of the investment funds was Romanian), and issues of law ... The issues of fact are ones which the Respondent bears the burden of proving according to the requisite standard, in order to sustain the claims of law it bases on them'); *Desert Line Projects LLC v Republic of Yemen*, ICSID Case No ARB/05/17, Award (6 February 2008) para 105; *G. Hamester v Republic of Ghana*, ICSID Case No. ARB/07/24, Award (18 June 2019) para 132.

[29] Article 14.9(2) of the India Model BIT of 2016 explicitly confirms this: 'The investor at all times bears the burden of establishing ... jurisdiction' https://www.mygov.in/sites/default/files/master_image/Model%20Text%20for%20the%20Indian%20Bilateral%20Investment%20Treaty.pdf.

[30] See eg *Generation Ukraine v Ukraine* (Merits) 10 ICSID Rep 236, 272/15.7 ('This [the denial of benefits clause in the US/Ukraine BIT] is not, as the Respondent appears to have assumed, a jurisdictional hurdle for the Claimant to overcome in the presentation of its case; instead it is a potential filter on the admissibility of claims which can be invoked by the respondent State'). In support: Zachary Douglas, *The International Law of Investment Claims* (CUP 2009) para 874 ('A jurisdictional requirement must be positively established by the claimant. A "denial of benefits" provision must be positively invoked by the respondent ... The burden of proof clearly falls upon the respondent host state and if that burden is discharged before the tribunal, then the claimant investor's claims must be dismissed ... It is thus a matter of admissibility.'

[31] See *Ahmadou Sadio Diallo (Republic of Guinea v Democratic Republic of the Congo)* (n 11) paras 44, 48, 74. See also ILC Report, John Dugard, International Law Commission, 'Third Report on Diplomatic Protection' UN Doc A/CN.4.523 (2002) para 19: '[T]he burden of proof in respect of the availability and effectiveness of local remedies will in most circumstances be on different parties. The respondent State will be required to prove that local remedies are available, while the burden of proof will be on the claimant State to show that such remedies are ineffective and futile.' See also *Chevron Corporation (USA) and Texaco Petroleum Corporation (USA) v Republic of Ecuador [I]* PCA Case No AA 277, Partial Award on the Merits (30 March 2001), para 329 ('A respondent State must prove that remedies exist before a claimant will be required to prove their ineffectiveness or futility or that resort to them has been unsuccessful') and *Dalia v France* (154/1996/773/974) (ECHR 19 February 1998) paras 37 and 68.

3.3 The special case of international criminal law

International criminal law offers a deviation from the general rule that it is for respondents to carry the burden of persuasion for exceptions and defences. Given the presumption of innocence, linked to the gravity of being deprived of personal freedom once condemned of a crime, Article 66.2 of the Rome Statute of the International Criminal Court (ICC), for example, squarely puts the burden of proof on the prosecutor ('The onus is on the Prosecutor to prove the guilt of the accused'). Importantly, Article 67.1(i) further specifies that this onus never shifts to the accused, not even, apparently,[32] for exceptions or defences ('... the accused shall be entitled ... (i) Not to have imposed on him or her any reversal of the burden of proof or any onus of rebuttal').[33] The defendant may have a limited burden to *raise* a claim in defence or burden of *production* of evidence in respect of the constituent elements of a claim in defence (after which the burden of production may shift to the prosecutor). However, the real burden of proof always stays with the prosecutor so that, as the International Criminal Tribunal for the former Yugoslavia (ICTY) in *Delalić* found, 'at the conclusion of the proceedings, if there is any doubt that the Prosecution has established the case against the accused, the accused is entitled to the benefit of such doubt and, thus, acquittal'.[34]

The ICC Statute offers a second peculiarity as regards *admissibility* of a case. As pointed out in section 2, objections to admissibility must generally be *raised* by the respondent.[35] Article 19.1 of the Rome Statute explicitly provides, however, that '[t]he Court may, *on its own motion*, determine the admissibility of a case in accordance with article 17'.[36] Article 17, in turn, requires the ICC to determine that a case is inadmissible in certain situations where national proceedings are pending or have been concluded, following the ICC principle of complementarity (i.e. the overall priority of national over ICC proceedings). The burden of *raising* this admissibility defence may, therefore, rest on the Court. It stresses the importance of the principle of complementarity. However, this does not create an overall presumption of *inadmissibility* or shift the real burden of proof as regards admissibility to the prosecutor to demonstrate, for example, that national proceedings have *not* been initiated.[37] Similar to the admissibility objection of exhaustion of domestic remedies discussed earlier,[38] the burden of *production* may shift (e.g. once the defendant has submitted evidence that the case is 'being investigated ... by a State', the burden of production may shift to the prosecutor to show that the state is 'unwilling or unable genuinely to carry out the investigation'[39]). However, as is the

[32] In other criminal law regimes there may be presumptions against the accused. The International Criminal Tribunal for the former Yugoslavia (ICTY), for example, held that there was a presumption of sanity. The burden of proof was, therefore, on the defendant 'to rebut the presumption of sanity'. See *Prosecutor v Delalić and Others* (Judgment) ICTY Case No IT-96-21 (16 November 1998) para 1158.

[33] See Geert-Jan A Knoops, *DeKnops in Contemporary International Criminal Law* (2nd edn Martinus Nijhoff 2008) 260 ('the burden rests squarely on the prosecutor to prove guilt beyond a reasonable doubt, and clearly the accused must never be required to discharge a similar onus with respect to establishing his or her innocence, which equally applies to the establishing of defences').

[34] *Prosecutor v Delalić and Others* (n 32) para 603.

[35] See text at n 11, which also provides exceptions to this general rule.

[36] Emphasis added.

[37] That there is no presumption of inadmissibility see, for example, *Prosecutor v Germain Katanga and Others* (Judgment) ICC-01/04-01/07-1497 (25 September 2009) para 82 (art 17(1)(b) 'comprises two cumulative elements that have to be fulfilled for a case to be inadmissible: the case must have been investigated, and the State having jurisdiction must have "decided not to prosecute"').

[38] See text at n 31. See also text at notes 21 (on necessity defence) and 29 (on jurisdictional objections).

[39] ICC Statute art 17.1(a).

general rule for all objections to admissibility, the real burden of proof or burden of persuasion stays with the party relying on the objection so that, in the end, when all the evidence has been submitted by all parties but it remains in equipoise, the defendant loses (i.e. the objection is dismissed and the case proceeds). As the Appeals Chamber of the ICC found in *Muthaura and Others*, '[i]f a State challenges the admissibility of a case, it must provide the Court with evidence with a sufficient degree of specificity and probative value that demonstrates that it is indeed investigating the case'.[40]

4 Exceptions versus Exemptions (or Alternative Rules)

The distinction between exceptions (burden of proof on the respondent) and exemptions (burden of proof on the claimant) is firmly established (although not uncontested[41]) in WTO jurisprudence. It has intuitive value, even though the Appellate Body (AB) itself admits that the 'distinction may not always be evident or readily applicable'.[42] When faced with a rule exception relation, both the rule and the exception (or affirmative defence) apply to a given fact pattern. As a result, the rule is, at least prima facie, breached (breach to be established by the claimant) but the limited exception to the rule (to be established by the respondent) nonetheless allows for the measure or conduct. In contrast, when faced with a rule exemption relation, the exemption (carve-out, reservation, or alternative rule) excludes a situation from the scope of application of the rule: the rule applies to one set of situations; the exemption or alternative rule applies (as a positive rule or autonomous right) to another set of situations; rule and exemption never apply to the same facts. As a result, it is for the claimant to demonstrate that the rule it claims is violated applies and that the exemption (or alternative rule) does not apply.

The exception–exemption distinction has two other consequences in addition to the burden of proof. First, if something is an exemption in the form of an autonomous right or alternative rule—think of Article 3.3 of the SPS Agreement or Article 2.4 of the Technical Barriers to Trade (TBT) Agreement, which, as an alternative rule, not as an exception, allows WTO members to deviate from international standards when certain conditions are met—the exemption is a provision *that can be violated* and lead to responsibility. In *EC—Hormones*, for example, the EC was found to be in violation of Article 3.3 of the SPS Agreement. An exception provision, in contrast, justifies breach of another provision; it can never, by itself, be violated. A respondent cannot, for example, violate Article XX of the GATT; at worst, it does not meet the conditions in Article XX so that its breach of, say, Article III of the GATT cannot be justified. This also means that, as noted earlier, if a provision is an exemption or alternative rule, rather than an exception, the claimant must allege a violation of the exemption or alternative rule. Failure to do so would simply lead to the tribunal finding that the general rule (say, Article 3.1 of the SPS Agreement requiring WTO members to base their

[40] *Prosecutor v Francis Kirimi Muthaura and Others* (Judgment) ICC-01/09-02/11 OA (30 August 2011) para 2.

[41] For a critique see Michelle T Grando, *Evidence, Proof, and Fact-Finding WTO Dispute Settlement* (OUP 2009) 181–84.

[42] Appellate Body Report, *EC—Tariff Preferences* (n 14) para 88. The Appellate Body defines the distinction as follows: 'In cases where one provision permits, in certain circumstances, behaviour that would otherwise be inconsistent with an obligation in another provision, and one of the two provisions refers to the other provision, the Appellate Body has found that the complaining party bears the burden of establishing that a challenged measure is inconsistent with the provision permitting particular behaviour [i.e. that the provision is an *exemption*] *only* where one of the provisions suggests that the obligation is not applicable to the said measure.'

sanitary measures on international standards) does not apply, without a finding on breach or compliance with the exemption or alternative rule.[43]

Secondly, where a provision is an exception, one would expect the tribunal to examine, first of all, whether a rule is breached *before* checking whether an exception can justify this breach. As a matter of judicial economy, if there is no breach in the first place, there is no need to examine the exception. A WTO panel, for example, will first examine whether there is a breach of, say, Article III of the GATT (national treatment) before assessing whether such breach can be justified under Article XX of the GATT. Other tribunals have not followed this sequence.[44] In the *Oil Platforms* case, for example, the ICJ first assessed whether the United States could rely on essential security under Article XX of the Treaty of Amity (a question the Court answered in the negative). Only after that did the Court turn to the obligation in Article X of the Treaty on freedom of commerce and navigation (where the Court found that the United States did *not* breach this obligation in the first place). Since there was no breach in the first place, there was technically no need for the Court to address essential security under Article XX. The Court must have had strong reasons to want to address use of force and Article XX no matter what (remember that, in 2003, use of force in the wake of the 9/11 terrorist attacks in the United States was highly controversial).[45]

For exemptions or reservations, in contrast, one could expect the tribunal to analyse first whether the exemption/reservation/alternative rule applies since, if it does apply, the general rule is not applicable in the first place. Only after a finding that the exemption or *lex specialis* does *not* apply would one expect the tribunal to turn to the question of whether the general rule is breached. In *Mobil v Canada*, however, where Article 1108 of the NAFTA set out non-conforming measures not subject to Article 1106 performance requirements, the tribunal first examined whether Article 1106 was violated and only afterwards turned to Article 1108 reservations.[46]

Before other tribunals, the exception–exemption distinction plays little or no role. In the ICJ *Whaling* case, for example, the core question was whether Japan's whaling activities were covered by Article VIII of the International Whaling Convention allowing for special permit whaling for purposes of scientific research. Article VIII itself states that 'the killing, taking, and treating of whales in accordance with the provisions of this Article *shall be exempt* from the operation of this Convention' (emphasis added). Japan argued that this was an exemption (with presumably the burden of proof on the claimant, Australia); in turn, Australia argued that it was a limited exception (with presumably the burden of proof on the respondent, Japan).[47] But neither the parties, nor ultimately the ICJ, explicitly linked this to the burden of proof.[48] Burden of proof was not even mentioned. Although Article VIII itself and some

[43] See n 14 above.

[44] Another good example is *Continental v Argentina*, where the tribunal explained the reasons supporting its choice to discuss the exceptions invoked by Argentina before the claims of breach as follows: 'The pervasive nature of these general exceptions, which Argentina raises against all claims of Continental, might be such as to absolve Argentina, in whole or in part, from the alleged breaches and from the ensuing responsibility to pay damages' (*Continental Casualty Company v Argentine Republic*, ICSID Case No ARB/03/9, Award (5 September 2008) para 161).

[45] In *Case Concerning Military and Paramilitary Activities in and against Nicaragua (Nicaragua v United States of America)* (Merits, Judgment) [1986] ICJ Rep 14, in contrast, the ICJ first examined whether the treaty was prima facie breached and only subsequently assessed what it called the 'exception' on essential security in art XXI of the 1956 Treaty (I.C.J. Reports 1986, p. 140, para 280).

[46] *Mobil v Canada*, ICSID Case No ARV(AF)/07/4, Decision on Liability (22 May 2012).

[47] *Whaling in the Antarctic (Australia v Japan: New Zealand intervening)* (Judgment) [2014] ICJ Rep 226, paras 52 and 53, respectively.

[48] In the *Nicaragua* case (n 45), the ICJ found that the essential security clause in art XXI of the 1956 Treaty is an 'exception' but did not mention the exception-exemption dichotomy.

of the findings of the ICJ would seem to indicate that Article VIII is an exemption[49] (with the burden of proof on the claimant, Australia), in subsequent findings the ICJ seemed to place the burden of proof on the respondent.[50] Similarly, although the ICJ in *Oil Platforms* seemed to read Article XX of the Treaty of Amity as an exception (or affirmative defence) rather than an exemption, the Court did not discuss the exception–exemption distinction.[51] Another example is *Mobil v Canada*. Much of the Decision (and Dissent) in that case was about whether Article 1108 of the NAFTA (entitled 'Reservations and Exceptions') covered certain Canadian measures listed in Article 1108 as 'non-conforming measures' that would otherwise be in violation of Article 1106 of the NAFTA prohibiting certain performance requirements. Yet, neither the tribunal nor the dissenting arbitrator discussed the distinction between exceptions and exemptions or explicitly allocated or even discussed the burden of proof. The majority found that the Article 1108 reservation did not apply and reached the conclusion that Canada had therefore violated its commitments on performance requirements under Article 1106;[52] the Dissent came to the opposite conclusion.[53]

The lack of reference to the burden of proof in *Oil Platforms, Whaling*, and *Mobil* is not in and of itself a problem or error of law. Indeed, burden of proof matters only in exceptional cases where the evidence is in equipoise. If it is not, and the tribunal is convinced one way or the other, who bears the burden of proof (i.e. who is the victim of doubt) plays no practical role. If anything, it is WTO jurisprudence that too often overindulges in complex analyses on burden of proof that neither add clarity to the exercise nor ultimately have practical importance.

5 Proving Facts, Not Law

Importantly, what does it mean to have the burden of proving, for example, that an exception applies? The tribunal 'knows the law' (*iura novit curia*) so it is not for either party to convince or persuade the tribunal of what the law means.[54] If the law in question is treaty law, that is

[49] ibid paras 55, 230, and 233.

[50] ibid para 141 ('There is no evidence that Japan has examined whether it would be feasible to combine a smaller lethal take ...'); para 185 ('the purpose of ... inquiry is not to second-guess the scientific judgments made by individual scientists or by Japan, but rather to examine whether Japan ... has demonstrated a reasonable basis for annual sample sizes ...'); para 227 ('the Court considers that JARPA II involves activities that can broadly be characterized as scientific research ... but that the evidence does not establish that the programme's design and implementation are reasonable in relation to achieving its stated objectives').

[51] *Oil Platforms*, supra note 20, para 32 ('It is the contention of the United States that the actions complained of by Iran were measures necessary to protect the essential security interests of the United States, and that accordingly, if those actions would otherwise have been breaches of Article X, paragraph 1, of the Treaty, which the United States denies, the effect of Article XX, paragraph 1 (d), is that they are justified under the terms of the Treaty itself, and thus do not constitute breaches of it') and para 33 ('it is now for the Court to interpret and apply that subparagraph, inasmuch as such a defence is asserted by the United States'). On other occasions, art XX seemed portrayed as an exemption or alternative rule see para 36: 'In the present case the United States has argued that Article XX, paragraph 1(d), of the 1955 Treaty is not a limitation on Article X, paragraph 1, nor yet a derogation from it; and that it is a substantive provision that determines, defines and delimits the obligations of the parties, simultaneously with and on the same level as Article X, paragraph 1.' In its judgment on preliminary objections (*Case Concerning Oil Platforms*, Judgment of 12 December 1996, para 20), the ICJ states that art XX 'does not restrict its jurisdiction' and is, instead, 'a possible defence on the merits'. However, the Court did not specify what type of defence on the merits it is, e.g. an exemption or an exception.

[52] *Mobil v Canada* (n 43).

[53] ibid Partial Dissenting Opinion by Prof Philippe Sands QC.

[54] See e.g. Appellate Body Report, *EC—Tariff Preferences* (n 14) para 105 ('[I]t is not the responsibility of the [party invoking a WTO provision] to provide us with the legal interpretation to be given to [that] particular provision').

a matter of treaty interpretation and the tribunal can come up with its own legal arguments. Facts, in contrast, must be raised and proven by the parties (except where tribunals have investigative powers to collect evidence themselves[55]). If the decision-making process has three steps—(i) establishing the facts, (ii) determining what the law is, and (iii) applying the law to the facts—then the burden of proof applies only to steps (i) and (iii). Put differently, stating that a respondent has the burden of proving an exception means that the respondent must establish *the facts required for the exception to be complied with*. This is, for example, what Article 24(1) of the UNCITRAL Arbitration Rules explicitly provides: '[e]ach party shall have the burden of proving the facts relied on *to support his claim or defence*' (emphasis added).

In other words, that respondents have the burden of proof under Article XX of the GATT or Article 25 of the ILC means that it is up to the respondent to establish that *its measure meets the requirements of*, for example, Article XX(b) of the GATT as a measure necessary to protect human health, or Article 25 of the ILC as a measure taken in a situation of 'necessity'. In this respect, the statement that it is for the party alleging a fact to prove it—without linking that fact to requirements under a claim—can be misleading. If it were to refer to timing, for example, the party *first invoking* that domestic remedies have (or have not) been exhausted, it would invite strategic litigation and may delay proceedings or affect due process. If the statement were, instead, meant to allocate the burden of proof in a time-neutral fashion, it risks to not resolve anything: if a claimant–investor alleges that it has US nationality, while the respondent state is of the view that the investor is not a US national but is Belgian, is it for the claimant to prove US nationality (the fact it invoked) or for the state to prove absence of US nationality or the existence of Belgian nationality (the facts that party is invoking)? Rather, in this example, since nationality is a matter of jurisdiction *ratione personae*, it is for the claimant to demonstrate that all jurisdictional requirements are met (e.g. that it does have US nationality).

6 Techniques to Produce and Evaluate Evidence (Burden of Production) versus Standard (Level or Quantum) of Proof

That the respondent has the burden of proof under, for example, an exception does not mean that the claimant is absolved from submitting evidence or arguments. Both parties have a duty to cooperate and to submit relevant evidence. When they refuse, adverse inferences can be drawn and may even discharge the burden of proof. Even when a respondent does not have the burden of proof, it may—and in most cases will—submit evidence or allege facts that, if proven, will support its case, for example, support a finding that no breach occurred.[56] Even then, however, the ultimate burden of persuasion remains on the claimant to prove that a breach did occur.

[55] e.g. pursuant to the ex officio powers under art 43 of the ICSID Convention, the SPS/TBT Agreements (and DSU Appendix) allowing WTO panels to appoint independent experts or Annex V to the SCM Agreement for the collection of evidence in actionable subsidy cases.

[56] See Panel Report, *Japan—Measures Affecting the Importation of Apples*, WT/DS245/R (adopted 10 December 2003), DSR 2003:IX, p. 4481, at para 8.168, putting the burden on defendant Japan to prove a fact it alleged (that fire blight bacteria carried by an infected US apple could be transferred to a host plant in Japan by means of rain splash) even though this occurred under a claim for which the US had the burden of proof. See also Appellate Body Report, *Japan—Measures Affecting the Importation of Apples*, WT/DS245/AB/R (adopted 10 December 2003), DSR 2003:IX, 4391, at para 157.

6.1 Prima facie case and shifting burdens of production

Some tribunals organize the process of producing arguments and evidence in the form of a genuine ping-pong match, whereby the burden shifts from one party to the other, and back. Under Article XX exceptions, for example (for which the burden of proof rests on the respondent), it is, first, for the respondent to establish a prima facie case that its measure *is* 'necessary' to protect, say, health (step 1); if the respondent succeeds, it is up to the claimant to raise an alternative measure that the respondent could have enacted (step 2); once the claimant has done so, however, it is, again, for the respondent to demonstrate that the suggested alternative does, for example, *not* meet its appropriate level of health protection or is *not* reasonably available (step 3); if the respondent succeeds, the measure is justified under the Article XX(b) exception (subject to meeting also the conditions in the *chapeau* of Article XX).[57]

There are two ways to interpret this back-and-forth. A first approach is to say that the prima facie case of necessity that the respondent must originally establish (step 1) actually discharges the respondent's real burden of proof, after which that burden (the burden of persuasion) shifts to the claimant (for step 2 of the process regarding alternative measures) etc. The problem with this approach is that, at no time during the proceedings, parties are informed about when the burden shifts or when the process has moved from step 1 to step 2, and from step 2 to step 3. Only in its final report, ex post, does the Panel describe what happened. This can raise fundamental due process concerns: a party may not know whether or at what time it carries the burden of persuasion.

Under a second approach, the prima facie case merely shifts the burden of production (not the burden of persuasion[58]) from the respondent to the claimant; the real burden of proof under the Article XX exception remains with the respondent and at the end of the ping-pong match (after all three steps) the ultimate question is: has the respondent convinced the tribunal that its measure is necessary to protect, for example, health under Article XX(b) of the GATT.[59] This second approach is both practically and conceptually more attractive.[60]

[57] In contrast, unlike under GATT art XX, 'under Article 2.2 of the TBT Agreement, a complainant must make a *prima facie* case that its proposed alternative measure is indeed reasonably available' (Appellate Body Reports, *United States—Certain Country of Origin Labelling (COOL) Requirements—Recourse to Article 21.5 of the DSU by Canada and Mexico*, WT/DS384/AB/RW/WT/DS386/AB/RW (adopted 29 May 2015) para 5.338). But 'taking into account that the specific details of implementation may depend on the capacity and particular circumstances of the implementing Member in question, it would appear incongruous to expect a complainant, under Article 2.2 of the TBT Agreement, to provide detailed information on how a proposed alternative would be implemented by the respondent in practice, and precise and comprehensive estimates of the cost that such implementation would entail'. As a result, 'once a complainant has established *prima facie* that the proposed alternative is reasonably available to the respondent, it would be for the respondent to adduce specific evidence showing that associated costs would be prohibitive, or that technical difficulties would be so substantial that implementation of such an alternative would entail an undue burden for the Member in question'.

[58] Except when faced with a legal presumption as in art 10.3 of the WTO Agreement on Agriculture or art 3.8 of the DSU or strict liability rules which presume liability as soon as harm is proven unless the company can show that the damage was caused exclusively by another person (as set out in the Ecuadorian Constitution of 2008 in respect of environmental damage, discussed in *Perenco v Ecuador*, ICSID Case No ARB/08/6, Interim Decision (11 August 2015).

[59] This is similar to the position defended above in respect of jurisdictional objections (see text at n 29) and the admissibility objection of exhaustion of domestic remedies (supra text at note 31). See also text at n 21.

[60] See Joost Pauwelyn, 'Evidence, Proof and Persuasion in WTO Dispute Settlement, Who Bears the Burden?' (1998) 1 Journal of International Economic Law 227, 235, and 252 ff. In support: John Barcelo, 'Burden of Proof, Prima Facie Case and Presumption in WTO Dispute Settlement' (2009) 22 Cornell International Law Journal 23, 24 and references in n 1; Georges Abi-Saab, 'L'Organe de règlement des différends de l'OMC, Commentaire' in H Ruiz Fabri and J-M Sorel (eds), *La preuve devant les jurisdictions internationales* (Pedone 2007) 97–103, 100: the ping-pong game of shifting burdens 'me paraît assez artificiel et très peu convaincante. Car, pour moi, la charge de preuve ... reste toujours la même, incombant à celui qui avance la prétention'). See also *Rompetrol Group NV*

Similarly, in the recent *Bilcon v Canada* Award, the tribunal found that 'Bilcon had the affirmative burden of proving' the constituent elements for breach by Canada of NAFTA Article 1102 national treatment: (i) according of treatment by Canada to Bilcon and Canadian investors; that is (ii) 'less favorable' for Bilcon; in the presence of (iii) 'like circumstances'.[61] However, once the claimant–investor makes a prima facie case under this three-pronged test, 'the onus is on the host state to show that a measure is still sustainable within the terms of Article 1102', for example, because the discriminatory treatment identified is 'not sufficiently linked to nationality, but merely an incidental effect of the reasonable pursuit of domestic policy objectives'.[62] Did the *Bilcon* tribunal thereby shift the real burden of proof from Bilcon to Canada? Or, rather, did the tribunal merely shift the burden of production from Bilcon to Canada[63] with the real burden of proof remaining on Bilcon throughout? Here too the second approach seems the better one.[64]

6.2 Standard or quantum of proof

When it comes to standard or quantum of proof (including for claims in defence) the general default option taken by international tribunals, if addressed at all, seems to be 'preponderance of the evidence' or 'balance of probabilities'.[65] This typically means 'more probable than not' or more than 50 per cent probable.[66] In some instances, international tribunals have opted for a lower standard of prima facie evidence.[67] They have also lowered the standard in

v Romania, ICSID Case No ARB/06/3, Award (6 May 2013) para 178: 'if, according to basic principle, it is for the one party, or for the other, to establish a particular factual assertion, that will remain the position throughout the forensic process, starting from when the assertion is first put forward and all the way through to the end.... the Tribunal is not enamoured of arguments setting out to show that a burden of proof can under certain circumstances shift from the party that originally bore it to the other party, and then perhaps in appropriate circumstances shift back again to the original party'.

[61] *Bilcon v Canada*, PCA Case No 2009-04, Award on Jurisdiction and Liability (17 March 2015) para 718.

[62] ibid paras 720 and 723.

[63] A reason to shift this burden of production from claimant to host state is, arguably, as the tribunal stated (ibid para 723): '[i]t is the host state that is in a position to identify and substantiate the case, in terms of its own laws, policies and circumstances, that an apparently discriminatory measure is in fact compliant with the "national treatment" norm set out in Article 1102.'

[64] Similar to *Bilcon*'s approach to NAFTA national treatment, under the TBT Agreement art 2.1 national treatment (for which the burden of proof rests on the claimant) the Appellate Body found that it is, first, on the claimant to demonstrate that the products compared are 'like' *and* that the challenged measure has a detrimental impact on imports; thereafter, it is for the respondent to show that the detrimental impact 'stems exclusively from a legitimate regulatory distinction'. If the respondent succeeds, no violation of art 2.1 is found (Appellate Body Report, *United States—Measures Concerning the Importation, Marketing and Sale of Tuna and Tuna Products*, WT/DS381/AB/R (adopted 13 June 2012) DSR 2012:IV, 1837, at para 216). The subsequent art 21.5 compliance panel in this dispute (Appellate Body Report, *United States—Measures Concerning the Importation, Marketing and Sale of Tuna and Tuna Products—Recourse to Article 21.5 of the DSU by Mexico*, WT/DS381/AB/RW and Add.1 (adopted 3 December 2015) paras 7.51 ff) was unclear; however, whether this means that the burden of proof for all elements under TBT art 2.1 is on claimants; or whether the burden of proving a 'legitimate regulatory distinction' is actually on the respondent. As noted above, the better approach is to leave the real burden of proof for all constituent elements of breach of TBT art 2.1 on the claimant, but to shift the burden of production to the respondent once the claimant has proven (a prima facie case of) detrimental impact on like imports. It is then for respondent to produce arguments and evidence that this detrimental impact 'stems exclusively from a legitimate regulatory distinction'.

[65] See e.g. Separate Opinion of Vice-President Wolfrum, *M/V Saiga No 2 Case* (1 July 1999), at para 12. In support: *Emmis v Hungary*, ICSID Case No ARB/12/2, Award (16 April 2014) para 171; *Marion Unglaube v Republic of Costa Rica*, ICSID Case No ARB/08/1, Award (16 May 2012) para 34.

[66] Barcelo (n 60) 30.

[67] See e.g. the burden on claimants at the jurisdictional phase in ISDS cases to make only a prima facie showing of treaty breach as this involves questions of fact that go to the merits and which a tribunal must normally not prejudge in the jurisdictional phase (see *Emmis v Hungary*, ICSID Case No ARB/12/2, Award (16 April 2014) paras 171–72). When the International Tribunal for the Law of the Sea applied a similar prima facie evidence approach

some cases where the party was required to prove a negative[68] or where evidence was hard to obtain.[69] In other cases, given the gravity of claims or defences made, tribunals adopted a higher standard such as 'fully conclusive',[70] 'clear and convincing evidence',[71] or even evidence 'beyond reasonable doubt'.[72] Overall, however, international tribunals have remained rather silent on the standard of proof, thereby following a more civil law tradition that refers, without more, to *l'intime conviction du juge*.[73]

An outlier is, once again, international criminal law where, for a conviction, 'the Court must be convinced of the guilt of the accused beyond reasonable doubt'.[74] This means that when an accused argues a defence (which, as discussed earlier, does not, at least not before the ICC, shift the burden of proof), such defence will be maintained, and the defendant must be acquitted if the evidence submitted in defence induces 'a reasonable doubt as to whether [the accused] version might not be true, rather than that of the Prosecution'; that is, the evidence in defence 'should be enough to suggest a reasonable possibility'.[75] In contrast, for matters where the accused (rather than the prosecutor) has the burden of proof (e.g. when a defendant argues that a case is inadmissible before the ICC[76]), the quantum of proof is set at the lower, default standard of preponderance of the evidence.[77]

in the *M/V Saiga No 2 Case*, this was recognised clearly by one judge to entail a lower standard of proof than usual (Separate Opinion of Vice-President Wolfrum, *M/V Saiga No 2 Case* (1 July 1999), at para 12).

[68] See *Nicaragua Case* (n 45) para 147 and *Ahmadou Sadio Diallo (Republic of Guinea v Democratic Republic of the Congo)* (Judgment) [2010] ICJ Rep 639, para 55.

[69] This approach was adopted by the Iran–US Claims Tribunal in the *Sola Tiles Case*, where it was held that due to the difficulties of the plaintiff in obtaining evidence of documents located in Iran, the standard of proof could be somewhat lowered (14 Iran–US CTR 224 para 52). In the same vein see Eritrea Ethiopia Claims Commission, Eritrea's Claim 17, Partial Award (1 July 2003).

[70] See *Application of the Convention on the Prevention and Punishment of the Crime of Genocide (Bosnia and Herzegovina v Serbia and Montenegro)* (Judgment) [2007] ICJ Rep 43, para 209: 'The Court has long recognized that claims against a State involving charges of exceptional gravity must be proved by evidence that is fully conclusive (cf *Corfu Channel (United Kingdom v Albania)* (Judgment) [1949] ICJ Rep 4, 17). The Court requires that it be fully convinced that allegations made in the proceedings, that the crime of genocide or the other acts enumerated in art III have been committed, have been clearly established. The same standard applies to the proof of attribution for such acts.' See also *Oil Platforms (Islamic Republic of Iran v United States of America)* (Separate Opinion of Judge Higgins) (n 24) para 33 (referring to 'a general agreement that the graver the charge the more confidence must there be in the evidence relied on'). In the same vein see Eritrea Ethiopia Claims Commission, Eritrea's Claim 17, Partial Award (1 July 2003), para 46 ('Particularly in light of the gravity of some of the claims advanced, the Commission will require clear and convincing evidence in support of its findings').

[71] In respect of claims of corruption in international arbitration see *EDF (Services) Ltd. v Romania*, ICSID Case No ARB/05/13, Award (8 October 2009, para 221. Contra: *Metal-Tech v Uzbekistan*, applying also for allegations of corruption a 'with reasonable certainty' standard and, in the process, admitting 'circumstantial evidence'.

[72] In cases of alleged violation of the prohibition of torture under art 3 of the European Convention on Human Rights, the standard of proof is 'beyond reasonable doubt' (*Ireland v UK*, 5310/71 ECHR 1 (18 January 1976, para 161).

[73] In support: *Oil Platforms (Islamic Republic of Iran v United States of America*) (Separate Opinion of Judge Higgins) (n 24) 234.

[74] ICC Statute art 66.3.

[75] *Prosecutor v Delalić and Others* (n 32) para 603.

[76] See text at n 40. In criminal regimes, other than that of the ICC, there may also be presumptions against the accused. See supra note 32 in respect of the defence of insanity. In that case, for the accused to discharge his or her burden of proof, it is generally sufficient to meet a preponderance of the evidence standard. See Knoops (n 33) 261 ('The major difference with respect to the onus of proof of the prosecution is that a defendant fulfills the "burden of proof", underlying a defence, on a balance of probabilities—the same standard as that of a plaintiff in a civil action—without the requirement of proving beyond reasonable doubt').

[77] See Informal Expert Paper, 'The Principle of Complementarity in Practice' ICC-OTP (2003) para 52 ('As the issue in complementarity is one of admissibility before a particular forum, rather than the objective and subjective elements of a particular crime, the appropriate burden is the simple balance of probabilities, rather than any higher standard such as "proof beyond a reasonable doubt" ').

Finally, what is the quantum of proof required in WTO dispute settlement where, as discussed above, there is a prevailing reference to prima facie case—be it for claims of breach, or exceptions—which, once established, triggers an elaborate game of shifting burdens (of production)? The Appellate Body has clarified that 'a *prima facie* case is one which, in the absence of effective refutation … requires a panel, as a matter of law, to rule in favour of the … party presenting the *prima facie* case'.[78] This clarification tells us that once a prima facie case is established (and not effectively refuted), it can not only shift the burden of production but also discharge the real burden of proof. In other words, a prima facie case seems to be the standard or quantum of proof in at least some WTO cases. But this clarification does not tell us *what* is needed to establish a prima facie case in the first place. It does not tell us, for example, whether it requires merely a scintilla of evidence, prima facie evidence, substantial evidence, a preponderance of the evidence, or any of the higher standards mentioned above (e.g. evidence beyond reasonable doubt). The AB itself confirmed that 'precisely how much and precisely what kind of evidence will be required to establish such a presumption [or prima facie case] will necessarily vary from measure to measure, provision to provision, and case to case'.[79]

Although the French translation of prima facie case in official WTO reports is *un commencement de preuve* (a translation that has been criticized by an Appellate Member as wrong[80]), it is hard to imagine that a mere scintilla of evidence or mere prima facie evidence would be enough not just to shift the burden of production (that may well be the case) but also formally to discharge the real burden of proof or persuasion. If so, it would set a remarkably low standard of proof for finding breach of a WTO treaty commitment or compliance with a WTO exception. The better option is to set the standard of proof in WTO dispute settlement (which, in some cases, will mean the establishment of a prima facie case, not sufficiently refuted, but in general should be a test to be applied once all the evidence is in[81]), at the default standard of 'preponderance of the evidence' or 'balance of probabilities'[82] unless there are exceptional reasons to use a lower or higher standard, along the lines followed by other international tribunals.[83]

7 The Neutrality of Treaty Interpretation but Increasing Importance of Standard of Review

Questions of burden and standard of proof for claims in defence must be clearly distinguished from treaty interpretation and the question of whether, for example, exceptions must be interpreted narrowly. There is a clear trend amongst a variety of international tribunals to interpret exceptions 'neutrally' like any other treaty provision, neither broadly nor

[78] Appellate Body Report, *EC Measures Concerning Meat and Meat Products (Hormones)*, WT/DS26/AB/R, WT/DS48/AB/R (adopted 13 February 1998) DSR 1998:I, 135, para 104.

[79] Appellate Body Report, *United States—Measure Affecting Imports of Woven Wool Shirts and Blouses from India*, WT/DS33/AB/R (adopted 23 May 1997) and Corr.1, DSR 1997:I, 323, at 4.

[80] Abi-Saab (n 60) 101.

[81] See n 59.

[82] See n 65. In support: David Unterhalter, *The Burden of Proof in WTO Dispute Settlement* in Merit E Janow, Victoria Donaldson, and Alan Yanovich (eds), The WTO: Governance, Dispute Settlement and Developing Countries (Juris Publishing 2008) 543, 552 ('there seems little reason not to adopt a standard that is clear and well understood in other contexts, the most obvious candidate being proof on a balance of probabilities').

[83] See nn 67–72 above.

narrowly.[84] The ICJ in the *Whaling* case, for example, stated that 'taking into account the Preamble and other relevant provisions of the Convention ... the Court observes that neither a restrictive nor an expansive interpretation of Article VIII [on whaling for purposes of scientific research] is justified'.[85] Similarly, in respect of jurisdiction and compromissory clauses, Judge Higgins famously stated that 'the Court has no judicial policy of being either liberal or strict in deciding the scope of compromissory clauses: they are judicial decisions like any other'.[86]

This was not always the case and to this day some tribunals continue to interpret defences narrowly,[87] especially necessity under customary international law[88] (although they may thereby conflate the strict *substantive* conditions under ILC Article 25 necessity, with a restrictive approach to treaty interpretation for all exceptions as such[89]).

Finally, burden and standard of proof must be distinguished from standard of review (*le critère d'examen*). Whereas burden of proof in respect of, for example, GATT or BIT exceptions can make it harder for regulating countries to justify their policies (when in doubt, the regulation is not justified), recent trends in respect of standard of review go in the other direction: they stress the deference to be given to regulating countries, along the lines of the famous 'margin of appreciation' championed by the European Court of Human Rights.[90] A telling example in this respect is the ICJ ruling in the *Whaling* case. As noted earlier, the ICJ never explicitly allocated burden of proof under Article VIII of the Convention (on whaling for purposes of scientific research), although on occasion it seemed to put the burden on the defendant, Japan. Far more important, however, was the Court's finding on standard of review. Japan had argued, early in the proceedings, that 'the Court is limited, when exercising its power of review, to ascertaining whether the determination [by Japan under Article VIII scientific research] was 'arbitrary or capricious', 'manifestly unreasonable', or made in bad faith'.[91] The Court rejected this extremely deferential approach and opted for the following standard of review: 'the Court will consider if the killing, taking and treating of whales is "for purposes of" scientific research by examining whether, in the use of lethal methods, *the programme's design*

[84] See Appellate Body Report, *United States—Standards for Reformulated and Conventional Gasoline*, WT/DS2/AB/R (adopted 20 May 1996) DSR 1996:I, 3, applying standard rules of treaty interpretation in the VCLT to the exception in GATT art XX; *Mobil v Canada*, ICSID Case No ARV(AF)/07/4, Decision on Liability (22 May 2012) para 255; *Aguas del Tunari SA v Bolivia*, ICSID Case No ARB/02/3, Decision on Respondent's Objections to Jurisdiction (21 October 2005) para 91.

[85] *Whaling* case (n 47) para 58.

[86] *Oil Platforms (Islamic Republic of Iran v United States of America)* (Separate Opinion of Judge Higgins) (n 24) para 35.

[87] See *Noble Ventures Inc v Romania*, ICSID Case No ARB/01/11, Award (12 October 2005) para 55; *Enron Creditors Recovery Corporation (formerly Enron Corporation) and Ponderosa Assets LP v Argentine Republic*, ICSID Case No ARB/01/3, Award (22 May 2007) para 331 ('the Tribunal must first note that the object and purpose of the Treaty is, as a general proposition, to apply in situations of economic difficulty and hardship that require the protection of the international guaranteed rights of its beneficiaries. To this extent, any interpretation resulting in an escape route from the obligations defined [in casu, art XI of the treaty on essential security] cannot be easily reconciled with that object and purpose. Accordingly, a restrictive interpretation of any such alternative is mandatory'). For another teleological interpretation but going in the other direction see *Perenco v Ecuador*, ICSID Case No ARB/08/6, Interim Decision (11 August 2015) para 322: 'the Tribunal considers that the Constitution's focus on environmental protection means that when choosing between certain disputed (but reasonable) interpretations of the Ecuadorian regulatory regime, the interpretation which most favours the protection of the environment is to be preferred.'

[88] See *EDF v Argentina* (n 8) para 1171 ('Necessity must be construed strictly and objectively, not as an easy escape hatch for host states wishing to avoid treaty obligations which prove difficult').

[89] ILC art 25 may also be exceptional and invite a restrictive approach because of its formulation as a double negative ('necessity may not be invoked ... unless ...'), which is different from the formulation of most other defences.

[90] See e.g. *Case of A, B and C v Ireland* App no 25579/05 (Grand Chamber 16 December 2010) para 185.

[91] *Whaling* case (n 47) para 65.

and implementation are reasonable in relation to achieving its stated objectives. This standard of review is an objective one'.[92] This 'reasonableness' standard—more deferential than a so-called de novo review but less deferential than a self-judging provision or bad faith test[93] —is clearly inspired by the WTO Appellate Body's statement on standard of review under the SPS Agreement in *US—Continued Suspension*: 'the review power of a panel is not to determine whether the risk assessment undertaken by a WTO Member is correct, but rather to determine whether that risk assessment is *supported by coherent reasoning and respectable scientific evidence and is, in this sense, objectively justifiable*'.[94] Thus, restricting the review powers of WTO panels when examining health or safety measures under the WTO treaty (limiting it to a 'reasonableness test'), the AB gave more—not less—deference to regulating countries than traditionally understood. The ICJ followed in the AB's footsteps.

8 Conclusion

This contribution unpacks the, at first sight, obvious statement that the burden of proving a defence is on the party invoking it. It distinguishes six different 'claims in defence': (i) objections to jurisdiction, (ii) objections to admissibility, (iii) exemptions or alternative rules, (iv) absence of breach, (v) exceptions, and (vi) defences under secondary rules. For each of these six 'claims in defence', five types of 'burden' on the parties or tribunal are identified: (i) burden of raising a claim in defence, (ii) burden of production of evidence, (iii) burden of persuasion (or real burden of proof), (iv) standard or quantum of proof, and (v) standard of review. Although for some claims in defence some types of burden are on the defendant, this is certainly not the case for all.

- Defendants generally have the burden to *raise* objections to admissibility but not objections to jurisdiction (which the tribunal must examine at its own initiative). In addition, even if the burden of *persuasion* for admissibility objections generally rests on defendants, the burden of persuasion in respect of jurisdictional requirements generally rests on claimants.
- The burden of persuasion for *exceptions* and *defences* under secondary rules does fall on respondents (except before the international criminal court). However, it is for claimants to prove that a rule applies and not an *exemption* (reservation, carve-out, or alternative rule) or that the constituent elements for breach are met. The difference between exceptions and exemptions is well established in WTO jurisprudence. It needs more attention before other international tribunals.

Whereas the burden of *production* of evidence may shift within the examination of a single claim in defence (e.g. once a prima facie case is established), the burden of persuasion (or real burden of proof) does not shift. Where a party has the burden of persuasion under a claim in defence, it has the burden of proving the facts (not the law) required for that claim

[92] ibid para 67, emphasis added.

[93] See the Argentina ISDS cases rejecting that art XI in the US–Argentina BIT on essential security is a self-judging clause. See also *Nicaragua* case (n 45) for the security exception in art XXI of the 1956 Treaty.

[94] Appellate Body Report, *United States—Continued Suspension of Obligations in the EC—Hormones Dispute*, WT/DS320/AB/R (adopted 14 November 2008) DSR 2008:X, 3507, para 590. In *Whaling*, Japan itself ultimately relied on this WTO standard of review (n 47) para 66, quoting verbatim from the Appellate Body ruling) a standard that the ICJ broadly adopted at para 67.

in defence to succeed. Whereas a prima facie case may shift the burden of production (and in some cases, when not refuted, even discharge the burden of persuasion), it should not be generally equated with the quantum or standard of proof required to discharge the burden of persuasion. The fallback standard of proof before international tribunals is 'preponderance of the evidence' or 'balance of probabilities'. Yet, special cases may justify a lower or higher standard of proof (such as proof beyond reasonable doubt in international criminal proceedings). Increasing deference is provided to respondents by way of less intrusive standards of review (focused on reasonableness; margin of appreciation) and a rejection of the alleged rule that exceptions must, by definition, be interpreted restrictively.

Finally, given the increasing fact-intensive nature of disputes and thus enhanced importance of burden of proof issues (including for claims in defence), tribunals should clarify upfront (i) *who* has the burden of persuasion and (ii) what precise *standard* of proof applies (matters on which tribunals have been surprisingly silent), rather than describe formalistic ping-pong games of prima facie cases and shifting burdens of production, disclosed to the parties only ex post.

7

Derogation and Defeasibility in International Law

Andrea Dolcetti and Giovanni Battista Ratti***

1 Explicit and Implicit Exceptions in the Legal Domain

Every social practice involving rules shows that it is possible for general norms to be open to exceptions.[1] In the legal domain, exceptions can be explicitly identified by a given positive legal order. For example, Article 2043 of the Italian Civil Code expresses a general norm according to which one must redress the damage caused by his or her wrongdoing.[2] Article 2044 of the Italian Civil Code provides an *explicit exception* to the norm expressed by Article 2043, in terms of self-defence.[3] However, a general norm may also be open to an *implicit exception*. Usually, implicit exceptions cannot be identified prior to the application of a general norm to a particular case.[4] For example, Section 101 of Title 35 of the United States Code identifies the following criteria for patent eligibility: 'Whoever invents or discovers any new and useful process, machine, manufacture, or composition of matter, or any new and useful improvement thereof, may obtain a patent therefor, subject to the conditions and requirements of this title'.[5] In a 2013 case—*Association for Molecular Pathology v Myriad Genetics, Inc*—the Court held that Section 101 above contains an important implicit exception, according to which laws of nature, natural phenomena, and abstract ideas are not patentable.[6]

What is the difference between explicit and implicit exceptions in the legal domain? This section aims to explain what the 'implicit character' of implicit exceptions in the legal domain amounts to. In order to do so, we will clarify the difference between the formulation

* Junior Research Fellow in Constitutional Law, Trinity College, Oxford.
** Full Professor of Legal Philosophy, Tarello Institute for Legal Philosophy, Department of Law, University of Genoa. We would like to thank Lorand Bartels, Antonio Coco, Miles Jackson, Katie Johnston, Federica Paddeu, and Daniela Simone for their helpful comments on a previous version of this chapter.

[1] The existence and the nature of exceptions, as well as their interaction with rules, have attracted attention from moral philosophers. Several reasons why a person interested in moral phenomena should reflect upon the nature of exceptions are discussed in Leonard G Miller, 'Rules and Exceptions' (1956) 66 Ethics 262 .

[2] This is the Italian formulation of art 2043: 'Qualunque fatto doloso o colposo, che cagiona ad altri un danno ingiusto, obbliga colui che ha commesso il fatto a risarcire il danno.'

[3] This is the Italian formulation of art 2044: 'Non è responsabile chi cagiona il danno per legittima difesa di sé o di altri.'

[4] On the idea of legal defeasibility in the legal domain see Giovanni Sartor, 'Defeasibility in Legal Reasoning' (1993) 24 Rechtstheorie 281; Neil MacCormick, 'Defeasibility in Law and Logic' in Zenon Bańkowski, Ian White and Ulrike Hahn (eds), *Informatics and the Foundations of Legal Reasoning* (Kluwer 1995) 99–117; Frederick Schauer, 'On the Supposed Defeasibility of Legal Rules' (1998) 51 Current Legal Problems 223; Henry Prakken, 'Modelling Defeasibility in Law: Logic or Procedure?' (2001) 48 Fundamenta Informaticae 253; Jaap Hage, 'Law and Defeasibility' (2003) 11 Artificial Intelligence and Law 221; Henry Prakken and Giovanni Sartor, 'The Three Faces of Defeasibility in the Law' (2004) 17 Ratio Juris 118 ; David M Godden and Douglas Walton, 'Defeasibility in Judicial Opinion: Logical or Procedural?' (2008) 28 Informal Logic 6; Jordi Ferrer Beltrán and Giovanni B Ratti (eds), *The Logic of Legal Requirements* (Oxford University Press 2012).

[5] 35 USC § 101 (2012).

[6] For a discussion of this case, see: Wesley D Markham, 'How to Explain the "Implicit Exceptions" to Patent-Eligible Subject Matter' (2014) 16 Vanderbilt Journal of Entertainment and Technology Law 353.

Andrea Dolcetti and Giovanni Battista Ratti, *Derogation and Defeasibility in International Law* In: *Exceptions in International Law*. Edited by: Lorand Bartels and Federica Paddeu, Oxford University Press (2020).
DOI: 10.1093/oso/9780198789321.003.0007

of a legal norm and the legal norm itself (section 1.1). We will then distinguish between expressed (or explicit) norms; implicit norms; logically derived norms; and inferred norms (section1.2). Thirdly, we will recall Alf Ross' identification of three types of normative conflicts (or antinomies) (section1.3). These three sub-sections will help us develop a theoretical model that can explain the difference between explicit and implicit exceptions in the legal domain (section1.4).

1.1 Norms and norm-formulations

In legal discourse, norms (i.e., legal rules and principles) and norm-formulations (i.e., legal provisions) are seldom kept separate. The terms 'norm' and 'provision' are often used interchangeably to refer to norms and/or norm-formulations. The use of the terms 'norm' and 'provision' as synonymous may be motivated by a formalistic view on legal interpretation, according to which words have a 'proper' meaning that judges can 'discover'. From this perspective, there is a one-to-one correspondence between legal provisions and legal norms.[7] From a logical point of view, however, legal norms (legal rules and principles) and legal norm-formulations (legal provisions) should be distinguished and kept separate. Norm-formulations should be seen as segments of prescriptive language, that is to say a discourse whose principal function is to direct human behaviour. On the other hand, norms should be seen as the meaning-content of norm-formulations.[8] From this perspective, norms depend upon interpretation, in the sense that they are the result of an interpretative activity. Legal interpretation is the process that associates one or more meanings to one or more norm-formulations. It is often said that lawyers, judges, and legal scholars 'interpret legal norms'; in fact, from a logical point of view, they interpret legal provisions and legal norms follow from that interpretation.[9]

At the end of this section, we will develop a theoretical model that can explain the difference between explicit and implicit exceptions in the legal domain. This model capitalize on the logical gap between norms and norm-formulations. A key feature of our model is the idea that there is no one-to-one correspondence between norms and norm-formulations. This means that a legal provision may express more than one norm at the same time, both disjunctively and/or conjunctively. Further, a legal provision may express less than one norm—it may express a fragment of norm, as it were—or no norm at all. Conversely, a legal norm is not necessarily the meaning of just one norm-formulation; and it may be necessary to rely upon more than one legal provision to identify a legal norm. Finally, and this is an important point for the purposes of this chapter, a legal norm is not necessarily the expression of a norm-formulation, as it is possible for a legal system to include *implicit norms*.[10]

[7] See Riccardo Guastini, 'Ought-Sentences and Description of Rules' (1991) 4 Ratio Juris 308.

[8] Norms should be regarded as the prescriptive analogous of propositions in descriptive language—the key difference being that the former are expressed by prescriptive statements, whereas the latter are expressed by descriptive statements. Norms can be thought of as the meaning of legal provisions. As such, they are like propositions; however, unlike propositions, norms are prescriptive in character (and, for this reason, they cannot be said to be true or false). See Hans Kelsen, 'What Is the Pure Theory of Law?' (1960) 34 Tulane Law Review 269; Giovanni Tarello, *Diritto, enunciati, usi* (Il Mulino 1974); Carlos E Alchourrón and Eugenio Bulygin, 'The Expressive Conception of Norms' in Risto Hilpinen (ed), *New Studies in Deontic Logic* (Reidel 1981).

[9] Carlos E Alchourrón, 'Systematization and Change in the Science of Law' (1986) 10 Rechtstheorie 173: '... when jurists say, for example, that a legal norm has been given different judicial interpretations, it must be understood that they are referring to norm-formulations.'

[10] At least eight different cases of relationship between norms and norm-formulations can be identified. (1) A norm-formulation expresses only one norm. This is the only case, extremely rare in the practice, in which there is a bi-univocal relationship or one-to one correspondence between a norm and a norm-formulation.

1.2 Four classes of legal norms

In this sub-section we distinguish between four classes of legal norms: (i) expressed (or explicit) norms; (ii) implicit norms; (iii) logically derived norms; and (iv) inferred norms.

(i) The class of *expressed norms* comprises those norms whose norm-formulation is explicitly laid down in a legal source.[11]
(ii) The class of *implicit norms* comprises those norms whose norm-formulation has not been explicitly formulated in a legal source, but are, so to speak, 'free-floating' in the legal system.[12]
(iii) The class of *logically derived norms* comprises those norms (normally not expressed) which are the logical consequences of explicit and/or implicit norms.[13]
(iv) The class of *inferred norms* comprises those norms (normally not expressed) which are 'legitimately' inferred from explicit norms and/or implicit norms by using arguments other than strictly logical deductions.[14]

(2) A norm-formulation tolerates the disjunctive attribution of a plurality of norms. One and the same norm-formulation is assumed to express different norms according to different and conflicting interpretations. (3) A norm-formulation tolerates the conjunctive attribution of a plurality of norms. One and the same norm-formulation is assumed to express not just one norm, but several norms at the same time. (4) Two different norm-formulations are assumed to express the same norm (5) Two different norm-formulations are partially synonymous. In other words, one could say that they express two partially overlapping set of norms. (6) A norm-formulation expresses no norm, in the sense that, despite appearing in a normative text, it expresses something different from a norm (e.g. a declaration of will, a political programme, an invocation to gods, etc) (7) Several norm-formulations express, jointly, a norm. This means that each of those norm-formulations only expresses a fragment of a norm. (8) A norm is not the product of the attribution of meaning to one or more norm-formulations, but the product of an implication (entailment) from other norms, which are expressed by explicitly laid down norm-formulations. See Riccardo Guastini, 'Disposizione vs. Norma' in AA. VV., *Studi in onore di Giovanni Tarello, vol. II, Saggi teorico-giuridici* (Giuffrè 1987) 243 ff; see also Giovanni Tarello, *L'interpretazione della legge* (Giuffrè 1980).

[11] In the context of a state legal system, this could be a legal provision included, for example, in a statute, or in the constitution, or in secondary/delegated/regulatory legislation; as well as the formulation of the ratio of a binding precedent. In the context of international law, this could be a legal provision included, for example, in an international treaty.

[12] The inspiration for the term 'free-floating' comes from Matthew Kramer, 'Why the Axioms and Theorems of Arithmetic Are not Legal Norms' (2007) 27 Oxford Journal of Legal Studies 557 footote 9 and accompanying text. Kramer defines a 'free-floating norm' in the following way: 'The term 'free-floating' indicates that [the norm] N is not the product of a contemporaneous formally authoritative institution such as a foreign legal system or a sporting association or Harvard University'. We use the term 'free-floating' in a 'negative' way: in our view, norms that are free-floating cannot count on a pedigreed source and are not derivable, either logically or argumentatively, from pedigreed sources (or, better put, do not owe their status as valid norms to such a derivation). For the purposes of this chapter, the expression 'free-floating standards' denotes the complementary class of the union of the classes of those norms which are explicit, logically derivable, or otherwise inferred. So understood, this class contains customary rules. For these rules are not explicitly laid down in legal sources, nor derived or inferred from norms 'extracted' from such sources.

[13] In Chapter 2 of this volume, the expression 'derived rule' is used to refer to the combination of two rules into a third, derived rule that incorporates the exception. In that context, a derived rule has the following structure: If A, then B, unless E. In this chapter, we use the expression 'derived norm' to refer to a norm which is derived from another norm by means of logical deduction. As such, a derived norm may simply have the following structure: if A, then B.

[14] By 'legitimately' we understand 'according to the rules of inference, other than logical ones, admitted by the normative system at hand'. In many cases, such derivations are carried out by using additional premises, which often include doctrinal positions. See Riccardo Guastini, 'Juristenrecht: Inventing Rights, Wrongs, and Powers' in Jordi Ferrer Beltrán, José J Moreso, and Diego M Papayannis (eds), *Neutrality and Theory of Law* (Springer 2013) 147–59.

1.3 Three types of normative conflicts

In this sub-section we consider how norms may conflict with each other. Alf Ross offered a clear taxonomy of normative conflicts based upon three types of antinomies: total-total; total-partial, and partial-partial antinomies.[15]

A *total-total antinomy* occurs when a given normative system includes two norms such as 'If you drive while it is raining, you ought to reduce your driving speed' and 'If you drive while it is raining, you ought not to reduce your driving speed'.[16] As the antecedents of the two norms completely overlap, the two norms regulate the same conduct (i.e., driving when it is raining) in a conflicting way—hence, the total–total character of this antinomy.[17]

A *total-partial antinomy* occurs when a given normative system includes two norms such as 'If you drive while it is raining, you ought to reduce your speed' and 'If you drive while it is raining *and* you drive a 4WD vehicle, you ought not to reduce your speed'.[18] In this case, the conflict between the two norms emerges only in relation to the partial overlap between the antecedents of the two norms. This is a total-partial antinomy, because the antecedent of the second norm is totally included within the antecedent of the first, more generic norm.

A *partial-partial antinomy* occurs when a given normative system includes two norms such as 'If you drive while it is raining, you ought to reduce your speed' and 'If you drive a 4WD vehicle, you ought not to reduce your speed'.[19] In this case, we have a partial-partial antinomy because the antecedent of both norms overlaps only partially, as the two norms regulate in a conflicting way only the conduct of 'driving a 4WD vehicle while it is raining'.[20] This conduct is captured by the intersection of the antecedents of the two norms; there is no conflict in relation to the other conducts captured by the two antecedents: 'driving a 4WD vehicle while it is not raining', and 'not driving a 4WD vehicle while raining'.[21]

It should be noted that, from a logical point of view, normative conflicts are ultimately always total-total antinomies. For two norms are in conflict only when they bring about two outcomes that are completely incompatible in relation to the same conduct. For instance, one cannot understand that the norms 'All citizens ought to pay taxes' and 'All unemployed people ought not to pay taxes' are in conflict unless we derive the norm 'All unemployed citizens ought to pay taxes'—derived by enriching the antecedent of the first norm—and the norm 'All unemployed citizens ought not to pay taxes'—derived by enriching the antecedent of the second norm.[22] Saying that the two original norms are in conflict is just an elliptical way of saying that the two derived norms generate a total-total antinomy. In similar case, a normative conflict always occurs between logically derived norms.

We would like to conclude this section by showing how the notion that a normative conflict always occurs between logically derived norms can be applied to the three examples of normative conflicts mentioned above. In the case of a partial-partial antinomy, it is easy to

[15] Alf Ross, *On Law and Justice* (Stevens and Sons 1958) 128 ff.

[16] Here, 'ought not' is tantamount to 'may' in the sense that the negation of an obligation to φ is a permission not to φ.

[17] We can symbolize these norms in the following way: '$p \rightarrow Oq$' and '$p \rightarrow {\sim}Oq$'.

[18] In symbols: '$p \rightarrow Oq$' and '$p\&r \rightarrow {\sim}Oq$'.

[19] In symbols: '$p \rightarrow Oq$' and '$r \rightarrow {\sim}Oq$'.

[20] In symbols: '$p\&r$'.

[21] In symbols: '$p\&{\sim}r$' and '${\sim}p\&r$'.

[22] 'Enrichment' (or 'strengthening the antecedent') denotes the rule of inference according to which, given a certain legal conditional, any sentence whatsoever added to the antecedent does not alter the original relation between it and the consequent. In propositional logic, enrichment (or strengthening the antecedent) is symbolized as follows: $(p \rightarrow q) \rightarrow ((p\&r) \rightarrow q)$. As regards norms, we can symbolize it: (according to the so-called 'bridge conception' of normative conditionals): $(p \rightarrow Oq) \rightarrow ((p\&r) \rightarrow Oq)$.

see how the conflict occurs between two derived norms: 'If you drive *a 4WD vehicle* while it is raining, you ought to reduce your speed' and 'If you drive a 4WD vehicle *while it is raining*, you ought not to reduce your speed'. In the other two cases, it may be argued that the conflict occurs between an 'original norm' and a derived norm—in the case of a total-partial antinomy—or between two 'original norms'—in the case of a total-total antinomy. However, it should be remembered that a norm is always at least the logical consequence of itself.[23] This means that even in these two cases, a normative conflict should be seen, from a logical point of view, as a total-total antinomy between two derived norms.

1.4 What is the difference between explicit and implicit exceptions?

At the beginning of section 1, we mentioned Article 2044 of the Italian Civil Code as an example of an explicit exception in the legal domain. Now, we would like to revisit that example in light of the three ideas put forward in the previous sub-sections. First, the distinction between norms and norm-formulations.[24] Secondly, the distinction between (i) expressed (or explicit) norms; (ii) implicit norms; (iii) logically derived norms; and (iv) inferred norms.[25] Thirdly, the notion that a normative conflict is ultimately always a total-total antinomy between two derived norms.[26]

Our example of an explicit exception in the legal domain can be reconstructed as a particular kind of normative conflict. We have a general expressed norm and a more specific expressed norm. Both norms are expressed because their norm-formulation is expressly laid down by the legislator in Articles 2043 and 2044 of the Italian Civil Code. In symbols, the two norms can be represented in the following way:

> [Ne1] D→OR
> Ne1 should be read as 'If damage, then it is obligatory for the wrongdoer to redress the damage'
> [Ne2] D&S→~OR
> Ne2 should be read as 'If damage and self-defence, then it is not obligatory for the wrongdoer to redress the damage'.

From a logical point of view, it is easy to see the conflict between the two norms above. We just need to derive the norm [Nd1] D&S→OR, by enriching the antecedent of [Ne1]. We also know that, in light of the principle of identity, it is possible to derive the norm [Nd2] D&S→~OR from [Ne2].

> [Nd1] D&S→OR
> Nd1 should be read as 'If damage and self-defence, then it is obligatory for the wrongdoer to redress the damage'
> [Nd2] D&S→~OR
> Nd2 should be read as 'If damage and self-defence, then it is not obligatory for the wrongdoer to redress the damage'.

23 This is due to a possible formulation of the principle of identity: p→p.
24 See section 1.1.
25 See section 1.2.
26 See section 1.3.

We have now a conflict between the two derived norms [Nd1] and [Nd2]. This is a total-total antinomy between two derived norms; in this case, derived from two expressed norms [Ne1] and [Ne2]—two norms whose norm-formulations are explicitly formulated in a legal source. The antecedents of the two norms [Nd1] and [Nd2] capture the same conduct—that is, damage and self-defence (D&S); but the two norms attach to this conduct two incompatible normative consequences—that is, obligatory and non-obligatory redress of damage (OR and ~OR).

Saying that Article 2044 of the Italian Civil Code appends an explicit exception to Article 2043 of the same Code is an elliptical way of stating that the normative conflict between [Nd1] and [Nd2] has been resolved by giving priority to [Nd2]. Once the exception is recognized, [Ne1] D→OR is usually reformulated as [Ne1*] D&~S→OR.

This is how we explain, from a logical point of view, the existence of explicit exceptions. What about implicit exceptions? In the next sub-section, we will use our theoretical model to explain the difference between explicit and implicit exceptions.

1.4.1 Implicit exceptions in the legal domain

In the legal domain, these are situations that are frequently labelled under the heading of 'legal defeasibility'. Several commentators argue that general legal norms are defeasible in so far as they are open to *implicit* exceptions, which cannot be identified ex ante (i.e., prior to their application to a particular case). Our view is that legal defeasibility should be conceived of as a complex situation, in which a norm which is derived from an *implicit* norm is given priority over another norm, which is derived from an explicit/implicit norm.

In light of our theoretical model based upon the idea of normative conflict, implicit exceptions in the legal domain should be reconstructed as the result of the following reasoning. One identifies a conflict between two norms—let us call them Na and Nb. Norm Na is derived from a general norm, which is the norm considered to be open to an implicit exception. Norm Nb is derived from a more specific norm, which is the norm associated with the implicit exception. The key feature of this type of normative conflict is that Nb is derived from an implicit norm—that is, a norm whose norm-formulation is not explicitly formulated in a legal source. The existence of an implicit exception is recognized when Nb is given priority over Na (in relation to the overlap between the antecedents of Na and Nb).[27]

From a logical point of view, implicit exceptions can be explained as the solution of a particular type of normative conflict. In the case of implicit exceptions, the norms in conflict are derived norms. It is worth highlighting that this feature of the normative conflict that underpins implicit exceptions is also present, as seen above, in the normative conflict that underpins explicit exceptions. What is characteristic of implicit exceptions is that the norm associated with the implicit exception is derived from an *implicit* norm, whereas in the case of explicit exceptions the more specific norm is derived from an explicit norm. Since implicit norms are not linked to norm-formulations that are explicitly formulated in a legal source, implicit norms can be seen as free-floating standards, within or outside of the relevant legal system.[28]

[27] In order to capture more complex situations, this simple model can be developed by introducing chains of (logical and/or justifiable) derivation. Whatever complexity the model may have, its characteristic feature is the presence of two logically derived norms, one derived from an expressed norm and the other derived from an implicit norm, conflicting with each other.

[28] As free-floating standards, implicit norms do not have a written source (i.e. the source containing the norm-formulation associated with that norm) as the basis for their formal legal validity, in the sense that its first appearance in a judicial decision is not justified by resorting to a written source or formulation. Sometimes, the inferential

Our main suggestion in this first section is that exceptions to general legal norms should be seen as the result of a type of reasoning based upon the identification, and the solution, of a normative conflict. According to our model, the key difference between implicit and explicit exceptions depends upon the 'original' norm (associated with the exception) from which the norm that ultimately prevails in the conflict is derived. In the case of an explicit exception, the 'original' norm is an explicit norm, whereas in the case of an implicit exception the 'original norm' is an implicit norm. In the case of implicit exceptions, the general norm defeated by the more specific norm is usually an explicit norm, but it may be possible to have a conflict between two implicit norms.[29]

Our model explains the reasoning behind the introduction of an implicit exception to a general legal norm.[30] In the next two sections, we will apply this explanation to implicit exceptions in the context of international law. This will be a useful way to test the explanatory power of our model, as the examples considered in this first section came from domestic jurisdictions. Before considering the manifestation of explicit and implicit exceptions in international law, we would like to highlight that in all the cases in which norms are regarded as indefeasible, even when the possibility of an implicit exception is entertained, *the norm derived from the explicit norm ultimately prevails*. These cases are clearly not cases of legal defeasibility, although they may be characterized as cases of normative conflict between a general norm derived from an expressed legal standard and a more specific norm derived from an implicit legal standard. They can be called 'cases of *straight reasoned application*'. In these cases, a conflict is identified and considered, but it is solved in favour of the general norm derived from the explicit norm. The cases of straight reasoned application must be distinguished from the 'cases of *simple straight application*', where the possible conflict is neither identified nor discussed, so that the unreasoned favour for the explicit norm is consequently the outcome of its straight application. Cases of simple straight application occur whenever a norm is applied without taking into account possible legal reasons that would justify the disapplication of the norm.[31]

relation between the implicit original norm and the norm which is derived from it is mediated by other inferential passages. In particular, some free-floating standards, such as very broadly framed principles, need to be specified in order to be applied to particular cases. This means that they are used to generate new norms, usually not by means of deductive reasoning, but by means of other kinds of inference (mainly teleological ones, which are not deductive in character). Let it be noted, moreover, that free-floating standards are, in many cases, themselves the product of generalizing inferences. See Riccardo Guastini, *Interpretare e argomentare* (Giuffrè 2011); Giovanni B Ratti, 'An Analysis of Some Juristic Techniques for Handling Systematic Defects in the Law' in Thomas Bustamante and Christian Dahlman (eds), *Argument Types and Fallacies in Legal Reasoning* (Springer 2015) 151–77.

[29] Within the legal domain, there is the possibility that a conflict arises between two norms both derived from implicit free-floating standards. In this event, whatever norm prevails in the conflict is a norm derived from an implicit standard. This is a more analytical way of rephrasing the widespread tenet according to which free-floating legal standards are essentially open to exceptions.

[30] Recall Pufendorf's famous case of the Statute of the city of Bologna prohibiting 'letting blood in the streets' which was held not to apply to a surgeon performing emergency surgery. Here we have the explicit norm N0 about 'no letting blood in the streets' an implicit principle expressing norm N1 'save lives' the norm N2 derived from the norm N0 'If let blood & save lives, then it is obligatory to sanction' and the norm N3, derived from the implicit principle N1, which provides that 'If let blood & save lives, then it is obligatory not to sanction'. N3 is given priority over N2, making N0 defeasible. In this case, an exception was identified and appended to N0, so that it was obligatory to punish someone letting blood in the streets, unless this was necessary to save lives.

[31] Following Schauer, we would say that cases of simple straight application materialize whenever a norm is treated as opaque or resistant to its underlying reasons (or other more distant reasons) which, if taken into consideration, may bring about the disapplication of the norm.

2 Exceptions and Peremptory Norms of General International Law

Explicit and implicit exceptions can also be found in public international law, and the theoretical model outlined in the first section can help us understand these exceptions in a better way. An example of an explicit exception is Article XXI of the General Agreement on Tariffs and Trade (GATT), where exceptions regarding security of the parties are explicitly identified in relation to the application of the other parts of the treaty.

The *Anglo-Norwegian Fisheries* case provides a good example of an implicit exception. Notwithstanding the terminology used in the decision,[32] a logical analysis of the language of the Court shows that what is at stake here is the possibility of introducing an implicit exception into a general norm about territorial waters.[33] In this case, the United Kingdom requested the Court to decide whether Norway had used a legally acceptable method to draw the baseline from which its territorial sea should be measured. The United Kingdom argued that customary international law did not allow the length of a baseline drawn across a bay to be longer than ten miles. Norway argued that, on the other hand, the way in which its baseline was drawn was consistent with customary international law. There are two arguments that can be offered to undermine a general rule of customary international law: (1) that the disputed rule does not really exist *qua* customary rule; and (2) that the disputed rule is open to an implicit exception. In our view, both lines of reasoning are present in the judgment.

In the *Anglo-Norwegian Fisheries* case we have a claim about the existence of a general norm (i.e. a general rule of customary international law) stating that the drawing of baselines must not exceed ten miles from the coast—this was the argument put forward by the United Kingdom. This claim was rejected. As Bradley and Gulati observe: 'the primary holding of the case was that the alleged CIL rule did not exist. In the alternative, the Court briefly remarked that, had the rule existed, it would not have applied against Norway.'[34] The idea at work in the alternative line of reasoning is that general principles of international law would suggest that, when geographical specificities characterize a certain country, it would be permissible to draw straight baselines that exceed ten miles. This second line of reasoning is particularly interesting for the purposes of this chapter, since it can be explained as the recognition (and the solution) of a normative conflict—a conflict of the type analysed in the previous section. We recognize the existence of an implicit general norm [Ni1] B→O~E, according to which,

[32] 'This conception of an historic title is in consonance with the Norwegian Government's understanding of the general rules of international law. In its view, these rules of international law take into account the diversity of facts and, therefore, concede that the drawing of base-lines must be adapted to the special conditions obtaining in different regions. In its view, the system of delimitation applied in 1935, a system characterized by the use of straight lines, does not therefore infringe the general law; it is an adaptation rendered necessary by local conditions.' The key idea here is that of an adaptation of a general rule rendered necessary by specific conditions. This point is also present in the Separate Opinion of Judge Hsu Mo: 'It is necessary to emphasize the fact that Norway's method of delimiting the belt of her northern territorial sea by drawing straight lines between point and point, island and island, constitutes a deviation from what I believe to be a general rule of international law.' These are all rhetorical formulations that disguise a state of affairs—the identification of an implicit exception to a general norm—that our theoretical model of exceptions aims to reconstruct.

[33] As suggested by Orakhelashvili: '... the International Court affirmed the legality of straight baselines as the inner boundary of Norwegian territorial waters even though that regime deviated from the general regime of territorial waters and *the latter regime remained valid and unaffected on a general plane*. The judgment indicates that the regime of the territorial sea can be regulated in more than one way with regard to specific States or situations and that was based in that case on the attitudes of the States involved towards Norwegian baselines, their abstention and acquiescence. The overall reason for the finding in Norway's favour was that the baselines method was not contrary to international law, even though it was different from general international law.' Alexander Orakhelashvili, *Peremptory Norms in International Law* (Oxford University Press 2006) 70–71 (emphasis added).

[34] Curtis A Bradley and Mitu Gulati, 'Withdrawing from International Custom' (2010) 120 Yale Law Journal 235.

when drawing maritime borders, (B) it is obligatory (O) not to exceed ten miles (~E).[35] Then we have a more specific norm [Ni2] B&G→~O~E, according to which, when drawing maritime borders in the presence of geographical specificities (B&G), it is not obligatory (~O) not to exceed ten miles (~E).[36] As indicated by our theoretical model, it is now possible to derive the following two norms from [Ni1] and [Ni2]:

[Ndi1] B&G→O~E[37]
[Ndi2] B&G→~O~E[38]

The two norms [Ndi1] and [Ndi2] generate a total-total antinomy. By giving priority to [Ndi2] over [Ndi1], one recognizes an implicit exception to [Ni1] B→O~E, that is, the general rule of customary international law according to which when drawing maritime borders, it is obligatory not to exceed ten miles. The exception considering the presence of geographical specificities is implicit because [Ni2] is inferred from general principles of international law.

These two examples show how our model could be used to explain the reasoning behind the identification of explicit and implicit exception in international law. But international law offers an even more interesting phenomenon that could be used to further test the explanatory power of our theoretical model. This phenomenon is the existence of peremptory norms of general international law (i.e., *jus cogens*).

2.1 Peremptory norms of general international law

According to Article 53 of the Vienna Convention on the Law of Treaties (VCLT), peremptory norms are non-derogable (i.e., they are not liable to exceptions). Article 53 establishes that:

> A treaty is void if, at the time of its conclusion, it conflicts with a peremptory norm of general international law. For the purposes of the present Convention, a peremptory norm of general international law is a norm accepted and recognized by the international community of States as a whole as a norm *from which no derogation is permitted* and which can be modified only by a subsequent norm of general international law having the same character.[39]

It is not easy to categorize a norm as part of *jus cogens*. From a conceptual point of view, it seems that we have at least two independent criteria mentioned in Article 53: first, acceptance as a fundamental norm of the community of states; and, secondly, non-derogability.[40] The possible combinations of these two criteria are as follows:

[35] This norm is implicit because it is not expressed in any legal source, understood in a linguistic sense (instead, it is derived from customary international law).

[36] This norm is also implicit because it is not expressed in any legal source, understood in a linguistic sense (instead, it is derived from general principles of international law).

[37] [Ndi1] is derived from [Ni1] by enriching the antecedent of [Ni1]. On the 'enrichment' of the antecedent see n 22.

[38] Here, the principle of identity is applied—every norm entails itself.

[39] The 1969 Vienna Convention on the Law of Treaties1969, 1155 UNTS 331–53 (emphasis added).

[40] 'This is indeed how some jurists explain peremptory norms — as customary norms that need to be substantiated by practice and *opinio juris*. The relevant practice here is the practice of the international community as a whole (not merely a 'general practice'). In relation to the *opinio juris*, a double *opinio* is needed: (i) that the rule is

Criteria for *Jus Cogens* norms

	Acceptance	Non-Derogation
1.	+	+
2.	+	–
3.	–	+
4.	–	–

Amongst fundamental norms of international law, there are norms that are not subject to derogation (case 1—*jus cogens* norms properly so-called) and others that are liable to such derogation (case 2). There can also be norms that are not universally accepted, and are characterized as not subject to derogation (case 3), and norms that are neither universally accepted nor immune from derogation (case 4).

Now, fundamental norms of international law that are regarded as derogable cannot be norms of *jus cogens* under the definition provided by Article 53 of the VCLT.[41] It should be noted, however, that as a matter of cognitive interpretation—that is, an interpretation that seeks to identify all possible meanings of a legal provision—the expression 'from which no derogation is permitted' is ambiguous. This is because it is not clear whether this derogation refers to explicit or implicit exceptions (or both). We think that our model can help us shed some light on this issue.

3 Derogation and Defeasibility: A Logical Analysis of Article 53 of the VCLT

In this final section we use the theoretical model illustrated in section 1 to clarify the scope of the 'non-derogation clause' included in Article 53 of the VCLT. In doing so, we focus on the legal sources and the relevant norm-formulations connected with the norms that may be in conflict with *jus cogens*.

binding; and (ii) that it is a rule that is non-derogable. On this point see Hugh Thirlway, *The Sources of International Law* (Oxford University Press 2014).

[41] Non-derogability is not a property a rule has per se. That a norm N1 is not liable to derogation in light of a norm N2 depends on a norm N3 stating that N1 is not derogable. Article 53 is sometimes interpreted as a norm imposing the non-derogability of *jus cogens* norms on states and judicial bodies. The problem stemming from this interpretation is the following: can a higher-level norm depend on a lower-level norm regarding its non-derogability? As far as we can see, it is possible to answer this question in three ways. First, one may say that being a treaty norm, art 53 only applies to other treaties, and not to peremptory norms. So, the definition of peremptory norms contained in art 53 would be just a reference to a higher-level source, which is the real source of *jus cogens* norms and their non-derogability. This is because art 53 is part of a treaty, so it would be revisable based on an agreement of the parties; therefore, the norms of *jus cogens* would be peremptory in character as long as that agreement exists. This is, however, a *contradictio in adjecto* regarding the notion of *jus cogens* norms as superior norms of international law which are not liable to derogation by inferior norms. So, this argument would conclude, art 53 cannot be the source of the peremptory character of *jus cogens* norms, which find their source elsewhere. Secondly, one may argue that art 53 itself expresses a *jus cogens* norm, since it expressly formulates the widely accepted definition of peremptory norms as non-derogable norms and is universally accepted by the community of states. Thirdly, one may argue that not only does art 53 express a *jus cogens* norm, but it also expresses the norm which is conceptually the highest one, providing that other peremptory norms shall not be derogated. Here it is important to notice that, if art 53 is regarded as derogable, it would turn out not to be part of *jus cogens* (being derogable). By contrast, if it is regarded as not liable to derogation, it would be the highest peremptory norm, providing for the non-derogation of all peremptory norms (itself included).

In light of the Spanish version of the VCLT, it may be possible to argue that Article 53 *only* expresses a norm about the *invalidity* of treaty norms conflicting with *jus cogens*.[42] If so, Article 53 would *just* establish a *lex superior* principle for international law norms.[43] Nonetheless, it may be possible to rely upon other versions of the VCLT—e.g. the English and the French—to argue that the idea of derogation in the context of Article 53 has a wider reach. According to this broader interpretation, Article 53 would express a notion of *jus cogens* applicable beyond the law of treaties. In this case, the non-derogation clause in Article 53 would capture a characteristic feature of *jus cogens* norms, that is, the property of not admitting exceptions from hierarchically inferior sources. This would amount to a rejection of the *lex specialis* principle for peremptory norms. This last interpretation of Article 53's non-derogation clause emerges in the scholarly debate on exceptions to peremptory norms of general international law. It is this aspect of *jus cogens* norms that we would like to discuss in the rest of this chapter.

Consider the question of whether the prohibition of the use of force—often seen as the paradigm of a peremptory norm[44]—may be open to exceptions. Green has observed that: 'in the case of the prohibition of the use of force, exceptions to the rule not only exist, but are built into the very nature of the U.N. system.'[45] Now, the fact that explicit exceptions may be introduced into the norm prohibiting the use of force is not really a matter of derogation, if one reads Article 53 as referring only to *implicit exceptions*. If the exceptions at issue were both explicit and originated from other peremptory norms, one may even argue that there is no real derogation.[46] From this perspective, the solution of an alleged conflict between the norm prohibiting the use of force and the norm allowing the use of force for self-defence would be a norm according to which the use of force is prohibited, unless it is used in self-defence.[47] We can imagine a parallel universe in which Article 2(4) of the UN Charter

[42] In the Spanish version of the VCLT, art 53 is formulated as follows: 'Una norma imperativa de derecho internacional general es una norma que ... no admite acuerdo en contrario.' This is certainly what the VCLT intends also in the English language version. Article 53 starts by saying that: 'A treaty is void if, at the time of its conclusion, it conflicts with a peremptory norm of general international law.' See also Art 64, which provides: 'If a new peremptory norm of general international law emerges, any existing treaty which is in conflict with that norm becomes void and terminates.' What we suggest here is that, while the Spanish version only expresses the norm on invalidity, the English version (as well as the other versions we mention) expresses also a norm on non-derogation.

[43] See *Report of the Study Group of the International Law Commission*, finalized by Martti Koskenniemi, entitled 'The fragmentation of international law: difficulties arising from the diversification and expansion of international law'—A/CN.4/L.682.

[44] See art 2(4) of the UN Charter: 'All Members shall refrain in their international relations from the threat or use of force against the territorial integrity or political independence of any state, or in any other manner inconsistent with the Purposes of the United Nations'. For discussion on whether this is the source of the corresponding *jus cogens* norm, see James A Green, 'Questioning the Peremptory Status of the Prohibition of the Use of Force' (2011) 32 Michigan Journal of International Law 215.

[45] ibid 229.

[46] For a good discussion of *jus cogens* restrictions on the use of armed force see André de Hoogh, 'Jus Cogens and the Use of Armed Force' in Marc Weller, *The Oxford Handbook of the Use of Force in International Law* (Oxford University Press 2015) Pt VII—General Problems, ch 54 s III. In relation to specific exceptions as *jus cogens*, De Hoogh recognizes that '... one may therefore either argue that exceptions are (necessarily) part and parcel of the peremptory prohibition and as such limit its scope, or that such exceptions have independent status as peremptory norms and as such would prevail in the case of conflict.' ibid 1172.

[47] It should be noted that this is the approach endorsed by the ILC in the Articles on State Responsibility, in the Commentary to art 21 (at para 1). Article 51 of the UN Charter provides that: 'Nothing in the present Charter shall impair the inherent right of individual or collective self-defence if an armed attack occurs against a Member of the United Nations, until the Security Council has taken measures necessary to maintain international peace and security. Measures taken by Members in the exercise of this right of self-defence shall be immediately reported to the Security Council and shall not in any way affect the authority and responsibility of the Security Council under the present Charter to take at any time such action as it deems necessary in order to maintain or restore international peace and security'.

provides that the use of force is prohibited, unless in cases of self-defence; what is important here is that the norm formulated in this 'new' article would be same as the one identified by combining the current Articles 2(4) and 51 of the UN Charter.

From a logical point of view, the norms expressed by the provisions included in Articles 2(4) and 51 can be represented in the following way:[48]

[Ne3] R→O~F
[Ne4] R&S→~O~F

In light of our theoretical model, from these two norms it is possible to derive the following two norms:

[Nd3] R&S→O~F
[Nd4] R&S→~O~F

When we consider these last two norms together, we have a total-total antinomy. This normative conflict might be solved by giving priority to [Nd4] to [Nd3]. Once the exception about self-defence is recognized, [Ne3] can be reformulated in the following terms [Ne3*] R&~S→O~F. It should be noted that this norm is the norm that we would obtain by combining Articles 2(4) and 51 in order to include, in one norm-formulation, the prohibition of use of force and the negative condition of self-defence. There is a difference between the two styles of law-making; that is, combining legal provisions instead of enacting a legal provision that includes negative conditions. Nonetheless, from a logical point of view, there is no difference. International law scholarship sometimes does not seem to recognize this point. Green, for example, connects the peremptory status of the norm to the circumstance that its formulation contemplates all the explicit exceptions to the norm.[49] In our view, this is a misunderstanding resulting from a lack of appreciation of the difference between norms and norm-formulations. If one were to affirm that a norm of *jus cogens* is not subject to derogation, in the sense that it does not admit explicit exceptions, it would be easy to elude such a limit by introducing exceptions in the very formulation of the rule.

Let us clarify this last point with an example. Imagine a legal provision P stating that 'The use of force is prohibited, unless a state acts in self-defence'. One may suggest that this provision would be open to derogation only if a different explicit exception, external to the rule and to the condition of self-defence, were provided. An external exception could be—let us assume—preventing or stopping a genocide. We do not find such a suggestion convincing, because it assumes that the property of being open to derogation may be a property of legal provision P. Instead, being open to derogation is not a property of legal provisions, but rather of legal norms.[50] This means that, when legal norms are considered, the same normative consequences are consistent with both formulations of legal provision P above.

[48] R is for 'international relations' 'S' is for 'self-defence' and 'F' is for 'use of force'.

[49] Green suggests that: 'However, the fact that the prohibition of the use of force has agreed exceptions does not necessarily bar the norm from peremptory status as long as one is willing to see the rule in more expansive terms than it appears in art 2(4). If the norm being discussed here were framed in a way as to additionally include the exceptions to the prohibition, then its peremptory character could be preserved.' See Green (n 44) 230.

[50] For an analysis of the logical problems involved in the synchronic isomorphism of two logically equivalent sets of norms derived from different normative provisions see Eugenio Bulygin, *Essays in Legal Philosophy* (Oxford University Press 2015) 220 ff.

If our view on this point is correct, it follows that the idea of non-derogation in the context of Article 53 of the VCLT should not be seen as referring to explicit exceptions, since these exceptions can be listed amongst the explicit conditions of a norm. It should also be noted that Article 53 mentions the possibility for peremptory norms to be modified by other peremptory norms, so that explicit exceptions can certainly be introduced diachronically by means of introducing more specific norms partially overlapping with older norms. Therefore, we submit that the idea of non-derogation present in Article 53 should be seen as capturing implicit exceptions. Article 53 of the VCLT should be understood as stating that norms of *jus cogens* must be universally accepted and indefeasible, in the sense that they are not open to implicit exceptions. It should be stressed again that defeasibility and/or indefeasibility refer to norms, and not norm-formulations. Also, these two properties of norms depend on two factors: first, the existence of meta-norms stating that certain norms are (not) defeasible in either a substantial or a procedural way;[51] and, secondly, the importance of the legal construction of defeasible norms and the existence of various kinds of defeasibility in the legal domain. In the next two sub-sections, we will briefly expand on these two factors.

3.1 Meta-norms and defeasibility

There are two ways in which the defeasibility of legal norms can depend upon meta-norms. First, a legal system may include meta-norms, directed to judges, that define what norms can be regarded as defeasible, or indefeasible (and under what conditions). Article 53 appears to express a norm that characterizes peremptory norms as always indefeasible. Secondly, a legal system may include meta-norms that establish the conditions that must be satisfied to prove the existence of a determinate exception—this is what has been recently called 'procedural defeasibility'.[52] This means that, even if a given norm is treated as substantively defeasible, the allocation of the burden of proof solves, in many a case, the problem of its application, since procedural meta-norms impose (on those who claim that an exception exists) the burden of proving the occurrence of the exception.[53]

Procedural defeasibility may solve the problem of substantive defeasibility at the judicial level. Let us suppose that the prohibition of the use of force may be open to an exception regarding the so-called 'anticipatory self-defence' (i.e., the perception of an imminent attack by

[51] See Jorge L Rodríguez, 'Defeasibility and Burden of Proof' (2017) 47 Materiali per una storia della cultura giuridica 243.

[52] See Rodríguez (n 51) 257: 'In a trial the plaintiff will try to prove those operative facts of a rule that the secondary rules of the system allocate under her burden, and the other party either will not even allege the existence of an exception, or if she does, such a claim will have to be grounded on another rule specifying an incompatible normative solution regarded as hierarchically superior to the first, if she wants her claim not to be dismissed. Regardless of the fact that in the case in question other circumstances could have been introduced by the defendant as exceptions, and even regardless of the fact that the set of exceptions was not closed, the judge will be in a position to infer a conclusive solution to the case since the matters under discussion have been limited to those that have been proposed and proved (or not proved) by the parties. Thus, the secondary rules allocating between the parties the burden of proof and those stipulating rebuttable presumptions function as institutional devices oriented to bridge the limitations of information regarding the facts of a case and, at the same time, they restrict the scope of the problems posed by substantial and epistemic defeasibility of legal rules, were we to admit that they are defeasible in such senses.'

[53] In international law, we can find something of this sort in norms expressed by the third chapter of the Statute of the International Court of Justice—in particular, arts 48 and 52. The former provides that: 'The Court shall make orders for the conduct of the case, shall decide the form and time in which each party must conclude its arguments, and make all arrangements connected with the taking of evidence'; while the latter establishes that: 'After the Court has received the proofs and evidence within the time specified for the purpose, it may refuse to accept any further oral or written evidence that one party may desire to present unless the other side consents.'

another country). Let us also suppose that State A, which claims compensation for damage resulting from State B's use of force, cannot rebut the evidence B tendered of its perception of an imminent attack by A. Finally, let us suppose that State A can, at a later stage, prove that State B's perception was completely wrong. However, having received evidence within the time specified for the purpose, the Court refuses to accept any further evidence, since State B opposes it. Now, whether we happen to think that anticipatory self-defence is an exception to the norm on the prohibition of the use of force, in our example the question is settled in light of secondary rules of procedure and the allocation of the burden of proof. If State A seeks reparation from State B for its use of force, and State B proves an exception which is not, in turn, rebutted by State A, State B wins even if the scope of the norm regarding its possible implicit exceptions could not be determined in advance.

3.2 Construction of defeasible norms and several kinds of defeasibility in international law

In relation to the legal construction of defeasible norms and to the different kinds of defeasibility present in the legal domain, it is necessary to distinguish between expressed norms, whose norm-formulation is enshrined in relevant legal texts, and implicit norms, such as customary rules.

3.2.1 Expressed norms: internal versus external defeasibility

We have used our model to explain how a given expressed norm is made defeasible (i) by creating an antinomy between a norm derived from that expressed norm and another norm, derived from an implicit norm; and (ii) by giving priority to the latter derived norm over the norm derived from the expressed norm. We should add here that two different kinds of defeasibility are at play in the ordinary functioning of a legal system.[54] The first kind of defeasibility can be called 'internal defeasibility': this is the phenomenon we have analysed in the previous sections of the chapter. The second kind of defeasibility can be called 'external defeasibility', that is, the recognition of an implicit exception to a meta-norm that imposes, or authorizes, the application of another norm. The situation envisaged here is the following: we have a meta-norm N1 that imposes, or authorizes, the application of a norm N2 to the class of cases C; however, N2 is not applied to C because N1 is considered to be defeasible.

The existence of these two kinds of defeasibility can help us better understand the idea of derogation. In international law scholarship, it is often argued (especially from a doctrinal point of view) that substantive and procedural rules are different in kind, and that an alleged 'collision' (not conflict) between substantive *jus cogens* norms and procedural rules would not amount to an implicit exception. For example, according to Talmon:

> Substantive and procedural rules are not *ejusdem generis*; that is, they are not of the same kind. The two sets of rules address different matters. They have different contents and therefore do not impose incompatible obligations. While the former address the question of the lawfulness of a situation or conduct, the latter deal with rule interpretation, implementation, and enforcement. There may be indirect and occasional *collisions* between the two, but there is no logical *conflict* between substantive rules and rules of a procedural

[54] See Jordi Ferrer Beltrán and Giovanni B Ratti, 'Validity and Defeasibility in the Legal Domain' (2010) 29 Law and Philosophy 601.

> character. This is true for both the relationship between ordinary substantive and procedural rules and for the relationship between substantive rules of a *jus cogens* character and procedural rules. A *jus cogens* rule is one from which no derogation is permitted, but the application of a procedural rule does not amount to derogation from substantive rules of *jus cogens*. A procedural rule may hinder the application or enforcement of the *jus cogens* rule, but it does not derogate from its content.[55]

Talmon claims that when substantive and procedural norms collide, there is no derogation. This claim may be true if the colliding norms had a different *logical status* (e.g., regulative norms versus constitutive norms), but this is not the case. We find this view, based upon a separation between substantive and procedural norms, problematic, and we would like to suggest alternative explanations.

First, it may be possible to see the conflict between peremptory norms and procedural norms as a case of internal defeasibility. In this case, *jus cogens* norms would be defeated by immunity norms. Peremptory norms would be defeasible in the sense that they would be considered to be open to implicit exceptions introduced in light of unexpressed norms.

Secondly, it may be argued that what is defeasible here is not a set of peremptory norms, but rather the norms that impose the application of *jus cogens* norms to the case at hand. This is how the last part of the above quotation—'A procedural rule may hinder the application or enforcement of the *jus cogens* rule, but it does not derogate from its content'—may be read. It is true that in *Jurisdictional Immunities of the State (Germany v Italy: Greece Intervening)*, the ICJ appears to affirm that, between peremptory norms and rules on adjudication there is no possible conflict and, consequently, there is no derogation from peremptory norms when they are disapplied:

> A *jus cogens* rule is one from which no derogation is permitted but the rules which determine the scope and extent of jurisdiction and when that jurisdiction may be exercised do not derogate from those substantive rules which possess *jus cogens* status, nor is there anything inherent in the concept of *jus cogens* which would require their modification or would displace their application.[56]

However, from a logical point of view, peremptory norms are treated as externally defeasible, in the sense that norms which impose the application of peremptory norms are disapplied in favour of norms which grant states immunity from prosecution. Peremptory norms ought to be applied, unless there is a norm according to which the immunity of states bars such an application (implicit exception). What we would like to highlight here is that this is also a kind of derogation, as peremptory norms are displaced in favour of another norm. So, a *jus cogens* norm is not treated as really peremptory in this case, insofar as the distinction

[55] Stefan Talmon, 'Jus Cogens after Germany v. Italy: Substantive and Procedural Rules Distinguished' (2012) 25 Leiden Journal of International Law 986. This is a distinction which must not be confused with what we said earlier in relation to procedural defeasibility and the rules on the burden of proof, as Talmon emphasizes: 'Rules of a procedural nature or procedural rules are also not identical with the "rules of procedure", i.e., the rules governing administrative and judicial proceedings. The latter comprise all rules and laws governing the methods and mechanics of the legal and administrative process, including the filing of documents, evidentiary standards as well as modes and burden of proof, and the conduct of hearings. These rules of procedure are sometimes also described as "procedural law". The terms "rules of procedure" and "procedural law" describe a narrower concept than "rules of a procedural character". In particular, procedural rules are not limited to the rules set out in Chapter III of the ICJ Statute dealing with "Procedure" and the corresponding rules in the Rules of Court.' ibid 982.

[56] *Jurisdictional Immunities of the State (Germany v Italy: Greece intervening)* (Judgment) [2012] ICJ Rep 99, 141.

between procedural and substantive norms seems to be simply a smokescreen to identify an implicit exception that may lead one to derogate from a substantive *jus cogens* norm.

3.2.2 Customary norms and defeasibility

When considering customary norms, a major problem is that they are liable to be moulded flexibly according to changing patterns of behaviour.[57] Although, at first sight this may appear to be an empirical issue, it is in fact a conceptual issue. No series of past actions univocally determine the action that should 'correctly' follow in the series. If actions A, B, and C are regarded to be in accordance with (or constituting) customary norm N1, action D, which might be characterized by properties that are partially dissimilar from actions A, B, and C, may be characterized either as part of the pattern described by N1 or as an infringement of that pattern of behaviour. The vice of this piece of reasoning is conceptual indeterminacy.

This is the reason why a rule of customary international law should be conceived of as defeasible. For it is not possible to determine with absolute certainty whether a certain additional property which characterizes a given fact makes this fact lie within the scope of a given customary norm. This phenomenon frequently emerges in customary international law:

> there are entire areas of the *jus ad bellum* that are fiercely contested by states. Take, for example, the avowed rights of anticipatory and pre-emptive self-defence. Some states have consistently argued that there exists a right to use force in self-defence even before the occurrence of an armed attack, if such an attack is imminent (anticipatory self-defence). Other states have hotly disputed this claim. To this can be added the fact that it has also been argued-most notably by the United States-that military action may be taken even before the potential attack can be identified as being imminent (pre-emptive self-defence). There is no consensus among states or writers as to the legal validity of these possible manifestations of self-defence. [...] The fundamental question here, then, is: Can a *jus cogens* norm exist when its scope and the parameters for its application are so debated?[58]

In this example, we have a customary norm permitting self-defence. The issue is whether particular actions, qualified by additional properties (imminent attack, perception of a threat, etc), fall under this permission or not. It seems to us that one cannot univocally determine whether these properties constitute cases of implicit exceptions to the rule, or cases in which the rule must be applied. The problem here is not the existence of a customary rule—that a state can act in self-defence is not called into doubt. The key aspect of the example is that every customary norm has, for conceptual reasons, a debatable area of application, since any new case can be taken to be in accordance or in contrast with the previous rule. Consequently, all customary rules are potentially defeasible in this specific sense, and they must be always accommodated in relation to novel cases.[59] In light of this

[57] For an illuminating analysis of this problem see Frederick Schauer, 'Pitfalls in the interpretation of customary law' in Amanda Perreau-Saussine and James B Murphy, *The Nature of Customary Law* (Cambridge University Press 2007) 13–34; and Damiano Canale, 'Paradossi della consuetudine giuridica' in Silvia Zorzetto, (ed), *La consuetudine giuridica: teoria, storia, ambiti disciplinari* (ETS 2008) 109–136.

[58] Green (n 44) 236.

[59] Schauer explicitly applies this observation to customary international law: 'So when the interpreter of customary international law, for example, says that in this instance the practices of nations over some past period of years *stand* for this proposition now, it becomes permissible to ask what else those customs of the past might now be taken to stand for, and then to ask further why the selected interpretation was selected rather than some number of others that might have been equally consistent with the past decisions and the past acts, and thus, in the large, with the customs of the past'. Frederick Schauer, 'Pitfalls in the interpretation of customary law' in Amanda Perreau-Saussine and James B Murphy, *The Nature of Customary Law* (Cambridge University Press 2007) 25.

consideration, a new problem emerges in relation to Article 53 of the VCLT, since it may be argued that it is contradictory to have a customary norm which is, at the same time, universally accepted *and* peremptory. This is because, as we have just seen, a customary norm is, for conceptual reasons, always open to derogation. This is, however, a topic for another occasion.

PART II

EXCEPTIONS IN CUSTOMARY INTERNATIONAL LAW

8

The Compelling Law of *Jus Cogens* and Exceptions to Peremptory Norms

To Derogate or Not to Derogate, That Is the Question!

*André de Hoogh**

1 Introduction

The concept of *jus cogens* was introduced into positive international law by Article 53 of the Vienna Convention on the Law of Treaties (VCLT),[1] stipulating that a treaty is void if it conflicts with a peremptory norm of general international law. Under the VCLT, a peremptory norm must be accepted and recognized by the international community as a norm from which no derogation is permitted. Although the concept seems by now to have been positively embraced even by the International Court of Justice (ICJ),[2] its appearance has given rise to a spirited debate regarding many of its constitutive elements, legal consequences and implications.

One of the more thorny issues raised concerns the specification that a peremptory norm is one 'from which no derogation is permitted'. In view of the concept's attribute of non-derogability,[3] the problematic of exceptions to peremptory norms has been examined within the literature primarily with a view to establishing the compatibility of exceptions to the peremptory norm prohibiting the use of force (or alternatively that prohibiting aggression).[4]

* Associate Professor in International Law, University of Groningen. This chapter is based, in various ways, upon thoughts expressed in André de Hoogh, '*Jus Cogens* and the Use of Armed Force' in Marc Weller (ed), *The Oxford Handbook of the Use of Force in International Law* (OUP 2015) 1161.

[1] See art 53 of the Vienna Convention on the Law of Treaties 1969 (VCLT) (adopted 23 May 1969; in force 27 January 1980) 1155 UNTS 331; see also arts 64 (emergence of a new peremptory norm), 71 (legal consequences), and 66(a) in conjunction with art 65 (dispute settlement).

[2] *Armed Activities on the Territory of the Congo (New Application: 2002) (Democratic Republic of the Congo v Rwanda)* (Judgment) [2006] ICJ Rep 6, 31–33 [64]–[70]; *Application of the Convention on the Prevention and Punishment of the Crime of Genocide (Bosnia and Herzegovina v Serbia and Montenegro)* [2007] ICJ Rep 43, 104–105 [146]–[148] and 110–11 [161–62]; *Jurisdictional Immunities of the State (Germany v Italy: Greece Intervening)* [2012] ICJ Rep 99, 140–42 [92]–[97]; *Questions relating to the Obligation to Prosecute or Extradite (Senegal v Belgium)*]2012] ICJ Rep 422, 457 [99]; *Application of the Convention on the Prevention and Punishment of the Crime of Genocide (Croatia v Serbia)* [2015] ICJ Rep 3, 46–48 [87–88]. See also *North Sea Continental Shelf (Federal Republic of Germany v Denmark; Federal Republic of Germany v Netherlands)* (Judgment) [1969] ICJ Rep 3, 41–42 [72]; *Barcelona Traction, Light and Power Company, Limited* [1970] ICJ Rep 3, 32 [33]–[34]; *Military and Paramilitary Activities in and against Nicaragua (Nicaragua v United States of America)* (Judgment) [1986] ICJ Rep 14, 100–101 [190].

[3] In his reports, Tladi speaks of non-derogability being the (primary) consequence of the peremptory character of a norm: see Dire Tladi, 'First Report on *Jus Cogens*' (8 March 2016) A/CN.4/693, 7 [12], 38 [62], and [64]; and Dire Tladi, 'Second Report on *Jus Cogens*' (16 March 2017) A/CN.4/706, 19 [38], 32–33 [64], 36–37 [73].

[4] See generally Ulf Linderfalk, 'The Effect of *Jus Cogens* Norms: Whoever Opened Pandora's Box, Did You Ever Think about the Consequences?' (2008) 18 European Journal of International Law 853, 859–867; James A Green, 'Questioning the Peremptory Status of the Prohibition of the Use of Force' (2011) 32 Melbourne Journal of International Law 215; Sondre Torp Helmersen, 'The Prohibition of the Use of Force as *Jus Cogens*: Explaining Apparent Derogations' (2014) 61 *Netherlands International Law Review* 167; Alexander Orakhelashvili, 'Changing *Jus* Cogens through State Practice? The Case of the Prohibition of the Use of Force and Its Exceptions' in

André de Hoogh, *The Compelling Law of* Jus Cogens *and Exceptions to Peremptory Norms* In: *Exceptions in International Law*. Edited by: Lorand Bartels and Federica Paddeu, Oxford University Press (2020). © Lorand Bartels and Federica Paddeu.
DOI: 10.1093/oso/9780198789321.003.0008

However, the question of the compatibility with and hence (im)permissibility of exceptions may come up, in different guise, with respect to other accepted or asserted peremptory norms. This may be due, to an extent, to the fact that an exception to a (general) rule can be framed and formulated in different manners. Moreover, various issues may come up in view of the generality with which a norm is formulated, or the absolute character with which it may be endowed. Finally, whether an act or conduct conflicts with a peremptory norm may impact upon our perception whether an exception is permissible.

In order to structure the analysis, this contribution will proceed to discuss first some of the meanings attributed to the words derogation and exception (section 2). It will then proceed to consider whether an exception excludes the applicability of a general norm, and assess the validity of a proposition to this effect with respect to the main exceptions to the prohibition of the use of force as a *jus cogens* norm (section 3). This will be followed by some thoughts on circumstances precluding wrongfulness as exceptions that may justify or excuse certain conduct, and special attention will be paid to Article 26 of the Articles on the Responsibility of States for Internationally Wrongful Acts (ARSIWA),[5] which prevents the preclusion of wrongfulness of conduct 'not in conformity with an obligation arising under a peremptory norm'. In this context, the character of (specific) circumstances precluding wrongfulness—as inherent exception, excuse, or justification—will be investigated (section 4). Finally, section 5 will return to the issue of derogation.

2 Prologue: Derogation and Exception

A discussion of exceptions to peremptory norms requires, first of all, attention being paid to the interpretation of Article 53 of the VCLT, which stipulates:

> A treaty is void if, at the time of its conclusion, it conflicts with a peremptory norm of general international law. For purposes of the present Convention, a peremptory norm of general international law is a norm accepted and recognized by the international community of States as a whole as a norm from which no derogation is permitted and which can be modified only by a subsequent norm of general international law having the same character.

As such, establishing the meaning of this provision requires the application of the rules of interpretation as embodied in Articles 31 and 32 of the VCLT.

A useful starting point of any inquiry may be recourse to a dictionary. In the online Oxford dictionaries, insofar as relevant, the word 'derogation' is explained as 'an exemption from or relaxation of a rule of law'.[6] The verb 'to derogate from' is indicated to involve 'to detract from'

Marc Weller, *The Oxford Handbook of the Use of Force in International Law* (OUP 2015) 157; André de Hoogh, '*Jus Cogens* and the Use of Armed Force', 1165; and further Carin Kahgan, '*Jus Cogens* and the Inherent Right to Self-Defense' (1997) 3 *ILSA Journal of International & Comparative Law* 767; Ole Spiermann, 'Humanitarian Intervention as a Necessity and the Threat or Use of *Jus Cogens*' (2002) 71 Nordic Journal of International Law 523; Charles Leben, 'Obligations Relating to the Use of Force and Arising from Peremptory Norms of International Law' in James Crawford, Alain Pellet, and Simon Olleson (eds), *The Law of International Responsibility* (OUP 2010) 1197. See also Lauri Hannikainen, *Peremptory Norms (Jus Cogens) in International Law, Historical Development, Criteria, Present Status* (Finnish Lawyers' Publishing Company 1988) 323–56; and Olivier Corten, *The Law against War: The Prohibition on the Use of Force in Contemporary International Law* (Hart Publishing 2010) 198–213.

[5] Articles on Responsibility of States for Internationally Wrongful Acts (ARSIWA), annexed to UNGA Res 56/83 (28 January 2002) UN Doc A/RES/56/83.

[6] Oxford Dictionaries http://www.oxforddictionaries.com/definition/english/derogation.

or 'deviate from (a set of rules or agreed form of behaviour)'.[7] An 'exception' is said to mean 'a person or thing that is excluded from a general statement or does not follow a rule'.[8] The preposition 'except' entails 'not including; other than'; when taking the form of conjunction it will be 'used before a statement that forms an exception to one just made'; and the verb is used so as to 'specify as excluded from a category or group'.[9]

Taking all these meanings then in broad stride, a certain overlap does appear to exist between the possible meanings of the words derogation and exception. That particular overlap allows for an intriguing exploration of the concept of *jus cogens* as embodied in Article 53 of the VCLT, which makes reference to peremptory norms of general international law. *Jus cogens* rules are said to be, according to Article 53, norms 'from which no derogation is permitted'; hence their designation as 'peremptory norms' and the appellation as *jus cogens*. The word 'peremptory' is indicated to mean, in the dictionaries, 'insisting on immediate attention or obedience, especially in a brusquely imperious way' and also, in law, as 'not open to appeal or challenge' or 'final'.[10] '*Jus cogens*', the heading of Article 53 of the VCLT, is defined as 'the principles which form the norms of international law that cannot be set aside', coming from the Latin signifying 'compelling law'.[11]

When considering the meaning of derogation, the International Law Commission (ILC) in drawing up the provision on *jus cogens* appears to have had in mind the idea of exemption from a rule of law, as it asserted that the perspective that '... there is no rule of international law from which States cannot at their own free will contract out has become increasingly difficult to sustain ...'.[12] It concluded this initial claim by saying that '... to-day there are certain rules from which States are not competent to derogate at all by a treaty arrangement, and which may be changed only by a rule having the same character.'[13] At times, authors indicate that *jus cogens* sets a limit to the existing freedom of states to contract out of rules of (conventional and customary) international law,[14] and this has been argued to extend from conventional rules to (local, special, or general) rules of customary international law.[15] It may be noted that the freedom of states to displace rules of international law operates in both directions of the two most important primary sources of international law:[16] most commonly, rules of customary international law are substituted by treaties; rather more rarely, a treaty rule will be replaced by a rule of customary international law.[17]

[7] ibid.
[8] ibid.
[9] ibid.
[10] ibid https://en.oxforddictionaries.com/definition/peremptory.
[11] ibid https://en.oxforddictionaries.com/definition/jus_cogens.
[12] ILC, Commentary to art 50 (renumbered 53) VCLT, 248 [1] (and also [2]).
[13] ibid.
[14] See in this respect Helmersen (n 4) 170, pointing to VCLT art 30 as evidence of the possibility of contracting out of treaties; Robert Kolb, 'Observation sur l'évolution du concept de *jus cogens*' (2009) 113 *Revue Générale de Droit International Public* 837, 845 and 846–48; and de Hoogh, '*Jus Cogens* and the Use of Armed Force' (n 4) 1170.
[15] *Prosecutor v Anton Furundžija* (Judgment) ICTY-95-17/1-T (10 December 1998) [153] (see also [144]). Also Malcolm N Shaw, *International Law* (7th edn, OUP 2014) 89, indicating that derogation is barred for local or special custom.
[16] Occasionally the existence of such freedom is disputed and presumed absent unless stipulated by positive law: see Kammerhofer, *Uncertainty in International Law: A Kelsenian perspective* (Routledge 2011) 177–78 (also 135–37 and 154).
[17] Consider the recognition of the existence of an exclusive economic zone (EEZ), without supporting argument, by the ICJ even before the United Nations Convention on the Law of the Sea (UNCLOS) had entered into force, thus displacing certain rules concerning the high seas by those of the EEZ: *Continental Shelf (Tunisia v Libyan Arab Jamahiriya)* [1982] ICJ Rep 18, 73–74 [100].

Sometimes the basis for this freedom is sought in conflict solving maxims such as *lex specialis derogat legi generali*.[18] Yet while such a maxim may provide a solution as to which rule to apply, taking account of concrete circumstances and better reflecting the intent of the parties concerned,[19] it does not provide a rationale as to why states ought to be left with such freedom in the first place. That rationale may be found in the axiomatic sovereignty of states, providing political communities with independence of decision-making. This is consolidated by the fact that there is, in consequence, largely identity between states possessing the authority of law-making, both at the national and international level, and states as subjects of law being bound by the binding rules resulting therefrom.[20] Indeed, as that much maligned dictum of the Permanent Court of International Justice in *Lotus* aptly articulates: '[t]he rules of law binding upon states therefore emanate from their own free will . . .'[21] That free will, apparently, also entitles states to substitute an existing rule with another, preferred rule. Although not commented upon much, a derogation would most likely be applied only inter se in the mutual relations of the states concerned. Indeed, this could hardly be otherwise in view of their sovereignty, which entails the denial of any higher authority; the consequential equality of states produces the legal incapacity to make decisions or rules binding other states (*par in parem non habet imperium*). As much is, of course, demonstrated by the rules of the Vienna Convention concretizing the *pacta tertiis nec nocent nec prosunt* principle.[22]

One particular emanation of a potential overlap between the concepts of derogation and exception is the peremptory prohibition of the use of armed force in international relations, which admits of at least the exception of self-defence and arguably others too (e.g., humanitarian intervention, the protection of nationals). This raises the question as to how the exception of self-defence, and other potential exceptions, may be reconciled with the claim that the prohibition of the use of force constitutes a peremptory norm and thus does not admit any derogation. Different legal devices have been suggested to explain (away) the real or apparent contradictions between the peremptory prohibition and its (accepted or purported) exceptions: a restrictive interpretation of the word 'derogation' (see section 5 below); a restrictive interpretation of the peremptory prohibition itself (see section 4 below); and the proposition that exceptions limit the scope of applicability of a general rule, to which we turn next.

3 The Scope of Applicability of Rules: The Prohibition of the Use of Force and Its Exceptions

Nevertheless, there is a further need to clarify the exact meaning of the words 'derogation' and 'exception' in law; put differently, what exactly differentiates, from a legal perspective, a derogation from an exception. In this respect, Helmersen claims that an exception 'can be defined as "a special situation excluded from the coverage of an otherwise applicable rule"'.

[18] See e.g. *Nicaragua* (n 2) 137 [247], observing that treaty rules constitute *lex specialis* in relation to customary rules; ILC, 'Conclusions of the Study Group on the Fragmentation of International Law: Difficulties arising from the Diversification and Expansion of International Law' in *Report of the International Law Commission* adopted at its 58th session, A/61/10, 407, 409, points 8–9.

[19] ILC, 'Conclusions of the Study Group on the Fragmentation of International Law' (n 18) 409, point 9.

[20] See André de Hoogh, 'Regionalism and the Unity of International Law from a Positivist Perspective' in Mariano J Aznar and Mary E Footer (eds), *Select Proceedings of the European Society of International Law, vol. 2012/4* (Hart Publishing 2016) 51, 58–59.

[21] *The Case of the S.S. "Lotus"* (1927) PCIJ Rep Series A No 10, 18.

[22] VCLT arts 34–37.

Next, he advances the proposition that: 'Exceptions limit the scope of rules. This means that an apparent derogation that is covered by an exception is not a derogation, since it regulates something that is outside the scope of the rule.'[23]
However, he also quoted the definition of 'derogation' in the Random House Webster's Dictionary in Law, by J. Clapp, as 'limitations on the scope of something'.[24] In a way, a derogation is therefore also a kind of exception. Continuing his discussion, he then observes:

> Exceptions can be distinguished from derogations by their level of generality. An exception is at the same level of generality as the rules that it modifies ... The application of a derogation, on the other hand, will be limited to some of the parties that are bound by the rule in question; a 'derogation' between all parties should rather be considered an exception.[25]

Considering his reference to parties, one may assume that he is considering exceptions under a treaty, although his observations suggest all exceptions are removed from the scope of a rule; with respect to *jus cogens* he accordingly posits that exceptions to peremptory norms are not derogations, since one need not derogate from something outside the scope of the rule.[26] In essence then, Helmersen denies the applicability of a rule in case of exceptions.

His position involves the distinction, commented upon by Hage, Waltermann, and Arosemena, between applicability and application: certain facts must fall within the scope of the rule in order for it to be applicable, and only an applicable rule is one that may be applied to the facts.[27] As Hage, Waltermann, and Arosemena submit, the applicability of rules depends on scope conditions, which ordinarily are (an internal) part of the rule but may also be externally imposed (conditions related to personal, spatial, and temporal jurisdiction).[28] If the fulfilment of a scope condition is lacking, the rule is not applicable to the facts at hand.

Helmersen's construction then is to see various kinds of circumstances—self-defence, consent, force used under UNCLOS provisions, humanitarian intervention—as exceptions that limit the scope of the prohibition of the use of force.[29] Any of these circumstances, if present, would cause the prohibition to lack applicability. However, Helmersen's theoretical construct appears belaboured, if only because it starts from an assumption, a premise, that needs to be proven: that the exception limits the scope of the general rule, which consequently lacks applicability. Only if the validity of this premise can be ascertained by reference to the content of positive international law would the validity of the conclusion follow that an exception does not, indeed cannot, constitute a derogation.

The question may then be raised whether the Charter or customary international law qualify exceptions to the rule prohibiting states to have recourse to armed force as (negative) scope conditions whose fulfilment or non-fulfilment either affirms or excludes the applicability of the (general) rule. As a matter of interpretation, both from the viewpoint of the Charter and the construction of customary international law, this may be doubtful.

[23] Helmersen (n 4) 176.
[24] ibid 175, continuing with the observation that '[i]n the context of international law, derogations are specific acts or rules that diverge from and supplant the content of a more general rule. This is done by treaty or by consent.'
[25] ibid 175–76.
[26] ibid 176.
[27] Jaap Hage, Antonio Waltermann, and Gustavo Arosemena, ch 2 in this volume, 18–9.
[28] ibid—18, 22, and 29; see also discussion by Duarte d'Almeida, 'Defences in the Law of State Responsibility, A View from Jurisprudence', ch 10 in this volume, 181.
[29] Helmersen (n 4) respectively at 176–77, 177–78, 178–80, and 182. He also argues (at 180) that art 42 of the Charter requires further explanation as a possible exception to the customary prohibition of the use of force and (at 180–82) that various treaties providing for rights of intervention for the future have disputed validity.

Turning to the wording of Article 2(4) of the Charter, one may note that it stipulates that: 'All Members shall refrain in their international relations from the threat or use of force against the territorial integrity or political independence of any state, or in any other manner inconsistent with the Purposes of the United Nations.'[30]

Even though attempts have been made to argue that the prohibition is not all-encompassing,[31] authors have *grosso modo* maintained that states are generally prohibited from using force in their international relations.[32] The ICJ has had the opportunity to shed light on the interpretation of the prohibition of the use of force, but it has generally refrained from a close reading of Article 2(4) of the Charter.[33] Coming somewhat near, the Court observed in the case brought by the Congo (DRC) against Uganda that the latter had violated the sovereignty of the DRC and its territorial integrity, and went on to describe Uganda's military intervention as a grave violation of Article 2(4) of the Charter.[34] As there were no indications that Uganda was actually attempting to appropriate Congolese territory, the Court's pronouncement could be taken to support an interpretation equating 'territorial integrity' to 'territorial inviolability'.[35]

Although, as a matter of interpretation, this is far from persuasive, the phrase 'inconsistent with the purposes of the United Nations' cuts off any argument intended to limit the scope of the prohibition. Indeed, the US position during the San Francisco Conference, responding to the amendment that brought 'territorial integrity and political independence' into Article 2(4), observed that the intention of the original text had been to 'state in the broadest terms an absolute all-inclusive prohibition' and added that the phrase 'in any other manner' was 'designed to insure that there should be no loopholes'.[36] The reason why any possible loopholes are fully closed is that the primary purpose of the United Nations is the maintenance of international peace and security.[37] As such, any cross-border use of armed force, in and of itself, already results in a failure to maintain international peace and security and will therefore be inconsistent with that purpose.[38] The fact that the use of force may be pursued to further the cause of human rights, and could and would therefore be consistent with the UN's

[30] Charter of the United Nations (adopted 26 June 1945; in force 24 October 1945) https://treaties.un.org/doc/Publication/UNTS/No%20Volume/Part/un_charter.pdf.

[31] See e.g. Harold Hongju Koh, 'Syria and the Law of Humanitarian Intervention (Part III: A Reply)' *EJIL Talk!* (12 October 2013) https://www.ejiltalk.org/syria-and-the-law-of-humanitarian-intervention-part-iii-a-reply/#more-9613.

[32] Article 2(4) of the Charter appears to have some inherent limitation in that members are required to refrain from the threat or use of force 'in their international relations' only and, as such, does not cover the use of force in a domestic context. The use of force in a domestic setting is, however, not an exception, because the rule as formulated simply does not cover such use of force in the first place. As Helmersen (n 4) 176, observes: 'All legal rules have a (more or less clearly) defined scope. There will necessarily be much that is not covered by a given rule.' See further Albrecht Randelzhofer and Oliver Dörr, 'Article 2(4)' in Bruno Simma and others (eds), *The Charter of the United Nations: A Commentary, vol I* (3rd edn, OUP 2012) 200, 208 [14], and 208–18 [15]–[43].

[33] *Nicaragua* (n 2) 99–101 [188]–[190], referencing art 2(4) and determining the existence of the corresponding rule of customary international law; *Oil Platforms (Islamic Republic of Iran v United States of America)* [2003] ICJ Rep 161, 199 [78], concluding that the US had used armed force not qualifying as acts of self-defence (noting earlier (at 189 [57]) that the burden was on the US to show that it was the victim of an armed attack 'so as to justify it using armed force in self-defence'); *Armed Activities (Congo v Uganda)* (n 2) 223–27 [148–65].

[34] *Armed Activities (Congo v Uganda)* (n 2) 227 [165].

[35] In support of this interpretation see Randelzhofer and Dörr, 'Article 2(4)' (n 32) 215–16 [37]. See also, against, de Hoogh, *Obligations* Erga Omnes *and International Crimes, A Theoretical Inquiry into the Implementation and Enforcement of the International Responsibility of States* (Kluwer Law International 1996) 288–90; and André de Hoogh, 'The "Armed Activities" Case: Unasked Questions, Proper Answers' (2006) 1 *Hague Justice Journal* 47, 47–48.

[36] United Nations Conference on International Organization (UNCIO) vol VI, 335. The originally proposed formulation of art 2(4) was: 'Members shall refrain from the threat or use of force inconsistent with the Purposes of the United Nations.' Randelzhofer and Dörr, 'Article 2(4)' (n 32) 216 [38].

[37] Charter of the United Nations (n 30) art 1(1). Randelzhofer and Dörr, 'Article 2(4)' (n 32) 216 [38].

[38] See de Hoogh, *Obligations* Erga Omnes *and International Crimes* (n 35) 290–91. But see below on consent.

purpose to promote and encourage 'respect for human rights and fundamental freedoms',[39] will not negate its fundamental inconsistency with the UN's primary purpose to maintain international peace and security.

For various reasons, therefore, the language of Article 2(4) of the Charter is broadly interpreted as establishing a general rule prohibiting states from using of force against other states, and the ICJ has held the prohibition to be embodied in customary international law.[40] This general rule is applicable to any member that uses armed force across a border with another state: considering its language, no general or specific exceptions are carved out from the scope of the prohibition![41] However, if the general rule is applicable and prohibits any cross-border use of armed force, this raises the question in what manner to qualify recourse to armed force by states under the headings of self-defence, military action by the Security Council, and the use of armed force under its authority.[42] In this respect, one may wonder whether the language of other relevant provisions of the Charter (Articles 51 and 42), or the Council's practice on authorizations,[43] would dictate a different conclusion in that force resorted to were to exclude the applicability of the prohibition.

Starting with self-defence, Article 51 of the Charter specifies, in relevant part, that: '*Nothing in the present Charter* shall impair the inherent right of individual or collective self-defence if an armed attack occurs against a Member of the United Nations, until the Security Council has taken the measures necessary to maintain international peace and security...'[44]

The opening words of this provision might be read to imply that the presence of a situation of self-defence allows one simply to ignore the prohibition contained in Article 2(4) in respect of the state invoking self-defence. However, one may note that Article 2(4) of the Charter does not exempt the use of force in self-defence from its scope, even if Article 51 does start by saying that '[n]othing in the present Charter' shall impair the right to self-defence.[45] In a rather similar vein, Article XX of the General Agreement on Tariffs and Trade, dealing with 'general exceptions' to the trade in goods, provides that '[n]othing in this Agreement shall be construed to prevent the adoption or enforcement ... of measures' for certain purposes.[46] Textually then, these formulations do not testify to the inclusion of the exception within the rule itself; indeed, such exceptions apply in relation to the rules covered, but not per se as an

[39] Charter of the United Nations (n 30) art 1(3). Note the argument by Koh, (n 31), who observes that '[l]ike other originalist/textualist interpretations, the absolutist position does not acknowledge that the U.N. has multiple purposes –including protecting human rights, promoting regional security, and ending the scourge of war— instead flattening those purposes to one goal: the protection of sovereignty' and that '... the use of force in carefully limited circumstances can protect human rights without undermining the general prohibition against force'.

[40] *Nicaragua* (n 2) 99–102 [188–92].

[41] In an earlier contribution, I suggested a distinction between specific exceptions and general exceptions. The difference between the two would be that the former operate exclusively in relation to the prohibition of the use of force, whereas the latter may be invoked with respect to any rule imposing an obligation. See de Hoogh, '*Jus Cogens* and the Use of Armed Force' (n 4) 1165–75.

[42] As the ILC has ruled out necessity precluding the wrongfulness of the use of force, this circumstance will not be discussed further; but see text below relating to nn 105 to 110.

[43] Generally Niels Blokker, 'Outsourcing the Use of Force: Towards More Security Council Control of Authorized Operations?' in Marc Weller (ed), *The Oxford Handbook of the Use of Force in International Law* (OUP 2015) 202; Ian Johnstone, 'When the Security Council is Divided: Imprecise Authorizations, Implied Mandates, and the 'Unreasonable' Veto' in Marc Weller (ed), *The Oxford Handbook of the Use of Force in International Law* (OUP 2015) 227.

[44] Charter of the United Nations (n 30) art 51 (emphasis added).

[45] Otherwise, in support, one could further point to the qualification of the right of self-defence as 'inherent', often considered suggestive of some pre-positive natural law origin. In *Nicaragua* (n 2) 102–103 [193], the Court rather interpreted the word inherent to be indicative of its customary international law origin.

[46] General Agreement on Tariffs and Trade (adopted 30 October 1947, in force provisionally 1 January 1948) (1947) 55 UNTS 194.

integral part restricting their substantive scope; in other words, they appear to be superimposed upon them.

Some support for the view that self-defence is excluded from the scope of the prohibition may be seen in the Court's observation in the *Nicaragua* case that:

> If a State acts in a way prima facie incompatible with a recognized rule, but defends its conduct by appealing to exceptions or justifications contained within the rule itself, then whether or not the State's conduct is in fact justifiable on that basis, the significance of that attitude is to confirm rather than to weaken the rule.[47]

The reference to 'exceptions or justifications contained within the rule itself' is interesting, since it might be taken to show a disposition by the Court to see exceptions as part and parcel of the rule. Yet, as we shall see below (section 4), this pronouncement, taken acontextually, would misrepresent its approach to general rules and exceptions within the judgment at large. Be that as it may, it has been claimed by the ILC that:[48]

> Article 51 of the Charter of the United Nations preserves *a State's 'inherent right' of self-defence* in the face of an armed attack and *forms part of the definition of the obligation to refrain from the threat or use of force laid down* in Article 2, paragraph 4. Thus, *a State exercising its inherent right of self-defence* as referred to in Article 51 of the Charter *is not, even potentially, in breach of Article 2, paragraph 4.*

One might argue in corroboration of this view the Court's reversal, without further explanation, of the order in which the prohibition and self-defence are examined in *Armed Activities*. In that case, the Court first scrutinized whether Uganda's invocation of the right of self-defence was warranted in light of the conditions set for the exercise of that right, before coming to the conclusion that Uganda's military intervention in the DRC constituted a grave violation of Article 2(4).[49] The explanation given by judge Tomka[50] for this reversal—quoting the text of Article 51—is that 'a lawful exercise of the right to self-defence cannot constitute the breach of any relevant article of the Charter', and he then contends:[51]

> The prohibition on the use of force cannot be read without having regard to the Charter provisions on self-defence. The provisions on self-defence, in fact, delineate the scope of rules prohibiting the use of force. If a measure in question constitutes a lawful measure of self-defence, it necessarily falls outside the ambit of the prohibition. In other words, the prohibition of the use of force is not applicable to the use of force in lawfully exercised self-defence.

[47] *Nicaragua* (n 2) 98 [186].

[48] Commentary to art 21 ARSIWA, in Report of the International Law Commission on the work of its fifty-third session (2001) A/56/10 (ILC Report 2001) 74 [1] (footnote omitted; emphasis added). A similar kind of argument is made by Stefan Kadelbach, 'Genesis, Function and Identification of *Jus Cogens* Norms' (2015) 46 *Netherlands Yearbook of International Law* 147, 162, to the effect that the binding effect of *jus cogens* norms is absolute, but that such norms admit of 'inherent exceptions, like self-defence with respect to the use of force'; and by Sten Verhoeven, *Norms of* Jus Cogens *in International Law: A Positivist and Constitutionalist Approach* (PhD Leuven 2011) 120–22 [128 and 131], 146 [160].

[49] *Armed Activities (Congo v Uganda)* (n 2) 227 [165].

[50] See e.g. Verhoeven (n 48) 265–66 [281], considering for this reason also the right of self-defence to be part of *jus cogens*.

[51] *Armed Activities (Congo v Uganda)* (n 2) (Separate Opinion of Judge Tomka) 351, 354–55 [10]–[11].

Although the reasoning is appealing, these observations miss the mark in several important and rather crucial respects.

First, Judge Tomka, in making his argument on the applicability of the prohibition limits this position to 'lawful' measures of self-defence and 'lawfully' exercised self-defence. Although he does not further specify how to establish such lawfulness, this presupposes that where the measures concerned cannot be labelled as 'lawful' self-defence they would fall within the scope of the prohibition. One may presume that such will be the case if, for instance, a claim of self-defence would not be predicated upon an armed attack and possibly also if the measures concerned would fail to comply with conditions set for the exercise of the right of self-defence, such as the tests of necessity and/or proportionality.[52]

Secondly, the exercise of the right of self-defence relies on the precondition of an armed attack—a *conditio sine qua non*—whose existence needs to be ascertained for any recourse to armed force to be lawful in the first place. Until and unless the existence of an armed attack is established, recourse to force by a state must be presumed to fall within the scope of the prohibition of the use of force in Article 2(4) and customary international law. In view of the horizontal structure prevalent within international relations, with each state determining for itself its legal position vis-à-vis other states,[53] and in the absence of an authoritative decision of (primarily) the Security Council, rebuttal of that presumption may be demanding at worst, challenging on the whole, and facile in exceptional cases at best.

Thirdly, an armed attack must involve, of necessity, a use of force unlawful under Article 2(4) and/or customary international law.[54] This constraint is necessary in order to prevent the logical regression of a state being able to invoke self-defence against an otherwise lawful recourse to armed force by another state. If an armed attack as *conditio sine qua non*, the *prima causa* of self-defence, could involve a lawful use of armed force, there would be no prospect to judge either party's recourse to armed force as unlawful; hence, this would lead to an impasse and the consequent inability to rule on all kinds of related matters. This argument also explains the difficulty of fitting the armed activities of non-state actors within the concept of armed attack, since (most) non-state actors are not bound under international law by the rules banning the use of force in international relations.[55] This, in turn, has led to many difficulties in establishing the standard by which to judge whether the armed activities of non-state actors may be equated to an armed attack by a state, whether through attribution, substantial involvement, due diligence, unable, or unwilling tests (or none of those).[56]

Fourthly and finally, the precondition of armed attack is itself obscured by cloudy ambiguities that make its utility in determining the lawfulness of a claim of self-defence tenuous or even precarious. Leaving aside such claims as to the availability under international law of self-defence for preventive, pre-emptive, anticipatory, or interceptive purposes, the use of different terms in the Charter—force, armed attack, breach of the peace, and act of aggression—has led many to consider the concept of armed attack to require the unlawful use of force to reach a certain threshold of severity.[57]

[52] Two conditions fulfilment of which has been held to be required under customary international law: *Nicaragua* (n 2) 103 [194], and further 122–23 [237].

[53] *Case Concerning the Air Service Agreement of 27 March 1946 between the United States and France* (Arbitral Award) (2006) 28 RIAA 417, 443 [81], sometimes referred to as the principle of auto-interpretation or auto-determination.

[54] See André de Hoogh, 'Restrictivist Reasoning on the *Ratione Personae* Dimension of Armed Attacks' (2016) 29 *Leiden Journal of International Law* 19, 22.

[55] ibid 22–23.

[56] ibid 25–33.

[57] Albrecht Randelzhofer and Georg Nolte, 'Article 51' in Bruno Simma and others (eds), *The Charter of the United Nations: A Commentary, vol I* (3rd edn, OUP 2012) 1397, 1401–403 [6–8] and 1409–10 [20–21], with further

In *Nicaragua*, the Court spoke of less grave and most grave uses of force, the latter constituting an armed attack,[58] and later specified that the armed activities of non-state actors ought to be of a scale and effect similar to an armed attack engaged in by regular armed forces rather than a frontier incident.[59] Although the Court has been less forthright in upholding the gravity requirement in later cases, considering (without much conviction) the possibility of the mining of a single military vessel or a number of incidents spread out over time to amount to an armed attack,[60] the uncertainties in this respect militate against viewing the exception of self-defence as excluding the applicability of the prohibition. Indeed, the reference to self-defence is quite often accompanied by the depiction of 'justification' or 'justified' (see section 4 below). However, if the prohibition of the use of force were not to be applicable in the first place, no justification would be required in any event.

Turning to the Security Council, Article 42 of the Charter provides for the legal power of the Council to initiate military action. However, it ought to be noted that this provision provides for action *by the Security Council* rather than the member states. The initial thought behind this power was that the member states would make armed forces, matériel and all kinds of assistance available to the Council (Articles 43 and 45), and that the Council would direct military action through the Military Staff Committee (Articles 46-47 and 45). A determination of the actor involved—the Security Council or the member(s)—is critical, as the prohibition contained in Article 2(4) is addressed to the members. The prohibition is therefore not applicable to military action by and under control of the Council. In essence, the Security Council has exercised this power by the creation of UN peacekeeping forces with peace enforcement mandates.[61]

However, to the extent that the Security Council were to take military action against a non-member state, the equivalent rules of customary international law would be applicable. As the prohibition of the use of armed force is also embodied in customary international law,[62] the United Nations and its organs must be considered equally bound. This is so since states in creating an international organization cannot derogate from rules of customary international law in relation to non-members.[63] The provision of Article 2(6), evidencing the UN's universal vocation to ensure international peace and security even in respect of non-members,[64] cannot be read to give the Security Council legal powers of decision-making[65] going beyond what may be justified under customary international law.[66]

references; and generally Jan Klabbers, 'Intervention, Armed Intervention, Armed Attack, Threat to the Peace, Act of Aggression, and Threat or Use of Force: What's the Difference?' in Marc Weller (ed), *The Oxford Handbook of the Use of Force in International Law* (OUP 2015) 488; and this is also discounting the suggestions made in the literature as to the availability of self-defence in relation to cyber-attacks: see generally Michael N Schmitt (ed), *Tallinn Manual 2.0 on the International Law Applicable to Cyber Operations* (2nd edn, CUP 2017).

[58] *Nicaragua* (n 2) 101 [191].

[59] ibid 103–104 [195].

[60] *Oil Platforms* (n 33) 195–96 [72]; *Armed Activities (Congo v Uganda)* (n 2) 219–20 [131]–[135] and 222–23 [144]–[146].

[61] For early example see SC Resolution 161, S/RES/169 (1961) [4]; for a more recent example see SC Resolution 2098, S/RES/2098 (2013) [12]. Arguably, although more likely an example of UN coordination of action in collective self-defence, the action in Korea could be seen as an exercise of military enforcement powers: see SC Resolutions 82–85, S/RES/82, S/RES/83, S/RES/84, S/RES/85 (1950).

[62] *Nicaragua* (n 2) 99–101 [188]–[190].

[63] As follows from the relative effect of treaties (VCLT, arts 34–37). On this point, in support Stefan Talmon, 'Article 2(6)' in Bruno Simma and others (eds), *The Charter of the United Nations: A Commentary, vol I* (3rd edn, OUP 2012) 252–79 [28–29], 261–63 [35] and 265–66 [41].

[64] Generally, Talmon (n 63) 265–66 [39–43].

[65] In support, ibid 263 [35].

[66] In support, Linderfalk, 'The Effect of *Jus Cogens* Norms' (n 4) 863–64; and Talmon (n 63) 265–66 [41] and n 93, although his contribution as a whole goes against the grain of the argument here.

However, the situation is markedly different when member states, whether acting directly or through (regional) organizations, have recourse to armed force after being authorized to this effect by the Security Council. In such a case, armed action is neither under the control of the Security Council, notwithstanding its option to cancel the authorization (subject to the veto), nor can it be said to be undertaken by the Council.[67] Furthermore, the Council's authorization is normally granted for specific purpose(s), however wide-ranging such may be, and this suggests that action going beyond such purpose(s) would still be covered by the prohibition.[68] More specifically, in the absence of a legal basis for military action accepted under international law, authorization by the Security Council is required precisely because in its absence the armed activities concerned would violate the prohibition. Hence, an authorization by the Council provides a justification under international law to engage in action ordinarily covered by the prohibition on the use of armed force.

In conclusion, exceptions to a general rule do not per se exclude the applicability of that general rule. Furthermore, an inquiry into the specific exceptions to the prohibition of the use of armed force as accepted under international law also does not show this to be the case. Armed action by and under control of the Security Council comes closest in that the prohibition of the use of armed force as laid down in the Charter is not applicable in such a case. However, this is not because such action constitutes an exception excluded from the scope of the prohibition, but because the prohibition is applicable only to UN members and not to the United Nations as such. In other words, the general rule contains a scope limitation *ratione personae*. Bringing the discussion back to *jus cogens*, if exceptions do not limit the scope of applicability of the general rule prohibiting the use of armed force, then these may (possibly) amount to derogation from the peremptory prohibition.

4 Circumstances Precluding Wrongfulness and Justifications: Peremptory Norms and Exceptions

Whether circumstances precluding wrongfulness have a bearing upon the applicability of the rules affected upon their invocation is open to debate. The ILC, in its Articles on the Responsibility of States, made a choice to consider various circumstances to preclude the wrongfulness of certain conduct upon the legal construction that the circumstances concerned rendered an obligation, either temporarily or definitively, inoperative.[69] To put this in a logical chain: no obligation (suspended)—no breach (possible)—no internationally wrongful act—no responsibility. In all of this, no reference is made to a denial of the applicability of relevant rules of international law, other than to note that the circumstances 'do not annul or terminate the obligation', but instead 'provide a justification or excuse for

[67] Contrary, *Behrami and Behrami v France, and Saramati v France, Germany and Norway* (ECHR) Grand Chamber, Decision as to Admissibility of Application nos 71412/01 and 78166/01 (2 May 2007) [132–41], in which the Court held that the Security Council retained ultimate authority and control and that the conduct concerned was therefore attributable to the UN.

[68] Consider the debate of whether the authorization provided by the Council regarding Libya to protect civilians, or civilian populated areas, under threat of attack permitted action in support of the rebels and the overthrow of the Gaddafi-led government: SC Resolution 1973, S/RES/1973 (17 March 2011) [4]. Generally Constantine Antonopoulos, 'The "Legitimacy" to "Legitimise": The Security Council Action under Resolution 1973 (2011)' (2012) 14 *International Community Law Review* 359.

[69] See Sandra Szurek, 'The Notion of Circumstances Precluding Wrongfulness' in James Crawford, Alain Pellet, and Simon Olleson (eds), *The Law of International Responsibility* (OUP 2010) 427, 434 (footnote omitted), who observes at 435: 'It has not been claimed that the rule or obligation effectively disappears, even temporarily ... even in the case of force majeure.' She continues: 'Rather the notion of circumstance precluding wrongfulness is concerned with situations in which the obligation is continuing but responsibility cannot be invoked where certain circumstances exist.'

non-performance while the circumstance in question subsists'.[70] The ILC considered that the circumstances have no relevance to 'the constituent requirements of the obligation' but operate in a way similar to 'defences or excuses in internal legal systems'.[71]

In a more theoretical fashion, taking examples from criminal law as a starting point, Duarte d'Almeida asserts a distinction between *P*-facts and *D*-facts, whereby the former indicates facts that need to be present for a decision on the merits to be correct, whereas the latter concerns facts that need to be absent for such a decision to be correct.[72] The actual presence of *D*-facts, however, signifies the availability of a defence and hence the possibility of justification or excuse.[73] Refining his reasoning, he further specifies that *P*-facts may involve the necessity of proving that something is absent, a negative constituent element then, for example having to prove absence of consent in order to establish rape.[74] Transposing his reasoning to the law of state responsibility, he discusses whether circumstances precluding wrongfulness should not be seen as negative elements of the primary rules rather than acting as secondary rules in the nature of defences, eventually coming to the conclusion that they can be, indeed are, both.[75]

In this context, he deplores the absence in international law of the notion of offence or prima facie wrong.[76] Furthermore, he asserts a distinction among the possible defences between justifications and excuses, whereby the former appear both as negative qualifications of obligations (under primary rules) and as secondary rules, whereas the latter only come into play as secondary rules.[77] Regarding justifications he argues that, if present, the conduct concerned is permissible, whereas Paddeu observes that as a justification is based on 'a permission of the legal order to engage in certain conduct', this 'leads to the conclusion that the conduct is lawful'.[78] To say that the conduct concerned is permissible or lawful is perhaps a bridge too far; after all, there is a difference between, on the one hand, a (primary) permissive rule laying down a right to engage in conduct rendering it lawful per se and, on the other hand, a (secondary) permissive rule granting a right to engage in conduct that is otherwise prohibited. As such, rather than qualifying such conduct as permissible or lawful, it would be preferable to call such conduct, considering the circumstances ruling at the time, justifiable or justified.

Although the Articles on the Responsibility of States do not as such enunciate the notion of a prima facie wrong, there are at least some indications that suggest that this is implied.

[70] Commentary to ch V of Pt 1, ILC Report 2001, 71 [2], adding that they function 'as a shield rather than a sword'.

[71] ibid 71 [7].

[72] Duarte d'Almeida, Defences in the Law of State Responsibility, A View from Jurisprudence, ch 10 in this volume, 180.

[73] ibid 184.

[74] ibid 180–1.

[75] ibid 194–7.

[76] ibid 190–3, at the end pointing to the notion of *Tatbestand* in German criminal law theory or *tipo* in Portuguese, Spanish, or Italian criminal law theory. In a similar vein, see Paddeu, 'Clarifying the Concept of Circumstances Precluding Wrongfulness (Justifications) in International Law', ch 11 in this volume, 208–9.

[77] D'Almeida, Defences in the Law of State Responsibility, A View from Jurisprudence, ch 10 in this volume, 195–7.

[78] ibid 195; see Paddeu, 'Clarifying the Concept of Circumstances Precluding Wrongfulness (Justifications) in International Law', ch 11 in this volume, 211. Earlier on, Duarte d'Almeida explained the difference between justification and excuse in criminal law as meaning that a justification renders the conduct permissible, whereas an excuse concerns impermissible conduct by a person considered not culpable (184–6); for Paddeu, 211 (see also text up to n 55), '[a]n excuse, instead, does not constitute a permission to engage in certain conduct and, for this reason, it does not affect the illegality of conduct; the excuse serves only to exclude the consequences that follow from that illegality for the defendant.'

In its commentaries, the ILC regularly refers to conduct that would 'otherwise' be unlawful or internationally wrongful, or not in conformity with an international obligation.[79] This allows for the inference that when a circumstance precluding wrongfulness is present and invoked the requirements to conclude to the existence of an internationally wrongful act laid down in Article 2 of the ARSIWA could be, or indeed are, in fact met.[80] From a logical perspective then, the ILC's construction of the constituent elements embodied in Article 2 of the ARSIWA being determinative of an internationally wrongful act without cross-reference to the circumstances precluding wrongfulness is flawed.[81] For purposes of Article 2, the absence of any circumstance precluding wrongfulness should then have been included as a constituent element of an internationally wrongful act (in effect, a negative *P*-fact in Duarte d'Almeida's construction).

Although the notion of a prima facie wrong cannot be found in any explicit manner in the provisions of the Articles on the Responsibility of States, there are in fact a few telling examples to be found in case law.[82] In *Nicaragua*, the Court, when discussing the methodology of establishing a rule of customary international law, mentioned that '[i]f a State acts in a way prima facie *incompatible with a recognized rule*, but defends its conduct by appealing to exceptions or justifications contained within the rule itself', this confirms the existence of the rule.[83] With respect to certain acts (laying of mines in Nicaragua's internal and territorial waters; attacks on Nicaraguan ports, oil installations, and a naval base) attributable to the United States, the Court held: '[t]hese activities constitute infringements of the principle of the prohibition of the use of force, defined earlier, unless they are justified by circumstances which exclude their unlawfulness . . .'.[84] Considering especially the United States' support to the *contras*, in terms of training and arming, it then found with respect to the 'customary international law principle of non-use of force':[85]

> . . . that, subject to the question whether the action of the United States might be justified as an exercise of the right of self-defence, *the United States has committed a prima facie violation of that principle by its assistance to the contras in Nicaragua*, by 'organizing or encouraging the organization of irregular forces or armed bands . . . for incursion into the territory of another State', and 'participating in acts of civil strife . . . in another State', in the terms of General Assembly resolution 2625 (XXV).

[79] Commentary to art 2 ARSIWA, ILC Report 2001, 36 [11]; Commentary to ch V of Pt 1, ibid 71 [1]; Commentary to art 20 ARSIWA, ibid 72 [3] and 74 [10]; Commentary to art 22 ARSIWA, ibid 75 [2]; Commentary to art 23 ARSIWA, ibid 76 [1]; Commentary to art 24 ARSIWA, ibid 79 [5]; Commentary to art 27 ARSIWA, 8 ibid 6 [5]; Commentary to ch II of Pt Three, ibid 128 [1 and 3]; Commentary to art 49 ARSIWA, ibid 130 [6]. *Gabčíkovo-Nagymaros Project (Hungary/Slovakia)* [1997] ICJ Rep 7, 55 [80].

[80] Indeed, the ILC's observation that circumstances precluding wrongfulness lack relevance for the constituent requirements of the obligation suggests as much: see Commentary to ch V of Pt 1, ILC Report 2001, 71 [7]. See further Paddeu, 'Clarifying the Concept of Circumstances Precluding Wrongfulness (Justifications) in International Law', ch 11 in this volume, 207–209, but arguing that establishing the incompatibility of conduct with what is required by an obligation entails a factual determination and not per se also the legal qualification of breach or unlawfulness.

[81] In the same manner, ibid 209.

[82] The examples discussed in this section are from ICJ jurisprudence; for examples taken from other jurisdictions ibid 204.

[83] *Nicaragua* (n 2) 98 [186] (emphasis added); in relation to non-intervention, ibid 108–109 [207].

[84] ibid 118 [227].

[85] ibid 118–19 [228] (emphasis added). In relation to non-intervention see ibid 126 [246], where the Court mentions 'prima facie acts of intervention' that might be justified on some legal ground.

Indeed, as to the Nicaraguan complaints regarding the Treaty of Friendship, Commerce and Navigation,[86] the Court first investigated whether the act complained of *appeared* to be well founded, before considering whether the security exception might justify those acts.[87] The Court reverted to this matter in *Oil Platforms*, in discussing the order of investigation of questions of interpretation and application of the bilateral Treaty of Amity, Economic Relations, and Consular Rights.[88] It referred back to *Nicaragua* and observed, not altogether accurately, that there it had first examined whether a prima facie breach of that treaty had been committed before turning to the question of whether exceptions under the treaty could be invoked to justify such conduct.[89]

All in all, then, rather than regarding exceptions or circumstances precluding wrongfulness as substantive (*ratione materiae*) limitations to the scope of a general rule, this suggests that the conduct concerned should be understood to fall under the scope of two different rules both applicable in the circumstances at hand. As argued by Hage, Waltermann, and Arosemena, this implies that:[90] '[a]n exception to a rule in a case is defined as the situation in which a rule is applicable to, but nevertheless not applied to the case.' Moreover, they point out that applicability must be determined, aside from possible territorial, temporal and personal limitations to the rule, by the case satisfying 'the ordinary conditions of the rule'.[91]

The ordinary conditions of the rule, in this instance the prohibition of the use of force, are that the conduct involves the use of armed force, taking place in the international relations of the state, and that it be against the territorial integrity or political independence of another state or inconsistent with the purposes of the UN. Self-defence would clearly fulfil the first two conditions, but the third requires further argument. Leaving aside whether to support a narrow or broad interpretation of 'territorial integrity' or 'political independence', one might be tempted to argue that self-defence is not inconsistent with the purpose 'to maintain international peace and security'. As such, however, the legal construction would not be that the rule prohibiting force is not applicable, but that the conduct concerned would not involve a breach of obligation in the first place. As a result, the use of armed force as an exercise of the right of self-defence would not require justification in any way.

However, the ICJ case law on the use of force and self-defence simply does not testify to such a construction. Thus, the most directly relevant cases are replete with references to self-defence (potentially) justifying armed or military activities that would otherwise constitute a violation of the prohibition of the use of force.[92] Returning to the subject of this contribution, this then suggests—on the assumption that the prohibition of the use of force constitutes a peremptory norm—that peremptory norms allow for justification and hence that exceptions to rules of *jus cogens* may be admissible, notwithstanding their attribute of non-derogability.

[86] Treaty of Friendship, Commerce and Navigation (adopted 21 January 1956, in force 24 May 1958) (1956) 367 UNTS 3.

[87] In *Nicaragua* (n 2) 136 [272], 140 [280], the Court found that certain acts were in contradiction with the terms of the treaty, subject to the question of justification.

[88] Treaty of Amity, Economic Relations, and Consular Rights (adopted 15 August 1955, in force 16 June 1957) (1955) 284 UNTS 93.

[89] *Oil Platforms* (n 33) 179–80 [35] (see also 202–203 [88]), referring to *Nicaragua* (n 2) 140 [280] (where the Court does not, in actual fact, use the term 'prima facie breach').

[90] Hage, Waltermann, and Arosemena, ch 2 in this volume, 34 and 18–9.

[91] ibid 18, 22.

[92] *Nicaragua* (n 2) 118–21 [228–29 and 232–33], 128 [252], 141–42 [282] and 146 [292] (dictum no 2); *Oil Platforms* (n 33) 180–81 [37], 185–87 [48 and 51], 193–94 [67], 195–96 [72], and 198 [76]; *Legal Consequences of the Construction of a Wall in the Occupied Palestinian Territory* [2004] ICJ Rep 136, 194 [139]; *Armed Activities (Congo v Uganda)* (n 2) 213 [106], 215 [108], 215 [112], and 269 [304].

But, taking a step back, the status of the prohibition of the use of force as a peremptory norm has been questioned,[93] and obviously denial of that status would obviate the need to account for possible discrepancies between a peremptory prohibition and the existence of exceptions thereto. The assumption mentioned itself suffers from the fact that, over the years, the scope of the peremptory prohibition has alternatively been related to the use of force generally or to that of aggression in particular. Indeed, the ILC itself, in its commentary on *jus cogens* in its draft on the law of treaties, noted that:[94] '... the law of the Charter concerning the prohibition of the use of force in itself constitutes a conspicuous example of a rule in international law having the character of *jus cogens*.' However, in its projects on the law of responsibility of states and of international organizations, the Commission consistently opted to make reference instead to the prohibition of aggression as a peremptory norm.[95]

Now, if there really were no real difference in substance between the prohibition of the use of force and the prohibition of aggression, then all of the same complications would apply as discussed previously. Over and above these, however, one would also be confronted with the affirmation, in the Definition of Aggression adopted by the General Assembly, that:[96] '[n]o consideration of whatever nature, whether political, economic, military or otherwise, may serve as a justification for aggression.' By ruling out justifications, this assertion would also appear to exclude the possibility of exceptions to the prohibition of aggression. A contextual reading of the Definition allows one to wave away this suggestion, as one of its clauses saves cases where the use of force would be lawful under the Charter (Article 6) and aggression itself seems to be predominantly, if not exclusively (Article 1), defined by reference to first uses of force (Article 2).

Nevertheless, it does appear that the notion of aggression embodies something fundamentally different from the (mere) use of force. The Definition itself, in the preamble, makes mention that aggression is 'the most serious and dangerous form of the illegal use of force', and most of the examples set forth in Article 3 appear to imply a certain gravity and scale of the force resorted to.[97] In a similar vein, when discussing 'armed attack' (in French: *agression armée*) and the sending of armed bands under Article 3(g) of the Definition in *Nicaragua*, the Court required their activities to be of a 'scale and effects' in order to be equated to an attack by regular armed forces.[98] Finally, the amendments to the Rome Statute define an act of aggression as a manifest violation of the Charter by reason of its 'character, gravity and scale'.[99]

In this respect, one may note that the ILC has limited some of the legal consequences for breaches of peremptory norms to those which are 'serious'.[100] The Commission has specified that a serious breach entails 'a gross or systematic failure' to fulfil the obligation (Article

[93] Generally Green, 'Questioning the Peremptory Status of the Prohibition of the Use of Force' (n 4).

[94] Commentary to art 50 (renumbered 53) (n 12) 247 [1] (see also 248 [3]).

[95] Commentary to art 26 ARSIWA, ILC Report 2001, 85 [5]; Commentary to art 40 ARSIWA, ibid 112–13 [4 and 8]; Commentary to art 41 ARSIWA, ibid 116 [14]; Commentary to art 26 DARIO, in Report of the General Assembly on the work of its sixty-third session (2011) A/66/10, 53 [2]; Commentary to art 41 DARIO, ibid 66 [1]; see also *Barcelona Traction* (n 2) 32 [34], where the Court speaks of the 'outlawing of acts of aggression'; and draft art 19 of the Draft articles on State Responsibility, ILC Yearbook 1980, vol II (2) 30, qualifying 'a serious breach of an international obligation of essential importance for the maintenance of international peace and security, such as that prohibiting aggression' as an international crime (of State).

[96] GA Resolution 3314, A/RES/3314 (XXIX) (14 December 1974) Annex, Definition of Aggression, art 5(1).

[97] Note also that art 2 provides that the Security Council may judge aggression not to have been committed for lack of 'sufficient gravity'.

[98] *Nicaragua* (n 2) 103 [195].

[99] Amendments to the Rome Statute of the International Criminal Court on the Crime of Aggression (adopted 11 June 2010) 2922 UNTS 9, art 8 *bis*.

[100] DARIO arts 40–41.

40(2) ARSIWA). In its commentary, the Commission referred to the scale or character of a breach, and observed that 'a certain order of magnitude is necessary'.[101] In referencing the gross and/or systematic character of the breach, the Commission stated that:[102]

> To be regarded as systematic, a violation would have to be carried out in an organized and deliberate way. In contrast, the term 'gross' refers to the intensity of the violation or its effects; it denotes violations of a flagrant nature, amounting to a direct and outright assault on the values protected by the rule. The terms are not of course mutually exclusive; serious breaches will usually be both systematic and gross. Factors which may establish the seriousness of a violation would include the intent to violate the norm; the scope and number of individual violations; and the gravity of their consequences for the victims. It must also be borne in mind that some of the peremptory norms in question, most notably the prohibitions of aggression and genocide, by their very nature require an intentional violation on a large scale.

Of course, matters of gravity, scale, and effects only account for a difference in degree and not one in kind. The latter would have to be sought rather in the character of an act of aggression, which carries with it overtones of malevolence and malice. Aggression might be distinguished then by requiring the use of force concerned to be motivated by an *animus aggressionis* or otherwise being resorted to for unlawful and improper purposes.[103] The early work of the ILC on 'state of necessity' as a circumstance precluding wrongfulness advanced the view that aggression constituted a qualified violation of the prohibition of the use of force. In its 1980 commentary, the Commission made reference to examples where necessity had been invoked to justify the annexation (in whole or in part) or occupation of the territory of another state, and qualified such actions as 'an assault on the very existence of a State or on the integrity of its territory or the independent exercise of its sovereignty'.[104] It specified that any use of armed force for such an assault on the sovereignty of another state 'indisputably comes within the meaning of the term "aggression" and, as such, is subject to a prohibition of *jus cogens* ...'.[105] After quoting Article 5(1) of the Definition of Aggression, barring any kind of justification, the Commission opined that necessity as a justification could not preclude the wrongfulness of a use of force constituting aggression.[106]

The Commission, however, went considerably further in arguing that not all conduct infringing the territorial sovereignty of a state would constitute aggression or a breach of *jus cogens*, and claimed that such actions in the territory of another state:[107]

> ... although they may sometimes be of a coercive nature, *serve only limited intentions and purposes bearing no relation to the purposes characteristic of a true act of aggression*. These would include, for instance, some incursions into foreign territory to forestall harmful operations by an armed group which was preparing to attack the territory of the State, or in pursuit of an armed band or gang of criminals who had crossed the frontier and perhaps had their base in that foreign territory, or to protect the lives of nationals or other persons

[101] Commentary to ch Three of Pt Two ARSIWA, ILC Report 2001, 110 [1].
[102] ibid Commentary to art 40 ARSIWA, 113 [8] (footnote omitted).
[103] On *animus aggressionis*, in relation to individual responsibility, see Yoram Dinstein, *War, Aggression and Self-Defence* (5th edn, CUP 2012) 146.
[104] Commentary to former art 33 ARSIWA, ILC Yearbook 1980, vol II (2) 42–43 [22].
[105] ibid.
[106] ibid.
[107] ibid 43–44 [23].

> attacked or detained by hostile forces or groups not under the authority and control of the State, or to eliminate or neutralize a source of troubles which threatened to occur or to spread across the frontier. The common feature of these cases is, first, the existence of grave and imminent danger to the State, to some of its nationals or simply to human beings—a danger of which the territory of the foreign State is either the theatre or the place of origin, and which the foreign State has a duty to avert by its own action, but which its unwillingness or inability to act allows to continue. Another common feature is the limited character of the actions in question, as regards both duration and the means employed, in keeping with their purpose, which is restricted to eliminating the perceived danger.

After these rather suggestive observations, the Commission then declined to take position on the question of whether the Charter implicitly excludes the invocation of necessity to all conduct inconsistent with the prohibition of the use of force.[108]

Although the ILC back-pedalled on this particular point in its second reading and completion of the ARSIWA in 2001,[109] a more general point may be made here regarding the nature of norms of *jus cogens*. If the prohibition of aggression (with gravity and purpose requirements in order to determine its violation) constitutes a peremptory norm, rather than the prohibition of the use of force more generally, then the argument can be made that *jus cogens* norms are absolute in character and do not permit invocation of any kind of justification (as is claimed for aggression).[110] This legal construction would also take away much of the force of the argument by Leben that two types of peremptory norms exist: simple and reinforced.[111] In his view, simple peremptory norms would not exclude sanctions imposed by a central authority, whereas reinforced peremptory norms would prohibit certain acts in all circumstances.[112] If *jus cogens* status is accorded to the prohibition of aggression, as discussed above, such a distinction would lack validity.

For certain other peremptory norms, this denial of possible justification, suggesting their absolute character, has been explicitly provided in a relevant treaty. One example is the prohibition

[108] ibid 44–45 [24].

[109] Commentary to art 25 ARSIWA, ILC Report 2001, 84 [21]; discussed earlier in de Hoogh, '*Jus Cogens* and the Use of Armed Force' (n 4) 1168–70.

[110] See Alexander Orakhelashvili, *Peremptory Norms in International Law* (OUP 2008) 67–72, arguing that peremptory norms are absolute and unconditional in character. Tladi, 'First Report' (n 3) 38 [63], observes that: 'Firstly, *jus cogens* norms are universally applicable. Secondly, *jus cogens* norms are superior to other norms of international law. Finally, *jus cogens* norms serve to protect the fundamental values of the international community ...'. See also Tladi, 'Second Report' (n 3) 37–38 [74]. If peremptory norms are absolute in character, this might explain why the right to life is not generally mentioned in listings of peremptory norms, since the right to life appears subject to exceptions and justification in case of infringement. Nevertheless, recently Christof Heyns and Thomas Probert, 'Securing the Right to Life: A Cornerstone of the Human Rights System', *EJILTalk!* (11 May 2016) https://www.ejiltalk.org/securing-the-right-to-life-a-cornerstone-of-the-human-rights-system/, claimed: 'The right to life is a well-established and developed part of international law, in treaties, custom, and general principles, and, in its core elements, in the rules of *jus cogens*.' See further Paul Harpur, 'The Evolving Nature of the Right To Life: The Impact of Positive Human Rights Obligations' (2007) 9 *University of Notre Dame Australia Law Review* 95, 106–110; and Kadelbach (n 48) 157, pointing to the case law of the Inter-American Court of Human Rights considering the right to life to be part of *jus cogens*. Otherwise, although the right to life is listed as non-derogable in art 4 of the International Covenant on Civil and Political Rights (ICCPR) (adopted 16 December 1966, in force 23 March 1976) (1966) 999 UNTS 171, the ILC observed: 'Nor would it be correct to say that a provision in a treaty possesses the character of *jus cogens* merely because the parties have stipulated that no derogation from that provision is to be permitted, so that another treaty which conflicted with that provision would be void. Such a stipulation may be inserted in any treaty with respect to any subject matter for any reasons which may seem good to the parties.' Commentary to art 50 (renumbered 53) (n 12) 248 [2]. See further Verhoeven (n 48) 146–50 [161–62]; Thomas Kleinlein, '*Jus Cogens* as the "Highest Law"? Peremptory Norms and Legal Hierarchies' (2015) 46 *Netherlands Yearbook of International Law* 173, 189–91; and Kimberley Trapp, 'Human Rights Exceptions', ch 17 in this volume, 312–321.

[111] Leben (n 4) 1197, 1202.

[112] ibid.

of torture, regarding which Article 2(2) of the Convention against Torture stipulates that: '*[n]o exceptional circumstances whatsoever*, whether a state of war or a threat of war, internal political instability or any other public emergency, *may be invoked as a justification of torture*.'[113] In a similar vein, the preamble of the Convention on the Elimination of Racial Discrimination states that its parties are: '[c]onvinced that any doctrine of superiority based on racial differentiation is scientifically false, morally condemnable, socially unjust and dangerous, and *that there is no justification for racial discrimination, in theory or in practice, anywhere*.'[114]

More particularly, the ILC itself adopted Article 26 of the ARSIWA, in which it is stipulated that: '[n]othing in this chapter precludes the wrongfulness of any act of a State which is not in conformity with an obligation arising under a peremptory norm of general international law.'[115] Only limited reference is made by the Commission to examples, one of which is that a counter-genocide cannot be justified as a countermeasure.[116] No further argument is to be found in the commentary as to the relationship between self-defence and the peremptory norm prohibiting aggression.[117]

The commentary does make reference to consent, indicating that one state cannot release another from obligations under peremptory norms, such as those related to genocide and torture.[118] However, it continues to observe that consent may at times be relevant for the application of peremptory norms, noting that a state may validly consent to 'a foreign military presence on its territory for a lawful purpose'.[119] Indeed, the prohibitions of the use of armed force and of intervention do not appear to stand in the way of a state consenting to an actual use of force on its territory.[120] Different legal constructions are possible to explain why consent to a 'foreign military presence' on a state's territory, or even an actual use of force by a foreign state within such territory, would not present any difficulty with respect to the peremptory prohibition. One explanation would be, discussed above, that the peremptory prohibition concerns aggression rather than the use of armed force more generally.

A second explanation might be that consent does not operate as a circumstance precluding wrongfulness, but rather constitutes an inherent element of any primary rule (a negative *P*-fact, in Duarte d'Almeida's perspective). Therefore, if consent is validly given, as Article 20 of the ARSIWA stipulates,[121] the rule would not apply in the first place and no obligation exists that could be violated. Clearly, this construction might explain why a foreign military presence or even an actual use of armed force on a state's territory would not fall

[113] Convention against Torture and Other Cruel, Inhuman or Degrading Treatment or Punishment (adopted 10 December 1984, in force 26 June 1987) (1984) 1465 UNTS 85 (emphasis added).

[114] International Convention on the Elimination of All Forms of Racial Discrimination (adopted 7 March 1966, in force 4 January 1969) (1966) 660 UNTS 195 (emphasis added).

[115] See also art 26 DARIO.

[116] Commentary to art 26 ARSIWA (n 95) 85 [4].

[117] If aggression were not to be qualified by gravity and purpose requirements, further argument would be necessary; however, even in such a case the ILC might cling to its view that action in self-defence 'is not, even potentially, in breach of Article 2, paragraph 4'. Commentary to art 21 ARSIWA (n 48) 74 [1].

[118] Commentary to art 26 ARSIWA (n 95) 85 [6].

[119] ibid; see also Commentary to art 20 ARSIWA (n 79) 73–74 [9].

[120] See James Crawford, 'Second Report on State Responsibility' (1999) 2(1) Yearbook of the International Law Commission 3, 63 [240(b)]; Affef Ben Mansour, 'Circumstances Precluding Wrongfulness in the ILC Articles on State Responsibility: Consent' in James Crawford, Alain Pellet, and Simon Olleson (eds), *The Law of International Responsibility* (OUP 2010) 439, 447, claiming that the practice related to consent suggests that the prohibition of the use of armed force is not peremptory in character; and Spiermann (n 4) 535. In *Armed Activities (Congo v Uganda)* (n 2) 196–97 [45–47], the Court found that consent had been given, but did not specifically examine its validity.

[121] As Vaughan Lowe, 'Precluding Wrongfulness or Responsibility: A Plea for Excuses' (1999) 10 European Journal of International Law 405, 407 observes: 'In a legal system based on consent, the binding force of a rule may be removed by the consent of the states concerned.'

foul of the peremptory prohibition. However, as Lowe has pointed out, this is based on the assumption that the law is a bilateral affair 'of concern only to the state that is the actor, and the state that is, as it were, acted upon—the "victim" state'.[122] As such, this construction could certainly not apply to peremptory norms which are human rights based—such as the prohibitions of genocide, slavery, racial discrimination, and torture—since these rules do not generally operate in the bilateral relations of states (even if at times foreign nationals may be affected, eventually allowing for the exercise of the right of diplomatic protection).

Although the commentary of the ILC to Article 20 affirms that consent may be given in advance,[123] issues arise with respect to intervention clauses in treaties.[124] Although the claim has been made that provisions establishing powers of armed intervention for international organizations do not contravene Article 26 of the ARSIWA and would not result in a 'coercive use of force',[125] this view has its difficulties. When consent is not provided in concrete circumstances, an armed intervention against a state might be resorted to without the agreement of its current government.[126] Indeed, the underlying purpose and main interpretative element of the prohibition of Article 2(4) of the Charter, through its reference to the purposes of the United Nations, concern the maintenance of international peace and security; the use of armed force without the contemporary assent of a state's government will invite (armed) opposition or even armed conflict and jeopardizes the achievement of this purpose.

A third explanation could be that when a state consents to the stationing of foreign troops in its territory, and in their use of force, this simply does not amount to a 'breach' of obligation under the prohibition of Article 2(4) of the Charter to begin with. Thus, as a use of force consented to by a state would neither be against the territorial integrity or political independence of that state, nor inconsistent with the UN's purposes, it would not be, in the words of Article 12 of the ARSIWA, 'not in conformity with what is required' by the obligation concerned.[127] Whether this argument pertains under customary international law may be open to doubt.

Before coming to a conclusion, it is to be noted that the circumstances precluding wrongfulness accepted under customary international law are general exceptions in that the preclusion of wrongfulness may, in principle, relate to any kind of conduct taking place in varied situations. This is different only for self-defence, which constitutes a specific exception, since that circumstance can only be invoked in response to qualified violations of the prohibition of the use of force and precludes the wrongfulness primarily of the use of armed force (rather than any other type of conduct).[128]

The distinction between general and specific exceptions is relevant because of the requirement stipulated in Article 53 of the VCLT that peremptory norms may be modified only by a

[122] ibid.

[123] Commentary to art 20 ARSIWA (n 79) 73 [3].

[124] Article 10 of the Protocol relating to the Mechanism for Conflict Prevention, Management, Resolution, Peace-Keeping and Security (adopted 10 December 1999) http://www.comm.ecowas.int/sec/index.php?id=ap101299&lang=en; see art 4(h) of the Constitutive Act of the Africa Union (adopted 11 July 2000, in force 26 May 2001) (2000) 2158 UNTS 3. See also art IV, second sentence of the 1960 Treaty of Guarantee (on Cyprus) (adopted 16 August 1960, in force 16 August 1960) (1960) 382 UNTS 3.

[125] Ademola Abass, 'Consent Precluding International Responsibility: A Critical Analysis' (2004) 53 The *International and Comparative Law Quarterly* 211, 223–24, claiming that a consensual use of force cannot pursue aggressive purposes (at 224) and that not every obligation under art 2(4) of the Charter is peremptory (at 225). See also Helmersen (n 4) 180–82, highlighting a distinction in this respect between permanent and ad hoc consent.

[126] In this sense see Corten(n 4) 254–55. For an example see e.g. Antenor Hallo de Wolf, 'Rattling Sabers to Save Democracy in The Gambia' *EJILTalk!* (1 February 2017) https://www.ejiltalk.org/rattling-sabers-to-save-democracy-in-the-gambia/.

[127] See de Hoogh, 'The "Armed Activities" Case' (n 35) 47–48.

[128] The distinction between general and specific exceptions was suggested earlier by this author. See de Hoogh '*Jus Cogens* and the Use of Armed Force' (n 4) 1165–70.

norm having the same character.[129] As none of the circumstances precluding wrongfulness, with the possible exception of self-defence, has the status of *jus cogens*,[130] this may provide some explanation as to why the ILC introduced Article 26 of the ARSIWA in the first place. Modification of a peremptory norm would appear to be at hand especially if a new exception were to limit the applicability of a *jus cogens* rule or if a new justification or excuse to such a rule were to be accepted. However, it is hard to see in what manner legal rights or faculties, such as those entailed by the circumstances precluding wrongfulness, would obtain the status of *jus cogens*.[131] As the main attribute of a peremptory norm is its non-derogability, this sits uneasily with the generally optional character of invoking and/or exercising rights or faculties.

This section has found that generally accepted circumstances precluding wrongfulness may not be invoked when the conduct concerned amounts to a breach of obligation under a peremptory norm, and that it is a characteristic of norms of *jus cogens* that they do not admit of justification. This finding is predicated upon the premise that *jus cogens* status is reserved to the prohibition of aggression, rather than the prohibition of the use of force, since its breach presupposes a level of gravity and malevolent purpose. Other, human rights based, peremptory norms similarly do not admit of justification.

5 Epilogue: Back to Derogation

Most rules of international law are in the nature of *jus dispositivum*, meaning that they may be displaced by states acting in their relations inter se.[132] As recounted above (section 1), the possibility of derogating from existing rules of international law is often described as the option of contracting out from those rules. At times, the foundation for this option is said to be the maxim *lex specialis derogat legi generali*,[133] although improperly so since the choice of states to replace a rule will regularly not be motivated by having tailor-made, special rules for their particular situation. Instead, they may rather prefer to have a radically different rule or perhaps even have no rule at all.[134]

To an extent this ties up with certain remarks by the ILC in its commentary on the provision that became Article 53, that peremptory norms block derogation 'even by agreement between particular States'.[135] Moreover, the Commission also considered that modification of a peremptory norm would most likely take place by 'general multilateral convention', subject to the condition that such a change could only take place by a later norm having peremptory character.[136] In the opinion of the Commission, such a general multilateral convention

129 Generally Orakhelashvili, *Peremptory Norms in International Law* (n 110) 127–30.

130 This may be verified also by reference to the Articles on the Responsibility of States, since arts 23(2)(b), 25(2)(a), and 50 envisage the possibility of excluding the invocability of certain circumstances. On self-defence as *jus cogens* see n 49 above.

131 See Paddeu, 'Clarifying the Concept of Circumstances Precluding Wrongfulness (Justifications) in International Law', ch 11 in this volume, 206, who considers circumstances precluding wrongfulness to constitute 'permissions of the legal order'.

132 Gerald Gray Fitzmaurice, 'Third Report on the Law of Treaties' (1958) 2 Yearbook of the International Law Commission 20, 40–41 [76]; Tladi, 'First Report' (n 3) 38–41 [64–66].

133 See Report of the Study Group of the International Law Commission, 'Fragmentation of International Law: Difficulties Arising from the Diversification and Expansion of International Law' A/CN.4/L.682 (13 April 2006) 44–46 [78]–[83]; *Nicaragua* (n 2) 137 [274]; and *North Sea Continental Shelf (Federal Republic of Germany v Denmark; Federal Republic of Germany v Netherlands)* (n 2) [72].

134 See de Hoogh, 'Regionalism and the Unity of International Law from a Positivist Perspective' (n 20) 58–9.

135 Commentary to art 50 (renumbered 53) (n 12) 248 [2 and 4].

136 ibid 248 [4].

would 'fall outside the scope of the article' (on *jus cogens*).[137] This then may be taken to support Helmersen's claim that exceptions operate as between all parties rather than between only some of them.[138] However, how is one to determine that a rule constitutes an exception, operating between all, rather than a prohibited derogation?

In order to justify the admissibility of exceptions to peremptory norms, perhaps something else, some kind of addition, needs to be read into the concept of derogation as embodied in Article 53 of the VCLT. Conceivably, an additional criterion might come to the rescue, namely whether the purported exception relates to an existing state of affairs, and hence would constitute a *mala fide* contracting out rather than instituting a new exception intended for future use and unrelated, as of yet, to any concrete circumstances. The point, then, would not be plain and simple that peremptory norms impose a restriction on the legal capacity of states to substitute an existing rule by a new one limited to a particular circle of states. Instead, rules of *jus cogens* would (only) bar states from legalizing conduct that would otherwise constitute an actual or intended violation of international law under a pre-existing rule of customary international law.

Of course, the Vienna Convention envisages this as a matter of (attempt at) derogation in treaty form, and specifies that the ensuing legal consequence—the treaty will be, or becomes, void—only occurs when a 'conflict' exists between the treaty and the peremptory norm concerned.[139] This feature then, that derogation encompasses not merely the displacement of a rule but also an attempted legalization of concrete conduct, may further explain, a fortiori, the limitation imposed in Article 26 of the ARSIWA that the wrongfulness of conduct will not be precluded if it is not in compliance with an obligation under a peremptory norm.

The ILC's commentary to an extent provides evidence of this when it clarifies that circumstances precluding wrongfulness 'do not authorize or excuse derogations from a peremptory norm'.[140] This suggests that, ordinarily, a circumstance precluding wrongfulness as an exception generally available to justify or excuse otherwise wrongful conduct would constitute a 'derogation' from a peremptory norm. As such, an exception generally available to states could only truly escape a charge of derogation if, as in Helmersen's construction, it were to limit the scope of applicability of the peremptory prohibition and the conduct covered under that exception would therefore fall outside that scope. Existing specific exceptions to the prohibition of the use of force, such as the right of self-defence and military action authorized by the Security Council, seem to avoid qualification as derogation.

New specific exceptions, whether to the prohibition of the use of force or other peremptory prohibitions, face difficult hurdles. First, under customary international law, states would have to act in violation of the peremptory prohibition concerned in order to generate

[137] ibid. Tladi, 'First Report' (n 3) 28 [55], takes this observation regarding multilateral treaties to indicate that multilateral treaties are excluded as a basis for *jus cogens* rules, since those must be norms of 'general international law'. An alternative reading here could be that such a multilateral treaty, intent upon modifying an existing *jus cogens* norm, would not fall foul of that norm. As such, the new multilateral treaty would not fall within the scope of the article, as ordinarily it would due to conflict with an existing peremptory norm.

[138] Helmersen (n 4) 175–76, but note that he also observes that '... derogations are specific acts or rules that diverge from and supplant the content of a more general rule. This is done by treaty or by consent.' See further Kleinlein (n 110) 191–93.

[139] On conflict of norms see Joost Pauwelyn, *Conflict of Norms in Public International Law: How WTO Law Relates to Other Rules of International Law* (CUP 2003) 164–88; Kammerhofer (n 16) 141–46; Robert Kolb, 'Conflits entre normes de jus cogens' in *Droit du pouvoir, pouvoir du droit: mélanges offerts à Jean Salmon* (Bruylant 2007) 481, 483; and François Boudreault, 'Identifying Conflicts of Norms: The ICJ Approach in the Case of the *Jurisdictional Immunities of the State (Germany* v. *Italy: Greece Intervening)*' (2012) 25 *Leiden Journal of International Law* 1003.

[140] Commentary to art 26 ARSIWA (n 95) 85 [4].

state practice forming the nucleus of a possible new exception. For rules in the nature of *jus dispositivum* this is a process that is perfectly possible, for as the Court observed in *Nicaragua* 'reliance on a novel right or unprecedented exception to the principle' of non-intervention could lead to a change in customary international law 'if shared in principle by other States'.[141] However, such examples of state practice would violate existing rules and one should probably expect an overall negative response by other states when peremptory prohibitions are at stake.[142]

Secondly, since exceptions may be regarded as derogations, this would entail that the exception must have *jus cogens* status in view of the requirement stipulated in Article 53 of the VCLT that a peremptory norm may only be modified by another norm having the same character. This is, as recounted above, a rather difficult legal construction, considering that exceptions tend to offer rights or faculties to engage in certain conduct and it remains unclear how such a right or faculty would constitute compelling law or not admit of derogation.[143] Even though at times the right of self-defence is considered to also constitute a *jus cogens* rule in order to account for a possible derogation from the prohibition of the use of force,[144] other legal constructions appear more convincing, such as considering the peremptory prohibition to relate to aggression rather than the use of force generally. This then leaves, as the ILC suggested, possible modification by introducing an exception to a peremptory norm by way of general multilateral convention; of course, in such a case, the grant of *jus cogens* status for a new exception to an existing peremptory norm would have to be in explicit terms.

5.1 Concluding observations

The current contribution has explored the extent to which peremptory norms may be subjected to exceptions, considering that Article 53 of the VCLT stipulates that peremptory norms do not permit of derogation. Prime among the discussion has been the prohibition of the use of force in international relations, since that prohibition admits certain accepted exceptions—in particular, self-defence, Security Council authorization, and consent. Different legal constructions may be entertained to explain the exceptions of the right of

[141] *Nicaragua* (n 2) 108–109 [207]. The Court also observed, 98 [186], that '[i]f a State acts in a way prima facie incompatible with a recognized rule, but defends its conduct by appealing to exceptions or justifications contained within the rule itself, then whether or not the State's conduct is in fact justifiable on that basis, the significance of that attitude is to confirm rather than to weaken the rule.'

[142] Compare the observation by Orakhelashvili, 'Changing *Jus* Cogens through State Practice' (n 4) 174–75, that '[c]laims in favour of extra-Charter exceptions have always been incoherent to constitute valid state practice for purposes of custom-creation, and has fallen short of commanding he support of states to produce an amending peremptory norm under Article 53 VCLT. All this practice has been fragmented and not general; or inconsistent in relation to the same state, same incident, or as between multiple states; or it has consolidated within a group of states but has been rebuffed by the rest of the community of states.' See also Linderfalk, 'The Effect of *Jus Cogens* Norms' (n 4) 862–63 and 864–67; and Cezary Mik, 'Jus Cogens in Contemporary International Law' (2013) 33 *Polish Yearbook of International Law* 27, 42–45.

[143] Kleinlein (n 110) 192, pertinently observes in this respect (footnotes omitted): 'In order to establish a genuine conflict and a substantial hierarchy between *jus cogens* and state immunity, a peremptory norm would need to create a positive obligation, for instance, to put torturers on trial or to compensate torture victims. However, this would need to be demonstrated. It should not be taken for granted that *jus cogens* demands 'affirmative action'. Even if positive obligations to enforce the prohibition existed, it could be questioned whether they share the peremptory status. Rather, the peremptory character may be limited to the so-called negative obligations of states.' See also Cathryn Costello and Michelle Foster, 'Non-Refoulement as Custom and *Jus Cogens*? Putting the Prohibition to the Test' (2015) 46 *Netherlands Yearbook of International Law* 273, 322–23.

[144] Orakhelashvili, 'Changing *Jus* Cogens through State Practice' (n 4) 165. See further discussion by Green, 'Questioning the Peremptory Status of the Prohibition of the Use of Force' (n 4) 229–36.

self-defence, recourse to force pursuant to an authorization by the Security Council or pursuant to consent of the territorial state in terms of their compatibility with the peremptory prohibition of the use of force.

One particular legal construction is to see exceptions as limiting the scope of applicability of the general rule, which would therefore mean that conduct covered by an exception is consequently removed from that scope and for that reason does not constitute derogation from an existing peremptory norm. Although the construction is logically coherent, an interpretation and analysis of positive international law regarding the regulation of the use of armed force does not (fully) support it. As such, it does not provide an adequate explanation as to the legal admissibility of exceptions to peremptory prohibitions.

Alternatively, the exceptions to the prohibitions of the use of force could be explained by instead considering only part of that prohibition to have obtained *jus cogens* status. In this respect, it has been noted that although ILC in its commentary on the law of treaties referred to the prohibition of the use of force, later on in its commentaries on the law of responsibility it has consistently referenced the prohibition of aggression. Thus, if aggression were to be seen and interpreted more narrowly than the use of armed force generally, for instance by imposing gravity and purpose requirements, this could be taken to support the proposition that *jus cogens* prohibitions are absolute in character and do not permit of exceptions. Existing exceptions would then be considered not to fall foul of the peremptory prohibition, since conduct covered by such exceptions could not be qualified as aggression.

Setting aside the problematic of self-defence, other circumstances precluding wrongfulness are considered as exceptions generally available in relation to conduct that would otherwise have to be qualified as internationally wrongful. The ILC has specified in Article 26 of the ARSIWA that such circumstances do not preclude the wrongfulness of conduct that is not in conformity with a peremptory norm. Its commentary to that provision suggests that invoking a circumstance precluding wrongfulness in relation to conduct covered by a *jus cogens* rule does amount to derogation (excepting consent in relation to the prohibition of the use of force).

A final, viable legal construction could be to interpret the word derogation restrictively, not merely to bar displacement between particular states of a peremptory norm by another rule. Instead, derogation would occur only if this substitution were to result from a desire and intention to legalize unlawful conduct already underway or contemplated for the near future. However, introducing new exceptions to peremptory norms through the process of customary international law will come up against two important hurdles. First, states would have to engage in practice in violation of the peremptory prohibition concerned and such practice is unlikely to meet with favourable responses from other states. Secondly, a new exception, as a modification of an existing peremptory norm, would have to be accorded *jus cogens* status itself. To overcome such formidable hurdles, one would almost inevitably have to have recourse, as the ILC suggested, to the process of drafting a multilateral treaty open to all states. A tall order indeed, both politically and legally.

9
Exceptions
Self-defence as an Exception to the Prohibition on the Use of Force

*Iain Scobbie**

1 The Normality of the Use of Armed Force before the Twentieth Century—War as Natural, Noble, and Necessary

Just war theories stretch back into antiquity but, from a Western perspective, reached their apex in Scholastic Roman Catholic theology of the late fifteenth and early sixteenth centuries, exemplified in the work of authors such as St Thomas Aquinas, Francisco de Vitoria, and Francisco Suárez, and subsequently in the ostensibly more secular natural law of Grotius.[1] Just war theories did not aim at the elimination of war as a legitimate international activity, but only tried to put constraints on its outbreak—'for where judicial settlement fails, war begins'.[2] Before the twentieth century, recourse to armed force was not seen as exceptional in international relations, but accepted as a normal part of the affairs of state. It was seen as natural, noble, and necessary.

Some social theorists, for example, Adam Ferguson, who was one of the leading figures of the Scottish Enlightenment in the eighteenth century, were convinced that war could be creative as well as destructive, as conflict could play a beneficial role in both the development of social institutions and of individuals,[3] as 'he who has never struggled with his fellow-creatures, is a stranger to half the sentiments of mankind'.[4] Alexander Broadie ascribed this belief to Ferguson's nine years' service as a chaplain to the Black Watch regiment, and his

* Professor of Public International Law and Co-Director of the Manchester International Law Centre, University of Manchester.

[1] For overviews of these theories see e.g. David Bederman, *International Law in Antiquity* (Cambridge University Press 2001) 208–27; Robert J Delahunty and John Yoo, 'From Just War to False Peace' (2012–2013) 13 Chicago Journal of International Law 1; GIAD Draper, 'The Interaction of Christianity and Chivalry in the Historic Development of the Law of War' (1965) 46 International Review of the Red Cross 3, and his 'The Origins of the Just War Tradition' 'The Christian and War' 'Penitential Discipline and Public Wars in the Middle Ages' and 'Grotius' Place in the Development of Legal Ideas about War' in Michael A Meyer and Hilaire McCoubrey (eds), *Reflections on Law and Armed Conflicts: The Selected Works on the Laws of War by the Late Professor Colonel GIAD Draper, OBE* (Kluwer 1998); the paper on Grotius is more readily available in Hedley Bull, Benedict Kingsbury, and Adam Roberts (eds), *Hugo Grotius and International Relations* (Clarendon Press 1992) 177; Arthur Nussbaum, 'Just War—a Legal Concept?' (1943) 42 Michigan Law Review 453; Mary Ellen O'Connell, 'Peace and War' in Bardo Fassbender and Anne Peters (eds), *The Oxford Handbook of the History of International Law* (Oxford University Press 2012) 272, 273–77; and Ivo Rens, 'Grotius et la Doctrine Traditionnelle de la "Guerre Juste"' in Alfred Dufour, Peter Haggenmacher, and Jiří Toman (eds), *Grotius et l'Ordre Juridique International* (Payot 1985) 67.

[2] Grotius, *De Iure Belli ac Pacis* [*The Rights of War and Peace*] (1625, Richard Tuck (ed), Liberty Fund 2005) Bk II, ch 1, § 2.

[3] See Adam Ferguson, *An Essay on the History of Civil Society* (1767, Duncan Forbes (ed), Edinburgh University Press 1966) xvii–xix (introduction by Forbes).

[4] ibid Pt I, §iv, 'Of the Principles of War and Dissension' 24.

Iain Scobbie, *Exceptions* In: *Exceptions in International Law*. Edited by: Lorand Bartels and Federica Paddeu, Oxford University Press (2020). © Lorand Bartels and Federica Paddeu. DOI: 10.1093/oso/9780198789321.003.0009

view that responsibility for national security should lie with the population as a whole, and not merely a professional military class.[5]

In common with other Scottish Enlightenment figures, Ferguson denied both the existence of a utopian state of nature which preceded the formation of human societies and the foundational postulate of a social contract.[6] Societies were simply a matter of fact: 'Mankind are to be taken in groupes, as they have always subsisted.'[7] This was a question of human instinct, as mankind: 'has one set of dispositions which refer to his animal preservations, and to the continuance of his race; another which lead to society, and by inlisting him on the side of one tribe or community, frequently engage him in war and contention with the rest of mankind.'[8]

For Ferguson, conflict between human groups was simply natural—'the frequent wars, or rather the perpetual hostilities, which take place among rude nations and separate clans, discover how much our species is disposed to opposition, as well as to concert.'[9] War and conflict, however, can encourage virtue—such as the warrior's self-denial in defence of his country—but may also have a generative function:

> Without the rivalship of nations, and the practice of war, civil society itself could scarcely have found an object, or a form. Mankind might have traded without any formal convention, but they cannot be safe without a national concert. The necessity of a public defence, has given rise to many departments of state . . .[10]

Thus, Ferguson considered that, in the nature of things, although war was unavoidable it could bring benefits to societies. External threats provided the impetus for the formation of societies, and a reason for social cohesion, as the perception of a common danger united a society, suppressed internal dissent, and maintained social peace.[11]

Some viewed war not simply as natural, but also as noble. For instance, James Lorimer recounted a letter written by Helmuth von Moltke, who was chief of staff of the Prussian Army for thirty years from 1857, when he received a copy of the 1880 *Oxford Manual of the Laws of War*.[12] In terms reminiscent of Ferguson, von Moltke wrote:

> Perpetual peace is a dream, and is not even a beautiful dream. War is an element in the order of the world ordained by God. In it the noblest virtues of mankind are developed: courage and the abnegation of self, faithfulness to duty, and the spirit of sacrifice: the soldier gives his life. Without war the world would stagnate and lose itself in materialism.[13]

[5] Alexander Broadie, 'Adam Ferguson, Classical Republicanism and the Imperative of Modernity' in Neil Walker (ed), *MacCormick's Scotland* (Edinburgh University Press 2012) 107, 119–21.

[6] For a 'classic' overview of the approach of Scottish Enlightenment writers on this matter see Gladys Bryson, *Man and Society: the Scottish Inquiry of the Eighteenth Century* (Princeton University Press 1945) ch 6.

[7] Ferguson (n 3) Pt I, §i, 'Of the Question Relating to the State of Nature' 4.

[8] ibid Pt I, §ii, 'Of the Principles of Self-Preservation' 11.

[9] ibid Pt I, §iv, 21.

[10] ibid Pt I, §iv, 24.

[11] ibid Pt I, §iv, 24; and also Pt II, §iii, 'Of Rude Nations under the Impression of Property and Interests' 104.

[12] The manual was drafted by Gustave Moynier and adopted unanimously by the Institut de Droit International https://www.icrc.org/ihl/INTRO/140?OpenDocument.

[13] Helmuth Karl Bernhard Graf von Moltke, as quoted in James Lorimer, *The Institutes of the Law of Nations, vol II* (Blackwood 1884, facsimile reprint Elibron Classics 2006) 22.

On this Lorimer cuttingly remarked: 'How does Count von Moltke explain the fact that materialism has flourished in Germany, since his two great wars, as it never did at any previous period of the intellectual life of his country?'[14]

While von Moltke's claim that war is consecrated by God stands in stark contrast with theological just war theories, it was very much in the spirit of the times, exemplified a century earlier in the work of Emmerich de Vattel, who made the decisive break with just war theories and argued that war was necessary—'Vattel's entire discussion of the subject brings home the degeneration of the inherited doctrine'.[15] The Vattellian tradition emphasized the state as the primary actor and bearer of values in international relations, and the pre-eminent values were those that concerned the state. This is manifest in the text of *Droit de Gens*,[16] where Vattel emphasized that it is the duty of the sovereign to protect the state's interests:

> Every one is at liberty to recede from his right, to relinquish a just subject of complaint, and to forget an injury. But the ruler of a nation is not, in this respect, so free as a private individual... The representative of a nation, the sovereign, must not consult his own gratification, or suffer himself to be guided by his private inclinations. All his actions must be directed to the greatest advantage of the state... The rights of the nation are a property of which the sovereign is only the trustee; and he ought not to dispose of them in any other manner than he has reason to presume the nation herself would dispose of them.[17]

If a dispute threatened an essential right of the state, then any thought of resort to a peaceful mode of dispute settlement was redundant and the state 'will, in such a quarrel, exert her utmost efforts, exhaust every resource, and gloriously lavish her blood to the last drop if necessary... and if fortune prove unfavourable, a free people will prefer death to servitude'.[18] Vattel was clear that the state was essentially at liberty to determine if it considered a dispute threatened or encroached upon its essential interests and whether it should resort to war in their defence:

> it belongs to each nation to judge whether her situation will admit of pacific measures, before she has recourse to arms. Now, as the voluntary law of nations ordains, that, for these reasons, we should esteem lawful whatever a nation thinks proper to do in virtue of her natural liberty... by that same voluntary law, nations are bound to consider as lawful the conduct of that power who suddenly takes up arms in a doubtful cause, and attempts to force his enemy to come to terms, without having previously tried pacific measures.[19]

Although Grotius and other traditional just war theorists tried to limit resort to war, Vattel effectively threw off any shackles that just war theories sought to impose, despite paying lip service to the idea.[20] For Vattel, each state possessed autonomy and sovereignty, which

[14] Lorimer, *Institutes* (n 13) Vol II, 22 n 1.
[15] Nussbaum (n 1) 471.
[16] Emmerich de Vattel, *Droit des Gens: ou, Principes de la Loi Naturelle Appliqués à la Conduite et aux Affaires des Nations et des Souverains* (1758). The edition used, edited by Béla Kapossy and Richard Whatmore, is based on the 1797 English translation, *The Law of Nations, or the Principles of Natural Law Applied to the Conduct and to the Affairs of Nations and of Sovereigns* (Liberty Fund 2008).
[17] Vattel (n 16) Bk II, 'Of a Nation Considered in its Relations to Others' ch xviii, 'Of the Mode of Terminating Disputes Between Nations' §325.
[18] ibid Bk II, xviii, § 332.
[19] ibid xviii, § 335.
[20] ibid Bk III, 'Of war' ch iii, 'Of the Just Causes of War'.

carried with them the necessity to prosecute its perceived national and vital interests through the use of force as it thought fit. Like Ferguson, Vattel thought that the unity and survival of the state required, in principle, the inclusion of the whole population in the conduct of war as 'society cannot otherwise be maintained; and this concurrence for the common defence is one of the principal objects of every political association'.[21]

In *Perpetual Peace*, Immanuel Kant complained that 'Grotius, Pufendorf, Vattel and the rest (sorry comforters that they are) are still dutifully quoted in *justification* of military aggression', even though their arguments had no legal force because states were 'not subject to a common external constraint'.[22] He did not differentiate between the ambiguities and malleabilities of just war theories and the realism (or perhaps cynicism) of Vattel in the relative efficacy of their ability to constrain war, and saw them as inimical to his goal of perpetual peace. But Vattel's perspective on war proved to be more influential during the nineteenth century. Philip Allott claimed that Vattel's *Droit des gens*: 'was on the desk of every diplomat for a century or more. It was a book which formed the minds of those who formed international reality, the international reality which is still our reality today'.[23]

Allott argued that Vattel supplied the philosophical foundations of 'international unsociety', a morality-free world governed by and tailored to the interests of states, or perhaps more accurately to the interests of ruling national élites (the *hofmafia*),[24] rather than to the interests of humanity as a whole, 'a state of nature of the most exciting kind, in which the survival of the fittest is decided by an intoxicating mixture of urbane diplomacy and mass murder'.[25]

2 Collective Security, War, and Armed Conflict

In contrast, the doctrine of collective security—the rejection of war as an inevitable aspect of international affairs, as a phenomenon that was neither natural, noble, nor necessary—is a relatively recent development. In the aftermath of the First World War, the 'war to end all wars', this crystallized the desires of popular peace movements which had sought to replace the use of armed force as a method of settling international disputes with recourse to law and international adjudication.[26]

[21] ibid Bk III, ch ii, 'Of the Instruments of War—the Raising of Troops, &c,—their Commanders, or the Subordinate Powers in War' § 8.

[22] Immanuel Kant, *Perpetual Peace: a Philosophical Sketch* [*Kant's Political Writings*] (1795, Hans Reiss (ed), (Cambridge University Press 1970) Second Definitive Article 93, 103.

[23] Philip J Allott, *The Health of Nations: Society and Law Beyond the State* (Cambridge University Press 2002) 416, §14.45.

[24] ibid ch 13, 'International Law and the International Hofmafia' and also his *Towards the International Rule of Law: Essays in Integrated Constitutional Theory* (Cameron May 2005) ch 8, 'The Emerging International Aristocracy'. The term *hofmafia* is drawn from the diplomatic machinations of royal and aristocratic courts and translates as 'court-mafia'; see Allott (n 23) 384, §13.9.

[25] Allott (n 23) 295, §10.11.

[26] See e.g. Ruhl J Bartlett, *The League to Enforce Peace* (University of North Carolina Press 1944) chs 1–4; Donald S Birn, *The League of Nations Union 1918–1945* (Clarendon Press 1981) ch 1; and on the point of international judicial process in particular, David D Caron, 'War and International Adjudication: Reflections on the 1899 Peace Conference' (2000) 94 American Journal of International Law 4; Mark W Janis, 'Protestants, Progress and Peace: Enthusiasm for an International Court in Early Nineteenth-Century America' in Mark W Janis (ed), *The Influence of Religion on the Development of International Law* (Nijhoff 1991) 223, and *The American Tradition of International Law: Great Expectations 1789–1914* (Oxford University Press 2004) 94–116 and 134–54, and his *America and the Law of Nations 1776-1939* (Oxford University Press 2010) ch 4; Cecelia Lynch, 'Peace Movements, Civil Society, and the Development of International Law' in Bardo Fassbender and Anne Peters (eds), *The Oxford Handbook of the History of International Law* (Oxford University Press 2012) 198; and Michla Pomerance, *The United States and the World Court as a 'Supreme Court of the Nations': Dreams, Illusions and Disillusion* (Nijhoff 1996) ch 1.

George Egerton has described the doctrine of collective security as 'the central myth of the twentieth century liberal internationalist ideology'.[27] Egerton does not use 'myth' as a term with pejorative connotations, or to denote something fictitious; rather, a 'myth' is a notion that encapsulates and communicates an underlying political ideology, its values, and beliefs. In the aftermath of the First World War the myth of collective security was fashioned as the cornerstone of the League of Nations system as only this, an apparent guarantee of peace, could ascribe sense and value to the privations suffered during the war. The League was seen as 'a cause, perhaps the only cause, capable of giving satisfying moral and ideological direction in the wake of the Great War and its personal and social tragedies'.[28] The necessity to create a League as an integral part of the post-First World War settlement in order to restructure the international system, bolster international peace, and promote the spread of democracy was central to United States' President Wilson's vision for peace-making, even before the United States entered into the war.[29] Wilson's 'sense of personal responsibility ... transformed him into a passionate believer in the absolute necessity of transforming international law and organization and make it the principal justification for the loss of life of the Great War'.[30] The primordial importance of the League in this scheme was underlined in a letter from United States Supreme Court Justice John Hessin Clarke to Wilson in November 1919. He wrote that, if it were not created, 'the sacrifices of the great war will have been, in large measure, made in vain'.[31] Egerton sees this desire as the international projection of a myth associated with classical liberalism, the myth of the social contract—that 'the natural state of anarchy and war would be ended by consensual structuring of an international political and legal order'.[32]

The League, of course, did not prohibit recourse to armed force in international relations but merely placed restraints on resort to war.[33] Only in 1928, in the Pact of Paris, did states agree to 'renounce [war] as an instrument of national policy',[34] but this did not dispel ideas about the persistent normality of warfare. Writing during the Second World War in 1943, Georg Schwarzenberger commented: 'For a generation which has witnessed two World Wars in its lifetime, the assumption of peace as the normal state of international relations is much more problematical'[35] because:

> In a system of power politics, war is not an unhappy incident or an incalculable catastrophe, but the culminating point in a rising scale of pressure, the last resort of power

[27] George W Egerton, 'Great Britain and the League of Nations: Collective Security as Myth and History' in UN Library/Graduate Institute of International Studies, *The League of Nations in Retrospect: Proceedings of the Symposium* (de Gruyter 1983) 95, 96.

[28] George W Egerton, 'Collective Security as Political Myth: Liberal Internationalism and the League of Nations in Politics and History' (1983) 5 The International History Review 496, 506.

[29] On President Wilson's vision see Thomas J Knock, *To End All Wars: Woodrow Wilson and the Quest for a New World Order* (Oxford University Press 1992) *passim*, but especially at 95–98, ch 7, 123–28, 148–54, 160–66, 189–93, ch 11 and ch 12: see also Leonard V Smith, 'The Wilsonian Challenge to International Law' (2011) 13 Journal of the History of International Law 179.

[30] Janis, *America and the Law of Nations* (n 26) 173; see 167–75 generally: see also e.g. Knock (n 29) 193 and 262.

[31] Quoted in Knock (n 29) 190.

[32] Egerton, 'Collective Security' (n 28) 502; and 'Great Britain' (n 27) 98.

[33] See arts 11, 12, and 16 of the Covenant of the League of Nations.

[34] Article 1 of the 1928 General Treaty for the Renunciation of War—also known as the Kellogg-Briand Pact or Pact of Paris—94 League of Nations Treaty Series 57. For a survey of the development of the prohibition on the use of force by States in international relations from the conclusion of the Covenant to the conclusion of the Charter see Ian Brownlie, *International Law and the Use of Force by States* (Clarendon Press 1963), chs 4 and 5.

[35] Georg Schwarzenberger, 'Jus Pacis ac Belli? Prolegomena to a Sociology of International Law' (1943) 37 American Journal of International Law 460, 466.

> politics when diplomacy fails to achieve its objects by the threat of force or the application of less drastic forms of pressure.[36]

This reflects Schwarzenberger's rejection of idealist natural law doctrine where peace was seen as the normal state of affairs which was secured by just war doctrine. He denied that this was the case,[37] and claimed that peace 'is nothing but the interval between the dynamic periods in which previous systems of power politics undergo a process of confirmation or transformation'. As peace was the result of force, force was necessary to uphold the peace, and so he concluded that there was no intrinsic difference between peace and war.[38]

The contemporary formulation of collective security, however, reaches further than acts of 'war' as Article 2(4) of the UN Charter prohibits any 'threat or use of force against the territorial integrity or political independence of any State, or in any other manner inconsistent with the Purposes of the United Nations'. This was underpinned by a similar concern to ensure international peace. The preamble to the Charter expressly declares the desire 'to save succeeding generations from the scourge of war, which twice in our lifetime has brought untold sorrow to mankind'.

This aim was underlined in the award in the *Dalmai Cement* case,[39] which arose as a result of hostilities between India and Pakistan in September 1965. Although no formal declaration of war had been made during the initial phase of the conflict in Kashmir, nor when India subsequently attacked Pakistan, the President of Pakistan stated on the radio that it was at war with India, and then the Indian Prime Minister claimed that the situation was one of 'full-scale war', although this claim was later withdrawn.[40] Pierre Lalive, the sole arbiter in an International Chamber of Commerce Arbitral Tribunal, affirmed the view that not all armed conflicts constitute 'war', and that hostile acts did not necessarily amount to 'war' in the legal sense.[41] He erected an effective presumption against the outbreak of 'war' by holding that the fact that the opposing parties to the conflict were United Nations Members was significant. Lalive ruled that their obligations under the Charter were relevant as to whether a state of war existed:

> This minimum effect [of United Nations Membership] may be described as follows: in case of doubt as to the answer to be given to that question [whether a state of war existed], the answer should be negative rather than affirmative, for the existence of a state of war can certainly not be presumed between Members of the [United Nations]. On the contrary, it must be presumed, *in dubio*, that each Member State, if and when it is using force, intends to use it in a manner which is consistent with its obligations under the Charter (especially under Article 2(4)).

Lalive held that it followed that if United Nations members must be presumed not to use force in breach of the Charter, a fortiori they must be presumed not to intend to resort to war,

[36] ibid 466.
[37] ibid' 465–67.
[38] ibid' 479.
[39] *Dalmai Cement Ltd v National Bank of Pakistan (Jurisdiction Judgment)* (1976) 67 ILR 611.
[40] For a summary account of these events see Arnold D McNair and Arthur D Watts, *The Legal Effects of War* (Cambridge University Press 1966, 4th edn) 457–458; and Christopher Greenwood, 'The Concept of War in Modern International Law' (1987) 36 International and Comparative Law Quarterly 283, 292–293.
[41] *Dalmai Cement Ltd v National Bank of Pakistan (Jurisdiction Judgment)* (n 39) 611 at 615, para 7: here, Lalive expressly adopted as authoritative the position set out in ch 1 of McNair and Watts (n 42).

and that the President of Pakistan's reference to 'war' in his radio broadcast should not be interpreted as referring to war in a technical legal sense.[42]

The exact contours of the Article 2(4) prohibition on the use of force are, however, notoriously contested,[43] as are those of its purported principal exception, the right to self-defence enshrined in Article 51 of the Charter,[44] which provides in part: 'Nothing in the present Charter shall impair the inherent right of individual or collective self-defence if an armed attack occurs against a Member of the United Nations, until the Security Council has taken measures necessary to maintain international peace and security.'

Notions of collective security and self-defence have, however, mutated through time, responding to states' changing security concerns. In particular, since 1945, an evident shift has been from concerns arising from threats of inter-state violence to the suppression of perceived threats against established domestic or regional political orders arising from 'terrorism' and acts of organized non-state armed groups. This change in focus raises an acute question: if self-defence is an exception to the general prohibition on the use of force imposed by international law, what are its proper parameters?

3 When Is the Use of Armed Force by a State Justified as an Exception?

3.1 The nature of exceptions

A prior question that must be addressed is the conceptual or analytical nature of an exception to a 'rule'. Various explanations are given in this volume. For example, Valentin Jeutner defines rules as legal norms which provide a default framework for the legal classification of a given act. An exception is a norm that provides for a deviation from a default classification in specified circumstances and the substitution of an alternative classification.[45] Robert Kolb offers a different explanation, distinguishing between derogations and exceptions. A derogation arises when a general rule of international law is replaced by another rule which governs

[42] *Dalmai Cement Ltd v National Bank of Pakistan (Jurisdiction Judgment)* (n 39) 619–20, paras 25–27: quotation at 619, para 27. For a discussion of the problem of defining 'war' in a technical or legal sense see Iain Scobbie, 'War' in Jean d'Aspremont and Sahib Singh (eds), *Concepts for International Law—Contributions to Disciplinary Thought* (Edward Elgar Publishing 2019).

[43] The literature on this is voluminous, but see e.g. Albrecht Randelzhofer and Oliver Dörr, 'Commentary to Article 2(4)' in Bruno Simma, Daniel-Erasmus Khan, Georg Nolte, and Andreas Paulus (eds), *The Charter of the United Nations: a Commentary, vol I* (3rd edn, Oxford University Press 2012) 200; Brownlie (n 34); Thomas M Franck, 'Who Killed Article 2(4)? Or, Changing Norms Governing the Use of Force by States' (1970) 64 American Journal of International Law 809, and his *Recourse to Force: State Action Against Threats and Armed Attacks* (Cambridge University Press 2002); Christine Gray, *International Law and the Use of Force* (3rd edn, Oxford University Press 2008); David McKeever, 'The Contribution of the International Court of Justice to the Law on the Use of Force: Missed Opportunities or Unrealistic Expectations?' (2009) 78 Nordic Journal of International Law 361; and Tom Ruys, 'The Meaning of "Force" and the Boundaries of the *Jus ad Bellum*: Are Minimal Uses of "Force" Excluded from UN Charter Article 2(4)?' (2014) 108 American Journal of International Law 159.

[44] Again, the literature is voluminous. See e.g. Albrecht Randelzhofer and Georg Nolte, 'Commentary to Article 51' in Bruno Simma, Daniel-Erasmus Khan, Georg Nolte, and Andreas Paulus (eds), *The Charter of the United Nations: a Commentary, vol II* (3rd edn, Oxford University Press 2012) 1396, 1414–19, paras 31–41; Derek W Bowett, *Self-Defence in International Law* (Manchester University Press 1958); James A Green, *The International Court of Justice and Self-Defence in International Law* (Hart Publishing 2009); Tom Ruys, *'Armed Attack' and Article 51 of the UN Charter* (Cambridge University Press 2010); Iain Scobbie, 'Words My Mother Never Taught Me: "In Defense of the International Court"' (2005) 99 American Journal of International Law 76; and Kinga Tibori Szabó, *Anticipatory Action in Self-Defence: Essence and Limits under International Law* (TMC Asser Press 2011).

[45] Valentin Jeutner, 'Both the Rule and the Exception: the Concept of a Legal Dilemma and the Survival of the State': Chapter 13.

the legal relationships existing between a restricted set of parties.[46] The latter only determines these parties' relationships inter se, leaving unaffected the continued legal validity of the general rule in all other relationships. If the category of exceptions is construed widely, it may encompass derogations because the essence of an exception is that there are circumstances when a rule does not apply, but still remains formally in force. More narrowly, the term 'exception' indicates that a rule, while formally valid, will not apply because another rule 'carves out from it',[47] or limits the scope of its application. Kolb comments that this is not an interplay between a general rule and a more specialist one which applies inter partes between specific actors, although substantively the exception may be narrower or more specialized *ratione materiae*.[48]

Jaap Hage, Antonia Waltermann, and Gustavo Arosemena adhere to a similar core concept to that of Jeutner and Kolb: an exception occurs when a rule is applicable to a situation but is nevertheless not applied and yet remains legally valid. Adopting an argumentative framework, they posit the notion of contributory reasons: reasons which either argue for or against a given conclusion. If a rule is applicable to a case, then this is a contributory reason for applying it, but an exception may arise if the application of the rule is thought to give rise to undesirable consequences because this would either violate its purpose; or lead to legal consequences which are incompatible with the consequences of another applicable rule (rule conflict); or harm values or goals that were not or insufficiently taken into account when the rule was created.

Hage, Waltermann, and Arosemena also propose the notion of a 'derived rule', where an apparent conflict between rules is removed by reformulating them into one rule, thus removing an exception. They give the example that the perceived conflict between Articles 2(4) and 42 of the UN Charter, the blanket prohibition of the use of force and the lawful use of force authorized by the Security Council, may be removed by reformulation, namely that the use of force is prohibited unless authorized by the Security Council. This derived rule avoids the need to invoke an exception as the prohibition is not applicable if the Security Council has authorized force: 'If a rule seems to have an exception, why not say that the rule was not formulated properly, and that it actually has an additional condition namely that the exceptional circumstances are absent?'[49]

Nevertheless Hage, Waltermann, and Arosemena continue that while the notion of derived rules allows for syllogistic legal reasoning, the consequent eradication of exceptions neglects an important function of exceptions, namely the distribution of the burden of proof within an argument. They argue that the syllogistic model of legal argument should be replaced with a view of the legal system as a dialogic practice between the parties who offer reasons why a given rule should or not should apply in a given situation. They note that there are three possible outcomes once the parties have adduced their reasons: the reasons for application of the rule outweigh the reasons against; the reasons against application outweigh the reasons for; or the reasons for and against balance each other out. The burden of proof is critical in the third situation, which:

[46] For an alternative explanation of derogation in the context of international human rights law treaties see Jorge E Viñuales, 'Seven Ways of Escaping a Rule: Of Exceptions and their Avatars in International Law' §1.5: Chapter 5.

[47] On 'carve-outs' see ibid §1.3. Chapter 5.

[48] Robert Kolb, 'The Construction of the *Rebis Sic Stantibus* Clause in Different Phases of International Law—Exception, Rule or Remote Spectator?' Chapter 15.

[49] Jaap Hage, Antonio Waltermann, and Gustavo Arosemena, 'Logical Tools for International Law' s 10: Chapter 2.

> should either lead to an outcome that favours the proponent, or to an outcome that favours the opponent. In the former case we say that the burden of proof lies with the opponent, because if the opponent does not want the rule to apply, he must make sure that the balance of reasons does not end in a draw. In the latter case we say that the burden of proof lies with the proponent, because then the proponent has an interest in avoiding a draw in the balance of reasons.[50]

The burden of argument shifts as the preponderant weight of argument shifts. The connection between exceptions and the burden of proof cannot be captured if exceptions are abolished by seeing the legal system in terms of derived rules.

While these accounts of exceptions have some utility, they lack a close engagement with analytical concerns regarding legal system structure. It is arguable that these explanations are predicated on an inadequate deontic array because they focus on 'rules', but other elements of a legal system might also be relevant in the construction of 'exceptions'. Exceptions to the operation of rules could conceivably arise from the influence of a principle of general application or from the existence of a countervailing legal relationship peculiar to two or between a restricted group of states.

While the latter seems self-evident, and arises simply as a result of the predominantly *ius dispositivum* structure of international law (although Kolb would see this as a derogation than an exception), the former might require demonstration. Consider the normative function of the principle of self-determination in moulding aspects of the law of armed conflict in the late 1970s. Article 1(4) of the 1977 Additional Protocol I to the1949 Geneva Conventions provides that its application, and consequently the application of the Geneva Conventions themselves, encompasses wars of national liberation, namely: 'armed conflicts in which peoples are fighting against colonial domination and alien occupation and against racist régimes in the exercise of their right of self-determination . . .'[51]
For states party to Additional Protocol I, this has effectively reclassified conflicts not of an international character[52] as international armed conflicts, thus excepting wars of national liberation from the former category while making them subject to the legal régime applicable in the latter.

Similarly, Article 44(3) of Additional Protocol I initially restates the fundamental rule that combatants have a duty to distinguish themselves from the civilian population but, again under the influence of self-determination, this is immediately made subject to an exception in its second sentence: 'Recognizing, however, that there are situations in armed conflicts where, owing to the nature of the hostilities an armed combatant cannot so distinguish himself, he shall retain his status as a combatant, provided that, in such situations, he carries his arms openly . . .'[53]

The ICRC *Commentary* notes that 'guerrilla fighters . . . are the chief concern of this provision'[54] and the Report of the Rapporteur to the Diplomatic Conference stated that this

[50] Hage, Waltermann, and Arosemena, 'Logical Tools' 'Logical Tools' s.11. Chapter 2.

[51] For an account of the influence of self-determination in the drafting of this provision see Yves Sandoz, Christophe Swinarski, and Bruno Zimmermann (eds), *Commentary on the Additional Protocols of 8 June 1977 to the Geneva Conventions of 12 August 1949* (ICRC/Nijhoff 1987) 41–56, §§66–118; Hans-Peter Gasser, 'An Appeal for Ratification by the United States (1987) 81 American Journal of International Law 912, 916–18; and Heather Wilson, *International Law and the Use of Force by National Liberation Movements* (Clarendon Press 1988) 127–30 and 162–68.

[52] See Sandoz and others (n 51) 47, §§89–90.

[53] On this provision see ibid 527–37, §§1691–715; and Wilson (n 51) 173–78.

[54] Sandoz and others (n 51) 527, §1592.

exception could apply in occupied territory and wars of national liberation, a view expressly endorsed by many of the Conference delegations;[55] for example, on signing the Protocol, the United Kingdom (UK) made an interpretative declaration that Article 44(3) could *only* apply in these situations.[56]

Furthermore, situations which are at least akin to exceptions may arise from the influence of non-normative elements which are deemed to be relevant to the operation of a legal system, such as standards which are essentially statements of factual considerations. Consider the doctrine of the margin of appreciation employed by some international courts, which utilizes factual assessments of societal attitudes to determine the legitimate application of international human rights law in specific domestic jurisdictions, but which anticipates their variable rather than uniform application. This doctrine was developed judicially by the European Court of Human Rights and is not mentioned in the text of the European Convention, although its Protocol 15 (24 June 2013), which is not yet in force, will add a new paragraph to the Convention's preamble, which notes that the parties have the primary responsibility to secure their rights and freedoms but that in doing so 'they enjoy a margin of appreciation, subject to the supervisory jurisdiction of the European Court of Human Rights'.[57]

One of the early cases in which the Court developed this doctrine, *Handyside v United Kingdom*, dealt with an allegedly obscene publication suppressed by the UK and the compatibility of this action with the Convention's right of freedom of expression. The Court noted that the UK had acted to protect public morals, which was a legitimate aim, but the issue was whether the action taken was necessary to further that aim. The Court ruled:

> the machinery of protection established by the Convention is subsidiary to the national systems safeguarding human rights ... The Convention leaves to each Contracting State, in the first place, the task of securing the rights and liberties it enshrines ... In particular, it is not possible to find in the domestic law of the various Contracting States a uniform European conception of morals. The view taken by their respective laws of the requirements of morals varies from time to time and from place to place ... By reason of their direct and continuous contact with the vital forces of their countries, State authorities are in principle in a better position than the international judge to give an opinion on the exact content of these requirements as well as on the 'necessity' of a 'restriction' or 'penalty' intended to meet them ... [I]t is for the national authorities to make the initial assessment of the reality of the pressing social need implied by the notion of 'necessity' in this context ...[58]

These examples at least indicate that exceptions to rules might arise from the operation of elements of a legal system which are not themselves 'rules'. If this is correct, then

[55] ibid 529–30, §1698.

[56] Quoted in ibid 530, n.43.

[57] Text available at https://rm.coe.int/1680084831. For academic commentary on the doctrine see e.g. Steven Greer, 'The Interpretation of the European Convention on Human Rights: Universal Principle or Margin of Appreciation?' (2010) 3 UCL Human Rights Review 1; Jan Kratochvíl, 'The Inflation of the Margin of Appreciation by the European Court of Human Rights' (2011) 29 Netherlands Quarterly of Human Rights 324; George Letsas, 'Two Concepts of the Margin of Appreciation' (2006) 26 Oxford Journal of Legal Studies 705; Dominic McGoldrick, 'A Defence of the Margin of Appreciation and an Argument for its Application by the Human Rights Committee' (2016) 65 International and Comparative Law Quarterly 21; and Yuval Shany, 'Towards a General Margin of Appreciation Doctrine in International Law' (2005) 16 European Journal of International Law 907.

[58] *Handyside v United Kingdom* App no 5493/72 (7 December 1976) para 48, http://hudoc.echr.coe.int/eng?i=001-57499.

it is submitted that Hage, Waltermann, and Arosemena's notion of 'derived rules' requires reconsideration.

Further, their example 'the use of force is prohibited unless authorised by the Security Council' is substantively incomplete on its own terms: one would obviously have to add 'or unless justified by a lawful act of self-defence which may take place before the Security Council has had a chance to authorise this action'. To this some might add 'or by humanitarian intervention or a forcible exercise of the responsibility to protect', which Hage, Waltermann, and Arosemena see as an interpretation of the Charter prohibition on the use of force rather than an exception to it.[59] The contours of self-defence, and both the validity and scope of humanitarian intervention and forcible responsibility to protect, are contested issues: does this mean that to state the derived rule fully one would have to enumerate all exceptions and their possible interpretations within the body of the rule itself?[60] Would a derived rule formulation of any internationally wrongful act necessarily include a statement of all circumstances precluding wrongfulness, to say nothing of the rules of attribution and the potential consequences of the delict? How elaborate would derived rules need to be in order to ensure the inclusion of all possible exceptions? Would this entail indicating all systemic connections related to a 'rule', including relevant principles and standards? Would it entail a mapping of the legal system, or at least a significant section of it, and how could this proposal deal with particular legal relations between actors which alter or derogate from general international law?

The concept of derived rules simply appears to be over-inclusive. An alternative approach may be found in Joseph Raz's notion of the individuation of norms which is based on the idea that every act situation is the core of a separate law.[61] Individuation requires that a balance is drawn between two conflicting considerations: the definition of 'small and manageable units of law' which, nevertheless, are 'relatively self-contained and self-explanatory so that each contains a significant part of the law'.[62] Accordingly, individuated norms should not be over-repetitive, where each one contains parts of other laws, but should be fairly simple, both structurally and substantively: 'It should not be formed ... in such a way that a very large proportion of the legal material of a system would have to be scrutinized in order to discover the content of any one law.'[63]

This seems to be where the notion of derived rules falls short, akin to the schemes of individuation proposed by Bentham and Kelsen which Raz criticizes. Derived rules are not 'relatively self-contained' but could be seen to combine unrelated ideas into one law, or normative statement. In contrast, the focus of an individuated norm is on a single act-situation—'the performance of a certain act by certain persons in certain circumstances'.[64]

Kolb argues that an exception entails that a rule will not apply because another 'carves out from it' or limits the scope of its application, noting that the exception may have a narrower substantive ambit.[65] The idea that an exception may be narrower could point to a notion not unlike *lex specialis*. It may be that the circumstances of an exception's act situation, when the

[59] See Hage, Waltermann, and Arosemena, 'Logical Tools' (n 49) s 8.3. Chapter 2.

[60] Compare James A Green, 'Questioning the Peremptory Status of the Prohibition on the Use of Force' (2010–2011) 32 Michigan Journal of International Law 215, 229–36.

[61] See Joseph Raz, *The Concept of a Legal System: An Introduction to the Theory of Legal System* (2nd edn, Clarendon Press 1980) 76, 144: individuation is discussed at 140 ff.

[62] ibid 115.

[63] ibid 142–44: quotation at 143–44, terminal note omitted.

[64] ibid 144.

[65] Kolb, 'Rebus Sic Stantibus' (n 48) cross reference required.

exception becomes operative, are more restricted than those of the rule whose application it limits, but that might raise the problem of identifying when this occurs.

This is a difficulty some commentators have encountered with the operation of the doctrine of *lex specialis*. There is a general tendency in contemporary doctrine to cast doubt on its ability to provide a coherent and principled solution to potential conflicts between norms.[66] The doctrine's application is claimed to be dependent on context rather than principle, and is unable to provide clear and unequivocal solutions to potential norm conflicts in international law because the legal system on the whole lacks hierarchical structure and the relationships between both sources of law and substantive norms are undefined. Anja Lindroos summarized these difficulties as follows:

> the application of *lex specialis* faces difficulties when we need to determine the relationship between two different normative orders or rules deriving from different areas of law, such as environmental norms and trade norms ... If two specialised norms stand side by side, the *lex specialis* maxim cannot be applied, given its inability to establish whether environmental protection is more special than human rights law, the law of the sea, or trade law.
>
> As the maxim is a mechanic principle without a clear content it does not provide guidance in determining what is general and what is special. This is the second difficulty faced in the application of *lex specialis* to different normative orders. Giving priority to a special norm within the system of unclear norm relations in which a decision cannot rely on such relations, the decision actually relies on political or other considerations ... Basing a decision only on a juridical logic such as *lex specialis* is rarely possible in the international legal system ...
>
> Thirdly, *lex specialis* is in some sense a contextual principle. It is difficult to use when determining conflicts between two normative orders *in abstracto*, and is, instead, more suited to the determination of relations between two norms in a concrete case.[67]

An analogous difficulty might apply to the rule-exception relationship. There might be circumstances in which it could be difficult to determine which is which. Consider this banal example:[68] in states where the drinking of alcohol is not prohibited but is nevertheless regulated by law, usually by imposing a minimum age limit for alcohol consumption, a licencing system for those who wish to sell alcohol, and by levying tax on alcoholic drinks, it may nonetheless be prohibited in public places such as parks or streets, but which is the 'rule' and which the 'exception'? Is the rule the prohibition of drinking in public places and the exception that drinking is not prohibited elsewhere, or is the rule the general privilege that people have to drink alcohol with the exception that one should not do so in public?[69] Which proposition 'carves out' the other? When is an 'exception' an exception?

[66] See e.g. Anja Lindroos, 'Addressing Norm Conflicts in a Fragmented Legal System: The Doctrine of *Lex Specialis*' (2005) 74 Nordic Journal of International Law 27; Jörg Kammerhofer, 'Unearthing Structural Uncertainty through Neo-Kelsenian Consistency: Conflict of Norms in International Law' (2005) www.esil-sedi.eu/sites/default/files/Kammerhofer.pdf; Nancie Prud'homme, 'Lex Specialis: Oversimplifying a More Complex and Multifaceted Relationship?' (2007) 40 Israel Law Review 355; Iain Scobbie, 'Principle or Pragmatics? The Relationship Between Human Rights Law and the Law of Armed Conflict' (2010) 14 Journal of Conflict and Security Law 449; and also 'Human Rights Protection During Armed Conflict: What, When and for Whom?' in Erika de Wet and Jann Kleffner (eds), *Convergence and Conflicts of Human Rights and International Humanitarian Law in Military Operations* (Pretoria University Law Press 2014) 3.

[67] Lindroos (n 66) 41–42.

[68] I have used this example before. See Iain Scobbie, 'The Theorist as Judge: Hersch Lauterpacht's Concept of the International Judicial Function' (1997) 8 European Journal of International Law 264, 294–96.

[69] The term 'privilege' should be understood in terms of Hohfeld's classification: see Wesley N Hohfeld, *Fundamental Legal Conceptions as Applied in Judicial Reasoning* (1919, reprinted Greenwood Press 1964).

Some legal propositions are clearly exceptions as they obviously modify the application of a rule in defined circumstances—a possible example being self-defence as an exception to the general prohibition on the use of force in international relations—but the classification of others might not be so clear-cut. For example, are circumstances which preclude wrongfulness exceptions to the rule(s) determining the ascription of state responsibility, or should they be seen as countervailing propositions which displace the operation of another norm? This idea harks back to Raz's theory of individuation, that the applicability of a given legal proposition is determined by the specific act situation which mandates or authorizes 'the performance of a certain act by certain persons in certain circumstances'. Self-defence is not only an exception to the prohibition on the use of force but also a circumstance precluding wrongfulness as Article 21 of the Articles on State Responsibility makes clear: 'The wrongfulness of an act of State is precluded if the act constitutes a lawful measure of self-defence taken in conformity with the Charter of the United Nations.'[70]

The classification of a normative proposition could depend on context, thus self-defence may be seen as an exception to the prohibition on the use of force because there is a relation of dependency with the 'principal' norm. In contrast, self-defence in the context of precluding state responsibility could be seen as a countervailing legal proposition because it operates with a degree of autonomy from the primary rules in issue.

Why is this important? It is generally accepted that the interpretation of the scope of the exception is constrained by the import of the principal norm. Quite simply, an exception must remain within the ambit of the principal rule's underpinning policy or of the value it embodies: the exception must not defeat the purpose of the rule; otherwise there arises the risk that the normative situation is reversed with the exception becoming the rule and the rule the exception. Thus, in the *Nicaragua* case, in discussing the identification of customary international law, the International Court observed that state practice should 'in general' be consistent and that practice which was inconsistent with a rule should be regarded as a breach of that rule rather than the emergence of a new rule. Further:

> If a State acts in a way prima facie incompatible with a recognized rule, but defends its conduct by appealing to exceptions or justifications contained within the rule itself, then whether or not that State's conduct is in fact justifiable on that basis, the significance of that attitude is to confirm rather than to weaken the rule.[71]

Further, the recognition of the existence of countervailing propositions amounts to a rejection of a Cartesian model of law in favour of one based in rhetoric and argumentation where normative propositions are not automatically applied in a deductive fashion. The Cartesian model is one which:

> tends to be modelled on the more elementary operations of arithmetic and physics: it is desired that decisions should conform to weighing, measuring or calculating. The judge apportioning to each his due in accordance with the law can be assimilated to those advanced machines which indicate the total the customer is to pay by multiplying the quantity of

[70] For commentary see James Crawford, *State Responsibility: The General Part* (Cambridge University Press 2013) 274–83, 289–92; and, more generally, Federica Paddeu, 'Clarifying the Concept of Circumstances Precluding Wrongfulness (Justifications) in International Law' Chapter 11; and Viñuales, 'Seven Ways' (n 46) §§1.7–1.8. Chapter 5.

[71] *Case Concerning Military and Paramilitary Activities in and against Nicaragua (Nicaragua v United States of America)* (Merits, Judgment) [1986] ICJ Rep 14, 98, para 186 (*Nicaragua* case).

> goods delivered by the price per unit. The total is just because the account is correct and no one questions either the accuracy of the machine or the price per unit. On this view the perfect judge would be like an infallible machine, giving the answer when furnished with the elements of the problem ... This is the view of formal justice, the very formalism of which confers on it a logical structure encouraging correct deduction and more particularly the use of the syllogism ... The ideal of juridical positivism would be a legal system so well worked out, laws so clear and complete, that ultimately law could be administered by an automaton.[72]

Perelman's mantra that 'the judge is not a calculating machine' may be extended to encompass legal reasoning generally where the outcome of a transaction does not simply depend on proof of operative facts. The choice of grounds is critical in the construction and justification of any legal argument of relative complexity, and in this process countervailing propositions are competing argumentatively plausible, or possible, normative classifications or analyses of a given act situation. This approach is akin to Hage, Waltermann, and Arosemena's dialogical model but it perhaps places more emphasis on the inevitability of choice in selecting propositions, and differs from them in rejecting their notion of derived rules in favour of individuation and in the claim that propositions may compete for application.

3.2 Self-defence and the *Nicaragua* case

Currently, the principal judicial exposition of the law of self-defence is that contained in the merits judgment of the *Nicaragua* case,[73] in which the International Court of Justice underlined its exceptional nature.[74] The principal basis of jurisdiction in the *Nicaragua* proceedings were the declarations made by Nicaragua and the United States under Article 36(2) of the Statute of the ICJ, which provides:

> The states parties to the present Statute may at any time declare that they recognize as compulsory *ipso facto* and without special agreement, in relation to any other state accepting the same obligation, the jurisdiction of the Court in all legal disputes concerning:
>
> a. the interpretation of a treaty;
> b. any question of international law;
> c. the existence of any fact which, if established, would constitute a breach of an international obligation;

[72] Chaïm Perelman, *The Idea of Justice and the Problem of Argument* (Routledge and Kegan Paul 1963) 62–63 (note omitted): see also 101, and 146–47. For commentary on Perelman see e.g. Alan G Gross and Ray D Dearin, *Chaim Perelman* (SUNY Press: Albany: 2003), Roland Schmetz, *L'argumentation selon Perelman: pour une Raison au Coeur de la Rhétorique* (Presses Universitaires de Namur: Namur: 2000); and Iain Scobbie, 'Rhetoric, Persuasion, and Interpretation in International Law' in Andrea Bianchi, Daniel Peat, and Matthew Windsor (eds), *Interpretation in International Law* (Oxford University Press 2015) 61.

[73] *Nicaragua* case (n 71) 14. Self-defence has been considered by the ICJ in subsequent cases, principally *Oil Platforms (Islamic Republic of Iran v. United States of America)* (Judgment) [2003] ICJ Rep 803; *Legal Consequences of the Construction of a Wall in the Occupied Palestinian Territory* (Advisory Opinion) [2004] ICJ Rep 136; and *Armed Activities on the Territory of the Congo (New Application: 2002) (Democratic Republic of the Congo v Rwanda)* (Judgment) [2006] ICJ Rep 6, 168.

[74] See *Nicaragua* case (n 71) 102–103, paras 193, 110, 210, and 211.

d. the nature or extent of the reparation to be made for the breach of an international obligation.

The United States' declaration contained a multilateral treaty reservation which excluded from its consent to jurisdiction: 'disputes arising under a multilateral treaty, unless (1) all parties to the treaty affected by the decision are also parties to the case before the Court, or (2) the United States of America specially agrees to jurisdiction'.[75]

The United States relied on this reservation with the consequence that the Court could not base any rulings on multilateral treaties which Nicaragua had invoked in support of its claims.[76] These included the UN Charter,[77] thus precluding the Court from focusing directly on the interpretation of Article 51. Nevertheless, it observed that the UN Charter did not comprehensively regulate the use of force in international relations and that the Article 51 reference to self-defence as an 'inherent right' (or, in the French text, «droit naturel») which 'nothing in the present Charter shall impair' was a reference to pre-existing customary international law. The meaning of Article 51 was thus dependent on this customary law 'even if its present content has been confirmed and influenced by the Charter'. In particular, Article 51 did not determine all aspects of self-defence, and made no mention of the requirements of necessity and proportionality which are inherent in customary law. Further:

> a definition of the "armed attack" which, if found to exist, authorizes the exercise of the "inherent right" of self-defence, is not provided in the Charter, and is not part of treaty law. It cannot therefore be held that Article 51 is a provision which "subsumes and supervenes" customary international law. It rather demonstrates that in the field in question ... customary international law continues to exist alongside treaty law. The areas governed by the two sources thus do not overlap exactly, and the rules do not have the same content.[78]

But here lies the problem. Conventional and customary rules have a different normative basis and, as the International Court observed in the *Nicaragua* case itself:

> There are a number of reasons for considering that, even if two norms belonging to two sources of international law appear identical in content, and even if the States in question are bound by these rules both on the level of treaty-law and on that of customary international law, these retain a separate existence ... Rules which are identical in treaty law and in customary international law are also distinguishable by reference to the methods of interpretation and application.[79]

This is a problematic ruling: the International Court simply declared that self-defence has an autonomous existence in both treaty and custom but it is neither candid nor clear on the relationship between the two. In conceptual terms, these different sources refer to different

[75] Quoted in *Case concerning Military and Paramilitary Activities in and against Nicaragua* (Jurisdiction of the Court and Admissibility of the Application Procedure(s): Questions of jurisdiction and/or admissibility) [1984] ICJ Rep 392, 421–22, para 67: for the Court's discussion of the multilateral treaties reservation see 421–26, paras 67–76. See also Stanimir A Alexandrov, *Reservations in Unilateral Declarations Accepting the Compulsory Jurisdiction of the International Court of Justice* (Nijhoff 1995) 112–19; and Vanda Lamm, 'The Multilateral Treaty Reservation Revisited' (2006) 47 Acta Juridica Hungarica 331.

[76] *Nicaragua* case (n 71) 92, para 172.

[77] ibid 118, para 228.

[78] ibid 94, para 176.

[79] ibid 95, para 178.

legal institutions which are rooted in different constitutive, interpretative, and terminative rules[80]—for example, desuetude is a doctrine that applies only to treaties and, moreover, it does not lie in simple non-use. Obsolescence per se is not a recognized ground for treaty termination. Desuetude requires evidence of the parties' intention and consent to abandon the treaty.[81] An analogous consideration applies to the extinction of a doctrine rooted in customary international law. States must be seen to adopt a position which contradicts their previous practice in order to extinguish the rule through the emergence of contrary custom. Similarly, the consequences of material breach and *exceptio inadimplenti* only concern treaties.[82] Although Article 31(3)(c) of the Vienna Convention on the Law of Treaties mandates that the interpretation of a treaty must take into account 'any relevant rules of international law applicable in the relations between the parties', and thus any relevant rules of customary law,[83] does the converse hold, as a matter of principle, in the interpretation of customary rules? What is the relationship between norms drawn from these different sources of international law which deal with the same substantive issues? As Schachter points out, treaties and custom are not merely alternative sources of international law, but they are also competitive.[84] Where customary and conventional rules deal with the same substantive issue but might be argued to impose different obligations, which should prevail?[85] Presumptively, it seems apparent that if not all the actors in a given situation are parties to the relevant convention then customary law should take preference, but if all are parties should we assume that the principles of *pacta sunt servanda* and possibly *lex specialis* dictate that the conventional formulation of the obligation applies, possibly to the complete exclusion of the customary? Or might there be circumstances in which the doctrine of *lex posterior* requires the application of a customary norm which has superseded an earlier conventional provision? Complex doctrinal questions exist which are not answered simply by the bare affirmation that treaties must be interpreted in the light of any relevant rules of customary international law.

With regard to the prohibition on the use of force we can effectively assume that every state concerned is a party to the UN Charter. In cases of purported self-defence, when states present innovative claims which are not manifestly inconsistent with established law but which might potentially extend the boundaries of this exception to the prohibition on the

[80] On legal institutions see Neil MacCormick, *Rhetoric and the Rule of Law: A Theory of Legal Reasoning* (Oxford University Press 2005) ch 1, and his *Institutions of Law: An Essay in Legal Theory* (Oxford University Press 2007); and Iain Scobbie, 'Legal Theory as a Source: Institutional Facts and the Identification of International Law' in Samantha Besson and Jean d'Aspremont (eds), *The Oxford Handbook of the Sources of International Law* (Oxford University Press 2017) 493.

[81] On desuetude see e.g. Guillaume Le Floch, 'La Désuétude en Droit International Public' (2007) 111 Revue Générale de Droit International Public 609; Michael J Glennon, 'How International Rules Die' (2004) 93 Georgetown Law Journal 939; Robert Kolb, 'La Désuétude en Droit International Public' (2007) 111 Revue Générale de Droit International Public 111; and Athanassios Vamvoukos, *Termination of Treaties in International Law: The Doctrines of* Rebus Sic Stantibus *and Desuetude* (Clarendon Press 1985) Pt II.

[82] See Malgosia Fitzmaurice, 'Aspects of the Law Relating to Material Breach of Treaty' in Malgosia Fitzmaurice and Olufemi Elias, *Contemporary Issues in the Law of Treaties* (Eleven International Publishing 2005) 123; and her 'Angst of the *Exceptio Inadimplenti Non Est Adimplendum* in International Law' Chapter 15, although there she notes [text to her current note 37] that Gerald Fitzmaurice in his Fourth Report (1959) as ILC Rapporteur on the law of treaties argued that the *exeptio inadimplenti* doctrine is a general principle applicable to all international obligations, and not simply those arising under treaty relationships. This appears to be a minority opinion.

[83] On art 31(3)(c) see Campbell McLachlan, 'The Principle of Systemic Integration and Article 31(3)(c) of the Vienna Convention' (2005) 54 International and Comparative Law Quarterly 279.

[84] Oscar Schachter, 'Entangled Treaty and Custom' in Yoram Dinstein (ed), *International Law at a Time of Perplexity: Essays in Honour of Shabtai Rosenne* (Nijhoff 1989) 717, 720.

[85] For an overview of some of the issues implicated in this question see e.g. Nancy Kontou, *The Termination and Revision of Treaties in the Light of New Customary International Law* (Clarendon Press 1994) 19–36.

use of force, is this practice relevant to the creation of a new understanding of the customary rule, or is it relevant to a new interpretation of the conventional Charter rule? If the latter, then presumably this claim should be understood as subsequent practice relevant to the interpretation of the Charter *qua* treaty, but if the former, following the dual element approach adopted by the International Law Commission (ILC) in its current work on the identification of customary international law,[86] then this practice must be accompanied by an *opinio juris* in order to assert any normative significance. Is the nature of the claim being advanced always clear and unambiguous?

An additional potentially relevant consideration in determining the interplay of custom and Charter obligations in relation to self-defence is Article 103 of the Charter, which provides: 'In the event of a conflict between the obligations of the Members of the United Nations under the present Charter and their obligations under any other international agreement, their obligations under the present Charter shall prevail.'

The terms of Article 103 suggest that it only applies to treaties and not to customary international law. This is supported by the *travaux préparatoires* of the Charter. Despite an initial observation by Venezuela which implied that the Charter should prevail over any inconsistent obligations of member states,[87] and the view expressed by the Soviet representative, Golunsky, in the Co-ordination Committee of the San Francisco Conference that the draft Article prepared by the Advisory Committee of Jurists encompassed obligations other than treaties,[88] the Co-ordination Committee itself replaced the phrase 'any other obligations to which they are subject' with the more restrictive 'their obligations under any other international agreement'.[89]

Andreas Paulus and Johann Leiss nevertheless argue that the predominant interpretation of Article 103 is extensive and covers customary international law. They caution that the pre-eminence of the Charter over custom must be distinguished from its further development by way of agreed reinterpretation: 'In such an event, the law of the Charter itself is modified, and its (previous) norms can thus not prevail over the new rule modifying it. Nevertheless, such modification is rare and requires universal acceptance.'[90]

Paulus and Leiss query what is meant by 'a conflict' for the purposes of Article 103, noting that divergent understandings may be reconciled through interpretation,[91] but that where this is not possible the impact of Article 103 is situational with the consequence that the relevant Charter obligation pre-empts the operation of the conflicting norm in the circumstances of the case. Only where: 'a norm stands in clear contrast *ipso iure* with the Charter, however, Art. 103 might lead to its de facto nullity as the state of conflict is of permanent character and the rule must not be implemented.'[92]

[86] See Michael Wood, *First Report on Formation and Evidence of Customary International Law*, A/CN.4/663 (17 May 2013); *Second Report on Identification of Customary International Law*, A/CN.4/672 (22 May 2014); *Third Report on Identification of Customary International Law*, A/CN.4/682 (27 March 2015); *Fourth Report on Identification of Customary International Law*, A/CN.4/695 (8 March 2016); and International Law Commission, *Report on the Work of the Sixty-Eighth Session*, A/71/10 (2016), ch 5. Draft Conclusion 2 adopted by the Commission in 2016 provides: 'To determine the existence and content of a rule of customary international law, it is necessary to ascertain whether there is a general practice that is accepted as law (*opinio juris*)' A/71/10, 76.

[87] See (1945) 3 UN Conference on International Organization Documents 223 and 226.

[88] See (1945) 17 UNCIO Docs 112–13.

[89] ibid Docs 382 and 19 UNCIO Docs 376: see also Alix Toublanc, 'L'Article 103 et la Valeur Juridique de la Charte des Nations Unies' (2004) 108 Revue Générale de Droit International Public 439, 446–50.

[90] Andreas Paulus and Johann Ruben Leiss, 'Commentary to Article 103' in Bruno Simma, Daniel-Erasmus Khan, Georg Nolte, and Andreas Paulus (eds), *The Charter of the United Nations: a Commentary, vol II* (3rd edn, Oxford University Press 2012) 2110, 2133, para 69: see generally ibid 2132–33, paras 66–69, and also 2116, para 9, and 2117, para 14.

[91] See Paulus and Leiss (n 90) 2121–32, paras 29–36.

[92] ibid 2136, para 78: see 2135–36, paras 75–80.

Regarding novel claims which appear to push the boundaries of accepted notions of the exception of self-defence, it might argued be that there is little or no practical difference whether the claim is made as one of the reinterpretation of Article 51 of the Charter or an extension of its customary equivalent. As noted, Paulus and Leiss argue that an accepted re-interpretation of a Charter provision is dependent on its 'universal acceptance' by member states. The conditions for the modification of a customary norm are perhaps less stringent, but where the norm is of general application, such as that of self-defence, a high threshold of consensus is still required. In relation to the practice element of custom formation, Draft Conclusion Eight on the Identification of Customary International Law adopted by the ILC in 2016 provides in part: 'The relevant practice must be general, meaning that it must be sufficiently widespread and representative, as well as consistent.'[93]

In its commentary to Draft Conclusion Eight, the Commission noted the practice concerned must be adopted by 'a sufficiently large and representative number of States' and 'must exhibit consistency' in such a way that makes it possible 'to discern a constant and uniform usage'.[94] This is not a precise science, capable of being expressed in the abstract—'The requirement that the practice be "widespread and representative" does not lend itself to exact formulations, as circumstances may vary greatly from one case to another'. The Commission gives the example of the law of diplomatic relations, an issue 'in which all States regularly engage', as one in which relevant practice 'would have to be widely exhibited', but it is important that the participating states 'are representative of the various geographical regions and/or various interests at stake'.[95] Even if all states do not 'regularly engage' in the exercise of self-defence, it is nonetheless an issue in which all have a direct interest, and consequently novel claims regarding its parameters under customary international law must be generally supported in order to become established. Further, novel customary claims should not undermine the rationale of the rule itself. As the International Court observed in the *Nicaragua* case:

> It is not to be expected that in the practice of States the application of the rules in question should have been perfect... The Court does not consider that, for a rule to be established as customary, the corresponding practice must be in absolutely rigorous conformity with the rule. In order to deduce the existence of customary rules, the Court deems it sufficient that the conduct of States should, in general, be consistent with such rules.[96]

Having said that, the proposition that practice in relation to self-defence can contribute to the development or modification of customary international law outside the parameters of the UN Charter is problematic. Given the ubiquity of UN membership, it is difficult to see how state practice could do so because, as the International Court ruled in the *North Sea Continental Shelf* cases, in identifying customary international law where there is a related or parallel conventional obligation, the critical practice is that of states which are not parties to the instrument in question. States parties, on the other hand, must be presumed to be acting in the performance of their treaty commitments, and thus '[f]rom their action no inference could legitimately be drawn as to the existence of a rule of customary international law'.[97]

[93] International Law Commission, *Report on the Work of the Sixty-Eighth Session*, A/71/10 (2016) 77 and 94.
[94] ibid 94, para 2.
[95] ibid 94–95, para 3.
[96] *Nicaragua* case (n 71) 98, para 186.
[97] *North Sea Continental Shelf* cases *(Germany v Denmark and Germany v the Netherlands)* (Judgment) [1969] ICJ Rep 1 3, 43, para 76.

Accordingly, in relation to the development of the substantive content of customary self-defence, the practice of UN member states is confronted by the Baxter paradox:

> As the number of parties to a treaty increases, it becomes more difficult to demonstrate what is the state of customary international law *dehors* the treaty... As express acceptance of the treaty increases, the number of States not parties whose practice is relevant diminishes. There will be less scope for the development of international law *dehors* the treaty.[98]

On this point, the fact that custom and treaty are different legal institutions is relevant: while practice in the performance of a treaty may not contribute to custom formation or development, treaty commitments may contribute to the content of custom. In the *Nicaragua* case, the Court ruled that it was bound to take into account the UN Charter and that of the Organization of American States, to which the United States was party 'in ascertaining the content of the customary international law which the United States is also alleged to have infringed'.[99]

Further, if one accepts Paulus and Leiss' argument that the predominant interpretation of Article 103 is extensive and encompasses customary international law, then if divergent understandings between alleged customary claims and Charter exigencies cannot be reconciled, the purported customary norm is pre-empted by the relevant Charter provisions, failing the 'universal acceptance' of this proposition as a Charter reinterpretation.

3.3 Extensive claims of self-defence beyond the state

The obvious contemporary issue which appears to push the boundaries of self-defence is the claim made by some states that self-defence may legitimately be invoked against non-state armed groups, which are invariably classified as terrorist organizations.[100] Before the

[98] Richard Baxter, 'Treaties and Custom' (1970) 129 Recueil des Cours 27, 73; see also 64 and 96, and also his 'Multilateral Treaties as Evidence of Customary International Law' (1965–66) 41 British Yearbook of International Law 275, 296–97 and 299; compare Theodor Meron, *Human Rights and Humanitarian Norms as Customary Law* (Clarendon Press 1989) 50–57, and his 'Revival of Customary Humanitarian Law' (2005) 99 American Journal of International Law 817, 833; and Schachter, 'Entangled Treaty and Custom' (n 84) 725.

[99] *Nicaragua* case (n 71) 97, para 183.

[100] On this question in general see e.g. Karine Bannelier-Christakis, 'Military Interventions against ISIS in Iraq, Syria and Libya, and the Legal Basis of Consent' (2016) 29 Leiden Journal of International Law 743; Stephanie A Barbour and Zoe A Salzman, '"The Tangled Web": the Right of Self-Defense Against Non-State Actors in the *Armed Activities* Case' IILJ Emerging Scholars Paper (2007) 1; Daniel Bethlehem, 'Self-Defense Against an Imminent or Actual Armed Attack by Nonstate Actors' (2012) 106 American Journal of International Law 770; Jutta Brunnée and Stephen J Toope, 'Self-Defence Against Non-State Actors: Are Powerful States Willing but Unable to Change International Law?' (2018) 67 International and Comparative Law Quarterly 263; Antonio Cassese, 'Terrorism Is Also Disrupting Some Crucial Legal Categories of International Law' (2001) 12 European Journal of International Law 993; Olivier Corten, 'The "Unwilling or Unable" Test: Has It Been and Could It Be, Accepted?' (2016) 29 Leiden Journal of International Law 777; Anthony Dworkin, 'Drones and Targeted Killing: Defining a European Position' ECFR Policy Brief (3 July 2013) http://www.ecfr.eu/page/-/ECFR84_DRONES_BRIEF.pdf; Norman M Fedr, 'Reading the UN Charter Connotatively: Toward a New Definition of Armed Attack' (1987) New York University Journal of International Law and Politics 395; Michael J Glennon, 'Law, Power, and Principles' (2013) 107 American Journal of International Law 378; Christine Gray, 'The Bush Doctrine Revisited: the 2006 National Security Strategy of the USA' (2006) 5 Chinese Journal of International Law 555, and Gray, *Use of Force* (n 43) 193–53; Marcelo G Kohen, 'The Use of Force by the United States after the End of the Cold War, and its Impact on International Law' in Michael Byers and Georg Nolte (eds), *United States Hegemony and the Foundations of International Law* (Cambridge University Press 2003) 197 and the subsequent comments by Thomas M Franck (264), Jochen A Frowein (274), and Daniel Thürer (277); Ady Niv, 'The International Court of Justice Under the Scrutiny of Article 51' (2005–2006) 2 Israel Defense Forces Law Review 173; Mary Ellen O'Connell, 'Dangerous Departures' (2013) 107 American Journal of International Law 380; Federica Paddeu, 'Use of Force Against Non-State Actors and the Circumstance Precluding Wrongfulness of Self-Defence' (2017), 30 Leiden Journal

terrorist attacks of 11 September 2001, the legal position seemed clear, as laid out by the International Court in the *Nicaragua* case. While the fundamental principle governing the use of force in international relations is embodied in Article 2(4), to which the right of self-defence expressed in Article 51 ostensibly constitutes an exception, the terms these articles employ do not correspond exactly—a 'threat or use of force' is not equivalent to an 'armed attack'. The latter is a much narrower concept, and not all breaches of Article 2(4) give rise to a right of self-defence.[101]

This was expressly recognized by the International Court in *Nicaragua* in its adoption of the 'scale and effects' doctrine. The Court conceded that it was necessary 'to distinguish the most grave forms of the use of force (those constituting an armed attack) from other less grave forms'.[102] The Court ruled:

> There appears now to be general agreement on the nature of the acts which can be treated as constituting armed attacks. In particular, it may be considered to be agreed that an armed attack must be understood as including not only action by regular armed forces across an international border, but also 'the sending by or on behalf of a State of armed bands, groups, irregulars or mercenaries, which carry out acts of armed force against another State of such gravity as to amount to' (*inter alia*) an actual armed attack conducted by regular forces, 'or its substantial involvement therein' ... The Court sees no reason to deny that, in customary law, the prohibition of armed attacks may apply to the sending by a State of armed bands to the territory of another State, if such an operation, because of its scale and effects, would have been classified as an armed attack rather than a mere frontier incident had it been carried out by regular armed forces.[103]

Accordingly, in determining whether hostile acts by non-state forces amount to an armed attack which would justify the invocation of self-defence against the state in whose territory they are based, the determining factor is the involvement or complicity of that state in those acts. But under the *Nicaragua* doctrine, the plea of self-defence is invoked against that state, and not against the non-state armed group as such.

Although there had been a few earlier incidents in which states had claimed to use force against a non-state entity on the basis of self-defence, such as Israel's 1985 attack on the Tunis headquarters of the PLO in response to Palestinian attacks on Israelis abroad (condemned as an act of aggression against Tunisia by the Security Council in resolution 573 (1985) by a vote of 14–0–1), the catalyst for purported change came with the 11 September 2001 attacks on the United States. While Security Council resolutions 1368 (12 September 2001) and 1373 (28 September 2001), adopted in response to these attacks, recognized 'the inherent right of

of International Law 93; Gabor Rona and Raha Wala, 'No Thank You to a Radical Rewrite of the *Jus ad Bellum*' (2013) 107 American Journal of International Law 386; Ruys *'Armed Attack'* (n 44) 419–510; Scobbie, 'Words my Mother Never Taught Me' (n 44); Kinga Tibori Szabó, 'Self-Defence and the United States Policy on Drone Strikes' (2015) 20 Journal of Conflict and Security Law 381; Nicholas Tsagourias, 'Self-Defence Against Non-State Actors: The Interaction between Self-Defence as a Primary Rule and Self-Defence as a Secondary Rule' (2016) 29 Leiden Journal of International Law 801; Elizabeth Wilmshurst, 'The Chatham House Principles of International Law on the Use of Force in Self-Defence' (2006) 55 International and Comparative Law Quarterly 963 https://www.chathamhouse.org/publications/papers/view/108106; and Elizabeth Wilmshurst and Michael Wood, 'Self-Defense Against Non-State Actors: Reflections on the "Bethlehem Principles"' (2013) 107 American Journal of International Law 390.

101 See e.g. Randelzhofer and Nolte (n 44) 1401–1403, paras 6–8.
102 *Nicaragua* case (n 71) 101, para 191.
103 ibid 103, para 195.

individual or collective self-defence in accordance with the Charter', which some states saw as justification for armed action against non-state armed groups as such, commentary is divided on whether the parameters set out in *Nicaragua* have changed.[104]

In its subsequent jurisprudence, the International Court has effectively upheld the *Nicaragua* position, in both the *Legal consequences of the construction of a wall* advisory opinion,[105] and in the *Armed Activities (DRC v Uganda)* case[106]—although in the latter it continued:

> the Court finds that the legal and factual circumstances for the exercise of a right of self-defence by Uganda against the DRC were not present. Accordingly, the Court has no need to respond to the contentions of the Parties as to whether and under what conditions contemporary international law provides for a right of self-defence against large-scale attacks by irregular forces.[107]

In both proceedings, some judges dissented from the view adopted by the Court regarding the continued validity of *Nicaragua*, namely Judges Buergenthal,[108] Kooijmans,[109] and Higgins in the *Legal Consequences of the Construction of a Wall* opinion. Judge Higgins commented that she could not agree with all of the Court's rulings on self-defence in paragraph 139 of the opinion, and in particular the restriction it imposed that an 'armed attack' in terms of Article 51 solely concerned an attack by one state upon another. She stated:

> There is, with respect, nothing in the text of Article 51 of the Charter that *thus* stipulates that self-defence is only available when an armed attack is made by a State. *That* qualification is rather a result of the Court so determining in [the *Nicaragua* case] ... While accepting, as I must, that this is to be regarded as a statement of the law as it now stands, I maintain all the reservations that I have expressed elsewhere.[110]

Similarly, Judges Kooijmans[111] and Simma[112] criticized the *Nicaragua* position in the *Armed Activities (DRC v Uganda)* case. Judge Simma commented:

> 8. ... I submit that the Court should have taken the opportunity presented by the present case to clarify the state of the law on a highly controversial matter which is marked by great

[104] See e.g. Bethlehem (n 100) 774; Cassese (n 100) 996–98; Kohen (n 100) 204–10; Randelzhofer and Nolte (n 44) 1416–18, paras 35–39; Ruys *'Armed Attack'* (n 44) 419–85; Thürer, 'Comment' 279–81: but compare Gray, 'Bush Doctrine' (n 100) 571 and Gray, *Use of Force* (n 43) 198–99, 227–53; and Frowein, 'Comment' 274–75; and contra, Franck, 'Comment' 268–74; Wilmshurst(n 100) 969–71 (Principle F); and Wilmshurst and Wood (n 100) 393.

[105] *Legal Consequences of the Construction of a Wall on Occupied Palestinian Territory* (Advisory Opinion) [2004] ICJ Rep 136, 194, para 139 (*Wall Opinion* case): but compare Gray, *Use of Force* (n 43) 135–36.

[106] *Armed Activities on the Territory of the Congo (Democratic Republic of the Congo v Uganda)* (Judgment) [2005] ICJ Rep 168, 222–23, paras 146–47.

[107] ibid 223, para 147.

[108] *Legal Consequences of the Construction of a Wall on Occupied Palestinian Territory* (Declaration of Judge Buergenthal) [2004] ICJ Rep 240, 241–43, paras 5–7.

[109] ibid (Separate Opinion of Judge Kooijmans) 219, 229–30, paras 35–36.

[110] ibid (Separate Opinion of Judge Higgins) 207, 215, para 33. Judge Higgins' reservations had earlier been expressed in her *Problems and Process: International Law and How We Use It* (Clarendon Press 1994) 250–51.

[111] *Armed Activities on the Territory of the Congo (Democratic Republic of the Congo v Uganda)* (Separate opinion of Judge Kooijmans) [2005] ICJ Rep 306, 311–15, paras 20–32.

[112] *Armed Activities on the Territory of the Congo (Democratic Republic of the Congo v Uganda)* (Separate Opinion of Judge Simma) [2005] ICJ Rep 334, 335–37, paras 5–11.

controversy and confusion—not the least because it was the Court itself that has substantially contributed to this confusion by its *Nicaragua* Judgment of two decades ago ...

11. Such a restrictive reading of Article 51 might well have reflected the state, or rather the prevailing interpretation, of the international law on self-defence for a long time. However, in the light of more recent developments not only in State practice but also with regard to accompanying *opinio juris*, it ought urgently to be reconsidered, also by the Court. As is well known, these developments were triggered by the terrorist attacks of September 11, in the wake of which claims that Article 51 also covers defensive measures against terrorist groups have been received far more favourably by the international community than other extensive rereadings of the relevant Charter provisions ... Security Council resolutions 1368 (2001) and 1373 (2001) cannot but be read as affirmations of the view that large-scale attacks by non-State actors can qualify as 'armed attacks' within the meaning of Article 51.[113]

This observation appears to conflate the *Nicaragua* bifurcation, namely that the customary and conventional law on self-defence are autonomous and subject to different systemic rules of interpretation and application. Can practice simultaneously be undertaken in pursuit of a treaty obligation (Article 51) and relevant to its interpretation, while also being relevant to the manipulation of a customary norm (practice plus *opinio juris*)? I have my doubts as each retains an autonomous and separate existence and, following the *North Sea Continental Shelf* cases, treaty parties must be presumed to act in performance of their treaty obligations and no inference may legitimately be drawn from this regarding custom.[114] A further consideration when the UN Charter is in play is the Baxter paradox: can there be any practice beyond the Charter relevant to custom?

As noted, in the *Armed Activities (DRC v Uganda)* case, the Court ruled that there was 'no need' for it to answer the parties' arguments 'as to whether and under what conditions contemporary international law provides for a right of self-defence against large-scale attacks by irregular forces'.[115] There is, however, some evidence of an emerging scholarly consensus in favour of the legitimacy of claims that states might invoke self-defence against non-state actors directly,[116] but this proposition is not without doctrinal controversy.[117] It is, however, another matter if this proposition finds sufficient support in state practice and opinion to ground a plausible claim that it forms part of customary international law. Reliance is often placed on the *Caroline* incident to argue that custom recognizes the right of self-defence against non-state armed groups, but in the mid-nineteenth century there were no restrictions on the use of force by states and so to interpret it as an example of a plea of self-defence, as this would be understood in contemporary international law, is misplaced. The *Caroline* is better understood in terms of the doctrine of necessity.[118] Moreover, if one accepts Paulus

113 ibid 336, para 8, and 337, para 11.

114 *North Sea Continental Shelf* cases (n 97) 43, para 76.

115 *Armed Activities (DRC v Uganda)* case (n 111) 223, para 147.

116 See e.g. Bethlehem (n 100) 772 and 774; Wilmshurst (n 100) 969–71 (Principle F); and Wilmshurst and Wood (n 100) 393.

117 See e.g. Corten (n 100) 795–96; Gray, *Use of Force* (n 43) 227–28; Ruys *'Armed Attack'* (n 44) 485–89; Randelzhofer and Nolte (n 44) 1414–19, paras 31–41.

118 See e.g. James Crawford, *The International Law Commission's Articles on State Responsibility: Introduction, Text and Commentaries* (Cambridge University Press 2002), 'Commentary to Article 25' 178, 179–80, para 5, and Crawford, *State Responsibility: The General Part* (n 70) 309–10. See also Jean-Marc Thouvenin, 'Circumstances Precluding Wrongfulness in the ILC Articles on State Responsibility: Self-defence' in James Crawford, Alain Pellet, and Simon Olleson (eds), *The Law of International Responsibility* (Oxford University Press 2010) 455, 456–59.

and Leiss' position that a novel interpretation of the UN Charter requires universal acceptance, then this required unanimity is simply lacking. As Christine Gray notes, the ICJ's refusal to rule on this point in both the *Wall* advisory opinion and *Armed Activities* case illustrates the divisive nature of this issue and the uncertain state of the law.[119]

Having said that, if a state takes armed action against a non-state armed group within its own territory, it is difficult to see how this may be classified as self-defence as that is an exception to the prohibition of the use of force in international, not internal, relations. The plea only appears to be relevant when a state uses force against a non-state actor which is located within the territory of another state, without the latter's invitation or consent. A contested and controversial issue is whether a state may take action in self-defence against a non-state armed group which is based in the territory of another state if it deems the latter is unable or unwilling to take effective action to contain or terminate actual or threatened attacks by the non-state armed group in question.[120] A related issue is the identification of standards of imminence in relation to anticipatory self-defence. The 2006 Chatham House Principles on the Use of Force in Self-Defence provide that force may only be used in self-defence where this is necessary to end an attack or avert an imminent attack: there must be no practical alternative to the use of force that is likely to be effective. In assessing the imminence of an attack, reference should be made to the gravity of the attack, the attacker's capability, and the nature of the threat posed—'In this sense, necessity will determine imminence: it must be necessary to act before it is too late'.[121] Olivier Corten traces the express formulation of the 'unable or unwilling' doctrine to the 2006 Chatham House Principles,[122] which expressed the view that: 'The right to use force in self-defence is an inherent right and is not dependent upon any prior breach of international law by the state in the territory of which defensive force is used.'[123]

This proposition hinges on the notion of an 'inherent right', but what does this mean? Rights are not autonomous but are correlative to duties,[124] so either this proposition is a *non sequitur* as it detaches the assertion of the right of self-defence from the breach of any corresponding duty, or this is an appeal to some pre-emptive 'natural' right which has a higher or privileged normative status.[125] Neither appears convincing.

The 'unable or unwilling' doctrine gained greater prominence and elaboration in the principles formulated by Daniel Bethlehem in 2012 concerning *self-defense against an imminent or actual armed attack by non-state actors*.[126] Bethlehem argued that academic commentary on self-defence has had little impact on governmental and military decision-makers, as it has not resulted in a clear set of principles which addresses operational circumstances effectively and that are sensitive to practical realities. Bethlehem formulated his proposed sixteen principles following discussions with legal advisers from foreign

119 Gray, 'Bush Doctrine' (n 100) 571.

120 For a range of opinion on this matter see e.g. Bannelier-Christakis (n 100); Bethlehem (n 100) 776; Brunnée and Toope (n 100); Corten (n 100); Glennon, 'Law, Power, and Principles' (n 100); O'Connell, 'Dangerous Departures' (n 100); Randelzhofer and Nolte (n 44) 1418–19, para 41 and 1427, para 61; Ruys *'Armed Attack'* (n 44) 502–507; Tibori Szabó, 'US Policy on Drone Strikes' (n 100) 391–92; Tsagourias(n 100) 808–13; Wilmshurst (n 100) 970–71; and Wilmshurst and Wood (n 100) 393.

121 Wilmshurst (n 100) 996–68: quotation at 968.

122 Corten (n 100) 778 n 6, referring to Wilmshurst (n 100) 970, Principle F.

123 Wilmshurst (n 100) 970.

124 See Hohfeld (n 69).

125 On the latter point, compare Higgins, *Problems and Process* (n 110), 20–21.

126 See Bethlehem (n 100) 776–77, Principles 10–13.

and defence ministries and the military from a number of states who had had operational experience.[127]

The Bethlehem Principles cover issues including the criteria for imminence and the 'unable or unwilling' doctrine and attracted immediate criticism in academic journals. For example, Elizabeth Wilmshurst and Michael Wood, while endorsing the 'unable or unwilling' doctrine but noting that it is controversial, observed that attempts within the UN to secure agreement on the principles governing self-defence have been unsuccessful, citing in particular General Assembly Resolution 60/1 (2005), operative paragraph 79 of which reaffirmed 'that the relevant provisions of the Charter are sufficient to address the full range of threats to international peace and security' and which stressed 'the importance of acting in accordance with the purposes and principles of the Charter'.[128] Wilmshurst and Wood comment that the discussions which underpinned the Bethlehem Principles 'no doubt anticipated that a select group of governmental representatives might reach agreement among themselves when the UN membership as a whole could not'.[129] This criticism was echoed by Michael Glennon, who argued that the Principles attempted to substitute the *opinio juris* of powerful states for the practice of all[130] and also by Mary-Ellen O'Connell, who thought them based on the misconception that international law lacks sufficiently clear principles to govern the use of force against non-state actors and was an attempt to rewrite the law to legitimize unlawful practices undertaken by a few states.[131]

One state which has embraced an extended understanding of standards of imminence and the 'unable or unwilling' doctrine is the UK.[132] This is implicit in the statement made by then Prime Minister David Cameron in the House of Commons on 7 September 2015 regarding the targeted killing by a Royal Air Force drone of UK nationals, including Reyaad Khan, who were alleged to be members of the Islamic State armed group, involved in plotting terrorist attacks in the UK and other states. He said that, as 'their intention was the murder of British citizens':

> We took this action because there was no alternative. In this area, there is no Government we can work with; we have no military on the ground to detain those preparing plots; and there was nothing to suggest that Reyaad Khan would ever leave Syria or desist from his desire to murder us at home, so we had no way of preventing his planned attacks on our country without taking direct action ...
>
> ... the action we took was entirely lawful. The Attorney General was consulted and was clear that there would be a clear legal basis for action in international law. We were exercising the UK's inherent right to self-defence. There was clear evidence of these individuals planning and directing armed attacks against the UK. These were part of a series of actual and foiled attempts to attack the UK and our allies, and given the prevailing circumstances

[127] ibid. See also Victor Kattan, 'Furthering the "war on terrorism" through international law: How the United States and the United Kingdom resurrected the Bush doctrine on using preventative military force to combat terrorism' (2018) 5 Journal on the Use of Force and International Law 97, particularly 112–123.

[128] General Assembly resolution 60/1, *2005 World Summit Outcome*, A/RES/60/1 (16 September 2005).

[129] Wilmshurst and Wood (n 100) 391.

[130] Glennon, 'Law, Power, and Principles' (n 100) 378.

[131] O'Connell, 'Dangerous Departures' (n 100) 380, and also 384–85.

[132] Brian Egan, then legal adviser to the US Department of State, has also endorsed this doctrine, citing the Bethlehem Principles in his address to the annual meeting of the American Society of International Law in April 2016; see Brian Egan, 'International Law, Legal Diplomacy, and the Counter-ISIL Campaign: Some Observations' (2016) 92 International Law Studies 235, 238–41; and also Kattan, 'Furthering the "war on terrorism"' (n 127) *passim*.

> in Syria, the airstrike was the only feasible means of effectively disrupting the attacks that had been planned and directed. It was therefore necessary and proportionate for the individual self-defence of the United Kingdom.[133]

This incident appears to be consonant with the view expressed by the then Attorney-General, Lord Goldsmith, before the House of Lords on 21 April 2004 that: 'It must be right that states are able to act in self-defence in circumstances where there is evidence of further imminent attacks by terrorist groups, even if there is no specific evidence of where such an attack will take place or of the precise nature of the attack.'[134]

As Gray tartly comments, 'such a wide view deprives the requirement of "imminence" of any content',[135] and further argues that there is no international consensus on the legality of anticipatory self-defence.[136] This nonetheless remains the settled view of the UK government. On 11 January 2017, the Attorney General, Jeremy Wright, set out the government's understanding of self-defence 'in greater detail than the Government has before' in connection with 'our need to defend ourselves against new and evolving types of threats from non-state actors'.[137] Expressly classifying self-defence as an exception to the Article 2(4) prohibition on the use of force,[138] his primary focus was on the notion of imminence in anticipatory self-defence. Arguing that the principles of the law of imminence originate in the *Caroline* incident, 'the way the law is applied has not stood still since 1837', and international terrorism has led the international community to apply the law to new circumstances.[139] Invoking the Chatham House Principles on the Use of Force in Self-Defence, Wright noted that for action taken in self-defence to be necessary, law enforcement measures must be insufficient to deal with the perceived threat: 'But the situation we face today does not always allow for the possibility of using criminal law enforcement measures to stop attacks—when attacks are planned from outside our territory and where the host state is unable or unwilling to act.'[140]

In setting out the UK government's position on the meaning of 'imminence' in relation to terrorist threats, Wright not only referred to the Chatham House Principles, but based himself squarely on the Bethlehem Principles concerning self-defence against an imminent or actual armed attack by non-state actors. He reiterated that the Bethlehem Principles had been informed by 'detailed official-level discussions' and expressly endorsed Principle 8, which enumerated a non-exhaustive list of factors that should be taken into account in

[133] House of Commons Debates (7 September 2015) vol 599, cols 25–26: see also the House of Lords and House of Commons Joint Committee on Human Rights Second Report of Session 2015–16, *The Government's Policy on the Use of Drones for Targeted Killing*, HL Paper 141/HC 574 (10 May 2016), chs 3 and 5; and Intelligence and Security Committee of Parliament, *UK Lethal Drone Strikes in Syria*, HC 1152 (26 April 2017).

[134] See 'United Kingdom Materials on International Law' (2004) 75 British Yearbook of International Law 822–23.

[135] Gray, *Use of Force* (n 43) 215.

[136] See Gray, 'Bush Doctrine' (n 100) 566 and Gray, *Use of Force* (n 43) 160–65; see also Wilmshurst (n 100) 964–65 (Principle A).

[137] Jeremy Wright, 'The Modern Law of Self-defence' International Institute of Strategic Studies (London, 11 January 2017) 1 https://www.gov.uk/government/uploads/system/uploads/attachment_data/file/583171/170111_Imminence_Speech_.pdf. These remarks have been endorsed by the Australian government. In April 2017, the Australian Attorney-General, George Brandis, delivered a lecture entitled 'The Right of Self-Defence against Imminent Armed Attack in International Law' at the University of Queensland, during the course of which he referred to Wright's speech and commented: '[t]he Australian Government agrees with the position stated by my United Kingdom counterpart'. See https://www.ejiltalk.org/the-right-of-self-defence-against-imminent-armed-attack-in-international-law/.

[138] Wright, 'Self-defence' (n 137) 6.

[139] ibid 9.

[140] ibid 10.

assessing whether an anticipated attack is imminent, as well as an observation by Bethlehem which is redolent of the statement made by Lord Goldsmith in April 2004, namely:

> [t]he absence of specific evidence of where an attack will take place or of the precise nature of an attack does not preclude a conclusion that an armed attack is imminent for the purposes of the exercise of a right of self-defense, provided that there is a reasonable and objective basis for concluding that an armed attack is imminent.[141]

This doctrine is reminiscent of an old advertising campaign for a leading brand of vermouth: it is the Martini doctrine of self-defence, justifying recourse to force against non-state armed groups 'anytime, any place, anywhere'.

The position espoused by the UK does not reflect settled law. In 2014, Ben Emmerson, the Human Rights Council's Special Rapporteur on the Promotion and Protection of Human Rights and Fundamental Freedoms while Countering Terrorism, stated in his annual report that there are:

> a number of legal issues on which there is currently no clear international consensus, or where current practices and interpretations appear to challenge established legal norms ... Legal uncertainty in relation to the interpretation and application of the core principles of international law governing the use of deadly force in counter-terrorism operations leaves dangerous latitude for differences of practice by States.[142]

The issues which he identified as giving rise to 'an urgent and imperative need to reach a consensus between states' included the 'unable and unwilling' doctrine, and whether states were entitled to undertake pre-emptive military operations against a non-state armed group situated on the territory of another without the latter's consent if it thought that there was an imminent risk of attack and, if so, 'how is imminence to be defined?'[143] He invited Member States to express their views on these questions before the twenty-seventh session of the Human Rights Council,[144] but in his 2017 Report he noted that no formal answers had been received, although recent developments 'may offer some embryonic direction',[145] which included the January 2017 Wright speech but on which Emmerson offered no comment.[146] It goes without saying that even if the Wright speech offers 'some embryonic direction', this is far from constituting established law.

Leaving the normative uncertainty of the 'unable or unwilling' doctrine and the purported reinterpretation of the requirement of 'imminence' to one side, what are the implications of these alleged developments for the structural core value of collective security? In particular, does the 'unable or unwilling' doctrine destroy or fatally compromise collective security expressed in the prohibition of the use of force in international relations: in short, does it fulfil the *Nicaragua* test that a claimed exception must be consistent with its 'parent' rule?

[141] ibid 17, quoting Bethlehem (n 100) 776.

[142] Ben Emmerson, *Report of the Special Rapporteur on the Promotion and Protection of Human Rights and Fundamental Freedoms while Countering Terrorism*, A/HRC/25/59 (11 March 2014) 18, para 70.

[143] ibid 18–19, para 71(a)(b).

[144] ibid 19, para 72.

[145] Ben Emmerson, *Report of the Special Rapporteur on the Promotion and Protection of Human Rights and Fundamental Freedoms while Countering Terrorism*, A/HRC/34/61 (21 February 2017) 8, para 25.

[146] ibid 9–10, para 28.

The ICJ did not provide an elaborate account of this requirement, and arguably a narrow focus on mere 'local' consistency is inadequate. This could lead to an atomized approach where rules and their exceptions are examined in isolation, detached from wider principles, values, and the context of the legal system which risks introducing (at least latent) structural inconsistencies because the evaluation of the legitimacy, including the consequences, of the exception lacks systemic location. Just as a claimed exception must not efface the efficacy of the parent rule, nor should it prejudice the effective operation of others. While exceptions by their nature may be seen to introduce apparent inconsistencies into the rules of a legal system, they should be consonant with the aims and values of the legal system as a whole, or at least with related normative areas. In MacCormick's terms, a novel claim to an exception raises an issue of second-order reasoning, and its legal acceptability is dependent not only on whether it is coherent with the content of the existing legal system, but also whether it is consistent with (at least) related rules, and also that it is a solution which is universalizable:

> Decisions are not justified in terms of their direct immediate effect on the parties alone (that is when hard cases make bad law), but in terms of an acceptable proposition of law that covers the present case and is therefore available for other like cases (hence satisfying the demand of justice that like cases be treated alike).[147]

To assess the validity of a novel legal issue or claim, such as the 'unable or unwilling' doctrine, MacCormick argues that it must not contradict established rules but also be demonstrably supported by established principles or 'by reasonably close analogy with established rules of law where some statable principle sustains the relevancy of the analogy'.[148] Fulfilling these requirements is necessary, but not sufficient or conclusive as MacCormick's theory is ultimately consequentialist in which an important aspect is the effect the given decision might have on behaviour and its consonance with the values embodied in the legal system:

> It is against these very values that we test and eliminate rival rulings in problematic cases. In considering the juridical consequences of a ruling by way of its implications for hypothetical cases, we discover whether a ruling commits us to universally treating as right deeds that subvert or fail of sufficient respect for the values at stake, or to treating as wrong forms of conduct which include no such subversion or failure. Either consequence is unacceptable.[149]

If these requirements are met, then this serves as some guarantee that the content of the legal system is integrated with a degree of integrity, rather than constitute an atomized set of rules or wilderness of single instances.

Contemporary concerns with the question of the use of force, and self-defence as an exception to the use of force, have mutated since the conclusion of the First World War and the creation of the League of Nations and the formulation of the doctrine of collective security,

[147] MacCormick, *Rhetoric and the Rule of Law* (n 80) 103. This explanation draws on the views set out by MacCormick in *Legal Reasoning and Legal Theory* (Clarendon Press 1978), as reformulated in *Rhetoric and the Rule of Law* and, to a lesser extent, his *Practical Reason in Law and Morality* (Oxford University Press 2008).

[148] MacCormick, *Rhetoric and the Rule of Law* (n 80) 104.

[149] ibid 114. On this aspect of MacCormick's theory see ch 6 and, for commentary, see Maksymilian Del Mar, 'The Forward-Looking Requirement of Formal Justice: Neil MacCormick on Consequentialist Reasoning' (2015) 6 Jurisprudence 429; Bernard Rudden, 'Consequences' (1979) 24 Juridical Review 193; Giovanni Sartor, 'Syllogism and Defeasibility: a Comment on Neil MacCormick's Rhetoric and the Rule of Law' (2008) 59 Northern Ireland Legal Quarterly 21.

and since the Second World War, the creation of the United Nations, and the prohibition on the use of force in Article 2(4). Concern has taken on a new guise with the focus now placed on the use of force against non-state actors.

Contemporary armed conflict may often be seen to involve two types of asymmetry, one of which might be termed performative and the other structural. These terms are only intended to be illustrative, rather than doctrinal or philosophical. The performative asymmetry is the practice of asymmetric warfare and the possibilities it affords to parties to an armed conflict, whether states or non-state armed groups, to bypass or nullify an adversary's strengths and exploit any perceived weaknesses by relying on dissimilarities in strategy, organization, and capacity. It is often claimed that hostile acts of non-state armed groups gain advantage from the asymmetric nature of their operations when contrasted with those conventionally undertaken by a state, and thus pose a performatively asymmetric threat as they aim to avoid the opponent's strengths while exploiting its weaknesses to obtain a disproportionate result.

Structural asymmetry refers to the biases encoded within the structure and substance of international law. These undoubtedly favour states, as states make international law, and the law they make tends, on the whole, to favour their interests. Allott would ascribe this to the influence of Vattel, which has resulted in the situation that 'international law is left speaking to governments the words that governments want to hear'.[150] Of course, states often have different values and policies that they want to embody in international law, but it is none the less true that the law arises from the interaction of states.

The 'unable or unwilling' doctrine is manifestly an attempt to counter the performative asymmetry which might exist in a non-international armed conflict between a state and a non-state armed group which has a transnational spatial dimension, but clear structural support for the doctrine is currently absent. As Emmerson noted, like purported reinterpretations of imminence, the doctrine is (at best) embryonic: no clear state consensus supports it. Accordingly, it can neither form part of the customary international law of self-defence nor amount to an authoritative reinterpretation of the 'parallel' conventional right contained in Article 51 of the UN Charter, particularly if, as Paulus and Leiss maintain, a reinterpretation requires 'universal acceptance' by member states. Is this simply an attempt by a coalition of the powerful to push for change?[151]

For a century, since the end of the First World War, the foundational premise of the international legal and political system has been the doctrine of collective security, initially expressed in the restraints placed on recourse to war in the League Covenant, extended to the renunciation of war as an instrument of national policy in the Pact of Paris, and ultimately culminating in the prohibition on the use of force contained in Article 2(4) of the UN Charter. This strengthening and extension of the ambit of collective security is the background assumption of contemporary international law. The 'unable or unwilling' doctrine is not consonant with the values embedded in and underpinning the over-arching principle of collective security because it contemplates the unilateral extra-territorial use of force by states. Arguably it stands in such a stark conflict with this principle, conventionally expressed in Article 2(4), that it cannot be seen as a legitimate extension of the interpretation of its exception, Article 51, and must be precluded by virtue of the operation of Article 103. As a purported exception to Article 2(4), and its underlying premise of collective security, the 'unable or unwilling' doctrine constitutes a commitment 'to universally treating as right

[150] Philip J Allott, *Eunomia: New Order for a New World* (Oxford University Press 1990) 296, §16.1.

[151] See e.g. Brunnée and Toope (n 100); Corten (n 100); Glennon, 'Law, Power, and Principles' (n 100) 378; O'Connell, 'Dangerous Departures' (n 100) 380; Wilmshurst and Wood (n 100) 391.

deeds that subvert or fail of sufficient respect for the values at stake' and thus fatally falls short of MacCormick's test of legitimacy and acceptability. The doctrine cannot be implemented universally by all states given disparities of power and politics, unless the inevitable inequality of opportunity and ability of action is simply disregarded and subsumed by conventional notions of formal equality. Quite simply, if the 'unable or unwilling' doctrine is accepted as an authoritative aspect of customary self-defence and of the interpretation of Article 51, does this entail that the exception has effaced the rule?

These recent purported developments in the interpretation of the exception of self-defence raise the possibility that the core value of collective security is at risk of being critically undermined so that Egerton's 'myth' of collective security is in danger of becoming no longer an embodiment of a cohesive community value but degenerates into a discarded and dead fiction which, at best, is paid only lip service. A potential danger is that international law is standing on the brink of reverting to a clash between the exigencies and restraints of collective security and the view espoused by Ferguson that armed conflict is simply natural or, in Schwarzenberger's terms, that it is simply 'the culminating point in a rising scale of pressure, the last resort of power politics when diplomacy fails to achieve its objects'. If so, have the 'sacrifices of the great war', and of many more since, simply been made in vain?

10

Defences in the Law of State Responsibility

A View from Jurisprudence

*Luís Duarte d'Almeida**

1 Introduction

Ongoing discussions among international lawyers on defences in state responsibility have close analogies with debates in two other fields: debates in general legal theory on defeasibility in law, and debates in criminal law theory (and philosophy) on the elements of criminal responsibility. The similarities are not surprising. But it is striking how little cross-fertilization there seems to have been. For jurisprudence and criminal law scholars have developed a number of points and distinctions that international law theorists working on defences should find helpful. That, at least, is how things look like to someone coming to learn about the controversies in international law having first gained some familiarity with the insights from those other disciplines.

My goal in this chapter is to illustrate these claims. I cannot provide comprehensive pictures of the debates, but I will concentrate on issues whose discussion may prove especially useful to international law theorists. The chapter has three main sections. Section 2 looks at the role and status of defences in legal decision-making from the point of view of general legal theory, and section 3 does the same from the point of view of criminal law theory. In both cases, I will not merely introduce the relevant issues, but also, drawing on some of my own previous work, recommend specific solutions to particular problems. And then, in section 4, I will suggest—not too immodestly, I hope—that the points made in the preceding sections can help to answer some persistent questions surrounding defences in the law of state responsibility.

2 Lessons from Legal Theory

2.1 'Defences': an ambiguous term

Let us start by being clear about the very notion of a defence. It is not a specifically legal notion. It is just as prominent, for example, in the context of moral responsibility. But my focus will be on the legal domain, and particularly on criminal responsibility. Of course, the model of criminal responsibility can only go so far in assisting us with understanding the law of state responsibility. But it is a useful model as far as it goes.

The word 'defence' is multiply ambiguous. Sometimes it is used to refer to a certain type of facts that, if raised and successfully established, mandate an acquittal. This is the sense in

* University of Edinburgh.

Luís Duarte d'Almeida, *Defences in the Law of State Responsibility* In: *Exceptions in International Law.* Edited by: Lorand Bartels and Federica Paddeu, Oxford University Press (2020). © Lorand Bartels and Federica Paddeu.
DOI: 10.1093/oso/9780198789321.003.0010

which self-defence, for example, is said to be a 'defence' in murder. But the word 'defence' can also be used to refer to one characteristic way in which relevant facts may be brought to the attention of a decision maker in the course of the legal process. This is the sense in which a defendant can be said to offer a certain fact *as* a 'defence' *to* a claim or charge. In this second sense of the term, we can say that self-defence (a 'defence' in the first sense of the term) is a fact that can be offered *as a defence*—as a procedural reply *to* a criminal charge—in a case of murder.

That is one source of ambiguity. Yet even if we confine ourselves to what I have just called the 'first' sense, the scope with which the word is used can still vary, and that too calls for disambiguation. Sometimes 'defence' is used to refer to *any* fact that will, when successfully established, mandate an acquittal. In this broad, all-encompassing sense, the word extends, for example, to purely procedural obstacles to conviction, such as limitation bars, lack of jurisdiction, or a defendant's immunity from trial. But the term can also be used in a narrower sense covering only facts (a) whose presence (or absence) bears on the *merits* of the issue of liability, and (b) which, moreover, do not amount to a denial that the relevant offence-elements are satisfied.[1]

My concern throughout this chapter is with defences in this narrower sense—which is the sense in which they are properly contrasted with the criminal 'offences'. To prevent confusion, then, let us fix some terminology.

2.2 *P*-facts and *D*-facts

I will speak of '*D*-facts' to refer to facts of the relevant type: facts—like self-defence in murder—that need to be *absent* in order for a certain decision—like a decision to convict a criminal defendant—to be correct on the merits. And I will speak of '*P*-facts' to refer to facts—like those that constitute the elements of criminal offences—that need to be *present* in order for a certain decision to be correct on the merits. (The distinction between these two types of facts, *P*-facts and *D*-facts, is not, of course, specific to the criminal law.)

Note that the distinction between the two types of facts is always relative to a certain type of decision or judgment.

2.3 A puzzle

I said that the difference between *P*-facts and *D*-facts in the domain of the criminal law—the difference between offences and defences—is that the former must be present, and the latter absent, for the decision to convict the defendant to be warranted. Compare self-defence in murder with, say, consent in rape. Each plays a different role. The former is a defence, but the latter is not. We would say, not that consent is a defence in rape, but that *absence of consent* is an element—a 'negative' element—of the corresponding offence. Unlike self-defence, then, consent is not a *D*-fact. Rather, its negation is a *P*-fact.

Or so we are used to thinking and saying. But are we right to draw such a distinction? In fact, can the distinction even be consistently maintained? Could we not say that consent—the

[1] I say more on the meaning of 'defence', and on what a working definition of the term should encompass, in 'Defining "Defences"' in Andrew Dyson, James Goudkamp, and Frederick Wilmot-Smith (eds), *Defences in Tort* (Hart Publishing 2015) 35–52.

supposed negation of a *P*-fact—is something that must be *absent* if a conviction in trespass or rape is to be warranted? Or, conversely, that *absence of self-defence*—the supposed negation of a *D*-fact—is something that must be *present* in order for a conviction in murder to be correct? And does that not show that there really is no difference—our initial intuitions and linguistic practices notwithstanding—between the two kinds of facts?

Some theorists have thought so. Glanville Williams, for example, thought that we are bound to acknowledge that there really is 'no intrinsic difference between the elements of an offence and an exception (or defence) to that offence'. His point was that 'the negative of an element of an offence can be regarded as an exception, and the negative of an exception can be regarded as an element of the offence'. Therefore 'a rule that is subject to an exception is only partly true if stated without the exception ... The exception is, rationally regarded, part and parcel of the rule'.[2]

Williams was not alone in adopting this view, which I will dub 'incorporationism'. According to incorporationism, the rule setting out the conditions on which a conviction depends can be represented as having the following structure, in which '*a*' and '*b*' stand for the elements of the relevant criminal offence, '*x*', '*y*', and '*z*' for the admissible defences, and '*C*' can be read as 'the court should convict':

(1) If *a* and *b* and *not-x* and *not-y* and *not-z*, then *C*.

The point—the incorporationists' point—is that the *absence* of each of the admissible defences plays precisely the same role that the *presence* of each of the relevant offence-elements: they are elements of the antecedent of the relevant rule. Moreover, there is nothing preventing an *offence* from having—as in the example of rape—'negative' elements, and in that case the structure of the corresponding rule shows clearly that there is no distinction between the kind of fact ('*c*') which, like consent in rape, *negates* a *negative* offence-element, and the kind of fact ('*x*') which, like self-defence in murder, we would call a 'defence':

(2) If *a* and *b* and *not-c* and *not-x* and *not-y* and *not-z*, then *C*.

Not everyone agrees with the incorporationist account of defences, though—nor should we. We ought not to be so quick to abandon the thought that there *is* some relevant difference to be drawn between offences and defences, between *P*-facts and *D*-facts. How then is the difference to be explained? Some theorists, dissatisfied with the incorporationist proposal, have tried to make sense of the contrast by saying that defences have the nature of *exceptions*: they are facts that stand, as it were, 'outside' the relevant rules, but which, when present, prevent the relevant rules from applying.[3] Some of those theorists suggest that we think of the rules that govern judgments of criminal liability as having the following structure, which purports to differentiate between *P*-facts, positive or negative ('*a*', '*b*', '*not-c*'), and *D*-facts ('*x*', '*y*', '*z*'):

(3) If *a* and *b* and *not-c*, then *C*, unless *x* or *y* or *z*.[4]

There is something to this suggestion: whilst negative offence-elements ('*not-c*') are facts that need to be positively established if the conviction is to be warranted, defences ('*x*', '*y*', '*z*') are

[2] See Glanville Williams, 'The Logic of "Exceptions"' (1988) 47 Cambridge Law Journal 261, 277–78.

[3] See e.g. Claire Oakes Finkelstein, 'When the Rule Swallows the Exception' in Linda Meyer (ed), *Rules and Reasoning: Essays in Honour of Fred Schauer* (Hart Publishing 1999) 145–75 at 149–50.

[4] See HLA Hart, 'The Ascription of Responsibility and Rights' (1949) 49 Proceedings of the Aristotelian Society 171, 174.

facts that constrain decision-making only when they do come up in the relevant context.[5] This, then, is an insight worth preserving. The problem is that it is not adequately captured in formulation (3). Indeed, since 'C, unless *x* or *y* or *z*' entails 'if C, then *not-x* and *not-y* and *not-z*', formulation (3) seems to collapse back into incorporationism. It is also hard to see that 'If *a* and *b* and *not-c*, then C' would give us a satisfactory rendition of the relevant rule; for we can always ask for a *complete*, all-things-considered formulation of the facts on which the conviction depends, and at least in contexts in which there is a closed catalogue of defences it seems we would again end up with the incorporationist proposal. Which, of course, was Williams's point: 'a rule that is subject to an exception is only partly true if stated without the exception'.[6]

Neither of these common approaches, then, is good enough. Each lacks precisely what the other provides. Is there a way out?

2.4 The proof-based account

The reason that the incorporationist proposal fails to adequately capture the difference between *P*-facts and *D*-facts is that it is unable to discriminate between two senses in which a relevant fact can be said to be 'absent' in a given decision-making context. Incorporationists work under a binary scheme. They distinguish only, for any fact *F*, between *F* and *not-F*. In the legal context, however, our judgments depend, not on whether the relevant facts *are* the case, but on whether they have been established (or 'proved', as I will say) in the relevant decision-making context. There is room, therefore, to draw a fourfold distinction. For any fact *F*, it can be that:

A. *F* is proved.
B. *Not-F* is proved.
C. *F* is *not* proved.
D. *Not-F* is *not* proved.

This framework enables us to capture the difference between the sense in which consent must be 'absent' in a case of rape, and the sense in which self-defence must be 'absent' in a case of murder. The former must be absent in the sense that its *negation* must *be* proved; the latter must be absent in the sense that *it* must *not* be proved. This also does justice to the insight that defences matter only if and when they actually emerge—if and when they are actually established—in the relevant decision-making context.

[5] See John F Horty, 'Nonmonotonic Logic' in L Goble (ed), *The Blackwell Guide to Philosophical Logic* (Blackwell 2001) 341.

[6] See the passages accompanying n 2 above. Williams was not alone; other authors who endorse the incorporationist strategy include JL Mackie, 'Responsibility and Language' (1955) 33 Australasian Journal of Philosophy 143, 146–47; George Nakhnikian, 'Contemporary Ethical Theories and Jurisprudence' (1957) 2 Natural Law Forum 4, 26 (on the 'formal' equivalence of 'P-conditions' and 'negated D-conditions'); Richard E Susskind, *Expert Systems in Law: A Jurisprudential Inquiry* (Clarendon Press 1987) 196; Neil MacCormick, 'Defeasibility in Law and Logic' in Zenon Bańkowski, Ian White, and Ulrike Hahn (eds), *Informatics and the Foundations of Legal Reasoning* (Kluwer 1995) 100; Fernando Atria, *On Law and Legal Reasoning* (Hart Publishing 2001) 124–25, 137–38; Richard HS Tur, 'Defeasibilism' (2001) 21 Oxford Journal of Legal Studies 355, 359–60, 367; or Wilfrid J Waluchow, 'Defeasibility and Legal Positivism' in Jordi Ferrer Beltrán and Giovanni Battista Ratti (eds), *The Logic of Legal Requirements: Essays on Defeasibility* (Oxford University Press 2012) 260.

Here, then, is how the structure of the rule setting out the conditions of a correct conviction can be represented (with '*a*', '*b*', and '*not-c*' standing, as before, for offence-elements or *P*-facts; and '*x*', '*y*', and '*z*' for defences or *D*-facts):

(4) If it is *proved that* (*a* and *b* and *not-c*) and it is *not proved that* (*x* or *y* or *z*), then *C*.

It turns out, therefore, that our intuitive resistance to the incorporationist view—according to which there is no difference between *P*-facts and *D*-facts—is well grounded. There is a significant difference. *P*-facts are facts—positive or negative—on whose ascertainment the relevant decision depends, whereas *D*-facts are facts—positive or negative—on whose *non*-ascertainment the relevant decision depends.

This is just the roughest of summaries of an account of defences—the 'proof-based' account—that I have defended at length elsewhere.[7] Unlike the alternative accounts described in the previous subsection, the proof-based account is able to accommodate in a coherent way our seemingly conflicting pre-theoretical intuitions on defences. It also brings out the fact that defences are a by-product of our need to reach decisions under conditions of uncertainty. In a world of omniscient decision-makers there would be no need, and indeed no room, for the distinction between *P*-facts and *D*-facts.

The proof-based account also carries important practical consequences. The most important of these concerns the allocation of burdens of proof. Lawyers, courts, and even legislators sometimes speak as if one sensible way of determining which party should carry the burden of proof relative to a certain fact is to ask whether that fact is a defence. If the proof-based account is right, however, this is a wild goose chase. To say that a fact is a defence—a *D*-fact—*just is* to say that the defendant is burdened with the corresponding proof. (And to say that a party carries the 'burden of proof' with regard to a certain fact just is to say that unless that fact is proved, that party will fail.) Put another way: debates about who should carry the burden of proof about a certain circumstance *are* debates about whether that circumstance should be treated as a *D*-fact, or its negation as a *P*-fact instead. So the circumstance's status as either a *P*-fact or a *D*-fact cannot itself be a criterion on the basis of which to allocate the burden.

2.5 Summing up

What matters for my present purposes is not so much that the proof-based account of defences be perceived as persuasive. What matters now is that the nature of the jurisprudential debate on defences be clearly understood.

The issue is how to explain a difference between two types of facts—a difference that lawyers recognize and speak of as significant, and which is present across many branches of law. In the criminal law, it is expressed as the difference between offences and defences. But it is the same contrast that shows up, for example, in tort law (where the 'elements' of a tort are contrasted with the relevant defences), in contract, and in many other areas of substantive law. It is a distinction that is characteristically present whenever matters of responsibility arise. Both kinds of facts, which I have called '*P*-facts' and '*D*-facts', feature in the conditions of the rules governing the ascription of responsibility and of liability to certain consequences (including sanctions). At the intuitive level, the claim is that the absence of a *P*-fact

[7] See Luís Duarte d'Almeida, *Allowing for Exceptions: A Theory of Defences and Defeasibility in Law* (Oxford University Press 2015).

is 'something quite different' from the absence of a *D*-fact.[8] The jurisprudential challenge is to articulate the framework that vindicates that intuition as well as our well-established practices.

3 Lessons from Criminal Law Theory

3.1 Justifications and excuses as two kinds of *D*-facts

Having focused so far on the distinction between criminal offences and defences to highlight some important jurisprudential points, I want now to turn to some other, related distinctions relied on by criminal law theorists to account for some salient features of our systems of criminal responsibility. One such distinction is between two kinds of defences: justifications and excuses.

All defences—all *D*-facts—are alike in the effect they bring about. They all mandate a verdict of acquittal (or, at any rate, a decision favourable to the defendant). But it does not follow that the reason why they mandate this verdict is the same for every defence. Indeed, the classification of defences into justifications and excuses is an attempt to distinguish two importantly different types of reasons why an acquittal may be warranted on substantive grounds even if the defendant has been shown to have committed an offence. Some *D*-facts, like self-defence in murder, are said to *justify* the defendant's conduct: although the defendant's action (e.g., killing another person) does meet the description of a criminal offence, the fact that it has been performed in self-defence makes it legally permissible. Some other *D*-facts, by contrast, do not render the action permissible, but show the agent not to be culpable of performing it: the action remains impermissible, but the agent has an *excuse*, which gives us a reason of a different sort to acquit him.

This again is a superficial presentation; the distinction between justifications and excuses, although widely used, is far from being fully clear or unproblematic. What is well known, or at least widely accepted, is that *there is* a distinction. What the distinction ultimately comes down to is something on which different theorists take different views, but my concern here is not with the minutiae of these debates. My concern is to highlight a couple of important points about the role the contrast plays within the frame of a theory of responsibility.

3.2 'Elements' of responsibility and theories of responsibility

As I just noted, the distinction between justifications and excuses provides a way of accounting for the reasons why different types of *D*-facts have the acquittal-warranting effect that they have. Obviously, then, this distinction is perfectly compatible with the distinction between offences and defences. The fact that some of the admissible defences ('*x*', '*y*') in a given decision-making context are to be classified as justifications, and some ('*z*') as excuses, does not upset the accuracy of the model with which the structure of the relevant rule can—as we saw in section 2—be displayed:

(4) If it is *proved that* (*a* and *b* and *not-c*) and it is *not proved that* (*x* or *y* or *z*), then *C*.

[8] This is Hart's phrase: see n 4 at 174.

My reason for emphasizing this point is that, on the back of the distinction between justifications and excuses, many criminal law theorists—including those who subscribe to the dominant Continental approach to criminal law, the German *Verbrechenslehre*—endorse what they call a tripartite 'definition' of the notion of a crime. They analyse this notion in terms of a conjunction of three positive 'elements': (a) the offence-elements (i.e., the elements of what German criminal law theorists call the *Tatbestand*); (b) legal wrongfulness (*Rechtswidrigkeit*); and (c) blameworthiness or culpability (*Schuld*).

Importantly, this tripartite 'definition' of a crime is not to be construed as an *alternative* to the bipartite breakdown of the relevant facts into offences and defences.[9] As we saw in section 2, the distinction between offences and defences—*P*-facts and *D*-facts—classifies relevant facts according to the way in which their presence or absence bears on the correctness of a court's decision to either convict and acquit. And it is not a parochial or jurisdiction-specific distinction; it is just as much a feature of Continental (including German) criminal law and procedure as it is of Anglo-American criminal law and procedure. There, as elsewhere, the admissible defences are facts that, if established, mandate an acquittal, but whose absence does *not* have to be ascertained for the court to convict correctly; and there, as elsewhere, what needs to be established is that the elements of the offence are present. By contrast, the theoretical 'definition' of a crime into those three 'elements'—offence-elements, wrongfulness, and blameworthiness—does not purport to track the relevant facts or represent the way in which their presence or absence bears on the correctness of a court's decision to either convict and acquit. 'Wrongfulness', for example, is *not* the name of any operative or material fact that actually needs to be ascertained for a conviction to be warranted. So the tripartite definition of a crime does not purport to supplant or replace the bipartite offence/defence distinction. What it does purport to do is to offer is a theoretical explanation of why these two types of material facts, *P*-facts and *D*-facts, have the responsibility-warranting or responsibility-precluding effects that they do.

Now, theorists who adopt the tripartite definition of a crime adopt the distinction between justifications and excuses. How so? By saying that each type of *D*-fact 'precludes' the satisfaction of one of the three 'elements' in the definition. Justifications are *D*-facts that preclude the *wrongfulness* of the defendant's action. Excuses are *D*-facts that preclude the agent's *culpability*. That much is clear. But endorsers of the tripartite account also purport to explain why certain other facts—the *P*-facts—are such that, if they are ascertained and no other relevant facts are ascertained, then the correct decision is to convict. The tripartite definition, in other words, involves an attempt—whether good or bad is now beside the point—to provide an explanation of the *relation* between *P*-facts and *D*-facts in the criminal law. What then do these theorists say about the *first* definitional 'element'? How do they explain why *P*-facts should have the effect that they do?

3.3 *P*-facts, *D*-facts, and 'prima facie' vs 'all things considered' wrongfulness

The dominant account of the relevance of *P*-facts—offences—within the frame of this 'tripartite' definition is in terms of *prima facie* legal wrongfulness. What does that mean? We should take care not to get confused. A justified action, such as a killing done in self-defence,

[9] I explain this at much greater length in ch 9 of Duarte d'Almeida, *Allowing for Exceptions* (n 7) especially at 219–34.

is a legally permissible—a lawful—action. But that does not imply that it is a legally neutral or indeed legally irrelevant action. In this context, 'permissible' expresses an all-things-considered deontic evaluation of a given course of action. But there are other ways in which that course of action can be normatively evaluated and deemed to constitute a wrong.

How can a permissible action still be a wrong? One popular explanation appeals to reasons. Criminal offences, some theorists suggest, are types of action that we have, according to the law, particularly strong reasons *not* to perform—actions against which there are 'legally recognised reasons'—and, indeed, reasons that suffice to call the action a *wrong*.[10] This does not mean that there is, all things considered, a duty not to perform it. The action may still be all things considered permissible: it may be justified. But the point is that reasons that count *against* the action are still 'in place', as it were: they remain 'genuine', *pro tanto* reasons against performing the action, even if, on the balance of reasons, the action is not impermissible. That is what these theorists call a 'prima facie' wrong. Note that the phrase 'prima facie' is being used, not in the evidential sense (perhaps more familiar to lawyers) that means something like 'at first sight', but to refer to a wrong that *is* and *remains* a wrong even in the face of justification. A 'prima facie' wrong that is *not* justified is called an 'all things considered wrong'; but a justified wrong *remains a wrong*, even when it is, all things considered, permissible.

Whether or not a reasons-based account along these lines is ultimately defensible, it certainly is true that an action that is all things considered permissible is not ipso facto an action against which there cannot be strong reasons—let alone an action against which nothing can be said. It is a mistake to think that the law cannot take an unfavourable view of actions that it ultimately permits. And it does seem plausible that the difference between neutral or irrelevant actions—actions not even described as criminal offences to begin with—and actions that are marked as *offences* even if they may turn out to be justified, is a difference to be explained in terms of the different normative stances that the law takes towards them. To give a famous example, the law must surely draw some *normative* difference between the killing of a mosquito and the killing of a man in self-defence; for the latter killing, unlike the former, is a *P*-fact.[11]

This carries an interesting implication regarding those defences that are classified as justifications. At the level of the *identification of the facts on whose presence or absence a criminal conviction depends*, justifications, as we have seen, stand *apart from offences*, and together with excuses, as *D*-facts. But at the level of the *theoretical explanation of why they should carry the liability-preventing effect that they do*, justifications—or their absence—stand *alongside* offences, and apart from excuses: for crimes are actions that the law regards as wrongful all things considered, and all-things-considered wrongfulness is a matter of an action being *both* (a) an offence, and thus an action on which the law takes an unfavourable normative view, and (b) not justified.

There is nothing inconsistent about this dual view of justifications. Those are just two different types of claims, made at two different levels of analysis and explanation. One is a claim about the way in which the presence or absence of justifications constrains decision-making

[10] See e.g. John Gardner, *Justifications and Reasons* (Oxford University Press 1996), 'In Defence of Defences' (Oxford University Press 2002), and 'Fletcher on Offences and Defences' (Oxford University Press 2004), all reprinted in his *Offences and Defences: Selected Essays in the Philosophy of Criminal Law* (Oxford University Press 2007); and RA Duff, *Answering for Crime: Responsibility and Liability in the Criminal Law* (Hart Publishing 2007).

[11] The example is from Hans Welzel, 'Die Regelung von Vorsatz und Irrtum im Strafrecht als legislatorisches Problem' (1955) 67 Zeitschrift für die gesamte Strafrechtswissenschaft 196, 211; it is echoed in George Fletcher, *Rethinking Criminal Law* (1978, Oxford University Press 2000) 561.

in the criminal context. The other is part of a theoretical explanation of why justifications should constrain decision-making in that way. The two are perfectly compatible.

It is true, however, that it can be easy to lose sight of the distinction between these two levels of discourse about responsibility. And that, as we will see in section 4, can give rise to some apparent paradoxes.

3.4 Primary and secondary rules

One equally popular way of further explaining this dual role played by justifications is by appealing to a distinction between two types of *rules*, both of which would be at play in the criminal law: (a) primary, duty-imposing rules, addressed to everyone; and (b) secondary rules, addressed to legal officials, and courts in particular, specifying the conditions under which someone should be liable to certain consequences that come with the infringement of a primary rule.[12] Secondary rules are 'secondary' in the sense that the consequences that they stipulate or trigger—paradigmatically, punishment—presuppose that a duty-imposing rule has been broken.

How does this distinction help us to understand the dual status of justifications? It is at the level of *secondary* rules that justifications can be seen to be defences or *D*-facts. Indeed, the very notion of a defence is a notion that comes up *only* at the level of the secondary rules—whose structure, as I have pointed out above, can be displayed as follows:

(4) If it is *proved that* (*a* and *b* and *not-c*) and it is *not proved that* (*x* or *y* or *z*), then *C*.

Primary rules have a different structure. They are best conceived as requirements of the following form (where 'φ' stands for a type of action):

(5) It is forbidden to φ.

Here there is no room for any distinction between *P*-facts and *D*-facts. All we have is a certain course of action that is legally proscribed. But if a circumstance *x* is a justificatory defence—that is, if it is both (at the level of the secondary rule) a defence, and (like self-defence in murder) a justification—then its negation will form part of the description of the relevant action φ that is the content of the primary prohibition: and the reason is that, as we have also seen above, no justified action is legally forbidden.

I hope this is clear enough, but for avoidance of doubt let me sound two notes of caution. The first is that the point of adopting this distinction between those two types of rules is not that one should be turning to primary *rather than* to secondary rules in order to understand the role of justification (or indeed in order to understand criminal responsibility more generally). The point is that a complete account of the role of justifications will avail itself of both notions. Justifications are *both* defences within the frame of secondary rules, *and* circumstances that render permissible, all things considered, actions that satisfy an offence definition, with the result that such actions fall outside the scope of any primary rule.

[12] This can be traced back to Karl Binding's 1872 distinction between the penal *law* (the *Strafgesetz*) specifying the conditions on which the imposition of a criminal sanctions depends, and the prescriptive *norm*, addressed to the legal subjects, and the infringement of which the *Strafgesetz* is said to presuppose: see Karl Binding, *Die Normen und ihre Übertretung: Eine Untersuchung über die Rechtsmässige Handlung und die Arten des Delikts. Erster Band: Normen und Strafgesetze* (Wilhelm Englemann 1872) 6–14, 23–31.

The second note of caution concerns the idea, which I have already mentioned, that defences—*D*-facts—can be characterized as exceptions *to* rules, as considerations that stand 'outside' the applicable rules and which will, when present, prevent such rules from applying.[13] What rules would these be? The primary rules? The secondary rules? The answer is 'neither'. Defences are emphatically *not* exceptions *to* the fully spelled-out primary rules; and of course they cannot be exceptions *to* the fully spelled-out secondary rules (which *include*, as part of the conditions of their application, the absence of admissible exceptions). What then can those who speak of defences as exceptions *to* rules mean?

What they have in mind is a 'rule' formulated *at the level of* the secondary rules—but one that directly links the *P*-facts with the relevant consequences:

(4*) If it is *proved that* (*a* and *b* and *not-c*), then *C*.

Clearly, however, this 'rule' could not be taken to specify sufficient conditions for the consequence. It has to be meant instead as a 'defeasible' rule (which is how it is sometimes characterized), a rule *to* which there can be exceptions. But whether or not one wants to speak of 'rules' of this sort—my own view is that we would do well to stick to the unpacked version in (4)—the point now is that these would be instances of neither primary rules proscribing certain types of action, nor fully spelled-out secondary rules setting out the conditions of correct ascriptions of responsibility.

3.5 The crucial role of the notion of an offence

As may have become clear in the course of the preceding discussion, it is not only justifications that enjoy a dual status in theoretical accounts of criminal responsibility. The same is true of the facts that constitute elements of criminal offences. At the level of the *secondary* rules, offences are the relevant *P*-facts: those facts which, if successfully established, will warrant a conviction unless some defence is also established. At the level of the theoretical explanation of why it is that such facts should have this conviction-warranting status, offences are taken by many theorists, as I pointed out, to be actions or omissions, the commission of which amounts to a prima facie wrong. Let me reiterate that this is not the same as saying that there is, all things considered, a legal duty not to perform such actions or omissions; an action or omission that satisfies the elements of an offence may still be justified. But—again—what a justification precludes is the judgment that the action of omission is all things considered wrongful, not the judgment that there are, according to the law, strong reasons *not* to perform it.

4 Applying the Lessons to the Law of State Responsibility

4.1 *P*-facts and *D*-facts in the law of state responsibility

I remarked that the distinction between *P*-facts and *D*-facts is not specific to the criminal law, but a more important point is that the distinction is also not specific to decision-making

[13] See text accompanying n 3 above.

contexts—like the judicial one—whose proceedings are institutionally governed by authoritative rules. In fact, as I also pointed out, the distinction between *P*-facts and *D*-facts is not even a uniquely *legal* distinction. It presents itself in exactly the same way, for example, in the context of our everyday practices of holding each other responsible.

The reason I mention this is that one might be tempted to think that the proof-based account of defences, apt though it may be in the context of the criminal trial, cannot be of much use in explaining the role of defences in the law of state responsibility. After all, the adjudication of disputes between states by an international court or tribunal is neither the only nor the primary context in which the issue of state responsibility is appropriately raised.

But this worry would be misplaced. Consider a state that claims—however informally—that some other state should be held responsible for some breach of an international obligation. How is such a claim to be assessed? What are its success conditions? There will be some relevant facts that form the basis of the claim—namely, the facts that constitute the conduct which is, according to the claimant state, attributable to the state being held responsible—and which will need to be established; and it also has to be the case that none of the admissible defences is shown to apply. But this is just another instance of the basic distinction between two classes of relevant facts, *P*-facts and *D*-facts. The distinction is present even in the absence of settled rules (e.g. rules on what constitutes admissible evidence, or laying down particular standards of proof) specifying what exactly counts as 'showing' or 'establishing' a relevant fact.

What this means is that the same model that I have been using to represent the structure of the secondary rules that govern criminal liability can also be used to display the rules that govern the international responsibility of states. We may substitute 'shown' for the more formal-sounding 'proved'; but we can use, as before, '*a*', '*b*', '*not-c*', and so on, to stand for the relevant *P*-facts, and '*x*', '*y*', and so on, to stand for the admissible defences:

(4') If it is *shown that* (*a* and *b* and *not-c*) and *not shown that* (*x* or *y* or *z*), then *C*

Here we can take '*C*' to stand for the claim that whatever consequences of international responsibility happen to be applicable in the relevant context should indeed be implemented.

4.2 *D*-facts and 'circumstances precluding wrongfulness'

The six 'circumstances precluding wrongfulness' codified in Chapter V of the International Law Commission's Articles on Responsibility of States for Internationally Wrongful Acts (ARSIWA) are a catalogue of admissible defences; and I do not think I can overemphasize the point that the status of these circumstances *as defences*—as *D-facts*—is something completely independent of their status as circumstances that 'preclude wrongfulness'.

To say that these six circumstances—consent, self-defence, countermeasures, force majeure, distress, necessity—are defences is, as we know from the discussion in section 2, to make a point about the *way* in which their presence or absence affects the relevant judgments about the international responsibility of a state: it is to say that such circumstances are *D*-facts rather than negative *P*-facts. By contrast, to say that they are circumstances that 'preclude' the wrongfulness of the relevant act is, as we know from the discussion in section 3, to make a point about the *reason* that any of those circumstances should have the responsibility-preventing effect that it does.

My impression, however, is that these two points are often conflated in the relevant literature. There are international law theorists who seem to think that the status of any given circumstance as a defence is something that turns on its status (or lack thereof) as a circumstance that precludes wrongfulness. I will give some examples below, but it should already be clear why this view must be mistaken.

Indeed, there is no reason that international law scholars should blindly endorse the ARSIWA's own classification of the six defences as circumstances that *do* all of them preclude wrongfulness. It may have been Roberto Ago's view that that is the common effect of the relevant circumstances.[14] It may be James Crawford's view that 'on balance ... [no] categorical distinction needs to be made as between the circumstances to be covered by chapter V', and that no explicit distinction should be drawn 'between justifications (such as self-defence), which preclude wrongfulness, and excuses (such as necessity), which may have some lesser effect'.[15] But international law theorists are free, of course, to take a different view—as some have.[16] It is open to them to hold that as a matter of sound theory, the responsibility-preventing consequences of at least some of the six ARSIWA circumstances is indeed to be explained in terms of their exculpatory rather than justificatory effect. But that, again—this is my point—would be a matter of providing a theoretical account of why it is that these defences should have the effect that they do. That the six circumstances *are* defences—*D*-facts—is not in issue; on the contrary: it is something that must be presupposed by both sides in the debate.

4.3 A plea for offences

Although there is, as I have just noted, some debate among international law theorists about how to classify the admissible defences, there seems to be little awareness that there is a cognate question to be asked with regard to *P*-facts. As we saw in section 3, however, theorists of responsibility do not just need to account for how the notion of legal wrongfulness relates to the admissible *D*-facts. They also need to explain how it relates to the relevant *P*-facts.

What are the relevant *P*-facts in the context of international responsibility? They are those facts that any state invoking the responsibility of another state needs to raise, and be prepared to establish, in order for its claim to be successful. Importantly, these are not facts whose ascertainment conclusively shows that there has been a breach of an international obligation. For the establishment of the relevant *P*-facts is compatible with there being a justification, and if there is a justification there will have been no breach of any international obligation. The *P*-facts, rather, are the exact analogue, in this domain, of what criminal law theorists call 'offences'. As far as I can see, however, international law theorists seem to have no similar term or notion. That is, it seems to me, a significant theoretical handicap.

The case for having the notion of an offence (or any equivalent notion) in one's conceptual toolkit is, as we saw in section 3, that the notion tracks a specific type of facts: those whose presence or absence constrains the relevant decisions (e.g. to convict or acquit) in a particular way, and whose role therefore needs to be accounted for by any theory of responsibility. We

[14] Eighth Report on State Responsibility, *Yearbook of the International Law Commission* (1979) vol II(1) para 55.

[15] Second Report on State Responsibility, *Yearbook of the International Law Commission* (1999) vol II(1) paras 231, 355.

[16] See e.g. Vaughan Lowe, 'Precluding Wrongfulness or Responsibility: A Plea for Excuses' (1999) 10 European Journal of International Law 405.

also saw that, on a popular view, criminal offences are actions or omissions that we have, according to the law, strong reason not to perform—they are actions that the law regards as prima facie wrongs. On that view, as I then mentioned, we need to draw a distinction between this notion of a prima facie wrong, and the notion of an action that is wrongful *all things considered*. Both are normative notions. Both express a negative evaluation of the relevant action. Only the latter, however, can be translated into the deontic language of what is legally 'impermissible'.

In international law, however, it seems that there is, for the most part, only *one* notion in play—the notion of an 'internationally wrongful act' of a state, in the language of Article 1 of the ARSIWA—which is supposed to somehow do double theoretical work. One rare instance in which something approximating the notion of an offence seems to be at play is in the opening commentary to Chapter V: 'Circumstances precluding wrongfulness ... are to be distinguished from the *constituent requirements of the obligation*, i.e. those elements which have to exist *for the issue of wrongfulness to arise in the first place* and which are in principle specified by the obligation itself.'[17]

This reference to the *constituent elements of the obligation*, and their definition as elements that 'have to exist'—that is, are necessary, though, presumably, not sufficient—'for the issue of wrongfulness to arise in the first place' seems to be an attempt, however unhelpfully phrased, to refer to the relevant *P*-facts.[18] It is echoed in Crawford's *State Responsibility*, where he writes that the class of admissible defences 'does not extend to *requirements necessary for a primary obligation to arise in the first place*'.[19] The language of 'constituent elements' is also used in the commentary to Article 2 of the ARSIWA (italics added): 'Article 2 specifies the conditions required to establish the existence of an internationally wrongful act of the State, i.e. the *constituent elements* of such an act.'

The use of this phrase is a step in the right direction, but fails to dispel confusion. Indeed, the passage just quoted from the commentary to Article 2, although it starts by employing this notion of the *constituent elements* of a wrongful act—a category which is not, one would presume, identical with the notion of an act that is *not justified*—goes on to assert that one of those constituent elements is in effect that the conduct *constitutes a breach of an international legal obligation*: 'Two elements are identified. First, the conduct in question must be attributable to the State under international law. Secondly, for responsibility to attach to the act of the State, the conduct must constitute a breach of an international legal obligation in force for that State at that time.'

But this can be true only if the question of whether the act is justified has already been asked *and answered* negatively. The point of isolating the 'constituent elements' of obligations, however, should be that of identifying types of act with regard to which it would *then* make sense to ask whether they are justified.

The same can be said of the excerpt, quoted above, from the introductory commentary to Chapter V of the ARSIWA.[20] Its attempt to single out the 'constituent requirements of the obligation' as those elements that need to be present 'for the issue of wrongfulness to arise in the first place' is undermined by the fact that the passage goes on to state that such elements

[17] Draft Articles on Responsibility of States for Internationally Wrongful Acts, with Commentaries (2001) para 7 of the opening commentary to ch V (italics added).

[18] That must also be the reason that Ago, in his Eighth Report, speaks of an act of a state done, for example, in self-defence, as an act that is 'not in conformity with the *terms* of an international obligation' even if it does conform with the *obligation* itself: see Eighth Report on State Responsibility (n 14) para 51.

[19] James Crawford, *State Responsibility: The General Part* (Cambridge University Press 2013) 275.

[20] See passage accompanying n 17 above.

are specified *by the obligation* itself—which circularly suggests that we *do* need to consider the question of whether the obligation has been breached (and thus to deal with 'the issue of wrongfulness') in order to determine whether the 'constituent requirements' are satisfied.

For one illustration of the dangers stemming from this inability to differentiate between the question of whether the relevant *P*-facts are present, and the further question of whether the corresponding act does amount to a breach of an international obligation, consider the following passage, from Giorgio Gaja's fourth Report on the responsibility of international organizations:

> A few commentators noted that the articles on responsibility of States for internationally wrongful acts in part one, chapter V, group some heterogeneous circumstances and, in particular, do not make a distinction between causes of justification and excuses. If that distinction were made, the first category would group circumstances which radically exclude wrongfulness, while the other circumstances would have a more limited effect and only exceptionally provide a shield against responsibility ... However, a cause of justification cannot appropriately be ranged among the circumstances precluding wrongfulness, because it would rule out any breach of an international obligation.[21]

Note this last sentence: a cause of justification is not appropriately classified as a circumstance 'precluding wrongfulness' *because* that 'would rule out any breach of an international obligation'. I take Gaja's point to be that breach of an international obligation is something that must be established in order for a claim in international responsibility to even get off the ground; and if *that* has to be established before the question of whether the state being held responsible can avail itself of a Chapter V defence, then no such defence can have the effect of ruling out any such breach; therefore, since justifications *do* rule out the breach of the relevant obligation, their inclusion in the Chapter V catalogue of defences is not strictly speaking appropriate.

This argument is mistaken, however, and the mistake is grounded precisely on the fact that the category 'breach of an international obligation' is being used to stand for the relevant *P*-facts—it is being used to stand for the analogue, in the international domain, of the notion of an 'offence'. What does need to be established in order for a claim in international responsibility to get off the ground is *not* that there was a breach of an international obligation. What needs to be established must be that there is a certain act attributable to a state—for example, the act of trespassing into another state—with regard to which it then makes sense to ask whether that state can avail itself of a defence. In this example, the facts that constitute the act of trespassing into another state are the relevant *P*-facts, the relevant 'offence'. That such an act has indeed been committed does not mean that it was impermissible, that the state did breach an obligation: the state may have a justification. But the act of trespass *itself* is such that it now gives rise to the question of whether the state being charged with having committed it can offer a justification. If the answer to this question is 'Yes', then the state has breached no obligation. But the relevant *P*-facts remain in place. They are, after all, the *object* of justification.

Why is it that the act of trespassing into another state's territory gives rise to the question of justification—why is it that it makes sense to ask what justification, if any, the trespassing state can offer? What is it that differentiates an act like trespass—an act the performance

[21] Fourth Report on Responsibility of International Organizations, *Yearbook of the International Law Commission* (2006) vol II(1) para 6, footnote omitted.

of which does get a claim in international responsibility off the ground *even if* the possibility remains that the trespassing state can offer a justification and thereby show that its act of trespass was permitted—from the myriad perfectly lawful acts that states perform on an everyday basis and which do not even raise the question of international responsibility to begin with?

This question is, of course, just like that well-known question—which criminal law theorists, as I mentioned in section 3, discuss—about the difference between killing someone in self-defence, and killing a mosquito.[22] It is the question about the difference between actions that constitute offences even if they are all things considered permissible, and actions that do not even constitute offences. And in the same way that criminal law theorists have sought to give principled accounts of this contrast, international law theorists need to be able to provide a sound theoretical explanation of the difference.

I see no reason why the reasons-based account that is popular among criminal law theorists could not equally apply to the international domain. One might then say that the act of trespassing into another state is an act that—just like an offence in the context of the criminal law—is prima facie wrong, and thus an act which, from the point of view of international law, states have strong *reason* not to perform. It is, therefore, an act that can be deemed permissible—all things considered lawful under international law—only if the trespassing state had stronger reasons that justify having its having committed it. My point, however, is not that this particular explanation—the reasons-based explanation—is the best available explanation of the contrast between offences and defences; perhaps it isn't. My point is that this is an explanatory task that international law theorists should be alert to, and, of course, address and try to solve.

As soon as we bring the notion of an 'offence' into the picture, Gaja's mistake becomes apparent, and his objection to classifying justifications as circumstances 'precluding wrongfulness' is deflated. The notion of an 'offence', then, or something like it, is one that international lawyers would do well to adopt. My suggestion is not that they should actually import the *word* 'offence' to refer to the relevant *P*-facts. After all, the term 'offence' carries the suggestion that there is something untoward about the relevant action, and this is likely to be an implication that states that do have a justification for performing the relevant actions would resist, for political reasons. But what matters is not that the word 'offence' be adopted. What matters is that *some* word or phrase be adopted to refer to the relevant facts, the relevant *P*-facts: some word of phrase that unambiguously identifies the relevant actions without carrying the inference that such actions must be all things considered prohibited. That is the function performed not just by the word 'offence' in Anglo-American criminal law theory, but by the word *Tatbestand* in German criminal law theory, or by the word *tipo* in Portuguese, Spanish, or Italian criminal law theory. It is also the function performed by the word 'tort' in Anglo-American tort law (the 'elements' of a tort, which form the basis of a claim in tort, do not include or pre-assess the absence of defences, justificatory, or otherwise[23]).

Perhaps 'constituent elements of responsibility', or even just 'constituent facts', would be suitably neutral phrases, with the added advantage of tracking language already used in the ARSIWA commentary. Whatever the label, what seems clear is that the law and theory of state responsibility is in need of such a notion.

[22] See the text accompanying n 11 above.

[23] See e.g. James Goudkamp, *Tort Law Defences* (Hart Publishing 2013) 8.

4.4 The status of specific D-facts

Some commonly offered arguments concerning the classification of specific defences in the law of state responsibility also seem to me confused. One question that international lawyers have addressed is whether some of the Chapter V circumstances are not best understood as negative elements of *primary rules*, rather than (as its inclusion in the Chapter V catalogue suggests) as defences proper. For example, the inclusion of self-defence in Chapter V has been criticized on the grounds that self-defence 'does not violate any international obligation whatsoever of any State':

> [T]he exclusion of the action in self-defence is part of the definition of the obligation itself. A State exercising its inherent right of self-defence ... is not, even potentially, in breach [of any obligation] ... and if the only effect of self-defence as a circumstance precluding wrongfulness is so to provide, then it should be deleted [from Chapter V][.][24]

Note that the point here is not that self-defence is not properly classified as a justification because it rules out the breach of an obligation. The point here, rather, is that self-defence is not properly classified *as a defence*—as a D-fact—justificatory or otherwise, because it rules out the breach of an obligation. The thought is that Chapter V, and the ARSIWA more generally, are concerned, not with the specification of *primary*, obligation-imposing rules, but only with the codification of *secondary rules* dealing with the breach of international obligations. This is a distinction on which the ARSIWA are said to be 'as a whole ... founded';[25] and, indeed, one reads in the Introduction to the 1980 draft articles that

> the purpose of the present draft articles is not to define the rules imposing on States, in one sector or another of inter-State relations, obligations whose breach can be a source of responsibility and which, in a certain sense, may be described as 'primary'. In preparing the present draft the Commission is undertaking solely to define those rules which, in contradistinction to the primary rules, may be described as 'secondary', inasmuch as they are aimed at determining the legal consequences of failure to fulfil obligations established by the 'primary' rules. Only these 'secondary' rules fall within the actual sphere of responsibility for internationally wrongful acts. A strict distinction in this respect is essential if the topic of international responsibility for internationally wrongful acts is to be placed in its proper perspective and viewed as a whole.[26]

If '*only* these "secondary" rules fall within the actual sphere of responsibility for international wrongful acts', and if justificatory circumstances like self-defence pertain to the domain of the primary rules instead, then they should not have been included in the catalogue of defences in Chapter V of the ARSIWA—or so the argument runs. Here is another version of the same argument:

> It might be said that, properly understood, the primary rule actually contains in itself all the conditions, qualifications, justifications or excuses applicable to it, so that the notion

[24] See the Second Report on State Responsibility (n 15) para 298.
[25] ibid para 9.
[26] Report of the Commission to the General Assembly on the work of its thirty-second session, *Yearbook of the International Law Commission* (1980) vol II(2) para 23.

> of 'conformity' with the obligation imposed by that rule entails that all these conditions or qualifications are met, and all possible justifications or excuses excluded ... [But] the circumstances precluding wrongfulness, dealt with in chapter V of the draft articles, are treated as secondary rules of a general character *and not as a presumptive part of every primary rule.*[27]

This contrast—a false contrast, as I will shortly explain—has also been relied upon to argue that consent, too, should *not* have been included in the Chapter V catalogue, the point being, again, as Szurek puts it, that consent 'belongs to primary rules and not to secondary rules on responsibility':[28]

> Is it possible to distinguish between, on the one hand, the issue of consent as an element in the application of a rule (which is accordingly part of the *definition* of the relevant obligation) and, on the other hand, the issue of consent as a basis for precluding the wrongfulness of conduct inconsistent with the obligation? ... [I]f consent must be given in advance ... then it may be asked whether the element of consent should not be seen as incorporated in the different primary rules ... [I]t seems that to treat consent in advance as a circumstance precluding wrongfulness is to confuse the content of the substantive obligation with the operation of the secondary rules of responsibility[.][29]

We are now in a position to see why this way of framing the relevant issues is neither correct not helpful. I will first address the very contrast between primary and secondary rules in international law—and the unwarranted assumption that a circumstance must be classified *either* as a negative qualification in a primary rule, *or* as an element of a secondary rule; and I will then look at the issues concerning the classification of these two specific defences: self-defence and consent.

4.4.1 Primary and secondary rules in international responsibility: getting the distinction right

The distinction between primary rules imposing obligations on states, and secondary rules specifying the conditions under which a state should be held responsible for the breach of a primary obligation, mirrors *exactly*—labels included—the distinction between two types of rules that, as we saw in section 3, criminal law theorists also rely on as part of the theoretical framework with which they explain criminal responsibility.

I then highlighted two important points regarding the distinction. The first was that it is at the level of the *secondary* rules that the bipartite distinction between offences and defences—*P*-facts and *D*-facts—is drawn. The second point was that at least some defences—those properly classified as justifications—are such that they render the relevant action all things considered lawful—legally permissible, and therefore not in breach of any primary rule—despite the fact that the action constitutes a criminal offence. What this means, as I also emphasized, is that such defences, justificatory defences, perform a dual role. They feature *both* as *D*-facts in secondary rules, *and* as negative qualifications in primary rules.[30]

[27] Second Report on State Responsibility (n 15) para 10 (italics added).

[28] Sandra Szurek, 'The Notion of Circumstances Precluding Wrongfulness' in James Crawford, Alain Pellet, and Simon Olleson (eds), *The Law of International Responsibility* (Oxford University Press 2010) 430, n 22.

[29] Second Report on State Responsibility (n 15) paras 238, 241.

[30] See in particular section 3.4 above.

The same holds, with no exceptions or caveats, in the context of international responsibility. It is a mistake to suppose that for any relevant fact *F*, it must be the case *either* that *F* is a defence in a secondary rule, *or* that the absence of *F* is an element in a primary rule. This mistake, however, is again one that international law theorists are not sufficiently alert to. Consider, for example, the following passage:

> If there is a particular field in which the existence of autonomous secondary rules can give rise to discussion, it is in the field of the circumstances precluding wrongfulness. In fact, insofar as these rules aim at excluding the wrongfulness of conduct and not the responsibility of the State for that conduct, as explained by Ago, then these rules are more appropriately regarded as being situated 'upstream', that is, they should be seen as forming an element of the primary rule in question.[31]

Why is this a false contrast—indeed a bundle of false contrasts? The reference to Ago is to the first Rapporteur's distinction, in his Eighth Report, between 'circumstances precluding *responsibility*' and 'circumstances precluding *wrongfulness*'.[32] But the passage quoted above suggests, wrongly, that this contrast is supposed to be exclusive. It isn't. Not every circumstance that precludes responsibility is necessarily a circumstance that precludes wrongfulness (and Ago means here, of course, all things considered wrongfulness: legal impermissibility). But every circumstance that precludes wrongfulness is necessarily a circumstance that precludes responsibility. (Ago says as much: 'for the purposes of the draft, any circumstance precluding the wrongfulness of an act necessarily has the effect of also precluding responsibility'.[33]) It follows that any rules that 'aim at excluding wrongfulness' are rules that aim at excluding responsibility as well.

The second false contrast in the passage quoted above is, of course, that of assuming that the question of how to classify justificatory defences is a question of whether they are 'more appropriately regarded as situated "upstream" ... as forming an element of the primary rule in question' than as elements of the relevant secondary rules. The answer, as I pointed out, is that they are *both*. No other explanation is 'appropriate'. It is true that defences can plausibly be said to come in two flavours, justifications and excuses. It is also true that those defences that are justifications can plausibly be said to constitute negative qualifications of obligations, whereas excuses are circumstances that come into play *only* at the level of secondary rules. But it does not follow, and it is not true, that defences that are justifications do not *also* come into play at the level of secondary rules. They do.

Perhaps one factor explaining this common confusion is the habit of referring to secondary rules as rules 'aimed at determining the legal consequences *of failure to fulfil obligations established by the "primary" rules*', to quote again from the 1980 Report of the International Law Commission.[34] Strictly speaking, however, this too is not correct. Secondary rules are *not* rules that come into play only when it has already been shown—or when it is assumed—that a primary rule has been breached. Secondary rules come into play also when there is a need to assess *whether* such a breach of a primary rule has really occurred, and, if so, whether the relevant consequences of responsibility should follow.

[31] Eric David, 'Primary and Secondary Rules' in James Crawford, Alain Pellet, and Simon Olleson (eds), *The Law of International Responsibility* (Oxford University Press 2010) 29 (footnote omitted).
[32] Eighth Report on State Responsibility (n 14) para 49.
[33] ibid para 49.
[34] Italics added; see passage accompanying n 26 above.

It is true that secondary rules are rules that govern the process of holding states accountable for certain actions; but ascertaining whether the state being held accountable has a valid justification, and can therefore correctly claim to have acted permissibly, is itself *part* of the process of holding them accountable. What needs to be established, or at least plausibly claimed, to trigger the process of accountability, and bring secondary rules into play, therefore, is *not* that a primary rule was breached. What is it then? By now the answer is clear. It is—what else?—that the relevant 'offence' (or whatever you want to call it) has been committed.

4.4.2 Self-defence

It should now also be easy to see where exactly some arguments about the status of specific defences go wrong. Consider the following passage by Eric David, on the classification of self-defence:

> [A] debate arose in relation to self-defence, which was also included [in the draft ARSIWA] as a circumstance precluding wrongfulness, *despite the fact that it does not really seem to constitute a secondary rule* ... [T]o say that acts taken by way of self-defence are in accordance with international law is to say that it is a substantive rule, a primary rule.[35]

David also alludes to a telling 1963 exchange between Grigory Tunkin and Roberto Ago. Tunkin objects to the classification of self-defence as a circumstance that precludes wrongfulness, on the grounds that if a state 'acted in self-defence, it was not acting wrongfully, and hence the question of its responsibility did not arise at all in that case'.[36] We already know why this is muddled; but Ago's reply is interesting:

> [H]e fully agreed that Mr. Tunkin was right from a theoretical point of view. A general right of self-defence was accepted in international law; but it had to be remembered that, under the United Nations system for example, recourse to force was not normally permitted, and accordingly it seemed to him that a special problem of self-defence as an excuse for contravening that rule might arise.[37]

David protests that this is a 'noncommittal reply'.[38] There is nothing noncommittal about it. Ago is right; he just lacks the terminology that would enable him to make his point more forcefully. Notice what he says: because the use of force is not normally permitted, then whenever a state does resort to force, the question of whether they have a defence arises. 'Not *normally* permitted': why the adverb? What he means is that the very use of force by a state—not use-of-force-not-in-self-defence, but use of force *tout court*—is a type of conduct that brings up the question of responsibility. It *raises*—rather than presupposes an answer to—the question of whether there are any defences. It works, in other words, just like an offence in criminal law; and what Ago lacked to make his point more rigorously and persuasively, was, again, a clear grasp of the importance of this notion—and a label to go with it.

[35] David, 'Primary and Secondary Rules' (n 31) 30, footnotes omitted (italics added).
[36] Report of the International Law Commission covering the work of its fifteenth session, *Yearbook of the International Law Commission* (1963) vol II, 233.
[37] ibid 237.
[38] David, 'Primary and Secondary Rules' (n 31) 31.

Ago was also right, by the way, to point out that it is 'from a *theoretical* point of view' that Tunkin's claim that a state that acts in self-defence 'is not acting wrongfully' can be said to be correct. (He was wrong, however, to call self-defence an 'excuse' rather than a 'justification'.) As we also saw in section 3, the thought that some defences (of which self-defence is the paradigm) preclude wrongfulness is part of a *theoretical* framework developed to account for—to explain at the theoretical level—why it is that such defences should have the liability-precluding effect that they do.

4.4.3 Consent

Similar problems affect debates on the status of consent. Consider the following excerpt, concerning 'the question of the place of consent in Chapter V':

> Consent given prior to the act may be construed as an agreement between the States to modify or suspend the norm in question. Put this way, the question of consent relates to the law of treaties and not to the law on responsibility (where the relevant primary norm derives from a treaty). Furthermore, consent is contained in several primary norms. In these circumstances, where State A consents to State B derogating from a norm, State B will simply be complying with the norm, and article 20 [of the ARS, which states that 'valid consent by a State to the commission of a given act by another State precludes the wrongfulness of that act . . . '] is not applicable.[39]

Mansour concludes that Article 20 must regulate 'a rare situation where consent is not an element of the norm in question'.[40] The underlying assumption is again that *because* wrongfulness (and thus the primary rules) presupposes absence of consent, consent cannot generally speaking be a matter for secondary rules—that it cannot be a defence.[41] I will not explain again why this contrast is a false one, and this view mistaken. But I would like to introduce one further distinction, specific to the issue of consent, of which international law theorists also seem to be insufficiently aware, and which might shed further light on this question.

We know that the supposedly exclusive contrast between consent as a defence (which means that absence of consent is an element in the secondary rule of responsibility), and consent as a justification (which means that absence of consent is an element in the primary, obligation-imposing rule) is a spurious contrast: if consent is a justification, then it is a defence. There is, however, a genuine contrast to be drawn between consent as a defence, and consent as a negative *P*-fact.

To explain the point, let me bring you back to examples from criminal law, and particularly examples like that of the criminal offence of rape, discussed above in section 2. We then saw that the very action that constitutes the criminal offence of rape is defined in such a way that *absence of consent* is one of its elements; consensual sexual penetration is simply not an instance of rape to begin with. Trespass is another example of the same kind, and indeed a particularly helpful one, since it has a direct equivalent in the domain of international responsibility. So, think of a state's international responsibility for trespassing into another state. Here too the relevant *P*-facts—the 'constituent elements' of the state's responsibility—*include*

[39] Affef Ben Mansour, 'Circumstances Precluding Wrongfulness in the ILC Articles on State Responsibility: Consent' in James Crawford, Alain Pellet, and Simon Olleson (eds), *The Law of International Responsibility* (Oxford University Press 2010) 445.

[40] ibid.

[41] See also David, 'Primary and Secondary Rules' (n 31) 29, expressing the same view on the specific topic of consent.

the fact that the state's entry into another state's territory has not been consented to. What then is the status of consent in examples like this? Is it a defence, a *D*-fact? The answer is 'No'; instead, *absence of consent* is a *P*-fact: it is a negative *P*-fact. That means that in examples like this consent is *also not* a justification. It is true that a state's *consented-to* transit through another state's territory is a permissible action, which means that it infringes no primary rule. But the reason it is permissible is that the action does not even meet the description of the sort of acts to which the rule applies. Consented-to entry into another state and consented-to sexual penetration are like the action of killing a mosquito, not like the action of killing another person in self-defence.[42]

This is not, however, the only role that consent can play. There are also cases in which consent does not negate any element of the relevant offence—cases, that is, in which *absence of consent* is not a *P*-fact—but in which the fact that the victim did consent gives the agent a justification, and renders the action permissible. Assault is perhaps a good example. Here consent has no bearing on the question of whether the offence definition is satisfied, but it can plausibly be taken to constitute a justification.[43] In such cases, then, consent is a defence, a *D*-fact; and although the consented-to action is, all things considered, a permissible, lawful action—and thus not a breach of any primary rule—the explanation of why this should be so is very different from the explanation of why consented-to sexual intercourse is also a permissible action.

This crucial distinction between two kinds of role that consent can play is actually highlighted in German criminal law theory by the use of two different nouns: *Einwilligung*, used to refer to consent when it plays the role of a justification; and *Einverständnis*, used to refer to consent in those cases in which the relevant offence—the relevant *Tatbestand*—includes *absence of consent* as one of its elements.[44] This is a helpful terminological distinction; and the underlying substantive point is that it is a mistake to ask about *the* status of consent in criminal law as if the question had a single, uniform answer.

It seems to me that this distinction between the two different roles that consent can play, too, is one that international law theorists might usefully embrace. It could assist them in understanding the proper scope of article 20 of the ARSIWA, and perhaps lead to a revision of the view that this article deals with a 'rare' situation; this is Mansour's adjective,[45] but a similar view is also endorsed, for example, by Crawford:

> [I]t is difficult to distinguish between consent as an element of the *definition* of a primary obligation and consent as a circumstance precluding the wrongfulness of the non-performance of that obligation ... Consent can be seen as being incorporated into particular primary rules, perhaps in different ways in different cases. It could thus have been deleted from the ARSIWA altogether. Against this, Pellet supported a comment by Addo that 'experience should prevail over logic', adding that 'the relevant experience and practice' supported retaining consent: there were both primary rules that could exclude it as a possibility and a general one that when a State consented not to apply a rule of positive law, 'the wrongfulness itself was expunged'. It is indeed possible to envisage cases where an obligation is formulated in absolute terms—without a qualification for consent—but

[42] This is again a reference to the text accompanying n 11 above.
[43] As it is, for example, in German criminal law: see § 228 of the StGB.
[44] See Michael Bohlander, *Principles of German Criminal Law* (Hart Publishing 2009) 77.
[45] See the text accompanying n 40 above.

> where consent nonetheless precludes the wrongfulness of an act. But it is hard to find any in practice.[46]

Surely it is not necessary—it never is—to embrace irrationality in the name of 'experience'. But I take Crawford's last sentence to be euphemistic; and we cannot take literally his concession that it is 'possible to envisage' cases in which consent precludes wrongfulness (and thus makes an action permissible) and yet is *not* incorporated into the relevant primary rules. Crawford's point, after all, is the logical point that since a consented-to action is always permissible, consent is to be seen as 'incorporated' into the relevant primary rules, and that *therefore* there is simply no conceptual room for wrongfulness-precluding consent at the level of the secondary rules. That is why Crawford thinks that consent *could have been deleted* from the ARSIWA.

It is a good thing, it seems to me, that consent was *not* deleted from the ARSIWA. Crawford's argument turns on the same misunderstanding of the distinction and relation between primary and secondary rules that I tried to dispel in subsection 4.4.1. Having said that, however, it *is* true that in several important types of cases consent will play a role having nothing to do with Article 20. Thus if a state sends its troops into the territory of another state with the latter's consent, the former has not breached any obligation; but in such a case consent is *not* properly classified as a circumstance precluding wrongfulness: rather, this is an instance in which absence of consent is a *P*-fact—a case of consent in the sense of *Einverständnis*, not of consent in the sense of *Einwilligung*.

This does not mean, however, that Article 20 is thereby devoid of applicability, as Crawford's argument implies. That is because Article 20 is not about consent in the sense of *Einverständnis*—it is not about the cases in which *absence of consent* is a *P*-fact. Article 20 is about consent in the sense of *Einwilligung*. It is about cases in which consent is a defence, a *D*-fact. The distinction is ignored, indeed lost, in Crawford's all-encompassing argument: he observes that

> [t]he examples of consent in the Draft Articles Commentary all relate to primary rules that are *not* formulated in absolute terms but instead allow the target state to validly consent to conduct that would otherwise constitute a breach: prohibitions on the exercise of jurisdiction on another state's territory, on the use of force against it, on intervention in its internal affairs and so on.[47]

It is true that all examples of consent—and this applies to consent in the sense of *Einwilligung* as well as to consent in the sense of *Einverständnis*—'relate' to primary rules which when formulated in absolute terms would specify absence of consent as an element. But that does not mean that the list of examples is homogeneous. Consider *use of force* against another state: here *absence of consent* is not plausibly classified as a negative *P*-fact, as a negative element of what we might think of as the relevant 'offence'. Rather, consent justifies the conduct: it renders it permissible *despite* the fact that it is an instance of use of force.

[46] See Crawford, *State Responsibility* (n 19) 288, footnotes omitted.
[47] See Crawford, *State Responsibility* (n 19) 288, footnote omitted.

4.5 The proof-based account: practical implications

I conclude with a couple of remarks reiterating the applicability of the proof-based account of defences—the account I both described and endorsed in subsection 2.4 above—to the domain of defences in the law of state responsibility.

We have already seen that the proof-based account discharges its explanatory task—the task of accounting for the different ways in which the presence or absence of *P*-facts and *D*-facts constrains decision-making in any given domain—by making clear that *P*-facts are facts that must be established, and *D*-facts facts that must *not* be established, in order for a certain decision or judgment to be correct. And I have also stressed, at the start of section 4, that the proof-based account is by no means restricted to decision-making contexts governed by formal rules allocating burdens of proof and specifying the relevant standards.

As I explained, the account carries practical consequences, because it controverts the traditional, but mistaken, view that it must be possible to identify which facts are defences, and which are *P*-facts, independently of any matters concerning the distribution of probative burdens. And it is not surprising to see that this traditional view also makes its appearance in the commentaries to the ARSIWA. Here is a passage from paragraph 8 of the opening commentary to Chapter V:

> Just as the articles do not deal with questions of the jurisdiction of courts or tribunals, so they do not deal with issues of evidence or the burden of proof. In a bilateral dispute over State responsibility, the onus of establishing responsibility lies in principle on the claimant State. Where conduct in conflict with an international obligation is attributable to a State and that State seeks to avoid its responsibility by relying on a circumstance under chapter V, however, the position changes and the onus lies on that State to justify or excuse its conduct. Indeed, it is often the case that only that State is fully aware of the facts which might excuse its non-performance.

I cannot deal here with all the misunderstandings on which this passage rests.[48] Note, however, that this passage assumes that it must be easy to identify what it is that a claimant state needs to establish in a bilateral dispute—while at the same time using extremely vague language to refer to it. It refers to the 'onus of establishing *responsibility*', but that cannot be right: for if it were right, then the claimant state would have to show, among other things, that no single one of the admissible defences was present—the claimant state would have to *disprove* each one of the admissible defences—and that, of course, is not the case, as indeed the passage itself recognizes further ahead. So the claimant state's burden is not that of establishing *responsibility*. What then? Is it the onus of establishing that there is some 'conduct in conflict with an international obligation' that can be attributed to the state being held responsible? If by 'conduct *in conflict* with an obligation' what is meant is 'conduct in breach of an international obligation', then the answer must also be negative, for that would entail that the claimant state would have to disprove exceptions.

So what is it that the claimant state has to prove? The answer is again that it must be the equivalent, in the international domain, of what criminal lawyers call the 'offence'—the relevant *P*-facts. But the relevant *P*-facts, if the proof-based account is right, *just are* those facts whose establishment is required for the claim to succeed—and defences *just are* those facts

48 I discuss the many mistakes of this popular conception of the burden of proof in ch 4 of *Allowing for Exceptions* (n 7) 83–134.

whose non-establishment is required for the claim to succeed. So insofar as the ARSIWA purport, as they clearly do, to draw a distinction between two classes of relevant facts—those that ground a claim, and the circumstances catalogued in Chapter V—the articles *do* deal with issues of the burden of proof. There is no other way to draw the distinction.

This also means that debates, among international law theorists or indeed judges, about *how* to allocate the burden of proof with regard to any given circumstance, can never be settled by asking whether that circumstance is a *P*-fact or a *D*-fact.[49] On the contrary, such debates *just are* debates about how to allocate the relevant burden of proof. Nor is it an argument against the proof-based account that scholars or courts *do* in fact disagree about how to allocate the burden of proof with regard to certain circumstances, and that different courts may take different views on such questions. (Such debates are more likely to emerge with regard to potential second-level defences—defences *to* defences—whose status is less likely to be consolidated in the legal and scholarly community.[50]) If there is no settled view on who should be burdened with the proof of a certain fact, then there is no settled view on whether that fact should be classified as a *P*-fact or as a *D*-fact instead.[51]

[49] See the discussion at the end of section 2.5 above.

[50] On defence 'levels' see Duarte d'Almeida, *Allowing for Exceptions* (n 7) 77–82.

[51] Thanks to Federica Paddeu for discussing some of these issues with me, for letting me see some of her unpublished work on defences in international law—I learned a lot from it—and for pointing me in the direction of the relevant literature. Thanks also to the participants in the Cambridge Conference on Exceptions in International Law, to the editors of this volume, and to Euan MacDonald, for questions and comments on an earlier draft.

11

Clarifying the Concept of Circumstances Precluding Wrongfulness (Justifications) in International Law

*Federica Paddeu**

1 Introduction

The Articles on the Responsibility of States for Internationally Wrongful Acts (ARSIWA)[1] include six circumstances precluding wrongfulness: consent, self-defence, countermeasures, *force majeure*, distress, and (state of) necessity.[2] All of the circumstances are, to a greater or lesser extent, recognized as part of customary international law. Neatly drafted, these provisions might give the impression that the topic of circumstances precluding wrongfulness is familiar and well-trodden. And yet, given the considerable substantive differences among the circumstances, some have questioned whether they can all be covered under the same 'wrongfulness preclusion' umbrella or, rather, whether some (or even all) of the circumstances may only preclude responsibility (leaving wrongfulness intact).[3] This is a question of classification, and an important one at that, which has so far received relatively scant attention from the scholarship. I have considered the question at length elsewhere,[4] but here I want to focus on the concept of preclusion of wrongfulness since this, as will be seen, has been the subject of some disagreement and uncertainty among courts and scholars alike.

The expression 'circumstance precluding wrongfulness' is now entrenched in the language of international law, from where one might infer familiarity by international actors with this notion. But it seems that this is only an intuitive familiarity; theorists would say it is a pre-theoretical familiarity. Most international actors would say they are familiar with the concept and know what it is for, but if pressed to explain, analytically, how it works and what its effects are (what we might term their 'operation'), the answers would reveal deep uncertainties. Ian Brownlie was correct when he observed in 2007 that:

> With hindsight, it was clear that in the context of the draft articles on responsibility of States for internationally wrongful acts, the question of justifications had never been properly worked out. With every new case that came before the ICJ and every new arbitration, it became increasingly clear that the subject was immature, yet the Commission had adopted

* John Tiley Fellow in Law, Queens' College; Fellow, Lauterpacht Centre for International Law, University of Cambridge. I am indebted to Fernando Lusa Bordin, Luís Duarte d'Almeida, André de Hoogh, Jaap Hage, and Francesco Messineo for their helpful comments on previous drafts of this contribution.

[1] International Law Commission (ILC), Articles on Responsibility of States for Internationally Wrongful Acts (ARSIWA) annexed to UNGA Res 56/83 (28 January 2002) UN Doc A /RES/56/83.

[2] ibid arts 20–25.

[3] See references in section 2.2 below.

[4] See Federica Paddeu, *Justification and Excuse in International Law: Concept and Theory of General Defences* (CUP 2018) chs 1–3.

Federica Paddeu, *Clarifying the Concept of Circumstances Precluding Wrongfulness (Justifications) in International Law* In: *Exceptions in International Law*. Edited by: Lorand Bartels and Federica Paddeu, Oxford University Press (2020). © Lorand Bartels and Federica Paddeu. DOI: 10.1093/oso/9780198789321.003.0011

> an 'emperor's new clothes' policy, so that it now had a splendid set of draft articles relating to justifications in the context of responsibility of States, which were very difficult to apply.[5]

Indeed, the Commentary to the ARSIWA does not provide an explanation of the operation of the circumstances. The Commentary simply states that the circumstances operate as 'justifications or excuses for non-performance'[6] and that they provide a 'shield against an otherwise well-founded claim for the breach of an international obligation'.[7] All we have is a metaphor (of a 'shield') applicable to what are rather different types of circumstances.[8]

Absent any guidance from the ARSIWA and their Commentary, it should be no surprise that the case law and the literature on the topic have so far provided different explanations of the operation of the circumstances and, in so doing, have used rather diverse language as well. Some examples illustrate this diversity. As far as case law is concerned, the *Rainbow Warrior* tribunal explained that the circumstances 'may exclude wrongfulness (and render the breach only apparent)'; the *LG&E v Argentina* tribunal held that the circumstances 'exclude under international law the wrongfulness of a state's act that violates an international obligation';[9] for the *Sempra v Argentina* Annulment Committee, a circumstance precluding wrongfulness 'presupposes that an act has been committed that is incompatible with the State's international obligations and is therefore "wrongful" ';[10] and for the ICJ in *Gabčíkovo-Nagymaros*, the circumstances did not mean that a state acted 'in accordance with its obligations', at most, they meant that the state would 'not incur international responsibility by acting as it did'.[11] All of these descriptions imply subtle, but important, differences. On the *Rainbow Warrior* approach, there would be no breach of international law (conduct is lawful), on the *Gabčíkovo-Nagymaros* approach there would be a wrongful act but no responsibility for it (conduct is unlawful), on the *LG&E* and *Sempra* approach there would be a ... non-wrongful breach or violation (conduct is not unlawful)?

A similarly broad range of views can be found in the literature. For example, on one view the circumstances 'temporally affect the effectiveness of the primary rule not complied with ... by releasing the State from the relevant obligations (exculpation)', with the result that 'there is no breach'.[12] On another view, an 'unlawful act *already exists* at the time when the secondary rules [the circumstances] intervene to erase their unlawfulness';[13] or, what

[5] Brownlie, 2877th meeting, 17 May 2006, (2006) Ybk Int L Commission, vol I, UN Doc A/CN.4/SER.A/2006, 70 [18]. Brownlie was a member of the ILC at the time of the second reading of the ARSIWA, in the years 1998–2001.

[6] Commentary to ch V of Pt 1, [2].

[7] Commentary to ch V of Pt 1, [1].

[8] The metaphor is particularly inapt, for the same image could be applied to jurisdictional objections or objections to the admissibility of a claim, for example. As such, the metaphor is unable to tell us much about the concept of circumstances precluding wrongfulness.

[9] *LG&E Energy Corp, LG&E Capital Corp, LG&E International Inc v Argentine Republic*, ICSID Case No ARB/02/1, Liability (3 October 2006) [249]. Similarly, *Metalpar SA and Buen Aire SA v Argentine Republic*, ICSID Case No ARB/03/5, Award (6 June 2008) [213]; *Continental Casualty Company v Argentine Republic*, ICSID Case No ARB/03/9, Award (5 September 2008) [166]; *Total SA v Argentine Republic*, ICSID Case No ARB/04/1, Liability (27 December 2010) [221].

[10] *Sempra Energy International v Argentine Republic*, ICSID Case No ARB/02/16, Annulment (29 June 2010) [220].

[11] *Gabčíkovo-Nagymaros Project (Hungary v Slovakia)* [1997] ICJ Rep 7, 39 [48].

[12] Tarcisio Gazzini, 'Foreign Investment and Measures Adopted on Grounds of Necessity: Toward a Common Understanding' (2010) 7(1) Transnational Dispute Management 6. This view was held by Special Rapporteur Ago and was endorsed in the first reading of the ARSIWA. It was, however, ultimately rejected: as the Commentary to ch V of Pt 1 indicates, the circumstances produce *no effect* on the validity and continued operation of the underlying obligation, at [2–4].

[13] Karine Bannelier and Théodore Christakis, '*Volenti non fit injuria*? Les effets du consentement à l'intervention militaire' (2004) 50 Annuaire Francaise de Droit International 102, 107 (emphasis in original). See also Sarah Cassella, *La nécessité en droit international* (Martinus Nijhoff 2011) 412.

is the same, that conduct covered by a circumstance precluding wrongfulness nevertheless amounts to a breach or a violation of international law.[14] On yet another view, the circumstances entail that the relevant conduct is 'unlawful with precluded wrongfulness'.[15] Finally, for others, the circumstances do not exclude the illegality of conduct, but only the responsibility of the state.[16]

Underlying the various statements above are two important aspects of the circumstances precluding wrongfulness. First is the question of whether a breach of international law exists even though a circumstance precluding wrongfulness may be available; in short, whether justified conduct nevertheless amounts to a breach of international law. Second is the question of the characterization of conduct covered by one of the circumstances (that is, justified conduct) as 'unlawful with precluded wrongfulness', non-wrongful, or variations thereof, or simply lawful. It is not clear, however, whether these two misunderstandings are simply the result of terminological imprecisions, or if they betray a deeper analytical problem, one concerning the understanding of how the circumstances 'work'.[17]

Whatever their origins, these two misunderstandings are troubling, for they may have important repercussions in practice. To begin with, they affect the availability of (legal) reactions to violations of the law. Take the case of the termination or suspension of a treaty owing to material breach under Article 60 of the Vienna Convention on the Law of Treaties (VCLT).[18] Can a state unilaterally terminate or suspend a treaty when the other treaty party's 'material breach' is covered by one of the circumstances? The first thing to note here is that the material breach *must be* a violation of the treaty—that is, it must be a wrongful act.[19] Thus, depending on how one characterizes conduct covered by a justification the entitlement in Article 60 may or may not be available.[20] If we accept that justified conduct nevertheless amounts to a breach of the treaty, then a treaty-party may invoke the material breach to unilaterally suspend or terminate the treaty. But if we consider that conduct covered by a justification is lawful, then the entitlement to terminate or suspend the treaty under Article 60 will not be available. Furthermore, given this binary option, what should be done when

[14] See in this sense the remarks by Giorgio Gaja, Fourth Report on Responsibility of International Organizations, UN Doc A/CN.4/564 and Add.1-2, (2006) Ybk Int L Commission, vol II(1), UN Doc A/CN.4/SER.A/2006/Add.1, 106 [6]; August Reinisch, 'Necessity in Investment Arbitration' (2010) 41 Netherlands Yearbook of International Law 137, 148–49. Neither of these scholars appear to suggest that they are concerned with circumstances precluding responsibility (or excuses) as opposed to circumstances precluding wrongfulness (or justifications).

[15] Martins Paparinskis, 'Circumstances Precluding Wrongfulness in International Investment Law' (2016) 31 ICSID Review 484, 491.

[16] See e.g. Nicholas Tsagourias, 'Self-Defence against Non-State Actors: The Interaction between Self-Defence as a Primary Rule and Self-Defence as a Secondary Rule' (2016) 29 Leiden Journal of Internatioal Law 801, 823–24; Tarcisio Gazzini, 'Necessity in International Investment Law: Some Critical Remarks on *CMS v Argentina*' (2008) 26 Journal of Energy and Natural Resources Law 450, 457–58.

[17] It is possible that these tribunals and scholars intended to say that the defences operate as excuses, in that they do not affect the illegality of the conduct in question but simply exclude the legal consequences of wrongfulness (i.e. responsibility) from arising (on which see section 2.2 below). Whether this is the case is unclear from the language used in these sources. This contribution will take these assertions at face value, which suggest that these sources are speaking about justifications (they use the expression 'circumstance precluding wrongfulness' and the language of 'preclusion of wrongfulness').

[18] Vienna Convention on the Law of Treaties (VCLT) (adopted 23 May 1969, in force 27 January 1980) (1969) 1155 UNTS 331. Article 60(3) states, in relevant part, that: 'A material breach of a treaty, for the purposes of this article, consists in: (a) a repudiation of the treaty not sanctioned by the present Convention; or (b) the violation of a provision essential to the accomplishment of the object or purpose of the treaty.'

[19] On which see generally Bruno Simma, 'Reflections on Article 60 of the Vienna Convention on the Law of Treaties and Its Background in General International Law' (1970) 20 Österreichische Zeitschrift für öffentliches Recht 5. That the conduct triggering VCLT art 60 must be wrongful is also implied in a more recent work by the same author: Bruno Simma and Christian Tams, 'Article 60 (1969)' in Olivier Corten and Pierre Klein (eds), *The Vienna Convention on the Law of Treaties: A Commentary* (OUP 2011) 1351.

[20] The following remarks assume that the conduct concerns a 'provision essential to the accomplishment of the object and purpose of the treaty'.

the conduct in question is characterized as 'unlawful with precluded wrongfulness'. Would the entitlement to terminate or suspend the treaty arise then? Another potential implication involves the potential concession of breach or of wrongdoing which may be implicit in the invocation of a circumstance precluding wrongfulness. Thus, in *Gabčíkovo-Nagymaros*, Slovakia argued that by invoking a circumstance precluding wrongfulness Hungary implicitly admitted to having committed a breach of international law, with the result that the claimant may not need to prove its claim. The correctness of Slovakia's position depends, once again, on whether justified conduct amounts to a breach of international law.

This chapter aims to clarify the concept of circumstance precluding wrongfulness in international law. It is hoped that, with this clarification, the two misunderstandings just mentioned may be dispelled. The argument will proceed in four steps. First, the chapter will provide some terminological and conceptual clarifications (section 2). As will be seen, circumstances precluding wrongfulness refer to permissions of the legal order to engage in certain conduct and, as a result, the conduct at issue is lawful; moreover, rather than involving a breach of international law, they specifically exclude that a breach has occurred. In these respects, circumstances precluding wrongfulness are to be distinguished from circumstances precluding responsibility which do not affect the fact that conduct is wrongful, although they exclude the legal consequences of responsibility arising therefrom. Secondly, the chapter will consider the analytical process by which the circumstances are applied and, as such, produce their exonerating effects (section 3). In short, it will consider the operation of the circumstances. To this end, it will rely on two theoretical models of defences discussed in Part I of this volume, which aim to represent the manner in which arguments about exceptions are formulated by lawyers and decision-makers. In particular, it will consider the account presented by Luís Duarte d'Almeida;[21] and the 'dialogic' model, explained by Jaap Hage, Antonia Waltermann, and Gustavo Arosemena.[22] Thirdly, and using the two models just discussed as an analytical framework, the chapter will assess the two misunderstandings mentioned above and show that these are mistaken (section 4). These clarifications made, it will then be possible, by way of conclusion, to answer the practical difficulties mentioned above (section 5).

Before proceeding, some disclaimers are necessary. First, this chapter will not contest (or consider the question of) the distinctiveness of the circumstances precluding wrongfulness. As various chapters in Part I of this book have shown, there is evidence in legal practice and broad agreement in the literature that there is a significant distinction between offences and defences, to use the terminology of domestic law, or between the circumstances and the 'constituent requirements of the obligation', in the language of the ARSIWA.[23] This chapter will take for granted that the circumstances in the ARSIWA are distinct from states' obligations; in other words, that they are *not* negative rule elements implicit in these obligations. Secondly, the chapter will focus on the concept of circumstances precluding wrongfulness only. That is to say that it will not address circumstances precluding responsibility. This should not be seen as an acknowledgement or endorsement of the view that all of the circumstances in the ARSIWA constitute circumstances precluding wrongfulness; that is a different and separate question on which this chapter will not take sides.[24] The purpose here

[21] See ch 10 in this book. For a more extensive explanation see Luís Duarte d'Almeida, *Allowing for Exceptions: A Theory of Defences and Defeasibility in Law* (OUP 2015).
[22] See ch 2 in this book.
[23] Commentary to ch V of Pt 1, [7].
[24] I have considered this question at length elsewhere; see Paddeu (n 4).

is simply to illuminate the concept and operation of those defences which can be classed as circumstances precluding wrongfulness.

2 Terminological and Conceptual Clarifications

The expression 'circumstance precluding wrongfulness' is seemingly self-explanatory. In the presence of one of these circumstances, conduct adopted by a state is not wrongful. But what exactly does this mean? As noted above, case law and literature have provided different, often byzantine and sometimes meaningless, ways to express this concept: none of the paraphrases of the expression 'not wrongful', of which a few were quoted in section 1, have actually been able to clarify the meaning of the concept of circumstance precluding wrongfulness.

The following two sub-sections attempt to make some terminological and conceptual clarifications (as far as these are possible) on the notions of internationally wrongful act, breach, circumstances precluding wrongfulness, and circumstances precluding responsibility, or as these two circumstances will be called in this chapter, justifications and excuses. These remarks will focus on international law and how all these terms are used in international legal practice. However, given the inconsistent and often confused use of the relevant terms in both practice and literature on international law, it will be necessary to have recourse to legal theoretical developments on analogous notions in domestic law settings. This should not be seen as an (unwarranted) attempt to transpose domestic law concepts to the international legal order, but only as an effort to gain greater conceptual awareness which may be useful in defining the international law notions.

This section first considers the notions of internationally wrongful act and breach (section 2.1), then the notions of justification and excuse (section 2.2) and, finally, it will consider the place of justifications in the primary/secondary rule framework developed by the Commission during the codification of the ARSIWA (section 2.3). This latter clarification is necessary because the claim has not infrequently been made that either justifications are not a part of the law of responsibility because they are primary rules (they are conduct-guiding) or that whatever defences are recognized in the law of responsibility must be excuses, because the law of responsibility consists of secondary rules only. As will be seen, both these arguments are flawed.

2.1 Internationally wrongful act and breach

The internationally wrongful act is the central pillar of the law of state responsibility: it is this typology of act that, according to Article 1 of the ARSIWA, 'entails the responsibility' of the state. The internationally wrongful act is then defined in Article 2 of the ARSIWA as an act or omission attributable to the state which constitutes a 'breach of an international obligation' of that state.[25] The internationally wrongful act is, therefore, composed of two basic elements: attribution and breach. The first element is further elaborated upon in Articles 4 to 11, establishing the rules of attribution, which determine when a given act or omission is the act or omission of the state.[26] The element of breach is further specified in Article 12,

[25] ARSIWA art 2.

[26] This chapter will not deal with questions of attribution and in its analysis it will assume that the requirement of attribution has been met.

which states that: '[t]here is a breach of an international obligation by a state when an act of that state is not in conformity with what is required of it by that obligation'. The combined reading of Articles 2 and 12 leads to the conclusion that any conduct which is not in conformity with an obligation of the state amounts to a breach thereof and, if attributable to that state, it constitutes an internationally wrongful act. In practice, it is indeed often the case that it is sufficient to ascertain that a given act of State A is not in conformity with what is required of that state by an international obligation to establish that a breach of the law, and therefore an internationally wrongful act, has been committed. A good illustration of this is the *Avena* case before the ICJ.[27] The case concerned the obligation to notify foreign nationals of their right to consular assistance, established in the Vienna Convention on Consular Relations (VCCR).[28] The Court found that, by failing to notify Mexican nationals of their right to consular assistance, the US had acted in a manner incompatible with its obligation under the VCCR. The Court thus concluded that there was a breach of the relevant treaty provision and, as such, the US had committed an internationally wrongful act.

Generalizing from the *Avena* case, one could conclude that all acts incompatible with obligations constitute breaches thereof. But there are two related problems with this conclusion. The first one is terminological: it assumes that the term 'breach' and the expression 'incompatible with an international obligation' are synonymous. The term 'breach' can indeed be used as a synonym of 'incompatibility with obligation'; that is, it can be used to describe the situation in which a state has failed to comply with what an obligation, arising under a given rule of international law, required it to do or not to do. But this sense of the term 'breach' does not reflect the common (let alone, the uniform) international legal usage. In international law, the term 'breach' carries a connotation of wrongfulness, in the sense that a 'breach of international law' is another way of describing an internationally wrongful act. Note that the term 'breach' is used to describe an *unlawful* non-performance of the relevant international legal rule, and not the fact of non-performance of the obligation as such. The latter is an important conceptual distinction, to which we will return shortly. For now, as a matter of terminology, it is important to note that precisely because the term 'breach' carries a connotation of wrongfulness then it is a mistake or, at the very least, confusing to use this same term to describe conduct that is 'non-wrongful' or, even worse, that is lawful.[29] A breach of an obligation is *more* than the factual incompatibility between conduct and obligation: it is an *unlawful* incompatibility. 'Breach' and 'incompatible with an obligation' are therefore not synonymous: the former is a legal qualification, the latter a factual description. Perhaps this distinction would be clearer if international law possessed a specific term to refer to the factual description of incompatibility between conduct and obligation.[30] The term 'breach' could certainly be repurposed in this way, so as to describe the factual situation of incompatibility. But given the way in which this term has been used in international legal practice, it would seem better to use an alternative expression. Duarte d'Almeida suggests speaking of the 'constituent elements' of responsibility, to follow the language in the ARSIWA's commentary; or, perhaps, in accordance with ICJ case law one could even speak of a 'prima facie' or

[27] See *Case Concerning Avena and Other Mexican Nationals (Mexico v United States of America)* (Judgment) [2004] ICJ Rep 12.

[28] Article 36(2) of the Vienna Convention on Consular Relations (1963) 596 UNTS 261.

[29] The same holds true for the term 'violation' which, although not used in the text of the ARSIWA, is often encountered in practice as a synonym of 'breach'.

[30] Thus, the Commentary to ch V of Pt 1 distinguishes between the 'constituent requirements of the obligation', namely 'those elements which have to exist for the issue of wrongfulness to arise in the first place', and the defences, at [7].

'apparent' breach to describe this factual situation.[31] Whatever the choice of terminology in this regard, the point is that 'incompatible with an obligation' and 'breach of obligation' are not synonymous.

The second problem is conceptual. If 'breach' refers to an unlawful incompatibility between conduct and obligation, then *surely* it will not be sufficient that the relevant conduct is incompatible with the obligation to reach a conclusion as to breach. For there may be cases in which the conduct of the state is both incompatible with what is required by the obligation and yet it is also not unlawful. Indeed, the conduct may be covered by a justification. The Commentary to Article 12 elaborates on this point: 'In order to conclude that there is a breach of an international obligation in any specific case, it will be necessary to take account of… the provisions of chapter V dealing with circumstances which may preclude the wrongfulness of an act of a State.'[32] That is, it will be necessary to ascertain that, in addition to an incompatibility between conduct and obligation, no justifications are present before it can be concluded that a breach has occurred.

A breach is therefore better defined as conduct which is incompatible with an obligation of the state and which is *not* covered by one of the justifications. This is not to say that a tribunal will need to ascertain that none of the circumstances precluding wrongfulness are present to establish a breach of international law. They may be required to do so only when prompted by the respondent.[33] However, when a justification is raised by the respondent, no conclusion can be reached as to the existence of a breach until it has been considered. The practice of international courts and tribunals supports this conclusion. Thus, in *Avena* the ICJ did not have to ascertain that there was no consent, no self-defence, and so on, in order to reach its conclusion as to the existence of a breach since none of these justifications was raised by the US. In turn, in *Interim Agreement* the Court considered whether the justifications raised by Greece against the Federal Yugoslav Republic of Macedonia's claim were met, before concluding as to the existence of a breach of the obligations at issue.[34] It follows from the above that conduct which is incompatible with an obligation can, therefore, be either a breach (in which case it is wrongful) or not (in which case it is lawful).

These terminological and conceptual differences are also supported theoretically. As Jaap Hage has explained, the determination of what amounts to a 'breach' of the law (in the sense of a wrongful incompatibility between conduct and any given rule of the legal system) cannot simply be derived from what a rule of the legal order says at any given time. That is, what an agent is legally obliged to do in any given circumstance is not derivable by a mere deductive step from the relevant legal rule. As Hage has demonstrated, there is a difference between the abstract and the general rule, the obligation arising under that rule for a specific agent and what, in the circumstances, the agent is legally obliged to do.[35] Of crucial importance in this context is the difference between the obligation arising from the rule and what an

[31] See section 4.1 below.

[32] ARSIWA art 12 Commentary, [12]. See also James Crawford, Second Report on State Responsibility, UN Doc A/CN.4/498/Add.2, (1999) Ybk Int L Commission, vol II(1), UN Doc A/CN.4/SER.A/1999/Add.1, 12, 13.

[33] There are certain situations in which a tribunal may be required to do this, for example, in cases of non-appearance of the respondent State. See e.g. art 53(2) of the ICJ Statute, which requires the Court to 'satisfy itself, not only that it has jurisdiction in accordance with Articles 36 and 37, but also that the claim is well founded in fact and law'. The Court has interpreted this mandate as a requirement also to consider possible defences. See e.g. the *Nicaragua* case, in which the Court considered (if briefly) the (potential) plea of countermeasures on behalf of the US: *Military and Paramilitary Activities in and against Nicaragua (Nicaragua v United States of America)* [1986] ICJ Rep 14, paras [249] and [252].

[34] *Application of the Interim Accord of 13 September 1995 (FYR Macedonia v Greece)* [2011] ICJ Rep 644.

[35] See Jaap Hage, 'The (Onto)Logical Structure of Law' in Michal Araszkiewicz and Krzysztof Pleszka (eds), *Logic in the Theory and Practice of Lawmaking* (Springer 2015) s 7.

actor is legally obliged to do in any given circumstance, insofar as 'having an obligation is not the last word concerning what one ought to do'.[36] Having an obligation is a reason to do the very thing required by the rule. A mandatory rule will therefore provide a reason to do a certain thing, whereas a prohibitory rule provides a reason not to do a certain thing. But what one legally ought to do depends, in any given situation, on the set of reasons relevant to that situation. What one legally ought to do is always relative to a set of reasons—reasons which are provided for by the obligation arising under the relevant rule and any other permissions relevant in the circumstances. These additional permissions include potential justifications, which provide reasons not to do a certain thing (when set against mandatory rules) or to do that very thing (when set against prohibitory rules). A justification thus constitutes a reason which collides with the obligation-based reason. To determine what an agent is legally obliged to do in the circumstances is therefore the result of the balancing or weighing of these two colliding reasons. In so far as the justification prevails, then the author (while having an obligation) will not be legally obliged to behave in accordance with the legal rule. As a result, acting in accordance with justification the agent, while acting in a manner incompatible with the obligation, does not breach the relevant legal rule.

By way of summary, then, a breach of international law attributable to a state constitutes an internationally wrongful act for which that state is responsible. To determine the existence of a breach it is not enough simply to attest to the existence of conduct of the state which is incompatible or not in conformity with what is required of it by an international obligation. Rather, as explained by the ILC in the Commentary to Article 12, the determination of the existence of a breach requires excluding the existence of justifications (at least, those that have been raised by the respondent state).

2.2 Justification and excuse

Now, what is a justification? To answer this question, it is perhaps useful to turn to the work of theorists in domestic law first, so as to better understand the notion of justification and then turn to international law which, as will be seen, attempted to articulate the notion of justification through the expression 'circumstance precluding wrongfulness'. Equally, although the focus of this chapter is exclusively on circumstances precluding wrongfulness or justifications, it is nevertheless useful to distinguish between these and circumstances precluding responsibility (or excuses). An awareness of this distinction will help better to appreciate the concept of circumstances precluding wrongfulness/justifications, as well as determine the language necessary in the discussion, analysis, and application of this concept.

Legal theorists and a significant number of domestic legal orders recognize (at least)[37] two different typologies of defences:[38] justifications and excuses. The American criminal law theorist Douglas Husak has provided the following definitions:

> Justifications are defenses that arise from properties or characteristics of acts; excuses are defenses that arise from properties or characteristics of actors. A defendant is justified

[36] ibid s 7.

[37] For additional types of defences see Douglas Husak, 'Beyond the Justification/Excuse Dichotomy' in Rowan Cruft and others (eds), *Crime, Punishment, and Responsibility: The Jurisprudence of Antony Duff* (OUP 2011) 141.

[38] The term 'defence' is used here in a narrow sense, as a reference to substantive arguments aimed at defeating a claim on the merits. That is exclusive of jurisdictional or other procedural bars invoked so as to prevent a tribunal from considering the merits of a dispute.

> when his *conduct* is not legally wrongful, even though it apparently violates a criminal law. A defendant is excused when *he* is not blameworthy or responsible for his conduct, even though it … violates the criminal law.[39]

Both defences exonerate, in the sense that, colloquially, they get the defendant 'off the hook'. But they do so for different reasons and produce different effects. A justification provides a permission of the legal order to engage in certain conduct and, therefore, leads to the conclusion that the conduct is lawful.[40] An excuse, instead, does not constitute a permission to engage in certain conduct and, for this reason, it does not affect the illegality of conduct; the excuse serves only to exclude the consequences that follow from that illegality for the defendant.

The definitions provided above represent the common core of agreement in respect of the meaning of these two terms. Indeed, few domestic lawyers would confuse or conflate these two terms—whether in continental or common law systems. What is more, the meaning attributed to these terms in legal systems tracks the meanings given to the same terms in moral philosophy and ordinary language.[41] Thus, Vaughan Lowe's assertion that '[n]o dramatist, no novelist would confuse them. No philosopher or theologian would conflate them.'[42] Yet—and regrettably so—international lawyers are often inattentive to this distinction, sometimes even claiming that it is not clear or that it remains unresolved. To be sure, there are disagreements at the margins,[43] but the core meaning of these concepts, as defined above, is no longer disputed. At its core, the distinction is both clear and resolved.[44]

It is possible that international lawyers' difficulties with these two concepts is (at least in part) attributable to the language chosen by the ILC in this regard. Instead of speaking of justification and excuse, the ILC (and, consequently, the ARSIWA) opted for the (cumbersome) expressions 'circumstances precluding wrongfulness' and 'circumstances precluding responsibility'. A close study of the ILC's work on this subject reveals that these two expressions were simply synonyms of the notions of justification and excuse. Thus, a 'circumstance precluding wrongfulness' prevents 'the characterization of the conduct of the State … as wrongful'.[45] In contrast, a 'circumstance precluding responsibility' excludes the legal consequences 'that would otherwise result from an act wrongful in itself'.[46] In the former case, the

[39] Douglas Husak, 'Justifications and the Criminal Liability of Accessories' (1989–1990) 80 Journal of Crim Law & Criminology 491, 496 (emphasis in original, footnotes omitted.)

[40] On justifications as permissions see Robert Schopp, *Justification Defenses and Just Convictions* (CUP 1998) 4–5.

[41] These definitions largely track the meaning of these notions in ordinary language. See in this respect the Oxford English Dictionary definitions of both words: justification is '[t]he action of justifying or showing something to be just, right, or proper; vindication of oneself or another' (3) and excuse is the 'attempt to clear (a person) wholly or partially from blame, without denying or justifying his imputed action' (I.1.a).

[42] Vaughan Lowe, 'Precluding Wrongfulness or Responsibility: A Plea for Excuses?' (1999) 10 European Journal of International Law 405, 406.

[43] For an overview see Kimberley Kessler Ferzan, 'Justification and Excuse' in John Deigh and David Dolinko (eds), *The Oxford Handbook of Philosophy of Criminal Law* (OUP 2011) 239.

[44] Indeed, the resolution of this debate was hailed as one of the successes of criminal law theory by Joshua Dressler during a meeting of the Criminal Law section of the American Association of Law Schools: see Mitchell Berman, 'Justification and Excuse, Law and Morality' (2003) 53 Duke Law Journal 1, 4. The question of whether the distinction is useful, or has any practical implications, is a separate and distinct one.

[45] Report of the Commission to the General Assembly on the work of its twenty-fifth session, UN Doc A/9010/Rev.1, (1973) Ybk Int L Commission, vol II, UN Doc A/CN.4/SER.A/1973/Add.1, 176 [12].

[46] ibid. See also Roberto Ago, Eighth Report on State Responsibility, UN Doc A/CN.4/318 and Add.1 to 4, (1979) Ybk Int L Commission, vol II(1), UN Doc A/CN.4/SER.A/1979/Add.1 (part 1), 27–29. In the literature see, inter alia, Dionisio Anzilotti, 'Corso di diritto internazionale' in *Opere di Dionisio Anzilotti* (reprint of 3rd edn originally published in 1927, CEDAM, 1955) 413; Peter Malanczuk, 'Countermeasures and Self-Defence as Circumstances Precluding Wrongfulness in the ILC Draft Articles on State Responsibility' (1983) 43 Zeitschrift für ausländisches öffentliches Recht und Völkerrecht ZaöRV 705, 713–15.

conduct is lawful (it does not constitute an internationally wrongful act);[47] in the latter it is wrongful but the normal consequences of wrongfulness (the legal relations of responsibility, the obligations of cessation, and reparation)[48] do not arise. The expression 'circumstance precluding wrongfulness' is therefore equivalent to the term 'justification', and 'circumstance precluding responsibility' the equivalent of the term 'excuse'. And, indeed, in doctrine and practice these equivalences are often assumed.[49]

Now, one could query whether all circumstances in the ARSIWA constitute justifications, whether they all constitute excuses, or whether they can be classified into these two categories. On this question, the position of the ARSIWA is less clear than it is often assumed. On first reading, the Commission (apparently) took the view that all the defences recognized in international law operated as justifications. This was the view forcefully defended by Special Rapporteur Ago, and the view which determined the terminology used in the text of the ARSIWA themselves (i.e. the language of 'preclusion of wrongfulness'). However, despite the adoption of the language of 'preclusion of wrongfulness', the Commission was not as assertive in its position that all the circumstances acted as justifications.[50] Indeed, tracing the discussions in the Commission during the first reading of the ARSIWA, it seems that the question was left unresolved and that it would be the subject of subsequent discussion.[51] But that subsequent discussion never occurred. Indeed, on second reading, Special Rapporteur Crawford raised the issue but decided that, on balance, the ARSIWA should not strictly classify the various circumstances as justifications or excuses. The Commission endorsed this suggestion, and no discussion on these two concepts therefore took place. So, the ARSIWA *do not* determine, definitely or definitively, the character of the individual circumstances therein recognized. It is in this light that the use of the expression 'circumstances precluding wrongfulness' in the title of Chapter V of Part One, and the use of the terms 'justification' and 'excuse' throughout the Commentary must be viewed: the use of these terms is neither an indication of the Commission's definitive views, nor an indication of the Commission's confusion as to the meaning of these terms. Rather, the work of the Commission strongly suggests that the character of each of the circumstances in the ARSIWA remains to be settled. Different views exist in this regard in the literature,[52] the merits of which are beyond

[47] As explained by the US in its pleadings in *Oil Platforms (Islamic Republic of Iran v United States of America)* (Judgment) [2003] ICJ Rep 161: '[t]he action taken under [a circumstance precluding wrongfulness] is not an internationally wrongful act; it is an internationally lawful act'. See US oral statement, *Oil Platforms*, CR 2003/12 (translation) (23 February 2003) [17.16].

[48] See ARSIWA arts 30 and 31.

[49] For an example from practice see *CMS Gas Transmission Company v Argentine Republic*, ICSID Case No ARB/01/8, Annulment (25 September 2007) [129–36]. In the literature see Helmut Aust, 'Circumstances Precluding Wrongfulness and Shared Responsibility' in André Nollkaemper and Ilias Plakokefalos (eds), *Principles of Shared Responsibility* (CUP 2014) 169.

[50] It is significant in this regard that the commentary to the draft ARSIWA adopted on first reading stated that the circumstances excluded wrongfulness 'in the normal case', thus leaving open the possibility that they may operate to exclude responsibility. See on this point Paddeu (n 4) ch 1, s 1.3.1.

[51] The ILC Report of 1973 records that only 'some members' of the Commission agreed with Ago's view 'for the time being': ILC Report, twenty-fifth session (n 46) 176, commentary to draft art 1, [12]. Ago's Eighth Report to the ILC in 1979, which tackled the question of the character of the defences, selectively quoted from the 1973 report, and asserted that the Commission 'had already had occasion to state its view' on the matter and that it had done so in agreement with Ago's view. He omitted from his reference the fact that only 'some members' had agreed and that, moreover, they had done so 'for the time being': Ago, 'Eighth Report' (n 46) [44]. The passage from Ago's report was subsequently copied verbatim in the 1979 Report: Report of the Commission on the work of its thirty-first session, UN Doc A/34/10, (1979) Ybk Int L Commission, vol II(2), UN Doc A/CN.4/SER.A/1979/Add.1 (Part 2), 106 [2].

[52] Arguing that all defences constitute justifications see Ago, 'Eighth Report' (n 46) 27 ff. Arguing that they all are (or should be) excuses see Lowe, 'Precluding Wrongfulness or Responsibility' (n 42); Brigitte Stern, 'The Elements of an Internationally Wrongful Act' in James Crawford and others (eds), *The Law of International Responsibility*

the scope of this chapter. All that can be said here is that the determination of the character of any given circumstance as a justification or an excuse is a complex process which, in the absence of clear legislative indication (in this case, clear evidence from the practice of states and *opinio juris*), will involve a study of the formulation of the circumstance, its rationale, and the theory underlying its exonerating effect.[53] That is to say, contrary to what is often argued as will be seen below, it involves *more* than a simple reference to the primary or secondary rule classification of the individual circumstance. Indeed, whether a defence is attributed primary or secondary rule characteristics depends on whether it is formulated as justification or an excuse, and not the other way around.

Leaving aside the question of the classification of the defences in the ARSIWA, the important point here is that the relevant terminology, and the accepted meanings of these terms, should not be determined by the language used in the ARSIWA. This document is not binding and, regardless of the authority with which it is treated, the language used therein is not and cannot constitute an impediment to the clarification of terminological questions and the further refinement of the law of responsibility in this area. Thus, if one were to hold that all (or any) circumstances in the ARSIWA operate as excuses, it would be incorrect to refer to these as 'circumstances precluding wrongfulness' (which is tantamount to using the term 'justification' to refer to 'excuses') simply because this is the expression used in that instrument.[54]

2.3 Justifications and the primary and secondary rule distinction

The ARSIWA are built upon a distinction between so-called primary and secondary rules. As explained in the Commentary to the ARSIWA, primary rules relate to the 'content of the international obligations',[55] whereas secondary rules refer to 'the general conditions under international law for the State to be considered responsible for wrongful actions or omissions, and the legal consequences which flow therefrom'.[56] Primary rules guide or direct state conduct; secondary rules determine when the primary rules have been breached and regulate the legal consequences that flow from that breach. This is a distinction which is not peculiar to international law. Duarte d'Almeida shows in his chapter how continental (especially German) criminal law theorists developed an analogous distinction as far back as the late 19th century.[57] Equally, in the common law world, this distinction is often reflected in the dichotomy between conduct rules and decision rules. As explained by Meir Dan-Cohen, law is a 'set of normative messages', in which conduct rules are 'directed at the general public and provide guidelines for conduct' and decision rules are 'directed at the officials and provide

(OUP 2010) 218. In favour of classification see Théodore Christakis, 'Les "circonstances excluant l'illicéité": une illusion optique?' in Olivier Corten and others (eds), *Droit du pouvoir, pouvoir du droit: Mélanges offerts à Jean Salmon* (Bruylant 2007); Giancarlo Scalese, *La rilevanza delle scusanti nella teoria dell'illecito internazionale* (Editoriale Scientifica 2008); Paddeu (n 4) ch 1, and the decision of the tribunal in *CMS (Annulment)* (n 49) [129–36].

[53] For an overview of the different approaches to the characterization of defences in domestic law see Ferzan, 'Justification and Excuse' (n 43) 253–55. In international law see Paddeu (n 4) ch 1, s 1.4.

[54] This is not to say that terms have universal and unchanging meanings. To be sure, the meaning of terms can change. However, insofar as the expressions 'justification' and 'excuse' and their international law analogues are currently used, both in the legal domain and in ordinary language, with the meanings described above, it would seem prudent to continue to use them in this way so as to ensure comprehension, certainty, and clarity.

[55] General Commentary to the ARSIWA, [1].

[56] ibid.

[57] Chapter 10 in this book, section 2.4.

guidelines for their decisions'.[58] These concepts, as can be seen, are very close to those of primary and secondary rules prevalent in international law.

The distinction between primary and secondary rules was introduced in the ILC's work on responsibility by Special Rapporteur Ago in the early 1960s, although the idea underlying the distinction was much older *also* in international law: it can be detected, for example, in Dionisio Anzilotti's *Teoria generale della responsabilità*, published in 1902,[59] and in Ago's own previous scholarly work.[60] Ago formulated this distinction as a methodology for codification through which the Commission might overcome the impasse reached by previous attempts to codify the law of responsibility from the standpoint of the law on the treatment of aliens.[61] The Commission, under this approach, should focus on codifying *only* the general principles of responsibility, that is, the secondary rules, and not the substantive obligations of states, or primary rules of international law. The distinction was, therefore, intended as a pragmatic solution to a problem of codification: it was an heuristic device that allowed the Commission to delimit the scope of the responsibility project. As Rolando Quadri put it, the distinction was not a reflection of 'the structure and functioning of the legal order', but rather 'a legislative technique or scientific convenience'.[62] To be sure, the Commission (and Ago, for that matter) did not intend the distinction to be a conceptual one, and indeed it was employed by the Commission pragmatically and not dogmatically.[63]

The Commission's main goal was the elaboration of a coherent and comprehensive system of state responsibility and for this reason it refrained from a formalist approach as to what should be included or excluded from the project. That is, the Commission did not exclude rules from the ARSIWA *because* they were primary or conduct-guiding. This was certainly a wise choice for, as Dan Cohen's 'acoustic separation' thought experiment shows, a legal order in which subjects only 'hear' the primary rules and decision-makers only 'hear' secondary rules cannot function properly. The behaviour of the law's subjects is equally influenced by primary *and* secondary rules and, similarly, decision-makers cannot apply secondary rules in a vacuum—these must be applied in the context of the primary rules. Thus, there are several provisions in the ARSIWA which can 'properly' be characterized as primary rules but which are nevertheless important for a complete statement of the law of responsibility. A clear example is that of Article 16 of the ARSIWA, on complicity, which itself imposes an obligation on states not to aid or assist in the commission of a wrongful act by another state.[64] The same can be said of justifications. Justifications, as was seen, constitute permissions of the legal order to engage in certain behaviour which would otherwise be prohibited by a rule

[58] Meir Dan-Cohen, 'Decision Rules and Conduct Rules: On Acoustic Separation in Law' (1985) 97 Harvard Law Review 625, 630. Similarly Peter Alldridge, 'Rules for Courts and Rules for Citizens' (1990) 10 Oxford Journal of Legal Studies 487; Paul Robinson, 'Rules of Conduct and Principles of Adjudication' (1990) 57 University of Chicago Law Review 729.

[59] Dionisio Anzilotti, *Teoria generale della responsabilità dello stato nel diritto internazionale* (Lumachi 1902).

[60] See e.g. Roberto Ago, 'Le délit international' (1939) 68 Recueil des Cours 415.

[61] James Crawford, *The International Law Commission's Articles on State Responsibility* (CUP 2002) 15.

[62] Rolando Quadri, 'Cours général de droit international public' (1964) 113 Recueil des Cours 237, 455. Quadri was critical of the distinction precisely *because* the two functions mentioned were often conflated by the Commission and in the scholarly literature alike.

[63] Thus, Ago warned the Commission that the distinction 'must be understood rather loosely': Roberto Ago, 1013th meeting, 2 July 1969, (1969) Ybk Int L Commission, vol I, UN Doc A/CN.4/Ser.A/1969, 117 [33]. The Commission, for its part, acknowledged that the distinction was not watertight; see Report, thirty-first session (n 51) 88 [63].

[64] ARSIWA art 16 Commentary, [9] (speaking of the 'obligation not to provide aid or assistance to facilitate the commission of an internationally wrongful act by another State ...').

of that same legal order; as such they are conduct-guiding.[65] The Commission was aware of this,[66] but it was understood that no responsibility project would be complete without them and, for this reason, they were included in the ARSIWA.[67]

The law of responsibility is thus not limited to secondary rules only. To be sure, the distinction between primary and secondary was instrumental in the codification effort of the ARSIWA and has been useful in practice as well. But it is fundamental to recognize that the law of responsibility also includes rules which may be characterized as primary. For this reason, it seems that a better way of understanding the scope of the ARSIWA and the law of responsibility more generally is that expounded by Daniel Bodansky and John Crook: '[w]hat defines the scope of the [ARSIWA] is not their 'secondary' status but their generality: the [ARSIWA] represent those areas where the ILC could identify and reach consensus on general propositions that can be applied more or less comprehensively across the entire range of international law.'[68]
Of course, this too will be an imperfect solution—it seems that most organizing principles will be imperfect in some or other way. At the very least, to think about the law of responsibility as concerned with general propositions applicable to the issue of responsibility 'across the entire range of international law' may help to overcome certain formalist arguments which do not help our understanding of the law of responsibility and could, most importantly, lead to the incorrect application of the relevant legal principles. In particular, these are arguments to the extent that certain rules are *not* part of the law of responsibility because they are primary and that certain rules are secondary because they are included in the law of responsibility.

For present purposes, two lessons can be drawn from the above remarks. The first is that arguments that any given rule does *not* belong to the ARSIWA *because* it is primary 'are not based on solid ground'.[69] Thus, it is not the case that justifications do not belong to the law on state responsibility because they are primary in character. The second is that no implications may be drawn from the presence of any given rule in the ARSIWA as to its primary or secondary character. This is an especially important clarification to make, since it is not uncommon to read in the scholarly literature on international law that *because* the ARSIWA constitute a codification of secondary rules (only), then any defences included in that document *therefore* constitute excuses.[70] Not only is this statement incorrect as a matter of the law

[65] See Eric David, 'Primary and Secondary Rules' in James Crawford and others (eds), *The Law of International Responsibility* (OUP 2010) 29. Indeed, Dan-Cohen considers justifications to possess mixed character: they are both conduct *and* decision rules: Dan-Cohen (n 58) 631.

[66] See, among others, comments by Eustathiades, 1013th meeting, 2 July 1969, (1969) Ybk Int L Commission, vol I, UN Doc A/CN.4/Ser.A/1969, 114 [9]; Riphagen, 1538th meeting, 24 May 1979, (1979) Ybk Int L Commission, vol I, UN Doc A/CN.4/SER.A/1979, 34 [11]; Reuter, 1538th meeting, 24 May 1979, (1979) Ybk Int L Commission, vol I, UN Doc A/CN.4/SER.A/1979, 35 [17].

[67] David (n 66) 32. A similar remark was made by the Italian representative in the Sixth Committee of the GA, during discussion on the ILC's Report on State Responsibility; see UNGA 6th Committee Summary Record 22nd Meeting (1 November 1999) GAOR 54th Session 6th Committee 22nd Meering UN Doc A/C.6/54/SR.22, [54].

[68] Daniel Bodansky and John Crook, 'Symposium: The ILC's State Responsibility Articles: Introduction and Overview' (2002) 96 American Journal of International Law 773, 780–801. As an interesting analogue to this argument, the criminal codes of many continental legal systems divide the criminal law into a general part (the general principles of responsibility) and a special part (detailing the specific crimes recognized in the legal order). In the common law, the distinction is adopted in the US Model Penal Code and was endorsed in England and Wales by Sir Glanville Williams in his work *Criminal Law: The General Part*, first published in 1953. The title of James Crawford's latest work on State responsibility, *State Responsibility: The General Part* (CUP 2013), is a nod in this direction too.

[69] Giorgio Gaja, 'Primary and Secondary Rules in the International Law of State Responsibility' (2014) 97 Rivista di diritto internazionale 981, 990–91.

[70] See e.g. Gazzini, 'Necessity in International Investment Law' (n 16) 457; Tsagourias, 'Self-Defence against Non-State Actors' (n 16).

of responsibility (as already explained), but it is *also* incorrect as a matter of the ILC's work on the circumstances which does not support the characterization of all the circumstances in Chapter V of Part One as excuses and, most importantly, as a matter of state practice.[71]

3 Explaining the Operation of Justifications

Having clarified the meaning of 'circumstance precluding wrongfulness' or 'justification', and their place in the law of state responsibility, it remains to investigate the analytical process through which they are applied to specific cases and perform their justifying effect.

Consider a situation involving the rule relating to territorial sovereignty. Under this rule, states (may)[72] have an obligation not to interfere with the territorial sovereignty of other states. Now, say that State A's police, chasing a suspect, enter the territory of State B and apprehend that suspect in State B's territory. State A's actions constitute an encroachment on territorial sovereignty: State A's police crossing over into State B's territory and apprehending a suspect constitutes an exercise of enforcement jurisdiction on State B's territory.[73] In order to determine whether State A has committed an internationally wrongful act, we need to apply the relevant rule; that is, the rule which specifies the obligation breached, to the specific circumstances of the case. As a general matter, the application of this rule involves the operation by means of which a decision-maker determines 'according to the interpretative findings in the specific set of facts ... specific juridical results'.[74] These juridical results vary depending on the rule in issue, in particular the content and scope of the obligation it imposes, and they may include an 'acknowledgement of breach of a norm' (that is, that there is an internationally wrongful act) as well as 'the determination of the juridical consequences to which the breach gives rise to'.[75] In the context of the law of responsibility, these legal consequences consist in the obligations of cessation and reparation.[76] Applying the rule to State A's conduct, it will be said that State A breached its obligation to respect State B's territorial sovereignty (acknowledgement of breach) and that, as a result, State A is under an obligation to provide reparation to State B in adequate form (determination of juridical consequences).

What happens when State A invokes a justification in respect of this behaviour? State A could say, for example, that it was in a situation of necessity: the suspect possessed

[71] The practice of States is unequivocal that consent, self-defence (in the sense of ARSIWA art 21), and countermeasures, for example, constitute justifications. With a few exceptions, the same can be said of the plea of necessity. For an elaboration of these points see Paddeu (n 4) ch 2 (consent) ch 3 (self-defence) ch 4 (countermeasures), and ch 6 (state of necessity).

[72] It is important to recall that the obligation is not derived from the rule as a matter of logical deduction. Whether the obligation arises for the State from the rule to begin with is dependent on the specific set of circumstances and the collection of rules and permissions applicable in any given case. In the present hypothetical example, it will be assumed that the obligation *is* derived for the State—namely, that there is no exclusionary reason which prevents the obligation from arising.

[73] On the territoriality of enforcement jurisdiction see *The SS 'Lotus' (France v Germany)* (Judgment) [1927] PCIJ Rep Series A No 10, 3, 18–19; *Arrest Warrant of 11 April 2002 (DRC v Belgium)* (Judgment) [2002] ICJ Rep 3; Separate Opinion of President Guillaume 35, 36 [4]; Joint Separate Opinion of Judges Higgins, Kooijmans and Buergenthal 63, 79 [54]; Dissenting Opinion of Judge Van den Wyngaert 137, 168 [49].

[74] Anastasios Gourgourinis, 'The Distinction between Interpretation and Application of Norms in International Adjudication' (2011) 2 *Journal of International Dispute Settlement* 31, 47.

[75] ibid. See also Georges Abi-Saab, 'Cours général de droit international public' (1987) 207 Recueil des Cours 9, 219.

[76] Other consequences may follow in other contexts as well. For example, within the law of treaties, a treaty imposed by the threat or use of force (a breach of the prohibition of force) carries the consequence of invalidity for the treaty in question: VCLT art 52. On which see Olivier Corten, 'Article 52 (1969)' in Corten and Klein (eds), *The Vienna Conventions on the Law of Treaties: A Commentary, vol* 2 (OUP 2011) 1201.

confidential information relating to its nuclear arsenal and intended to use it to detonate several nuclear heads (threatening an essential interest of State A and, possibly, of the international community), and the only way to prevent this from happening was to apprehend him with a minor police incursion into the territory of State B.[77] The justification of necessity gives State A permission to act in the circumstances. If State A complied with all the requirements of the plea, a decision-maker would have to conclude that, even though State A encroached upon State B's territory, the conduct was lawful.

In these circumstances, therefore, there is conduct which is at once incompatible with what is required by an international obligation *and* compatible with a permission of the legal order (the justification). It is possibly in an effort to reflect this that, as noted earlier, such conduct is described as 'non-wrongful' conduct or unlawful conduct with precluded wrongfulness, and so on. But these descriptions, as was stated in the introduction, are problematic. Section 2 explained why these descriptions are definitionally and conceptually problematic. Here, we examine why they are *analytically* mistaken. The next two sub-sections will employ two models for the representation of legal argumentation and decision-making to explain the manner in which justifications produce their exonerating effects: first, a model which relies on deductive argumentation (3.1) and, second, a model which employs a dialogic approach. Each model will be presented in general terms, and will then be applied to the extra-territorial enforcement hypothetical by way of illustration.[78] The point of this analysis is not that of determining which of these two models better describes judicial practice or of evaluating which one should be followed in judicial practice. Rather, insofar as they analytically render legal argumentation and decision-making about defences, these models will be relied upon in sections 4 and 5 to strengthen further the clarifications made in section 2 above, namely that justified conduct does *not* amount to a breach of the law and that justified conduct is lawful. In short, these models will not be used to describe but rather to rectify current misconceptions in the case law and literature. In this sense, they will be used to 'improve', in the sense described by Hage, Waltermann, and Arosemena,[79] our understanding of the defences.

3.1 Justifications and deductive reasoning

One way to represent legal reasoning is through deductive logic. According to Neil MacCormick, '[i]t is in the nature of a rule to provide that whenever a certain state of facts obtains, a given normative consequence is to follow therefrom.'[80] Thus, legal rules can be restated in the following form: 'If *OF*, then *NC*', where '*OF*' (the antecedent) stands for the operative facts contained in the rule and '*NC*' (the consequent) for the normative consequence attributed by the rule to those facts.[81] Legal reasoning, therefore, can take deductive form: if *OF* obtains in any given case, then *NC* follows.[82]

[77] For the formulation of the plea of necessity see ARSIWA art 25.

[78] Note that these approaches can be applied to both justification and, *mutatis mutandis*, excuse defences. When in respect of justifications, they will concern the 'acknowledgment of the breach' as the relevant juridical result of application; when in respect of excuses, they will concern the 'determination of legal consequences', namely responsibility, as the relevant juridical result of application.

[79] On this point see Hage, Waltermann, and Arosemena, ch 2 of this book, at section 1.2.

[80] Neil MacCormick, *Rhetoric and the Rule of Law: A Theory of Legal Reasoning* (OUP 2005) 24.

[81] ibid 24.

[82] ibid 32.

It is possible to use the legal syllogism to represent legal reasoning with defences. The facts that enliven justifications (or defences more generally) can be included in the 'if' clause (or antecedent) of the rule. More precisely, the *absence* of those facts can be included therein. Thus, the rule including the defence can be restated as follows: 'If OF and *no defence*, then NC'. This is precisely what Glanville Williams had maintained in his famous article 'The Logic of Exceptions'.[83] To take an example from international law, one could restate the prohibition on the use of force and the right of self-defence as follows: 'if there is a use of force [OF] and there is no self-defence, then there is a breach of international law'.[84] Now, the difficulty with this approach is that it essentially collapses the difference between rules and the defences: the defences (and exceptions more generally) simply become negative rule-elements. This was precisely Glanville Williams's point, for in his view there is nothing special about defences that sets them apart from the elements of the rule. But this need not be the case. As Luís Duarte d'Almeida has shown in his work, it *is* possible to employ deductive reasoning to represent defences and *still* avoid the elision between the rule-elements and the defence.

Duarte d'Almeida's proof-based account of defences provides a synthesis between two intuitions: that law allows for exceptions *and* that we can argue deductively from existing law. Duarte d'Almeida has thus drawn a distinction between two types of facts whose proof or absence of proof bears on the correct decision to be made. These are what he calls '*P*-facts' and '*D*-facts' facts. *P*-facts are those that must be proved for a certain decision to be correctly issued; *D*-facts, those that must be *not* proved for that decision to be correctly issued. In the domain of the criminal law, he explains the difference between offences and defences by characterizing the former as *P*-facts, and the latter as *D*-facts. But the distinction applies to the domain of international law as well. To put it in the language used in the ARSIWA, the 'constituent requirements of the obligation' are to be understood as *P*-facts,[85] whereas the circumstances precluding wrongfulness have the status of *D*-facts. Thus, as Duarte d'Almeida explains, the rule setting out the (sufficient) conditions under which the legal consequence can be drawn can be represented as follows:

> If it is *proved that* (*a* and *b* and *not-c*) and it is *not proved that* (*x* or *y* or *z*), then *C* (see Chapter 10, at 183),

where '"*a*", "*b*", and "*not-c*" stand, as before, for *P*-facts; and "*x*", "*y*", and "*z*" stand for defences or *D*-facts'.[86]

It follows that if the *D*-facts are proved, then we cannot derive on the basis of such a conditional the conclusion that *C* is the case. This account brings out that it is not necessary to prove the *absence* of D-facts. It is enough that—together with proof of the relevant *P*-facts—the presence of *D*-facts is *not* proved.[87]

In this model, justifications constitute *D*-facts and are, therefore, facts the presence of which must *not* be proved in order to conclude that a violation of the law has occurred. In the hypothetical scenario provided above, the rule protecting a state's territorial sovereignty

[83] Glanville Williams, 'The Logic of "Exceptions"' (1988) 47 Cambridge Law Journal 261.

[84] This seems to be the view taken by the ILC in respect of the relation between self-defence and the prohibition of force. See ARSIWA art 21 Commentary, [1].

[85] Commentary to ch V of Pt 1, [7].

[86] Duarte d'Almeida, in this volume, ch 10. This is a crude and simplistic statement of Duarte d'Almeida's sophisticated proof-based account of defences, a brief summary of which can be found in his own chapter in this volume. For his extensive analysis see Duarte d'Almeida (n 21) ch 3.

[87] On this point see generally Duarte d'Almeida (n 21) ch 4.

would provide the relevant *P*-facts, those whose proof is necessary for the decision that the rule had been breached to be correctly issued. In turn, the plea of state of necessity would provide a *D*-fact which, if proven, would prevent the decision from being correctly issued. Following this approach, the rule which a decision-maker would have to apply in the hypothetical scenario would read as follows:

> If (*a*) it is *proved that* a State organ exercised enforcement jurisdiction in the territory of another State, and (*b*) it is *not proved that* there existed a state of necessity,[88] then it is correct to decide that there was a breach of the latter State's territorial sovereignty (*C*).

Thus, it is necessary to prove that an enforcement agent of State A captured a suspect in the territory of State B in order to conclude that State A breached its obligation to respect State B's territorial sovereignty; and necessary, also, that the defence of necessity not be proved.

3.2 Justifications and dialogic reasoning

An alternative way of representing legal argument is as a dialogic practice.[89] Hage, Waltermann, and Arosemena explain this in their chapter in this volume, but it is worth quoting the relevant passage here as it may be useful for the present explanation. According to these authors, this representation of reasoning involves a

> dialogue between two parties: the one party, the proponent, wants to establish a particular legal consequence for a case and to do so it invokes a legal rule and wants it to apply. The other party, the opponent, does not want that consequence and therefore does not want the rule to be applied. Both proponent and opponent can adduce reasons: the proponent reasons why the rule should be applied, the opponent reasons why the rule should not be applied.[90]

What is at stake is whether the rule invoked by the proponent should be applied to the facts of the case. The distinction between applicability and application of rules is crucial for the understanding of this model. A rule is *applicable* whenever all of its conditions (rule elements or what the ARSIWA calls the 'constituent requirements' of the obligation) are met; a rule is *applied* to a set of facts when it attaches its consequences to that case.[91] As described earlier, in the present context these consequences are a finding of breach and the determination of responsibility. But the fact that a rule is applicable is not enough to decide that it should be applied. On the contrary, as these authors explain, applicability is only a contributory reason in favour of the application of the rule to the concrete case. But there may be reasons *against* its application.

[88] The conditions of the state of necessity contained in ARSIWA art 25 (that the state was protecting an essential interest from a grave and imminent peril, that its action was the only way to protect that interest, that the action did not infringe the essential interest of another State or of the international community as a whole, and that the State had not contributed to the situation of necessity) all constitute the relevant *D*-facts. For the sake of simplicity, these were not included in the statement of the rule in the text.

[89] For an overview see Jaap Hage, *Studies in Legal Logic* (Springer 2005) ch 8. Note that this approach is not incompatible with a deductive model, insofar as the application of the rule is concerned (once it is decided that there are no reasons defeating its application).

[90] Chapter 2 in this book, 32.

[91] ibid, 18–19.

These reasons may be of two kinds: exclusionary or colliding. In the case of exclusionary reasons, the reason 'makes that a fact that normally would count as a reason, does not count so anymore'.[92] An example of this is the patient who allows a surgeon to hurt him in the course of surgery. Exclusionary reasons block the derivation of a duty for the agent from the relevant rule. That is, where there is an exclusionary reason, the agent is *not* under an obligation to behave in accordance with the rule. Colliding reasons, instead, constitute reasons against performing or abstaining from performing a given action. As such, they do not block the generation of the obligation from the relevant rule; but the agent will be at the same time under a reason to perform an action (the obligation) and a reason not to perform that action. A balancing or weighing of reasons is therefore required, before it is possible to conclude what an actor has the duty to do (or ought to do) in the circumstances.[93] The result is that, although the actor may be under an obligation to do or not to do a certain thing, on the balance of reasons for and against that action, it ought not to do it.

Justifications belong to the latter category of reasons. Thus, in this model, justifications would provide reasons against the application of an applicable rule, more particularly they are reasons that can defeat the reasons in favour (they are defeating reasons). In the extraterritorial enforcement hypothetical scenario, the rule prohibiting trespass into a state's territory is the applicable rule and its applicability to the facts of the case provides a contributory reason to apply it. But State A's justification of necessity is a reason against the application of the rule. In the battle between the two reasons, the justification of necessity defeats the rule which, despite being applicable, is ultimately not applied to the concrete case. Thus, no finding of breach and responsibility can be made. Note, as this will become relevant later, that in this model the justification is not itself applied to the facts of the case: it is simply a reason against the application of the rule.

4 An Assessment

With linguistic and analytical clarifications made, it is now time to assess the two misunderstandings mentioned in the introduction: (i) the claim that justified conduct constitutes a breach of international law and (ii) the legal characterization of justified conduct as 'unlawful with precluded wrongfulness', or non-wrongful, or variations thereof.

4.1 Justified conduct and breach of international law

It is not uncommon to read in international legal materials that conduct covered by a justification nevertheless amounts to a breach of international law. Section 2 above clarified that, as a conceptual matter, a breach of international law, and therefore an internationally wrongful act, can only exist if no justifications are available.[94] Indeed, the very concept of a 'breach of international law', as this is explained in the ARSIWA and its Commentary,

[92] Jaap Hage, 'Facts, Values and Norms' in Sanne Taekema and others (eds), *Facts and Norms in Law* (Edward Elgar Publishing 2016) 3.2.

[93] ibid. On the difference between rules, obligations, and what an agent ought to do see also Hage, 'The (Onto) Logical Structure of Law' (n 35) section 7.

[94] According to Crawford: 'it is odd to say that a State has committed an internationally wrongful act when the circumstances are such as to preclude the wrongfulness of its act under international law'; see Crawford, 'Second Report on State Responsibility' (n 32) 13 [14].

includes consideration (and refutation) of the existence of justifications. *A contrario*, if a justification is available, then there will be no breach of international law.

This conclusion is borne out also by the two approaches to the operation of justifications explained in section 3. The first model clearly conveys the need to consider justifications before reaching a conclusion as to the existence of breach, by representing the decision-making process as involving a syllogism which includes both the requirements of the rule ('If R') as well as the absence of justifications ('and not-J') as the set of premises for the conclusion that a breach of the law has occurred.

The second model, in turn, schematically shows that a determination that the rule is *applicable* to the facts of the case is not equivalent to the *application* of that rule to those facts. Thus, a decision as to applicability is not equivalent to a finding of breach: the finding of breach can only be arrived at if the rule is actually applied to the facts. In simplified terms, at the stage where it is decided that a rule is applicable to the facts of the case, there is at most, an 'apparent' or 'prima facie' breach of obligation, to use the words of the ICJ in *Nicaragua*,[95] a possibility which may nevertheless be defeated or set aside by the justification. Indeed, the manner in which this expression is used by the ICJ, suggests that the notion of a 'prima facie breach' is evidential in nature insofar as it indicates that, at the relevant stage of the reasoning, it would appear, if no other considerations are relevant, that a breach of the law may have occurred.[96] An 'apparent' or 'prima facie' breach is a first-blush assessment, not a conclusion as to the existence of a breach.

4.2 Justified conduct as lawful conduct

The other common misapprehension in the case law and literature relates to the legal appraisal of justified conduct. Is this behaviour lawful, non-wrongful, or 'unlawful with precluded wrongfulness'?

It was said in section 2 that justifications involve permissions of the legal order to engage in conduct which would normally be prohibited. As permissible conduct, justified conduct is therefore lawful. Once again, the two models described in section 3 bear this out analytically as well. In the first model, this is because if the conditions of the justification are met then the tribunal can only (logically) conclude that the act is lawful. If the reasoning is represented in syllogistic form: 'if R and not-J, then U', where R stands for the requirements of the rule, J for the justification, and U for the conclusion as to the unlawfulness of conduct, then if J is present the conclusion as to unlawfulness cannot be derived. In the second model, illegality is the conclusion reached when the rule is actually *applied*. In this case the rule is applicable to the facts, but it is not applied because the justification constitutes a defeating reason (model 2). As a result, the legal conclusion of illegality cannot be reached.

It could be said that both models 1 and 2 lead to the conclusion that the conduct is not unlawful. This is either because the unlawfulness of the conduct cannot be derived from the premises, or because the application of the rule has been defeated by the justification. Strictly speaking, therefore, it could be concluded that the conduct is 'not unlawful'. It might thus be

[95] *Nicaragua* (n 33) [226], [228].

[96] Note that the expression 'prima facie wrong' is used by theorists in domestic law settings in a substantive sense, as a moral judgment to refer to conduct that there are reasons not to perform. See e.g. John Gardner, 'In Defence of Defences' in John Gardner (ed), *Offences and Defences: Selected Essays in the Philosophy of Criminal Law* (OUP 2007) 77. It does not appear that international lawyers have used the expression in this latter sense.

inferred that models 1 and 2 support the view of those scholars who speak of justified conduct as 'non-wrongful'. But such an inference, at least in respect of justifications that are recognized by the legal order (so, for explicit and not implicit exceptions), is incorrect.

Whether 'non-wrongful' is equivalent to 'lawful' depends on the view taken as to the categories of normative modality recognized in any given legal order. International law has traditionally operated on a 'logically bivalent view of normative modality: either prohibition or permission'.[97] This understanding underpinned, most recently, the ICJ's decision in *Kosovo*, in which the Court was asked whether a unilateral declaration of independence was in 'accordance with' international law and it answered that the declaration was not prohibited by international law.[98] On this view, therefore, to say that conduct is non-wrongful is the same as saying that it is lawful. But Judge Simma, in his Declaration in *Kosovo*, argued that permission and prohibition are insufficient categories to capture the multiple shades of the legal world and thus proposed additional normative modalities, including legal neutrality, tolerance, and non-prohibition.[99] On this latter view, it would not be possible to equate non-wrongfulness to legality, for the absence of prohibition need not necessarily correspond to the existence of a permission. That is to say, it is just as possible that, in the absence of a prohibition, the behaviour would be considered as legally neutral.[100] It is unnecessary, for present purposes, to enter into the merits of this debate because, insofar as justifications are concerned, these constitute permissions of the legal order to engage in certain conduct. As a result, even if the representation of reasoning in models 1 and 2 does not lead to the conclusion that the conduct is lawful, it remains the case that the conduct in question, in addition to not being a breach of the rule, is covered by a permission of the legal order. Conduct adopted in accordance with a justification is, therefore, lawful.

André de Hoogh disagrees with this conclusion. In his view, it is a 'bridge too far' to say that justified conduct is permissible or lawful. After all, he says, there is a 'difference between on the one hand a (primary) permissive rule laying down a right to engage in conduct and rendering it lawful per se, and on the other hand a (secondary) permissive rule granting a right to engage in conduct that is otherwise prohibited'.[101] De Hoogh would prefer to speak about 'justified' conduct in these circumstances, where 'justified' serves not just a descriptive function (namely, to attest to the fact that it is conduct covered by a justification) but also a normative one. This expression aims to set this behaviour apart from conduct lawful under primary rules, by comparison with which justified conduct is, one might say, only 'lawful-ish'. But as with the qualifier 'non-wrongful' considered earlier, to talk about 'justified conduct' in this normative sense does not solve the problems identified in the introduction to this chapter: can countermeasures be adopted against justified conduct in this sense; and

[97] Jörg Kammerhofer, 'Gaps, the Nuclear Weapons Advisory Opinion and the Structure of International Legal Argument Between Theory and Practice' (2010) 80 British Yearbook of International Law 333, 337.

[98] *Accordance with International Law of the Unilateral Declaration of Independence in Respect of Kosovo* (Advisory Opinion) [2010] ICJ Rep 403, 425 [56].

[99] ibid, Declaration of Judge Simma 478, 480–81 [8–9].

[100] The point is that not all behaviours are (or need to be) regulated by the legal order. For example, the killing of a mosquito. It is not prohibited by the legal order, but it would be strange to derive from this that the law *permits* the killing of mosquitoes. Some of the arguments presented before the ICJ in the *Kosovo* case supported the legal neutrality of unilateral declarations of independence (UDIs) under international law: there is no right to secede (outside of self-determination) and secession is not prohibited as such or by the principle of territorial integrity (which is applicable only as between States). See e.g. the argument of the United Kingdom (UK): ibid Written Statement of the United Kingdom (17 April 2009) ch 5. As the UK argued: 'it is one thing to say that there is no right to secede in international law and another to say that secession is contrary to international law' [5.17]; and 'international law neither authorises nor prohibits secession' [5.61]. On legal neutrality as a deontic mode see Ilmar Tammelo, 'On the Logical Openness of Legal Orders: A Modal Analysis of Law with Special Reference to the Logical Status of *Non Liquet* in International Law' (1959) 8 American Journal of Comparative Law 187, 194.

[101] Chapter 8 in this book, 138.

can justified conduct in this sense amount to a material breach of treaty under Article 60 of the VCLT? It is unclear. This said, the concern identified by de Hoogh is an important one relating to the normative messages of the law. If law is to be conduct-guiding, then surely it is important to convey that justified conduct is only exceptionally so, and that it would be better if it was not resorted to? This is where the lack in international law of a concept equivalent to that of 'offence' in domestic law, as noted by Duarte d'Almeida in his chapter, would become useful. Developing one such notion may perform the function that de Hoogh suggests: the conduct would be a *wrong*, but only a *pro tanto* one, for, all things considered, the conduct is lawful.[102] This solution would take care of the difficulty identified by de Hoogh, while at the same time avoiding the difficulties that arise from a normative concept of 'justified conduct'.

It is possible that, as for de Hoogh, the expression 'non-wrongful' (and its other avatars) as used by part of the case law and scholarship constitute an attempt to convey the undesirability of this type of behaviour. Indeed, this label is frequently used to describe conduct justified under the plea of necessity. This defence is currently formulated as a consequentialist-based justification in Article 25 of the ARSIWA, pursuant to which a state is permitted to act for the protection of its essential interests to the detriment of the (lesser) interests of an innocent third party. And while the protection of superior (essential) interests may be permissible, it is still seen as undesirable to obtain that protection by unilateral means and at the expense of an innocent party. Moreover, on account of the abuses that this notion historically gave rise to, action under a state of necessity, while permissible, is to be discouraged.[103] Similar considerations apply to countermeasures. Countermeasures are defined as permissible, although 'intrinsically wrongful',[104] measures adopted in response to a prior wrongful act by the target state. Of course, if the conduct is permitted as a countermeasure it cannot be unlawful, be it intrinsically or extrinsically. As with state of necessity, countermeasures are unilateral measures of enforcement and they, too, were abused in the past by powerful states against weaker states. Given this context, the expression 'intrinsic wrongfulness' may also be an attempt to convey the undesirability of resort to this type of measure. Be that as it may, to speak of acts of necessity as being 'non-wrongful' or of countermeasures as 'intrinsically wrongful' has no bearing on the *legal* characterization of both acts as permissible and, as such, lawful. At most, these labels constitute normative appraisals of the relevant conduct, be it from a moral, political, or other normative stance.[105]

102 Namely, one that there are reasons not to engage in and that, failing an overriding reason against, would be all things considered wrong to do. On 'all things considered' judgments, see e.g. Seth Lazar, *Sparing Civilians* (OUP 2015) 5; Adil Haque, *Morality and Law at War* (OUP 2017) 8. One might even speak of a 'prima facie breach' in this connection, as de Hoogh suggests (at fn 79). Note, as already mentioned, that the expression 'prima facie breach' can be used in both substantive and evidential or procedural senses. When used in the context described in the text, it takes on a substantive shade: it is a moral or other normative evaluation of conduct. This is not, it appears, the sense in which the ICJ used it in *Nicaragua* (n 33) where, as already noted, it was deployed in a procedural sense to denote a step in the reasoning of the Court.

103 The use of negative formulation in the text of ARSIWA art 25 ('Necessity may not be invoked ...) as well as the positioning of the defence in the list in ch V of Pt 1 (the last one in the list) both reflect the desire to discourage reliance on this defence and to stress that this is a defence of last resort.

104 See e.g. Denis Alland, 'The Definition of Countermeasures' in James Crawford and others (eds), *The Law of International Responsibility* (OUP 2010) 1135.

105 A thorough defence of the view that justified conduct need not be morally right (but indeed, can be morally wrong); see Berman (n 44). See also Suzanne Uniacke, *Permissible Killing: The Self-Defence Justification of Homicide* (Cambridge University Press 1994) 13–14. Further, Duarte d'Almeida, chapter 10 in this book. It is perhaps in this sense that Crawford's view that 'it cannot be said that a State which has evidently not acted in the manner required by a treaty or customary obligation in force for it has nonetheless acted "in conformity with" or "in accordance with" that obligation' must be read. See Crawford, 'Second Report on State Responsibility' (n 32) 13 [14].

5 Conclusion

The variety of expressions used in international case law and in the scholarly literature to describe the operation and effect of the 'circumstances precluding wrongfulness' seemed to corroborate Brownlie's view that the circumstances 'had never been properly worked out'.[106] Indeed, the language used in this regard suggested contradictory conclusions as to the effect of the circumstances: thus, for some the circumstances excluded the breach of international law, whereas for others the circumstances excluded wrongfulness but not the breach of international law; by the same token, for some the circumstances rendered conduct lawful, whereas for others justified conduct could only be classified as 'non-wrongful' or 'unlawful with precluded wrongfulness'. In essence, there seemed to be uncertainty as to whether a circumstance precluding wrongfulness excludes the breach of international law and whether conduct covered by one of the circumstances is lawful. These uncertainties are not inconsequential. As was said in the Introduction, how one understands the effect of the circumstances may determine whether justified conduct may nevertheless be considered as a material breach of a treaty for the purposes of Article 60 of the VCLT; and, whether the invocation of a justification implies a concession of wrongdoing.

It is unclear whether these differences in the understanding of the circumstances precluding wrongfulness are simply a matter of the incorrect and inconsistent use of the relevant terminology, or whether they betray a deeper analytical misunderstanding of how the circumstances 'work' and what their effect is. This study thus attempted to provide clarifications on both counts, showing that: (i) that the circumstances *preclude* a breach of international law and (ii) that, insofar as they constitute permissions of the legal order to engage in certain conduct, they result in the legality of the relevant conduct. As a result, it is now possible to conclude that since justified conduct does not constitute a breach of international law and is lawful, it cannot constitute a material breach in the sense of Article 60 of the VCLT. Similarly, the invocation of a justification does not amount to a concession of wrongdoing, for there can be no ascertainment of wrongdoing until *after* the justification has been considered. In *Nicaragua*, indeed, the Court only accepted that an invocation of a justification might involve a concession that the state engaged in certain conduct—but not of the legal qualification of that conduct as wrongful.[107]

[106] Brownlie (n 5) [18].
[107] *Nicaragua* (n 33) [74].

12

Freedom with Their Exception*

Jurisdiction and Immunity as Rule and Exception

*Eleni Methymaki*** *and Antonios Tzanakopoulos****

There is behaviour that is right; and there is behaviour that, though wrong, is understandable and excusable. The distinction between the two is the very stuff of classical tragedy.

V Lowe, 'Precluding Wrongfulness or Responsibility: A Plea for Excuses' (1999) 10 European Journal of International Law 405

And then there is behaviour that might be right or wrong, but it's not for you to say.

Eleni and Antonios

1 Introduction

Immunity is most usually described as a bar to the jurisdiction of the forum state, and thus seems to signify a set of exceptional circumstances in which jurisdiction, although present, may not be exercised.[1] According to Chief Justice Marshall in *The Schooner Exchange v McFaddon*, 'the jurisdiction of the nation within its own territory is necessarily exclusive and absolute ... susceptible of no limitation not imposed by itself'.[2] If the general rule then is that a state may exercise jurisdiction to prescribe and to enforce norms under specific circumstances,[3] the rule of immunity, barring the exercise of such jurisdiction in certain situations

* James Hetfield, Kirk Hammett, and Lars Ulrich, 'Eye of the Beholder' in Metallica, ... *And Justice for All* (Elektra, 1988). We thank Christian J Tams and the participants in the Cambridge Workshop on Exceptions and Defences for useful comments and suggestions. The usual disclaimer applies.

** Faculty of Law, University of Oxford. Eleni is grateful to the AG Leventis Foundation and the Foundation of Education and European Culture for generously supporting her LLM studies at the University of Cambridge during which period most of the work on the present chapter was undertaken.

*** Faculty of Law, University of Oxford.

[1] See e.g. *Natoniewski v Federal Republic of Germany*, Supreme Court of Poland, Case No 465/09 (29 October 2010), where the Supreme Court of Poland accepted that immunity is a procedural bar to jurisdiction, while also stating that it creates an exception to jurisdiction. Later in its decision the Court considered the question of jurisdiction to be a matter of admissibility, on which see section 6 below. See also *Al-Adsani v UK* App No 35763/97 (Judgment of 21 November 2001) para 48: 'The grant of immunity is to be seen not as qualifying a substantive right but as a procedural bar on the national courts' power to determine the right'; *Jones v Saudi Arabia* [2006] UKHL 26, para 33 (Lord Bingham); *Bencharbouche v Secretary of State for Foreign and Commonwealth Affairs; Libya v Janah* [2017] UKSC 62, paras 17–19 (Lord Sumption).

[2] *The Schooner Exchange v McFaddon*, 11 US 7 Cranch 116 (1812). The quote is open to interpretation, and the Court in that case appeared to grant immunity as a matter of comity rather than as a matter of international obligation. See also Lee Caplan, 'State Immunity, Human Rights and *Jus Cogens*: A Critique of the Normative Hierarchy Theory' (2003) 97 American Journal of International Law 741, 749–51.

[3] The law of jurisdiction itself 'determines how far, *ratione loci*, a State's laws might reach', 'it ensures that States, especially powerful States, do not assert jurisdiction over affairs which are the domain of other States', and it 'is closely related to the customary international law principles of non-intervention and sovereign equality of States'. See Cedric Ryngaert, *Jurisdiction in International Law* (2nd edn, OUP 2015) 6.

Eleni Methymaki and Antonios Tzanakopoulos, *Freedom with Their Exception* In: *Exceptions in International Law*. Edited by: Lorand Bartels and Federica Paddeu, Oxford University Press (2020).
DOI: 10.1093/oso/9780198789321.003.0012

otherwise falling within the ambit of the rules allowing the exercise of jurisdiction, appears very much as an exception. But then immunity itself is also a rule seemingly subject to exceptions, in particular with respect to non-sovereign acts (or non-sovereign property).[4] An exception to the exception signifies a return to the rule, in this particular case the rule allowing the exercise of jurisdiction.

In what follows, we will focus on sovereign (state) immunity, without delving into issues of immunity of state officials. We will focus further on immunity from jurisdiction, only occasionally bringing in issues pertaining to immunity from execution. We will try to ascertain whether the rule of sovereign immunity before the courts of foreign states constitutes an exception to the rules on jurisdiction. We will also seek to ascertain what the implications of such characterization may be, considering also that the rules of sovereign immunity (both from jurisdiction and from execution) are seemingly subject to exceptions themselves. Section 2 sets out our understanding of the differences between exceptions and defences in international law, and the particular characteristics of exceptions, with special reference to the rules of jurisdiction and immunity. Sections 3 and 4 discuss the positions taken by the International Law Commission (ILC), the International Court of Justice (ICJ), and the states in adopting the 2004 UN Convention on Jurisdictional Immunities of States and their Property (UNCJISP). Section 5 finally puts forward some of the potential implications of the characterization of the rules of immunity as exceptions to the rules regarding state jurisdiction. Section 6 concludes.

2 Exceptions and Defences: Some Conceptual Remarks

In our understanding, the difference between exceptions and defences in international law is essentially reflected in the difference between primary norms and secondary norms. Primary norms, in the sense adopted by the ILC in its Articles on State Responsibility and on the Responsibility of International Organizations,[5] are norms of international law that prescribe, proscribe, or permit certain conduct, establishing thus international rights and obligations.[6] In turn, secondary norms are norms that indicate the general conditions under international law for a state to be held responsible for the violation of a primary norm, and the legal consequences stemming therefrom.[7] This distinction is to some extent simplistic,

[4] State immunity was initially envisaged as an 'absolute' rule (or exception!) in the sense that whenever a state was involved in proceedings before domestic courts of another state, then the latter ought not to exercise their jurisdiction. Gradually, and given the increased engagement of states in commercial activities, the 'restrictive theory' of state immunity was adopted by the courts of several states, according to which the domestic courts were not obligated to grant immunity for non-sovereign acts (acts *jure gestionis*). For this evolution see generally ILC, 'Draft Articles on Jurisdictional Immunities of States and Their Property, with Commentaries' (1991) 2 Yearbook of the International Law Commission 12; see also Hersch Lauterpacht, 'The Problem of Jurisdictional Immunities of Foreign States' (1951) 28 British Yearbook of International Law 220; Sompong Sucharitkul, 'Immunity of Foreign States Before National Authorities' (1976-I) 149 Recueil des Cours 85; Ian Sinclair, 'The Law of Sovereign Immunity: Recent Developments' (1980-II) 167 Recueil des Cours 113; Peter Trooboff, 'Foreign State Immunity: Emerging Consensus on Principles' (1986-V) 200 Recueil des Cours 235; Christian Tomuschat, 'The International Law of State Immunity and Its Development by National Institutions' (2011) 44 Vanderbilt Journal of Transnational Law 1105; Hazel Fox and Philippa Webb, *The Law of State Immunity* (3rd edn, OUP 2013).

[5] ILC, 'Articles on the Responsibility of States for Internationally Wrongful Acts' (ARSIWA) (2001) 2(2) Yearbook of the International Law Commission, annex to GA Res 56/83 UN Doc A/56/49(Vol I)/Corr.4; ILC, 'Draft Articles on the Responsibility of International Organizations (DARIO)' (2011) 2(2) Yearbook of the International Law Commission, annex to GA Res 66/100.

[6] 'ARSIWA (n 5) with commentaries' (2001) 2(2) Yearbook of the International Law Commission 31, para 1; 'DARIO (n 5) with commentaries' (2011) 2(2) Yearbook of the International Law Commission 2, para 3.

[7] ibid.

and we admit so at the outset. It has, however, significant explanatory force. We concede that certain formally secondary norms, such as those regarding reparation, in fact act as primary norms at the secondary level: they establish rights and obligations consequential on the existence of an attributable breach of primary norms. As such, their operation in terms of the rule-exception structure is the same as that of primary norms; we discuss this briefly below.

An exception is a primary norm that operates to limit the scope of application of another, usually more general, primary norm. Essentially then, an exception is a carve-out from or limitation of the scope of application of another primary norm.[8] A defence, in contrast, is a norm that operates to preclude the wrongfulness of the violation of a primary norm, and thus responsibility for the relevant act.[9] As such, a defence is necessarily a secondary norm. In the case where an exception operates, the primary norm from which the exception carves out certain situations is not engaged at all, in the sense that it cannot be violated if the exception is operating.[10] A defence, on the other hand, presupposes the violation of a primary norm, and operates in the secondary regime of responsibility, in essence in order to preclude wrongfulness and thus responsibility, which would otherwise be engaged.

Certain formally secondary norms, such as those regarding reparation or countermeasures, for example, operate as primary norms on the secondary (responsibility) level. They require or permit certain conduct, or abstention from certain conduct, establishing (secondary) obligations of the responsible state, or even all states,[11] and secondary rights or faculties of the (directly or indirectly) injured state(s). These norms operate with respect to one another in the same way as primary norms: the general rule regarding the right (faculty) to take countermeasures in response to an internationally wrongful act, for example, is limited in its scope of application by more specific rules regarding obligations not affected by countermeasures (Article 50), conditions for resorting to countermeasures as well as obligations to suspend them (Article 52), and so on.

Very exceptionally, a norm, in its different iterations, may operate *both* as an exception *and* as a defence. For example, self-defence operates both as an exception to the prohibition of the use of force,[12] and as a defence, in the sense of a circumstance precluding the wrongfulness of an act other than the use of force.[13] Consent is also peculiar in the sense that it can be cast as an exception in certain cases, and as a defence in others: certain things are not unlawful if done with the consent of the state: the exercise of jurisdiction is an example. Others are unlawful, but consent operates to preclude wrongfulness. This could also be said of necessity. In essence, it all comes down to the content of the relevant primary norm, as this will help determine whether consent or necessity are cast as exceptions, as exclusions from the scope of application of the primary rule, or if they are only to operate at the secondary level to preclude wrongfulness of the act.

[8] cf also Jorge Viñuales's contribution in the present volume.

[9] For the debate on whether defences (as prescribed by the ILC in the ARSIWA) preclude the responsibility of the wrongdoing state or the wrongfulness of the act, see Federica Paddeu's contribution in the present volume.

[10] See also Federica Paddeu, 'Self-defence as a Circumstance Precluding Wrongfulness: Understanding Article 21 of the Articles on State Responsibility' (2015) 85 British Yearbook of International Law 90, 91.

[11] See eg the obligation not to recognize as lawful a situation created by a serious breach of an obligation arising under a peremptory norm of international law in ARSIWA art 41(2). See further Stefan Talmon, 'The Duty Not to "Recognise as Lawful" a Situation Created by the Illegal Use of Force or Other Serious Breaches of a *Jus Cogens* Obligation: An Obligation without Real Substance?' in Christian Tomuschat and Jean-Marc Thouvenin (eds), *The Fundamental Rules of the International Legal Order:* Jus Cogens *and Obligations* Erga Omnes (Martinus Nijhoff 2005).

[12] See UN Charter art 51.

[13] See ARSIWA art 21; see further generally Paddeu (n 10).

Usually, then, a particular norm with specific substantive normative content (i.e. with content prescribing, proscribing, or permitting certain conduct) which interacts with another such norm will have to be classified as either an exception or as a defence (depending on whether it operates at the primary or the secondary level). Still, there exist also norms without any independent 'normative charge'. These may affect the operation of primary norms, even though they cannot be classified as either exceptions or defences. Norms without such independent normative charge are mainly conflict resolution rules (such as *lex posterior* or *lex specialis*),[14] rules of interpretation (such as the ones reflected in Articles 31 and 32 of the Vienna Convention on the Law of Treaties, or principles of interpretation such as the principle of effectiveness and others[15]), or even interstitial norms (such as proportionality).[16]

Exceptions, rules of conflict resolution, rules of interpretation, and interstitial norms may all be seen as in some way moderating or regulating normative conflict.[17] However, the important distinction here is precisely that exceptions have specific normative content of primary norm quality, that is, in a way, they *are* the conflicting norm. All the other norms mentioned have no independent normative charge in the sense that they do not impose or require particular conduct on the part of the addressee. In fact, their addressee is not necessarily a state at all, but rather *any* interpreter of international law.

Further, it is useful to distinguish here between apparent and genuine normative conflicts. That two rules may seemingly be applicable in the same circumstances does not necessarily mean that the two rules conflict with one another, except at first glance. The apparent conflict may be easily resolved through relating one rule as an exception to the other; or through 'harmonious' or 'consistent' interpretation (interpreting one rule in harmony with the other);[18] or through the operation of an interstitial norm, such as proportionality. This will reveal the apparent conflict as never to have been a conflict at all. Only genuine conflicts will require the employment of rules of occasional (*lex specialis, lex posterior*) or normative hierarchy (*lex superior*)[19] in order to be resolved. Or such genuine conflicts may indeed be irresolvable. In this latter case, a state will simply have to decide which rule it will comply with and which it will violate, engaging its international responsibility.

This discussion may to some extent be theoretical. We could conceptualize an exception as a special rule operating to limit the application of the general rule in specific circumstances. If so, the exception would appear simply as an application of the *lex specialis* rule, a rule of occasional hierarchy that importantly operates not to strike down the general rule, but merely to suspend its operation in the specific circumstances and for as long as they pertain. The exception in this case will have relative operation in the sense that 'whatever is being "set aside" will continue to have an effect on the interpretation and application of the

[14] See e.g. ILC, 'Fragmentation of International Law: Difficulties Arising from the Diversification and Expansion of International Law', Report of the Study Group of the International Law Commission, UN Doc A/CN.4/L.682 (13 April 2006) para 56: 'The principle that special law derogates from general law is a widely accepted maxim of legal interpretation and technique for the resolution of normative conflicts'.

[15] Which, however, will in any case be anchored to the general rules of interpretation reflected in the VCLT; see also ILC, 'Fragmentation of International Law' (n 14) para 412.

[16] For the concept of interstitial norms see generally Vaughan Lowe, 'The Politics of Law-Making: Are the Method and Character of Norm Creation Changing?' in Michael Byers (ed), *The Role of Law in International Politics* (OUP 2000) 207, 213 ff.

[17] cf with respect to exceptions being used as tools to resolve conflicts between different rules or legal systems the contribution by Jaap Hage, Antonia Waltermann, and Gustavo Arosemena in the present volume.

[18] See ILC, 'Fragmentation of International Law' (n 14) paras 88 ff.

[19] For the terms see generally Emmanouel Roucounas, 'Engagements parallèles et contradictoires' (1987) 206 Recueil des Cours 9 ff.

exception'.[20] Or we could conceptualize the exception as merely conditioning the operation of another primary rule. We will return to the implications of such considerations in section 5 below.

In the context of jurisdiction and immunity, the starting point is necessarily the rules of jurisdiction as the set of primary norms establishing the power of the state to prescribe and to enforce rules.[21] The normative content of that set of norms is determined in the first instance, in the case of prescriptive jurisdiction by the variable limits of the domain réservé (that which is not prohibited is permitted) and in the case of enforcement jurisdiction primarily by reference to territoriality (enforcement is in the first instance only allowed within the territory of the state). The normative content determines the scope of application of the relevant set of norms, both substantively and locally. However, another set of primary norms, that of immunity from jurisdiction and enforcement, operates to exclude from the scope of application of the rules regarding jurisdiction certain acts and conduct (eg acts of a state) that would otherwise fall within that scope. In turn, the set of rules of immunity itself admits exceptions limiting its scope of application with respect to certain acts, such as, e.g., non-sovereign acts. This exception-to-the-exception signifies a return to the application of the rule, namely the rules regarding jurisdiction, the limitation of their scope of application now eliminated.

With this in mind, we will now survey the positions taken by the ILC, the International Court of Justice (section 3), and the states in adopting the 2004 UNCJISP (section 4), before re-evaluating our preliminary approach and discussing its implications in section 5.

3 The Positions of the ILC and the ICJ: Exceptions to the Exception?

Part III of the 2004 UNCJISP is entitled '[p]roceedings in which state immunity cannot be invoked', reflecting the position taken by the ILC in its relevant draft articles. This title was chosen, according to the ILC commentary, 'in order to reconcile the two positions' of the members of the Commission: some argued that there are certain circumstances and situations in international law in which state immunity is not recognized (these members advocated the title of '[L]imitations'), while others contended that state immunity is the rule in international law, and 'exceptions to that rule were made subject to the express consent of the State'.[22] This cryptic statement attempts to address the relationship between the circumstances in which state immunity does and does not apply. It was meant to 'bridge the doctrinal differences' expressed during the formulation of the draft articles on the matter.[23]

One is left wondering then what is the relationship between the rule of state immunity and the circumstances in which immunity is not considered applicable.[24] Moreover, and arising

[20] ILC 'Fragmentation of International Law' (n 14) para 103.

[21] See also Rosalyn Higgins, 'Certain Unresolved Aspects of the Law of State Immunity' (1982) 29 Netherlands International Law Review 265, 271; Sinclair (n 4) 215; Caplan (n 2) 744.

[22] ILC, 'Draft Articles on Jurisdictional Immunities of States and Their Property, with Commentaries' (n 4) 33, para 1.

[23] Rosanne van Alebeek, 'Part III: Proceedings in which State Immunity Cannot be Invoked. Introduction' in Roger O'Keefe, Christian J Tams, and Antonios Tzanakopoulos (eds), *The United Nations Convention on Jurisdictional Immunities of States and Their Properties: A Commentary* (OUP 2013) 153–66, 154.

[24] For example, one of the ILC members proposed during the deliberations of the Commission that a 'dual approach' be adopted, namely that there was no need for state immunity to be established as a general rule to which certain exceptions are applicable, but that the circumstances to which immunity applies and those that it does not should be researched: see ILC, 'Fourth Report on Jurisdictional Immunities of States and their Property'

as an underlying question, one wonders what is the relationship between the rules on immunity and the rules on state jurisdiction, both stemming directly from the concept of sovereignty and the related concept/consequence of sovereign equality.[25]

In its judgment in *Jurisdictional Immunities of the State* in 2012, the ICJ affirmed the customary status of the rule of state (otherwise, sovereign) immunity in international law.[26] It went on to state that the rule of state immunity

> derives from the principle of sovereign equality of States, which, as Article 2, paragraph 1, of the Charter of the United Nations makes clear, is one of the fundamental principles of the international legal order. This principle has to be viewed together with the principle that each State possesses sovereignty over its own territory and that there flows from that sovereignty the jurisdiction of the State over events and persons within that territory. *Exceptions to the immunity of the State represent a departure from the principle of sovereign equality. Immunity may represent a departure from the principle of territorial sovereignty and the jurisdiction that flows from it.*[27]

Two issues arise from the above-mentioned passage. First, the Court seems to embrace the view that immunity is the rule, and the circumstances to which it does not apply are exceptions to that rule. More importantly, these exceptions are as a matter of law considered 'departures' from the fundamental principle of sovereign equality itself. As the PCIJ stated in *SS Wimbledon*, restrictions or limitations upon the exercise of sovereignty must be restrictively construed.[28] Second, the Court does articulate the existence of some kind of relationship between the rule of state immunity and the rule of territorial jurisdiction of the state, but it avoids clearly characterizing immunity as an exception to territorial jurisdiction. It does, however, characterize immunity as a 'departure' from the principle of territorial sovereignty, a term it used immediately before to characterize exceptions to immunity. The Delphi Oracle might have been trusted to give a less ambiguous representation of the state of the art than the Court did in this instance. Nonetheless, the Court upheld its finding in *Arrest Warrant* that the rules on jurisdictional immunity are procedural in nature, and thus do not conflict with the substantive law that governs the lawfulness or unlawfulness of state conduct.[29]

by Mr Sompong Sucharitkul, Special Rapporteur, UN Doc A/CN.4/357 and Corr.1 (1982) 2(1) Yearbook of the International Law Commission 206, para 24. The Special Rapporteur, however, was not convinced that this was a wise proposal, since it could potentially leave a gap or a twilight zone in which uncertainty on whether immunity does or does not apply would continue to exist. He said this was an attempt 'to burn the candle at both ends' (ibid). cf *Bencharbouche* (n 1) para 39 (Lord Sumption).

[25] contra Caplan (n 2) 752–55.

[26] In *Jurisdictional Immunities of the State (Germany v Italy: Greece intervening)* (Judgment) [2012] ICJ Rep 99, neither Germany nor Italy disputed that immunity is generally granted as a matter of an international obligation and not just as a gesture of comity (ibid para 53). The Court then restated its well-established *North Sea Continental Shelf ((Federal Republic of Germany/Denmark; Federal Republic of Germany/Netherlands)* (Judgment) [1969] ICJ Rep 3) formula for the identification of customary international law and eventually concluded that practice shows that 'States generally proceed on the basis that there is a right to immunity under international law, together with a corresponding obligation on the part of other States to respect and give effect to that immunity'. See *Jurisdictional Immunities of the State* ibid para 56.

[27] ibid para 57 (emphasis added).

[28] *SS 'Wimbledon' (United Kingdom, France, Italy & Japan v Germany)* (Judgment) [1923] PCIJ Rep Series A No 1, 24–25. This finding of the Court is not unqualified, however, as the Court goes on to state the following: 'But the Court feels obliged to stop at the point where the so-called restrictive interpretation would be contrary to the plain terms of the article and would destroy what has been clearly granted'.

[29] *Jurisdictional Immunities of the State* (n 26) para 58; *Arrest Warrant of 11 April 2000 (Democratic Republic of the Congo v Belgium)* [2002] ICJ Rep 3, para 60.

The main point of difference between the parties in the *Jurisdictional Immunities of the State* case was the extent to which, and the circumstances under which, a state is entitled to sovereign immunity. There was no significant debate on the distinction between acts *jure imperii*, namely acts performed by the state in its capacity as a sovereign, and acts *jure gestionis*, that is, state acts performed in a non-sovereign capacity. Italy accepted the fact that the acts performed by the German armed forces during the Second World War should be considered sovereign acts of the state.[30] The Court for its part reiterated that, immunity being a norm of a procedural character, the lawfulness or unlawfulness of a given conduct may not alter the characterization of an act as a sovereign or non-sovereign. The determination of the character of an act as sovereign or not occurs before any consideration of the lawfulness of the relevant act.[31] Since there was no general disagreement between the parties as to whether immunity is to be granted for acts *jure imperii*, the Court went on to analyse whether there is any limitation to the granting of immunity for such acts, namely whether acts committed by the armed forces of a state during an armed conflict are always covered by immunity.[32] Therein lay the basic disagreement between the parties, since Germany was advocating that there is no limitation to sovereign immunity for acts *jure imperii*, whereas Italy's argument was based, first, on the so-called territorial tort exception to state immunity, and, secondly, on the fact that the conduct of the German armed forces amounted to violations of *jus cogens* rules.[33]

As regards the territorial tort exception, ie the exception to immunity for acts committed in the territory of the forum state and which have resulted in the death, personal injury or injury of nationals of the forum, the Court held that it was not applicable in the instance. Customary international law was found still to require that immunity be granted for torts committed in the territory of the forum state by the armed forces and other organs of another state in the course of an armed conflict.[34] It is noteworthy that the Court stated expressly that it did not need to address the issue of whether there is a 'tort exception' under customary international law which covers both acts *jure imperii* and acts *jure gestionis*.[35] Germany supported the view that the tort exception is only available for non-sovereign acts,[36] whereas Italy relied on the European Convention on State Immunity (ECSI), the UNCJISP, and state practice,[37] which make no distinction between sovereign and non-sovereign acts with respect to the tort exception.[38] This was also a major point of contention among the ILC

[30] *Jurisdictional Immunities of the State* (n 26) para 60. It has to be noted that the Court by-passed the issue of how international law treats the grant of immunity in cases of acts *jure gestionis* since the sovereign character of the acts in this case was not at dispute.

[31] ibid para 60.

[32] ibid para 61.

[33] ibid para 61.

[34] ibid para 75.

[35] ibid para 65.

[36] Germany's argument was that neither art 11 of the European Convention on State Immunity (adopted 16 May 1972, entered into force 11 June 1976) 1495 UNTS 182 (ECSI) nor art 12 of the United Nations Convention on Jurisdictional Immunities of States and their Property (adopted 2 December 2004, not yet in force) UN Doc A/RES/59/38, Annex (UNCJISP) reflected customary international law insofar as they denied immunity for acts *iure imperii* and that in any event neither of these articles was intended to apply to acts committed by state military forces. See *Jurisdictional Immunities of the State* (n 26) para 63.

[37] Italy's argument was that customary international law has evolved so as not to allow immunity for acts committed in the territory of the forum state and which have resulted in the death, personal injury or injury of nationals of the forum, even if the acts are sovereign acts in the course of an armed conflict. Italy based this argumentation on ECSI art 11, UNCJISP art 12, and the relevant domestic legislation adopted by nine states, for example see Foreign Sovereign Immunity Act, 28 USC §§1330, 1602–1611; UK, State Immunity Act 1978, 17 ILM (1978) 1123; Canada, State Immunity Act 1982, 21 ILM (1982) 798; Australia, Foreign States Immunity Act 1985, 25 ILM (1986) 715.

[38] *Jurisdictional Immunities of the State* (n 26) para 62.

members and the negotiating states in the long run-up to the adoption of the UNCJISP. The ILC commentary to Draft Article 12 recognizes that some states retain the distinction between *acts jure imperii* and *acts jure gestionis* when it comes to immunity from tort claims.[39] However, the ILC stressed that Draft Article 12 was intended to provide for no such distinction.[40] It would appear, thus, that as far as the tort exception in Article 12 of the UNCJISP covers also sovereign acts, it is not of customary status. The Court, however, did not pronounce on this.

With respect to Italy's second argument, namely that Germany was not entitled to jurisdictional immunity because of the special nature of the violations committed as violations of *jus cogens* norms, the Court made two important findings. First, since immunity is a procedural rule, and therefore preliminary in nature, it is a logical paradox to state that its being granted is dependent upon the nature of the violation committed by the foreign state. This is a matter for the merits phase and a domestic court having found a particular act to be immune would never get to the point of assessing the nature and the gravity of the violations regarding that act.[41] Notwithstanding this consideration, or perhaps because of it, the Court went on to examine whether an exception has emerged in international customary law depriving a state from immunity for acts constituting serious violations of international human rights law and international humanitarian law. It found that this was not the case at the current stage of development of international law.[42]

Second, the Court stated that, conceptually, there can be no normative clash between the rule of state immunity as such and certain rules of *jus cogens* status, because immunity is procedural in character, barring the exercise of jurisdiction over the conduct of the foreign state, whereas the relevant *jus cogens* rules are substantive in the sense that they regulate the conduct of the foreign state.[43]

Before elaborating on this point and discussing the Court's reasoning, a word needs to be said on the Court's finding regarding Germany's immunity from enforcement measures, specifically the ones imposed by Italian courts upon the Villa Vigoni. According to the Court, immunity from enforcement measures is even broader than the jurisdictional immunity that states enjoy before foreign courts.[44] The Court relied on Article 19 of the UNCJISP, although it again avoided pronouncing upon its customary status, in order to conclude that none of the circumstances provided for in Article 19 was present in the case at hand. Italy had thus violated Germany's immunity from enforcement.[45]

The fact that the Court upheld its finding in *Arrest Warrant* that state immunity is a rule of procedural nature and therefore not dependent upon the gravity or nature or *jus cogens* status of certain rules was more or less expected.[46] There are, however, two points of the

[39] ILC, 'Draft Articles on Jurisdictional Immunities of States and Their Property, with Commentaries' (n 4) 13, at 45, para 8.

[40] ibid. Joanne Foakes and Roger O'Keefe, 'Article 12' in O'Keefe, Tams, and Tzanakopoulos (n 23) 209–24, at 209 refer to art 12 as the 'odd one out' exactly because all other 'exceptions' of Part III are based on the non-sovereign character of certain state conduct; see also *Letelier v Republic of Chile*, 488 F Supp 665 (DDC 1980) 673 and *Schreiber v Canada* [2002] 3 SCR 269, 2002 SCC 62; contra *McElhinney v Ireland* App no 31253/96 (Grand Chamber, Judgment of 21 November 2001) para 38; *Margellos and Others v Federal Republic of Germany* Anotato Eidiko Diskastirio (Greek Special Supreme Court) 6/2002, 129 ILR (2007) 526.

[41] *Jurisdictional Immunities of the State* (n 26) paras 81–82.

[42] ibid para 91.

[43] ibid para 93.

[44] ibid para 113.

[45] ibid paras 115–19.

[46] Andrea Bianchi, 'On Certainty' *EJIL Talk!* (16 February 2012) https://www.ejiltalk.org/on-certainty/ (accessed 7 December 2017); see also Katherine Del Mar, 'The Effects of Framing International Legal Norms as Rules

Court's reasoning that deserve further consideration. First, the finding of the Court that state immunity, apart from not conflicting with the substantive rules governing the lawfulness of certain conduct, equally does not conflict with the duty of the responsible state to make reparation.[47] This statement seems to fit well with the Court's overall treatment of immunity as a procedural bar to jurisdiction. The Court, however, also states that 'the immunity from jurisdiction of Germany in accordance with international law may preclude judicial redress for the Italian nationals concerned'.[48] There is some incongruity here between Germany's obligation to make reparation and the right of the Italian nationals concerned to seek judicial redress regarding that reparation. However, it should be kept in mind that the obligation of Germany to make reparation for its wrongful conduct exists with respect to the injured state, namely Italy, and not necessarily with respect to the individual Italian nationals. If these have no capacity under international law to bring claims in their own name against Germany for the violations of the relevant rules of international law (even if these are *jus cogens*), they seem to have no independent and directly enforceable claim for reparation against Germany. To be sure, the Court found it 'unnecessary' to determine whether there was such a directly enforceable right for the individuals concerned.[49] In any event, the Court seems to be right in suggesting that the matter of reparation owed to Italy for violations also in the person of its nationals is subject to further negotiation between the two states.[50]

A second point which emerges clearly from the Court's judgment in *Jurisdictional Immunities of the State* is that immunity as a procedural bar to jurisdiction does not constitute a defence. It may seem trite to state this, but it seems also to be overlooked customarily in such cases where emotions run high. Immunity bars a state from exercising jurisdiction that it may otherwise have been able to exercise over certain acts, because these acts are the acts of another state. But this means nothing about the legality or otherwise of these acts, and thus the state invoking immunity may not invoke it as a defence for its acts, and will still be under the normal secondary obligations prescribed by the law of state responsibility as towards the injured state (and potentially states 'other than the injured state' in accordance with Article 48 of the ARSIWA). Thus, as a matter of international responsibility, the immune state will still be under the obligation to make reparation for the violations of international law committed[51] and, in the event that the norms violated have *jus cogens* status, under the aggravated regime set out by the ARSIWA.[52]

But what also emerges from the consideration of the positions of the ILC and the ICJ is that, while immunity is clearly not a defence, it remains unclear whether it is itself an exception to the rules regarding state jurisdiction (and thus its exceptions are

or Exceptions: State Immunity from Civil Jurisdiction' (2013) 15 International Common Law Review 143, 144, where she argues that the conclusions of the Court that there were no established exceptions to state immunity under customary international law for torts committed by armed forces and for violations of *jus cogens* rules was the 'direct output of an application of the rule-exceptions structure of the law governing State immunity'.

[47] *Jurisdictional Immunities of the State* (n 26) para 94.

[48] ibid para 104.

[49] ibid para 108.

[50] ibid para 104.

[51] ARSIWA art 31; see also Del Mar (n 46) 150–51.

[52] ARSIWA arts 40–41. This aggravated regime, however, does not impose any further secondary obligations on the responsible state: the latter is obligated, as any other responsible state, to cease the breach if it is continuing, to offer assurances and guarantees of non-repetition, and to offer reparation. The regime is rather aggravated for *all other states*, which are obligated to cooperate to bring the serious *jus cogens* violation to an end and not to recognize the situation created by it as lawful.

exceptions-to-the-exception), or whether it is considered as some sort of independent general rule admitting its own exceptions, or—what may amount to the same thing—limitations.[53] It would then be helpful to our inquiry to examine the stance taken by states regarding the matter during the negotiation and adoption of the main codification work on sovereign immunity, namely the UNJISP, as reflected in the normative framework and the legal principles of the convention.

4 The Position of States in the UNCJISP

Article 5 of the UNCJISP, in Part II of the Convention entitled 'General Principles', states the core rule that as soon as a legal entity qualifies as a state under Article 2 of the UNCJISP, it is entitled to immunity in respect of itself and its property.[54] As already discussed in section 3 above, the ILC in its commentary avoided espousing any specific legal theory regarding the 'exact nature and basis of immunity'.[55] It enumerated some of the relevant theories, ie that immunity constitutes an exception to the principle of territorial sovereignty and thus it 'should be substantiated in each specific case'; that it constitutes a general rule or general principle of international law, which in any event is not absolute and unqualified since in even its most extreme forms consent suffices to render the rule inapplicable; and finally that it constitutes a 'unitary rule'[56] inherently subject to its existing exceptions, in which case both immunity and non-immunity are part of the same rule: 'immunity exists along with its innate qualifications and limitations'.[57] The Commission thus adopted a 'basic principle' qualified by the provisions of the then draft articles, according to which in specific proceedings immunity cannot be invoked.[58]

As in the case of the *Jurisdictional Immunities* judgment, discussed above, Article 5 of the UNCJISP does not shed any light on the relationship of immunity to the rules regarding state jurisdiction; nor does it shed any light on the relationship of the general rule of immunity with potential exceptions. What it does do is to provide clearly for 'a procedural bar to judicial proceedings, rather than [for] the State's substantive non-liability under the municipal law applied by the court or the exemption from the application of that substantive law on it in the first place'.[59]

[53] As eg in the words of Lord Wilberforce in *I Congreso del Partido* (HL(E)) [1983] 1 AC 244, 262: 'It is necessary to start from first principle. The basis upon which one state is considered to be immune from the territorial jurisdiction of the courts of another state is that of "par in parem" which effectively means that the sovereign or governmental acts of one state are not matters upon which the courts of other states will adjudicate. The relevant *exception*, or *limitation*, which has been engrafted upon the principle of immunity of states, under the so called "restrictive theory" arises from the willingness of states to enter into commercial, or other private law, transactions with individuals' (emphasis added).

[54] Tom Grant, 'Article 5' in O'Keefe, Tams, and Tzanakopoulos (n 23) 99–104, at 99.

[55] ILC, 'Draft Articles on Jurisdictional Immunities of States and Their Property, with Commentaries' (n 4) 23, para 2. This is further reiterated in the Commission's commentary to Draft Article 10, where it indicates that the formulation of paragraph 1 was meant to be a compromise between the views considering the Article as an exception to the general rule of state immunity and those that supported that in these cases immunity simply cannot be invoked: ILC, 'Draft Articles on Jurisdictional Immunities of States and Their Property, with Commentaries' (n 4) 34, para 2.

[56] cf the contribution by Hage, Waltermann, and Arosemena in the present volume (n 17) where the authors argue that conflicting rules could be combined in one 'derived rule' without exceptions, and the combined rule will have the absence of the exception as one of its conditions.

[57] ILC, "Draft Articles on Jurisdictional Immunities of States and Their Property, with Commentaries' (n 4) 23, para 2.

[58] ibid para 3.

[59] Grant (n 54) 101; see also *Al-Adsani v UK* (n 1) para 48; *McElhinney v Ireland* (n 40) para 25.

This does little but to confirm that immunity is in any case not a defence, and may be characterized at best as an exception.

Part III of the UNCJISP sets out the 'exceptions' to the rule of state immunity. It seems that although previous state practice treated all 'exceptions' to state immunity as different iterations of the general 'exception' with respect to acts *jure gestionis*—understood primarily as private/commercial transactions,[60] the ILC in its work, and then the states in adopting the UNCJISP, took all these separate instances and formulated them as separate rules.[61] However, the first exceptions to the rule of immunity are arguably already found in Articles 7 to 9 of the UNCJISP, in Part II,[62] which deal with various iterations of consent (waiver) as exceptions to the rule of jurisdictional immunity. It can be argued that the exceptions in Part II are 'general' exceptions, while those in Part III are 'special', in that they relate specifically to the subject matter of the dispute at hand. In its commentary to Draft Article 7, the ILC stated that the absence or lack of consent is a 'distinct condition' for the grant of immunity.[63] Conditions for the application of a rule, however, are nothing but exceptions in a (slightly) different guise.[64] In any event, what they do is to limit the scope of application of the rule that they refer to.

Grant argues that under Article 5 of the UNCJISP as it is formulated 'a State is entitled to immunity for foreign jurisdiction unless it is not', that is, unless one of the exceptions to immunity enumerated in the remaining provisions of Parts II and III applies in the relevant proceedings.[65] This is also the view adopted by the ECSI and national legislation of various states on the matter. The practical consequences of this is that once a legal person before a court qualifies as a foreign 'state' under Article 2(1)(b) of the UNCJISP it is *presumed* to enjoy immunity;[66] and that the burden of proof lies then with the claimant to prove that a state is not immune from the proceedings, because one of the existing 'exceptions' is applicable. It is not for the state to prove that it is immune.[67] Article 5 also specifies that immunity is conditioned upon the provisions of the Convention, that is, subject to the specific 'exceptions' provided therein. This indicates that the exceptions are exhaustively enumerated.[68]

For her part, van Alebeek also argues that, from a structural point of view, Part III embodies a 'set of exceptions' to the immunity of states as envisaged by the Convention, as well as by the ECSI and by the national legislation of various states on the matter.[69] ILC Special

[60] See van Alebeek (n 23) 156, who argues convincingly that although Part III UNCJISP is not premised upon the distinction between acts *iure imperii* and acts *jure gestionis*, the distinction informs all but one of the 'exceptions' of Pt III, namely art 12 the 'tort exception' (on which see also section 3 above).

[61] See also Stephan Wittich, 'Article 2 (1)(c) and (2) and (3)' in O'Keefe, Tams, and Tzanakopoulos (n 23) 55–72, at 59 and 62, who states that this is especially true for cases under arts 12 (torts) and 13 (property-related rights).

[62] Roger O'Keefe, 'Part II: General Principles' in O'Keefe, Tams, and Tzanakopoulos (n 23) 97–98.

[63] See also 'Fourth Report of the Special Rapporteur' (n 24) 205, para 19.

[64] cf the 'unitary' or 'derived rule' theory in the contribution by Hage, Waltermann, and Arosemena in the present volume (n 17).

[65] Grant (n 54) 102; cf ILC, 'Preliminary Report on the Topic of Jurisdictional Immunities of States and Their Property' by Mr Sompong Sucharitkul, Special Rapporteur, UN Doc A/CN.4/323 (1979) 2(1) Yearbook of the International Law Commission 227, at 240, para 59: 'Whatever the legal foundation of the doctrine of State immunity . . . the principle of State immunity should be taken as a point of departure in any logical treatment of the topic. State immunity should be the general rule.'

[66] Grant (n 54) 103 (emphasis added).

[67] ibid; van Alebeek (n 23) 160.

[68] Grant (n 54) 103–4 and n 32 therein with further references on cases regarding exhaustiveness; van Alebeek (n 23) 157.

[69] cf van Alebeek (n 23) 154; cf 'Preliminary Report of the Special Rapporteur' (n 65) 241, para 69; 'Fourth Report of the Special Rapporteur' (n 24) 204, para 14.

Rapporteur Sucharitkul also advocated the 'limitative' nature of the exceptions; that is, they serve to 'restrict or limit the operation of a general rule of State immunity'.[70] However, almost in the same breath (a paragraph later) he stated that

> '[i]t is only in a manner of speaking that State immunity may be said to be restricted or limited, in the sense that it is not "absolute" or accorded in every type of circumstances, regardless of the capacity in which the State has acted or irrespective of the category of activities attributable to the state. The juridical basis for "non-immunity" may be described as the counterpart of the legal basis for "State immunity"'.[71]

Essentially what we see here is a constant oscillation between what is to be considered the general rule and what the exception. Even though most commentators are relatively comfortable in seeing immunity as the rule and its limitations, whether general (consent, waiver) or specific (subject matter) as exceptions, the ILC and the states in negotiating the UNCJISP can simply not make up their minds. There are a number of further relevant examples in the Convention.

With respect to Draft Article 11 on contracts of employment, the ILC comments that it 'covers an area commonly designated as contracts of employment, which has recently emerged as an *exception* to state immunity'.[72] The Commission does this even when it made a point of avoiding the term 'exception' and reiterating its ambivalent 'compromise' position in its commentary to Draft Article 10.[73] Notably, paragraph 1 of Draft Article 11 (and finally Article 11 of the UNCJISP) is formulated as a residual rule (like other provisions in the Convention), as states may agree to opt out of its application. During the discussion in the ILC, however, some members of the Commission argued that paragraph 1 should have been formulated as providing a general rule of immunity and then enumerate exceptions where immunity would not apply.[74] The provision was actually formulated the other way around, the commentary stating that 'paragraph 2 strives to establish and maintain an appropriate balance by introducing important limitations on the application of the *rule* of non-immunity'.[75] The circumstances enumerated in paragraph 2 are formulated as exceptions to the rule stated in paragraph 1.[76] O'Keefe and Foakes argue that within Article 11 there is also an implicit requirement of the *jure gestionis* character of the contract of employment in question, an argument derived *a contrario* from the exception in paragraph 2(a).[77] They further

[70] 'Fourth Report of the Special Rapporteur' (n 24) 207, para 31.

[71] ibid para 32. He then continues: 'Immunity operates as long as there is a legal basis for it. In the absence of such basis there is no immunity. Thus, the reverse for legal justification of "immunity" is the legal basis for "non-immunity" [ibid para 33] and then he argues that one way for justifying the non-recognition of immunity in a specific case is 'the absence or non existence of reasons or valid grounds for allowing State immunity in such a case' (ibid para 34).

[72] ILC, 'Draft Articles on Jurisdictional Immunities of States and Their Property, with Commentaries' (n 4) 41, para 1 (emphasis added); Joanne Foakes and Roger O'Keefe, 'Article 11' in O'Keefe, Tams, and Tzanakopoulos (n 23) 183–208, at 196.

[73] See n 55 above. The same is true for the commentary to draft article 12 which states: 'This article covers an exception to the general rule of state immunity' (ILC, 'Draft Articles on Jurisdictional Immunities of States and Their Property, with Commentaries' (n 4) 44, para 1) and later 'This exception to the rule of immunity is applicable only to cases or circumstances in which . . .' (ibid para 2).

[74] ibid 42, para 7.

[75] ibid para 8 (emphasis added).

[76] See also Foakes and O'Keefe (n 72) 184–85, 198.

[77] ibid 184.

argue for a restrictive interpretation of paragraph 2(a), calling in support the drafting history of the provision, which reveals 'successive attempts to narrow the scope of this exception to the exception to immunity'.[78]

The commentary on Draft Article 13 considers the provision as reflecting a well-established exception,[79] indeed an 'exception to immunity in its own right', regardless of the nature of the underlying contract or transaction,[80] while on Draft Article 14 (later Article 14 of the UNCJISP on intellectual and industrial property) the commentary states that [t]he *exception* provided in Article 14 appears to fall somewhere between the *exception* of "commercial transactions" provided in Article 10 and that of "ownership, possession and use of property" in Article 13'.[81] By contrast, paragraph 1 of Draft Article 15 (later Article 15 of the UNCJISP on participation in companies or other collective bodies) apparently establishes 'a *rule* of non-immunity'.[82]

Finally, with respect to immunity from execution, the Convention establishes a general rule of immunity of states from measures of constraint or execution, subject to very specific limitations.[83] The fact that there seems to be a more clear rule-exception relationship here is also apparent from the fact that both Article 18 and Article 19 of the UNCJISP are phrased in the negative, that is, 'No measure of constraint may be taken ... unless ...'. The negative wording practice is standard for formulating exceptions or defences in international law—although it is obvious that we are faced with an exception here. The negative wording is also widely considered as implying a restrictive interpretation of the negatively worded provision.[84]

What all this demonstrates is that there is no conceivable end to the whole rule/exception/exception to the exception—back to the rule/exception to the exception to the exception—back to the exception merry-go-round. It all depends on what will be selected as the first relevant rule, in order then to structure the rest of relevant primary rules accordingly as exceptions, exceptions to the exceptions, and so on.[85] It is a bit like maths, really: adding the negatives to get (back to) a positive. What is confirmed time and again throughout all the enumerated exceptions, whether put forward as exceptions to the immunity rule or 'non-immunity' rules, is that the courts of the forum state are presumed to have jurisdiction. One is left to wonder what better confirmation of what is in fact the general rule could there ever be.

[78] ibid 200.

[79] ILC, 'Draft Articles on Jurisdictional Immunities of States and Their Property, with Commentaries' (n 4) 46, para 2.

[80] Jörg Philipp Terhechte, 'Article 13' in O'Keefe, Tams, and Tzanakopoulos (n 23) 225–32, at 225.

[81] ILC, 'Draft Articles on Jurisdictional Immunities of States and Their Property, with Commentaries' (n 4) 47, para 2 (emphasis added).

[82] ibid 49, para 5 (emphasis added).

[83] ibid 56, para 3.

[84] See Mark E Villiger, *Commentary to the 1969 Vienna Convention on the Law of Treaties* (Martinus Nijhoff 2009) 770 in relation to VCLT art 62; *Gabčíkovo Nagymaros Project (Hungary/Slovakia)* (Judgment) [1997] ICJ Rep 7, paras 51–52; ARSIWA with commentaries (n 6) 83, para 14 in relation to ARSIWA art 25.

[85] cf James Crawford's discussion of Draft Article 12 proposed by SR Arangio-Ruiz in his 'Fourth Report on State Responsibility Concerning Countermeasures': 'Clause 12(3) was in effect an exception to an exception to an exception, and gave Article 12 an air of complexion, even convolution': James Crawford, 'Counter-measures as Interim Measures' (1994) 5 European Journal of International Law 65, 72.

5 Evaluation and Implications of Characterization

No clear picture emerges from the consideration of practice in sections 3 and 4 above. What does this mean for the presumptive position that, in the simplest terms, we should consider immunity as an exception to the rules of state jurisdiction, and that we should in turn consider exceptions from the rule of immunity as exceptions to the exception, signifying a return to the rule (ie the normal rules of state jurisdiction)?

There is no easy answer to this question. For that reason, we thought of testing our presumptive, and still not rebutted, position, against the potential implications of the characterization of immunity as an exception to the rules regarding jurisdiction. The main implications in our view relate to the question of consent and waiver (5.1), to the question of the burden of proof (5.2), and to the question of the interpretative principle *in dubio mitius* (5.3), which may be seen as stemming from the *SS Lotus* dictum on limitations on sovereignty not being lightly presumed.[86] These are treated here in turn.

5.1 Consent and waiver

One issue which may affect the characterization of immunity as an exception to jurisdiction is the fact that immunity may be waived by the state benefiting from it, whether explicitly or (in most cases also) implicitly, and that it is generally subject to that state's consent. Is it possible for an exception to be 'waived'? Or does this somehow indicate that if immunity can be waived then it is not really a true exception at all?

We cannot see why the latter would be the case. All rules of international law, apart from the rules of *jus cogens*, are more (custom) or less (treaty) *default* rules, rules that may be further contracted out of by consent of the states involved.[87] And while waiver may be seen as being a unilateral act of the state benefiting from immunity, this is only apparent. In reality it also presupposes the consent of the state exercising jurisdiction (through the acts of its courts, which are after all state organs). In the final analysis, if a state wishes to grant absolute immunity to another state by prohibiting its courts from exercising jurisdiction in a relevant case, no amount of waiving of that immunity by the state benefiting from it will necessarily result in the first state assuming jurisdiction.

In fact, it can even be argued that the possibility of waiver or contracting out by consent necessarily qualifies a particular norm as an exception to a more general norm, as without such more general norm there would be no rule to fall back to. This is to some extent regressive, as it will necessarily lead back to sovereignty as the *plénitude de pouvoir*. But, for one, that is what international law is about after all; and, for another, this is the immediate source of the rules of both jurisdiction and immunity.

[86] *SS 'Lotus' (France v Turkey)* (Judgment) [1927] PCIJ Rep Series A No 10, 3, 18.

[87] Note, however, that this is particularly complicated in treaties in certain cases: see especially the provisions of the VCLT on modification by *inter se* agreement; and it will even be impossible in cases of integral or interdependent obligations without the consent of all parties.

5.2 Burden of proof

One obvious implication of characterizing a particular rule as an exception to some other rule is the question of the burden of proof.[88] In accordance with the general principle *actori incumbit probatio*, also applicable in general international law,[89] the actor that invokes an exception to a rule should have the burden of proving it.[90] It was stated in section 4 above, when discussing the rule in Article 5 of the UNCJISP,[91] that a state only needs to prove that it is a state to enjoy immunity presumptively and thus reverse the burden of proof so that the other party to the dispute will have to prove the operation of an exception to that immunity. Might this suggest that immunity is a general rule rather than an exception, and that the characterization of a particular norm as a rule or an exception has implications for the burden of proof?

In our view, the answer to this question is no. Just like with any norm, a party invoking it will have to establish the facts that call the particular norm into application.[92] In the case of a state purporting to exercise jurisdiction, that state will need to establish the facts that call into application the rule of international law vesting it with jurisdiction. In the case of a party claiming the application of the rule of sovereign immunity in order to block the exercise of a state's jurisdiction (invoking thus an exception), the facts that need to be proven for the norm to be called into application are that the party invoking the rule is a state. A party then seeking to block the application of immunity (invoking an exception to the exception) would also have to prove the facts that render the particular 'rule of non-immunity', if you will, or the exception to the exception, applicable. As such, what we are talking about here are invocations or primary rules, the *Tatbestand* of which needs to be proven for each rule to apply. Their characterization as rules or exceptions is essentially of no consequence.

5.3 Restrictive interpretation

There is a commonly repeated argument in law that 'exceptions should be construed narrowly or restrictively'—and international law is no exception.[93] However, there is no basis

[88] See also the contribution of Joost Pauwelyn in the present volume.

[89] See e.g. Malcolm N Shaw, *Rosenne's Law and Practice of the International Court: 1920–2015, vol iii* (5th edn, Brill 2016) 1067; Chester Brown, *A Common Law of International Adjudication* (OUP 2007) 92–97.

[90] This was asserted early on by the PCIJ in *Eastern Greenland*, although in a slightly different guise: 'If it is alleged by one of the Parties that some unusual or exceptional meaning is to be attributed to it [the word 'Greenland'], it lies on that Party to establish its contention' (*Legal Status of Eastern Greenland* (Advisory Opinion) [1933] PCIJ Rep Series A/B No 53, 22, at 49).

[91] See text at nn 65–68.

[92] This was affirmed by the ICJ in *Nicaragua* when it stated that 'ultimately ... it is the litigant seeking to establish a fact who bears the burden of proving it'. See *Military and Paramilitary Activities in and against Nicaragua (Nicaragua v US)* (Jurisdiction and Admissibility) [1984] ICJ Rep 392, 437, para 101.

[93] For example, Judge Cançado Trindade argued in his Separate Opinion in the *Whaling* case discussing the scope of art VIII(1) of the International Convention on Regulation of Whaling: 'In my understanding, Article VIII(1) is not to be interpreted broadly, so as to go against the object and purpose of the normative framework of the Convention as a whole. Article VIII(1) appears as an *exception* to the normative framework of the ICRW, to be thus interpreted restrictively' (emphasis in original): *Whaling in the Antarctic (Australia v Japan: New Zealand intervening)* (Judgment, Separate Opinion of Judge Cançado Trindade) [2014] ICJ Rep 348, 356, para 21. For an early criticism of the principle of restrictive interpretation see Hersch Lauterpacht, 'Restrictive Interpretation and the Principle of Effectiveness in the Interpretation of Treaties' (1949) 26 British Yearbook of International Law 48.

for this argument, whether in international law or in any other area of the law.[94] An exception, just like any other primary rule, is to be interpreted on its own merits, and not in any way more restrictively because it is an exception—just like there is no interpretive rule requiring broad interpretations of general rules.[95] At best, what could be argued is that, in (seeming) accordance with *SS 'Lotus'*, limitations of sovereignty should be narrowly construed—the so-called *in dubio mitius* principle.[96] But all rules of international law are in some way a limitation of state sovereignty—the *plénitude de pouvoir*.[97] Indeed, the very act of assuming international obligations and thus limiting sovereignty is an emanation of sovereignty.[98] All primary norms are to be interpreted in accordance with the general rules of interpretation and on their own merits, irrespective of whether they may be cast as 'rules' or 'exceptions'.

6 Conclusion

In reality then, as emerges from our considerations above, there is nothing to be gained by characterising a particular norm as a rule or an exception. What remains important is the consideration of the scope of application and content of the primary rules, whether those providing for state jurisdiction, or those requiring the extension of immunity, or even those limiting immunity and allowing the exercise of previously barred jurisdiction.[99] At best, the only thing that seems to hinge on the rule-exception relationship between jurisdiction and immunity is that the consideration of immunity is a matter of admissibility rather than jurisdiction: the jurisdiction of the court may well be established over the act, but it ought not to be exercised in the circumstances.

Our analysis leaves us with few specific normative observations. First, it is apparent that the relationship between a certain rule and its exceptions is not static but may well change and evolve over time or even on a case-by-case basis.[100] Second, and as a direct consequence

[94] For more details see Pauwelyn's contribution in the present volume, especially section 7; cf Viñuales' contribution in the present volume discussing the treatment of art VIII(1) by the ICJ in the *Whaling* case and observing that '[t]he Court's approach may reflect some reluctance in recent years to take unnecessary principled positions' but later asserting that 'international courts and tribunals, while applying the usual rules of treaty interpretation do take into account the way in which some situations are placed beyond the scope of a treaty or a norm'. The ICJ in the *Whaling* case (n 93) rejected the argument that art VIII(1) of the International Convention on the Regulation of Whaling has to be narrowly construed ([2014] ICJ Rep 226, 252, paras 57–58).

[95] See also Pauwelyn's contribution in the present volume, at 104–105 and nn 84–86 therein, where he argues that: '[t]here is a clear trend amongst a variety of international tribunals to interpret exceptions "neutrally" like any other treaty provision, neither broadly nor narrowly.'

[96] In the *Dispute regarding Navigational and Related Rights (Costa Rica v Nicaragua)* (Judgment) [2009] ICJ Rep 213, eg, Nicaragua argued that Costa Rica's right of free navigation under art VI of the Treaty of Limits should be interpreted narrowly because it represents a limitation of Nicaragua's sovereignty over the San Juan river, the latter being the most important right conferred by the very same provision of the treaty in question (essentially thus a relationship of rule: Nicaragua's sovereignty over the river—to an exception: Costa Rica's rights with respect to navigation etc of the river). See also Robert Jennings and Arthur Watts, *Oppenheim's International Law: vol I, Peace* (9th edn, Longman 1992) 1278–79.

[97] The ICJ summarily rejected the Nicaraguan argument in *Dispute regarding Navigational and Related Rights* (n 96). See further Antonios Tzanakopoulos and Anna Ventouratou, 'Nicaragua in the International Court of Justice and the Law of Treaties' in Edgardo Sobenes and Benjamin Sampson (eds), *Nicaragua before the International Court of Justice: Impacts on International Law* (Springer 2018) section 2.2..

[98] *SS 'Wimbledon'* (n 28) 25; and see also n 28 above.

[99] For a similar analysis with respect to personal immunity of officials see Dapo Akande and Sangeeta Shah, 'Immunities of State Officials, International Crimes, and Foreign Domestic Courts' (2011) 21 European Journal of International Law 815, 841.

[100] cf Giovanni Sartor's contribution to the present volume on the 'dialectics between rules and exceptions'.

of the first observation, exceptions are primary rules of their own, without this being anything more than a change in terminology: the actual implications of this do not seem to be important. Simply put, exceptions are in themselves primary rules, which allow for further exceptions in the form of even more specific primary rules, and the merry-go-round simply continues.

13

Both the Rule and the Exception

The Concept of a Legal Dilemma and the Survival of the State

Valentin Jeutner

For the purposes of this chapter,[1] rules are defined as legal norms that control the legal classification of a given act by default. Exceptions are defined as legal norms that allow for the deviation from a rule and that control the legal classification of a given act in specific circumstances. In principle, all acts regulated by law[2] can be identified as being governed by a rule or by an exception. For example, as a rule, states may not use the facilities of other states on the moon.[3] However, in exceptional cases when human life is at risk, states may do so.[4] As a rule, warships may not board ships encountered on the high seas.[5] However, in exceptional circumstances ships not otherwise enjoying complete immunity[6] may be boarded.[7] In principle, states may not use force.[8] However, in exceptional circumstances states may do so, inter alia in pursuit of their right to self-defence.[9] This definition of the relationship between rules and exceptions differs from that put forward by other contributors to this collection.[10] Specifically, Iain Scobbie remarks that the definition offered here appears to 'lack a close engagement with analytical concerns regarding legal system structure'.[11] However, the accuracy of Scobbie's observation depends on the phenomenon the stipulative definition presented here intends to capture. While generally much is to be gained from an in-depth discussion of the various definitions of exceptions and rules, my contribution challenges a more fundamental assumption concerning 'legal system structure', one that is shared by most contributors to this collection (irrespective of how the respective authors chose to define rules and exceptions): the assumption that rules and exceptions are mutually exclusive.

[1] For an extended discussion of the questions considered in this chapter see Valentin Jeutner, *Irresolvable Norm Conflicts in International Law: The Concept of a Legal Dilemma* (OUP 2017). See also *Legality of the Threat or Use of Nuclear Weapons* (Advisory Opinion) [1996] ICJ Rep 226.

[2] This excludes instances of alegality—situations where conduct is not regulated by law at all.

[3] Agreement Governing the Activities of States on the Moon and Other Celestial Bodies (1979) 1363 UNTS 21, art 12(1).

[4] ibid art 12(3).

[5] United Nations Convention on the Law of the Sea (1982) 1833 UNTS 3, art 110(1).

[6] ibid arts 95–96.

[7] ibid art 110(1)(a).

[8] Charter of the United Nations (1945) 1 UNTS XVI, art 2(4).

[9] ibid art 51.

[10] Hage, Waltermann, and Arosemena observe, for example, that rules attach consequences to a factual situation when a factual situation satisfies the conditions regulation the applicability of the rule, and that exceptions disapply a rule despite a factual situation's satisfaction of the conditions regulating the applicability of the rule. See Jaap Hage, Antonia Waltermann, and Gustavo Arosemena, ch 2 in this volume, 11 to 13 Schauer, in turn, appears to hold the view that exceptions can respond to situations when 'the conditions for [the] application of the rule do not exist'. See Frederick Schauer, ch 4 in this volume, 57 to 59.

[11] Scobbie extends this observation also to the definitions provided by Hage, Waltermann, and Arosemena and Kolb. See the text accompanying footnotes 45–50 in Iain Scobbie, ch 9 in this volume .

Valentin Jeutner, *Both the Rule and the Exception* In: *Exceptions in International Law*. Edited by: Lorand Bartels and Federica Paddeu, Oxford University Press (2020). © Lorand Bartels and Federica Paddeu. DOI: 10.1093/oso/9780198789321.003.0013

In contradistinction to this assumption, I argue that there can be acts that are regulated by law that can and should be subsumed both under a rule and an exception; situations when legal norms conflict with each other in such a manner that the norm providing the rule is valid and applies despite the simultaneous validity and applicability of a competing norm providing an exception. I seek to test this thesis with reference to the question of whether a state may lawfully use a nuclear weapon to defend itself in extreme circumstances when that state's 'very survival [is] at stake'.[12]

The argument is divided into five parts. First, I will briefly introduce the notion of state survival. Secondly, I will introduce the rule that governs the conduct of a state whose survival is at stake. Thirdly, the exception applicable to such a situation will be considered. Based on the findings of the previous two sections, the fourth section will show that the particular constellation of rule and exception triggered by the notion of state survival is best characterized as an irresolvable conflict of norms. By way of synthesis, the fourth section will then attempt to reconceptualize the previously established conflict of norms as a legal dilemma which fulfils a distinct and beneficial function of law. The fifth and final section offers some concluding observations.

1 The Notion of State Survival

The notion of state survival raises fundamental questions concerning the relationship between (international) law and sovereignty. Indeed, it has been observed that the notion is 'as old as the science of international law itself'.[13] This is not surprising given that the character of the relationship between a legal order and its subject is never more critical than at times when the existence of the legal subject is itself at stake. In the *Nuclear Weapons* Advisory Opinion, the International Court of Justice (ICJ) raised the notion of the survival of a state by observing that, in the Court's considerations of the legality of the threat or use of nuclear weapons, 'the Court cannot lose sight of the fundamental right of every state to survival, and thus its right to resort to self-defence, in accordance with Article 51 of the Charter, when its survival is at stake'.[14] Despite the ICJ's reference to the notion of state survival, it is controversial whether the notion does or should have a particular or independent legal status.[15]

For our purposes, it suffices to treat the notion of state survival as a set of factual conditions referring to a state of affairs in which the continued existence of a state as a legal subject of international law is threatened to such an extent, and in such a manner, that resort to nuclear weapons 'constitutes the ultimate means by which [the state] can guarantee its survival'.[16] Neither the ICJ nor the states participating in the proceedings of the Advisory Opinion provided any details as to when situations of this kind could exist in practice. Possible scenarios may be situations when a state stands to lose one or more of the constituent features of statehood, including, for instance, the loss of population, territory, or government.[17] While it is possible to construe more or less far-fetched examples in this regard,

[12] *Legality of the Threat or Use of Nuclear Weapons* (n 1) [97].

[13] Marcelo G Kohen, 'The Notion of "State Survival" in International Law' in Laurence Boisson de Chazournes and Philippe Sands (eds), *International Law, the International Court of Justice and Nuclear Weapons* (CUP 1999) 294.

[14] *Legality of the Threat or Use of Nuclear Weapons* (n 1) [96].

[15] See generally Kohen (n 13).

[16] *Legality of the Threat or Use of Nuclear Weapons* (n 1) Separate Opinion of Judge Guillaume [8].

[17] Montevideo Convention on the Rights and Duties of States 1933 art 1.

many states[18] participating in the proceedings related to the ICJ's *Nuclear Weapons* Advisory Opinion were evidently concerned that such situations might exist. Notably, the drafters of the 1968 Nuclear Non-Proliferation Treaty[19] (NPT) may also be taken to have contemplated extreme situations of this kind. Employing slightly different terms, article X of the NPT provides that 'extraordinary events, related to the subject matter of [the NPT]' which jeopardize 'the supreme interests' of a state may entitle NPT parties to withdraw from the NPT.[20]

Against this background and assuming, if only for the sake of argument, that states may face extreme situations when their survival is at stake, the next two sections will consider whether situations of this kind should be covered by the rule or the exception.

2 The Rule: The Threat or Use of Nuclear Weapons Is Prohibited

According to the ICJ's decision in the *Nuclear Weapons* Advisory Opinion, the rule governing the threat or use of nuclear weapons is that 'the threat or use of nuclear weapons [is] generally ... contrary to the rules of international law applicable in armed conflict and in particular the principles and rules of humanitarian law'.[21] Earlier in the same opinion, the ICJ had confirmed that the invoked principles of humanitarian law consist chiefly of the principle of distinction between combatants and non-combatants, and the avoidance of unnecessary suffering.[22] Further, the ICJ stated that the respective principles are 'intransgressible'.[23] Specifically, with respect to the use of force in self-defence, the ICJ observed that measures which 'necessarily violate the principles of necessity and proportionality ... [are] unlawful under the law of the Charter'[24] and that any use of force that is 'contrary to Article 2, paragraph 4, of the United Nations Charter and that fails to meet all the requirements of Article 51, is unlawful'.[25] Thus, the general rule appears to be very clear: any threat or use of a nuclear weapon that violates 'intransgressible' principles of humanitarian law or the provisions of Articles 2(4) and 51 of the UN Charter, is unlawful.

The application of this rule to situations where a state's survival is at stake means that, even in extreme situations of self-defence, states could only use nuclear weapons lawfully if the proposed action met the requirements of Articles 2(4) and 51 of the UN Charter, and if the proposed action would not violate 'intransgressible' principles of humanitarian law.

[18] 'Written Statement of the Government of the United Kingdom to the International Court of Justice in Connection with a Request from the General Assembly of the United Nations for an Advisory Opinion on the Legality of the Threat or Use of Nuclear Weapons' para 3.71; 'Written Statement of the Government of India in Connection with a Request from the General Assembly of the United Nations for an Advisory Opinion on the Legality of the Threat or Use of Nuclear Weapons' 3; 'Oral Statement of HE Mr Berchmans Soedarmanto Kadarisman (Indonesia) in Connection with a Request from the General Assembly of the United Nations for an Advisory Opinion on the Legality of the Threat or Use of Nuclear Weapons, CR 95/25' paras 70–71; 'Oral Statement of Ms Federica Bigi (San Marino) in Connection with a Request from the General Assembly of the United Nations for an Advisory Opinion on the Legality of the Threat or Use of Nuclear Weapons, CR 95/31' 20.

[19] Treaty on the Non-Proliferation of Nuclear Weapons 1968, 729 UNTS 161.

[20] For additional examples of states attempting (mostly unsuccessfully) to invoke their imminent self-destruction as a reason to escape legal responsibility see Federica Paddeu, *Justification and Excuse in International Law: Concept and Theory of General Defences* (CUP 2017) 294–303.

[21] *Legality of the Threat or Use of Nuclear Weapons* (n 1) [105(2)(E)].

[22] ibid [78].

[23] ibid [79].

[24] ibid [48].

[25] ibid [105(2)(C)].

The argument that the rule, as identified above, covers such extreme situations, entails at least three immediately apparent benefits. First, and perhaps most importantly, it appears to correspond to contemporary international law, which does not, as such, contain an exception that would allow for the deviation from the stated rule just because a state confronts extreme circumstances that threaten its survival.[26] Secondly, insisting on the rule safeguards the protection of the cardinal principles of international humanitarian law at times of crisis when they are arguably most important. Thirdly, the refusal to acknowledge an exception for situations when a state's survival is at stake appears to keep the possibility of abusing any otherwise existing exception to a minimum.

At the same time, however, the insistence on the continued applicability of the rule in extreme circumstances when a state's survival is at stake can be highly problematic. First, although contemporary international law does not contain an explicit exception governing extreme self-defence scenarios, in the *Nuclear Weapons* Advisory Opinion the ICJ appeared to suggest that situations where a state's survival is at stake might have a special legal status—a status different from ordinary self-defence scenarios. This understanding of the ICJ's decision is supported by the fact that the second paragraph of paragraph 105(2)(E) of the ICJ's Advisory Opinion is introduced by the word 'However', which suggests that whatever follows constitutes a deviation from whatever preceded the term. Further, the fact that the second paragraph of paragraph 105(2)(E) refers to a very specific set of circumstances might support the thesis that the paragraph refers to an exception to the general prohibition.

Secondly, the refusal to acknowledge an exception in extreme situations means that states whose survival is at risk are by virtue of international law expected to risk losing their legal personality in return for complying with international law. Judge Fleischhauer stated most poignantly in this regard that 'no legal system is entitled to demand the self-abandonment, the suicide, of one of its subjects'.[27] Rejecting Judge Fleischhauer's observation could be problematic for a variety of public policy reasons, but it could also be problematic for a distinctly legal reason: if one accepts that a legal order derives its legitimacy vis-à-vis a given subject of that legal order from the fact that the legal order (domestic or international) confers a benefit upon that given subject, then a legal order loses its legitimacy the moment it expects the subject to sacrifice its legal personality—an act which represents the complete loss of the entirety of the subject's entitlements and, thus, an act which entails no benefit at all to the subject in question.[28]

Thirdly, insisting on the continued applicability of the rule could lead to the paradoxical situation that a victim state might be entitled to utilize its right to self-defence only up to a certain level of an attack's gravity. Once an attack becomes so severe that the victim state's survival is at risk and once an effective defence would require the taking of measures otherwise considered disproportionate, for example, the victim state would have no measures at its disposal that are both lawful and effective. Thus, it could be argued that even the insistence on the rule could be abused to the extent that an aggressor state's choice of weaponry could determine the victim state's ability to defend itself lawfully.

Given these problems, the next section considers whether international law does or should acknowledge an exception for situations when a state's survival is at stake.

[26] Kohen (n 13) 305.

[27] *Legality of the Threat or Use of Nuclear Weapons* (n 1), Separate Opinion of Judge Fleischhauer [5].

[28] For a domestic variant of this argument see Reinhard Merkel, '§14 Abs. 3 Luftsicherheitsgesetz: Wann und Warum Darf der Staat Töten?' (2007) 62 JuristenZeitung 373 and, in particular, 375.

3 The Exception: Extreme Self-defence When the Survival of the State Is at Stake

Having set out the general rule governing the threat or use of nuclear weapons, the ICJ then suggested that the general rule might not govern 'extreme circumstances, in which the very survival of a State would be at stake'.[29] However, the exact meaning of this sentence remains disputed.[30] If the ICJ intended to create an exception from the general rule it previously pronounced (rather than confirming a state's ability lawfully to resort to the use of a nuclear weapon when the state's survival is at stake), then the ICJ must have contemplated that a state fighting for survival may exceptionally be allowed to use a nuclear weapon in self-defence even if the otherwise applicable requirements conditioning the right to self-defence could not be met or even if the state's act results in the violation of one or both of the two cardinal and 'intransgressible' principles of international law.

At first sight, the benefits of such an exception correspond to the detriments related to the insistence on the rule considered above. The recognition of an exception arguably reflects the wording of the *Nuclear Weapons* Advisory Opinion's paragraph 105(2)(E) and it safeguards the legitimacy of international law by avoiding the expectation that states sacrifice their own legal personality in favour of complying with international legal norms. Finally, the recognition of an exception avoids the possibility that aggressor states can deprive victim states of their means of self-defence by choosing a modality of attack to which the victim state cannot respond by means that satisfy the requirements of the rule.

However, acknowledging an exception of the kind described here is also hugely problematic. First, the acknowledgement of an exception in situations when a state's survival is at stake would undermine the absolute nature of the cardinal norms of international humanitarian law and of the conditions governing the exercise of the right to self-defence. There would be a justified concern that questioning the absoluteness of the cornerstones of international humanitarian law and the prohibition of the use of force could open up a conceptual black hole that threatens to swallow and to consume the key pillars of the contemporary international legal order.

Secondly, an exception of this kind could be easily abused by states seeking to free themselves from the fetters of the law at times of crises. [31] This factor relates to the concerns conventionally raised with respect to the domestic concept of the state of exception and the concept's associations with unrestrained sovereign rule.[32]

Thirdly, the acknowledgement of the existence of an exception governing the use of force in extreme circumstances of self-defence could again lead to a loss of international law's legitimacy owing to international law's inability to reassert itself when it is needed most. Further, making an exception in the cited circumstances would amount to international law's sanctioning of acts that deviate from norms of international law thought to constitute the bedrock of the contemporary legal system.

[29] *Legality of the Threat or Use of Nuclear Weapons* (n 1) [105(2)(E)].

[30] Even and especially the ICJ's judges were divided on this point. Compare *Legality of the Threat or Use of Nuclear Weapons* (n 1), Separate Opinion of Judge Guillaume [9]; , Dissenting Opinion of Judge Koroma 558, 581; Separate Opinion of Judge Fleischhauer [6]; with Dissenting Opinion of Judge Shahabuddeen 376–77, 390, 391–97; Dissenting Opinion of Judge Schwebel 323–28 with Separate Opinion of Judge Ranjeva 303–304; and Dissenting Opinion of Judge Weeramantry 440, 495–96.

[31] See e.g. Georg Schwarzenberger, *The Fundamental Principles of International Law* (Academie de Droit International de la Haye 1955) 344; Kohen (n 13) 301–302.

[32] Carl Schmitt's state of exception is discussed in section 4.1 below.

Neither the rule nor the exception is particularly well placed to deal with the legal problem posed by the notion of state survival. Thus, in the next section I argue that it is possible to reconcile the wording of the ICJ's *Nuclear Weapons* Advisory Opinion with yet a third approach to the notion of state survival.

4 Superposition of Rule and Exception

As we have seen, each argument in favour of the applicability and validity of the rule invites counter-arguments in favour of the applicability and validity of the exception. It seems impossible to rationalize a decision in favour of either the rule or the exception without compromising international law's legitimacy and without sacrificing some of the most fundamental principles of international law. Against that background, I argue that situations of extreme self-defence where a state's survival is at stake should be governed by both the rule and the exception. This means that, as a matter of law, the threat or use of a nuclear weapon in the cited circumstances should be considered to be a 'legal dilemma' in the sense that the conduct in question is both permitted and prohibited and that obeying or applying one of the two norms necessarily entails the undue impairment of the other.[33] In practical terms, this means that international law does not provide legal subjects facing the contemplated extreme circumstances with 'one right answer'.

By insisting on the simultaneous validity and applicability of both the rule and the exception, international law would not even assist with the identification of a 'lesser evil'. Rather, flanked by the legal dilemma's two norms, the given legal subject would need to make its own decision and accept that its conduct will engage international legal responsibility irrespective of the norm it chooses to comply with, or, in the case of the non-utilization of a permissive norm,[34] that its conduct entails the foregoing of the exercise of a right.

It might not be immediately apparent how such a seemingly nonsensical suggestion could be any more desirable than the two options considered above. Indeed, it could inter alia be argued that the suggested solution is first, contradictory, secondly, that it undermines law's action-guiding nature, and, thirdly, that such a contradictory legal state could easily be abused. I will address each of these concerns before considering the benefits of the suggested solution.

4.1 Supposed detriments of the suggested solution

With respect to the first concern, some might argue[35] that legal dilemmas are conceptually inaccurate and illogical. Indeed, it could be argued that the acknowledgement of genuine irresolvable norm conflicts violates logic's law of non-contradiction.[36] The law of

[33] This is an abbreviated version of the definition of a legal dilemma put forward in my doctoral thesis, which provides that a 'legal dilemma exists when an actor confronts an irresolvable and unavoidable conflict between at least two legal norms so that obeying or applying one norm necessarily entails the undue impairment of the other'. See Jeutner (n 1) 20.

[34] For a more detailed consideration of conflicts between permissive and prescriptive norms see ibid 27–33.

[35] Kelsen dismisses the logical possibility of irresolvable norm conflicts, for example. See Hans Kelsen, *General Theory of Law and State* (Harvard University Press 1945) 374–75. See also Nicholas Rescher, *Paradoxes: Their Roots, Range, and Resolution* (Open Court 2001) 9; George P Fletcher, 'Paradoxes in Legal Thought' (1985) 85 Columbia Law Review 1263, 1264–65.

[36] The truth and/or necessity of the law of non-contradiction is disputed. See Graham Priest, 'What Is so Bad about Contradictions?' (1998) 95 Journal of Philosophy 410, 417.

non-contradiction stipulates inter alia that 'opposite assertions cannot be true at the same time'.[37] In the legal context, the explosion principle is one of the strongest arguments in favour of the law of non-contradiction. According to the explosion principle a true contradictory statement causes the statement's normative reference system (a legal system, for example) to degenerate into triviality where any statement is true. However, such concerns do not necessarily undermine the suggested solution for at least two reasons.

First, there are logical systems that are able to accommodate true contradictory statements. The law of non-contradiction and the explosion principle are by no means necessary principles of every logical system.[38] Paraconsistent conceptions of logic, for example, possess the ability to contain contradictions and can prevent the degeneration of a logical system into triviality. Indeed, von Wright acknowledges, for example, that the view that 'of "norm-logical-necessity" normative orders are gapless and free from contradiction' cannot be based on logic, but rather rests on certain '*normative* ideas'. Similarly, Luhmann admits that '[t]he world does not provide any guarantee for logical order and consistency of deductions',[39] but that legal systems are consistent merely to the extent that they positively stipulate for their own consistency.[40]

This means that the observation that dilemmatic declarations violate the laws of logic is contingent upon the adoption of a particular, contemporary logical system, which in turn relies on the acceptance of a specific metaphysical theory.[41] In legal contexts, it might on the whole appear to be desirable to preclude the possibility of genuine legal dilemmas.[42] However, I hope to show below[43] that there are also good reasons to allow for the possibility of genuine legal dilemmas in carefully delimitated situations.

In any event, the principles of formal logic cannot be transplanted automatically to the sphere of law since the validity of conclusions reached by applying principles of formal logic is limited to the sphere of formal logic. The validity or desirability of statements within a particular context such as international law cannot be established merely with reference to certain conclusions reached by applying principles belonging to a different context. When certain logical principles are applied to law, these principles need to be carefully incorporated in order to ensure that the utilization of logical principles does not undermine law's distinct procedures,[44] which respond, in particular, to the 'social

[37] Paula Gottlieb, 'Aristotle on Non-Contradiction' in Edward N Zalta (ed), *The Stanford Encyclopedia of Philosophy* (Stanford University Press 2015) http://plato.stanford.edu/archives/sum2015/entries/aristotle-noncontradiction/ (accessed 16 July 2015).

[38] See Georg Henrik von Wright, 'Deontic Logic: A Personal View' (1999) 12 Ratio Juris 26, 33.

[39] Niklas Luhmann, *Law as a Social System* (Fatima Kastner and others (eds), Klaus A Ziegert (tr), Oxford Socio-Legal Studies 2004) 286.

[40] This rationale can also be extended to the assumption of Hage, Waltermann, and Arosemena, who argue that owing to its 'nature', territory 'cannot belong to' two states 'at the same time' (see first paragraph of section 7.1, ch 2 in this volume). There is nothing about the inherent nature of territory that precludes it from being owned by more than one legal subject. In fact, there are various forms of co-ownership in both domestic and international law. It might well be that co-ownership might be precluded by the terms of a special agreement between disputing parties. However, there is certainly nothing 'in the nature' of territory as such that precludes it from belonging to two states.

[41] Eleftheriades makes a similar observation about von Wright's attitude towards normative inconsistency. Eleftheriadis observes that von Wright's view is 'linked to the purpose or rationale of any norm-giving project, not a logical point'. See Pavlos Z Eleftheriadis, *Legal Rights* (Oxford University Press 2008) 90. See also von Wright (n 38) 33.

[42] Various arguments of Hage, Waltermann, and Arosemena rely on this assumption, for example, see penultimate paragraph of section 10 and paragraphs 2–5 of section 11 in ch 2 in this volume.

[43] See section 4.2 below.

[44] See Dieter Krimphove, 'Grenzen Der Logik' (2013) 44 Rechtstheorie 315, 330–38.

dynamics'[45] of a given society and rely heavily on value judgments[46] rather than on logical deductions.[47]

While it might make sense to insist that particular logical systems degenerate into triviality in accordance with the explosion principle when and if true contradictions are tolerated. However, a contradiction in the realm of law by no means entails the disapplication of every other legal norm beyond a particular conflict. It entails, least of all of, the collapse of the entire legal system. Just because the use of a nuclear weapon in extreme circumstances of self-defence is both legal and illegal does not at all mean that any other legal statement is true. This is so not only because the inter-dependency of legal norms differs from that of logical norms, but also because legal contradictions can easily be contained by positing additional legal norms that can 'patch up' inconsistencies.[48] Indeed, deontic logicians have themselves observed that in the realm of law the coexistence of two mutually exclusive norms 'in itself, need not lead to trouble',[49] since legislators could 'take steps to remove the conflict'.[50] Thus, the utility of principles of formal logic in the sphere of law is limited and the mere fact that the proposal offered here might violate certain principles of formal logic cannot be an unqualified indicator of that proposal' undesirability.

With respect to the second concern related to law's action-guiding nature, it could be argued that describing the legality of the use of a nuclear weapon in circumstances when a state's survival is at stake as a legal dilemma, confronts decision-makers with unrealistic, impossible expectations as a result of which dilemmatic norms cease to engage with the motivational set of legal subjects. However, legal dilemmas do not confront decision-makers with impossible norms. Rather, a sovereign having to choose between the exercise of the right to self-defence and compliance with the prohibition of the use of nuclear force in the cited circumstances, faces two norms each of which the sovereign can perfectly comply with—separately but not concurrently. Dilemmatic situations thus differ from the scenario in the *Lighthouses Case*, for example, where Greece's de facto inability to restore and return the bombarded lighthouse was held to defeat Greece's obligation to do so.[51] In dilemmatic situations, decision-makers have an actual choice between two possible options.[52] That choice is not made impossible just because each alternative results in international legal responsibility of a state or the forgoing of the exercise of a right. This way, legal dilemmas leave room for sensible and rational decision-making processes that can seek to identify a preferable balance between competing norms. Similarly, legal dilemmas are not situations where legal

[45] Oren Perez, 'Law in the Air: A Prologue to the World of Legal Paradoxes' in Oren Perez and Gunther Teubner (eds), *Paradoxes and Inconsistencies in the Law* (Hart Publishing 2005) 16–17.

[46] Claus-Wilhelm Canaris, *Systemdenken und Systembegriff in der Jurisprudenz: Entwickelt am Beispiel des deutschen Privatrechts, vol 14* (Duncker & Humblot 1969) 29.

[47] See also the ILC's Report on Fragmentation which observed that 'any [legal] decision will involve interpretation and choice between alternative rule-formulations and meanings that cannot be pressed within the model of logical reasoning'. See Martti Koskenniemi, 'Fragmentation of International Law: Difficulties Arising from the Diversifications and Expansion of International Law, Report of the Study Group of the ILC, 58th Session, UN Doc A/CN.4/L.682' (2006) para 25. See also Lon L Fuller, *The Morality of Law* (Yale University Press 1969) 65–66; Gleider Hernandez, *The International Court of Justice and the Judicial Function* (Oxford University Press 2014) 278.

[48] Contractual or statutory severability clauses are, for example, designed specifically to contain legal defects to immediately affected clauses thereby preserving the validity of otherwise unaffected norms.

[49] Georg Henrik von Wright, 'Norms, Truth and Logic' in AA Martino (ed), *Deontic Logic, Computational Linguistics, and Legal Information Systems* (North-Holland 1982) 157–58.

[50] ibid.

[51] *Ottoman Empire Lighthouses Concession (Greece v France)* [1956] 12 RIAA 155, 219–20; James Crawford, *State Responsibility: The General Part* (Cambridge University Press 2013) 296.

[52] Potential objections based on the 'ought-implies-can' principle are thus unfounded in this regard. See Jeutner (n 1) 125–33.

actors are 'required to abide by some [ungraspable and unrecognizable] standard that hovers esoterically beyond [their] comprehension'.[53] In contrast, legal dilemmas arise in response to clearly identified norm conflicts whose occurrence is often (although certainly not always) predictable. That does not mean that predictable dilemmas are necessarily always avoidable or curable (at least ex post facto), but it does mean that decision-makers can take steps to prepare for their occurrence or try to prevent their occurrence.

Therefore, characterizing the use of a nuclear weapon in extreme circumstances of self-defence when a state's survival is at stake as a legal dilemma does engage with the motivational set of the legal subject. The legal actor's choice still matters:[54] a subject must choose which norm to apply or comply with and the awareness and acknowledgement of a legal dilemma may also influence an actor's behaviour before a particular legal dilemma occurs.

Finally, with respect to the third concern, regarding the risk of legal dilemmas being abused, it could be argued that deference to sovereign decision-makers in dilemmatic circumstances could lead to unfettered, sovereign decisionism, since law surrenders in light of an irresolvable norm conflict. One might fear that dilemmatic declarations could 'become all things to all States' [55] and that legal dilemmas could cause states to take the law into their own hands[56]—especially in the extreme circumstances contemplated here. In light of the fact, however, that legal dilemmas are still identified by law, that the competence of actors facing a legal dilemma is strictly limited to decide between the conflicting norms, and that they are legally accountable for any decision they make, these concerns are unfounded.

Compared to Carl Schmitt's classical conceptualization of the state of exception, for instance, legal dilemmas are not identified by sovereigns with reference to particular existing facts.[57] While Schmitt's state of exception[58] is triggered by 'extreme peril, a danger to the existence of the state, or the like'[59] and by events, which 'cannot be circumscribed factually and made to conform to a preformed law',[60] the conditions giving rise to legal dilemmas are different. There is no doubt that some legal dilemmas, especially the one considered here, concern situations where there is a 'danger to the existence of the state', but legal dilemmas are not in principle linked to a particular set of circumstances that undermine the ordinary framework of facts with respect to which the ordinary legal order is defined. Rather, the identification of a legal dilemma occurs in accordance with a predetermined, precise definition, and in accordance with particular legal tests.[61] In a state of exception it is the sovereign, and

[53] Matthew H Kramer, 'When Is There Not One Right Answer?' (2008) 53 American Journal of Jurisprudence 49, 55.

[54] Similarly, the ILC's Commentary on the Articles on Responsibility of States for Internationally Wrongful Acts observes that a legal subject 'acting under distress is not acting involuntarily'. See Commentary to the ILC Articles on Responsibility of States for Internationally Wrongful Acts, (2001) 2(2) Yearbook of the International Law Commission 31, art 24[1]. See also Paddeu (n 1) 84.

[55] Dapo Akande, 'Nuclear Weapons, Unclear Law? Deciphering the Nuclear Weapons Advisory Opinion of the International Court' (1998) 68 British Yearbook of International Law 165, 216; CF Amerasinghe, 'The Legality of the Use of or Threat to Use Nuclear Weapons' (1999) X Finnish Yearbook of International law 5, 44.

[56] Amerasinghe (n 55) 44; Hersch Lauterpacht, *The Function of Law in the International Community* (Clarendon Press 1933) 7.

[57] The link between exceptions and the question of how one decides on the exception is also discussed by Schauer in the first sentence of section 8 in ch 4 in this volume.

[58] Although Schmitt's *Ausnahmezustand* is usually discussed with reference to crises of various kinds, it should be noted that Schmitt intended the concept to have a more general meaning: 'the exception is to be understood to refer to a general concept in the theory of the state, and not merely to a construct applied to any emergency decree of state of siege.' See Carl Schmitt, *Political Theology: Four Chapters on the Concept of Sovereignty* (University of Chicago Press 1985) 15.

[59] ibid 6.

[60] ibid.

[61] Only if a norm conflict is irresolvable and unavoidable does a legal dilemma exist.

only the sovereign,[62] who determines 'when [the normal state of affairs is] disturbed'.[63] The existence of the state of exception is an inherently subjective question to the extent that the identification of whether or not a state of exception exists, depends on the actor tasked with making that determination. The question of the existence of a legal dilemma is, by contrast, an objective question to the extent that the identification of whether or not a legal dilemma exists does not inherently depend on the actor tasked with making that determination.

While it is true that legal dilemmas, just like states of exceptions,[64] which are not susceptible to codification,[65] can only be decided by means of a sovereign decision, decision-makers facing a dilemma can choose only to comply with either of the two conflicting norms. Sovereign decision-makers within a state of exception, by contrast, possess 'principally unlimited authority'[66] and decide what to do in a 'moment of indifference'[67] from a potentially 'infinite number of options'.[68] Compared to the 'unlimited authority' of a sovereign faced with a state of exception, the scope of the decision-making power of an actor faced with a legal dilemma is expressly limited to those conduct norms which form part of a particular dilemma. Dilemmas may certainly entail a 'moment of indifference'[69] regarding the comparative value of two or more conduct norms, and, in light of the limited assistance which reason can provide in dilemmatic cases, it might also be adequate to state that an actor's decision 'emanates from nothingness'[70] (at least from the law's point of view). Nonetheless, legal dilemmas concern a choice between two or more previously identified conduct norms, and they do not contain a notion of unlimited power. Therefore, the risk of abuse is much more limited compared to Schmitt's state of exception.

Finally, the desirability of legal dilemmas cannot be called into question by reference to states of exception as, crucially, actors facing a dilemma are legally accountable for their actions. It follows from Schmitt's conceptualization of the state of exception as a space, if not devoid of order,[71] then at least devoid of law, that a sovereign's conduct within a state of exception is not susceptible to legal sanction. As the entire legal order is suspended,[72] the sovereign's conduct does not engage a legal order's ordinary and regulatory functions.

[62] In *Die Diktatur*, which preceded *Political Theology*, Schmitt observed that at least historically the task of identifying the existence of a state of exception was kept distinct from the task of deciding what to do in a state of exception. See John P McCormick, 'The Dilemmas of Dictatorship: Carl Schmitt and Constitutional Emergency Powers' in David Dyzenhaus (ed), *Law as Politics* (Duke University Press 1998) 240.

[63] Schmitt (n 58) 9.

[64] ibid 15; Tracy B Strong, 'Foreword' in Carl Schmitt, *Political Theology: Four Chapters on the Concept of Sovereignty* (George Schwab (tr), University of Chicago Press 2005) xii.

[65] Schmitt (n 58) 13; Lars Vinx, 'Carl Schmitt' in Edward N Zalta (ed), *The Stanford Encyclopedia of Philosophy* (Stanford University Press 2014) http://plato.stanford.edu/archives/win2014/entries/schmitt/ (accessed 24 November 2014).

[66] Schmitt (n 58) 12, 6–7. See also Oren Gross and Fionnuala Ní Aoláin, *Law in Times of Crisis: Emergency Powers in Theory and Practice* (Cambridge University Press 2006) 165.

[67] Schmitt (n 58) 30, 32; Hasso Hofmann, *Legitimität Gegen Legalität: Der Weg Der Politischen Philosophie Carl Schmitts* (Duncker & Humblot 2010) 52. See also William E Scheuerman, *Carl Schmitt: The End of Law* (Rowman & Littlefield 1999) 32–34.

[68] Thalin Zarmanian, 'Carl Schmitt and the Problem of Legal Order: From Domestic to International' (2006) 19 Leiden Journal of International Law 41, 49. Note, however, that sovereigns may be subject to certain teleological restrictions depending on whether they are sovereign or commissarial dictators see Carl Schmitt-Dorotić, *Die Diktatur: von den Anfängen des modernen Souveränitätsgedankens bis zum proletarischen Klassenkampf* (Duncker & Humblot 1921) 139–40, 145–46; Joseph J Bendersky, *Carl Schmitt: Theorist for the Reich* (Princeton University Press 2014) 33.

[69] Schmitt (n 58) 30, 32; Hofmann (n 67) 52. See also Scheuerman (n 67) 32–34.

[70] Schmitt (n 58) 32; Hofmann (n 67) 52.

[71] Schmitt (n 58) 12. See also Strong (n 64) xliii.

[72] Note the similarity between Schmitt's sovereign and Kierkegaard's Abraham with respect to Kierkegaard's concept of the 'suspension of the ethical' in this regard. See Søren Kierkegaard, *Fear and Trembling/Repetition* (Howard Vincent Hong and Edna Hatlestad Hong trs, Princeton University Press 1983) 59–60.

Indeed, while the sovereign is part of the legal system by deciding the state of exception, the sovereign simultaneously 'stands outside'[73] of the legal order.[74]

The situation with respect to legal dilemmas is very different. Here, the legal order is at no time suspended. A legal dilemma entails no more than the recognition of a confined legal question with respect to which law is unable to establish the comparative validity and applicability of a specific number of legal norms. However, the acknowledgement of such a dilemmatic state is of no consequence to the legal status of the conflicting conduct norms. A sovereign facing the choice between utilising the right to self-defence or complying with international humanitarian law's 'intransgressible' principles (which would render the use of nuclear force in circumstances of state survival unlawful) decides knowing that the state cannot escape the legal dilemma without forgoing the exercise of a right or accepting international legal responsibility for the violation of the prohibition of the use of nuclear weapons. The mere existence of a legal dilemma does not alter the applicable legal sanctions. The actor facing a dilemma is not 'standing outside' the legal order. This insistence on the continued application of sanctions, the resistance to arguments of necessity and the deliberate subjection of a sovereign actor to 'arguments from outside' may be one of the most controversial aspects of legal dilemmas. It is this feature, however, which makes the contrast between Schmitt's state of exception and legal dilemmas most apparent.

Beyond these three negative reasons in favour of the suggestion to characterize the use of nuclear weapons in extreme circumstances of self-defence as a legal dilemma, there are also at least three positive reasons to apply both the rule and the exception to such situations.

4.2 Benefits of the suggested solution

The application of both the rule and the exception to circumstances of extreme self-defence is desirable for at least three reasons. First, the suggested solution avoids the necessity of international law having to decide a conflict of norms which it is ill-equipped to decide. In circumstances of state survival, international law, and by extension, international judges would have to decide which of two of international law's most fundamental norms takes priority. Considering that the ICJ determined that contemporary international law does not contain rules that would be able to identify a priority between these conflicting norms (*Kollisionslücke*), judges facing this question would lack the competence to choose one norm over the other.[75] Thus, the acceptance of the simultaneous existence of the rule and the exception saves international law from overreaching its competence.

Secondly, the solution suggested here preserves international law's relevancy in circumstances when a state's survival is at stake. If one assumes, for example, that it is 'pragmatically unthinkable that a statesman might be deterred [by a legal prohibition] from using'[76] a nuclear weapon in a circumstance of extreme self-defence and if one assumes that the conflicting norm—the inherent right to self-defence—is of equal status as the weapon's

[73] Schmitt (n 58) 7. See also Giorgio Agamben, *State of Exception* (University of Chicago Press 2008) 35.

[74] As many have acknowledged, the Schmittian state of exception is paradoxical in the sense that the exception 'represents the inclusion and capture of a space that is neither outside nor inside' of the legal order (see Agamben (n 73) 35).

[75] This does not mean, of course, that judges would lack the competence to identify that they face an irresolvable norm conflict and to communicate as much. For an extended treatment of the question of judicial competence in connection with irresolvable norm conflicts see Jeutner (n 1) 102–16.

[76] Martti Koskenniemi, 'Case Analysis: Faith, Identity, and the Killing of the Innocent: International Lawyers and Nuclear Weapons' (1997) 10 Leiden Journal of International Law 137, 142.

prohibition, then one might conclude that 'an absolute prohibition would ... condem[n] the law to irrelevance'.[77] In such circumstances, it would seem as if the law would make an unjustified, and perhaps even unrealistic, choice in favour of the attacked state's compliance with the prohibition of nuclear weapons at the expense of the attacked state's destruction. Conversely, if the law unqualifiedly favoured the inherent right to self-defence under such circumstances, those at the receiving end of a nuclear strike might well question the relevance of international law with respect to its ability to protect their interests (which for the purposes of this argument are assumed to be of the same status as the inherent right to self-defence).

Classifying situations of this kind as legal dilemmas, however, ensures the relevancy of international law by granting both legal norms equal rank and by imposing the responsibility to choose between the two options on the decision-maker. In nuclear self-defence scenarios, legal dilemmas save courts from having to pronounce that a state is legally expected to commit suicide in the interest of international law. At the same time, dilemmas save courts from having to engage in brute 'calculations of utility'[78] that would sanction the violation of some of international humanitarian law's most fundamental norms subject to the satisfaction of particular, and easily abused, legal tests.[79] Dilemmatic declarations allow international law to tolerate a certain indecisiveness that leaves a space within which no decision-maker can hide behind precisely predefined categories of action[80] without providing reasons for his/her conduct. Indeed, the wedge which legal dilemmas drive between the values of law's conventional binary code creates a highly pressurized and unique space for truly considered sovereign judgments which lead to more legitimate decision-making processes and better substantive outcomes.

Finally, the insistence on the simultaneous validity and applicability of rule and exception can contribute towards the progressive development of international law. By acknowledging, rather than concealing, the existence of a legal dilemma, dilemmatic declarations provide sovereigns with the opportunity to consider the causes of a dilemma[81] 'open[ing] the way for a debate on illegality and legality'[82] of a particular dilemmatic situation. In the *Nuclear Weapons* Advisory Opinion, the ICJ explicitly encouraged states to reconsider the contemporary legal framework governing nuclear weapons by observing that:

> [i]n the long run, international law ... [is] ... bound to suffer from the continuing difference of views with regard to the legal status of weapons as deadly as nuclear weapons. It is

[77] ibid 142, 145, 146, 147. For a classic critique of international law's favour for seemingly utopian standards see Carr, who observes inter alia, that '[i]n theories of international law, utopia tends to predominate over reality to an extent unparalleled in other branches of jurisprudence.' See Edward Hallett Carr, *The Twenty Years' Crisis 1919-1939: An Introduction to the Study of International Relations* (2nd edn, Macmillan 1946).

[78] Thomas Nagel, *Mortal Questions* (Cambridge University Press 1979) 59.

[79] Koskenniemi (n 76) 152, 153. Chamberlain opposed the codification of the crime of aggression for similar reasons. See 'Contribution of Sir Austen Chamberlain to a Parliamentary Debate on International Peace and Disarmament' HC Deb 24 November 1927, vol 210 col 2105; Ian Brownlie, 'Some Legal Aspects of the Use of Nuclear Weapons' (1965) 14 International & Comparative Law Quarterly 437, 438.

[80] Precise legal definitions also lead to the possibility of drawing seemingly unworldly and, in any case unpicturesque, distinctions. In the *Nuclear Weapons* Advisory Opinion, for example, a distinction was drawn between 'horrendous suffering' (which is of no legal relevance) and 'unnecessary suffering' (which is of legal relevance). See *Legality of the Threat or Use of Nuclear Weapons* (n 1) Dissenting Opinion of Judge Higgins [13].

[81] Richard Nobles and David Schiff, 'Review of Paradoxes and Inconsistencies in the Law by Oren Perez; Gunther Teubner' (2007) 70 Modern Law Review 505, 510–11; Edward J Lemmon, 'Deontic Logic and the Logic of Imperatives' (1965) 8 Logique et Analyse 39, 39–61.

[82] *Legality of the Threat or Use of Nuclear Weapons* (n 1) Separate Opinion of Judge Ranjeva 303.

> consequently important to put an end to this state of affairs: the long-promised complete nuclear disarmament appears to be the most appropriate means of achieving that result.[83]

Dilemmatic declarations do not only alert states to the existence of an irresolvable norm conflict, they also invite states to revisit the causes of particular dilemmas by denying any precedential value to a decision-maker's decision and by refusing to suspend any applicable sanctions. Compared to the suggestion to issue *non liquet* declarations in response to serious norm conflicts,[84] a 'dilemmatic declaration' which insists on the continued applicability of sanctions provides states with a much stronger incentive to consider reforming a particular dilemmatic conflict. Similarly, in the context of moral dilemmas it has been argued that 'ascriptions of guilt' strengthen the 'impulse' to 'strive ... to prevent ... future conflicts from arising'.[85] Pauwelyn holds a different view. Pauwelyn argues that *non liquet* declarations 'may provide [an incentive] for *states* to fill the gap by normal law-making processes.'[86] However, whether or not a state has an incentive to 'fill the gap' depends on a given state's interests at stake. If paragraph 105(2)(E) of the *Nuclear Weapons* Advisory Opinion is interpreted as a *non liquet* declaration, for example, the nuclear powers may not have any incentive to resolve the underlying irresolvable norm conflict as they could rest assured that the use of nuclear weapons is lawful in accordance with the orthodox interpretation of the *Lotus* Principle.[87] In contradiction to *non liquet* declarations, dilemmatic declarations trigger, at least ideally, serious debates amongst the members of the international community of states concerning the desirability or curability of a given dilemma.

It is of course also possible that states realize that their opinions are divided to such an extent that a legal norm conflict cannot be rectified before relevant normative questions have been settled. For example, it could be argued that a comprehensive and absolute prohibition of nuclear weapons requires a considered engagement with the fundamental question of whether it is ultimately the sovereignty of states or the interests of individuals that should trump in scenarios of extreme self-defence. Sovereigns need to ask themselves whether it is desirable to live in a world where a very small number of states should possess the right to self-defence even at the expense of causing horrendous harm to civilians, or of rendering large portions of the planet uninhabitable. Conversely, states need seriously to consider whether sovereign states as subjects of the international legal order could be deprived of their right to self-defence, even at the expense of losing at least their legal personality; in other words, whether the legal order is prepared to expect states to submit to an attack rather than defend themselves.

These are difficult questions and contemporary international legal documents—themselves a product of that legal order which generated the dilemma in the first place—are not going to provide any definitive answers in this regard. Nonetheless, dilemmatic declarations can increase the chance of productive negotiations leading to sustainable solutions by pointing out that the conflicting norms are of equal rank, that no state's interest are inherently paramount,[88] and by avoiding prematurely prioritising one party's legal claim in

[83] ibid 98.

[84] See e.g. Jochen von Bernstorff, 'Hans Kelsen on Judicial Law-Making by International Courts and Tribunals: A Theory of Global Judicial Imperialism?' (2015) 14 The Law and Practice of International Courts and Tribunals 35, 49–50; Joost Pauwelyn, *Conflict of Norms in Public International Law* (Cambridge University Press 2003) 152, 419.

[85] Ruth Barcan Marcus, 'Moral Dilemmas and Consistency' (1980) 77 Journal of Philosophy 121, 131, 133.

[86] See Pauwelyn (n 84) 152.

[87] For a discussion of the links between *non liquet* declarations, the *Lotus* Principle, and Legal Dilemmas see Jeutner (n 1) 85–90.

[88] Robinson argues, for example, that the awareness that all available options are 'by some metric "flawed"' leads to discussions less dominated by 'ascriptions of bad faith, incompetence, hidden agendas, or moral shortcomings'

an ongoing dispute.[89] Similarly, the acceptance of the possibility of legal dilemmas in academic contexts can facilitate the 'adoption of an attitude that acknowledges the incompleteness of the results of one's inquiry',[90] which may encourage international legal academics, attempting to identify novel solutions to irresolvable norm conflicts, to be 'both more willing and more able to learn from the insights reached by others'.[91]

5 Conclusion

The notion of the survival of the state has the potential to shake the foundations of the international legal order. It forces international law to confront its core paradox relating to the possibility of a legal order consisting of individually sovereign entities. In principle, there are at least two ways of approaching this issue. First, one may insist on the continued applicability of ordinary legal mechanisms even and especially at times of extreme self-defence scenarios. This would require making a decision as to which of the two conflicting norms (the rule or the exception) takes precedence—a decision international law and its judges, I argue, are not competent to make. Alternatively, it could be argued that international law is ill-equipped to resolve its own inherent and systemic paradoxes. As a result, international law should recede when faced with situations of the kind contemplated by the ICJ in the *Nuclear Weapons* Advisory Opinion. My proposed solution seeks to combine both of these alternatives. On the one hand, it insists on the continued relevance and importance of international law even at times of extreme self-defence scenarios. Thereby, it avoids the creation of alegal territories within the international legal order. On the other hand, my solution also avoids the risk of international judicial law-making by insisting on the continued applicability of both the rule and the exception.

than by a 'more generous, more collegial, and more open-minded' atmosphere. See Darryl Robinson, 'Inescapable Dyads: Why the International Criminal Court Cannot Win' (2015) 28 Leiden Journal of International Law 323, 345.

[89] Specifically, in the context of water disputes, Scott notes, for example, that '[o]nce a State is certain about its rights, or part of them, these rights will stand in the way of easy agreement.' See Robert D Scott, 'Kansas v. Colorado Revisited' (1958) 52 American Journal of International Law 432, 454.

[90] Maksymilian Del Mar, 'Jurisprudential Inquiries between Discourse and Tradition: Towards the Incompleteness of Theoretical Pictures' (2009) 13 www.era.lib.ed.ac.uk/bitstream/handle/1842/3237/Del%20Mar%20PhD%20thesis%2008.pdf.

[91] ibid. See also Julie Dickson, 'Ours Is a Broad Church: Indirectly Evaluative Legal Philosophy as a Facet of Jurisprudential Inquiry' (2015) 6 Jurisprudence 207, 214–15, 230.

PART III

EXCEPTIONS IN TREATY LAW

14
Good Faith and the Exercise of Treaty-based Discretionary Powers

*Ulf Linderfalk**

1 Introduction

This contribution forms a first preliminary stage in a broader inquiry into the exercise of discretion in the application of international law. To suit the theme of this book, the topic of the contribution will have to be limited, however. This is why it will address issues concerning the exercise of discretionary powers *conferred under treaties* only. The concept of good faith will be used as a starting point of all analysis.

The significance of good faith for the performance of treaty-based obligations generally is emphasized in common Article 26 of the 1969 and 1986 Vienna Conventions on the Law of Treaties.[1] The article provides:

> *Article 26. Pacta Sunt Servanda*
> Every treaty in force is binding upon the parties to it and must be performed by them in good faith.

Scholars stress the foundational value of the concept of good faith in the law of treaties.[2] Some refer to the concept as 'a major pillar of treaty law'.[3] In the writing of others, it is described as the basis of the law of treaties;[4] indeed, an idea that 'pervades the whole of this branch of the law'.[5] As many would seem to have it, good faith is a 'general principle' of international law,[6] in the sense of an idea that inspires and feeds into the substance of treaties

* Ulf Linderfalk is Professor of International Law at the Faculty of Law, Lund University. He is the Editor-in-Chief of the *Nordic Journal of International Law*. Special thanks go to Eduardo Gill-Pedro and Valentin Jeutner—they are both highly appreciated discussion partners. Thanks go also to the Ragnar Söderberg Foundations for the financial support needed to complete this contribution.

[1] Vienna Convention on the Law of Treaties, adopted on 22 May 1969, 1155 UNTS 331; Vienna Convention on the Law of Treaties between States and International Organizations or between International Organizations, adopted on 21 March 1986, UN Doc A/CONF.129/15. At the time of writing, the Convention has not entered into force.

[2] Michel Virally, 'Review Essay: Good Faith in Public International Law' (1983) 77 American Journal of International Law) 130, 132.

[3] Kirsten Schmalenbach, 'Preamble' in Kirsten Schmalenbach and Oliver Dörr (eds), *Vienna Convention on the Law of Treaties. A Commentary* (Springer 2012) 9, 12.

[4] MK Yasseen, 'L'interprétation des traits d'après la Convention de Vienne sur le droit des traités' (1976) 151 Recueils des Cours 1, 22. See similarly Bin Cheng, *General Principles of Law as Applied by International Courts and Tribunals* (Stevens |& Sons 1953) 105.

[5] Shabtai Rosenne, *Developments in the Law of Treaties 1945-1986* (CUP 1989) 173.

[6] Georg Ress, 'The Interpretation of the Charter' in Bruno Simma and others (eds), *The Charter of the United Nations. A Commentary, vol 1* (2nd edn, OUP 2002) 13, 19; Robert Kolb, 'Article 2(2)' in Bruno Simma and others (eds), *The Charter of the United Nations. A Commentary, vol 1* (3rd edn, OUP 2012) 166t 169; Markus Kotzur, 'Good Faith (Bona Fides)' (2009) 4 *Encyclopedia of Public International Law* 508, 511; Hugh Thirlway, 'The Law and Procedure of the International Court of Justice, 1960-1989, Part One' (1989) 60 British Yearbook of International Law 4, 7 ff; John F O'Connor, *Good Faith in International Law* (Dartmouth 1991) 120–24.

Ulf Linderfalk, *Good Faith and the Exercise of Treaty-Based Discretionary Powers* In: *Exceptions in International Law*. Edited by: Lorand Bartels and Federica Paddeu, Oxford University Press (2020).
DOI: 10.1093/oso/9780198789321.003.0014

throughout.[7] This proposition is confirmed by the preamble to the two Vienna Conventions, which not only describes good faith as a 'universally recognized' principle, but also places it on a par with the principle of free consent and 'the *pacta sunt servanda* rule'.[8]

Now, if international lawyers recognize the importance of the principle of good faith for the understanding of the vast body of law laid down in international treaties, this does not tell us very much about the precise definition of this principle. If scholarly comments are to be trusted, the meaning of good faith bears on the idea of the importance of rationality and reason for the application of international law. More specifically, good faith is said to place an obligation on every party to a treaty to take into account the reasonable expectations of all others,[9] or an obligation to apply the treaty in a reasonable way,[10] or again an obligation to give the treaty a reasonable and equitable effect.[11] Good faith is said to signify an element of reasonableness;[12] it is said to call in substance for a non-arbitrary interpretation of a treaty;[13] it is said to help bring into effect a reasonable and non-abusive result of any treaty interpretation process,[14] or a result which is not manifestly absurd or unreasonable.[15]

As this contribution will rather put it, good faith stands for the idea of international law as a purposive endeavour. It insists upon the assumption that when states and international organizations enter into a treaty relationship, this is done to help bring about some particular state or states of affairs, such as the maintenance of international peace and security,[16] the reinforcement of mutual commitments with regard to judicial settlement,[17] or the development of just any stable and foreseeable pattern of conduct. Stated in the inverse, good faith insists upon the assumption that the creation of the treaty relationship was seen by the parties as something more than an end in itself. So interpreted, good faith makes sense of the very occurrence of a treaty,[18] in much the same way as the assumption of a communicative intention provides the necessary basis for the understanding of treaty language.[19]

[7] Roberto Kolb, 'Principles as Sources of International Law (With Special Reference to Good Faith)' (2006) 53 Netherlands International Law Review 1, 19, comp 7–8; Oliver Dörr, 'Article 18' in Kirsten Schmalenbach and Oliver Dörr (eds), *Vienna Convention on the Law of Treaties. A Commentary* (Springer 2012) 219, 220; Kirsten Schmalenbach, 'Article 26' in Kirsten Schmalenbach and Oliver Dörr (eds), *Vienna Convention on the Law of Treaties. A Commentary* (Springer 2012) 427, 435; Ian Sinclair, *The Vienna Convention on the Law of Treaties* (2nd edn, Manchester University Press 1984) 120; HE Zeitler, '"Good Faith" in the WTO Jurisprudence' (2005) 8 Journal of International Economic Law 724, citing the WTO Appellate Body; Virally (n 2) 132.

[8] As some would have it, indeed, the concept of good faith is the very foundation of the principle of *pacta sunt servanda*. For more on this topic see Jean Salmon, 'Article 26: Pacta sunt servanda' in Olivier Corten and Pierre Klein (eds), *The Vienna Convention on the Law of Treaties: A Commentary, vol 1* (OUP 2011) 659, 671–73.

[9] Kotzur (n 6) 509.

[10] Salmon (n 8) 679, citing the ICJ in *Case Concerning the Gabčíkovo-Nagymaros Project (Hungary v Slovakia)* (Judgment) [1997] ICJ Rep 7.

[11] Compare Gerald Fitzmaurice, who in his Fourth Report as Special Rapporteur on the Law of Treaties, wrote: 'A treaty must be carried out in good faith, and so as to give it a reasonable and equitable effect according to the correct interpretation of its terms.' Gerald Fitzmaurice, 'Fourth Report of the Special Rapporteur' (1959) 2 Yearbook of the International Law Commission 42.

[12] Richard Gardiner, *Treaty Interpretation* (OUP 2008) 151.

[13] Ress (n 6) 31.

[14] Yasseen (n 4) 23.

[15] Sinclair (n 7) 120.

[16] See art 1 of the Charter of the United Nations.

[17] *Case Concerning Border and Transborder Armed Actions (Nicaragua v Honduras)* (Jurisdiction and Admissibility, Judgment) [1988] ICJ Rep 69, para 46.

[18] See Virally (n 2) 132: 'The effects attached to the expressed will and, more broadly, to the behavior of international actors are conceivable only because it is assumed that they act in good faith and that what is apparent is in conformity with their real will. If this postulate is not taken for granted, the whole fabric of international law will collapse.'

[19] See Ulf Linderfalk, 'Is Treaty Interpretation an Art or a Science? International Law and Rational Decision-Making' (2015) 26 European Journal of International Law 169, 172–73; Ulf Linderfalk and Maria Hilling, 'The Use of OECD Commentaries as Interpretative Aids: The Static/Ambulatory-Approaches Debate Considered from the Perspective of International Law' (2015) 1 Nordic Tax Journal 34, 37–39.

A great many rules laid down in the two Vienna Conventions have been drafted to give this idea precise legal form. Obvious examples include the obligation not to defeat the object and purpose of a treaty prior to its entry into force;[20] the prohibition of reservations that are incompatible with the object and purpose of a treaty;[21] the obligation to reconciliate the different authenticated texts of multilingual treaties by adopting the meaning that helps best attain their object and purpose;[22] the provision that excludes any modification of a treaty incompatible with the effective execution of its principal object and purpose;[23] the prohibition of suspension of the operation of a treaty by agreement between some of its parties when suspension is incompatible with the object and purpose of the treaty;[24] and the requirement that a breach of a treaty may only be used as an excuse for terminating it, or suspending its operation, when it consists in the violation of a provision essential for the accomplishment of the object and purpose of the treaty.[25]

This contribution will take the argument one step further. If common Article 26 of the two Vienna Conventions is to be taken at face value, obviously, not only does the principle of good faith form a source of inspiration and an explanatory background to the vast body of law laid down in international treaties, but it also supplies a *norm* that calls for observance whenever treaty obligations are to be performed. It is a purpose of this contribution to conduct a study clarifying, at least partly, the scope of application of this norm. Methodologically, the study will be based on an analysis of international judicial practice; analysis will be limited to practice addressing issues concerning the exercise of treaty-based discretionary powers. As sections 2-9 will establish, consequently, the principle of good faith sets a limit to the application of any treaty rule that confers a discretionary power, whether on states, on an international court or tribunal, or an organ of an international organization. In each and every case of application, this limit is relative to the purpose of the particular rule conferring the power. The conclusion raises a series of fundamental questions of great interest for legal theory. It is a purpose of this contribution to initiate discussion on one of those questions: What is the precise relationship between treaties and the principle of good faith? As section 10 will suggest, although primarily, good faith can be viewed as a principle and not a rule of international law, there is good reason to describe it as an exception, at least as far as concerns its significance for the exercise of treaty-based discretionary powers.

2 The Obligation to Negotiate in Good Faith

Many treaties impose on treaty parties an obligation to negotiate. Such an obligation typically applies on the condition of the existence of some or other specific state of affairs, such as a dispute between two parties concerning the delimitation of continental shelf areas, or the planning of construction works that may affect navigation on some international watercourse, the protection of the environment of the river, or the quality of its waters. The obligation to negotiate may be explicitly stated, such as in the case of Article 5(1) of the Interim

[20] See Vienna Conventions common art 18.
[21] ibid common art 19(c).
[22] ibid common art 33, para 4.
[23] ibid common art 41, para 1(b).
[24] ibid common art 58, para 1(b).
[25] ibid common art 60, para 3(b).

Accord of 13 September 1995 between the Former Yugoslavian Republic of Macedonia (FYROM) and Greece:

> The Parties agree to continue negotiations under the auspices of the Secretary-General of the United Nations pursuant to Security Council resolution 845 (1993) with a view to reaching agreement on the difference described in that resolution and in Security Council resolution 817 (1993).[26]

It may follow implicitly, such as in the case of Article 6(1) of the 1958 Geneva Convention on the Continental Shelf: 'Where the same continental shelf is adjacent to the territories of two or more States whose coasts are opposite each other, the boundary of the continental shelf appertaining to such States shall be determined by agreement between them.'[27] As clarified by the International Court of Justice (ICJ) in *Delimitation of the Maritime Boundary in the Gulf of Maine Area*, Article 6(1) enshrines for states parties to the Geneva Convention an obligation to 'enter into negotiations with a view to arriving at an agreement'.[28]

Many of the 100 or so disputes settled by the ICJ entailed allegations that brought some treaty-based obligation to negotiate into focus.[29] In *Application of the Interim Accord of 13 September 1995*,[30] for example, the Court considered the respondent's allegation that the applicant had breached the obligation laid down in the just-quoted Article 5(1). The provision, although it clearly imposed on the Greek and the FYROM governments an obligation to 'continue negotiations', conferred on them the discretion to decide precisely how negotiations are to be conducted and when. Citing Article 26 of the 1969 Vienna Convention, the Court stressed that it is a requirement following implicitly from Article 5(1) that the parties negotiate in good faith.[31] As the Court noted, the obligation imposed 'is not only to enter into negotiations, but also to pursue them as far as possible, with a view to concluding agreements'.[32] No doubt, so understood, Article 5(1) of the Interim Accord did not impose on the parties the obligation to reach an agreement; nor did it require that lengthy negotiations be pursued of necessity. As the Court seemed very keen to convey, the provision entailed an obligation of conduct. In exercising the discretion conferred under Article 5(1), the parties would have to conduct themselves so as not to frustrate the object and purpose of the provision—the creation of conditions favourable to reaching an agreement. As clarified by the Court:

> States must conduct themselves so that the 'negotiations are meaningful'. This requirement is not satisfied, for example, where either of the parties 'insists upon its own

[26] 1891 UNTS 7.

[27] 499 UNTS 311.

[28] *Delimitation of the Maritime Boundary in the Gulf of Maine Area (Canada v United States of America)* (Judgment) [1984] ICJ Rep 246, para 91.

[29] See e.g. *Application of the Interim Accord of 13 September 1995 (The Former Republic of Macedonia v Greece)* (Judgment) [2011] ICJ Rep 644, paras 127–38; *Case Concerning Pulp Mills on the River Uruguay (Argentina v Uruguay)* (Judgment) [2010] ICJ Rep 14, paras 145–48; *Case Concerning the Gabčíkovo-Nagymaros Project* (n 10) paras 112, 132–42. In at least two cases the ICJ did consider the obligation to negotiate laid down in art 6(1) of the 1958 Geneva Convention on the Continental Shelf, but then only as a reflection of customary international law. See *North Sea Continental Shelf (Federal Republic of Germany v Denmark; Federal Republic of Germany v Netherlands)* (Judgment) [1969] ICJ Rep 3, para 85; *Delimitation of the Maritime Boundary in the Gulf of Maine Area* (n 28), paras 87, 112.

[30] *Application of the Interim Accord of 13 September 1995* (n 29).

[31] ibid para 131.

[32] ibid para 132. Quotes are from the PCIJ in Railway Traffic between Lithuania and Poland, Advisory Opinion of 15 October 1931, PCIJ Ser A/B No 42.

position without contemplating any modification of it' or where they obstruct negotiations, for example, by interrupting communications or causing delays in an unjustified manner or disregarding the procedures agreed upon. Negotiations with a view to reaching an agreement also imply that the parties should pay reasonable regard to the interests of the other.[33]

3 The Obligation to Seek to Obtain in Good Faith the Consent of Another Treaty Party

In the *Rainbow Warrior Arbitration*,[34] the arbitration tribunal considered allegations of a series of breaches of the agreement of 9 July 1986 concluded between the governments of France and New Zealand. According to the terms of the agreement: 'Major Mafart and Captain Prieur will be transferred to a French military facility on the island of Hao for a period of not less than three years. They will be prohibited from leaving the island for any reason, except with the mutual consent of the two Governments.'[35]

New Zealand requested the tribunal to declare, among other things, that France had acted contrary to the agreement by, first, removing Major Mafart and Captain Prieur from the island of Hao and, secondly, by failing to seek in good faith to obtain the consent of New Zealand to their removal. As far as concerns the removal of Captain Prieur, the tribunal found in favour of New Zealand on both counts. In so doing, the tribunal fully accepted New Zealand's proposed understanding of the agreement. The understanding was that the agreement imposed on France a twofold duty: first, France had the duty not to remove the two agents from the island of Hao failing consent of the government of New Zealand; and, secondly, whenever France considered that there was good reason to remove an agent from the island, it had the duty to seek to obtain in good faith the consent of New Zealand.

To explain its finding that France had failed to make efforts to seek to obtain in good faith the consent of New Zealand, the tribunal reiterated the events of 5 May 1989:

> [W]hen the French Republic notified the Ambassador of New Zealand on 5 May at 11.00 a.m. (French time), the latter was merely told that Mrs. Dominique Prieur's father, hospitalized for cancer treatment, was dying. Of course, it was explained that the New Zealand Government could verify 'the validity of this information' using a physician of its choice, but the telegram the French Minister of Foreign Affairs sent to the Embassy of France in Wellington on 5 May 1988 clearly stated that the decision to repatriate was final. And this singular announcement was addressed to New Zealand: 'After all, New Zealand should understand that it would be incomprehensible for both French and New Zealand opinion for the New Zealand Government to stand in the way of allowing Mrs. Prieur to see her father on his death bed ...'. Thus, New Zealand was really not asked for its approval, as compliance with France's obligations required, even under extremely urgent circumstances; it was indeed demanded so firmly that it was bound to provoke a strong reaction from New Zealand.[36]

[33] ibid para 132. References to earlier case law have been omitted.
[34] *Rainbow Warrior Arbitration (New Zealand v France)* (Decision) [1990] 20 UNRIAA 215.
[35] ibid para 13.
[36] ibid para 94.

The 1986 Agreement, obviously, conferred on the parties the discretion to decide jointly what would constitute a valid reason to remove an agent from the island, in the sense of the conditions that would have to obtain before New Zealand could give its consent. What the decision of the tribunal appears to imply is that this discretion would always have to be exercised for a purpose. Indeed, if France had the duty to obtain the consent of New Zealand, it can be seen to be the very point of this requirement that New Zealand be given both an opportunity and the sufficient time to make an informed decision in the matter.

4 The Duty to Pronounce in Good Faith on the Admission of Members to the UN

In *Admission of a State to Membership in the United Nations*,[37] the ICJ examined a request made by the UN General Assembly for an advisory opinion. The request asked the Court to clarify whether in virtue of Article 4 of the Charter of the United Nations, on the admission of a state to membership in the UN, a member of the organization was 'judicially entitled to make its consent to the admission dependent on conditions not expressly provided by paragraph 1 of the said Article'. Article 4 provides:

1. Membership in the United Nations is open to all other peace-loving states which accept the obligations contained in the present Charter and, in the judgment of the Organization, are able and willing to carry out these obligations.
2. The admission of any such state to membership in the United Nations will be effected by a decision of the General Assembly upon the recommendation of the Security Council.

As the Court held, states which fulfil the conditions stated in Article 4(1) are qualified for admission to membership. Article 4(1) provides not merely the necessary conditions for admission, but also the conditions which suffice. At the same time, obviously, Article 4(2) confers on members of the UN—acting either in the Security Council or in the General Assembly—the discretion to pronounce itself by its vote on whether, in particular cases, admission should be granted to a state or not. As the Court emphasized, that discretion would have to be exercised in good faith. Even though, potentially, many circumstances of fact may be considered by a member when determining whether to support the admission of a state to membership or not, circumstances are relevant only when connected with the conditions laid down in Article 4(1): 'Article 4 does not forbid the taking into account of any factor which it is possible reasonably and in good faith to the conditions laid down in that Article.'[38] In other words, as the Court sees it, to pronounce in good faith on the admission of a state to membership in the United Nations means to make an assessment of facts with a view to determining whether the stated conditions for membership are all fulfilled.

[37] *Conditions of Admission of a State to the United Nations (Article 4 of the Charter)* (Advisory Opinion) [1948] ICJ Rep 57.
[38] ibid 63.

5 The Duty to Elect in Good Faith Members to the IMCO Maritime Safety Committee

In *Constitution of the IMCO Maritime Safety Committee*,[39] the ICJ considered the lawfulness of the decision of the Assembly of the-then Inter-Governmental Maritime Consultative Organization (IMCO) electing members to another principal body of the organization, the Maritime Safety Committee. More specifically, the Court examined whether, in not electing Liberia and Panama, the Assembly had exceeded the discretionary powers conferred upon it under Article 28(a) of the Convention for the Establishment of IMCO. The provision reads:

> The Maritime Safety Committee shall consist of fourteen Members elected by the Assembly from the Members, governments of those nations having an important interest in maritime safety, of which not less than eight shall be the largest ship-owning nations, and the remainder shall be elected so as to ensure adequate representation of Members, governments of other nations with an important interest in maritime safety, such as nations interested in the supply of large numbers of crews or in the carriage of large numbers of berthed and unberthed passengers, and of major geographical areas.

As can be seen from the wording of Article 28(a), it confers a discretion on the Assembly of the IMCO. The provision leaves it to the Assembly to elect to the Maritime Safety Committee fourteen members of the organization, of which not less than eight shall be 'the largest ship-owning nations'. Contrary to the argument of some governments, as the Court held, this discretion did not extend as far as to enable the Assembly to choose itself the criteria to be used in determining whether members are among the 'eight largest ship-owning nations' or not. Such a construction would deprive the passage of all significance. What is more:

> [t]o give to the Article such a construction would mean that the structure built into the Article to ensure the predominance on the Committee of 'the' largest ship-owning nations in the ratio of at least eight to six would be undermined and would collapse. The Court is unable to accept an interpretation which would have such a result.[40]

The Court found it apparent that in instructing the Assembly to elect the 'eight largest ship-owning nations', Article 28(a) implied the application of a specific basis of measurement—that of registered tonnage. This interpretation was said by the Court to be consistent also 'with the general purpose of the Convention and the special functions of the Maritime Safety Committee':

> The Organization established by the Convention is a consultative one only, and the Maritime Safety Committee is the body which has the duty to consider matters within the scope of the Organization and of recommending through the Council and the Assembly to Member States, proposals for maritime regulation. In order effectively to carry out these recommendations and to promote maritime safety in its numerous and varied aspects, the co-operation of those States who exercise jurisdiction over a large portion of the world's existing tonnage is essential.[41]

[39] *Constitution of the Maritime Safety Committee of the Inter-Governmental Maritime Consultative Organization* (Advisory Opinion) [1960] ICJ Rep 149.
[40] ibid 166.
[41] ibid 170–71.

Careful readers will note that in no part of the Opinion does the Court make explicit reference to good faith. However, as this contribution suggests, the line of reasoning applied by the Court is in all relevant respects similar to its reasoning in *Conditions of Admission of a State to Membership in the United Nations*. In *Constitution of the IMCO Maritime Safety Committee*, as in the Opinion given twelve years earlier, the Court pored over the application of a treaty provision, which conferred a discretion on an organ of an international organization. It reached once again the conclusion that discretion must be exercised so as not to leave a result which is inimical to the purpose of the provision—in this case, the promotion of maritime safety.

6 The Obligation to Implement in Good Faith a Judgment of the ICJ

In the recent *Certain Activities Carried out by Nicaragua in the Border Area*,[42] the ICJ found that Nicaragua had breached several international obligations owed to Costa Rica, including the principle of territorial sovereignty, and the right of navigation laid down in the 1958 Treaty of Limits. It found that Nicaragua had the obligation to compensate Costa Rica for material damages caused by its unlawful activities on Costa Rican territory. It declined, however, the request that the Court order Nicaragua to provide appropriate assurances and guarantees of non-repetition of its unlawful conduct.[43] In so doing, it followed what by now would seem to be a firmly established practice of the Court.[44] As the Court explained:

> 'there is no reason to suppose that a State whose act or conduct has been declared wrongful by the Court will repeat that act or conduct in the future, since its good faith must be presumed' and therefore assurances and guarantees of non-repetition will be ordered only 'in special circumstances'.[45]

To clarify its position fully, the Court could have added reference to Article 59 of the ICJ Statute. According to this provision, in contentious cases a judgment of the Court has binding force between the disputing parties in respect of the particular case. What makes Article 59 relevant to this contribution is the fact that it leaves to each of the disputing parties to decide themselves precisely how to implement a judgment. In exercising this discretion—this is what the statement of the Court implies—parties must remain faithful to the purpose of the provision: to avoid the repetition of internationally wrongful conduct. In other words, if two states have agreed to accept the compulsory jurisdiction of the ICJ, a judgment will entail the obligation that they accommodate their future behaviour with it, so as to avoid the repetition of conduct declared by the judgment to be internationally wrongful. It is for this

[42] *Certain Activities Carried Out by Nicaragua in the Border Area (Costa Rica v Nicaragua); Construction of a Road in Costa Rica Along the San Juan River (Nicaragua v Costa Rica)* (Judgment) [2015] ICJ Rep 665http://www.icj-cij.org.

[43] ibid paras 140–41.

[44] See e.g. *Request for Interpretation of the judgment of 15 June 1962 in the Case Concerning the Temple of Preah Vihear (Cambodia v Thailand)* (Judgment) [2013] ICJ Rep 281, para 99; *Application of the Interim Accord of 13 September* 1995 (n 30) para 168; *Case Concerning Pulp Mills on the River Uruguay* (n 29) para 278; *Dispute Regarding Navigational and Related Rights (Costa Rica v Nicaragua)* (Judgment) [2009] ICJ Rep 213, para 150.

[45] *Certain Activities Carried Out by Nicaragua in the Border* Area (n 42) para 141. Quotes are from the decision of the ICJ in *Navigational and Related Rights* (n 44).

reason that the Court sees no need to order specifically that Nicaragua provides appropriate assurances and guarantees of non-repetition of Nicaragua's unlawful conduct.

7 The Duty to Interpret Treaties in Good Faith

In *Navigational and Related Rights*,[46] the ICJ interpreted Article VI of the Treaty of Limits concluded by Costa Rica and Nicaragua in 1858, applying for that purpose customary international law 'as reflected in Articles 31 and 32 of the 1969 Vienna Convention on the Law of Treaties'.[47] Article VI established Nicaragua's dominion and sovereign jurisdiction over the waters of the San José river. At the same time, it affirmed Costa Rica's right to navigate the lower course of the river for purposes of commerce ('con objetos de comercio'). Nicaragua argued that the ordinary meaning of 'comercio' excluded all services, such as passenger transport, 'because in 1858 the word "commerce" [Sp. "comercio"] necessarily meant trade in goods and did not extend to services, the inclusion of services being a very recent development'.[48]

The interesting thing with this argument is that Article 31(1) of the Vienna Convention leaves the definition of 'the ordinary meaning' to the discretion of the interpreter.[49] It does not say whether the terms of a treaty are to be interpreted in accordance with their ordinary meaning at the time of the conclusion of the treaty or their ordinary meaning at the time of interpretation. Acting in line with the pattern established in sections 2 to 6 of this contribution, the interpreter would not be free to make this choice at will. He or she would have to continue efforts to fulfil the purpose of Articles 31 and 32 of the Vienna Convention—to establish the intention of the parties to the treaty.

In *Navigational and Related Rights*, the ICJ took this approach precisely. It began with affirming that, as a matter of principle, 'the terms used in a treaty must be interpreted in light of what is determined to have been the parties' common intention, which is, by definition, contemporaneous with the treaty's conclusion'.[50] As it immediately added, however, it did not necessarily follow that no account should ever be taken of the ordinary meaning of a treaty at the time of interpretation. More often than commonly realized, treaty parties use terms to refer generically, that is, to a class (or genus) of entities or states of affairs; 'comercio' presented an example of precisely such a generically referring expression. It referred to a class, the extension of which is defined by Costa Rica and Nicaragua only indirectly, by reliance on an institutional practice, in this case the language activities of Spanish-speaking people in general. Since, obviously, the parties were aware that, in common language, the usage of the word 'comercio' was likely to evolve over time, and since the 1858 Treaty had been entered into by the parties for a very long period, as the Court held, 'comercio' should be interpreted in light of the Spanish language now in current use, and not the language used in 1858.[51]

[46] *Dispute Regarding Navigational and Related Rights* (n 44).
[47] ibid para 47.
[48] ibid para 58.
[49] Symptomatically, the choice between contemporaneous and historical meaning is often said to be a matter of good faith. See e.g. György Haraszti, *Some Fundamental Problems of the Law of Treaties* (Akadémiai Kiadó 1973) 169.
[50] *Dispute Regarding Navigational and Related Rights* (n 44) para 63.
[51] ibid para 70.

8 The Duty to Refuse in Good Faith a Request for Assistance in Criminal Matters

In *Certain Questions of Mutual Assistance in Criminal Matters*,[52] the ICJ considered allegations of breaches of the 1986 Convention on Mutual Assistance in Criminal Matters between France and Djibouti.[53] More specifically, it considered the allegation that France had violated its obligation to afford assistance by not having executed a letter rogatory sent by a Djibouti investigating judge, requesting the transmission of a series of documents. France, for its part, invoked the possibility of refusing assistance provided by Article 2(c) of the Convention:

> Judicial assistance may be refused:
>
> (c) *If the requested State considers* that execution of the request is likely to impair its sovereignty, security, public policy or other essential interests.[54]

The Court began its examination of Article 2(c) by commenting upon a remark of the respondent categorizing the provision as a 'self-judging clause'. It observed that:

> while it is correct, as France claims, that the terms of Article 2 provide a State to which a request for assistance has been made with a very considerable discretion, this exercise of discretion is still subject to the obligation of good faith codified in Article 26 of the 1969 Vienna Convention on the Law of Treaties ... This requires it to be shown that the reasons for refusal to execute the letter rogatory fell within those allowed for in Article 2.[55]

What the Court seems to be saying is that, in order to understand Article 2(c) correctly, not too much emphasis should be placed on the mere wording of the phrase 'If the requested State considers'. While Article 2(c) leaves it up to France in the first place to assess whether the execution of a request for judicial assistance is likely to impair its sovereignty, security, public policy, or other essential interests, there is a limit to this discretion. The discretion conferred upon France under Article 2(c) does not extend so far as to make the assessment purely a question for the judgment of France alone. That would lead to a result inimical to the most basic of reasons for at all having a treaty such as that between France and Djibouti: not leaving it up to each of the two parties to conduct their relations at will. Good faith required that if France refused to execute a letter rogatory requesting judicial assistance, it fell on France to establish that it so acted for reasons that came within any of the categories stated in Article 2.

9 The Obligation Not to Exercise Treaty Rights Abusively

'Treaty abuse' and 'abuse of right' are concepts that have become increasingly more popular in the practice of international law over the last ten to fifteen years.[56] Applied especially in

[52] *Certain Questions of Mutual Assistance in Criminal Matters (Djibouti v France)* (Judgment) [2008] ICJ Rep 179.

[53] 1695 UNTS 298.

[54] Emphasis added.

[55] *Certain Questions of Mutual Assistance in Criminal Matters* (n 52) para 145.

[56] See generally Ulf Linderfalk, 'The Concept of Treaty Abuse: On the Exercise of Legal Discretion' http://ssrn.com/abstract=2526051.

the sphere of international economic law,[57] the two concepts figure prominently in several cases decided by ICSID tribunals under the 1965 Washington Convention. The single case of *Phoenix Action Ltd v Czech Republic* very neatly illustrates their relevance for the topic of this contribution.[58]

In this case, a company (Phoenix) registered under the laws of Israel complained about the treatment given by the Czech Republic to two Czech companies fully owned by Phoenix. As the respondent argued, because Phoenix had acquired the two companies 'for the precise purpose of bringing their pre-existing and purely domestic disputes before an international judicial body … the Tribunal should look beyond the shell of the corporate claimant'.[59] It should deal with the two companies as they would have to deal with any investment made by a Czech national in the Czech Republic. This argument prompted the tribunal to consider in detail the scope of the jurisdiction *ratione materiae* conferred upon it under Article 25 of the 1965 Washington Convention.[60] According to this provision:

> The jurisdiction of the Centre shall extend to any legal dispute arising directly out of an investment, between a Contracting State (or any constituent subdivision or agency of a Contracting State designated to the Centre by that State) and a national of another Contracting State, which the parties to the dispute consent in writing to submit to the Centre.

The tribunal noted that it was not the intention of the drafters of the ICSID Convention to confer upon parties the discretion to define for themselves, by the conclusion of bilateral investment treaties (BITs), what disputes should come within the jurisdiction of ICSID:

> There is nothing like a total discretion, even if the definition developed by ICSID case law is quite broad and encompassing. There are indeed some basic criteria and parties are not free to decide in BITs that anything—like a sale of goods or a dowry for example—is an investment.[61]

Among the criteria that limited the discretion of parties to the Washington Convention, the tribunal stressed in particular the purpose of the ICSID system.[62] As the tribunal observed:

> The ICSID Convention/BIT system is not deemed to protect economic transactions undertaken and performed with *the sole purpose* of taking advantage of the rights contained in such instruments, without any significant economic activity, which is the fundamental prerequisite of any investor's protection. Such transactions must be considered as an abuse of the system.

[57] See e.g. *Phoenix Action Ltd v Czech Republic*, ICSID Case No ARB/06/5, Award (2009); *Autopista Concesionada de Venezuela, CA v Bolivarian Republic of Venezuela*, ICSID Case No ARB/00/5, Decision on Jurisdiction (2001); *Tokios Tokelės v Ukraine*, ICSID Case No ARB/02/18, Decision on Jurisdiction (2004); *Aguas del Tunari SA v Republic of Bolivia*, ICSID Case No ARB/02/3, Decision on Respondent's Objections to Jurisdiction (2005) *Mobil Corporation, Venezuela Holdings BV and Others v Bolivarian Republic of Venezuela*, ICSID Case No ARB/07/27, Decision on Jurisdiction (2010); *Tidewater Inc and Others v Bolivarian Republic of Venezuela*, ICSID Case No ARB/10/5, Decision on Jurisdiction (2013); *ConocoPhilips Petrozuata BV and Others v Bolivarian Republic of Venezuela*, ICSID Case No ARB/07/30, Decision on Jurisdiction and the Merits (2013).

[58] *Phoenix Action Ltd v Czech Republic* (n 57).

[59] ibid para 34.

[60] 575 UNTS 159.

[61] *Phoenix Action Ltd v Czech Republic* (n 57) para 82.

[62] ibid paras 87–92.

Interestingly, good faith would seem to have been the reason of the tribunal for so bringing the application of Article 25 to bear on the concept of treaty abuse:

> The purpose of the international mechanism of protection of investment through ICSID arbitration cannot be to protect investments made in violation of the laws of the host State or investments not made in good faith, obtained for example through misrepresentations, concealments or corruption, or amounting to an abuse of the international ICSID arbitration system.[63]

This observation helps understanding the triad represented by the principle of good faith, the concept of treaty abuse, and the treaty purpose. Stated in terms of the particular case: (i) The purpose of the Washington Convention is '"to facilitate the settlement of disputes between states and foreign investors' with a view to "stimulating a larger flow of private international capital into countries which wish to attract it"'.[64] (ii) Every treaty rule that confers a discretion upon its parties includes an implicit obligation not to exercise this discretion abusively. (iii) This obligation follows from the principle of good faith, which requires that discretion be exercised so as not to leave a result, which is inimical to the purpose of the provision conferring it. (iv) Consequently, 'if the sole purpose of an economic transaction is to pursue an ICSID claim, without any intent to perform any economic activity in the host country, such transaction cannot be considered as a protected investment'.[65]

10 Good Faith and Its Relationship with Treaty Rules Conferring Discretion

Sections 2 to 9 of this contribution established two propositions:

- The principle of good faith sets a limit to the exercise of any treaty-based discretionary power.
- In each and every case of application, this limit is relative to the purpose of the particular rule conferring the power.

The propositions are fully consistent with the common scholarly description of the concept of good faith as related to ideas of rationality and reason. If good faith means that international law should be viewed as a purposive endeavour, then obviously, to exercise a discretionary power in good faith means to exercise it for a purpose. Stated in the inverse, to accept the unlimited exercise of a discretionary power is to accept that this power is sometimes exercised either unreasonably (i.e. for any purpose), or arbitrarily (i.e. for no purpose at all).

The generality of the two propositions should be noted. The claim is that the principle of good faith sets a limit to the application of treaty rules conferring a discretion, *whether they explicitly refer to the principle or not*. It is true that in at least two of the cases perused in sections 2 to 9,[66] it is possible to explain the importance given to the principle of good faith

[63] ibid para 100.

[64] ibid para 88. Quotes are from the Report of the Executive Directors on the ICSID Convention (18 March 1965).

[65] ibid *Phoenix Action Ltd v Czech Republic* (n 57) para 93.

[66] *Admission of a State to Membership in the United Nations* (n 37); *Certain Activities Carried out by Nicaragua in the Border Area* (n 42).

by reference to Article 2(2) of the Charter of the UN. According to this provision, members of the organization 'shall fulfil in good faith the obligations assumed by them in accordance with the present Charter'.[67] Similarly, in *Navigational and Related Rights*, it is possible to explain the ordinary meaning conferred on the expression 'comercio' by reference to the law laid down in Article 31 of the 1969 Vienna Convention, which explicitly calls for the interpretation of treaties in good faith. However, in the greater part of the judicial practice considered, no similar reference to an explicit treaty provision can be made. When all is said and done, consequently, there is certainly good reason to concur in the position indicated by the ICJ in *Application of the Interim Accord of 13 September 1995*, and by the ICSID tribunal in *Phoenix*: the principle of good faith forms implicitly a part of every treaty provision. The two propositions have been phrased so as to reflect this observation.

Now, the generality of the claim begs a crucial question: In what sense is the principle of good faith implicit in treaty provisions conferring a discretionary power? Clearly it is not implicit in the sense of the doctrine of implied powers. When the principle of good faith is applied, it is to justify legal propositions that cannot be similarly justified by reference to the doctrine of implied powers. This is to say, the scope of application of the two norms are different. First, whereas the doctrine of implied powers is invoked to confer powers that are not explicitly provided, the principle of good faith operates the other way around—it reduces the scope of powers indicated by the explicit words of treaty provisions. More fundamentally, however, whereas the doctrine of implied powers is a principle of treaty interpretation applied only on very strict conditions—according to common Article 32 of the two Vienna Conventions, the meaning conveyed by the explicit terms of a treaty must be 'manifestly absurd or unreasonable'—the principle of good faith is not subject to similar constraints. This is because the application of the principle of good faith is secondary to the application of each and all norms of treaty interpretation, including the doctrine of implied powers. The principle forms a safety valve. It serves to guarantee that the application of a treaty always brings a teleologically correct outcome. Comparison can be made with Article 33(4) of the two Vienna Conventions: 'Except where a particular text prevails in accordance with paragraph 1, when a comparison of the authentic texts discloses a difference of meaning which the application of articles 31 and 32 does not remove, the meaning which best reconciles the texts, having regard to the object and purpose of the treaty, shall be adopted.'

As argued in this contribution, the principle of good faith is implicit in treaty provisions in much the same sense as many provisions of the two Vienna Conventions incorporating the assumption of the existence of some or other party intention.[68] Common Article 19(b), for example, rests on the assumption that if a treaty includes a provision that explicitly allows particular categories of reservations, this provision implicitly shows that it was the intention of the parties to exclude reservation of other categories. Common Article 30 rests on the

[67] Note that, according to art 92 of the Charter of the UN, the Statute of the ICJ 'forms an integral part' of the Charter.

[68] It should be noted that this contribution does not use the word 'implicit' in the way that it is used by Andrea Dolcetti and Giovanni Battista Ratti in their contribution to this book. Dolcetti and Ratti make a distinction between 'expressed' and 'implicit' norms. For them, '[t]he class of *implicit norms* comprises those norms whose norm-formulation have not been expressly formulated by the law-giver, but are "free-floating" in the legal system.' As this author understands things, the assumption of an obligation to perform a treaty in good faith is expressed implicitly in the conclusion of a treaty by two or more parties in much the same way as the proposition that the captain of a ship may not always be sober can be conveyed by the following brief entry in the ship's log: 'Today, Captain stayed sober.' The mere existence of a treaty provision expresses the obligation to perform this provision in good faith, although it may not do so explicitly, by drawing on the lexicon and grammar of a language. For further reading on this topic see Ulf Linderfalk, 'What Are the Functions of the General Principles? Good Faith and International Legal Pragmatics' (2018) 78 *Zeitschrift für ausländisches öffentliches Recht und Völkerrect*, 1–31.

assumption that if states or organizations conclude two consecutive treaties, to the extent that the two treaties are not compatible with one another, the conclusion of the later treaty implicitly shows that parties preferred the later treaty over the earlier. In parallel to provisions such as these, it would seem natural to argue that if states or international organizations enter into a treaty relationship with one another, the mere fact of the existence of this relationship implicitly shows that it was their intention to perform the treaty in good faith. This conclusion paves the way for a discussion on the relationship between the principle of good faith and a treaty rule conferring a discretion.

As this contribution suggests, there are good reasons to construe this relationship as one between a rule and an exception.[69] In making this suggestion, the contribution does not imply the introduction of a new definition of the concept of an exception. As the contribution fully recognizes, whereas rules may provide exceptions to rules, principles may not. The right of self-defence laid down in Article 51 of the Charter of the United Nations forms an exception to the prohibition on the use of force provided in Article 2(4) of the Charter. The right of hot pursuit forms an exception to the rule that ships navigating on the high seas are subject to the exclusive jurisdiction of the flag state. The principle of good faith, *generally conceived*, does not similarly form an exception to a treaty rule conferring a discretion.

What this contribution suggests is that international lawyers should conceive of the principle of good faith more concretely. It proposes a construction of the principle that brings out its particular significance for the application of treaty-based discretionary powers along the lines of the following two rules:

1. If a discretionary power conferred under a treaty provision is exercised by a party so as to leave a result which is inimical to the purpose of that provision, then that party is performing the provision contrary to the requirement of good faith.
2. If a treaty provision is performed by a party contrary to the requirement of good faith, then this party would have to bear the consequences for not acting in conformity with the provision.

The former norm is a constitutive rule. It defines the concept of good faith for purposes of the exercise of any treaty-based discretionary power. The second norm is a regulative rule. It provides the legal consequences of any treaty performance defined by the constitutive rule as contrary to the principle of good faith.

Several good reasons support this construction. First, the combination of the regulative and constitutive rule clarifies the relationship between the principle of good faith and a treaty rule conferring discretion. If the principle of good faith does not itself form an exception to a treaty rule conferring discretion, then at least the proposed regulative rule does. Perhaps this character of the regulative rule comes out more clearly when phrasing it, instead using a deontic modality: No discretionary power conferred under a treaty provision may be exercised so as to leave a result which is inimical to the purpose of that provision.

Secondly, the construction makes explicit the particular structure underlying this part of international law. As the proposed constitutive rule reads, it forms something of a meddling bridge between the abstract and the concrete dimensions of law—the principle of good faith and the regulative rule, respectively. Thus, the construction emphasizes the

[69] This contribution fully shares the definition of the concept of an exception adopted in the contribution to this book by Jaap Hage, Antonia Waltermann, and Gustavo Arosemena: 'We have defined an exception as the situation in which a rule is applicable to a case, but is nevertheless not applied to this case.'

inductive-deductive nature of legal reasoning. Starting from the proposed constitutive-regulative rule set-up, rather than from the abstract principle of good faith, or a down-to-earth regulative rule such as the prohibition of abuse of rights, international lawyers should have an easier time discussing both the function of the principle of good faith in international law generally and the particular legal consequences of the principle.

Thirdly, the construction helps to clarify what the ICJ has several times emphasized, namely that 'the principle of good faith is not itself a source of obligation where none would otherwise exist'.[70] Any loose talk about the principle of good faith may suggest that it operates in much the same way as equitable principles in the resolution of maritime delimitation disputes. It does not.[71] The normative effect of an equitable principle depends on what other principles are applicable to the resolution of a maritime delimitation dispute. The outcome of the dispute is determined on the overall balance of all applicable principles. The normative effect of the principle of good faith, however, depends on the existence of some communicative behaviour on the part of a state or international organization.[72] Applied to the topic of this contribution, the normative effect of the good faith principle presupposes the existence of a treaty rule conferring discretion. Obviously, to suggest that the principle of good faith be construed as an exception is to assume the existence of a rule to which the exception can apply. As Frederick Schauer puts it in his contribution to this book, 'defeasibility is not a property of rules themselves'.

Fourthly, the construction clarifies the significance of the principle of good faith in a pluralist international legal order. The principle of good faith helps to ensure that decisions reached in the exercise of a legal discretion conferred under a treaty are coherent with the goals of 'the legal microcosm' created by that very treaty. It does not presuppose anything like the existence of universal values or goals set by the international community as a whole. Consequently, if the meaning of good faith bears on the idea of the importance of rationality for the application of international law, then this is only in a limited sense of international law. The assumed rational agents are the parties to the treaty only. The rationality of international law in a broad sense is ensured by other means, such as the categorization of some rules of international law as *jus cogens*.[73]

[70] See *Case Concerning Border and Transborder Armed Actions* (n 17) para 94; *Case Concerning the Land and Maritime Boundary between Cameroon and Nigeria (Cameroon v Nigeria)* (Preliminary Objections, Judgment) [1998] ICJ Rep 275, para 39.

[71] See Kolb (n 7) 13–25.

[72] ibid.

[73] In his contribution to this book, Frederick Schauer makes a distinction between 'internal' and 'external' forms of defeat of a rule. Drawing upon this terminology, the principle of good faith allows for an internal form of defeat of a rule.

15

The Construction of the *Rebus Sic Stantibus* Clause in International Law

Exception, Rule, or Remote Spectator?

*Robert Kolb**

1 Introductory Remarks

With the consolidation of the *pacta sunt servanda* principle during the times of European Enlightenment and its introduction into the modern law of nations,[1] the cornerstone for the 'sanctity' and 'stability' of treaties was laid. This evolution was necessary to give the nascent law of nations among independent states—in the so-called Westphalian system—a solid ground. As a law of coordination between equal entities, international law could not produce its positive law through 'vertical' legislation. It had to channel its sources through 'horizontal' agreements and accepted practices. In such a context, it is fundamental that agreements are binding and stable. As stated as early as in the eighteenth century, without good faith and the binding nature of commitments among states, there can be no law of nations at all.[2] But the question then also appeared as to possible exceptions to the principle of *pacta sunt servanda*.

It stands to reason that *pacta sunt servanda* is not an absolute rule knowing of no exceptions, even if it is logically non-derogable, which is another matter altogether.[3] There are commitments which need not or must not be honoured, either on account of breach by the other party, of coercion in the phase of conclusion, or precisely of changed circumstances. The private law of contracts provides good examples of such exceptions. Once *pacta sunt servanda* is established in a legal order as the main principle providing for treaty stability, it seems that any limitation on its reach must be considered as an 'exception'. From there flow certain normative conclusions, e.g. that it has to be narrowly interpreted.[4] But is this rule/exception frame necessarily true? Are there no other forms of interaction between the principle and its limitations? Does the history of international law not provide examples of this? The following pages will be devoted to a concise analysis of this point.

Before plunging into the matter, some terminological clarification is necessary.[5] First, 'exceptions' have to be distinguished from 'derogations'. A derogation consists of the replacement of a general rule by a particular one applicable between a restricted set of parties. The

* Professor of Public International Law at the University of Geneva.

[1] See Robert Kolb, *The Law of Treaties, An Introduction* (Edward Elgar Publishing 2016) 8 ff.

[2] Cornelius van Bynkershoek, *Quaestiones Juris Publici* (1737) Bk II, ch X: 'Pacta privatorum tuetur ius civils, pacta principum bona fides. Hanc si tollis, tollis mutua inter principes commercia ... quin et tollis ipsum ius gentium'.

[3] See e.g. Georges Perrin, 'La nécessité et les dangers du *jus cogens*' in Christophe Swinarski (ed), *Essays in Honor of Jean Pictet* (Martinus Nijhoff 1984) 751; Ian Sinclair, *The Vienna Convention on the Law of Treaties* (2nd edn, Manchester University Press 1984) 207, 215, 222.

[4] On the reach of this principle of narrow interpretation of exceptions in international law, see Robert Kolb, *Interprétation et creation du droit international* (2006) 673 ff.

[5] For a discussion of 'exceptions' in general see chs 2–5, 9, and 10, among others, in this volume.

Robert Kolb, *The Construction of the* Rebus Sic Stantibus *Clause in Different Phases of International Law* In: *Exceptions in International Law*. Edited by: Lorand Bartels and Federica Paddeu, Oxford University Press (2020). © Lorand Bartels and Federica Paddeu. DOI: 10.1093/oso/9780198789321.003.0015

general rule continues to exist and regulates the relationships between all the subjects not parties to the restricted legal act; and the latter prevails in the relationship of the latter parties. There is thus a split in the legal regime: some rights and obligations apply to some parties and other rights and obligations to other parties. The *lex specialis* rule is an example of this state of affairs. Thus, the general customary rule continues to apply to states at large, but a special derogatory agreement prevails in the inter se dealings of the states parties to it. The term 'abrogation' concerns the termination of a general or special rule by the subjects bound by that rule (i.e. by the 'legislator'). The rule thereby ceases to apply to all its subjects. Conversely, the term 'exception' can have wider or narrower meanings. In its widest meaning, it refers to all circumstances in which a rule will not apply, while remaining formally in force. In this perspective, derogation is covered,[6] but abrogation is not. In a narrower sense, an exception conveys the idea that a rule will not apply at all, while still in force, because *another rule* is carved out from it; or that its application is limited by *another rule* which delimits in some way the proper scope of application of the former. Contrary to derogations, here there is not the interplay between a general and a more special law *ratione personarum*. The exception is situated on the same level of primary legal positions as the rule itself (but it may admittedly be more special *ratione materiae*). A distinct question is whether the rule contains in its own normative description a limitation or exception (e.g. the military necessity clauses built into some rules of the law of armed conflicts[7]) or whether the exception is situated in another, external, rule of the legal order and the limitation is the result of an interpretation and adjustment of the relative reach of both norms (e.g. the conflict between the obligation to perform treaty obligations and the exception under Article 103 of the UN Charter[8]). In short, derogation is a 'vertical matter', and exceptions are a 'horizontal matter'. Finally, it is known that the decision on whether the exception is applicable entails delicate and important issues of power. It has been stressed in some quarters that he who decides authoritatively on the exception, especially in times of crisis, is the true sovereign.[9]

We may now turn to the construction of the *rebus sic stantibus* clause in the context of the rule/exception frame.

2 The Phase of Classical International Law

The *rebus sic stantibus* clause, or fundamental change of circumstances rule, has a long-standing pedigree in international law. Its reach with regard to the idea of 'exceptions' has dramatically changed over time. In the phase of classical international law (nineteenth century up to 1919, or even up to 1945), there were three fundamental approaches to the clause.[10] Each one had its own characteristic relation to the concept of exceptions. It is to be noted that this was a phase when the foundations of international law were not yet solidly in place. There remained many controversial questions on very fundamental matters. The

[6] See e.g. Gérard Cornu, *Vocabulaire juridique* (9th edn, 2011) 423.

[7] See, eg, Art 23(g) of the Convention (IV) respecting the Laws and Customs of War on Land and its annex: Regulations concerning the Laws and Customs of War on Land. The Hague, 18 October 1907 (https://ihl-databases.icrc.org/ihl/INTRO/195).

[8] Which reads as follows: 'In the event of a conflict between the obligations of the Members of the United Nations under the present Charter and their obligations under any other international agreement, their obligations under the present Charter shall prevail.'

[9] See Carl Schmitt, *Politische Theologie, Vier Kapitel zur Lehre von der Souveränität* (1922) 9 ff. And on this position, see generally M Caserta, *La decisione sovrana: politica e autorità fra Thomas Hobbes e Carl Schmitt* (1996).

[10] See Chesney Hill, *The Doctrine 'Rebus Sic Stantibus' in International Law* (1934) 7 ff; Cornelia Rabl-Blaser, *Die clausula rebus sic stantibus im Völkerrecht* (2012) 47 ff.

treatment of the *rebus sic stantibus* clause, which raises essential questions as to the construction of international law, was but an aspect of this search for progressive clarification.

First, there were authors negating the existence of the *rebus sic stantibus* clause in positive international law. For these authors, the doctrine did not in all logic represent an exception to the *pacta sunt servanda*-rule, which remained unaltered. Secondly, a series of authors construed the clause under the colour of some private law analogies. The matter is then one of interpreting the implied will of the parties or of exercising an equitable judicial function with regard to adjustment. The rule is here an exception with regard to *pacta sunt servanda*. Since the normative contours of the *rebus sic stantibus* doctrine remained highly imprecise, the exceptional regime it designated was considered dangerous for the main rule itself. In a sense, the exception was not fully domesticated by the legal order. There was thus a fear that 'he who decides' on this exception, that is, the single states—could be more sovereign than was wished to concede. Finally,, there were authors construing the *rebus sic stantibus* doctrine as a particular legal device of international law in accordance with the unique peculiarities of the latter. The Hegelian German doctrines of E. Kaufmann and C. Bilfinger are here particularly interesting. They dominated in the increasingly successful right-wing thinking of the inter-war times in their country. The clause ceases here to be an exception so as to become itself a fully-fledged rule. At best, *pacta sunt servanda* and *clausula* are both objective legal rules which must be mutually adjusted. But in some conceptions, the *clausula* is rather the rule and *pacta sunt servanda* rather the exception. To sum up: negation—no exception; private law analogies—exception; special *rebus sic stantibus* doctrine in international law—rule against rule. These three categories will now be presented.

First, we discuss the negation of the *rebus sic stantibus* clause. For a series of authors, the *rebus sic stantibus* clause was a political and not a legal maxim.[11] The conditions of its use could not be objectivized in international law to the minimum degree necessary for giving it a legal cloth. Moreover, international practice, where the clause had been often invoked, did not show, in this view, that the argument of its application had been accepted in a single case. Therefore, the doctrine lacked any firm standing in customary international law.[12] Finally, the doctrine carried with it a series of problems of legal policy. These problems made it unacceptable in international law, on account of the particularities of the latter. In the first place, its potential for unleashing instability was considered to be too great, in particular with regard to the fundamental stabilizing function of international treaties.[13] The latter are the main form of 'international legislation'. The intentions of the parties, when concluding a treaty, are precisely to create a certain degree of certainty—which would be lost by a doctrine referring to the great array of regularly occurring changes of circumstances.[14] Dynamism would completely outweigh stability. This is made all the graver by the lack of a standing judge in international law.[15] Arbitration was at that time still in its infancy; and it was burdened with the 'vital interest'

[11] See e.g. Albert Zorn, *Grundzüge des Völkerrechts* (2nd edn, 1903) 147–48; Gabriele Salvioli, 'Sulla clausula rebus sic stantibus nei trattati internazionali' (1914) 3 Rivista di diritto internazionale 275; Sir Hersch Lauterpacht, 'Règles générales du droit de la paix' (1937) 62 RCADI 303 ff and Sir Hersch Lauterpacht, *Private Law Sources and Analogies in International Law* (1927) 169.

[12] See e.g. A Cavaglieri, 'Règles générales du droit de la paix'(1929) 26 RCADI 537. The author adds that the invocation of the *rebus sic stantibus* clause can, however, lead to a negotiation which may alter a treaty by common consent. Other authors accepted that the principle is one of interpretation of the implied will of the parties, and beyond can serve only as an incentive for political negotiation and revision of treaties by consent: see e.g. William W Bishop, 'General Course of Public International Law' (1965) 115 RCADI 361.

[13] But it has also been said that the absence of a *rebus sic stantibus* doctrine allows one party to the treaty to refuse as abusively and unilaterally any modification of the treaty even when this seems to be necessary on account of gravely modified circumstances. See Henri Rolin, 'Les principes de droit international public' (1950) 77 RCADI 439.

[14] See Heinrich Lammasch, *Das Völkerrecht nach dem Kriege* (1917) 151.

[15] Lauterpacht, *Private Law Sources and Analogies in International Law* (n 11) 169–70. See also Hans Kelsen, 'Théorie du droit international public' (1953) 84 RCADI 162–64.

exception clauses.[16] In the second place, the result of the foregoing would be to multiply disputes and terse relations—possibly also war—between states trying to free themselves unilaterally from their treaty commitments. This danger was considered to be unacceptable at a time when the effort to develop an international law of peace loomed large. Overall, if this line of argument is followed this type of exception to *pacta sunt servanda* disappears. The principle *pacta sunt servanda* can be affected by other exceptions, such as termination of agreements by withdrawal or on account of breach, or by some circumstances precluding wrongfulness, but not by the non-existent *rebus sic stantibus* clause.

Secondly, we discuss private law analogies. For a second series of authors, as much as contracts must sometimes be adapted to fundamentally shifting circumstances in municipal law, so also must international treaties be adapted to shifting circumstances in international life. In both legal orders factual situations may change to a degree that the upholding of conventional commitments becomes highly inequitable and impracticable. International law must address these issues, if it does not want to remain irrelevant when the relevant situations occur. The main matrix for the application of the *rebus sic stantibus* clause is then found in the centuries-old experience of the municipal law of contracts, from where some fruitful analogies can be drawn. The most classically positivistic approach was to consider the clause an inherent and tacit part of the main agreement (subjective construction).[17] The parties always intend to agree that their common bond shall apply only to the extent that the circumstances do not fundamentally change. In case of a dispute, the party relying on the clause or the judge must therefore operate on the basis of the tacit intention of the parties and determine whether the change was of such a nature that the intention to maintain the treaty could not be implied. This approach then easily merged into a theory of reasonable expectations and equitable interpretation. The interpreter takes here some distance from the fictional intention of the concrete parties and considers rather the position of typical and reasonable parties as well as equitable arguments (no reasonable party would ...).[18] There was also the rule-oriented approach, independent from intentions (objective construction).[19] Under this conception, the doctrine of *rebus sic stantibus* is a rule of the legal order. It enjoins the legal operator to accept an exception to *pacta sunt servanda* when a change of circumstances has produced such an unforeseen and supplementary onus for one party to the treaty that performance can no longer be required in good faith. This is the case when the relevant obligations have been completely altered to the detriment of one party. In all of these legal constructions, *pacta sunt servanda* is taken as the main principle and as a starting point. The *rebus sic stantibus* clause or doctrine of *rebus sic stantibus* carves out an exception. The reach of the exception is narrower the better and more strictly the criteria for its application are defined; conversely, it is larger the looser and broader the criteria of its application are described. In most of the monographs of the classical phase of international law, as much as in the state practice of that time,[20] the criteria remain ill-defined and rather vague. They hover

[16] For a critique of these clauses, see e.g. Sir Hersch Lauterpacht, *The Function of Law in the International Community* (1933) 3 ff, 26 ff; Hans Kelsen and Robert W Tucker, *Principles of International Law* (2nd edn, 1966) 290–91; Gerald Fitzmaurice, 'The General Principles of International Law Considered from the Standpoint of the Rule of Law' (1957) 92 RCADI 59 ff; see also J H Ralston, *International Arbitration from Athens to Locarno* (1929) 31 ff.

[17] See e.g. William Edward Hall, *A Treatise on International Law* (8th edn, 1924) 407.

[18] Hill (n 10) 77.

[19] See e.g. John Fischer Williams, 'The Permanence of Treaties. The Doctrine of Rebus Sic Stantibus, and Article 19 of the Covenant of the League of Nations' (1928) 22 AJIL 94, 103.

[20] For a thorough analysis of this practice see Rabl-Blaser (n 10) 138 ff.

between various equitable considerations about what can reasonably be demanded and what can reasonably be implied in the will of the parties. All these criteria may be suitable for a judge; he or she can progressively lend precision to them in jurisprudence. On the level of self-judging qualifications by each state,[21] the room for arguing the exception manifestly increases. Since the doctrine was not yet legally digested in this phase of development of international law, the *rebus sic stantibus* clause implied a potentially significant 'exception' put at the heart of the legal system, that is, around the binding force of treaties. Reflecting that for the dominant positivistic theories of the time all international law flowed from agreements and treaties, the tremendous reach of the exception becomes palpable. The fear to see the 'exception' bolster itself to the level of a crypto-rule of paramount reach explains the great suspicion the *rebus sic stantibus* clause continued to arouse in many quarters—especially in the inter-war period with its virulent agitation against the peace settlement of Versailles. Finally, we note that the exception comes from outside the rule. It is not inherent in *pacta sunt servanda*. Rather, the latter principle has to be adjusted with another one, be it of interpretation or of substantive law, whereby in certain circumstances an exception will be conceded and the duty of performance may disappear.

Thirdly, we discuss a peculiar *rebus sic stantibus* clause for international law. The most interesting theories are embedded within a certain conception of international law as a whole. The *rebus sic stantibus* clause looms large as a signpost of its character and reach. These are theories influenced by the Hegelian perception of the state as being the highest legal-political reality on earth. International law is inferior to the state and its internal law. It is considered to be an external projection of the state and remaining subject to its shifting wills, which it cannot ultimately constrain. The most coherent and powerful explanation of the *rebus sic stantibus* clause in this context is the one by E. Kaufmann.[22] We shall concentrate on it more extensively here, since it is representative of a common belief in German political quarters on the right wing.

Kaufmann considers that all legal orders are of either of the following two types: 'law of subordination' (state, social law) or 'law of coordination' (international law, individual law).[23] He gives a special meaning to the concept of 'law of coordination'. It is not the same as the one used in the Anglo-Saxon world in the context of the 'common consent of nations' as the basis for a common bond between equals.[24] For Kaufmann, international law is a singular, purely 'individual-oriented law' (*Individualrecht*).[25] By this he means that international law is based merely on the will and interests of the individual state and that the latter remains pre-eminent in case of conflict. The state binds itself under the condition that the interests it pursues continue to be granted by the international engagements incurred; if these interests are jeopardized or undercut by the international obligations assumed, the latter cease to bind the state.[26] The state can then denounce the agreement with immediate effect.[27] Thus, the *rebus sic stantibus* clause is inherent in the legal order and is placed at its very apex. The result is, moreover, that international law's basis is the self-obligation of each state;[28] in all

[21] Which is the rule under international law. See Pierre Klein, 'Les prétentions des Etats à la mise en œuvre unilatérale du droit international' (2010) 43 RBDI 141 ff.

[22] Erich Kaufmann, *Das Wesen des Völkerrechts und die Clausula rebus sic stantibus* (1911).

[23] ibid 128.

[24] On this doctrine see Antonio Truyol y Serra and Robert Kolb, *Doctrines sur le fondement du droit des gens* (2007) 69–70.

[25] Kaufmann, *Das Wesen des Völkerrechts und die Clausula rebus sic stantibus* (n 22) VI, 69.

[26] ibid 59, 204.

[27] ibid 59, 221.

[28] ibid 61 ff.

coherence, the latter remains free to unbind itself at any time. International law is there for the state, which is the ultimate moral reality in the world, not the state for international law. The state is in this way placed above its treaties;[29] its self-preservation is the highest right under international law.[30]

The character of international law as 'individual law' further entails that, contrary to municipal law, which is a law of subordination, it has no specific aim in itself. There are no supra-individual values which it protects; there is no international community; no superior moral criterion to the one of the single state and its interests.[31] The consequence is that international law lacks a substantive criterion, necessary in all legal orders, as to how to distribute the scarce resources, that is, power, wealth, richness, etc. Since there is no superior power establishing the criteria for this distribution through legal processes, the solution has to accrue through the maxim: 'only he who can, may' (*nur wer kann darf*).[32] Hence, in international law power and law are identified.[33] Unilateral action creates facts; these facts are covered and justified by international law. The state will thus acquire its position in world history by increasing its power and by exercising it. Moreover, it will have to be prudent and vigilant with regard to the power of others: no law will protect it; only its power will form a shield. In the event of a conflict of interests on distributional issues, war will ultimately decide. War is an instrument of law, not simply of power; it proves one's place in the world's moral order; only those who are strong enough to win their cause have a moral justification for this cause.[34] This is also why a world state is not possible. Because there is no outside concurring power, the mechanism of competition described would disappear. The order thus created would quickly be petrified and become sterile.[35] History must continue to be made out of irrationality, that is, of striving, risking, and winning.[36] The *rebus sic stantibus* clause is the main tool to ensure that history is not stultified.[37]

With regard to the *rebus sic stantibus* clause, Kaufmann proposes the most radical doctrine. It must be admitted that it is a grandiose sketch of an international law unheard of up to the time of publication of this small and influential monograph in 1911. As can be seen, the *rebus sic stantibus* clause ceases to be an exception. Perhaps it is a rule, as is *pacta sunt servanda*, and both are then concurring in their respective spheres of application,[38] one being mainly called upon to limit the other. More precisely, *pacta sunt servanda* has priority (and is consequently the rule) in the most frequent cases where the interests of the state command to uphold the international obligation. Conversely, the *rebus sic stantibus* clause has priority (and is consequently the rule) in the restricted domain of important or vital interests of the state. In the result, international law is not fully binding law. It is law placed under some resolutory condition, that is, that a certain situation does not become contrary to the interests of the engaged state. In the latter case, the state can denounce its international commitments at any time by relying on the principle of the *rebus sic stantibus* clause. The *rebus*

[29] ibid 181.
[30] ibid 182, 192, 195, 204 ff.
[31] ibid 179.
[32] ibid 151.
[33] ibid 153.
[34] ibid 151–53.
[35] ibid 136.
[36] ibid 231.
[37] ibid 64–65.
[38] This was still Kaufmann's position in 1935. See Erich Kaufmann, 'Règles générales du droit de la paix' (1935) 54 RCADI 517: '[L]e principe de la clause *rebus sic stantibus*, loin d'être une dérogation au principe *pacta sunt servanda* fait partie de son contenu.'

sic stantibus clause is at the apex of the system: it, and not *pacta sunt servanda*, controls the gates of what is binding and what is not binding in international law. Note that vital interests are not linked only to territory or armies. Each type of obligation can at a certain moment conflict with important state interests.[39] In short, the clause here functionally takes the place *pacta sunt servanda* has in the consent-based positivistic theories of international law. It is the Archimedean point for the basis of obligation or non-obligation in the international legal order.

In order to be complete, we must emphasize that Kaufmann insists that there are some inherent limits to the invocation of the *rebus sic stantibus* clause, so that abuse is not to be feared. He claims first that only changes of circumstances 'destroying' the state's interests can lead to the liberation of the state under the *rebus sic stantibus* doctrine, not any type of change.[40] In most cases, moreover, there is a solidarity of interest in maintaining the international regime, e.g. in the cointext of exchange of mail (the Universal Postal Union) or in other matters of non-political cooperation. There is also the fear of reprisals and other reactions by the party suffering from the invocation of *rebus sic stantibus*, tempering the propensity to invoke the clause.[41] In actual fact, the *rebus sic stantibus* clause will therefore, according to Kaufmann, be less intrusive than it might first appear.

Carl Bilfinger, who was to become a Nazi international lawyer, picked up and developed this theory further. According to his conception, international society is based on systems of equilibria of power, that is, on a basic political and not a legal fact.[42] International law cannot fully regulate this primary fact of power. International law is composed of two separate circles:[43] technical, humanitarian, or private (non-political) matters, where it will produce functioning norms; and political matters, such as alliances, pacts of non-aggression, peace treaties, war, reprisals, and the like, where it will remain under the control of political forces. The term 'political' designates all the domain which is related to the very existence of the state.[44] Vital interests of states are at stake here. The rules of international law differ in both spheres of regulation. In particular, in political matters, a faculty of denunciation of treaties at all times, the availability of the *rebus sic stantibus* clause and the non-mandatory arbitration of disputes is granted to each state. Thus, a treaty is not simply law because it contains legal obligations; it depends on the fundamental bases of the international community of states with the bipartition of matters presented.[45] A provision in international law contrary to the independence of states in political matters is void and inapplicable.[46] In other words, international law is limited by the independence of states. Finally, there is the question of change (so-called peaceful change). In the absence of a super-state, it is difficult to adapt international law to changing realities. From there flows the particular importance of the *rebus sic stantibus* clause.[47] However, it is wrong to oppose stability (*pacta sunt servanda*) and dynamism (*clausula*). In reality, there is one single norm equilibrating the static and the dynamic element.[48] *Pacta sunt servanda* does not extend at all to inapplicable treaties (i.e. the ones contrary to the independence and vital interests of the state). The *rebus sic stantibus* clause opens the way to a faculty of unilateral denunciation of such obsolescent obligations.[49]

[39] Kaufmann, *Das Wesen des Völkerrechts und die Clausula rebus sic stantibus* (n 22) 220.
[40] ibid 59.
[41] ibid 220–21.
[42] Carl Bilfinger, 'Les bases fondamentales de la Communauté des Etats' (1938) 63 RCADI 138.
[43] ibid 141 ff. See also Carl Bilfinger, 'Betrachtungen über politisches Recht' (1929) 1 ZaöRV 57 ff.
[44] Bilfinger, 'Les bases fondamentales de la Communauté des Etats' (n 42) 144.
[45] ibid 150.
[46] ibid 198.
[47] ibid 205.
[48] ibid 206.
[49] ibid 209.

The main function of the *rebus sic stantibus* clause is to ensure the necessary dynamism of international law and its adaptability to changing power constellations.[50]

As can be seen, Bilfinger follows in the footsteps of Kaufmann. The essential differences between both German authors are the more rigid and categorical bipartition between political and non-political law by Bilfinger. It is easy to see that in this bipartition properly so-called international law can exist only in non-political matters, where it is not to be expected that the independence, honour, or vital interests of states could be affected. In the field of political international law, all obligations are political rather than legal: the rule *pacta sunt servanda* does not prevail over independence and vital interests as self-judged by any single state. One of the main instruments to achieve this *capitis diminutio* of international law is the *rebus sic stantibus* clause. It ensures significant dynamism, which ultimately means freedom from legal constraint. Therefore, states cannot rely on the binding nature of political commitments. They have to remain vigilant—*vigilanti jus est scriptum*!, Kaufmann often writes—and preserve their interests by marshalling superior power. The race for power and armaments is inevitable.

Of interest for our subject matter is the conception according to which *pacta sunt servanda* and *clausula* are not opposites. There is no rule and exception relationship. Both positions express one single rule dominating the political law of nations. Concretely, this means that the *clausula* is at least as much 'rule' and not exception as is *pacta sunt servanda*; and, in the context of political law, the *rebus sic stantibus* clause may well be more the rule than the exception. At least conceptually, the *rebus sic stantibus* clause is the primary principle protecting the independence and self-preservation of the state. And self-preservation is the highest legal value. *Pacta sunt servanda*, in this area, gives way and follows suit: it will be honoured only as long as the interests of the states so command. From *pacta sunt servanda* we move towards the rule that agreements can or could be honoured, if … (*pacta servare possumus*). The binding force of international law is denied in its core. These are the laws of political international law. In the contexts of non-political law, all is reversed.

Overall, the *rebus sic stantibus* clause plays in these last theories a distinctively different role from the one under the legal cloth of 'private law' analogy.

3 The Phase of Codification: the Vienna Convention on the Law of Treaties of 1969

From the emphasis placed in this chapter on historical analysis rather than on the exegesis of the positive law of the day, this section is brief. As is well known, the Vienna Convention on the Law of Treaties (VCLT) of 1969[51] eventually codified the *rebus sic stantibus* clause in its Article 62.[52] The main characteristic of the regulation is that the *rebus sic stantibus* clause is now given a precise legal cloth. From our perspective, three things are to be noted.

[50] ibid 221.

[51] For some short reflections on this codification of the law see Robert Ago, 'Droit des traités à la lumière de la Convention de Vienne—Introduction' (1971) 134 RCADI 297.

[52] The text of this provision reads as follows:

1. A fundamental change of circumstances which has occurred with regard to those existing at the time of the conclusion of a treaty, and which was not foreseen by the parties, may not be invoked as a ground for terminating or withdrawing from the treaty unless:
   (a) the existence of those circumstances constituted an essential basis of the consent of the parties to be bound by the treaty; and
   (b) the effect of the change is radically to transform the extent of obligations still to be performed under the treaty.

First, the *rebus sic stantibus* clause is cast in the complexion of a narrowly defined exception. This is mainly evidenced by the fact that, among the provisions on termination of treaties, the International Law Commission (ILC) has chosen, and the Conference maintained, a negative formulation. According to the text of Article 62 a state may *not* invoke the change of circumstances unless[53] we note that the same formulation has been chosen in the law of state responsibility for the 'state of necessity' (circumstance precluding wrongfulness, Article 25 of the ILC Articles on State Responsibility of 2001).[54] The reason for this negative formulation is that the state of necessity had an equally troubled historical record as the *rebus sic stantibus* clause. It had been used in a 'Hegelian' cloth in order to cast away the binding nature of 'disturbing' international legal obligations, for example, the Belgian neutrality in 1914. This negative formulation is meant to carry with it the prevalence of restrictive interpretation: exceptions are to be narrowly construed.

Secondly, comparing the legal conditions listed in Article 62 for the applicability of the doctrine *rebus sic stantibus* with the ones upheld in writings of the nineteenth and the beginning of the twentieth century, one sees a notable increase in precision. The conditions to be fulfilled are described as precisely as possible; they are cumulative; and they are given some normative addition in the extensive ILC Commentary to Article 62.[55] The doctrine is presented as an objective rule of international law and not as an implied condition of the parties' will.

Thirdly, the conditions are so strict that since 1969 the *rebus sic stantibus* clause has not been invoked a single time with success in international litigation.[56] The *rebus sic stantibus* clause has also rarely been invoked in state practice when compared with the nineteenth century. At this now remote time, the invocation of the clause was frequent and treaties were sometimes amended or terminated on its account, even if the process remained political and ambiguous. This state of affairs provides evidence of the progressive strengthening of the legal hold exercised by international law. In a sense, the codification of the VCLT of 1969 has achieved the domestication of the *rebus sic stantibus* clause. It has so much tuned it down to the exigencies of law and of the stability of treaties that the doctrine has to a large extent become toothless. The old distinction between political and non-political treaties has been completely given up.

2. A fundamental change of circumstances may not be invoked as a ground for terminating or withdrawing from a treaty:
   (a) if the treaty establishes a boundary; or
   (b) if the fundamental change is the result of a breach by the party invoking it either of an obligation under the treaty or of any other international obligation owed to any other party to the treaty.
3. If, under the foregoing paragraphs, a party may invoke a fundamental change of circumstances as a ground for terminating or withdrawing from a treaty it may also invoke the change as a ground for suspending the operation of the treaty.

On this key provision see e.g. Malcolm Shaw and Caroline Fournet, 'Article 62' in Olivier Corten and Pierre Klein (eds), *The Vienna Convention on the Law of Treaties, A Commentary, vol II* (2011) 1411 ff; Mark E Villiger, *Commentary on the 1969 Vienna Convention on the Law of Treaties* (2009) 762 ff (with an extensive bibliography); Thomas Giegerich, 'Article 62' in Olivier Dörr and K Schmalenbach (eds), *Vienna Convention on the Law of Treaties, A Commentary* (2012) 1067 ff.

[53] 'A fundamental change of circumstances ... may not be invoked as a ground for terminating or withdrawing from the treaty unless . . ': Article 62, Vienna Convention on the Law of Treaties of 1969.

[54] For the latter see James Crawford, *The International Commission's Articles on State Responsibility* (2002) 178 ff.

[55] See ILC, 'Commentary to Article 62' (1966) 2 Yearbook of the International Law Commission 256 ff, art 59 as it then was.

[56] On the salient aspects of this practice see Rabl-Blaser (n 10) 261 ff.

It is apparent that the logic of the *rebus sic stantibus* clause as an exception to *pacta sunt servanda* has now reached its apogee. *Pacta sunt servanda* is seen as the 'lifeblood' of international law. The *rebus sic stantibus* clause is a dangerous exception to it, with its potential for open-ended dynamism and heroic unilateral rejection of commitments. It must be reduced in such a way as not to allow abusive subjective interpretations, offending against the international rule of law.[57] The termination of treaty obligations on account of change must be sought under other rules of the law of treaties. These are a sort of *leges speciales* to the general *rebus sic stantibus* clause: termination or suspension on account of breach; on account of withdrawal (where permitted); on account of war; on account of a new agreement (revision or derogatory agreements); and so on. It appears that, in the modern context, these substitutes function well and that there is hardly a need for the general saving clause of the *rebus sic stantibus* clause—which still arouses some ill-feeling among international lawyers. To frame an argument under the *rebus sic stantibus* clause is to risk losing some empathy by the opposing party and by any judge. Consequently a state would today show some hesitation and disinclination to invoke the *rebus sic stantibus* clause, so much is that linked up with an argument seemingly contesting the binding nature of treaties and so exacting are the conditions to be fulfilled for securing success. Should one shoulder great legal difficulties for a morally stigmatizing argument? In one word, the exception-logic under the *rebus sic stantibus* clause cannot be pushed any further.

4 Conclusion

The conclusion of this contribution is that the *rebus sic stantibus* clause has undergone important changes in its legal clothing. In the phase of classical international law, its legal standing and construction was uncertain. If it was often invoked in a shifting practice, some authors confined it to a merely political argument leading possibly, if there was some form of agreement, to a revision or termination of treaties. For another school of thought, the municipal law experience of contract law showed that the *rebus sic stantibus* clause had to be constructed in international law as an exception to the *pacta sunt servanda* principle, since it was inequitable to insist on the binding force of obligations whatever circumstances—profoundly changing the mutual dealings—had in fact occurred. However, the law of treaties was not yet developed to the point to support a fully-fledged and reflected *rebus sic stantibus* doctrine, gifted with a set of precisely and narrowly defined conditions. Thus, the exception of the *rebus sic stantibus* clause tended to loom large—probably too large. Finally, there were schools of thought for which the *rebus sic stantibus* clause designated the greater or lesser area of an international law of 'vital interests'. Within that law, the escape clause of the *rebus sic stantibus* clause was as much the rule as *pacta sunt servanda* itself—if it was not even the main rule, with *pacta sunt servanda* featuring as the exception.

The process of codification of the VCLT brought to an end this phase of uncertainty and turmoil. It fixed the law in clear terms, and, as far as the formerly monstrous *rebus sic stantibus* clause is concerned, eventually laid it to rest. The conditions of the doctrine are now so narrowly defined, and the modern setting of international society

[57] See Giegerich (n 52) 1069.

has so much evolved, that the *rebus sic stantibus* clause has only rarely been invoked in international practice and, even more so, never with forensic success. Overall, the *clausula* has thus passed from heroic Hercules to gently civilized Melpomene … and, with the latter, paradoxically said definitively farewell to its tragic and grandiose phase of youth.

16

Angst of the *Exceptio Inadimplenti Non Est Adimplendum* in International Law

*Malgosia Fitzmaurice**

1 Introduction

The legal character of the *exceptio inadimplenti non est adimplendum* or *exceptio inadimpleti contractus* is one of those institutions in international law the legal character of which remains somewhat shrouded in mystery.[1] In broad brushstrokes, the *exceptio* implies that 'a condition for one party's compliance with a synallagmatic obligation is the continued compliance of the other party with that obligation'.[2]

There are a myriad of unresolved issues concerning the *exceptio* which are both of a theoretical and practical nature. As will be explained in the last part of this chapter, there are different forms of the *exceptio*—a fact which is frequently overlooked. Similarly, the relationship of the *exceptio* with the rules on countermeasures and material breach of a treaty are very unclear and have yet to be examined and analysed in depth. From a more theoretical point of view, it is interesting to explore whether the *exceptio* belongs to general principles of law as enshrined in Article 38(1)(c) of the Statute of the International Court of Justice (ICJ) or, rather, whether it should be approached as 'essentially a principle relating to cognate obligations', which exist more often in treaty obligations.[3]

This chapter will be structured in the following way. After this introduction, section 2 will deal with the notion of the *exceptio*. It comprises two sub-sections on (2.1) domestic legal systems and (2.2–2.4) the international level, analysing the work of the International Law Commission (ILC). The third section will be devoted to the relevant case law, while the fourth section will explore the relationship between the law of treaties and the law of state responsibility with regard to the *exceptio*. The fifth section will be devoted to theoretical considerations concerning the legal character of the *exceptio*.

* Professor of Public International Law, Queen Mary University of London, m.fitzmaurice@qmul.ac.uk. All internet references were last accessed on 22 August 2017, when this contribution was completed. The author would like to thank Dr Marco Longobardo for his invaluable comments on the final draft of this chapter.

[1] On this topic see generally James Crawford, 'Second Report on State Responsibility' A/CN.4498/Add.2 (1999) paras 314–29; Danae Azaria, 'Exception of Non-Performance' Max Planck Encyclopedia of Public International Law (2015) http://opil.ouplaw.com/view/10.1093/law:epil/9780199231690/law-9780199231690-e2130; James Crawford and Simon Olleson, 'The Exception of Non-Performance: Links between the Law of Treaties and the Law of State Responsibility' (2000) 21 Australian Yearbook of International Law 55; Filippo Fontanelli, 'The Invocation of the Exception of Non-Performance: A Case Study on the Role and Application of General Principles in International Law of Contractual Origin' (2012) 1 Cambridge Journal of International and Comparative Law 119; Serena Forlati, 'Reactions to Non-Performance of Treaties in International Law' (2012) 25 Leiden Journal of International Law 759.

[2] Crawford, 'Second Report' (n 1) para 314.

[3] Donald W Greig, 'Reciprocity, Proportionality and the Law of Treaties' (1994) 34 Virginia Journal of International Law 295, 400.

Malgosia Fitzmaurice, *Angst of the* Exceptio Inadimplenti Non Est Adimplendum *in International Law* In: *Exceptions in International Law*. Edited by: Lorand Bartels and Federica Paddeu, Oxford University Press (2020). DOI: 10.1093/oso/9780198789321.003.0016

2 The Notion of the *Exceptio Inadimplenti Non Est Adimplendum* in Domestic Legal Systems and in International Law

2.1 The *exceptio* in domestic legal systems

This sub-section is devoted to the question of whether *exceptio* exists in domestic *fora* in both civil and common law systems.

As a starting point, it should be noted that the institution of the *exceptio* is not found in the sources of Roman law. The interpreters of Roman law elaborate the theory of the *exceptio non adimpleti* from the sources pertaining to contracts with *argentarii* (bankers). The classical Roman law includes the *exceptio mercis non traditiae*, which, however, did not exist in the context of sale contracts. These contracts operated on the basis of good faith, which is considered to be sufficient in granting protection to a party who suspended its performance of a contract.[4] In Roman law, in relation to contracts of sale and, generally, in the context of actions in contract, the operation of good faith always allowed and justified the legitimate suspension of performance.[5]

The principle of the defence of non-performance can be found in many legal systems and traditions of Continental Europe.[6] The same rule is applied in states which adopted the German legal tradition, such as the Japanese[7] and the Chinese[8] Civil Codes. The Austrian Civil Code includes this principle in relation to exchange and sale.[9] The French Code Civil does not include a special provision on '*l'exception d'inéxecution*' but this can be derived from other provisions relating to sales,[10] barter,[11] and deposit.[12] From 1914, French case law has applied this principle to all contracts creating bilateral obligations. The French theory of exception of non-performance is particularly interesting as it has similar features to its construct in international law. The most important theory concerning this principle was elaborated by Henri Capitant.[13] This theory is premised on the idea that that the obligation of each party finds its reason in the performance of the other party. Therefore, in accordance with Article 1131 of the Code Civil, the non-performance of one party cancels the basis of the performance of the other and the obligation becomes without effect.[14] This theory was criticized on the ground that Article 1131 of the Code Civil pertains only to the initial validity of contracts and that the absence of cause is the nullity of the contract (not its suspension). It is argued that such an interpretation limits the operation of contracts exclusively to perfectly synallagmatic contracts.[15] Another explanation of the exception in the French law is that it should be approached as arising either from implied will of the parties or from the nature and common origins of reciprocal obligations. Under the first of these theories (which resembles the English construct), the exception stems from the interpretation of the agreement

[4] On this topic see generally Francesco Parisi, Marta Cenini, and Barbara Luppi, 'Enforcing Bilateral Promises: A Comparative Law and Economics Perspective' (2013) 2 European Review of Private Law 423, 431.

[5] ibid.

[6] See e.g. the German Bürgerliches Gesetzbuch (BGB) s 320; the Spanish Código Civil art 1426; the Swiss Code des Obligations art 82; and the Italian *Codice Civile* art 1460.

[7] See Civil Code, art 533.

[8] See Uniform Contract Law of the People's Republic of China (UCL) art 68.

[9] See s 1652 on exchange, applied to sale by s 1060, cited in Parisi, Cenini, and Luppi (n 4) 431–32.

[10] See Code Civil arts 1612 and 1652.

[11] ibid art 1704.

[12] ibid art 1948.

[13] Henri Capitant, *De la Cause des Obligations* (Dalloz 1923), as cited in Crawford and Olleson (n 1) 68.

[14] Crawford and Olleson (n 1) 68.

[15] ibid.

of the parties, which results in concluding that each party has consented to perform only if the other party also performed.[16] According to the other more comprehensive theory, the principle of non-performance is extended to other reciprocal relationships involving an imperfectly synallagmatic contract and also to relationships where there is no contract at all but only obligations of restitution resulting from the declaration of nullity or judicial resolution of contract, allowing one party to refuse to return to the performance of the other party until the other party is ready to rerun the performance received. Therefore, in the French legal system the maxim *inadimplenti non est adimplendum* has a wider construct.[17] However, the clear and fast differentiation of the application of the exception in French law is rather difficult as there are other competing institutions applied in French courts which overlap, such as the *compensation* and then the right of *retention*, which may be regarded as a sub-category of the exception (however, only within the legal context of property). As is explained, as a general rule, in the case of bilateral breaches, the judge establishes which breach prevails to ascertain which one is justified. The court analyses the behaviour of the parties in its entirety to determine which party is liable for the most relevant breaches, which resulted in provoking the behaviour of the other party 'and the consequent alternation of the contractual synallagma'.[18] Having determined which party breached the contract first,[19] the rules on damages and restitution are applicable. In cases of the impossibility of the determination of who was responsible for the most relevant breaches, breaches are considered to be equivalent and in some states (such as the Philippines, Article 1192 of the Civil Code), the contract will be extinguished with both parties bearing their respective costs. In Italy, in a similar situation, the judge cannot extinguish the contract but can declare the rejection of both claims owing to the lack of facts supporting therm. The opposite solution is adopted in the French legal system, where the judger can declare the termination of the contract (Article 1184 of the French Code Civil) of the parties for 'mutual and shared torts'.[20]

The most important feature of the *exceptio* in civil legal systems is that it is considered in a different way from the termination of the obligation. Rather, the *exceptio* is seen as a circumstance precluding wrongfulness.[21] Crawford, in his Second Report on State Responsibility, relies on Treitel, according to whom

> [t]ermination brings to an end each party's duty to perform, though the circumstances making the remedy available may give the injured party a right to damages; it also gives the injured party a right to the return of his own performance on restoring what he has received under the contract. The exception does not produce these effects, but only gives rise to what has been called a 'waiting position'. It is a 'dilatory plea' which does not terminate the contract but merely entitles the injured party for the time being to refuse to perform his part.[22]

In common law systems, the maxim *inadimplenti non est adimplendum* is not used or known but, as Crawford and Olleson explain, 'parallel effects are produced by an analysis of the

[16] ibid.
[17] ibid.
[18] Parisi, Cenini, and Luppi (n 4) 432.
[19] Crawford and Olleson (n 1) 71.
[20] Parisi, Cenini, and Luppi (n 4) 432–33.
[21] Crawford, 'Second Report' (n 1) para 318.
[22] GH Treitel, *Remedies for Breach of Contract. A Comparative Account* (Clarendon Press 1987) 310–11, cited in Crawford, 'Second Report' (n 1) para 318.

obligation of the parties, leading to the conclusion that the performance of each party's obligation is subject to the "condition" of performance by the other party'.[23] The same result can be achieved by the means of the interpretation. Since the eighteenth century, British courts, absent express terms assigning an order of performance, have tended to classify the obligation of each party as being interdependent, that is, each party agreed to perform only if the other party did. A similar legal position was adopted in the United States in the case of an 'exchange of promises' (which is a contract where the performance of both sides is due at some point in the future). If the analysis of the contract suggests that the obligations of both parties are to be performed simultaneously, non-performance of one party results in the lack of the corresponding performance of the other party. Such non-performance does not incur liability, as it caused no breach. Similarly to the French system, there are other legal institutions which have approximate legal characteristics, such as a situation of termination or rescission for breach, which makes their clear separation from exception of non-performance difficult to distinguish.

In conclusion, it may be said that there are significant differences between civil and common legal systems regarding the defence of non-performance and that, in a civil law regime, it is much better developed. However, even this short outline clearly evidences that such an *exceptio* is a principle of domestic legal regimes both in civil law and, to some extent, in common law regimes.

2.2 The *exceptio* in international law: general introduction

This sub-section is mostly devoted to the work of the International Law Commission (ILC) on the subject of the *exceptio*, although the ILC has not addressed it extensively. In general brushstrokes, it may be said that, similarly to domestic law, the legal character of the exception of non-performance in international law is based on the premise that performance of an obligation is permitted to be withheld if the other party has failed to perform the same or a related obligation.[24] Accordingly, the exception benefits only the innocent party, which is entitled to suspend its treaty obligations, while the other party is still required to implement its obligations under the treaty. The most important feature of such obligations is that they are based on synallagma and that their performance is conditioned upon the performance of the same obligation, or of another of a different kind.[25] The *exceptio* straddles both the law of treaties and the law of state responsibility. For this reason, this topic was debated by the ILC during its works both on the codification of the 1969 Vienna Convention on the Law of Treaties and on the codification of the 2001 Articles on State Responsibility. James Crawford, dealing with the *exceptio* in his Second Report on State Responsibility, has emphasized the underlying domestic law concepts of this principle.[26]

However, the exception is recognized also in specific areas of international law, such as in international commercial law. Article 80 of the 1980 UNCITRAL Convention on Contracts for the International Sale of Goods provides simply that '[a] party may not rely on a failure of the other party to perform, to the extent that such failure was caused by the first party's

[23] Crawford and Olleson (n 1) 70.

[24] Danae Azaria, *Treaties on Transit of Energy via Pipelines and Countermeasures* (Oxford University Press 2005) 151–52. See also *Application of the Interim Accord of 13 September 1995 (The former Yugoslav Republic of Macedonia v Greece)* (Separate Opinion of Judge Simma) [2011] ICJ Rep 695.

[25] Azaria (n 24) 152.

[26] Crawford 'Second Report' (n 1) paras 318–19.

act or omission'.[27] As Crawford observed, this formulation appears to indicate that, for the purposes of Article 80, it is not relevant whether the act or omission which caused the non-performance was or was not wrongful.[28] The *exceptio* is also included in the UNIDROIT Principles of International Commercial Contracts. According to Article 7.1, '[w]here the parties are to perform simultaneously, either party may withhold performance', in a situation where the other party has not performed.[29]

The lack of agreement—bordering open confusion—regarding the precise legal nature of this concept is clear from the discussions within the ILC at the time of the codification of the rules of state responsibility where it was mooted that the *exceptio* be retained as Article 30 bis of the Articles—a suggestion which failed to reach consensus.[30] It was suggested that this exception has a character similar to countermeasures and *force majeure*, and that it usually appears in synallagmatic relations.[31] In the context of the law of treaties, according to the ILC, the *exceptio* does not pertain to the performance of a treaty per se, but rather, it is relevant in cases where, without suspension or termination of a treaty, a state is nonetheless released from the performance of some treaty obligations due to certain circumstances.[32] The inclusion of a special provision relating to non-performance of treaty obligations in the VCLT was accepted and emerged as Article 60 of the VCLT, which is confined to 'material breaches'. The consequences of breach of obligation generally were left to be addressed in the Articles on State Responsibility.[33] Crawford and Olleson express the view that the *exceptio* (which might conceivably be applicable in the case of non-material breaches) 'has fallen between the two instruments'.[34]

The 'material breach' of a treaty is defined in Article 60(3) of the VCLT. According to this provision, a material breach 'consists in (a) [a] repudiation of the treaty not sanctioned by the [VCLT] or (b) [t]he violation of a provision essential to the accomplishment of the object or purpose of the treaty'. In other words, separate possibilities are envisaged for the occurrence of a material breach; conditions (a) and (b) are not to be taken as cumulative.[35] According to Article 60(1) of the VCLT, in cases of a material breach of a bilateral treaty by one party, the other may not only terminate the treaty, but also suspend it in whole or in part. In the case of a multilateral treaty, the only possibility for a party aggrieved by a material breach is to suspend the treaty in its relations with the defaulting state, since termination is a matter concerning all the parties to the treaty.[36] There are also three substantive differences between Article 60 of the VCLT and the *exceptio*. Article 60 relates only to material breaches, whilst the *exceptio* pertains to breaches of every kind; Article 60 allows the suspension of the whole treaty, or any combination of its provisions, whereas the *exceptio* only allows non-performance of the same or a closely related obligation; finally, the exception is not subject to the formal procedure for suspension in Article 65 of the VCLT, whereas material breach is.[37]

[27] 1489 UNTS 3.

[28] Crawford 'Second Report' (n 1) para 319.

[29] ibid.

[30] Part 1 of the Draft Articles was adopted in 'Report of the Commission to the General Assembly on the work of its thirty-second session' (1980) 2(2) Yearbook of the International Law Commission. See also James Crawford, 'Revising the Draft Articles on State Responsibility' (1999) 10 European Journal of International Law 435, 456–57.

[31] Crawford, 'Second Report' (n 1) paras 314–29.

[32] ibid para 324.

[33] Sir Gerald Fitzmaurice, 'Second Report on the Law of Treaties' (1957) 2 Yearbook of the International Law Commission 57.

[34] Crawford and Olleson (n 1) 66.

[35] Mohammed M Gomaa, *Suspension of Termination of Treaties on Grounds of Breach* (Martinus Nijhoff Publishers 1996) 25.

[36] Crawford, 'Second Report' (n 1) para 324.

[37] ibid para 325.

Although proportionality is not one of the conditions specified in Article 60 for responding to material breach, it has been suggested that proportionality is relevant for the application of Article 60 by virtue of (i) the restrictive definition of material breach and (ii) the limitations that are imposed on recourse to suspension and termination, which are such as to render it 'not a disproportionate response'.[38]

Whereas material breach has its *sedes materiae* in a treaty, countermeasures are responses of states relating to a breach of a treaty outside the realm of the law of treaties. Article 49 of the 2001 Articles on State Responsibility for Internationally Wrongful Acts (ARSIWA) defines the object of countermeasures. Countermeasures are limited to the non-performance for the time being of international obligations of the state taking the measures towards the responsible state, and shall, as far as possible, be taken in such a way as to permit the resumption of performance of the obligations in question (Article 49(2)). The measures taken must be proportionate or commensurate to the injury suffered, and there are also other stringent conditions attached to their use (Article 49(3)). Similarly to Article 60(2)(c) of the VCLT, Articles 42 and 48 of the ARSIWA concern the invocation of responsibility by a state other than the injured state. It entitles such states to demand cessation of the breach and that reparation be made to the injured state or the beneficiaries of the obligation breached. Crawford noted that, although the *exceptio* has a much more limited application than countermeasures, it is free from the limitations linked to countermeasures since it 'is a more specific response to a particular breach, lacking the opprobrium often associated with countermeasures'.[39] As Crawford observed, even a legal system rejecting countermeasures, self-help other than in self-defence, and reprisals, may still find a role for the *exceptio*.[40] The ILC has already rejected the category of reciprocal countermeasures beforehand during its codification of the law on state responsibility, as a distinct category of countermeasures on the ground that 'they did not deserve special treatment'.[41]

2.3 The International Law Commission and the *exceptio*

As already mentioned, the ILC discussed the exception on a number of occasions, both in the framework of the law of the treaties and of the law of state responsibility.

For instance, during the work on the codification of the law of treaties, Gerald Fitzmaurice discussed the existence of the principle of *exceptio* within the framework of 'circumstances justifying non-performance'. However, the Special Rapporteur was hesitant to define the *exceptio* as either a justification *ab extra* on the ground of a general rule of international law, or *ab intra* on the basis of the treaty, which is implied in it by international law.[42] He formulated this principle very widely as based on reciprocity and justified by continuing non-performance.[43] Integral obligations are excluded from the operation of this principle.

[38] Gomaa (n 35) 119 and 121. In his view, proportionality is automatically applied when the measures contained wherein are activated. This is achieved by virtue of combined effect of the relationship between paras 1, 2, and 3 of ARSIWSA art 60.

[39] Crawford, 'Second Report' (n 1) para 323.

[40] ibid.

[41] See (1992) 2(2) Yearbook of the International Law Commission 151.

[42] Sir Gerald Fitzmaurice, 'Fourth Report on the Law of Treaties' (1959) 2 Yearbook of the International Law Commission 45–46.

[43] ibid: 'By virtue of the principle of reciprocity, and except in the case of the class of [multilateral treaties of the 'integral' type . . . where the force of the obligation is self-existent, absolute and inherent for each party, irrespective and independently of performance by the others], non-performance of a treaty obligation by one party to the

Gerald Fitzmaurice approached it as a general principle of law not confined only to the law of treaties.[44]

Fitzmaurice's successor, Sir Humphrey Waldock did not comment on Fitzmaurice's report by virtue of the separation of the law of treaties and the law of state responsibility (Article 73 of the VCLT). However, this topic was undertaken within the remit of the law of state responsibility by Mr Riphagen, according to whom

> Subject to articles 11 to 13, the injured State is entitled, by way of reciprocity to suspend the performance of its obligations towards the State which has committed an internationally wrongful act, if such obligations correspond to, or are directly connected with, the obligation breached.[45]

Further, Arangio-Ruiz debated the *exceptio* within the law of countermeasures, noting, however, definitional difficulties and some practical problems arising from the separation between the law of treaties (treaty suspension and termination) and the law of state responsibility.[46]

2.4 International case law on the *exceptio*

The *exceptio* has been debated in some cases before international courts and tribunals. The analysis of the relevant case law may prove useful in order to better understand the nature of the *exceptio* and its place in contemporary international law.

The application of the *exceptio* first arose in the case *Diversion of Water from the Meuse (Netherlands v Belgium)* before the Permanent Court of International Justice (PCIJ).[47] One of the grounds for lodging the case was the Netherlands' complaint regarding Belgium's taking of water for irrigation and other purposes from a particular lock on the Belgian side of the Meuse, which was said to be in contravention of a bilateral treaty of 1863. Belgium argued that its use of the locks was lawful considering that the Netherlands also used those locks for similar purposes. The Court agreed with Belgium and stated that: 'the Court finds it difficult to admit that the Netherlands are now warranted in complaining of the construction and operation of a lock of which they themselves set an example in the past.'[48] Belgium

treaty will, so long as such non-performance continues, justify an equivalent and corresponding non-performance by the other party or parties.'

[44] ibid 70: '[T]here is a general international law rule of reciprocity entailing that the failure of one State to perform its international obligations in a particular respect will either entitle other States to proceed to a corresponding non-performance in relation to that State, or will at any rate disentitle that State from objecting to such corresponding non- performance.'

[45] Willem Riphagen, 'Fifth Report' (1984) 2(1) Yearbook of the International Law Commission 3. See also the draft commentary in Willem Riphagen, 'Sixth Report' (1985) 2(1) Yearbook of the International Law Commission 10, 11.

[46] According to Arangio-Ruiz, 'The problem involved here is to see whether practice may justify a distinction of such "conventional" measures as treaty suspension and termination from countermeasures in general not only for merely descriptive reasons but in view of the legal regime to be codified or otherwise adopted by way of progressive development. As well as the question of the so-called "reciprocity measures" in general, the issues relating to these two 'conventional' measures—issues connected with the relationship between the law of treaties and the law of State responsibility—will have to be the object of further study before any draft articles are formulated.' See Arangio-Ruiz, 'Third Report' (1991) 2(1) Yearbook of the International Law Commission 35.

[47] *Diversion of Water from the Meuse (Netherlands v Belgium)* (1937) PCIJ Series A/B No 70, 4, 31.

[48] ibid 25.

also made a subsidiary claim that 'by constructing certain works contrary to the terms of the Treaty, the Applicant has forfeited the right to invoke the Treaty against the Respondent';[49] however, in his Separate Opinion, Judge Altamira rejected the idea that the obligations of the two parties are synallagmatic, concluding that those treaty obligations 'must be observed irrespective of the others, and the fulfilment of the others cannot excuse the non-fulfilment of one'.[50] Judges Anzilotti and Hudson expressed their disagreement regarding the majority's view on this issue. The Opinion of Judge Anzilotti is very interesting, not only because he mentioned expressly, as clearly as possible in that case, the principle of *inadimplenti non est adimplendum* ('just, so equitable, so universally recognized, that it must be applied in international relations also'), but also because he defined it as a general principle of law within the meaning of Article 38 of the ICJ Statue.[51] This approach was shared by Judge Hudson, according to whom

> It would seem to be an important principle of equity that where two parties have assumed an identical or a reciprocal obligation, one party which is engaged in a continuing non-performance of that obligation should not be permitted to take advantage of a similar non-performance of that obligation by the other party. The principle finds expression in the so-called maxims of equity which exercised great influence in the creative period of the development of the Anglo-American law…
>
> A very similar principle was received into Roman law … The *exceptio non adimpleti contractus* required a claimant to prove that he had performed or offered to perform his obligation … The general principle is one of which an international tribunal should make a very sparing application … [i]n a proper case, and with scrupulous regard for the limitations which are necessary, a tribunal bound by international law ought not to shrink from applying a principle of such obvious fairness.[52]

In another case, the ICJ addressed this topic in the context of the material breach of a treaty. In the *ICAO Council* case, the ICJ approached this principle with caution, and maintained the view that one party's allegations that a material breach has been committed does not permit the unilateral termination or suspension of a treaty under Article 60 of the VCLT. The principle *inadimplenti non est adimplendum* was raised by Judge de Castro in his separate opinion. While discussing material breach of a treaty enshrined in Article 60 of the VCLT, Judge de Castro made the following statement in a footnote:

> It not should be overlooked that the rule [an injured party's entitlement to invoke the breach as a ground for suspending or terminating a treaty in accordance with Article 60] opens the possibility of raising the *exceptio inadimpleti non est adimplendum*. The breach of an obligation is not the cause of the invalidity or termination of the treaty. It is a source of responsibility and of new obligations or sanctions. Alongside this, it is the material breach of a treaty which entitles the injured party to invoke it in order to terminate or suspend the operation of the treaty.[53]

[49] ibid 8.
[50] ibid 43.
[51] ibid (Separate Opinion of Judge Anzilotti) 50.
[52] ibid (Separate Opinion of Judge Hudson) 70.
[53] *Case Concerning the Appeal Relating to the Jurisdiction of the ICAO Council* (Separate Opinion of Judge Castro) [1972] ICJ Rep 46, 116, 128.

Judge de Castro further mentioned this principle in connection with the discussion of the legal character of Article 60, which in his view was

> a principle which follows from the contractual nature of treaties … The rules of international law are not outside treaties, they give legal force to treaty rules … Article 60 is a complement and the sanction of the principle *pacta sunt servanda*. It is the breach of rights or obligations having their source in the agreement which lies at the root of the *exceptio non adimpleti*.[54]

Implicitly, the principle of reciprocity in the case of non-performance (or, one can say, the *exceptio*) was invoked during the *Oil Platforms* case, although only during the pleadings and not in the Court's judgment. Counsel for the United States, Stephen Mathias, pleaded the breach by Iran of a reciprocal obligation of the 1955 Treaty of Friendship, which allegedly prevented Iran from objecting to the corresponding non-performance on the part of the United States. The United States argued that 'the consequence of Iran's own wrongful conduct is that Iran may not invoke the 1955 Treaty'.[55] The US Counsel relied also on the *River Meuse* case.[56] It was also submitted that the US actions were the result of an unlawful action by Iran under the 1955 Treaty of Amity.[57] Mr Mathias did not suggest that measures adopted by the US were either countermeasures or actions in response to a material breach of a treaty.[58] In his argument, Mr Mathias relied on the statement of Fitzmaurice that 'the failure of one state to perform its international obligations in particular respect will … disentitle that State from objecting to … corresponding non-performance'.[59] Accordingly, in this case it appears that the argument of non-performance was based exclusively on the construct of the *exceptio*.

More recently, the *exceptio* was invoked extensively before the ICJ in the dispute between the Former Yugoslav Republic (FYR) of Macedonia and Greece.[60] 'Macedonia' is the name of an historical and geographical region that extends mainly between Greece, Bulgaria, and the FYR Macedonia. Greece objected to the use of the name by the FYR Macedonia of one of Greek administrative regions. The 1995 Interim Accord was supposed to normalize the relationship between Greece and the FYR Macedonia. Greece, inter alia, agreed not to object to the FYR Macedonia's applications to join international organizations, as long as the latter applied under the provisional designation stated in paragraph 2 of Security Council Resolution 817 (1993), namely as 'the former Yugoslav Republic of Macedonia' (Article 11(1)). This provision resulted in the FYR Macedonia's application to the ICJ. Macedonia wished to accede to NATO during the 2008 Bucharest Summit—under its provisional designation, that is, the FYR Macedonia (as envisaged in the Interim Accord) following the accession of the number of other international organizations under this designation. Such invitation was not extended. The FYR Macedonia accused Greece of objecting to its accession to NATO, and

[54] ibid 129.
[55] *Oil Platforms (Islamic Republic of Iran v United States of America)* Mr Stephan Mathias, Oral Arguments, Public Sitting (5 March 2003) Verbatim Record CR 2003/18, para 26.9.
[56] ibid para 26.4.
[57] ibid para 26.7.
[58] ibid para 26.9.
[59] ibid para 26.25.
[60] *Application of the Interim Accord of 13 September 1995 (The former Yugoslav Republic of Macedonia v Greece)* (Judgment) [2011] ICJ Rep 644. On this case see Antonios Tzanakopoulos, 'Legality of Veto to NATO Accession: Comment on the ICJ's Decision in the Dispute between FYR Macedonia and Greece' *EJIL Talk!* (7 December 2011).

filed an application to the ICJ, alleging that Greece had violated its obligation not to object under Article 11(1) of the Interim Accord, given that the FYR Macedonia had sought to accede to NATO under its provisional designation. In this case there were attempts on the part of the respondent Greece to invoke the *exceptio non adimpleti* (together with material breach of a treaty of obligations, in particular Article 60(3)(b), and with countermeasures) as subsidiary defences, in order to justify its apparent disregard regarding its obligations under the Interim Accord. The arguments of Greece and FRY Macedonia will be presented in some detail. Anticipating some arguments of Greece, the FYR Macedonia alleged (i) that '[t]he Respondent's non-performance cannot be explained on the basis of a Suspension of Article 11(1) of the Interim Accord for material breach'—thus basing itself on Article 60 of the 1969 Vienna Convention on the Law of Treaties—and (ii) that '[t]he Respondent's violation of Article 11(1) cannot be excused as a lawful countermeasure to a precedent wrongful act by the Applicant'.[61] Greece argued that it did not rely on one or the other ground. In respect to the FYR Macedonia's argument that Greece could invoke Article 60 of the VCLT, Greece noted that it has never claimed any intent to suspend or terminate in whole or in part the operation of the Interim Accord. Greece alleged that it had steadily and consistently maintained that the Accord is in force and ought to be fully respected; in particular, Greece stated that it respected the Interim Accord, on the basis of the principle *pacta sunt servanda*.[62] As a subsidiary argument Greece invoked the more general principle of reciprocity, according to which *non adimpleti non est adimplendum*, 'which means that as long as the FYROM does not comply with its obligations under the 1995 Accord, Greece is entitled not to comply with its own obligations under the same instrument'.[63] Unlike counter-measures, the purpose of which is to induce a state which is responsible for an internationally wrongful act to comply with its obligations under Part 2 (Article 49 para 1 of the ARSIWA), 'the *exceptio* is a defence which can be invoked at any time in response to a claim by another State'. Greece further stated that

> [t]he *exceptio inadimpleti contractus* must not be confused with the ground for suspension and termination of a treaty dealt with in Article 60 of the Vienna Convention or with countermeasures (even though the conditions for recourse to countermeasures are also met). It is merely a defence against a claim of non-performance of a conventional obligation.[64]

Greece further argued that these three international law institutions have a common purpose: all of them are lawful responses to unlawful conduct by another state. The conditions triggering the exception of non-performance are different from and less strict than the conditions for suspending a treaty or precluding wrongfulness by way of countermeasures.[65] The *exceptio* is broader than Article 60 of the Vienna Convention leading to the suspension or termination of the treaty[66] since the *exceptio* suspends the execution of the injured party's obligation only, which is the counterpart or the reciprocal engagement of the non-performed obligation.[67] Suspension under Article 60 of the VCLT suspends the execution of the obligations of the treaty for both parties, while termination puts an end to them definitively. Greece

[61] *Memorial of FYR Macedonia*, III, paras 94–100 www.icj-cij.org/files/case-related/142/16354.pdf.
[62] *Counter-Memorial of Greece*, para 8(2) www.icj-cij.org/files/case-related/142/16356.pdf.
[63] ibid paras 8(2) and (3).
[64] ibid para 8(6).
[65] ibid para 8(7).
[66] ibid para 8(10).
[67] ibid para 8(13).

argued that '[i]t would be paradoxical that the victim of a treaty breach has no choice but to suspend or terminate it'.[68] The result of the application of the *exceptio* is that the treaty will remain in force between the parties but the injured party will be able to withhold the execution of its own obligations, which are synallagmatic to the ones not performed by the other party. The next step would be recourse to the procedures under material breach of a treaty (Article 60 of the 1969 VCLT).[69]

The *exceptio* is also different from a countermeasure as it is a specific feature of certain mutual or synallagmatic obligations and not a circumstance precluding wrongfulness, as explained by Special Rapporteur on State Responsibility James Crawford.[70] Furthermore, in the cases of termination or suspension under the principle *inadimplenti non est adimplendum*, proportionality is substituted by a more specific criterion, namely by the typically synallagmatic principle of *quid pro quo (corrispettivo)*.[71] The *exceptio* is based on the principle of reciprocity and can be invoked at any time, even during judicial or arbitral proceedings, without giving prior notice of default to the non-performing party.[72] The *exceptio* clearly does not belong to the law of treaties, as codified in the VCLT. It is characterized by the flexibility in respect of reciprocal obligations. It accords the opportunity for the injured party to use the defences offered in case of breaches of treaty obligations, not only as an immediate response to the wrongdoing but also as a defence during proceedings initiated by the wrongdoer.[73] In the case at hand, Greece argued that the FYR Macedonia could not ask Greece to fulfil its obligations under Article 11(1) of the Interim Accord as the FYR Macedonia had not fulfilled its own obligations. Following this reasoning, Greece could raise the *exceptio* as a defence at the merits stage.

The applicant doubted the character of the *exceptio* as a general principle of international law. It also rejected the argument that its own obligations under the Interim Accord were to be regarded as synallagmatic with the respondent's obligation stipulated in Article 11(1) of the Accord. Furthermore, the applicant did not accept that the *exceptio* could justify non-performance under the law of state responsibility.[74] The applicant also argued that Article 60 of the VCLT provides the set of rules relating to material breaches of treaties and that the *exceptio* is not recognized under the law of state responsibility. It is noteworthy that the respondent changed its argument. Initially, it argued that it was not seeking the suspension of the Interim Accord in part or in whole according to the 1969 VCLT, but later it took the position that a partial suspension of the Interim Accord under Article 60 of the 1969 VCLT was justified owing to the materiality of the breaches.[75] The respondent acknowledged the procedural requirements of Article 65 but argued that if a state is suspending a part of a

[68] ibid para 8(11).

[69] ibid para 8(15).

[70] ILC, 'Draft Articles on Responsibility of States for Internationally Wrongful Acts, with Commentaries' (2001) 2(2) Yearbook of the International Law Commission 72. See also Bruno Simma and Christian J Tams, 'Article 60: 1969 Vienna Convention' in Olivier Corten and Pierre Klein (eds), *The Vienna Conventions on the Law of Treaties* (OUP 2011) 1351, 1354: 'resort to countermeasures aims at compelling the defaulting State to cease its violation of international law and/or restore the situation that would have existed had there been no such violation. In contrast, reactions under the treaty law principle of *inadimplenti non est adimplendum* aim at remedying a situation in which the balance of rights and obligations within a treaty relationship has been upset due to a prior breach by the defaulting State.'

[71] *Counter-Memorial of Greece* (n 62) para 8(19).

[72] ICSID, *Klöckner Industrie-anlagen GMBH and Others v Republic of Cameroon*, Merits (21 October 1983) 144 ILR 152, cited in *Counter-Memorial of Greece* (n 62) para 8(22).

[73] *Counter-Memorial of Greece* (n 62) para 8(2).

[74] *Application of the Interim Accord of 13 September 1995 (The former Yugoslav Republic of Macedonia v Greece)* (n 60) paras 115–17.

[75] ibid para 118.

treaty as a response to another party alleging its violation, ex ante notice is not required.[76] The applicant argued that the respondent never contended material breach or the reliance on Article 60 of the 1969 VCLT prior to the Bucharest meeting or in its Memorial. The applicant also reminded the Court of the procedural requirements of Article 65. During the proceedings the respondent evolved its position in relation to countermeasures. It argued that any failure to comply with its obligations under the Interim Accord could be justified as a countermeasure. Initially, the respondent stated that it did not claim that any objection to the applicant's admission to NATO was justified as a countermeasure. At a later stage of proceedings, the respondent stated that its supposed objection would fulfil the requirements for countermeasures. The respondent described the defence as 'doubly subsidiary', meaning that it would play a role only if the Court found the respondent to be in breach of the Interim Accord and if it concluded that the *exceptio* did not preclude the wrongfulness of the respondent's conduct.[77] The respondent discussed countermeasures in light of the requirements reflected in the ARSIWA. It asserted that the applicant's violations were serious and that the respondent's responses were consistent with the conditions of the ASR. In the view of the applicant, none of these requirements was met.[78]

The Court proceeded to analyse the respondent's allegations relating to breaches of various articles of the Interim Accord. Having done that, the Court concluded that the respondent has established only one such breach.[79] Having reviewed the respondent's allegations of breaches by the applicant, the Court addressed the respondent's contention that the *exceptio*, as defined by the respondent, precluded the Court from finding that the respondent had breached its obligation under Article 11(1) of the Interim Accord. According to the Court, since the respondent had failed 'to establish that the conditions which it has itself asserted would be necessary for the application of the *exceptio* have been satisfied in this case', that is, with one exception the respondent failed to prove the breaches of the Interim Accord by the applicant, the Court found it unnecessary to determine whether that doctrine formed part of contemporary international law.[80]

As to the allegations regarding a material breach of the treaty, the Court recalled that the only breach which has been established was the display of a symbol in violation of Article 7(2) of the Interim Accord, which, in the Court's opinion, was an incident that could not be regarded as a material breach under Article 60 of the VCLT. The Court considered that the respondent had failed to establish that the action taken in 2008 in connection with the applicant's application to NATO was a response to the breach of Article 7(2), approximately four years earlier. Thus, 'the Court does not accept that the Respondent's action was capable of falling within Article 60 of the 1969 Vienna Convention'.[81] In relation to countermeasures, the respondent argued that its objection to the applicant's admission to NATO could be justified as a proportionate countermeasure in response to breaches of the Interim Accord by the applicant. However, in light of the breach of only one provision by the applicant, the Court rejected the respondent's claim that its objection could be justified as a countermeasure (precluding the wrongfulness of the respondent's objection to the applicant's admission to NATO). Accordingly, the Court found there was no reason to consider any of

[76] *Counter-Memorial of Greece* (n 62) paras 8(15) and (19).

[77] *Application of the Interim Accord of 13 September 1995 (The former Yugoslav Republic of Macedonia v Greece)* (n 60) para 120.

[78] ibid para 121.

[79] ibid para 160.

[80] ibid para 161.

[81] ibid para 163.

the additional arguments advanced by the parties with respect to the law governing countermeasures and, for the foregoing reasons, the additional justifications submitted by the respondent failed.[82]

There is also yet another point to make concerning the *Interim Accord* case. As described and analysed above, Greece put forward three supplementary defences: *exceptio non adimpleti*; material breach (Article 60 VCLT); and countermeasures, as responses to alleged breaches of the Interim Accord by Macedonia, switching from one to the other. In the view of the present author, these defences and their changes were not at all well substantiated. The respondent in this case followed the system of 'pick and choose', rather than a rationally founded use of defences. We may ask why an alleged non-material breach which was responded to by the use of *exceptio* changed into a material breach and subsequently triggered recourse to Article 60 of the 1969 VCLT. By the same token, the respondent then changed the argument in order to rely on countermeasures as a medium of the response to the breach of a treaty, thus not only switching defences again without any substantiation, but altogether leaving the realm of the primary rules of international law (the law of treaties) and moving to secondary rules of international law (the law of state responsibility).

This case has also shed some light on the required burden of proof in relation to the *exceptio*. In Roman law, the burden of proof regarding the invocation of this contractual principle was borne by the defendant.[83] In the *Interim Accord* case, Greece, the defendant, followed the principle of the burden of proof in Roman law, asserting that the Republic of Macedonia was in breach of the bulk of its obligation arising from the Interim Award, and that the Greek conduct adopted at the Bucharest Summit was a mere response to these breaches. If these assertions had proved true, the situation would have been that the Interim Accord was not functioning at all. However, some scholars have contested the Greek position: for instance, Deskoski raised some doubts regarding the evidentiary value of this subsidiary defence in this case. He supports the view expressed by Counsel for Macedonia that the *exceptio* is not a general principle of international law and that the formal conditions for the invocation of the breach of a treaty under Article 60 of the VCLT and countermeasures under the law of state responsibility were not fulfilled. Even if such a subsidiary defence was formally allowed to be triggered by Greece, it had no evidence to support its contention that breaches of the Interim Accord by Macedonia actually occurred.[84] Therefore, it can be stated that, as a self-standing defence, the burden of proof regarding the *exceptio* must be borne by the defendant.

3 Interim Conclusions

The debate in the ILC described and analysed above and the relevant case law clearly indicate angst surrounding the institution of the *exceptio* in international law. Not only is its place within the remit of the law of treaties and state responsibility, as well as its role and usefulness

[82] *Application of the Interim Accord of 13 September 1995 (the Former Yugoslav Republic of Macedonia v Greece)* (n 60) para 164.

[83] William Warwick Buckland (revised by P Stein), *A Text-Book of Roman Law from Augustus to Justinian* (3rd edn, CUP 1968, internet edition 2009) 498. In many treatises on civil law it is submitted that the *exceptio* may be submitted at any time and without the authorization of the judge. See the views of the French doctrine of civil law discussed in ICSID, *Klöckner Industrie-anlagen GMBH and Others v Republic of Cameroon* (n 83) 211–12.

[84] Toni Deskoski, 'Macedonian–Greek Relations and the Judgment of 5 December 2011' in Rüdiger Wolfrum, Maja Seršić, and Trpimir Šošić (eds), *Contemporary Developments in International Law: Essays in Honour of Budislav Vukas* (Brill/Nijhoff 2015) 26, 35–36.

shrouded in mystery, but even its classification is unclear. Crawford has distinguished a narrower form of this principle formulated by the PCIJ in the *Factory at Chorzów (Jurisdiction)* case[85] that a party ought not to be able to benefit from its own wrong as in the following way and in Article 80 of the UNCITRAL Convention on Contracts for the International Sale of Goods as it requires the existence of a causal link between the breach of the obligation of one party and non-performance by the other. The second, broader type is concerned with synallagmatic or interdependent obligations, with each seen as in effect a counterpart of the other as it was expressed by Judge Hudson in *Diversion of Waters from the Meuse*, by Sir Gerald Fitzmaurice and in Article 7.1.3 of the UNIDROIT Principles of International Commercial Contracts.[86] The only common features of the different types of the *exceptio* appear to be legitimate non-performance of the party to an obligation as a response to continuous and sustained non-performance of the other party. It also may be said that that it is based on the principle of equity.

As to the origins of this principle in international law, it may be said that there is a prevailing view that the exception has originated in domestic legal systems (civil law systems having the most developed and sophisticated form of it). It is a fairly flexible form of defence of non-performance as the procedural requirements are absent, in contrast with material breach of a treaty, which is subject to rigorous procedural conditions according to the VCLT. The question of whether the exception is an institution of the law of treaties or of the law of state responsibility appears unclear, as demonstrated by the aforementioned remarks of Judge de Castro, who defined the *exceptio non adimpleti* as having its roots in the breach of rights and obligations deriving from an agreement. Some authors treat an *exceptio* as an institution of the law of treaties; other authors consider that Article 60 of the VCLT is sufficient in addressing material breaches of the law of treaties, arguing that the law of state responsibility addresses 'non-material breaches' (and thus excluding the exception from the realm of the law of treaties).[87]

The *Interim Accord* and *Oil Platforms* cases (the latter indirectly and to a lesser extent) are the only two cases in which the *exceptio* constituted a separate argument by a party to a dispute. Only in the *River Meuse* case was there a timid attempt on the part of Belgium to rely on this principle as a subsidiary argument. In all other cases it was only judges who, in their separate and dissenting opinions, analysed this principle as one possibly underlying some of the legal issues presented by the parties to the case. In 2011, Judge Simma declared the *exceptio* dead in light of the emergence of the sophisticated and mature Article 60 of the 1969 VCLT,[88] departing from his earlier views that such an exception could fill the gap between material and non-material breaches.[89] In his view, Article 60 'is truly exhaustive, that is, totally eclipsing the earlier non-written law of the functional synallagma operating behind treaties'.[90] Judge Simma favours the view that, at present, non-material breaches in the law of treaties are remedied by recourse to countermeasures. He also was of the view that

[85] *Factory at Chorzów (Jurisdiction)* [1927] PCIJ Series A, No 9, 3: 'It is ... a principle generally accepted in the jurisprudence of international arbitration as well as by municipal courts, that one Party cannot avail himself of the fact that the other has not fulfilled some obligation or has not had recourse to some means of redress if the former Party has, by some illegal act, prevented the latter from fulfilling the obligation in question, or from having recourse to the tribunal which would have been open to him.'

[86] Crawford, 'Second Report' (n 1) para 326.

[87] Azaria (n 24) 152.

[88] Separate Opinion of Judge Simma (n 24).

[89] Bruno Simma, 'Reflections on Article 60 of the Vienna Convention on the Law of Treaties and its Background in General International Law' (1970) 20 Österreichische Zeitschrift für öffentliches Recht 5, 59–60.

[90] Separate Opinion of Judge Simma (n 24) para 20.

'State responsibility has nothing to do with the maxim *inadimplenti non est adimplendum*'.[91] According to Fontanelli, this position is based on a narrow understanding of the synallagma between the respective obligations of the parties on which the *exceptio* is based, an irrelevant equipment in the regime of countermeasures and the assumption that withholding of one's performance under the *exceptio* equals treaty suspension, thus falling under the remit of the VCLT. According to Judge Simma, countermeasures entailing a refusal to perform a bilateral treaty may appear to be like a suspension but are not the same.[92]

The present author agrees that the exception has been subsumed by Article 60. However, even if the *exceptio* is indeed dead, it was an heroic death, because it left the heritage of reciprocal (*do ut des*) synallagmatic obligations, which underlie the relationship between states and which to some extent provided a solid foundation for the formulation of Article 60 of the 1969 VCLT.

However, an argument may be suggested that *exceptio* is not entirely dead and may still perform a useful role in cases of breaches of international treaty obligations which do not lend themselves to be remedied either by the law of treaties or by recourse to the measures available in state responsibility. There may be situations that escape the formal confines of the both regimes (the law of treaties and the law of state responsibility) when there are two reciprocal obligations, in some ways dependent on each other, but which do not fill the bill of recourse to codified justifications. Similar treaties may not provide express provisions dealing with such eventualities. In situations of this type, the legal solutions depend also on the interpretation of the treaty.[93] States may resort to the exception, or may depend on a construct of an interdependent obligation. Azaria presents an example of the applicability of such an exception. Russia may be entitled not to perform its expert obligations towards Ukraine, until the latter has performed its transit obligations, providing that the performance of one obligation is conditioned upon the performance of the other. Material breach of a treaty and the application of countermeasures can only be effected upon fulfilment of many procedural conditions which are absent from the application of the *exceptio*.[94] Further, there is no requirement of proportionality, which is replaced by *quid quo pro* in the exception of non-performance, as non-performance means in this institution the time of performance has not arrived yet, rather than robustly inducing compliance.[95]

Finally, the operation of the *exceptio* can be reviewed within the typology of treaty obligations set out by Fitzmaurice (providing that we assume that it belongs to the realm of the law of treaties). He typified the obligations stemming from the law of treaties into three categories: reciprocal (or concessionary), integral,[96] and interdependent.[97] In broad brushstrokes, reciprocal multilateral treaties are those 'providing for a mutual interchange of benefits between the parties, with rights and obligations for each involving specific treatment at the hands of and towards each of the others individually' (the 1961 Vienna Convention on Diplomatic Relations).[98] Integral multilateral are those 'where the force of the obligation is self-existent, absolute and inherent for each party' [99] directed 'towards all the world rather

[91] ibid.
[92] Fontanelli (n 1) 131.
[93] On the application of the exception to these cases see Hartmut Hillgenberg, 'A Fresh Look at Soft Law' (1999) 10 European Journal of International Law 499, 509 and 512–13.
[94] Azaria (n 24) 152.
[95] ibid 152.
[96] Fitzmaurice, 'Second Report' (n 33) art 18, para 2.
[97] ibid art 29.1(iii).
[98] Sir Gerald Fitzmaurice, 'Third Report' (1958) 2 Yearbook of the International Law Commission art 18, para 2.
[99] ibid arts 27 and 19.

than towards particular parties[100] and 'do not lend themselves to differential application, but must be applied integrally' (the 1948 Genocide Convention).[101] The reciprocal treaties could be suspended or terminated as a result of fundamental breach.[102] Integral treaties could not be terminated or suspended by the other parties as a result of breach, as the 'juridical force of the obligation is inherent, and not dependent on a corresponding performance by the other parties to the treaty'.[103] Interdependent treaties are those where 'the participation of all the parties is a condition of the obligatory force of the treaty' (disarmament treaties).[104] In case of fundamental breach, interdependent treaties can be terminated in their entirety by the other parties since for these treaties 'performance by any party is necessarily dependent on an equal or corresponding performance by all the other parties'.[105]

Crawford noted that the *exceptio* will not be applicable to the integral type of treaties, (i.e. where performance is not premised on reciprocity). It could not justify a breach of the rules relating to the use of force or, more generally, a breach of *jus cogens*. It could have no application to obligations *erga omnes* (e.g. obligations in the field of human rights, humanitarian law, or international criminal law).[106] These exclusions of the applicability of the *exceptio* are in line with the provisions of Article 60 of the VCLT (material breach of treaty) which does not allow suspension or termination of treaties in the event of a material breach in relation to 'the protection of the human person contained in treaties of a humanitarian character, in particular to provisions prohibiting any form of reprisals against persons protected by such treaties' (Article 60(5)). Therefore, they follow international law principles.

4 Theoretical Considerations

As explained in the introduction to this chapter, from a more theoretical point of view the question may be posed whether the *exceptio* belongs to general principles of law as enshrined in Article 38(1)(c) of the Statute of the ICJ; or whether it should be approached as 'essentially a principle relating to cognate obligations', which exists more often in treaty obligations' as suggested by Greig. In his view, the *exceptio* (although it can be treated as a general principle of law) is better approached as

> essentially a principle relating to cognate obligations which are more often to be found ... in treaty relationships. By their very nature such obligations cannot arise independently. Accordingly, it would make more sense to regard the principle as forming part of the law of treaties within which it has its main field of application. Viewed in this light, it is regrettable that thisprinciple was not expressed in the Vienna Convention. However, there is an alternative analysis. It is possible to regard the interrelated obligations ... as carrying an implied promise of reciprocity: the performance of one is dependent upon performance of the other. It is thus feasible to ascribe the link between the obligation and its consequences to the intention of the parties. It is then an issue of fact as to whether the link exists.[107]

[100] Fitzmaurice, 'Second Report' (n 33) 54.
[101] ibid 55.
[102] ibid art 19.
[103] ibid art 19(iv).
[104] ibid art 29.1(iii).
[105] ibid art 19.1(ii)(b).
[106] Crawford, 'Second Report' (n 1) para 327.
[107] Greig (n 3) 400. See also the analysis of his views by Crawford and Olleson (n 1) 56–58.

Therefore, in Greig's view, the *exceptio* relates to obligations which are generically alike, linked together, depending on the on the intention of the parties. Such an approach rules out the possibility of treating the *exceptio* as a general principle of law within the meaning of Article 38 of the ICJ Statute.

Crawford and Olleson analysed and synthesized Greig's theoretical approach to the *exceptio* within the framework of his broader approach to the issues of proportionality and reciprocity in international law. Greig submitted several grounds justifying his preference of this approach to the *exceptio* rather than as a general principle of law. Greig singled out the intention of the parties as the basis of the operation of the principle; therefore, there is no need to question the omission of the exception from the VCLT. In addition, the reliance on intention of the parties in formulating the exception so that it derives from the intention of the parties to create interdependent obligations, the recourse to countermeasures is not necessary in order to justify non-performance.[108] According to Greig, such an interrelationship of obligations is dependent upon the intentions of the parties creating them, and, accordingly, even if these obligations are not embodied in a treaty in formal sense, they constitute a treaty between the concerned states.[109] Greig expressed concern that the provisions regarding countermeasures in the Draft Articles on State Responsibility (Articles 8 and 9) can impinge on the VCLT 'by providing an extraneous ground for non-performance of a treaty'.[110] The third advantage of such an interpretation is that the integrity of the VCLT can be preserved[111] and it would enhance the operation of Article 42(2) of the VCLT, which suggests that any suspension or termination of a treaty may only be conducted in accordance with the provisions of the Vienna Convention (including Article 60). The suspension of treaty rights could be available either under the VCLT or because it was an intention of the parties to create reciprocally interdependent rights:[112] 'Therefore, "extraneous ground" for non-performance of treaty obligations provided by the rules of countermeasures would seem to undermine this provision, and indeed the whole system of the Vienna Convention.'[113]

The process of 'diluting of the law' of treaties, against which Greig warned, has not been observed in practice. There are several cases that emphasize correlation and coexistence between the rules of the law of treaties and those of state responsibility. As Crawford and Olleson observed in the *Air Services* arbitration,[114] the arbitral tribunal 'upheld the view that countermeasures could justify non-performance of a treaty obligation'.[115] Similarly, the decision of the arbitral tribunal in the *Rainbow Warrior* case[116] clarified that 'the regimes of the law of treaties and state responsibility were applicable sequentially to the same situation and that the "circumstances precluding wrongfulness" contained in the draft articles could provide an excuse for the non-performance of a treaty obligation'.[117] In the *Gabčíkovo-Nagymaros Project* case,[118] the Court held the view that non-performance of a treaty, adopted as a reaction to a prior breach of that treaty, could be justified as a countermeasure, and this

[108] Greig (n 3) 400; Crawford and Olleson (n 1) 57.
[109] Greig (n 3) 400.
[110] ibid.
[111] ibid.
[112] ibid 401.
[113] ibid; Crawford and Olleson (n 1) 57.
[114] *Case Concerning the Air Services Agreement of 27 March 1946 (United States of America v France)* (1979) 18 RIAA 417.
[115] Crawford and Olleson (n 1) 57.
[116] *Case Concerning the Difference between New Zealand and France Concerning the Interpretation or Application of two Agreements, Concluded on 9 July 1986 between the Two States and which Related to the Problems Arising from the* Rainbow Warrior *Affair (New Zealand v France)* (1990) 20 RIAA 217.
[117] Crawford and Olleson (n 1) 57.
[118] *Gabčíkovo-Nagymaros Project (Hungary v Slovakia)* (Judgment) [1997] ICJ Rep 7, paras 84–85.

quite apart from the conditions for suspension of a treaty under Article 60 of the Vienna Convention.[119] In the 2001 Articles on State Responsibility, countermeasures are based on the premise that the temporary non-performance of an unconnected treaty obligation may be justified as a response to the breach by a state of one of its obligations, subject to fulfilment of the relevant requirements and conditions.[120] Therefore, the present author agrees with Crawford and Olleson that 'Greig's view of the autonomy of the law of treaty performance under the Vienna Convention has not been sustained. At the same time, however, his analysis of the exception of non-performance should be regarded as essentially correct.'[121]

Since the theoretical basis for the *exceptio* was based on total autonomy of the law of treaties, which in fact does not exist, the theoretical basis for the *exceptio* have to be found elsewhere. It may be suggested that the *exceptio* can be treated as a general principle of law.

The question of general principles of law was robustly discussed at the forum of the Advisory Committee of Jurists who drafted the Statute of the ICJ.[122] Lord Phillimore explained that the general principles of law referred to in Article 38(3) were those 'which are accepted by all nations in *foro domestico*, such as certain principles of procedure, the principle of good faith, and the principle of *res judicata*, etc'.[123] These principles were also discussed within the paradigm of *non liquet*, that is, a situation where the Court has no legal grounds to adjudicate the case under either conventional or customary law. The possibility of such a situation was recognized by the members of the Committee.[124] The mainstream view was that *non liquet* is not a desirable position for a Court and therefore general principles of law were included in Article 38. It was observed that: '[t]he characteristic of general principles is clear: they apply directly when there is no conventional or customary rule of international law governing on a matter.'[125] Judges Anzilotti and Hudson in the *River Meuse* case approached the *exceptio* as general principles of law within the meaning of Article 38 of the Statute of the ICJ. However, in their view it embodied an idea of justice and equity in general, thus making this principle rather vague and too abstract, broad, and ill-defined to be relied upon in the judicial proceedings in order to fill the gap of the customary international law and the law of treaties. In general, it may be said regarding general principles of law that their status and content is vague and cannot be ascertained without any doubt[126] and that their notion has been used in doctrine and in practice in a rather loose, imprecise, and inconsistent manner.[127]

It is true that the *exceptio* exists in domestic law systems, and it is commonly acknowledged that general principles of international law derive from domestic law.[128] As explained above, however, there is no consistency in its legal construct and application in legal regimes

[119] Crawford and Olleson (n 1) 57.

[120] ibid.

[121] ibid 58.

[122] *Procès-verbaux* of the proceedings of the Committee (16 June–24 July 1920) with Annexes, Advisory Committee of Jurists Annex No 3 (van Langenhuysen Brothers 1920). On general principles of law see: Mads Andenas, Malgosia Fitzmaurice, Attila Tanzi, and Jan Wouters (eds), *General Principles and the Coherence of International Law* (Brill/Nijhoff 2011).

[123] ibid 335.

[124] ibid 296–97 (Hagerup), 307–308, 311–12 (Loder), 312–13, 317, 335–36 (de Lapradelle).

[125] Fontanelli (n 1) 127. See also ILC Study Group on Fragmentation, Full Report, UN Doc A/CN/4/L.682 (2006) paras 462 ff.

[126] Maria Panezi, 'Sources in Law in Transition. Revisiting General Principles of Law' (2007) Ancilla Juris 66.

[127] Vladimir Vlado Degan, *Sources of International Law* (Martinus Nijhoff Publishers 1991) 17.

[128] There were, however, examples of the application of general principles by the ICJ which are not part of municipal law systems (see e.g. *Corfu Channel (United Kingdom of Great Britain and Northern Ireland v Albania)* (Judgment) [1949] ICJ Rep 4, 22; *Reservations to the Convention on the Prevention and Punishment of the Crime of Genocide* (Advisory Opinion) [1951] ICJ Rep 15, 21).

of civil and common law. Moreover, it has been suggested that international treaties and domestic contracts have different functions and, thus, rules envisaged for domestic contracts cannot be transplanted in the law of treaties without considering the 'legislative' function of treaties in international law.[129] There is also a view expressed that, owing to their auxiliary character, the role of general principles of law as a main source of general international law has to a certain extent lost its significance.[130]

Therefore, in this author's view, it would be very difficult to classify the *exceptio* as a general principle of international law or as a rule of international law.

It may be said that the *exceptio* is based on good faith, which legal character is also quite vague. Reinhold turned to the theory of Dworkin to define the legal character of good faith.[131] According to Dworkin's theory, in which there is a conceptual difference between rules and principles, the *exceptio* cannot be treated as a rule. Rules are absolute and, wherever a rule is relevant, it is decisive. Principles serve as a guide in the decision-making process.[132] However, according to Dworkin, judges are obligated to turn to principles in the absence of rules.[133] Therefore, the court may resort to moral reasoning when deciding the case.[134] Since the exception is based on good faith, it may be argued that its role in international law is similar. In international law good faith cannot generally be the source of obligations or constitute a sole ground for decisions by judicial bodies.[135] Reinhold suggests that good faith 'serves a mediatory role between a rule and a principle', as it has an important role in the determination of obligations but generally is not a source of such obligations.[136] Therefore, the role of the exception (like good faith itself) can only play a more limited role in international law, contrary to national law where principles, under certain circumstances, can stand as a sole ground for adjudication, as Dworkin stated.

Crawford and Olleson expressed a harsher view, according to which the *exceptio* 'has not established an independent place as a rule or principle of international law'.[137] Good faith and the notion of reciprocity which underlie the exception are not enough to include it in the category of 'general principles of law'.[138] The above authors observe that the 'rather embryonic and under-theorised character of the exception in international law can be seen, for example, in the persistent confusion between the distinct institutions of termination (or suspension) of treaties for material breach and the various circumstances precluding wrongfulness in the law of state responsibility, especially countermeasures', as well as in various texts which articulate the exception for the purposes of international contracts.[139]

[129] See Thomas Giegerich, 'Article 60' in Oliver Dörr and Kirsten Schmalenbach (eds), *The Vienna Convention on the Law of Treaties: A Commentary* (Springer 2012) 1021, 1022.

[130] Malcolm Shaw, *International Law* (CUP 2014) 70.

[131] Steven Reinhold, 'Good Faith in International Law' (2013) 2 UCL Journal of Law and Jurisprudence 40.

[132] Ronald Dworkin, *Taking Rights Seriously* (Harvard University Press 1977) 25.

[133] ibid 82.

[134] ibid 72. Dworkin gives an example of *Riggs v Palmer* (1889), in which the court adjudged a case in which a grandson murdered his grandfather to collect the inheritance. There were no written statutes preventing him from the inheritance but the court found that he could not inherit on the grounds of moral reasoning that there is a principle that no one should be permitted to profit from his own wrongdoing. See on this Frederick Schauer, 'Rules, Defeasibility, and the Psychology of Exceptions', ch 4 in this volume.

[135] On the good faith principle in international law see generally Robert Kolb, *Good Faith in International Law* (Hart Publishing 2017).

[136] Reinhold (n 131) 2. In relation to international law, Dworkin analysed good faith in so far as it concerned human rights, see in particular Ronald Dworkin, *Justice for Hedgehogs* (Cambridge: The Belknap Press of Harvard University Press, 2011), 335–36.

[137] Crawford and Olleson (n 1) 73.

[138] ibid.

[139] See section 2 above.

The continuing debate on the role of the *exceptio* does not appear to render a definite answer as to its role, both in national and international law systems. Doubts remain regarding whether the *exceptio* is a rule of law, simply a rather vague principle based on good faith (or equity), or some embodiment of fairness. It should be borne in mind that, in the French legal system, the *exceptio* does not exist in the civil code but nevertheless is relied on in judicial proceedings, as a corollary of good faith. The roots of the *exceptio* in good faith flow from the idea 'that mutual obligations are dependent on each other and must, therefore, be carried out at one and the same time' and is based on a premise of 'the situation of equilibrium between the parties, which should have existed at the moment of contract formation, is thus maintained at the time of its performance'. [140]

5 Concluding Remarks

As evidenced in this chapter, the position of the *exceptio* causes angst. It appears to simulate an institution of the law of state responsibility. However, the suspension of a treaty on this basis is not a countermeasure; nor is it a construct belonging to Article 60 of the VCLT. The *exceptio* was not included in ILC's codifications as a sub-category of reciprocal countermeasures. As Crawford noted,

> The underlying problem is that, a broad view of the *exceptio* may produce escalating non-compliance, negating for practical purposes the continuing effect of obligation ... [t]he justification for non-compliance with synallagmatic obligations should be resolved (a) by the law relating to the suspension or termination of these obligations (which is sufficient to deal with most problems of treaty obligations), and (b) by the law of countermeasures.[141]

In this author's opinion, the legal character of *exceptio* is very vague since it is not a general principle of law under Article 38 of the ICJ Statute and, owing to its generality, it cannot fill the gaps left by a lack of corresponding treaty or customary international law norms. Even its character as a principle (in Dworkin's meaning) is doubtful. It may be seen, as Reinhold suggests, as a legal construct in between a rule and a principle.

However, the view that the *exceptio* in international law is completely dead is exaggerated, although its existence appears to be elusive. The reasonable explanation of the *exceptio* is that it falls within the remit of circumstances precluding wrongfulness, not as a sub-category of countermeasures but a separate kind, although rather amorphous, and therefore difficult to apply. In general, *exceptio inadimplenti non est adimplendum* has a distinctly nostalgic feeling about it.

[140] Philip O'Neill, Nawaf Salam, 'Is the *Exceptio Non Adimpleti Contractus* Part of the New *Lex Mercatoria*' in Emmanuel Gaillard (ed), *Transnational Rules in International Commercial Arbitration* (ICC Publishing 1993) 147, 152.

[141] Crawford, 'Second Report' (n 1) para 110, referring to *Factory at Chorzów* (n 85).

17
Exemptions, Qualifications, Derogations, and Excuses in International Human Rights Law

*Kimberley Trapp**

1 Introduction

International human rights law[1] recognizes a core of rights that are absolute. These rights protect human dignity and integrity and are not subject to any qualification, whether in the form of an exception or derogation (within international human rights law treaty regimes) or defence (under general international law). The prohibition of torture and slavery are very clear examples.[2] Most other human rights, however, including the right to life, are subject to some form of qualification. These qualifications might take the form of limitations to the scope of the right or the scope of the rights protection (for the purposes of balancing competing individual rights-based interests against public interests), or in the form of a temporally limited suspension of the obligation to respect the right or the secondary obligations which flow from responsibility for breach of the right (for the purposes of effectively responding to emergencies). In each case, the qualification carves out a space for the exercise of regulatory authority or executive power that is relatively free from the constraints otherwise imposed by a broad conception of human rights, in the interests of achieving some legitimate aim—and have in common an instrumentalist approach to human rights protection.

This chapter explores the different layers of qualification applicable to three international human rights law treaty regimes, in particular the ICCPR, the ECHR, and the ACHR—with a view to outlining a typology of qualifications and the interactions between them. One of these qualifications is better qualified as an exemption (at least formally), in that it defines the scope of the rule. Other qualifications will amount to exceptions properly so-called, in that they are primary rules which carve out a space that is free from the restrictions otherwise imposed by the rule. The final qualification explored in this chapter is in the form of a defence—it operates to limit the consequences which would normally flow from a breach of the rule. Despite these differences, this chapter argues that qualifications in international human rights law exist on a spectrum or continuum. Even though formally qualifications

* Professor of Public International Law, UCL, Faculty of Laws. k.trapp@ucl.ac.uk.

[1] The focus of this chapter will be on the three human rights treaty regimes which expressly allow for derogations—the International Covenant on Civil and Political Rights (1966) 999 UNTS 171, entry into force 23 March 1976 (ICCPR); the European Convention on Human Rights (1950) 213 UNTS 221, entry into force 3 September 1953 (ECHR), and the American Convention on Human Rights (1969) OAS Off Rec OEA/Ser.L/V/ ll.23, doc 21, rev 6, entry into force 18 July 1978 (ACHR)—and are subject to some form of monitoring mechanism (whether a court with compulsory jurisdiction or a treaty monitoring body to which the state party must report).

[2] Within international human rights law treaty regimes, the prohibition of torture and slavery is framed in absolute terms and expressly excluded from applicable derogation provisions (discussed in section 4below). Under general international law, the practice of torture or slavery cannot be the subject of any circumstance precluding wrongfulness in virtue of their characterization as a *jus cogens* (peremptory) norm, pursuant to art 26 of the ILC Articles on Responsibility of States for Internationally Wrongful Acts (ILC ARSIWA), in Report of the International Law Commission on the work of its fifty-third session, UN Doc A/56/10 (2001) 31.

Kimberley Trapp, *Exemptions, Qualifications, Derogations, and Excuses in International Human Rights Law* In: *Exceptions in International Law*. Edited by: Lorand Bartels and Federica Paddeu, Oxford University Press (2020). © Lorand Bartels and Federica Paddeu. DOI: 10.1093/oso/9780198789321.003.0017

operate at different levels (e.g. some are primary rules internal to the particular international human rights law regime, while others are secondary rules which operate at the level of general international law),[3] the different qualifications overlap or bleed into each other, and the structure of analysis in respect of each qualification can be relied on to inform the others' application on the basis of principles of systemic interpretation.[4]

2 Typology of 'Exceptions' Applicable to International Human Rights Law

All types of qualification which operate in the international human rights law context are in a broad sense instrumentalist—they enable the exercise of regulatory authority or executive power that is potentially or actually otherwise inconsistent with individual human rights interests, to the extent necessary either to facilitate living in community (balancing the protection of individual rights against the public interest), or to respond to crisis (with a view to restoring non-crisis or 'normal' conditions). Despite this common foundation, however, four types of qualification are ordinarily distinguished:

1. *Limited rights:* The human rights interest does not fall within the scope of a protected right (exemptions, which reflect the public interest, define the scope of the primary rule) (section 3.1.1 below).
2. *Qualified Rights:* The human rights interest falls within the scope of the primary rule (a protected right), but in circumstances that are defined within the primary rule, the limitation to the right is permissible in order to achieve legitimate aims (protecting public interests) (section 3.1.2 below).[5]
3. *Derogations:* Thehuman rights interest falls within the scope of the primary rule (a protected right), but in circumstances that are defined by a separate primary rule (which is nevertheless internal to the relevant international human rights law treaty regime), the state's obligation to respect that right is temporarily (for so long as the derogation triggering situation persists) waived[6] (section 4 below).
4. *Excuses:* The human rights interest falls within the scope of a primary rule (a protected right), the state's obligation to respect that right has not been waived and the right

[3] Primary rules of international law consist of the substantive international obligations of states under customary and treaty law (of particular relevance for present purposes, international human rights law treaty obligations), while secondary rules are of general application (of particular relevance for present purposes, the rules of state responsibility which bear on the identification of a breach of the primary rules and the consequences of any such breach). See James Crawford, 'Introduction' in James Crawford (ed), *The International Law Commission's Articles on State Responsibility: Introduction, Text and Commentaries* (CUP 2002) 16 (Commentary to ILC Articles on State Responsibility).

[4] See e.g. Vienna Convention on the Law of Treaties (1969) 1155 UNTS 331 (entry into force 27 January 1980) art 31(3)(c).

[5] In his contribution to this edited volume Chapter 5, Jorge Viñuales treats these two first types of qualification together as 'specific carve-outs or exemptions', describing them as responding 'to a specific reason, such as the protection of a specific interest considered as being of overriding importance as compared to the goals pursued by the norm or set of norms'. See J Viñuales, 'Seven ways of escaping a rule: Of exceptions and their avatars in international law' in L Bartels and F Paddeu (eds), *Exceptions and Defences in International Law* (OUP 2017) 65, §2.2. They are treated separately in this chapter on international human rights law because they are, in principle, subject to different forms of analysis and engage international human rights law treaty monitoring mechanisms differently—although, as set out further below, the difference is indeed more theoretical than practical.

[6] Of course, on jurisprudential grounds, some might contest whether it is even possible to have a right without a corresponding obligation to respect that right. For the purposes of avoiding this chapter falling into a black hole of jurisprudence, it will be assumed that international law and international human rights law now accepts that individuals are rights bearers, even in the presence of derogations and circumstances precluding wrongfulness.

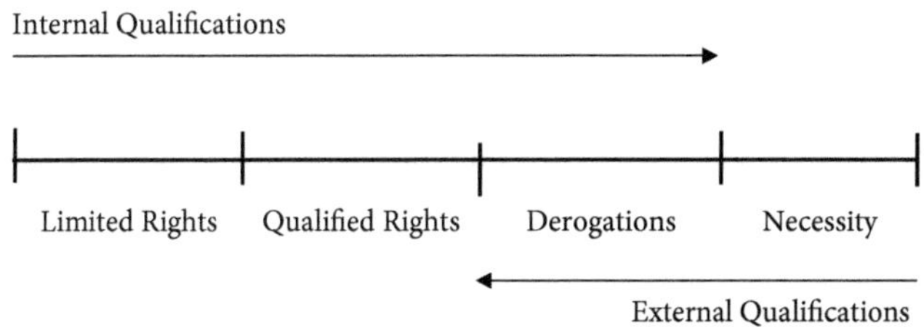

Figure 17.1 Human rights 'continuum'

has been breached, but in circumstances defined by a secondary rule, the obligations which normally attach to a breach[7] temporarily (for so long as the excuse triggering situation persists) do not follow from the breach [Section 5 below].

These qualifications exist along a continuum (illustrated below in Figure 17.1) that creates space for human rights inconsistent exercises of regulatory authority or executive power in the interests of a legitimate aim, each new qualification moving further along the continuum from the core of the right (defined through its scope). These four categories may also be analysed as reflecting two types of qualification which apply to international human rights obligations along this continuum: qualifications that are internal to relevant international human rights law treaty regimes and those that are external to them. The first three qualifications outlined above are internal to the international human rights law treaty regimes, while the fourth is external. The 'internal/external' nature of the qualifications is co-extensive with the distinction between primary rules of international law (in the case at hand, sourced from specialized treaty regimes) and secondary rules which are of general application and are creatures of customary international law. This latter distinction in respect of the source of the qualifications results in their being subject to differential monitoring. While internal qualifications (as primary treaty rules) remain subject to scrutiny by the relevant human rights treaty monitoring bodies or courts, external qualifications are ordinarily subject to the general international law mechanisms of state responsibility and courts of general jurisdiction (like the International Court of Justice).[8]

3 Internal Qualifications

Each of the international human rights law treaties explored in this chapter adopt the three 'internal qualification' approaches to the relationship between individual rights protection and the legitimate aims pursued by governments, as illustrated in the continuum above.

[7] In particular, cessation and the obligation to make reparations. See ILC ARSIWA arts 30, 31.

[8] It is possible, on the basis of a doctrine of incidental jurisdiction, that human rights courts and treaty monitoring bodies might exercise jurisdiction over external qualifications, but in practice there are no examples of such exercise.

3.1 Limited rights versus qualified rights

3.1.1 Limited rights

The first such approach might formally be qualified as an exemption,[9] in that the recognition of legitimate aims in the exercise of regulatory authority or executive power (which can be pursued unrestricted by human rights interests) is built into the scope of the right—the right is *limited*. The approach involves the identification of a human rights *interest* in general terms (life or liberty for instance), and the exemption of either specific government action, or generally defined government action (all of which is instrumental in protecting a public interest) from the scope of the *right* protecting that *interest*. In principle, the regulatory conduct or exercise of executive power which falls within the scope of an exemption does not engage the protected right—and because it falls outside the 'rule', it is in no need of an 'exception'.[10]

The ECHR, for instance, recognizes a broad interest in liberty, but excludes *specific* deprivations of liberty from the scope of the right (a deprivation of liberty as a result of lawful detention after conviction by a competent court, for instance).[11] In the case of the ECHR, the balance between public interest and individual rights is determined a priori. The ICCPR and the ACHR, on the other hand, recognize a broad interest in liberty from which a *general* exemption (non-arbitrary deprivations) is carved out.[12] The balance between public interest and individual rights is not determined a priori—as the contours of 'arbitrary' require definition. The same approach is taken in respect of the right to life, in that deaths which are contemplated in Article 2(2) of the ECHR, or deaths which are non-arbitrary under Article 6(1) of the ICCPR and Article 4(1) of the ACHR, do not engage the right to life. These deprivations of life fall outside the scope of the *right* to life as defined by the international human rights law treaties, and therefore need not be covered by an exception in order to remain lawful. Having said so, as argued in Section (iii) below, the distinction between exemptions from the rule and exceptions to the rule in the international human rights law context can be illusory.

3.1.2 Qualified rights

The second approach to accommodating legitimate aims within a rights based framework are better qualified as an exception, in the sense that the government action falls within the scope of the right (and would be prohibited as a breach of that right), but the limitation imposed on the right is permitted in the circumstances. All three human rights treaties under consideration provide for these so-called 'qualified rights',[13] in addition to providing for rights which do not permit any qualification (like the right to be free from torture, discussed

[9] See Joost Pauwelyn, 'Defenses and the Burden of Proof in International Law' in L Bartels and F Paddeu (eds) *Exceptions and Defences in International Law* (OUP 2017) 88, for a discussion of the distinction between exemptions and exceptions and the consequences thereof in respect of the burden of proof.

[10] In their contribution to this edited volume, Jaap Hage, Antonia Waltermann, and Gustavo Arosemena articulate this same point regarding 'limited rights' as a question of rule applicability (to be distinguished from exceptions, which are engaged in the *application* of the rule). See Jaap Hage, Antonia Waltermann, and Gustavo Arosemena, 'Exceptions in International Law' in L Bartels and F Paddeu (eds) *Exceptions and Defences in International Law* (OUP 2017) 11, §§ 5 and 8.2. The language of human rights 'interests' which are exempted from the scope of a protected 'right' is used in this chapter to reflect our intuition that certain State conduct limits human freedoms and interests broadly understood, even if those interests are not legally protected.

[11] ECHR art 5(1).

[12] ICCPR art 9(1).

[13] Rosalyn Higgins refers to these rights as subject to 'clawbacks' and treats them as on the same spectrum as derogations—discussed further below. See Rosalyn Higgins, 'Derogation under Human Rights Treaties' (1976) British Yearbook of International Law 281. Cf Tom R Hickman, 'Between Human Rights and the Rule of Law' (2005) 68 Modern Law Review 655, 658–59.

above). Qualified rights are defined generally (e.g. the rights to respect for private life; to freedom of thought, conscience, and religion; to freedom of expression, association, and movement),[14] but are subject to permissive limitations as are necessary to pursue legitimate aims.[15] Some of these limitations assume that rights are exercised within a community context, that the other members of the community are equivalently rights entitled, and that an absolute approach to certain rights is the enemy of community living. As Sir Hersch Lauterpacht put it, '[i]t is axiomatic that the natural rights of the individual find a necessary limit in the natural rights of other persons.'[16] As such, limitations on relevant human rights might be imposed where the right's unfettered exercise would be to the detriment of the exercise of the right by other members of the community. Equally, such rights might be limited where the maximal exercise of the right would be to the detriment of important public interests like order, health, or morals.

For instance, Article 9(1) of the ECHR provides broadly for freedom of thought, conscience, and religion, while paragraph (2) provides that:

> No restrictions shall be placed on the exercise of these rights other than such as are prescribed by law and are necessary in a democratic society in the interests of national security or public safety, for the prevention of disorder or crime, for the protection of health or morals or for the protection of the rights and freedoms of others. This Article shall not prevent the imposition of lawful restrictions on the exercise of these rights by members of the armed forces, of the police or of the administration of the State.

What is involved in respect of qualified rights is a balancing of interests—between the individual's interest in respect for their rights claim and the community's interest in coextensive rights assertions or other important public interests.[17] The scope of the permissible restriction of the human right concerned is based on its proportionality to the legitimate aim pursued. The courts and treaty monitoring bodies attached to the international human rights law treaties that are the subject of this study measure proportionality in varying ways—including by considering: (i) whether the human rights limiting measure is rationally connected to the legitimate aim; (ii) whether the measure is the least restrictive alternative available to achieve the legitimate aim; and (iii) the proportionality *stricto sensu* of the measure—whether the detriment to the person whose human rights are limited is excessive in relation to the benefits of pursuing the legitimate aim.[18]

[14] See e.g. ICCPR arts 17–22; ECHR arts 8–11; ACHR arts 12, 13, 15, 16, 21, and 22.

[15] ibid. The 'legitimate aims' recognized in the three international human rights law treaties which are the subject of this study are very similar and include, in varying combinations: national security, public safety, the prevention of disorder or crime, the protection of public order, health, and morals, or for the protection of the rights and freedoms of others.

[16] Sir Hersch Lauterpacht, *International Law and Human Rights* (Stevens & Sons 1950) 366.

[17] See e.g. *Grand Hatton and Others v United Kingdom* App no 36022/97 (ECtHR (GC) 7 July 2003)—in which the Court notes that qualified rights call for a balance to be struck 'between the competing interests of the individual . . . and the community as a whole'. For a critique of balancing individual rights as against public interests see Baak Cali, 'Balancing Human Rights? Methodological Problems with Weights, Scales and Proportions' (2007) 29 Human Rights Quarterly 251, 259–60, arguing in particular that human rights protection need not be conceptualized as a zero-sum game.

[18] See eg Human Rights Committee, General Comment No 27 (1999) UN Doc CCPR/C/21/Rev.1/Add.9, para 14 (in reference to freedom of movement); *Murillo and Others v Costa Rica (In Vitro Fertilization)* (IACtHR 28 November 2012) para 273. For an analysis of the approach to proportionality taken by the European Court of Human Rights (ECtHR), (which is a less structured analysis) see Yutaka Arai-Takahashi, 'Structural Principles: Proportionality' in Dinah Shelton (ed), *The Oxford Handbook of Human Rights Law* (OUP 2014) ch 19, 454–56.

3.2 A distinction without a difference?

On one view, these two techniques for accommodating a sphere of government action undertaken in pursuit of legitimate aims are (at least) formally different, in that one is an exemption defining the very scope of the rule (or right), while the other defines the rule (or right) broadly, and then 'claws back' a sphere of activity free from the restrictions otherwise imposed by the rule (which rule is nevertheless engaged by the relevant activity). An exercise of regulatory authority or executive power which is excluded from the scope of a right is not even potentially in breach of the obligation to respect that right, and is therefore in no need of an exception to carve out a space for the lawful exercise of that authority or power.

On another view, this is a distinction without a difference. First, the 'qualification' in 'qualified rights' is in one important sense also about scope, in that the breadth of the *claimed rights protection* cannot be accommodated in a democratic society. In the case of both limited rights subject to exemptions and qualified rights subject to exceptions, an applicant is making a claim that a particular human rights interest has been engaged (whether it is a liberty interest or a freedom of expression interest), and the relevant court or treaty monitoring body is making a determination about the scope of protection afforded that interest. Indeed, the reasoning involved in both cases can be all but identical, as discussed further below.

A possible difference between these two approaches in the sphere of human rights, however, might be in reference to the role courts or human rights treaty monitoring bodies ought to play. In the case of limited rights explored in sub-section 3.1.1 above, the primary norm distinguishes between situations to which the rule applies and situations to which it does not—and all that should remain for the court or treaty monitoring body to do is apply the primary norm—the reasoning might be described as 'algorithmic'. The 'legislators' (or treaty negotiating states) have made the value judgments. In the case of qualified rights explored in sub-section 3.1.2, the individual's interest in respect for their rights claim is balanced against the interests represented by the clawbacks or exceptions.[19] The 'legislators' have left it open for courts or human rights treaty monitoring bodies to determine the scope of protection through a balancing of competing interests on the basis of a proportionality analysis. But again, this difference should not be exaggerated. In cases bearing on limited rights (for instance the right to life or liberty as discussed below), courts or international human rights law treaty monitoring bodies engage in the proportionality reasoning which is a principal feature of the human rights calculus in respect of qualified rights and exceptions. In these cases, there is a balancing of human rights interests against legitimate aims, as defined by the relevant context or regime, but for the purposes of defining the scope of the rule (right) rather than the scope of the protection.

3.3 Regime interaction

One example of a 'balancing of interests' approach in the context of defining the scope of a right emerges as a result of the interaction between international human rights law and international humanitarian law in respect of the right to life. Courts have repeatedly held either that international humanitarian law is a *lex specialis* in respect of the right to life,[20] or that

[19] See e.g. Cali (n 17) fn 31.

[20] See e.g. *Legality of the Threat or Use of Nuclear Weapons* (Advisory Opinion) [1996] ICJ Rep 226, paras 24–25. In its subsequent *DRC v Uganda* decision, the Court reiterated its approach to the relationship between international human rights law and international humanitarian law, but dropped the reference to *lex specialis*. See *Case*

international human rights law is to be interpreted *in light of* international humanitarian law based on Article 31(3)(c) of the Vienna Convention on the Law of Treaties 1969 (VCLT).[21] In either event, international humanitarian law does not displace international human rights law at the regime level, but does (for the most part) displace international human rights law at the normative level in respect of the right to life. The result is that an international humanitarian law compliant deprivation of life is also an international human rights law compliant deprivation of life (and an international humanitarian law non-compliant deprivation of life is an international human rights law non-compliant deprivation of life). An international humanitarian law compliant deprivation of life is determined either on the basis of status (combatants or civilians directly participating in hostilities) or through a proportionality assessment—in particular whether incidental loss of civilian life would be excessive in relation to the concrete and direct military advantage anticipated from the attack resulting in the deprivation of life.[22] As regards the proportionality analysis, the rule in effect defines a legitimate aim (gaining a military advantage) and requires that any limitations to otherwise applicable protections be proportionate to achieving that legitimate aim. This is precisely the same balancing of interests which is characteristic of qualified rights and their exceptions[23] —but it is applied in the context of determining the scope of a right, because the right to life (once engaged) is not subject to qualification. While international humanitarian law obviously takes into account a broader range of legitimate aims than international human rights law (for instance the gaining of military advantage which is not an international human rights law recognized legitimate aim), the structure of the reasoning is nevertheless the same.

3.4 Proportionality analysis in rights of qualified scope

In non-regime interaction cases regarding the scope of a right, the courts will also engage in a balancing of interests. Famously, in *Austin v Commissioner of Police for the Metropolis*,[24] the House of Lords held that kettling individuals for over seven hours on public order grounds did not amount to a restriction on liberty which engaged Article 5 of the ECHR. Clearly, being detained for more than seven hours engages an individual's *interest* in liberty, and the question for the Lords was whether it engaged their *right* to liberty. Kettling on public order grounds does not fall within the list of exemptions provided for in Article 5 (detention after conviction; arrest or detention for non-compliance with a court order; arrest or detention for the purposes of bringing person before a competent court etc). As a result, if the right to

Concerning Armed Activities on the Territory of the Congo (Democratic Republic of the Congo v Uganda) (Judgment) [2005] ICJ Rep 168, para 216. The Inter-American Commission on Human Rights has adopted the position of the ICJ. See *Coard v United States* (I/ACommHR, Report no 109/99, 29 September 1999) para 42.

[21] Adopting the systemic interpretation approach is the ECtHR (*Hassan v UK* App no 29750/09 (ECtHR (GC) 16 September 2014) para 104, and the Human Rights Committee in its General Comment No 31 (The Nature of the General Legal Obligation Imposed on States Parties to the Covenant) (2004) UN Doc CCPR/C/21/Rev.1/Add 13, para 11.

[22] Protocol Additional to the Geneva Conventions of 12 August 1949, and Relating to the Protection of Victims of International Armed Conflicts (1977) 1125 UNTS 3 (entry into force 7 December 1978) art 51(5)(b).

[23] The proportionality *stricto sensu* test applied by international human rights courts and monitoring bodies has been aptly summarized as 'measuring the relative intensity of the interference with the importance of the aim sought'. Stavros Tsakyrakis, 'Proportionality: An Assault on Human Rights?' (2009) 7 International Journal of Constitutional Law 468, 474.

[24] [2007] EWCA Civ 989, affirmed by the ECtHR in *Austin v UK* App no 39692/09 (ECtHR (GC) 15 March 2012).

liberty was engaged by kettling, it was also breached. To arrive at their conclusion that the right was not engaged, the Lords reasoned that, although Article 5 is an absolute right (subject to exemptions, but not exceptions), a pragmatic approach was necessary when deciding on the scope of the right. In particular, the Lords looked to the aim of the confinement—and reasoned that, although Article 5 of the Convention does not refer to the interests of public safety or the protection of public order as cases in which a person might be deprived of her liberty, importance had to be attached to such factors in determining whether there had been a breach of Article 5 so that competing fundamental rights might be reconciled with each other.[25] This balancing of individual rights as against the public interest is precisely what occurs in respect of exceptions to qualified international human rights law treaty rights, and yet the House of Lords engaged in this reasoning for the purposes of determining the scope of the right to liberty itself. The Lords concluded that the ambit given to Article 5, in respect of crowd control measures resorted to for public order and public safety reasons, has to 'take account of the rights of the individual as well as the interests of the community [… and that such measures will fall outside the ambit of Article 5 provided that they] are proportionate to the situation which has made them necessary'.[26] In so doing, the Lords in effect treated a limited right (subject only to expressly determined exemptions) as a qualified right (which permits the balancing of competing interests). The Human Rights Committee similarly characterizes the international human rights law calculus in respect of the right to liberty in terms of its proportionality, even though the right is one that subject to a limitation in scope (non-arbitrary detentions are exempted from the scope of the right), as distinguished from a qualified right subject to exceptions: 'The notion of "arbitrariness" is not to be equated with "against the law", but must be interpreted more broadly to include elements of inappropriateness, injustice, lack of predictability and due process of law, *as well as elements of reasonableness, necessity and proportionality*'.[27]

The structure of this analysis—the identification of legitimate aims which potentially justify limitations to a rights interest, and measuring the proportionality of the limiting measure as against that legitimate aim, is identical to the structure of analysis in reference to qualified rights. It is simply that, in respect of limited rights (rights qualified as to scope and subject to exemptions), the analysis simultaneously determines whether the right has been engaged and whether there has been a breach. There is indeed a formal difference between exemptions and exceptions as a matter of principle, but in the international human rights law context the distinction is *significantly* more fluid, with at least exemptions bleeding into exceptions insofar as the structure of analysis is concerned.

4 Derogations

All three international human rights law treaty regimes which are the subject of this study allow states to derogate from some of their human rights obligations for the limited purposes

[25] *Austin* (n 24) para 34 (Lord Hope, with Lords Scott, Walker, Carswell, and Neuberger concurring).

[26] ibid. This approach—one in which the pursuit of a legitimate aim (which does not fall within the list of stated exemptions in respect of limited rights) is permitted to proportionately(ish) limit a limited right is also evident in the counter-terrorism context. See Helen Fenwick and Gavin Phillipson, 'Covert Derogations and Judicial Deference: Redefining Liberty and Due Process Rights in Counterterrorism Law and Beyond' (2011) 56 McGill Law Journal 863, 870–71 for a very thoughtful critique of this approach.

[27] Emphasis added. Human Rights Committee, General Comment No 35 'Liberty and Security of Person' (2014) UN Doc CCPR/C/GC/35art 9, para 12.

of responding to crisis.[28] The ECHR and the ICCPR allow for measures which derogate from the obligation to respect (certain) human rights in times of 'public emergency [which threatens] the life of the nation', the ECHR and the ACHR allow for derogations in 'time of war', and the ACHR allows for derogation in times of 'public danger, or other emergency that threatens the independence or security of a State Party'. In each case, the state party may 'take measures derogating from [its] obligations [under the relevant Convention] to the extent strictly required by the exigencies of the situation'.[29]

While the effect of a derogation is not dissimilar from that of an exception to a qualified right, in that a freedom of action that would not otherwise exist is created, the mechanism for achieving this result is different. In particular, in respect of derogations, the primary rule continues to prohibit the relevant government action, but the obligation to respect that primary rule is suspended (or waived) in virtue of the derogation. In the case of an exception to qualified rights, an exercise of regulatory authority or executive power which falls within the scope of the exception is not prohibited—the entire calculus takes place within the context of the substantive primary rule defining the right. Derogations, on the other hand, are an 'internal/external' qualification—internal to the human rights regime (and therefore still a primary rule), but external to the particular primary rule (right) in question.

There is also a temporal distinction between exceptions to qualified rights and derogations. An exception carves out a space for government action from the rights protection which space can exist on a permanent basis provided that the balancing of interests at play does not shift. A derogation, by contrast, is intended to be a temporary measure to respond to a particular crisis which has arisen. In effect, exceptions to qualified rights are a vehicle for government action which *maintains* peace, order, and a balance between competing interests, while derogation clauses are a vehicle for government action which *restores* peace and order.[30] As a result, qualified rights (and their exceptions), operate as a matter of course—governments balance respect for the fullest possible conception of the right as against competing public interests, and exercise their regulatory authority in keeping with that balance. Derogations are meant to be *exceptional* and *temporary*.[31] This difference, however, is

[28] ECHR art 15; ICCPR art 4; ACHR art 27. There was much debate during the negotiation of both the ICCPR and the ECHR regarding whether a general derogation clause was necessary, given the availability of exceptions in reference to qualified rights, many of which recognized permissive limitations for the purposes of protecting 'national security' or 'public order'. These exceptions were considered to 'take care of situations which might arise in time of war or national emergency'. See United Nations Secretary-General, 'Annotation of the Draft Covenant on Human Rights' UN Doc A/2929 (1955) ch V pt II (arts 2 to 5) para 36. See also European Commission on Human Rights, 'Preparatory work on Article 15 of the European Convention on Human Rights' Information document prepared by the Secretariat of the Commission at the request of the President of the Commission (22 May 1956) 5. However, it was also argued that: '[t]here might . . . be instances of extraordinary peril or crisis, not in time of war, when derogation from obligations assumed under a convention would become essential for the *safety of the people and the existence of the nation*. These situations would not fall within the scope of the limitations provided for in the various articles of the covenant, nor could they be adequately covered by a general limitations clause.' UN Doc A/2929 (1995) para 37. The latter view won the day.

[29] ICCPR art 4,; ECHR art 15; ACHR art 27. The ACHR makes it clear that 'strictly required' is not only a substantive limitation on derogating measures, but also a temporal limitation.

[30] See e.g. International Law Association (ILA), 'The Paris Minimum Standards of Human Rights Norms in a State of Emergency' Report of the 61st Conference (Paris), section A.3(a); *Brannigan and McBride v United Kingdom* App nos 14553/89, 14554/89 (ECtHR 25 May 1993) para 34.

[31] Both the derogation triggering situation *and* the measures adopted in response thereto were originally understood to be temporary and exceptional. See eg *The Greek Case* App Nos 3321–3323, 3344/67 (ECommHR Report of 1969) para 158, identifying that the 'the crisis or danger must be exceptional' as one of the elements of a public emergency which might justify the invocation of a derogation; Human Rights Committee (HRC), General Comment No 29 (2001) UN Doc CCPR/C/21/Rev.1/Add.1, para 2, holding that derogating measures must be of an 'exceptional and temporary nature' (accepted by the ECtHR in *A and Others v United Kingdom* App no 3455/05 (ECtHR (GC) 19 February 2009). The ECtHR, however, at least in respect of the temporal nature of the derogation

perhaps in danger of becoming more theoretical than practical, as the tendency in the post-9/11 world has been to govern as though in a permanent state of emergency.[32]

Where a derogation validly operates, the obligation to respect the right is temporarily waived or suspended. As a result, the consequence of a derogation has been described in somewhat similar terms to that of denunciation—which is to say that a derogation 'take[s] a State outside the human rights regime'.[33] While derogations do indeed create a space for regulatory conduct and executive action within which the relevant human rights obligation does not restrict conduct as it would *sans* derogation, it is too far to claim that derogations take a state outside the human rights regime.[34] In particular, the lawfulness of the derogation itself—including whether the conditions of its invocability have been met, and the extent to which a state has in fact restricted its human rights inconsistent conduct to the sphere of freedom provided by the derogation (defined in reference to whether the measure is 'strictly required by the exigencies of the situation'), is fully subject to review within the relevant human rights regime. It is certainly true that a derogation changes the nature of the human rights regime's engagement—it is not measuring compliance of government action with substantive human rights, but the validity of the derogation and the compliance of the government action with that valid derogation. But given that the strict necessity of each and every measure which would otherwise be inconsistent with human rights obligations is fully subject to human rights monitoring mechanisms,[35] it seems rather a stretch to speak of states acting outside the human rights regime. They act within the regime, even while inconsistently with the normative human rights obligations provided therein.

That derogations are also subject to the scrutiny of relevant international human rights law monitoring bodies (as is the case with exceptions), however, is a similarity that obscures a relatively important distinction. In particular, institutionally, courts are very comfortable with balancing interests against each other, and making determinations on the proportionality of measures as referenced against the objective or aim of that measure or the underlying interest otherwise being protected by that measure. Limitations to qualified rights can therefore be subject to fairly robust judicial scrutiny. Derogations, , on the other hand, involve both a judgment as regards a security situation—whether there is a public emergency or other threat to the life of a nation—and a balancing of the measures limiting rights as against the legitimate aim of restoring the pre-emergency situation. The first element of this analysis is precisely the sort of calculus in respect of which courts and treaty monitoring bodies suffer a confidence crisis, underpinned by claims about particular spheres of institutional competence. Courts give governments a rather large margin of appreciation in determining the

triggering situation, has accepted that emergencies may be entrenched or rather more long term. *A and Others v UK* (ibid) para 178, citing *Ireland v United Kingdom*, App no 5310/71 (ECtHR 18 January 1978).

[32] For a very interesting discussion of this phenomenon see Oren Gross and Fionnuala Ní Aoláin, *Law in Times of Crisis: Emergency Powers in Theory and Practice* (CUP 2006) ch 4 and 281–83.

[33] Hickman (n 13), 665.

[34] Arguing persuasively *against* the existence of 'legal black holes' in respect of emergencies, whereby State conduct is taken outside the legal order see David Dyzenhaus, 'Schmitt v. Dicey: Are States of Emergency Inside or Outside the Legal Order?' (2006) Cardozo Law Review 2005.

[35] Courts and human rights treaty monitoring bodies have been somewhat uneven in distinguishing between the 'strictly required' standard of derogations, and the necessity of limitations in respect of qualified rights (framed in terms of proportionality). Compare eg *Handyside v United Kingdom* App no 5493/72 (ECtHR 7 December 1976) para 48, in which the Court suggests that the art 15 'strictly required' standard is synonymous with 'indispensable' (and is, on that basis, to be distinguished from the 'necessary' standard vis-à-vis qualified rights, which evokes proportionality), with the UN Human Rights Committee's General Comment No 29, in which it considers that proportionality is the standard which applies to both the derogation provision ('strictly required') and qualified rights ('necessary') in the ICCPR. See HRC, General Comment No 29 (n 31) para 4.

existence of a derogation triggering situation, even if they are more robust in their analysis of the necessity of the measures adopted in response.[36] This judicial discomfort with interference in determinations regarding derogation triggering situations is partially a reflection of the source of that determination. In respect of qualified rights subject to exceptions, it will in large measure be the legislature which determines the balance to be achieved between a legitimate aim (protecting public health for instance) and respect for individual human rights interests. A derogation, however, even if ratified by the legislature, will more commonly be triggered by the executive, in whose power making a determination as to the existence of a 'public emergency [threatening/which threatens] the life of the nation' will lie. And courts have long been institutionally disposed, through the operation of various domestic law doctrines, to be very slow to interfere in the exercise of executive or prerogative powers, particularly where such powers touch on questions of national security.[37]

Having said all this, there is a large measure of overlap between the structure of an exception and the structure of a derogation. Both define legitimate aims for the exercise of regulatory authority or executive power that is otherwise inconsistent with protected human rights interests, and indeed there may be some overlap in the aims recognized to be legitimate insofar as some qualified rights recognize national security as one such aim.[38] In addition, like qualified rights, derogations are purely instrumental—the human rights limitations must be rationally connected to the legitimate aim, and 'strictly required' to meet that aim. The 'strictly required' analysis in respect of derogations overlaps with the elements of a proportionality analysis in respect of qualified rights,[39] even if the derogation standard is often held to be stricter.[40] There is therefore not very much space on the spectrum of international human rights law qualifications between exceptions (to qualified rights) and derogations—at least insofar as the structure of analysis is concerned. There is perhaps more space between

[36] On the determination that a derogation triggering situation exists see eg *Ireland v UK* (n 31), where the Court held that: 'It falls in the first place to each contracting state, with its responsibility for "the life of [its] nation", to determine whether that life is threatened by a "public emergency" and, if so, how far it is necessary to go in attempting to overcome the emergency. By reason of their direct and continuous contact with the pressing needs of the moment, the national authorities are in principle in a better position than the international judge to decide both on the presence of such an emergency and on the nature and scope of derogations necessary to avert it. In this matter [art 15(1)] leaves the authorities a wide margin of appreciation' (para 207). While the courts have maintained an attitude of deference to the executive insofar as determinations regarding the existence of a threat to the life of the nation are concerned (which deference has been the subject of much criticism see eg Gross and Ní Aoláin (n 32) 280 ff), there is more robust review of whether the measures adopted are 'strictly required by the exigencies of the situation'. See eg *A and Others v Secretary of State for the Home Department* [2005] UKHL 71; *A and Others v United Kingdom* (n 31).

[37] See eg *CCSU v Minister for Civil Service* [1985] AC 374; *R (Corner House Research) v Director of the Serious Fraud Office* [2008] UKHL 60.

[38] The UK's derogation lodged following the 9/11 terrorist attacks identified a 'threat to ... national security' as the derogation triggering situation. While the UK's approach was confirmed (or at least tolerated) by the ECtHR in its *A and Others* decision (n 31), there is a not unreasonable argument to be made that national security, already a basis for limiting human rights in respect of certain qualified rights, should not be double counted as a derogation triggering situation. See e.g. Ed Bates, 'A "Public Emergency Threatening the Life of the Nation"? The United Kingdom's Derogation from the European Convention on Human Rights of 18 December and the "A" Case' (2006) 76 British Yearbook of International Law 245, 251. The UK's derogation was principally in respect of the right to liberty, however, which is not a qualified right. As a result, a derogation is the only emergency measure available to restrict liberty in response to genuine threats to national security.

[39] See n 18 and accompanying text for a discussion of the elements of the proportionality analysis in reference to qualified rights. In respect of 'strictly required' under derogation clauses see eg *Aksoy v Turkey* App No 21987/93 (ECtHR 18 December 1996) para 23 (in which the Court examines whether lesser measures might have been sufficient to respond to the emergency situation); *Jorge Landinelli Silva v Uruguay* Communication No R.8/34, UN Doc Supp No 40 (A/36/40) 130 (1981) para 8.2 (in which the Human Rights Committee considered the breath of the measures adopted and held them to be beyond what was 'strictly required').

[40] See n 36.

limited rights subject to exemptions (explored in section 3.1.1 above) and derogations, where the derogation clause might have a direct impact—in permitting limitations to the exercise of a right that otherwise does not admit such limitations once it is engaged. Again, however, this direct impact is somewhat minimized by the approaches to limited rights explored above. In particular, the fact that a balancing of interests (for the purposes of meeting legitimate aims which are not expressly addressed in the relevant rule) can take place in respect of limited rights[41] means that interests like security might be taken into account at the stage of defining the scope of a right, reducing the need for a derogation. Furthermore, in virtue of the regime interaction principles examined in section 3.2 above (which apply to limited rights), international humanitarian law, as an applicable *lex specialis*,[42] accommodates some of the state interests that are reflected in derogation clauses.[43] Consider, for instance, the difference between the ECHR, on the one hand, and the ACHR and the ICCPR on the other. In respect of the right to life, the ECHR exempts particular government conduct from the scope of the right (and international humanitarian law compliant incidental civilian deaths in the context of an armed conflict is *not* one of the exemptions), while the ACHR and the ICCPR exempt non-arbitrary deprivations of life (with 'non-arbitrary' tracking international humanitarian law compliance in respect of deprivations of life resulting from armed conflict). To accommodate this difference, there is also a difference in the derogation provisions of the ECHR as compared to the ACHR and the ICCPR. The ECHR permits no derogations to the right to life 'except in respect of deaths resulting from lawful acts of war',[44] while the ACHR and the ICCPR permit no derogations to the right to life, full stop. The scope of the right to life under the ACHR and the ICCPR are defined in reference to a standard which accommodates some forms of government action in emergency situations (in particular those resulting from armed conflict), and as a result, the derogation clause need not *also* accommodate such emergency situations. The scope of the ECHR right to life, however, does not accommodate armed conflict type emergencies, leaving this work to be done by the derogation clause. Both the ICCPR and the ECHR address the right to life and wartime deaths to the same effect, but relying on different 'qualification' mechanisms. There is nothing inherent or necessary in these concerns being addressed through defining the scope of a right or permitting derogations—it is a formal difference, of course, but not necessarily a substantive one.[45]

What remains to be determined, insofar as international human rights law qualifications are concerned, is whether necessity, as a circumstance precluding wrongfulness in the ILC's Articles on State Responsibility,[46] is the final qualification to human rights along the

[41] See nn 24–27 and accompanying discussion.

[42] Alternatively, international humanitarian law might be characterized as a regime which informs the interpretation of a limited right qualified as to scope. See nn 21–22.

[43] Indeed, international humanitarian law accommodates State interests on a broader basis than derogation provisions in that the security interests of a small subset of a nation—like the armed forces—form the basis of the limitation on a right in the international humanitarian law regime interaction context, while this is not necessarily so in the derogation context. See section 4 below for further discussion.

[44] ECHR art 15(2).

[45] Some of the chapters in this edited volume suggest that there may be normative consequences to (or litigation strategies attempting to derive normative consequences from) the distinction between a rule which incorporates its exception and a rule whose exceptions are addressed separately, in particular as regards the burden of proof. See Frederick Schauer, 'Rules, Defeasibility, and the Psychology of Exceptions' in L Bartels and F Paddeu (eds) *Exceptions and Defences in International Law* (OUP 2017), §5; Viñuales (n 5) sections 2.2 and 2.3. In the international human rights law context, given the inequality of arms between the applicant human right victim and the respondent State, strict rules on burdens of proof are not appropriate. For instance, the ECtHR has held that certain human rights cases do not 'lend themselves to a rigorous application of the principle whereby a person who alleges something must prove that allegation'. See *Bazorkina v Russia* App no 69481/01 (ECtHR 27 July 2006) para 170.

[46] ILC ARSIWA (n 2) ch V.

continuum. Part of the answer to that question involves an exploration of the applicability of derogations to situations of extraterritorial armed conflict, as set out below.

4.1 The approach to derogations in extraterritorial armed conflicts

Article 15 of the ECHR and Article 27 of the ACHR expressly recognize that derogations can apply to 'time of war'. Article 4 of the ICCPR, on the other hand, does not expressly reference war. It is clear from the drafting history of the provision, however, that war was envisaged as a derogation triggering situation, but that states objected to the optics of expressly contemplating war in a UN treaty.[47] This chapter will proceed on the basis that the applicability of derogations to 'war'—a formalistic concept which is no longer a relevant feature of the legal landscape—extends to the modern (post-Second World War) concept of 'armed conflict', most clearly in cases where the conflict takes place in the territory of the state invoking a derogation.[48] Indeed, the only state practice to date of invoking derogation clauses as a result of armed conflict have been in reference to armed conflicts within the invoking state's territory.[49]

It remains an open question, however, whether derogation clauses cover extraterritorial armed conflicts—in particular armed conflicts in which a state is acting in protection of its domestic security interests through an armed conflict which it pursues *abroad*.[50] There are suggestions in some of the international human rights law case law that derogation clauses ought not apply in such circumstances, in particular, two decisions by the UK's highest court. In *Al-Jedda*, Lord Bingham noted that:

> It is hard to think that these conditions could ever be met when a state had chosen to conduct an overseas peacekeeping operation, however dangerous the conditions, from which it could withdraw. The Secretary of State does not contend that the UK could exercise its power to derogate in Iraq (although he does not accept that it could not). It has not been the practice of states to derogate in such situations, and since subsequent practice in the application of a treaty may (under article 31(3)(b) of the Vienna Convention) be taken into account in interpreting the treaty it seems proper to regard article 15 as inapplicable.[51]

[47] In his guide to the *travaux préparatoires* of the ICCPR, Bossuyt explains that 'it was felt that the covenant should not envisage, even by implication, the possibility of war, as the United Nations was established with the object of preventing war'. Marc Bossuyt, *Guide to the 'Travaux Préparatoires' of the International Covenant on Civil and Political Rights* (Martinus Nijhoff 1987) 86.

[48] The Human Rights Committee, in setting out the availability of derogations, makes it clear that situations of armed conflict might amount to a derogation triggering situation: 'The Covenant requires that even during an armed conflict measures derogating from the Covenant are allowed only if and to the extent that the situation constitutes a threat to the life of the nation.' HRC, General Comment No 29 (n 31) para 3.

[49] See Marko Milanovic, 'Extraterritorial Derogations from Human Rights Treaties in Armed Conflict' in Nehal Bhuta (ed), *Collected Courses of the Academy of European Law* (OUP 2015). The UK may be the first State to invoke a derogation in respect of an extra-territorial armed conflicts. At the time of writing, Theresa May—the un-elected Conservative Prime Minister of the UK—announced that the UK would derogate from the ECHR in future overseas armed conflicts. 'Government to protect Armed Forces from persistent legal claims in future overseas operations' 4 October 2016, https://www.gov.uk/government/news/government-to-protect-armed-forces-from-persistent-legal-claims-in-future-overseas-operations.

[50] This section assumes that international human rights law treaties apply extra-territorially to armed conflicts (in respect of at least some State conduct), as determined by all three international human rights law courts and treaty monitoring bodies explored in this chapter: *Coard v United States* (n 20) para 38; Human Rights Committee General Comment No 31 (2004) para 11; *Hassan v United Kingdom* (n 21) para 101.

[51] *R (Al-Jedda) v Secretary of State for Defence* [2007] UKHL 58, para 38.

To similar effect, Lord Hope had this to say in the House of Lords *Smith* opinion:

> [T]he phrase "threatening the life of the nation" suggests that the power to derogate under this article is available only in an exceptional situation of crisis or emergency which affects the whole population and constitutes a threat to the organised life of the community of which the state is composed .... I do not think therefore that it would be right to assume that concern about the practical consequences in situations such as those with which we are dealing in this case can be answered by exercising the power to derogate. The circumstances in which that power can properly be exercised are far removed from those where operations are undertaken overseas with a view to eliminating or controlling threats to the nation's security. The jurisprudence of the Strasbourg court shows that there are other ways in which such concerns may be met.[52]

The International Court of Justice, however, seems to allow for the possibility that derogations are permissible in extraterritorial armed conflicts, in its general statement that 'the protection offered by human rights conventions does not cease in case of armed conflict, save through the effect of provisions for derogation of the kind to be found in Article 4 of the International Covenant on Civil and Political Rights'.[53] The Court makes no reference to whether it is contemplating armed conflicts within the invoking state's own territory or beyond, but the facts under contemplation in each case (Israel's limitations on human rights in occupied territory and the use of nuclear weapons—presumably abroad) suggest it may have had the applicability of derogations beyond the invoking state's territory in mind.

The matter obviously remains contested, but there may be very good reason for the Lords' intuition that derogations ought not apply to (at least some features of) extraterritorial armed conflicts—particularly those in which the state is protecting domestic security interests in its armed conflict abroad. While not articulated in these terms by the Lords—the problem is with identifying the relevant derogation 'situation' in complex factual contexts (like those of an extraterritorial armed conflict).

4.2 The 'one situation/two situation' problem

Extra-territorial armed conflicts potentially result in a disconnect between the derogation triggering situation and the situation to which the human rights limiting measure responds. It is clear from the language of the derogation clauses, however, that they contemplate *one* situation which *both* triggers the derogation and to which the relevant human rights limiting measures respond. In relevant part, derogation clauses read:

> In time of [war, public danger, or public emergency threatening the life of the nation/independence or security of a State Party], [the State parties to the present Convention] may take measures derogating from [their] obligations under [the present Convention] to the extent [strictly] required by the exigencies of *the* situation ...[54]

[52] *R (Smith and Others) v Ministry of Defence* [2013] UKSC 41, paras 59–60.

[53] *Legal Consequences of the Construction of a Wall in the Occupied Palestinian Territory* (Advisory Opinion) [2004] ICJ Rep 136, para 106; *Legality of the Threat or Use of Nuclear Weapons* (Advisory Opinion) [1996] ICJ Reports 226, para 25.

[54] Emphasis added and seen 31. Indeed, human rights courts or treaty monitoring bodies have often used language suggesting that the single situation (that which triggers the derogation and to which the relevant measures respond) must be within the *very* territory of the State invoking the derogation. See eg the decision in *Lawless v*

In respect of Security Council authorized humanitarian interventions,[55] initial phases of operations may well fall outside the scope of international human rights law treaties entirely, even if the human rights 'interests' of those on the ground would be considered to be engaged. And there is no need to search for a derogation triggering situation in cases where the international human rights law treaty regime doesn't apply, as derogation clauses obviously do not contemplate situations which are beyond the jurisdiction of the derogation invoking state. A State's conduct, which is otherwise inconsistent with the human rights interests of individuals beyond its jurisdiction, is in no need of an exception or derogation from a legal perspective—and humanitarian interventions carried out through aerial campaigns (for instance in Kosovo and Libya) have to date been judged by at least the European Court of Human Rights to be excluded from the scope of international human rights law treaties.[56]

But, in respect of humanitarian intervention operations which do fall within the scope of application of international human rights law treaties, because individuals in the territory subject to the intervention fall within the intervening state's jurisdiction, there will in fact be *two* emergency situations, one of which threatens two separate constituencies. First, there is the humanitarian catastrophe which occasioned the armed intervention (which does not require a derogation until troops are on the ground exercising some form of effective control over territory or control over individuals such that the derogation invoking state has jurisdiction), which is the first situation. Secondly, there is the emergency situation created by the armed conflict or intervention itself (as distinguished from the situation which occasioned the armed conflict or intervention, which might also have been a situation of armed conflict), which is the second situation . In respect of the latter, there are two separate constituencies threatened by the armed conflict: first, residents of the territory in which there is an armed conflict (situation 2A); and, secondly, the intervening armed forces (situation2B).

Ireland (n 53) para 28: 'an exceptional situation of crisis or emergency which affects the whole population and constitutes a threat to the organized life of the community of which the State is composed.' As the point has never been decided in quite such definitive terms, and the scope of application of human rights treaties (through the concept of 'jurisdiction') is constantly being expanded extra-territorially, this section will proceed on the basis that an extra-territorial situation could amount to a derogation triggering situation.

[55] A humanitarian intervention involves State A engaging in an armed conflict in State B's territory, not in defence of its own (or another State's) security interests, but in the interests of State B's civilian population (because the Government of State B is either unwilling or unable to protect its own civilian population, or because that Government is the source of the threat to the civilian population). For present purposes, and to side-step entirely the debate regarding the lawfulness of such interventions on a unilateral (or coalition) basis (see e.g. WM Reisman, 'Unilateral Action and the Transformations of the World Constitutive Process: The Special Problem of Humanitarian Intervention' (2000) 11 EJIL 3; Monica Hakimi, 'Toward a Legal Theory on the Responsibility to Protect' (2014) 39 Yale Journal of International Law 247; Harold H Koh, 'Syria and the Law of Humanitarian Intervention (Part II: International Law and the Way Forward)' *EJIL:Talk!* (4 October 2013) http://www.ejiltalk.org/syria-and-the-law-of-humanitarian-intervention-part-ii-international-law-and-the-way-forward/ ; Sir Daniel Bethlehem, 'Stepping Back a Moment: The Legal Basis in Favour of a Principle of Humanitarian Intervention' *EJIL:Talk!* (12 September 2013) http://www.ejiltalk.org/stepping-back-a-moment-the-legal-basis-in-favour-of-a-principle-of-humanitarian-intervention/), this chapter will assume that the intervention in State B has been authorized by the Security Council acting in exercise of its primary responsibility for international peace and security under ch VII of the UN Charter. See UN Charter arts 39 and 42.

[56] See in particular *Banković and Others v Belgium and Others* App no 52207/99 (ECtHR (GC) 12 December 2001) paras 59–82. This decision has rightly been the subject of sustained criticism, but subsequent ECtHR decisions have left untouched the basic principle that aerial attacks do not amount to an exercise of jurisdiction for the purposes of international human rights law treaty obligations. See *Al-Skeini and Others v United Kingdom* App no 55721/07 (ECtHR (GC) 7 July 2011) paras 109–50. In a recent United Kingdom (UK) Court of Appeal decision, Lord Justice Lloyd-Jones left it open for the ECtHR to step back from its position in *Banković*, such that a use of lethal force (even via aerial campaign) would in and of itself amount to the exercise of jurisdiction triggering human rights obligations. See *Al-Saadoon and Others v Secretary of State for Defence* [2016] EWCA Civ 811. At the time of writing, the decision had not been appealed to the UK Supreme Court.

While the first situation and situation 2A may well give rise to a valid derogation to which human rights limitations could be tailored (both of which will be a 'public emergency [which threatens] the life of the nation', in particular the nation that is victim of the humanitarian catastrophe and in whose interests the armed intervention is being fought), situation 2B could not, for the reasons set out below. And yet some of the human rights limitations adopted in humanitarian interventions will respond to situation 2B—and to the extent that they do, there is a disconnect between a valid derogation triggering situation and the situation to which particular human rights limiting measures respond.

The second type of conflict to consider is that in which a state is exercising its Article 51 UN Charter right of self-defence.[57] We will assume that State A is the victim of an armed attack (actual or imminent), and State B is both the source of the armed attack (actual or imminent) and the state in whose territory armed conflict is waged in defensive response. There might be several stages of such an armed conflict, including active combat operations (during which time State A's armed forces are fighting first and foremost in defence of State A's interests and, secondly, with a view to their own 'force protection'); and potentially occupation of State B. During occupation of State B, State A has an international humanitarian law obligation to 'take all the measures in [its] power to restore, and ensure, as far as possible, public order and safety, while respecting, unless absolutely prevented, the laws in force in the country',[58] in the interests of the local population. State A might also be taking measures necessary for its own security at home (to the extent that the threat of further armed attack remains from individuals within State B's territory) and its security as an occupying power (including detaining individuals who threaten the security of State A as an occupying power, as is permitted under the Fourth Geneva Convention).[59]

In such cases, the situation which threatens the life of the nation is the armed attack (actual or imminent) suffered in State A's territory, but the exigency creating situation (which calls for limitations on human rights) will in part be that of the armed conflict abroad (in particular the threat to the armed forces of State A during combat operations and to State A's security interests as an occupying power, as permissibly protected pursuant to the Fourth Geneva Convention, during any subsequent occupation). But based on the pronouncements of international human rights law treaty bodies and regional international human rights law courts, the armed conflict abroad (as distinguished from the armed attack in the derogating state's territory) cannot subsequently be characterized as the derogation triggering situation. This is because international human rights law treaty bodies and courts have held that derogation triggering situations must threaten the life of the 'whole' nation, or the 'whole' population of the area to which the declaration applies—not a small subset thereof (like the armed forces fighting in a foreign armed conflict).[60]

[57] This chapter will not examine armed conflicts in which State A is engaging in armed conflict in collective self-defence of State C, in State B's territory and pursuant to art 51 of the UN Charter. This type of extraterritorial armed conflict raises similar issues to those explored in reference to individual self-defence, but with the complicating factor of a third state's interests in the mix.

[58] Convention (IV) Respecting the Laws and Customs of War on Land and its annex: Regulations concerning the Laws and Customs of War on Land (The Hague, 18 October 1907) Annex: Regulations respecting the laws and customs of war on land, Section III: Military Authority over the Territory of the Hostile State art 43.

[59] Geneva Convention Relative to the Protection of Civilian Persons in Time of War of 12 August 1949 (Fourth Geneva Convention) 7 UNTS 287 art 78.

[60] See ECOSOC, 'Siracusa Principles on the Limitation and Derogation Provisions in the International Covenant on Civil and Political Rights' UN Doc E/CN.4/1985/4, Annex (1985) para 39. See also ILA, 'The Paris Minimum Standards' (n 30) Section A.1(b); *Lawless v Ireland (No 3)* App no 332/57 (ECtHR 1 July 1961). But see ILC, Commentary to ILC ARSIWA (n 3) art 21, para 3—in which the ILC concludes that '[h]uman rights treaties contain derogation provisions for times of public emergency, including actions taken in self-defence.' The Commentaries do not elaborate on this statement, and indeed say nothing about whether the 'actions taken in

The difficulty is best perceived when we remind ourselves that derogations permit the imposition of human rights limitations for the purposes of responding to an emergency situation and to *restore* conditions of normalcy. In the case of foreign armed conflicts, there will always be one situation which does not admit restoration to normalcy—and that is the situation of the armed forces participating in the armed conflict (whose interests may well need protecting during active combat operations and any subsequent occupation through limitations to human rights protection). The state engaging in an armed conflict abroad, in limiting human rights, is in part always responding to threats to its own security interests (which security interests are those created by the armed conflict, not those which might have triggered derogation by threatening the life of the nation domestically). And those security interests are the interests of a small subset of the nation (in particular, the armed forces) which do not have a 'normal' because, if those particular interests are engaged, it is always in a situation of conflict and emergency. Even where the derogation invoking state is principally acting to restore normalcy to the community whose rights are being limited and in whose territory the armed conflict is being waged (in situations of humanitarian intervention and any subsequent occupation), the derogating state will *also* in part be responding to a threat to its own security interests (in the sense of armed forces protection during active combat operations or its security interests as an occupying power). But the threat to its armed forces, being a subset of the 'nation as a whole', is not an 'emergency threatening the life of the nation' which might validly trigger a derogation. Again, there is a disconnect between the valid derogation triggering situation and the situation to which particular human rights limiting measures respond.

The 'one situation/two situation' problem, discussed above, suggests that derogation provisions ought not be available in respect of at least some features of extraterritorial armed conflicts. In particular, derogations should be unavailable where the triggering situation is a threat to the civilian population of foreign states (as is the case of the armed conflict phase of humanitarian interventions), but the interests protected by human rights limiting measures are those of the intervening and derogation invoking state's armed forces; or where the human rights limiting measures respond to the security interests of the armed forces which are *created by* the armed conflict. For principally pragmatic reasons, and perhaps counter-intuitively, this is not necessarily a *positive* human rights outcome. There is arguably a greater human rights benefit in permitting states to invoke derogations during extraterritorial armed conflicts, implicitly accepting that the human rights regime applies (in a way that is reviewable by human rights courts and treaty monitoring bodies), than there is in derogations being inapplicable, resulting in the continued (and rather stubborn) refusal of states engaging in these extraterritorial armed conflicts to accept the applicability of human rights law.[61] Necessity, as a defence or excuse under general international law, may be available in respect of extraterritorial armed conflicts to respond partially to this concern, as explored in section 2.1.3 below.

self-defence' are those a State might take in its own territory (for instance preventative detention of residents who are suspected of assisting invading forces, as would be permitted under the Fourth Geneva Convention (n 59)), or those it might take extraterritorially.

[61] See Milanovic (n 49).

5 External Exceptions: Circumstances Precluding Wrongfulness

Necessity is a 'circumstance precluding wrongfulness' in the ILC's Articles on State Responsibility. Article 25 of the ILC's Articles provides that:

1. Necessity may not be invoked by a State as a ground for precluding the wrongfulness of an act not in conformity with an international obligation of that State unless the act:
   a) is the only way for the State to safeguard an essential interest against a grave and imminent peril; and
   b) does not seriously impair an essential interest of the State or States towards which the obligation exists, or of the international community as a whole.
2. In any case, necessity may not be invoked by a State as a ground for precluding wrongfulness if:
   a) the international obligation in question excludes the possibility of invoking necessity; or
   b) the State has contributed to the situation of necessity.

As far as the ILC is concerned, 'necessity' does not render the relevant conduct lawful (or at least not unlawful) as a matter of the applicable primary rules, as do exceptions and derogations. Rather, it temporarily suspends the consequences of wrongfulness—in particular the obligations (derived from the secondary rules of state responsibility) to cease the wrongful conduct and to make full reparation.[62] Unlike derogations, which waive the obligation to comply with the primary rule (the right) in advance, necessity excuses a breach after the fact[63] —but the relevant conduct nevertheless remains a breach. Like derogations, however, necessity is autonomous from the primary rule which defines the right in question, although unlike derogations—it is also outside the scope of the primary regime entirely, falling squarely within the secondary rules of state responsibility. On these bases, necessity as a circumstance precluding wrongfulness is best characterized as a defence, not an exception. While this is certainly a formal difference, it is perhaps *only* that.

There are more points of overlap in respect of derogations and necessity as a circumstance precluding wrongfulness applied to a human rights context than points of divergence:[64]

1. Like derogations, necessity as a circumstance precluding wrongfulness is temporally limited—it excludes the consequences of responsibility only for so long as the circumstance precluding wrongfulness triggering situation persists.

[62] See n 7.

[63] The Commentary to the ILC ARSIWA (n 3) (art 25, para 2) qualifies 'necessity' as a circumstance which 'excuse[s] the non-performance of an obligation'. There is, however, some debate in the literature as to whether this is an accurate characterization of 'necessity'. Federica Paddeu argues that 'necessity', in its guise as a circumstance precluding wrongfulness under the ILC ARSIWA, is in fact a justification (and not an excuse), in that it 'involve[s] a permission of the legal order to engage in conduct which would normally be prohibited [and as] permissible conduct, justified conduct is therefore lawful'. Federica Paddeu, 'Clarifying the Concept of Circumstances Precluding Wrongfulness (Justifications) in International Law' in L Bartels and F Paddeu (eds) *Exceptions and Defences in International Law* (OUP 2017) 203, § 4.2. While this is an important debate, particularly insofar as it affects the right of the state to terminate a treaty for material breach under VCLT art 60, termination for material breach is not generally accepted to be applicable in respect of international human rights law treaties. This chapter will therefore proceed on the basis of the framework set out in the ILC ARSIWA, mindful that the ILC failed to treat the distinction between excuses and justifications with any care. See also Viñuales (n 5) X, qualifying the circumstance precluding wrongfulness of 'necessity' as an excuse.

[64] See Joan F Hartman, 'Derogation from Human Rights Treaties in Public Emergencies' (1981) 22 Harvard Journal of International Law 1, 12–13, discussing the 'striking resemblances between the derogation clauses and the customary law doctrine of necessity'.

2. Both derogations and necessity as a circumstance precluding wrongfulness create the space for international human rights law non-compliant conduct on the basis of situations that are not generally applicable, but exceptional and particular to the circumstances of the invoking state. This is to be distinguished from exceptions, at least in the context of international human rights law, which principally address interests of a general (and ongoing) nature.
3. As is the case in respect of derogations, measures which are excused by necessity as a circumstance precluding wrongfulness have to be strictly tailored to the situation giving rise to its invocation. Human rights limiting measures adopted pursuant to a derogation need to be 'strictly required' to respond to the derogation triggering situation, which analysis involves a 'least restrictive means' approach.[65] Similarly, measures adopted in reliance on necessity as a circumstance precluding wrongfulness need to be 'the only way' to respond to the necessity triggering situation, which also involves an inquiry as to whether there are other means available.[66]
4. Derogation and necessity as a circumstance precluding wrongfulness (like exceptions to qualified rights) engage in a form of balancing of interests: The benefit that is sought through the relevant measure cannot be outweighed by the cost to those who suffer at the hands of the measure. Put another way, the situation which the measure seeks to avoid must be worse than the situation created by the measure itself.

The question remains whether necessity is an applicable circumstance precluding wrongfulness in respect of international human rights law treaty obligations, and particularly in respect of human rights limiting measures that may not fall within the scope of derogations (on the basis of the 'one situation/two situation' problem discussed above). The answer to this question involves consideration of two separate questions. The first is whether breaches of human rights norms might be excused by their necessity under the terms of Article 25 of the ILC Articles on State Responsibility (and related customary international law); and the second is whether—assuming its applicability—the application of Article 25 to human rights breaches is nevertheless excluded by the human rights regime and the *lex specialis* rule.[67]

5.1 Availability of necessity as a circumstance precluding wrongfulness as a matter of principle

The ILC Draft Articles on State Responsibility adopted on First Reading left little doubt that necessity could indeed preclude the wrongfulness of human rights breaching conduct (provided the human rights norm was not *jus cogens*[68])—in that it adopted a principally state centric approach to state responsibility.[69] The interests against which the availability of wrongfulness preclusion had to be measured were those of other states.

[65] See n 39.

[66] Commentary to ILC ARSIWA (n 3) art 25, para 15.

[67] ILC ARSIWA arts 25(2)(a) and 55 .

[68] Draft Articles on State Responsibility adopted on First Reading, Report of the ILC on the work of its Thirty-second session, UN Doc A/35/10 (1980) art 33(2)(a), reproduced in (1980) 2(2) Yearbook of the International Law Commission 30.

[69] See Cedric Ryngaert, 'State Responsibility, Necessity and Human Rights' (2010) 41 Netherlands Yearbook of International Law 79, 80.

Draft Article 33, adopted on First Reading, did not allow for the invocation of necessity as a circumstance precluding wrongfulness *unless*: 'the act did not seriously impair an essential interest of the State towards which the obligation existed'.[70]

While it might be argued that respect for the human rights of its nationals is an essential interest of a state, the result would nevertheless be that necessity might only be excluded as a circumstance precluding wrongfulness in reference to State A's breach of the human rights of State B's nationals. Necessity would be available as a circumstance precluding wrongfulness in respect of State's A's breach of the human rights of its own nationals.

This state-centricity of the article on necessity as a circumstance precluding wrongfulness, however, was not reflected in the final articles adopted by the ILC. Like the previous draft, Article 25 excludes necessity as a circumstance precluding wrongfulness in respect of *jus cogens* breaches, but it further excludes necessity as a circumstance precluding wrongfulness to the extent that the breaching act 'seriously impair[s] an essential interest of the State or States towards which the obligation exists, *or of the international community as a whole*'.[71]

Given the human rights obligations have long been characterized as *erga omnes*[72] and the increasingly central role human rights play in international law generally,[73] respect for such rights undoubtedly amounts to an essential interest of the international community as a whole. Necessity as a circumstance precluding wrongfulness, however, is only inapplicable where the measure adopted by the necessity invoking-State *seriously impairs* an essential interest (of another State or the international community as a whole). The Commentaries to the ILC Articles do not define 'serious impairment' of an interest, but there is perhaps a clue elsewhere in the Articles as to what serious impairment might entail. In the context of serious breaches of peremptory norms, the ILC Articles define serious breach as one which 'involves a gross or systematic failure'.[74] This undoubtedly precludes the kind of human rights breaches that are in fact contemplated as State practice of necessity as a circumstance precluding wrongfulness in the Commentaries (albeit practice which occurred at a time when international law did not yet protect human rights)—which make reference to some rather serious breaches of the non-derogable right to life (in the *Caroline Incident*) and the right to property (in the Anglo-Portuguese dispute of 1832).[75] But in respect of targeted and limited breaches of human rights (like the right to liberty for instance), engaged in for the strict purposes of responding to a grave and imminent peril, necessity is on its face available as a circumstance precluding wrongfulness. For present purposes, this means that human rights feature on both sides of the circumstance precluding wrongfulness calculus: they are the obligation in respect of which wrongfulness preclusion is sought through the invocation of

[70] Draft ILC Articles on State Responsibility adopted on First Reading (n 68) art 33(1)(b).

[71] Emphasis added. See ILC ARSIWA art 25(1)(b).

[72] The ICJ first characterized 'the principles and rules concerning the basic rights of the human person' as *erga omnes* in its *Barcelona Traction* decision (*Barcelona Traction, Light and Power Company Limited (Belgium v Spain)* (Judgment) [1970] ICJ Rep 1, 3, para 34.

[73] See eg Ruti Teitel, *Humanity's Law* (OUP 2011); Anne Peters, 'Humanity as the A and Ω of Sovereignty' (2003) 20 European Journal of International Law 513; Johan D van der Vyver, 'Sovereignty and Human Rights in Constitutional and International Law' (1991) 5 Emory International Law Review 321; and Michael Reisman, 'Sovereignty and Human Rights in Contemporary International Law' (1990) American Journal of International Law 866

[74] ILC ARSIWA art 40(2).

[75] Commentary to ILC ARSIWA (n 3) art 25, paras 4-5. While the precise measures adopted may well be beyond the reach of necessity as a circumstance precluding wrongfulness under the ILC ARSIWA as finally adopted, the triggering situations remain relevant.

necessity; and they are also the interest which must be outweighed by the circumstance precluding wrongfulness invoking State's necessity driven interests.[76]

In respect of the types of grave and imminent peril which might legitimately trigger the invocation of necessity as a circumstance precluding wrongfulness, the Commentaries highlight 'safeguarding the environment, preserving the very existence of the State and its people in time of public emergency, or ensuring the safety of a civilian population'.[77] The 'existence of the State' and 'public emergency' is evocative of the situations which might trigger a derogation.

The point for present purposes is that necessity can respond to emergency situations beyond those which might underpin the valid invocation of a derogation, in that there is nothing in Article 25 or the Commentary thereto which suggests that the responded to peril must be one that affects the 'nation as a whole'. As a result, extraterritorial human rights limitations occasioned by (for instance) a State's interests in armed forces protection or security interests in occupation (which interests a State could protect as a matter of IHL), but which fall outside the scope of limitations which are permissible on the basis of regime interaction[78] and would be excluded from the scope of derogations on the basis of the 'one situation / two situation' problem articulated above, may fall within the scope of necessity as a circumstance precluding wrongfulness. For instance, the Commentaries to the ILC Articles on State Responsibility consider State practice in which a necessity triggering peril included 'the pressing necessity of providing for the subsistence of certain contingents of troops engaged in quelling internal disturbances'[79] and 'the necessity of self-defence and self-preservation'.[80]

Furthermore, the ILC Articles define necessity triggering crises as those which affect the interests of the international community as a whole.[81] Necessity as a circumstance precluding wrongfulness therefore recognizes that a triggering situation might be one that affects the interests of third party states, those *not* immediately subject to the jurisdiction of the invoking state, and that as long as the measures are strictly necessary to protect those third party interests, the wrongfulness of the measures might be precluded. This has the effect of making necessity an available circumstance precluding wrongfulness for human rights limitations occasioned by (for instance) humanitarian intervention, particularly relevant should aerial campaigns ever be decided to engage the jurisdiction of the intervening state.[82]

5.2 The exclusion of necessity as a circumstance precluding wrongfulness on the basis of *lex specialis*?

Article 25(2)(a) stipulates that necessity may not be invoked as a circumstance precluding wrongfulness if 'the international obligation in question excludes the possibility of invoking

[76] While the language of art 25 suggests that there is no weighing of interests involved, and instead that serious impairment of an interest is an objectively determined and *absolute* bar to successful reliance on necessity as a circumstance precluding wrongfulness, the ILC Commentaries stipulate that: 'In other words, the interest relied on [in invoking necessity] must *outweigh* all other considerations, not merely from the point of view of the acting State but on a reasonable assessment of the *competing interests*, whether these are individual or collective' (emphasis added, Commentary to ILC ARSIWA (n 3) art 25, para 17).

[77] Commentary to ILC ARSIWA (n 3) art 25, para 14.

[78] See discussion in n 60.

[79] Commentary to ILC ARSIWA (n 3) art 25, para 4.

[80] ibid para 5.

[81] ibid para 15.

[82] See n 56.

necessity'.[83] The question remains, therefore, whether the internal qualifications to international human rights law treaties discussed in section 2 above (in particular, exemptions to limited rights, exceptions to qualified rights and derogations) are meant to exclude the operation of necessity as a circumstance precluding wrongfulness.

The International Court of Justice had the opportunity to address the applicability of necessity as a circumstance precluding wrongfulness to human rights breaches in its *Palestinian Wall* Advisory Opinion. The Court held that construction of the wall was in breach of the ICCPR—an international human rights law treaty which contains a derogation provision, and queried whether necessity, as a customary circumstance precluding wrongfulness, had been displaced thereby.[84] Presumably on the basis of judicial economy (in respect of its decision that the route of the wall was not the *only way* to safeguard against a grave and imminent peril and therefore did not meet the strict requirements of necessity as a circumstance precluding wrongfulness in any event), however, the Court declined to answer the question. In considering whether the conditions for invocation of necessity had been met, however, the Court implicitly accepts—at the very least—that the case *against* the continued applicability of necessity as a circumstance precluding wrongfulness in respect of international human rights law treaties is not open and shut.

The principal argument regarding the inapplicability of necessity as a circumstance precluding wrongfulness to human rights breaches, on the basis of both Article 25(2)(a) and the *lex specialis* principle, is that the exceptions to human rights treaties and derogation clauses 'occupy the field'—accounting fully for emergency situations which might legitimately give rise to limitations on human rights,[85] and that they have done so on the basis of an internal international human rights law calculus which is to be respected. And, indeed, to the extent that exceptions (insofar as they address national security and therefore at least potentially the type of essential interest which might be in grave and imminent peril) and derogations under international human rights law treaties cover the field that would otherwise be occupied by necessity as a circumstance precluding wrongfulness, there can be no doubt that necessity has been displaced. It has been argued above, however, that certain features of extraterritorial armed conflicts will be excluded from the scope of derogation clauses in virtue of the 'one situation/two situation' problem, and self-defence and force protection (for instance) are precisely the sort of circumstance envisioned by the ILC Commentaries as a necessity triggering situation.[86] As a result, in certain circumstances that are not covered by derogation clauses, but nevertheless potentially call for targeted human rights breaches to respond to a grave and imminent peril to an essential interest, the invocation of necessity as a circumstance precluding wrongfulness is not precluded by either Article 25(2)(a) or Article 55 of the ILC Articles on State Responsibility.

[83] To somewhat similar effect, art 55 of the ILC ARSIWA provides that: 'These articles do not apply where and to the extent that the conditions for the existence of an internationally wrongful act or the content or implementation of the international responsibility of a State are governed by special rules of international law. The Commentaries contemplate either inconsistency between the special and general rules, or a discernible intention (in the special rules) to exclude the general rules.' Commentary to ILC ARSIWA (n 3) art 55, para 4. There is certainly no inconsistency between the derogation provision and necessity—and the argument in reference to a discernible intention is as set out below.

[84] *Legal Consequences of the Construction of a Wall in the Occupied Palestinian Territory* (Advisory Opinion) (n 53) para 140.

[85] See Ryngaert (n 69) 88; Sarah Heathcote, 'Est-ce que l'état de nécessité est un principe de droit international coutumier?' (2007) 40 Revue belge de droit international 53, 60.

[86] See n 82.

6 Conclusion

There is a broad spectrum of permissible qualifications to human rights interests, all of which carve out a space for the exercise of regulatory authority or executive power that is free from the constraints otherwise imposed by a broad conception of human rights in the interests of achieving some legitimate aim. There is nothing inherent in the form relevant qualifications take—they may take the form of exemptions from the scope of the right, exceptions to the rights protection, or a temporally limited suspension of the obligation to respect the right or the secondary obligations which flow from responsibility for breach of the right. The same legitimate aim can be recognized in the human rights calculus at the stage of defining the scope of the right itself, at the stage of waiving the obligation to respect the right, or at the stage of suspending the consequences of wrongfulness. The distinction with serious consequence lies not in the form of the human rights qualification, or indeed in the nature of the analysis applied to determining its lawfulness, but in the competence of various courts and human rights bodies to determine that lawfulness. In respect of qualifications which are internal to human rights treaty systems, human rights limiting measures remain subject to scrutiny by human rights treaty monitoring bodies and courts. And at least in the European system, such scrutiny has insured that human rights interests are not obscured or even obliterated by the twenty-first century's all-consuming sense of crisis and emergency.

External qualifications, like necessity as a circumstance precluding wrongfulness, however, are ordinarily subject to the general international law mechanisms of state responsibility and courts of general jurisdiction (like the International Court of Justice). There is nothing which precludes human rights monitoring bodies and courts (like the European Court of Human Rights (ECtHR), which is determining a state's responsibility for breach of its treaty obligations) from looking to necessity as a circumstance precluding wrongfulness in cases where the permissible internal qualifications to human rights are inapplicable, but there is nevertheless a widely recognized legitimate aim behind the human rights limitation. It is certainly hoped, on the basis of a doctrine of incidental jurisdiction, that human rights courts and treaty monitoring bodies might exercise jurisdiction over external qualifications in such cases—for the sake of ensuring both that emergency measures remain subject to independent scrutiny and that the human rights paradigm remains at the centre of state action which affects the human condition.

18
Exceptions in Multilateral Environmental Agreements

*James Harrison**

1 Introduction

International environmental law is a field of law that calls for cooperation between states to achieve the collective aim of preventing and reducing harm to the natural environment. Precisely how to achieve this aim is the subject of various rules and principles, with their legal foundation in either customary international law or treaty law. Needless to say, international environmental law does not exist in a vacuum. States have many other interests that they must balance with their desire to protect the environment. The concept of sustainable development, an underpinning policy goal in this field of international law, recognizes that 'environmental protection shall constitute an integral part of the development process and cannot be considered in isolation from it'.[1] It follows that there is a need to balance environmental considerations against other elements of sustainable development, such as social policies or economic objectives.[2] Achieving such a balance is in large part a question of treaty design and it can be achieved in a number of ways.[3]

One technique to balance these different objectives is the incorporation of exceptions within a treaty, thus allowing a state to depart from the general rules in specific circumstances. It is the incorporation of exceptions into multilateral environmental agreements that is the focus of this chapter.[4]

The inclusion of exceptions in a treaty indicates what has been called by one author 'deviation tolerance'.[5] This is in part inspired by a desire to achieve broad participation in the treaty, in recognition of the fact that 'no country can be forced to sign'.[6] The opportunity for states to participate in a treaty, subject to exceptions, may also affect the depth of treaty commitments because it alleviates the need to agree upon the lowest common denominator in

* Professor of Environmental Law, University of Edinburgh School of Law. Email: james.harrison@ed.ac.uk.

1 Rio Declaration on Environment and Development 1992, Principle 4. See also *Case Concerning the Gabčíkovo-Nagymaros Project (Hungary v Slovakia)* (Judgment) [1997] ICJ Rep 7, para 140: 'This need to reconcile economic development with protection of the environment is aptly expressed in the concept of sustainable development.'

2 See e.g. Christina A Voigt, 'The Principle of Sustainable Development' in Christina Voigt (ed), *Rule of Law for Nature: New Dimensions and Ideas in Environmental Law* (Cambridge University Press 2013) 154.

3 See generally Andrew T Guzman, 'The Design of International Agreements' (2005) 16 European Journal of International Law 579, 588, emphasizing that different design choices are inter-related. See also Laurence R Helfer, 'Not Fully Committed? Reservations, Risk, and Treaty Design' 2006) 31 Yale Journal of International Law 367.

4 Exceptions may also apply to environmental rules in customary international law; see e.g. *Case Concerning Certain Activities in the Border Area and the Case Concerning Construction of a Road* [2015] ICJ Rep 665, paras 158–59. In that case, the very existence of an exception to the international customary law rule of environmental impact assessment was in dispute.

5 See Peter Sand, 'Commodity or Taboo? International Regulation of Trade in Endangered Species' (1997) Green Globe Yearbook 19, 22.

6 Lawrence E Susskind and Saleem H Ali, *Environmental Diplomacy* (2nd edn, Oxford University Press 2015) 34.

James Harrison, *Exceptions in Multilateral Environmental Agreements* In: *Exceptions in International Law*. Edited by: Lorand Bartels and Federica Paddeu, Oxford University Press (2020). © Lorand Bartels and Federica Paddeu.
DOI: 10.1093/oso/9780198789321.003.0018

order to promote participation.[7] Yet, the precise balance that is achieved will depend upon the form of the exceptions. Understanding the nature, scope and substance of exceptions is therefore important. This is particularly the case for environmental treaties, which generally have an integral character, meaning that all parties must perform their obligations if the objectives of the treaty are to be achieved.[8] Thus, the interpretation and application of exceptions to integral treaties have consequences for all parties to the treaty. It is for this reason that exceptions are also often subject to oversight in order to control their exercise and to ensure that they are not abused. This is an additional element of treaty design that must be taken into account when considering the incorporation of exceptions into an environmental treaty. Indeed, it will be demonstrated through the review of treaty practice in this chapter that states have given increasing attention to designing mechanisms for the purpose of controlling the exercise of exceptions.

One of the challenges of undertaking a study of exceptions in environmental treaties is that there are numerous agreements related to the protection of the environment[9] and each treaty contains its own set of exceptions that have been specifically drafted for the purposes of that treaty. Thus, it is difficult to speak of a common doctrine of exceptions that will apply across international environmental law. The chapter will therefore attempt a different exercise, namely classifying different types of exceptions that are found in multilateral environmental agreements and the various means through which states have sought to control the exercise of these exceptions.

2 Distinguishing Exceptions and Other Flexibility Devices in Multilateral Environmental Treaties

The establishment of an exception recognizes that the pursuit of a singular rule may not be desirable or justified in all circumstances and some flexibility is required. Even very early efforts at drafting international rules relating to the protection of natural resources acknowledged the need to take into account different objectives in the form of exceptions.[10]

Exceptions can pursue a number of different objectives and the precise details will depend upon the issues raised by a particular environmental treaty. Broadly speaking, it is common to observe exceptions that relate to economic or development objectives,[11] the protection of human life and health,[12] scientific research,[13] or the protection of certain cultural

[7] Edward T Swaine, 'Reserving' (2006) 31 Yale Journal of International Law 307, 331.

[8] In the words of Fitzmaurice, integral treaties contain obligations that are 'self-existent, absolute and inherent for each party ... [and] must be applied integrally'; International Law Commission, 'Third Report on the Law of Treaties by G.G. Fitzmaurice, Special Rapporteur' (1958) 2 Yearbook of the International Law Commission 21; see also Joost Pauwelyn, 'A Typology of Multilateral Treaty Obligations' (2003)14 European Journal of International Law 907.

[9] See e.g. http://www.informea.org/ (accessed 15 February 2016).

[10] See e.g. the treaty drafted by the tribunal in the *Bering Fur Seals* arbitration, art 8 of which included an exception relating to fur seal fishing by coastal 'Indians'; see Award between the United States and the United Kingdom relating to the rights of jurisdiction of the United States in the Bering's sea and the preservation of fur seals (15 August 1893) 18 Reports of International Arbitral Awards 263.

[11] See eg 1987 Montreal Protocol on the Protection of the Ozone Layer (Ozone Protocol) art 5.

[12] Stockholm Convention on Persistent Organic Pollutants 2001 (POPs Convention) Annex B Pt II, para 3; London Dumping Convention1972 art V(1); Antarctic Protocol on Environmental Protection 1991 (APEP) Annex I art 7, Annex III art 12, and Annex IV art 7; Bern Convention on the Conservation of Wildlife and Natural Habitats 1979 (adopted on 2 December 2011) (Bern Convention) art 9(1).

[13] International Convention on the Regulation of Whaling 1946 (ICRW) art VIII; Convention on Migratory Species 1979 (CMS) art III(5)(a); Agreement on the Conservation of Cetaceans of the Black Sea, Mediterranean

rights.[14] Such exceptions may apply to an entire instrument or to a particular rule. What all exceptions have in common is that they introduce flexibility into the treaty regime, by allowing states to pursue countervailing objectives in some circumstances. However, exceptions are just one type of flexibility mechanism that can be employed in the design of a treaty, alongside the use of soft norms[15] or the development of differential obligations.[16] Thus, it is worthwhile considering at the outset the key characteristics of exceptions that distinguish them from other flexibility devices.

The nature of exceptions is itself the subject of a varied and sometimes conflicting literature. Without dwelling on these theoretical debates, which are addressed elsewhere in this volume, an exception can be generally understood as 'a particular case which comes within the terms of a rule, but to which the rule is not applicable'.[17] From this definition, it appears that the key characteristic of an exception is the interrelationship of two norms: one norm or set of norms that prescribe a certain sort of behaviour and another norm that exempts specified behaviour from the first norm in certain circumstances. In the words of Oakes Finkelstein, 'an exception is a qualification of a rule that stands in a certain relation to it, namely it stands outside the rule it qualifies'.[18]

This understanding of exceptions allows us to distinguish exceptions from other flexibility devices used in multilateral environmental treaties. First, it allows us to distinguish exceptions from differential obligations, that is, rules that only apply to a particular category of states.[19] Secondly, it allows us to distinguish exceptions from open-textured rules that allow different factors to be taken into account and balanced in the interpretation of that rule.[20] Due diligence obligations are good examples of the latter rules, as they must be interpreted and applied taking into account all the relevant circumstances of a particular case.[21] Both of these types of norms play a similar function to exceptions, in that they allow a balancing of objectives in the process of treaty interpretation and application. Owing to their different nature, however, they will not be considered further in this chapter.

Even if we accept that exceptions involve the interrelationship of two norms, there are nevertheless several types of provisions commonly found in environmental treaties that could be categorized as exceptions. Whilst such norms share the common characteristic that they permit deviation from a more general rule in a specific circumstance, they otherwise have different features, which have implications for their interpretation and application in practice. The following sections of this chapter will address three different categories of exceptions, namely 'exclusions', 'reservations, objections and opt-out clauses', and 'ad hoc

Sea and Contiguous Atlantic Area 1996 (ACCOMBAMS) art 2(2); APEP (n 12) Annex II art 3(5); Bern Convention (n 12) art 9(1).

[14] CMS (n 13) art III(5)(c).

[15] Guzman (n 3) 583.

[16] See e.g. Lavanya Rajamani, *Differential Treatment in International Environmental Law* (OUP 2006).

[17] 'exception, n.' *OED Online*, Oxford University Press, September 2019, www.oed.com/view/Entry/65724. Accessed 29 November 2019.

[18] Claire Oakes Finkelstein, 'When the Rule Swallows the Exception' in Linda Meyer (ed), *Rules and Reasoning: Essays in Honour of Frederick Schauer* (Hart Publishing 1999) 150.

[19] See e.g. 1992 United Nations Framework Convention on Climate Change (UNFCCC) art 4(2), which only applies to 'developed country parties and other parties included in Annex I'.

[20] What Magraw refers to as 'contextual norms'; see Daniel Barstow Magraw, 'Legal Treatment of Developing Countries: Differential, Contextual and Absolute Norms' (1989) 1 Colombia Journal of International Environmental Law & Policy 69, 75.

[21] See e.g. International Law Commission, 'Draft Articles on Prevention on Transboundary Harm from Hazardous Activities, with commentaries' (2001) 2 Yearbook of the International Law Commission 148, art 3 and commentary thereto.

conditional rights'. As will be seen in the following analysis, there may be differences in the operation of these categories, but they have all been the subject of increasing oversight, as states have sought to place the exercise of exceptions under greater scrutiny and control. Each section will discuss the nature of such control mechanisms and the challenges that arise for states in seeking to ensure that exceptions are not abused.

3 Exclusions as Exceptions

3.1 The nature of exclusions

The first type of exception to be considered is an exclusion clause, which exempts a particular activity or issue from the scope of a treaty. Exclusions are also sometimes referred to as exemptions, carve-outs, or delineation clauses and they are common in environmental treaties. They qualify as an exception because the exclusion is usually found in a separate part of the treaty to the substantive rules to which they relate.

The Convention on International Trade in Endangered Species (CITES) illustrates the use of exclusions in an environmental context. This treaty regulates the international trade in species of plants and animals that are listed in appendices to the treaty. Certain permits are required from the importing or exporting state, depending on the level of threat posed to a particular species.[22] CITES contains a number of important exceptions, however, several of which take the form of exclusions. For example, Article VII(1) provides that 'the provisions of Articles III, IV, and V shall not apply to the transit or trans-shipment of specimens through or in the territory of a Party while the specimens remain in Customs control'. This provision modifies the scope of the primary obligations in the treaty and excludes certain types of activity from the treaty. Similarly, Article VII(2) provides an exclusion for specimens acquired before the provisions of Convention applied to that specimen and Article VII(3) exempts 'specimens that are personal or household effects'.

What differentiates exclusions from the other types of exceptions considered later in the chapter is that they automatically apply to all parties to the treaty, without the need for an individual party to invoke them in order to benefit from their terms. In other words, exclusions have a symmetrical effect. It follows that exclusions have significant implications for the effectiveness of a treaty regime because whole categories of activity are entirely excluded from the treaty.

3.2 Control and oversight of exclusions

Given that the scope of exclusions has important ramifications for the execution of a treaty, it is unsurprising that parties to environmental treaties have sought to ensure that they are not abused.

One way in which states have sought to control the use of treaty exemptions is through promoting the uniform interpretation of exclusion clauses, with a view to ensuring that practice on this matter is harmonized. This approach is demonstrated by CITES Conference Resolution 9.7, which recommends a restrictive interpretation of 'transit or transhipment

[22] Convention on International Trade in Endangered Species 1973 (CITES) art II.

of specimens'[23] for the purposes of the exclusion in Article VII(1) of the treaty. The CITES Conference of the Parties (COP) has also interpreted other exemptions in this way.[24] These interpretations are expressed as recommendations, suggesting that they are not legally binding,[25] but they nevertheless provide a common benchmark against which to judge the practice of parties in relation to the exemption.

Nor has the CITES COP limited itself to policing the scope of the exclusions. For example, Resolution 9.7 goes further and encourages states, despite the existence of the exclusion, to 'inspect, to the extent possible under national legislation, specimens in transit or being tran-shipped, to verify the presence of a valid CITES permit or certificate as required under the Convention or to obtain satisfactory proof of its existence'.[26] It also recommends that 'Parties adopt legislation allowing them to seize and confiscate specimens in transit or being tran-shipped without a valid permit or certificate or proof of existence thereof'.[27] In other words, this resolution urges parties to take action to prevent abuse, even though the matter falls beyond the scope of their treaty obligations as a matter of international law. This approach is also seen in CITES COP Resolution 13.6 on pre-Convention species, which explicitly recognizes 'the right of Parties . . . to apply stricter domestic measures to the import of specimens covered by the pre-Convention [exclusion]'[28] and encourages parties to regulate pre-Convention species. In the case of the exclusion of trade in personal and household effects, the relevant COP resolution also suggest that states can apply stricter domestic measures and even notes that parties could 'choose not to implement the exemption at all'.[29]

This subsequent practice of the treaty parties demonstrates that they maintain an interest in the subject matter of the exclusion, even though it technically falls outside the scope of the treaty. Yet, the existence of the exclusion as a matter of law dictates that further cooperation takes places on the political level through the use of non-binding formulations.

4 Reservations, Objections, and Opt-outs as Exceptions

4.1 The nature of reservations, objections, and opt-out clauses

Another way of accommodating a broader range of competing values is through the allowance of specific reservations to a treaty rule.[30] Reservations share the same functional goal of exceptions—to permit states to participate in a legal regime, whilst also allowing them to pursue other goals or values that are contrary to the substantive rules of the treaty.[31] Unlike exclusions, reservations must be expressly made by a particular state in order to gain the benefit of flexibility. Whilst the reservation will provide an exception for the reserving state, it will not affect the obligations of the other parties (given their integral nature) and so reservations are asymmetrical exceptions. If a state ever abandons its reservation, the ordinary rules of the treaty will then apply to that state. Otherwise, a reserving state is exempt from the relevant rules.

[23] CITES COP Resolution 9.7 (Rev.COP15) para (a).

[24] CITES COP Resolution 13.6 (Rev.COP16) paras (a)–(b); CITES COP Resolution 13.7 (Rev.COP16) Annex 1, Guidelines for interpretation of personal and household effects.

[25] Contrast with CITES COP Resolution 4.25 discussed below.

[26] CITES COP Resolution 9.7 para (b).

[27] ibid para (e).

[28] CITES COP Resolution 13.6 (Rev.COP16) preamble.

[29] CITES COP Resolution 13.7 (Rev.COP16) Annex 1 para 4.

[30] See Rajamani (n 16) 7.

[31] See Swaine (n 7) 328.

Reservations must normally be made at the time when a state consents to be bound by a treaty.[32] Consistent with their integral nature, environmental treaties generally eschew reservations to their core obligations.[33] However, the possibility of making reservations in multilateral environmental treaties does arise in connection with tacit amendment procedures, which are used to keep a treaty up-to-date. The ability to modify treaty rules using tacit amendment procedures is a common feature of many multilateral environmental treaties.[34] At the same time, many of these procedures also preserve the fundamental concept of consent in international law-making, by allowing for particular states to make an objection to the new rules. Given that an objection must be made within a certain period before the rules enter into force, they function as reservations. There are many examples of environmental treaties allowing objections to the development of new rules in this manner, including the International Convention on the Prevention of Pollution from Ships,[35] the Ballast Water Management Convention,[36] CITES,[37] the ICRW,[38] and many regional fisheries management treaties.[39]

Some treaties also include provisions that allow an individual state to exclude a certain issue from the application of a treaty, even after its entry into force. Such opt-out clauses are similar to reservations, in that they allow a state unilaterally to decide to derogate from the principal rules of the treaty and the derogation lasts for as long as the state deems it appropriate. An example is provided by the 1993 Agreement to Promote Compliance with International Conservation and Management Measures by Fishing Vessels on the High Seas. This treaty requires states to exercise a minimum level of flag state responsibility over fishing vessels flying their flag whilst fishing on the high seas and it also prohibits the transfer of a fishing vessel from one register to another register where there is evidence that the vessel has undermined the effectiveness of international conservation and management measures. Article I(1) provides that the agreement 'shall apply to all fishing vessels that are used or intended for fishing on the high seas', but Article II(2) then goes on to permit that 'a Party may exempt fishing vessels of less than 24 metres in length entitled to fly its flag from the application of the Agreement unless the Party determines that such an exemption would undermine the object and purpose of this Agreement'. Once invoked, all vessels from that state benefit from the protection of the opt-out for as long as the party maintains the exception in place.

[32] Article 2(d) of the Vienna Convention on the Law of Treaties (VCLT) 1969 defines a reservation as 'a unilateral statement, however phrased or named, made by a State, when signing, ratifying, accepting, approving or acceding to a treaty, whereby it purports to exclude or modify the legal effect of certain provisions of the treaty in their application to that state'.

[33] See e.g. Convention on Biological Diversity 1992 (CBD) art 37; Ozone Protocol (n 11) art 18.

[34] See Hans C Bugge, 'Twelve fundamental challenges in environmental law' in Christina Voigt (ed), *Rule of Law for Nature: New Dimensions and Ideas in Environmental Law* (Cambridge University Press 2013) 11, expressing the view that environmental law must be 'flexible so as to meet changing circumstances and new insight'.

[35] International Convention on the Prevention of Pollution from Ships1973/78 art 16.

[36] Ballast Water Management Convention art 19.

[37] CITES (n 22) art XV.

[38] ICRW (n 13) art 5(3).

[39] See eg Convention on the Conservation and Management of Fishery Resources in the South East Atlantic Ocean 2001 (SEAFO Convention) art 23(1). This treaty not only gives the right of a party to object to a measure adopted by the SEAFO Commission, but it also allows any other state to request of a review of the measure in light of an objection. As part of this review, other states can indicate that they no longer accept the measure, owing to the objection.

4.2 Political oversight of reservation and opt-out procedures

Despite their unilateral nature, reservations, objection procedures, and opt-out clauses can still be subject to some form of scrutiny by the other parties to the treaty. Treaty drafting practice demonstrates variations in the rules, procedures, and oversight mechanisms that have been employed for this purpose.

The POPs Convention provides a particularly interesting example of the development of institutional mechanisms to control the use of reservations and opt-out clauses. It does so by limiting the purpose of such exceptions and also establishing procedures to oversee their use.

The general objective of the POPs Convention is to restrict the manufacture, trade, and use of the persistent organic pollutants (POPs) that are listed in the Annex to the treaty. However, the general obligations to control POPs are also subject to a regime of exceptions. The most important exception for present purposes is the ability of states to make reservations (called exemptions) in relation to particular uses of individual POPs in accordance with a detailed scheme set out in the Annexes to the treaty. The permitted exceptions vary, depending on the chemical in question. Part I of Annex A lists the situations in which the production and use of certain chemicals may be exempted from the general duty to eliminate such chemicals. For example, parties are ordinarily required to prohibit the production and use of Chlordane, but Annex A continues to allow the use of Chlordane as a termiticide, insecticide, local ectoparasiticide, or as an additive to plywood adhesives, if a party has registered a specific exemption. To qualify for this exception, states must notify the secretariat of which specific exemptions they intend to claim at the time at which they become a party.[40] It is the temporal aspect of this exception that suggests it should be considered as a reservation. The secretariat to the Convention is required to keep a public register of such exceptions.[41]

The POPs Convention attempts to regulate the use of the specific exemptions by introducing a time limit on their application. Thus, specific exemptions only last for five years after the entry into force, unless states specify an earlier date, it is unilaterally withdrawn, or an extension is granted. It is the COP that has the power to decide whether an exemption shall be extended or not, based upon a report submitted by the party in which it should '[justify] its continuing need for registration of that exemption'.[42] In other words, without a positive decision of the COP, a party will not be able to continue with its exemption after five years.[43] This oversight mechanism thus provides a means of ensuring that exemptions are not abused and it promotes the ultimate aim of the Convention to promote the eventual elimination of these chemicals. In theory, reservations can be renewed multiple times, provided that the COP agrees. In practice, however, when the first set of exemptions came to be reviewed, no extensions were requested and therefore the review procedure was not utilized.[44] Indeed, the parties have actively encouraged the development of alternatives in order to reduce the need for the reservations.[45] Nevertheless, the review procedure will still be relevant in the future as new POPs are added to the annexes of the Convention, along with specific exemptions.

[40] POPs Convention (n 12) art 4(3).

[41] See also Decision SC-1/23: Format for the Register of Specific Exemptions.

[42] Article 4(6). See also COP Decision SC-1/24; COP Decision SC-2/3; COP Decision SC-3/3.

[43] It is not entirely clear how decisions of the COP are to be taken. The first meeting of the COP was unable to agree upon voting rules; see Report of the First Meeting of the Conference of the Parties to the Stockholm Convention, Document UNEP/POPS/COP.1/31, para 21.

[44] See Report of the Fourth Meeting of the Conference of the Parties to the Stockholm Convention, Document UNEP/POPS/COP.4/38, para 33. See also COP Decision SC-4/3: Exemptions.

[45] See e.g. COP Decision SC-7/1, para 4, encouraging states to take into consideration an expert review on lindane and alternatives in the treatment of head lice and scabies.

Another interesting feature of the procedure is that 'when there are no longer any Parties registered for a particular type of specific exemption, no new registrations may be made with respect to it'.[46] It follows that new parties will lose the right to make reservations, if the reservations of all existing parties have expired. This provision creates an incentive for states to become a party to the Convention at an early date, in order to benefit from the reservation system.

Even where parties have registered a reservation, Article 3(6) of the Convention requires that they:

> take appropriate measures to ensure that any production or use under such exemption or purpose is carried out in a manner that prevents or minimizes human exposure and release into the environment. For exempted uses or acceptable purposes that involve intentional release into the environment under conditions of normal use, such release shall be to the minimum extent necessary, taking into account any applicable standards and guidelines.

This provision is important because it reinforces that states are not completely discharged from taking action to protect the environment, despite the fact that they have registered an exemption. In other words, this provision attempts to ensure that environmental protection is still taken into account by states exercising an exception, even if the standards that apply may be lower than if they had not registered an exemption. Moreover, in contrast to the use of non-binding measures to encourage measures to fill the gaps left by carve-out clauses, discussed in the previous section, this is a legal obligation on parties to the POPs Convention.

The POPs Convention also contains an exception to restrictions on the production and use of dichloro-diphenyl-trichloroethane (DDT), this time in the form of an opt-out clause that parties may invoke at any time after they become a party.[47] As in the case of other POPs, the Convention seeks to ensure that this exception is subject to some monitoring and control. To this end, a separate DDT register of exceptions is established. Moreover, the Convention subjects the parties to certain minimum standards of conduct, despite their invocation of the exception. For those states that invoke the DDT opt-out, the use of this chemical is still explicitly required to be controlled in accordance with World Health Organization (WHO) recommendations and guidelines and the exception can only be relied upon when 'locally safe, effective and affordable alternatives are not available to the Party in question'.[48] Moreover, states should develop an action plan, which includes measures to implement suitable alternatives, methods and strategies to reduce the incidence of disease. The COP is required to evaluate the continued need for DDT for the purposes of disease vector control. In contrast to the other specific exemptions under the Stockholm Convention, however, the COP does not have the power to overrule the decision of countries to continue to produce or use DDT. There would therefore appear to be less control over the exemptions for this chemical compared to the other chemicals regulated by the Convention. This is a reflection of a different political choice concerning the balance between certain values underpinning each set of exceptions.

Even where a treaty does not contain explicit constraints on the use of reservations in its text, states have sometimes attempted to introduce some form of control through other means. In this context, we return again to CITES to provide us with an example. CITES

46 POPs Convention (n 12) art 4(9).
47 ibid Annex B, Part II, para 1.
48 ibid para 2.

itself places no conditions on the making of reservations, not even requiring a party to give reasons for its decision.[49] Nevertheless, CITES COP Resolution 4.25 seeks to introduce controls on the ability of states to make a reservation to CITES regime. First, it establishes an interpretation of the provision on reservations to the effect that 'if a species is deleted from one Appendix of the Convention and simultaneously included in another, the deletion shall render invalid any reservation that was in effect in relation to the species and, consequently, any Party that wishes to maintain a reservation in relation to the species must enter a new reservation in accordance with Article XV, paragraph 3, or Article XVI, paragraph 2'. The language of the resolution suggests that this is an agreed interpretation that must be given effect by the parties, and not a mere recommendation.[50] This does not necessarily limit the ability of a state to make a reservation, but it does require a party to take positive action to reaffirm its need for a reservation if a species moves from one appendix to another. Secondly, the resolution also encourages states to continue to take action for the conservation of species even if they have entered into a reservation. Thus, the COP recommends that 'any Party having entered a reservation with regard to any species included in Appendix I treat that species as if it were included in Appendix II for all purposes, including documentation and control' and it further 'calls on the Parties having entered reservations to nevertheless maintain and communicate statistical records on trade in the species concerned, as part of their annual reports, so that international trade in specimens of these species may be properly monitored'. Through adopting this resolution, the COP makes clear that it will continue to expect the reserving party to cooperate in order to achieve the overarching aims of the Convention. The use of the word 'recommends' suggests that this part of the resolution does not have legal effect. Nevertheless, it affirms that the registering of a reservation does not remove the state from the scrutiny of the other parties and reserving states are still expected to take some action in order to ensure that trade does not undermine the efforts of the other parties. Although not legally binding, such political mechanisms may be effective in practice if sufficient pressure can be brought to bear on a reserving party.[51]

4.3 Independent oversight of reservation and opt-out procedures

Some treaty regimes have gone one step further and attached detailed conditions to the ability of states to make reservations and subjected such conditions to oversight by an independent body. The drafting of regional fisheries management treaties illustrates a trend in this direction.

Most regional fisheries treaties establish institutions that are able to adopt conservation and management measures that are applicable to the fishing vessels of all parties. At the same time, these treaties tend to allow states to escape the application of measures by registering an objection, which prevents that decision from becoming binding for that state.[52] In practice, objection procedures have been widely used and some commentators have noted

[49] Gwyneth G Stewart, 'Enforcement Problems in the Endangered Species Convention: Reservations regarding the Reservations Clauses' (1981) 14 Cornell International Law Journal 429, 435.

[50] The resolution explicitly provides that 'the Conference of the Parties to the Convention AGREES that ...'. Contrast with the interpretations of the resolutions relating to exclusion clauses, discussed above, which use hortatory language.

[51] See e.g. Stewart (n 49) 448.

[52] See e.g. Convention on Future Multilateral Cooperation in North-East Atlantic Fisheries 1980 art 12(2).

their potential to undermine conservation measures adopted by the RFMOs by permitting free-riders.[53]

More recent treaties have sought to counter this problem by introducing limits on the ability of a state to make reservations to new conservation and management measures. For example, the 2010 Convention on the Conservation and Management of High Seas Fishery Resources in the South Pacific Ocean (SPO Convention) provides that 'the only admissible grounds for an objection are that the decision unjustifiably discriminates in form or in fact against the member of the Commission, or is inconsistent with the provisions of [the SPO] Convention or other relevant international law as reflected in the 1982 [Law of the Sea] Convention or the 1995 [Fish Stocks] Agreement'.[54] This provision thus limits the discretion of a member as to the reasons for making an objection. In addition, the Convention requires an objecting state to advise the executive secretary of 'alternative measures that are equivalent in effect to the decision to which it has objectives and have the same date of application'.[55] In other words, members cannot escape regulation completely and they must take some measures that seek to promote the goals of the Convention. Indeed, the SPO goes further and includes a mechanism whereby any objection is automatically considered by an independent review panel that is mandated to decide whether or not the objection is permissible and, if so, whether the proposed alternative measures are equivalent.[56] This procedure further limits the possibility of abuse of the objections procedure by introducing independent scrutiny of the objection and proposed alternative measures. In the first case to fall under this procedure, the review panel upheld an objection by the Russian Federation as falling within the permitted grounds, but it determined that the alternative measures proposed by Russia were not adequate because they failed to take into account the catches of other states.[57] Decisions of the review panel would appear to be binding, unless the states concerned choose to initiate dispute settlement proceedings under the Convention.[58] If dispute settlement proceedings were initiated, then the decision of the court or tribunal would be final and binding.

The SPO Convention is the only regional fisheries treaty to require the automatic consideration of an objection by a review panel. However, other regional fisheries treaties have introduced similar conditions on the use of objections and they would also appear to allow questions of compatibility to be submitted to international dispute settlement at the instigation of any party.[59] Even older regional fisheries treaties have been amended to include such review procedures[60] and the review conference of the United Nations Fish Stocks Agreement has explicitly called for states to 'ensure that post opt-out behavior is constrained by rules to prevent opting-out parties from undermining conservation, by establishing clear processes for dispute settlement and for the adoption of alternative measures with equivalent effect

[53] See discussion in Daniela Diz, *Fisheries Management in Areas beyond National Jurisdiction* (Martinus Nijhoff 2012) 128.

[54] Convention on the Conservation and Management of High Seas Fishery Resources in the South Pacific Ocean 2010 (SPO Convention) art 17(2)(c).

[55] ibid art 17(2)(b)(ii).

[56] ibid art 17(5) and Annex II.

[57] Review Panel established under the Convention on the Conservation and Management of High Seas Fishery Resources in the South Pacific Ocean, Findings and Recommendations of the Review Panel (5 July 2013). See discussion in Andrew Serdy, 'Implementing Article 28 of the UN Fish Stocks Agreement: The First Review of a Conservation Measure in the South Pacific Regional Fisheries Management Organization' (2016) 47 Ocean Development and International Law 1.

[58] SPO Convention (n 54) Annex II, para 10.

[59] See also the West and Central Pacific Fisheries (WCPF) Convention 2000 art 20; North Pacific Fisheries Convention 2012 art 9(c).

[60] See e.g. amendments to art XIV of the Convention on Cooperation in the North-West Atlantic, which entered into force in 2017.

that would be implemented in the interim'.[61] There would thus appear to be a trend in this sector suggesting an increasing willingness to submit disputes over the use of exceptions to independent review. In other words, there is a legalization of objection procedures, which is intended to strengthen the integrity of the relevant treaty.

6 Ad Hoc Conditional Rights as Exceptions

6.1 The nature of ad hoc conditional rights

Exceptions can also take the form of an ad hoc conditional right that may be invoked by a state if it wishes to carry out an action that would otherwise conflict with the terms of the treaty. The key characteristic of an ad hoc conditional right is that it must be invoked each time that it is required by the state concerned. Moreover, the state must demonstrate that it meets the conditions attached to the exception in order to benefit from the protection of the exception. It follows that ad hoc conditional rights are only intended to provide temporary shelter to a state from the application of the other rules of the treaty so long as the conditions continue to be met. Such a right can be considered as providing a defence to the merits of a claim[62] and it is up to the state invoking the right to demonstrate that the conditions are met in the circumstances of a particular case.

CITES provides an example of this type of exception in Article VII(7), which provides that 'a Management Authority of any State may waive the requirements of Articles III, IV and V and allow the movement without permits or certificates of specimens which form part of a travelling zoo, circus, menagerie, plant exhibition or other travelling exhibition'. In contrast to paragraph 1 of Article VII discussed above in the context of exclusions, this paragraph qualifies as an ad hoc conditional right because it must be invoked by the relevant state, as made clear from the language used, i.e. the state 'may waive' the requirements. Moreover, the nature of this provision as an ad hoc conditional right is made clear by the fact that the exporter or importer must be registered in order to qualify.[63] In other words, the exception must be invoked individually for each situation that a state wishes to exempt from the operation of the treaty.

It is for the drafters of a treaty to decide what form of institutional control is put in place to oversee the use of exceptions of this type. Treaty practice demonstrates different models that can be implemented by drafters in this respect, involving both advance and after-the-fact scrutiny. Furthermore, it will be seen that this sort of exception may also be open to judicial oversight.

[61] Report of the 2016 Resumed FSA Review Conference, Document A/CONF.210/2016/5 (1 August 2016) Outcomes, para B5(b).

[62] See e.g. *Oil Platforms (Islamic Republic of Iran v United States of America)* (Preliminary Objection, Judgment) [1996] ICJ Rep 803, para 20, characterizing an exception, *in casu*, art XX(1)(d) of the Iran–United States Treaty of Amity, as 'affording the Parties a possible defence on the merits to be used should the occasion arise'. In doing so, the Court rejected the argument of the United States that this was an exclusion of the matter from the scope of the treaty, thus precluding the jurisdiction of the Court in the first place.

[63] CITES (n 22) art VII(7).

6.2 Post hoc scrutiny of ad hoc conditional rights

The control of exceptions under the 1972 London Dumping Convention and its 1996 Protocol provide examples of the control of exceptions being exercised by the other parties to the treaty. These treaties regulate the disposal of waste at sea by prohibiting the dumping of certain substances and requiring an environmental impact assessment to be carried out for all other dumping. The treaties also recognize exceptions to these rules and the parties have established particular mechanisms to oversee the exercise of those exceptions.

First, Article V(1) of the Convention contains an exception for the protection of human life, providing that the prohibitions on the dumping of waste under Article IV 'shall not apply when it is necessary to secure the safety of human life or of vessels, aircraft, platforms or other man-made structures at sea in cases of force majeure caused by stress of weather, or in any other case which constitutes a danger to human life or a real threat to vessels, aircraft, platforms or other man-made structures at sea, if dumping appears to be the only way of averting the threat and if there is every probability that the damage consequent upon such duping will be less than would otherwise occur'. A very similar provision is found in the 1996 London Dumping Protocol[64] and such provisions are also common in other maritime treaties.[65] The London Dumping Convention tries to control the invocation of this exception by including a provision requiring that '[dumping under the permitted exceptional circumstances] ... shall be reported forthwith to the [International Maritime] Organization'.[66] The parties have explicitly acknowledged that the purpose of this mechanism is to 'ensure that the case of dumping was in fact in accordance with [the exception]'.[67] In order to allow the greatest scrutiny of action, the parties to the Convention have made clear that the report provided by the party 'should include the available information regarding the details of the situations (including date, time, location, material concerned, circumstances of the event), the necessity of the emergency dumping, and the actions undertaken so as to minimize the likelihood of damage to human or marine life'.[68] The treaty is silent on the timing of such a report, however. The term 'forthwith' could be interpreted in various ways, but the parties to the treaty appear to have accepted that the party concerned may have some discretion and the reporting may take place either before the dumping occurs or after-the-fact, depending on the urgency of the situation.[69] The International Maritime Organization (IMO), as the secretariat to the Convention, is required to convey such reports to the other parties. The Convention does not specify what action can be taken on the basis of such a report, but it would appear that the parties could play a role in considering and commenting on situations in which the exceptions are invoked, on the basis of their general role in overseeing the implementation of the Convention. Even though the parties would appear to have no explicit powers of sanction, the very fact of demanding transparency in the exercise of this exception

[64] London Dumping Protocol art 8(1).

[65] See also e.g. the Ballast Water Convention, Annex, Regulation A-3(1): 'the requirements of regulation B-3, or any measures adopted by a Party pursuant to Article 2.3 and Section C, shall not apply to ... the uptake or discharge of Ballast Water and Sediments necessary for the purpose of ensuring the safety of a ship in emergency situations or saving life at sea ...'. See Convention on the Protection of the Marine Environment of the Baltic Sea Area 1992 (Helsinki Convention, entered into force 17 January 2000) art 11(4).

[66] Convention on the Prevention of Marine Pollution by Dumping of Wastes and Other Matter 1972 (London Dumping Convention) art V(1).

[67] Procedures and Criteria for Determining and Addressing Emergency Situations as Referred to in arts 8 and 18.1.6 of the 1996 London Protocol, Document LC 28/15 Annex 11, para 2.1.

[68] ibid para 2.1; see also para 2.3.

[69] ibid para 2.2.

may itself provide a small incentive for parties to avoid abuse. Where excesses are detected, parties may use diplomatic methods in order to discourage further violations or employ some other method of oversight that may be available.[70]

Secondly, the London Dumping Convention also contains a more general health-related exception by providing that 'a Contracting Party may issue a special permit as an exception to article IV(1)(a), in emergencies, posing an unacceptable threat to human health, safety, or the marine environment and admitting no other feasible solution'.[71] This exception has been invoked on several occasions to justify dumping of fish waste that posed a risk to human health[72] and dredged material that had been removed in order to protect safety of navigation.[73] The treaty text suggests that a party invoking the exception must first consult other parties and the IMO, which shall in turn recommend appropriate procedures to the party concerned. However, in practice, the parties have not exercised their right to provide recommendations and they appear to have accepted post hoc reporting under this exception.[74] Indeed, given that the parties only meet once a year, it is difficult to see how they could exercise effective control over such emergency situations with sufficient urgency under existing institutional arrangements. It follows that this has also become, perhaps as a matter of pragmatism, a post hoc oversight mechanism, which only allows for limited control of the exception.

Similar control mechanisms are found in several conservation treaties.[75] For example, under the Bern Convention, parties are required to report every two years on their reliance on exceptions related to the picking of wild flora or the killing or capture of wild fauna.[76] The Convention specifies the details that must be contained in such reports and the standing committee established to oversee the implementation of the Convention has agreed that states should provide further information on the justification for any derogation, highlighting that exceptions should only be authorized where there is no other satisfactory solution and where the exception will not be detrimental to the survival of the species.[77] To satisfy this condition, states must report inter alia on the current status of a population and on the alternative measures that were considered prior to authorizing an exception.[78] Indeed, the standing committee has adopted guidance on what is meant by key terms in the exception in order to ensure that states do not abuse their rights.[79] Whilst the guidance leaves some room for discretion for states when invoking exceptions, it nevertheless emphasizes that the justification

[70] eg the London Dumping Protocol provides for compulsory arbitration in relation to disputes regarding its interpretation and application; London Dumping Protocol art 16. See below for a discussion of judicial oversight of exceptions.

[71] London Dumping Convention (n 66) art V(2); see also London Dumping Protocol art 8(1).

[72] 'Notification under Article 8.2 of the London Protocol regarding a case of emergency' (Canada), Document LC-LP.1/Circ.21 (2 July 2008); 'Notification under Article 8.2 of the London Protocol regarding a case of emergency' (Canada), Document LC-LP.1/Circ.38 (12 July 2010).

[73] 'Notification under Article 8.2 of the London Protocol regarding a case of emergency' (Canada), Document LC-LP.1/Circ.46 (14 September 2011); 'Notification under Article 8.2 of the London Protocol regarding a case of emergency' (Canada), Document LC-LP.1/Circ.57 (8 May 2013).

[74] 'Procedures and Criteria for Determining and Addressing Emergency Situations as Referred to in Articles 8 and 18.1.6 of the 1996 London Protocol' Document LC 28/15 Annex 11, para 3.1: 'in some cases, Article 8.2 emergencies are situations requiring action with a marked degree of urgency, and which may preclude thorough consultations and evaluations. In these cases, the Contracting Party would notify the Secretariat as to the actions taken.'

[75] See e.g. CMS (n 13) art V(7), which explicitly provides that 'the Parties shall as soon as possible inform the Secretariat of any exceptions made pursuant to paragraph 5 of this Article'.

[76] Bern Convention (n 12) art 9(2).

[77] See Revised Resolution No 2 (1993) on the scope of arts 8 and 9 of the Bern Convention (n 12) Appendix, para 6.

[78] ibid para 7.

[79] ibid.

must be 'objective and verifiable'[80] and the standing committee proactively considers reports from the parties at its biennial meetings in order to police compliance.

6.3 Prior scrutiny of ad hoc conditional rights

Other treaty regimes have sought to subject ad hoc conditional exceptions to prior scrutiny. An example is provided by the control of the scientific exception to the International Convention on the Regulation of Whaling (ICRW). This treaty permits states to issue special permits to its nationals to carry out whaling 'for purposes of scientific research'.[81] The Convention text itself requires a party that invokes this exception to 'report at once to the Commission all such authorizations which it has granted'.[82] At first sight, this would appear to be an after-the-fact procedure to allow the review of the exercise of exceptions, similar to the procedure of the London Dumping Convention and Protocol. However, developments in the regulations contained in the ICRW schedule have to some extent modified the nature of this obligation. Paragraph 30 of the schedule thus provides that '[a] Contracting Government shall provide the Secretary to the International Whaling Commission with proposed scientific permits before they are issued and in sufficient time to allow the Scientific Committee to review and comment on them'. The regulation goes on to specify the nature of the information that should be provided to the scientific committee for review. The scientific committee is composed of scientists nominated by the contracting parties, as well as other invited scientists. Thus, this review process seeks to ensure technical scrutiny of the exercise of an exception. Normally, reviews should take place at the annual meeting of the scientific committee, but the procedure allows for the information to be sent to members of the scientific committee by mail for comment and review in situations where permits would be granted prior to the next annual meeting. This addresses the issue of timeliness raised above. Review is automatic for each and every case. The scientific committee has established a more elaborate procedure, which guides its scrutiny of proposals for special permits.[83] However, the views of the scientific committee are not binding.[84] Ultimately, the state invoking the exception is left to decide whether to grant the exception. Similarly, resolutions adopted by the International Whaling Commission on the use of exceptions have limited legal effect, particularly when they are adopted by a majority.[85] It does not follow that the recommendations can be ignored, however. In this regard, the International Court of Justice (ICJ) has expressly noted that: 'States parties to the ICRW have a duty to co-operate with the IWC and the Scientific Committee and thus should give due regard to recommendations.'[86] Nevertheless, states are left with discretion and the control that is exercised by the ICRW institutions is thus limited.

[80] ibid para 7.
[81] ICRW (n 13) art VIII(1).
[82] ibid.
[83] Process for the Review of Special Permit Proposals and Research Results from Existing and Completed Permits (Revised Annex P) https://iwc.int/private/downloads/DhqsrQGoqMHB2Gn464sibw/Annex%20P%20updated.pdf (accessed 15 February 2016).
[84] *Whaling in the Antarctic (Australia v. Japan: New Zealand intervening)* (Judgment) [2014] ICJ Rep 226, para 47.
[85] ibid para 46.
[86] ibid para 83. Judges were divided on whether Japan had done so; see *Whaling in the Antarctic (Australia v Japan: New Zealand intervening)* (Judgment) (n 84) and the Separate Opinions of Judges Sebutinde (at 431), Bhandari (at 438), and Judge ad hoc Charlesworth (at 453).

6.4 Judicial review of ad hoc conditional rights

The nature of ad hoc conditional rights makes them particularly susceptible to review by international courts and tribunals because states must demonstrate that they meet certain conditions in order to benefit from the exception. *Whaling in the Antarctic* demonstrates the role that courts and tribunals may play in overseeing the exercise of ad hoc conditional rights and the types of questions that may arise when interpreting and applying such exceptions. The case concerned the invocation by Japan of the exception for scientific whaling in Article VIII of the ICRW, discussed above. Australia launched proceedings against Japan, arguing that the special permits issued by the Japanese government for its JARPA II whaling programme were not consistent with the conditions found in Article VIII.

As noted above, the drafters of the ICRW had explicitly included other review mechanisms in Article VIII and the relevant parts of the Annex, but the treaty did not explicitly foresee the possibility of a decision to invoke the exception being challenged before a court or tribunal. Thus, a key question faced by the Court was whether or not such a decision was subject to judicial review.

The starting point for the analysis of the text of Article VIII itself, which provides that:

> notwithstanding anything contained in this Convention, any Contracting Government may grant to any of its nationals a special permit authorizing that national to kill, take or treat whales for purposes of scientific research subject to such restrictions as to number and subject to other conditions as the Contracting Government thinks fit, and the killing, taking, and treating of whales in accordance with the provisions of this Article shall be exempt from the operation of this Convention.[87]

The parties to the dispute took different views as to how this provision should be interpreted. On the ordinary meaning of this text, it could be plausibly argued that Article VIII in fact establishes a self-judging exception that is not subject to any form of external review. Indeed, at the outset, Japan appeared to adopt this position, arguing that Article VIII served to shelter a state's decision to grant a special permit from any form of review.[88] However, subsequently, Japan appeared to concede that Article VIII could not be considered a completely self-judging exception.[89] It is therefore no surprise that the Court also adopted this position. What is interesting is the apparent recognition of several judges that the need for review, despite the language of the treaty, comes from its integral nature. Thus, Judge Sebutinde noted that '[t]he discretion afforded by Article VIII is thus an integral part of the collective regulatory mechanism and is necessarily limited in scope and character'.[90] Similarly, Judge Xue remarked that 'the fact that the discretional power of the Contracting Parties is derived from the regulating regime of the Convention [means that] it cannot be deemed unlimited'.[91] These comments suggest that a court or tribunal will require a very high level of evidence to support a claim that an exception is self-judging in the context of an integral treaty.[92]

[87] ICRW (n 13) art VIII(1).

[88] *Whaling in the Antarctic* (n 86) (Japanese Counter-Memorial), para 7.15 (footnotes omitted).

[89] See the discussion below on standard of review.

[90] *Whaling in the Antarctic (Australia v Japan: New Zealand intervening)* (Separate Opinion of Judge Sebutinde) 431 para 4.

[91] ibid (Separate Opinion of Judge Xue) 420, 422, para 7. See also para 9.

[92] Indeed, one can observe a general scepticism in international jurisprudence towards arguments in favour of self-judging or absolute exceptions for precisely this reason. See e.g. *Continental Casualty v Argentina*, ICSID Case

Acceptance of the appropriateness of review does not settle the question of the intensity of the review, however.[93] It is clear that the standard of review can vary enormously and the choice will have a significant bearing on the amount of discretion that will be left to a state when exercising an exception.[94] This raises important questions; as noted by Henckels, '[s]tandards of review reflect the allocation of authority between a legal system's primary decision-makers and its adjudicators, shape the balance of powers within a legal system, and in a supranational and international setting, the relationship between state responsibility and responsibility'.[95] A de novo standard of review, for example, means that the court steps into the shoes of the state invoking the exception and determines for itself what conduct would have been appropriate in the circumstances. This form of review assumes that the decision was a completely objective one and only capable of a single right answer. However, lower standards of review extend varying levels of discretion to the state making the decision.

Some treaties are explicit in the standard of review that is to be applied when determining whether an exception has been validly claimed. For example, Article V(1) of the London Dumping Convention, discussed above, would appear to set a high threshold by requiring that invocation of the exception is 'necessary' and 'the only way of averting the threat'. The use of other explicit terms, such as 'proportionate' or 'reasonable', may also give an indication of the standard of review that should be applied, although it must be acknowledged that these terms can be interpreted and applied with some flexibility in order to vary the level of scrutiny that is applied to a particular measure.[96]

Identifying the standard of review is even more complex when the treaty itself is silent, as was the case for the ICRW.[97] For its part, Australia described Article VIII as a conditional exception to the general rules under the ICRW, stating that 'it is only where the conditions for the operation of this exception are met, and in particular that the whaling activity is "for purposes of scientific research", that whaling in purported reliance on Article VIII will be lawful within the meaning of the Convention'.[98] In doing so, Australia proposed a high standard of review, requiring that a measure is 'appropriate and necessary for the purpose of the right (ie in furtherance of the interests which the right is intended to protect)'.[99] The standard of necessity, invoked here by Australia, is normally a strict one,

No ARB/03/9 (5 September 2008) para 187, referring to *Case Concerning Military and Paramilitary Activities in and against Nicaragua (Nicaragua v United States of America)* (Merits, Judgment) [1986] ICJ Rep 14, para 222; *Oil Platforms* (n 62) para 43.

[93] *Whaling in the Antarctic*, (n 86) para 67.

[94] See Stephen Tully, 'Objective Reasonableness' as a Standard for International Judicial Review' (2015) 6 Journal of International Dispute Settlement 546, 547.

[95] Caroline Henckels, 'Indirect Expropriation and the Right to Regulate: Revisiting Proportionality Analysis and the Standard of Review in Investor-State Arbitration' (2012) 15 Journal of International Economic Law 223, 239.

[96] See e.g. Jan H Jans, 'Proportionality Revisited' (2009) 27 Legal Issues in Economic Integration 239, 263: 'the proportionality principle does not have a specific form, but is flexible' and it can lead to 'more or less intrusive review'.

[97] ibid 241: 'In the absence of a stipulation in the relevant treaty, standards of review should reflect the contextual placement of a court or tribunal vis-à-vis other decision-makers within a politico-legal environment and the level of control delegated to adjudicators compared with the scope of power or discretion held by legislators and administrators.' See also Jan Bohanes and Nicolas Lockhart, 'Standard of Review in WTO Law' in Daniel Bethlehem, Isabelle Van Damme, Donald McRae, and Rodney Neufeld (eds), *The Oxford Handbook of International Trade Law* (Oxford University Press 2009) 38081.

[98] *Whaling in the Antarctic* (n 86) Australian Memorial, para 4.35.

[99] ibid para 4.61. See also para 5.126.

requiring a state to demonstrate that no other means were available to achieve its goals.[100] For its part, Japan advocated a less stringent standard of review, suggesting that only 'an arbitrary or capricious designation of a whaling expedition as a scientific expedition entitled to authorization by a special permit might be challenged on the basis that it lies outside Article VIII'.[101]

In its decision, the Court preferred the concept of reasonableness as the appropriate ground of review for the Japanese exception. In explaining how it would review the special permits issued by Japan, the Court said that it would 'consider whether the elements of a programme's design and implementation are reasonable in relation to its stated scientific objectives'.[102] Reasonableness as a ground of review looks to the reasons given for an action compared to the objectives of the right or exception, in order to ensure some relationship between the two.[103] It does not purport to decide whether the measure is the only way of achieving the objective, but only that there are coherent reasons behind the measures.[104] Thus, the concept of reasonableness accepts that states have some discretion in their choice of measures. The Court went on to identify a number of elements that it would assess for their reasonableness, namely

> decisions regarding the use of lethal methods; the scale of the programme's use of lethal sampling; the methodology used to select sample sizes; a comparison of the target sample sizes and the actual take; the time frame associated with a programme; the programme's scientific output; and the degree to which a programme co-ordinates its activities with related research projects'.[105]

On the basis of the evidence before it, the Court determined that there was not a sufficient relationship between the measure and its objectives. The approach of the Court would appear to be an appropriate one in the circumstances of the case, where the treaty provision suggested some discretion should be exercised by the state invoking the exception, but the nature of the treaty itself required some oversight. In other words, the Court's assessment seeks to balance the interests of the state invoking the exception and the other parties.[106] Indeed, one can imagine reasonableness being applied more broadly as a standard of review under environmental treaties, where there is no express indication that a stricter or more lenient standard of review should be adopted.[107]

[100] The concept of necessity is itself capable of different meanings, however; see *Korea—Beef*, Appellate Body Report, Document WT/DS161/AB/R, para 161.

[101] *Whaling in the Antarctic* (n 86) Japanese Counter-Memorial (n 88), para 7.16.

[102] *Whaling in the Antarctic* (n 86) para 88.

[103] ibid para 97. This has been described by the WTO Appellate Body as a 'means and ends relationship'; see *US—Shrimp*, Appellate Body Report, Document WT/DS58/AB/R, para 141.

[104] On the need for reasons to be coherent, see *Whaling in the Antarctic* (n 86) (Separate Opinion of Judge Xue) para 16.

[105] *Whaling in the Antarctic* (n 86) para 88. These criteria would appear to come from the Australian Memorial (n 98) para 4.36.

[106] Unsurprisingly, the Court's decision has been criticized as being both too strict and too lenient; see Tullio Scovazzi, 'Between Law and Science: Some Considerations Inspired by the Whaling in the Antarctic Judgment' (2015) 14 Questions of International Law 13, 26; Tully (n 94) 553; Alexander Proelss and Katherine Houghton, 'Protecting marine species' in Rosemary Rayfuse (ed), *Research Handbook on International Marine Environmental Law* (Edward Elgar Publishing 2015) 244. See also the dissenting opinion of Judge Owada in *Whaling in the Antarctic* (n 86) paras 37–40.

[107] In a different context, it has been held that 'like the exercise of any authority, the exercise of regulatory authority is always subject to the rule of reasonableness'; *La Bretagne Arbitration* (1986) 82 ILR 591, para 54. See also the *North Atlantic Coast Fisheries Case* (1910) 11 Reports of International Arbitral Awards 167; *Duzgit Integrity Arbitration*, PCA Case No 2014-07, Award (5 September 2016) para 209.

6 Conclusion

It can be seen from the wide range of examples discussed in this chapter that multilateral environmental agreements make regular use of exceptions in order to accommodate the different interests of states involved in the negotiation a treaty. Several types of exceptions are used to achieve flexibility, depending upon the particular circumstances of a treaty. This chapter has discussed three categories of exceptions, namely exclusions, reservation/opt-outs, and ad hoc conditional rights. The different categories can largely be distinguished based upon their effects on the underpinning treaty obligations. Exclusions have the greatest effect because they automatically exempt all states from the relevant treaty obligations. Reservations and opt-outs are narrower in their effect because they must be unilaterally declared by a party. Nevertheless, once reservations and opt-outs have been invoked, they exempt that state from complying with the relevant obligations for as long as they maintain the exception in place. Ad hoc conditional rights are the least intrusive form of exceptions because they can only be relied upon by a particular state for as long as certain conditions are met. These categories may provide treaty drafters with a conceptual framework within which to think about exceptions, although the precise scope and effect of a treaty will always depend upon its particular wording.

Many exceptions in environmental treaties are also accompanied by procedural mechanisms in order to oversee their exercise in practice. The prominence of these mechanisms in multilateral environmental agreements can be explained in part by the integral nature of most of these instruments—all other parties have an interest in ensuring that a state invoking an exception does not exercise it in such a way that jeopardizes the attainment of the treaty's ultimate objectives. Thus, the invocation of an exception does not necessarily exempt a state from having to cooperate with other parties to the treaty, even if they may not be under any legal obligations.

In practice, states have negotiated a variety of institutional mechanisms to oversee the interpretation and application of all types of exceptions. This may involve oversight and control by a political organ constituted under the treaty or it may involve the delegation of the task to an independent body. Nevertheless, many of the mechanisms remain weak and there continue to be calls for the tightening of oversight mechanisms to make it harder for individual states to circumvent the principal rules of a treaty.[108] Ultimately, prospects for treaty reform depend upon the political will of the parties. The nature of oversight mechanisms is as much a reflection of the balancing of values, as the agreement on permitting the exception in the first place.

The development of further institutional mechanisms by the other treaty parties is not the only way of achieving scrutiny over the exercise of exceptions. *Whaling in the Antarctic* provides an example where a court stepped in to provide independent scrutiny of the exercise of exceptions. Moreover, the case demonstrates that the lack of compulsory compromissory clauses in many environmental treaties is not necessarily an obstacle to judicial scrutiny if states can identify an alternative jurisdictional basis, in this case acceptance of the compulsory jurisdiction of the ICJ under its Statute. The use of adjudication may be particularly productive where exceptions are subject to

[108] Anastasia Telesetsky, 'After Whaling in the Antarctic: Amending Article VIII to Fix a Broken Treaty Regime' (2015) 30 International Journal of Marine and Coastal Law 700.

objective conditions that can be verified by a judicial body. There are also downsides to litigation, however. It is both costly and time-consuming and so courts and tribunals will usually only be able to exercise post facto control of exceptions. Therefore, litigation only really offers a last resort, where other oversight mechanisms are not available or ineffective.

19
Defences in International Criminal Law
Exceptions in International Law?

*Kai Ambos**

1 Conceptual Remarks

Defences operate in international criminal law—as in domestic criminal law—as substantive reasons to exclude individual criminal responsibility (substantive defences) or as procedural obstacles/bars to criminal prosecution (procedural defences). We return to the substantive/procedural distinction, as one (first) form of classification of defences, in a moment (section 2; see also Figure 19.1). On a meta level, defences operate as exceptions[1] to the (secondary)[2] rule expressed by the respective offence but they do not invalidate this rule—the prohibition *sub poena* by the offence—and they only entail its non-application.[3] This effect of non-application presupposes, of course, that the respective rule (offence) is applicable to the case in the first place, that is, applicability precedes (non-)application.[4]

Defences will normally be brought by the defence lawyer, although, conceptually, this is different in a non-adversarial, judge-led ('inquisitorial') criminal procedure where truth-seeking is the task of state organs, especially the judges. This procedural distinction has to be taken into account when discussing failure of proof defences and alibi (section 2.4).

But there is a more fundamental question: do 'the most serious crimes of international concern' (Article 1 of the ICC Statute) deserve any defence at all? This has indeed been questioned, and not only by some academics.[5] Thus, the Charter of the Nürnberg International

* The chapter draws on my *Treatise on International Criminal Law* (Oxford University Press 2013) ch VIII. From a comparative perspective see A Reed and M Bohlander (eds), *General Defences in Criminal Law* (Ashgate 2014). I thank Federica Paddeu and Alexander Heinze for valuable comments, as well as Muriel Nißle for editorial assistance.

[1] From a meta perspective see the contribution of Giovanni Sartor and Jaap Hage, Antonia Waltermann, and Gustavo Arosemena, both in this volume; *contra* the concept of 'self-subsisting' exceptions, especially as introduced by criminal statutes, as being absurd and illogical Glanville Williams, 'The Logic of "Exceptions"' (1988) 47 Cambridge Law Journal 261, 273 ff (but this position is predicated on an 'incorporationist' view; see n 77 below and accompanying text).

[2] On the distinction between primary and secondary rules in this regard see Luís Duarte d'Almeida (section 2.4) in this volume (referring to Binding's famous distinction between primary duty-imposing rules addressed to everyone and secondary rules addressed to the law enforcement officials and specifying the consequences of the violation of the primary rules).

[3] See Jaap Hage, Antonia Waltermann, and Gustavo Arosemena (section 1) in this volume.

[4] ibid at 9.

[5] cf e.g. Caroline Fournet, 'When the Child Surpasses the Father: Admissible Defences in International Criminal Law' (2008) 8 International Criminal Law Review 510 and Elies van Sliedregt, *Criminal Responsibility* (Oxford University Press 2012) 213; Douglas Guilfoyle, *International Criminal Law* (Oxford University Press 2016) 364; but see also the discussion during the 2240th meeting of the International Law Commission (ILC) (1996) 1 *Yearbook of International Law Commission* 48 59–60.

Kai Ambos, *Defences in International Criminal Law* In: *Exceptions in International Law*. Edited by: Lorand Bartels and Federica Paddeu, Oxford University Press (2020). © Lorand Bartels and Federica Paddeu.
DOI: 10.1093/oso/9780198789321.003.0019

Military Tribunal (IMT) does not expressly provide for the exclusion of criminal responsibility, the same applies to the Charter of the Tokyo International Military Tribunal for the Far East (IMTFE), the Statute of the International Criminal Tribunal for the former Yugoslavia (ICTY), the Statute of the International Criminal Tribunal for Rwanda (ICTR), and the Statute for the Special Court for Sierra Leone (SCSL).[6] In a similar vein, it has been argued that in international criminal law defences may only excuse but—for principled reasons—not justify a conduct[7] —on the underlying distinction of justification and excuse see below (section 2.3)—and that certain kinds of defences, including self-defence, duress, or mistake of law should, at any rate, be inadmissible.[8]

While these approaches have, at first sight, a certain appeal, on second thought it becomes clear that they fail to capture the legal nature and structure of international *crimes* fully, as opposed to international wrongs like human rights violations. In fact, international crimes—from a structural perspective—do not significantly differ from ordinary national crimes. The existence of both is predicated on a verdict of guilt against the respective defendant, which in turn is based on the unlawfulness of his conduct. Both the unlawfulness and the guilt presuppose the absence of defences. Thus, defences are, in principle, applicable in international criminal law as they are in national criminal law, although they are indeed—as O'Keefe rightly points out—'the least developed aspect of substantive international criminal law'.[9] Of course, the gravity of the relevant crimes has to be taken into account when interpreting the defences and their individual elements.[10]

2 Classification of Defences

Defences vary from each other with regard to their rationale, their social meaning, their legal consequences, and for other reasons. Their classification[11] is no end in itself but reveals conceptual differences between these defences and may therefore contribute to their better understanding and proper interpretation.[12] Thus, the following differentiation criteria with a special focus on international criminal law may be suggested (see also Figure 19.1).

[6] Roger O'Keefe, *International Criminal Law* (Oxford University Press 2015) 210–11.

[7] Gert-Jan Alexander Knoops, *Defenses in Contemporary International Criminal Law* (2nd edn, Martinus Nijhoff Publishers 2008) 22–23, who only wants to make an exception for self-defence.

[8] In this vein see Fournet (n 5) 526–30; Annemieke van Verseveld, *Mistake of Law* (TMC Asser Press 2012) 9; with a special view on the insanity defence Olaoluwa Olusanya, 'Punishing Mentally Incapable Offenders under Supranational Criminal Law' in Roelof Haveman and Olaoluwa Olusanya (eds), *Sentencing and Sanctioning in Supranational Criminal Law* (Intersentia 2006) 122. In particular reference to the admissibility of self-defence in international criminal law see section 2.3 below and—with more detail—Ambos (n *) 336.

[9] O'Keefe (n 6) 224.

[10] Albin Eser, '"Defences" in War Crime Trials' in Y Dinstein and M Tabory (eds), *War Crimes in International Law* (Kluwer Law International 1996) 252–53; Harmen van der Wilt, 'Justifications and Excuses in International Criminal Law: An Assessment of the Case-law of the ICTY' in B Swart, A Zahar, and G Sluiter (eds), *The Legacy of the International Criminal Tribunal for the Former Yugoslavia* (Oxford University Press 2009) 276; in the same vein see Christiane Nill-Theobald, *'Defences' bei Kriegsverbrechen am Beispiel Deutschlands und der USA, Max Planck Institute for Foreign and International Criminal Law* (Edition Iuscrim 1998) 58.

[11] See e.g. the overview of the different classification schemes by Douglas N Husak, 'The Serial View of Criminal Law Defences' (1992) 3 Criminal Law Forum 371.

[12] In this vein see also Paul H Robinson, *Criminal Law Defenses* (West Publishing 1984) 63.

2.1 Substantive and procedural defences

A primary distinction has to be made between *substantive* and *procedural* defences.[13] The former relate to specific features or conditions of the conduct in question, which make it lawful or negate the actor's blameworthiness;[14] the presence of these conditions 'bears on the merits of the issue of liability'.[15] Thus, substantive defences always require the examination of the alleged facts.[16] Only after the gathering and consideration of evidence does it become clear whether or not the defendant has indeed acted pursuant to a substantive defence, for example, self-defence or owing to mental illness.

By contrast, *procedural* defences challenge—more broadly—*any* fact which is a prerequisite for a conviction,[17] for example the jurisdiction and the right of a court to try an accused.[18] In his seminal two volume treatise on defences, Paul H. Robinson recognizes a category of non-exculpatory defences which are based not on the innocence or blamelessness of the suspect, but on public policy considerations.[19] This group includes the legality principle (*nullum crimen sine lege*), the *ne bis in idem* principle, immunities, the statute of limitations, amnesties, pardons and other waiver of punishment, unfitness to plead, and abuse of process, as well as the exclusion of jurisdiction over juveniles.[20] The objective of such procedural defences is not to justify the conduct or to excuse the actor but to exempt him from criminal prosecution, regardless of his culpability. Unlike substantive defences, procedural defences hinder all investigative and procedural measures, including the examination of the alleged facts.[21]

Here, a fundamental question arises: does the underlying assumption—interests of criminal justice must take second place to other public policy considerations—also apply to international criminal law? Can the central purpose of international criminal law, that is, to ensure that 'the most serious crimes of concern to the international community' do not remain 'unpunished',[22] really be pushed to a second place by nebulous 'policy considerations'

[13] See also Ilias Bantekas and Susan Nash, *International Criminal Law* (3rd edn, Routledge-Cavendish 2007) 52; Ilias Bantekas, 'Defences in International Criminal Law' in D McGoldrick, P Rowe, and E Donnelly (eds), *The Permanent International Criminal Court—Legal and Policy Issues* (Hart Publishing 2004) 264; Robert Cryer, 'Defences/Grounds for Excluding Criminal Responsibility' in R Cryer and others (eds), *An Introduction to International Criminal Law and Procedure* (Cambridge University Press 2014) 398; Massimo Scaliotti, 'Defences before the International Criminal Court: Substantive Grounds for Excluding Criminal Responsibility: Part 1' (2001) 1 International Criminal Law Review 111; Eser, '"Defences" in War Crime Trials' (n 10) 251; Thomas Weigend, 'Germany' in K Heller and M Dubber (eds), *The Handbook of Comparative Criminal Law* (Stanford Law Books 2011) 269; implicitly also Reinhard Merkel, 'Gründe für den Ausschluss der Strafbarkeit im Völkerstrafrecht' (2002) 114 Zeitschrift für die gesamte Strafrechtswissenschaft 441; Kai Ambos, *Internationales Strafrecht* (5th edn, CH Beck 2018) § 7 mn 77; van Sliedregt, *Criminal Responsibility* (n 5) 215; from a more abstract perspective see also Duarte d'Almeida (section 1.1) in this volume.

[14] Kai Ambos, 'Defences in International Criminal Law' in B S Brown (ed), *Research Handbook on International Criminal Law* (Edward Elgar Publishing 2011) 300. This implies a distinction between justification and excuses which is analysed below.

[15] Duarte d'Almeida (section 1.1) in this volume.

[16] Scaliotti (n 13) 111; cf also Kimberly Kessler Ferzan, 'Justification and Excuse' in J Deigh and D Dolinko (eds), *The Oxford Handbook of Philosophy of Criminal Law* (Oxford University Press 2011) 241.

[17] Duarte d'Almeida (section 1.1) in this volume.

[18] Ambos, 'Defences in International Criminal Law' (n 14) 300; cf also Eser, '"Defences" in War Crime Trials' (n 10) 253.

[19] Robinson, *Criminal Law Defenses* (n 12) 103; Paul H Robinson, 'Criminal Law Defenses: A Systematic Analysis' (1982) 82 *Columbia Law Review* 229. In the same Eugene R vein Milhizer, 'Justification and Excuse: What They Were, What They Are, and What They Ought to Be' (2004) 78 St John's Law Review 810; Law Reform Commission, *Defences in Criminal Law* (2009) mn 1.12; Mitchell N Berman and Ian P Farrell, 'Provocation Manslaughter as Partial Justification and Partial Excuse' (2011) 52 *William & Mary Law Review* 1046.

[20] See also Bantekas (n 13) 264 and Robinson, *Criminal Law Defenses* (n 12) 103, who qualify most of these jurisdictional limitations as non-exculpatory defences.

[21] Scaliotti (n 13) 111. See also Robinson, *Criminal Law Defenses* (n 12) 501.

[22] ICC Statute, preamble, para 4.

implicit in procedural defences? Would such an exception not strikingly contravene the customary law duty to prosecute international core crimes?

To answer this question, one would first have to clarify if the said duty to prosecute international core crimes exists in international law in the first place. Before the adoption and entry into force of the ICC Statute, this was still controversial.[23] While such a duty may convincingly be inferred from treaty obligations, for example, under the Genocide, Geneva, or Torture Conventions, for the respective crimes of genocide, grave breaches, and torture,[24] it is limited to the state parties of these treaties[25] and, of course, *ratione materiae*, to the crimes mentioned. Beyond that, it is controversial to what extent such a duty may flow from customary international law[26] or general principles of law.[27] As to the former, it is difficult to adduce state practice to that effect,[28] and the latter meets with criticism since it seemingly attempts to overcome the lacking or even contrary state practice by just ignoring it.[29] However, the duty to respect and ensure and the right to remedy provisions of general human rights treaties[30] do *not necessarily*—contrary to the dominant opinion in the doctrine[31] and the case law of the Inter-American Court of Human Rights (IACHR)[32]—entail an obligation of criminal prosecution, since the rights may also be 'ensured' through other mechanisms, and such mechanisms may constitute 'remedies' within the meaning of these provisions.[33] In addition, it is controversial whether the general obligation to protect

[23] See for a detailed discussion regarding the situation before the ICC Statute Kai Ambos, *Impunidad y derecho penal internacional* (2nd edn, Ad-Hoc 1999) 66–121; Kai Ambos, 'Völkerrechtliche Bestrafungspflichten bei schweren Menschenrechtsverletzungen' (1999) 37 Archiv des Völkerrechts 319 ff. The subsequent literature overwhelmingly recognizes a duty to prosecute: John Dugard, 'Possible Conflicts of Jurisdiction with Truth Commissions' in Antonio Cassese, P Gaeta, and J Jones (eds), *The Rome Statute of the International Criminal Court* (CH Beck 2002) 696–97; Catalina Botero and Esteban Restrepo, 'Estándares internacionales y procesos de transición en Colombia' in Angelika Rettberg (ed), *Entre el perdón y el paredón: preguntas y dilemas de la justicia transicional* (Ediciones Uniandes 2005) 26–33; for identifying a 'trend' towards such a duty seeKarlijn van der Voort and Marten Zwanenburg, 'From "raison d'état" to "état de droit international": Amnesties and the French Implementation of the Rome Statute' (2001) 1 International Criminal Law Review 316, 324; for a partial duty depending on the crime see Helmut Gropengießer and Jörg Meißner, 'Amnesties and the Rome Statute of the International Criminal Court' (2005) 5 *International Criminal Law Review* 272.

[24] See e.g. John Dugard, 'Dealing with Crimes of a Past Regime. Is Amnesty Still an Option?' (1999) 12 *Leiden Journal of International Law* 1004; Jessica Gavron, 'Amnesties in the Light of Developments in International Law and the Establishment of the International Criminal Court' (2002) 51 *International and Comparative Law Quarterly* 92; Carsten Stahn, 'Complementary, Amnesties and Alternative Forms of Justice. Some Interpretative Guidelines for the International Criminal Court' (2005) 3 *Journal of International Criminal Justice* 703; for a general duty to exercise jurisdiction for all war crimes see Laura M Olson, 'Provoking the Dragon on the Patio. Matters of Transitional Justice: Penal Repression vs. Amnesties' (2006) 88 *International Review of the Red Cross* 279. For further references see Kai Ambos, 'The Legal Framework of Transitional Justice: A Systematic Study with a Special Focus on the Role of the ICC' in Kai Ambos, J Large, and M Wierda (eds), *Building a Future on Peace and Justice* (Springer 2009) 30 with n 64.

[25] Ambos, 'The Legal Framework of Transitional Justice' (n 24) 30.

[26] cf ICJ Statute art 38(b).

[27] ibid art 38(c).

[28] See e.g. Angelika Schlunck, *Amnesty versus Accountability: Third Party Intervention Dealing with Gross Human Rights Violations in Internal and International Conflicts* (Verlag Spitz 2000) 49, concluding that such a state practice can only be identified with regard to genocide; for a 'developing obligation' to prosecute crimes against humanity see Louise Mallinder, 'Can Amnesties and International Justice be Reconciled?' (2007) 1 International Journal of Transitional Justice 214. For an earlier critique see also Ambos, *Impunidad y derecho penal internacional* (n 23) 328–35.

[29] Ambos, *Impunidad y derecho penal internacional* (n 23) 332–35.

[30] See e.g. ICCPR art 2(1) and (3).

[31] See ibid with further references; see also on ICCPR art 2(3) van der Voort and Zwanenburg (n 23) 322; Olson (n 24) 282–83.

[32] See e.g. *Almonacid-Arellano and Others v Chile*, IACHR Series C No 154, IHRL 1538 (26 September 2006) para 110: 'La obligación conforme al derecho internacional de enjuiciar y, si se les declara culpables, castigar a los perpetradores de determinados crímenes internacionales, entre los que se cuentan los crímenes de lesa humanidad, se desprende de la obligación de garantía consagrada en el artículo 1.1 de la Convención Americana … Como consecuencia de esta obligación los Estados deben prevenir, investigar y sancionar toda violación … '. For further references see Ambos, 'The Legal Framework of Transitional Justice' (n 24) 30 with n 68.

[33] As to the argument that an effective remedy need not necessarily be a criminal prosecution see Schlunck (n 28) 44–45; Gavron (n 24) 99 with n 42.

human rights effectively entails the active prosecution of perpetrators, given that human rights treaties also pretend to protect these same perpetrators by way of fair trial provisions and other substantive rights.[34]

Be that as it may, the ICC Statute advanced the debate considerably, because with its entry into force it can now safely be said—on the basis of paragraphs 4–6 of its preamble[35]—that at least a state party to this treaty is obliged to prosecute the crimes covered by the Statute.[36] Non-state parties may be bound either by a specific treaty obligation or by the combined effect of the pre-ICC Statute instruments and the ICC Statute. Indeed, the Statute has reinforced the customary law duty in that it expresses—as a kind of *Verbalpraxis*[37]—the general acceptance of such a duty with regard to the ICC crimes (genocide, crimes against humanity, war crimes, and the crime of aggression). This duty will be further strengthened and consolidated with the increasing number of ICC state parties.[38] It follows from the very rationale of the international criminal justice system[39] that the duty to prosecute core crimes cannot exist solely on the national level. Rather, it is the central aim of international tribunals to ensure that the most heinous crimes do not go unpunished.

If a duty to prosecute international core crimes exists, it follows, arguably, as a corollary that these crimes *cannot be exempted* from punishment by procedural defences, in particular by amnesty-like provisions.[40] The same result follows from a *rule of law* argument: if the law provides for a duty to prosecute, then the rule of law entails a prohibition of amnesty[41] and other procedural defences, and as such constitutes a limit to politics;[42] otherwise, the very legal and social order to be protected by the rule of law would be undermined and, instead, a culture of impunity created or promoted.[43] In fact, the rule of law argument entails a host of

[34] See also on this contradiction Gerhard Werle and Florian Jeßberger, *Principles of International Criminal Law* (3rd edn, Oxford University Press 2014) mn 202.

[35] Paragraph 4 of the preamble was previously quoted above (n 22). Paras 5 and 6 read: '*Determined* to put an end to impunity for the perpetrators of these crimes and thus to contribute to the prevention of such crimes, *Recalling* that it is the duty of every State to exercise its criminal jurisdiction over those responsible for international crimes . . .'.

[36] See also Schlunck (n 28) 30; Ambos, *Internationales Strafrecht* (n 13) § 7 mn 109; see in the same vein Mohamed M el Zeidy, 'The Principle of Complementarity: A New Machinery to Implement International Criminal Law' (2002) 32 Michigan Journal of International Law 947, who even considers these crimes as *jus cogens* norms. For a general (emerging) duty to prosecute the ICC crimes see Darryl Robinson, 'Serving the Interests of Justice: Amnesties, Truth Commissions and the International Criminal Court' (2003) 14 European Journal of International Law 491.

[37] See also Helmut Kreicker, 'Völkerstrafrecht im Ländervergleich' in A Eser, U Sieber, and H Kreicker (eds), *Nationale Strafverfolgung völkerrechtlicher Verbrechen. National Prosecution of International Crimes* (Duncker & Humblot 2006) 12–13, 305.

[38] See in more detail and with further references Ambos, 'The Legal Framework of Transitional Justice' (n 24) 29–31.

[39] On this system see Ambos (n *) 56 with n 27.

[40] See for a discussion Kai Ambos, *Straflosigkeit von Menschenrechtsverletzungen* (Edition Iuscrim 1997) 209–27; Ambos, *Impunidad y derecho penal internacional* (n 23) 126–47; many writers argue in favour of such an inference e.g. Douglas Cassel, 'Lessons from the Americas: Guidelines for International Response to Amnesties for Atrocities' (1996) 59 Law and Contemporary Problems 210; Kreicker (n 37) 305–306. For further references see Ambos, 'The Legal Framework of Transitional Justice' (n 24) 31–33.

[41] Generally on the rule of law argument in this context see Schlunck (n 28) 24–26, 62; see also the statement of R Badinter, Rapporteur of the French Senate's Commission on Constitutional Law, stressing that an amnesty for international core crimes could simple not be envisaged in a state that respected the rule of law (quoted in van der Voort and Zwanenburg (n 23) 337).

[42] Ruti G Teitel, *Transitional Justice* (Oxford University Press 2000) 21–22, 59; see also Olson (n 24) 278–79.

[43] See Garth Meintjes, 'Post Conflict Justice Issues: Restoring order and Justice. Report of the Rapporteur' in C Joyner (ed), *Reining in Impunity for International Crimes and Serious Violations of fundamental Human Rights. Proceedings of the siracusa Conference, 17–21 September, 1998* (Erès 1998) 462; David A Crocker, 'Punishment, Reconciliatoin, and Democratic Deliberation' (2002) 5 Buffalo Criminal Law Review 538 and Ronald C Slye, 'The Legitimacy of Amnesties Under International Law and General Principles of Anglo-American law: Is a Ligitimate Amnesty Possible?' (2002) 43 Virginia Journal of International Law 197; cf also Héctor Olásolo, 'The Prosecutor of the ICC Before the Initiation of Investigations: A Quasi-Judicial or a Political body?' (2003) 3 International Criminal Law Review 144.

other arguments in favour of prosecution typically known from the debate on the purposes of punishment:[44] non-prosecution would undermine the effectiveness of criminal law deterrence,[45] whereas prosecution reinstates the victims' status as fellow citizens,[46] conveys the right message to perpetrators but also to the society in general (negative special and general prevention), and reasserts the values of a given society (positive general prevention).[47] The reinforcement of values such as the right to life, physical integrity, and liberty has a stabilizing effect for new democratic systems[48] and shows the moral dimension of the issue.[49]

However, despite all these forceful arguments in favour of prosecution, the respective duty constitutes a *principle* rather than a hard and fixed rule,[50] and as such permits—strictly defined—exceptions.[51] Thus, the general duty to prosecute international crimes does not forbid procedural defences per se, but requires that they are strictly limited to instances in which non-prosecution is acceptable or even demanded by higher interests, for example, by the overall fairness and integrity of the international criminal justice system.

2.2 Full and partial defences

Another fundamental classification refers to the *legal consequences* of a defence. Full or perfect[52] defences preclude the actor's criminal liability entirely, that is, they result in an *acquittal*.[53] In contrast, in case of a partial or imperfect[54] defence, the perpetrator is convicted but his *punishment mitigated*.[55]

[44] On this debate see Ambos (n *) 67 ff.

[45] Crocker (n 43) 536–37; Robinson, 'Serving the Interests of Justice' (n 36) 489; Rodrigo Uprimny and María Paula Saffon, 'Justicia transnacional y justicia restaurative: tensiones y complementariedades' in Angelika Rettberg (ed), *Entre el perdón y el paredón: preguntas y dilemas de la justicia transicional* (Ediciones Uniandes 2005) 225–26; Olson (n 24) 291.

[46] Similarly Jaime Malamud-Goti, 'Transitional Government in the Breach: Why Punish State Criminals?' in N Kritz (ed), *Transitional Justice* (Institute of Peace Press 1995) 199 ff; Juan Ernesto Méndez, 'National Reconciliation, Transnational Justice and the International Criminal Court' (2001) 15 Ethics International Affairs 31; cf also Stefanie Bock, *Das Opfer vor dem Internationalen Strafgerichtshof* (Duncker & Humblot 2010) 198–201 with further references; on a possible therapeutic effect see Pierre Hazan, 'Measuring the Impact of Punishment and Forgiveness: A Framework for Evaluating Transitional Justice' (2006) 88 International Review of the Red Cross 39.

[47] See also Michael P Scharf and Nigel Rodley, 'International Law Principles on Accountability' in M C Bassiouni (ed), *Post-Conflict Justice* (Transnational Publishers 2002) 90–91; Teitel (n 42) 28 and 67; Méndez (n 46) 31–32; Gropengießer and Meißner (n 23) 279; Uprimny and Saffon (n 45) 225–26; Diane F Orentlicher, 'Settling Accounts Revisited: Reconciling Global Norms with Local Agency' (2007) *1* International Journal of Transitional Justice 15; crit Danilo Zolo, 'Peace Trough Criminal Law?' (2004) 2 Journal of International Criminal Justice 734 ('retributive conception of criminal punishment can hardly be reconciled with any project of social peacemaking').

[48] Teitel (n 42) 67; Alex Boraine, *A Country Unmasked, Inside South Africa's Truth and Reconciliation Commission* (Oxford University Press 2001) 280–81; Uprimny and Saffon (n 45) 226.

[49] Robinson, 'Serving the Interests of Justice' (n 36) 489–90.

[50] I follow here R Alexy's distinction between (flexible) principles and (strict) rules (cf Robert Alexy, *Theorie der Grundrechte* (Frankfurt a.M.: Suhrkamp 1986) 71 ff;English translation Julian Rivers, *A Theory of Constitutional Rights* (Oxford University Press 2002) 44 ff). See also Gropengießer and Meißner (n 23) 276: 'in principle'; Stahn (n 24) 701: 'generally incompatible'.

[51] Ambos, 'The Legal Framework of Transitional Justice' (n 24) 32.

[52] Matthew Lippman, *Criminal Law* (3rd edn, Sage 2013) 213.

[53] Knoops (n 7) 112; Douglas N Husak, *The Philosophy of Criminal Law* (Oxford University Press 2010) 311; Hein D Wolswijk, 'Provocation and Diminished Responsibility in Dutch Homicide Law' in A Reed and M Bohlander (eds), *Loss of Control and Diminished Responsibility—Domestic, Comparative and International Perspectives* (Ashgate 2011) 329; cf also Julia Tolmie, 'Is the Partial Defence an Endangered Defence? Recent Proposals to Abolish Provocation' (2005) 122 New Zealand Law Reports 26 and *Delalić and Others* (Judgment) ICTY IT-96-21-A (20 February 2001) para 582.

[54] Lippman (n 52) 213.

[55] Knoops (n 7) 112; Husak, *The Philosophy of Criminal Law* (n 53) 313; Wolswijk (n 53) 330; cf also John Gardner, 'Justifications and Reasons' in A P Simester and A TH Smith (eds), *Harm and Culpability* (Clarendon Press 2003) 107.

This raises the question of the way in which partial defences differ from (other) mitigating factors. Some authors argue that, while the latter are only relevant for determining the severity of a sentence, partial defences result in the conviction for a different, separate (lesser) offence, although all elements of the more serious offence are fulfilled.[56] Take the most prominent example of the traditional common law defence of *provocation* (in modern English law replaced by 'loss of control').[57] If raised successfully, the perpetrator is convicted for manslaughter instead of murder.[58] The rationale of this partial defence is to exclude the mandatory sentence for the more serious offence, for example, the death penalty or life imprisonment.[59] A more sophisticated explanation is offered by Douglas Husak, who argues that partial defences are a kind of mitigating factor, which apply if the defendant deserves a lesser punishment. Thus, they constitute *desert-based mitigating circumstances*.[60] Accordingly, the perpetrator who acted under a threat (falling short of duress), on committing a crime, deserves a mitigation of punishment.[61]

Article 31 of the ICC Statute refers only to grounds excluding (not diminishing) criminal responsibility, that is, it recognizes *full defences* only.[62] However, pursuant to the ICC Rules of Procedure and Evidence (RPE), in situations falling short of full defences, mitigation is possible.[63] This is a reasonable approach, given that international criminal law does neither provide for mandatory sentences nor for appropriate lesser offences.[64] As a consequence, one should limit the use of the term 'defences' to those which have a fully exclusionary effect entailing an acquittal and speak of mere causes of factors of mitigation in case of 'partial' defences.

2.3 Justifications and excuses

Substantive defences may be subdivided further in justifications and excuses.[65] This differentiation originates in the civil law tradition,[66] in particular in the Germanic tripartite

[56] Berman and Farrell (n 19) 1045. In the same vein see Jeremy Horder, *Excusing Crime* (Oxford University Press 2006) 143–46.

[57] See generally Berman and Farrell (n 19) 1027 ff.

[58] In more detail see Berman and Farrell (n 19) 1045–65; Tolmie (n 53) 26; Arie Freiberg and Felicity Stewart, 'Beyond the Partial Excuse: Australasian Approaches to Provocation as a Sentencing Factor' in J V Roberts (ed), *Mitigation and Aggravation at Sentencing* (Cambridge University Press 2011) 102; cf also Horder (n 56) 102.

[59] *Delalić and Others* (n 53) para 590; Jens Watzek, *Rechtfertigung und Entschuldigung im englischen Strafrecht—Eine Strukturanalyse der allgemeinen Strafbarkeitsvoraussetzungen aus deutscher Perspektive* (Edition Iuscrim 1997) 246; Peter Krug, 'The Emerging mental Incapacity Defense in International Criminal Law' (2000) 99 American Journal of International Law 330; Sander Janssen, 'Mental Condition Defences in Supranational Criminal Law' (2004) 4 International Criminal Law Review 87; Andrew J Ashworth, *Principles of Criminal Law* (6th edn, Oxford University Press 2009) 250; Alan Reed and Nicola Wake, 'Anglo-American Perspectives on Partial Defences: Something Old, Something Borrowed, and Something New' in A Reed and M Bohlander (eds), *Loss of Control and Diminished Responsibility—Domestic, Comparative and International Perspectives* (Ashgate 2011) 183–84.

[60] Husak, *The Philosophy of Criminal Law* (n 53) 312–13.

[61] ibid 328; cf also Cryer (n 13) 399.

[62] cf Cryer (n 13) 399; more generally O'Keefe (n 6) 210, 211. This is overlooked by Bantekas and Nash (n 13) 70 (arguing that it is uncertain whether the insanity defence 'may serve as a complete or partial defence').

[63] See ICC RPE rule 145(2)(a)(i),which qualifies 'circumstances falling short of constituting grounds for exclusion of criminal responsibility, such as substantially diminished mental capacity or duress' as mitigating factors.

[64] *Delalić and Others* (n 53) para 590; John Cubbon, 'Diminished Responsibility and Loss of Control' in A Reed and M Bohlander (eds), *Loss of Control and Diminished Responsibility—Domestic, Comparative and International Perspectives* (Ashgate 2011) 369; cf also Krug (n 59) 331.

[65] See also Guilfoyle (n 5) 361; Nicola Lacey, Celia Wells, and Oliver Quick, *Reconstructing Criminal Law* (Cambridge University Press 2010) 120; also Duarte d'Almeida (section 2.1) in this volume.

[66] Antonio Cassese, 'Justification and Excuses in International Criminal Law' in Antonio Cassese, P Gaeta and J Jones (eds), *The Rome Statute of the International Criminal Law* (CH Beck 2002) 951; Cryer (n

structure of crime (distinguishing between offence definition, wrongdoing, and culpability).[67] In this system, the distinction between justifications and excuses is mandatory, since the former negate the wrongdoing while the latter exclude the actor's culpability.[68] The distinction has also received increasing support across the common law systems[69] and can be found in the Model Penal Code (MPC).[70]

According to this view, a *justification* excludes criminal responsibility for an act which fulfils the elements of the offence definition (actus reus) but is lawful because the actor acted on the basis of a permissive norm, for example, self-defence, which precludes the *actus reus*.[71] Thus, in case of a justification, society tolerates, approves or even encourages the

13) 398–99; van der Wilt (n 10) 276; Jens D Ohlin, 'Justifications and Excuses' in Antonio Cassese (ed), *The Oxford Companion to International Criminal Justice* (Oxford University Press 2009) 318; see also Ambos, 'Defences in International Criminal Law' (n 14) 300.

[67] George P Fletcher, 'The Influence of the Common law and Civil Law Traditions on International Criminal Law' in Antonio Cassese (ed), *The Oxford Companion to International Criminal Justice* (Oxford University Press 2009) 105; concurring George Mousourakis, 'Justification and Excuse' (1998) 7 Tilburg Foreign Law Review 50. As to the tripartite structure of crime cf also George P Fletcher, *Basic Concepts of Criminal Law* (Oxford University Press 1998) 101; Mohamed Elewa Badar, 'Mens rea: Mistake of Law & Mistake of Fact in German Criminal Law: A Survey for International Criminal Tribunals' (2005) 5 International Criminal Law Review 215; Claus Roxin, *Strafrecht: Allgemeiner Teil Band I* (4th edn, CH Beck 2006) § 10 mn. 1–29; Michael Bohlander, *Principles of German Criminal Law* (Hart Publishing 2008) 16–18; also Kai Ambos, 'Toward a Universal System of Crime: Comments on George Fletcher's Grammar of Criminal Law' (2007) 28 Cardozo Law Review 2647, 2650–52.

[68] See only Fletcher, 'The Influence of the Common law and Civil Law Traditions on International Criminal Law' (n 67) 105; Jean Pradel, *Droit Pénal Comparé* (3rd edn, Dalloz 2008), mn 99; van Sliedregt, *Criminal Responsibility* (n 5) 216; Guilfoyle (n 5) 362; crit Lacey, Wells, and Quick (n 65) 120.

[69] See e.g. Kent Greenawalt, 'The Perplexing Borders of Justification and Excuse' (1984) 84 Columbia Law Review 1897; Jonathan Herring, *Criminal Law: Text, Cases and Materials* (5th edn, Oxford University Press 2012) 711; Knoops (n 7) 22; Lippman (n 52) 212; Robinson, *Criminal Law Defenses* (n 12) § 24 (justifications) and § 25 (excuses); Kent Roach, 'Canada' in K J Heller and M D Dubber (eds), *Handbook of Comparative Criminal Law* (Stanford University Press 2011) 114; Stanley Yeo, 'India' in K J Heller and M D Dubber (eds), *Handbook of Comparative Criminal Law* (Stanford University Press 2011) 299; cf also Kai Ambos, *Der Allgemeine Teil des Völkerstrafrechts: Ansätze einer Dogmatisierung* (2nd edn, Duncker & Humblot 2004) 826–27; Cryer (n 13) 399 with n 4; Bantekas (n 13) 266; for an overview of the historical development of the distinction between justifications and excuses in the common law tradition see Watzek (n 59) 74–80; Mousourakis (n 67) 45–47 and Milhizer (n 19) 730–95. The distinction is also recognized in Iran (Silvia Tellenbach, 'Iran' in K J Heller and M D Dubber (eds), *The Handbook of Comparative Criminal Law* (Oxford University Press 2011) 332) and Japan (John Owen Haley, 'Japan' in K J Heller and M D Dubber (eds), *The Handbook of Comparative Criminal Law* (Oxford University Press 2011) 403); but not in Russia (Friedrich-Christian Schroeder, 'Die Straftatausschließungsgründe des russischen Rechts im Lichte der deutschen Strafrechtsdogmatik' (2011) 123 Zeitschrift für die gesamte Strafrechtswissenschaft 90), and Israel (Itzhak Kugler in 'Israel' in K J Heller and M D Dubber (eds), *The Handbook of Comparative Criminal Law* (Oxford University Press 2011) 376).

[70] MPC § 1.13(9) reads as follows: '"element of an offense" means (i) such conduct or (ii) such attendant circumstances or (iii) such a result of conduct as ... (c) negatives an *excuse or justification* for such conduct;' (emphasis added). See, however, also David Ormerod, *Smith and Hogan's Criminal Law* (13th edn, Oxford University Press 2011) 271, who argues that 'Anglo-American criminal law has never expressly recognized these distinctions'; in a similar vein see Andrew J Ashworth, 'United Kingdom' in K J Heller and M D Dubber (eds), *The Handbook of Comparative Criminal Law* (Oxford University Press 2011) 541; cf also Albin Eser, 'Die Unterscheidung von Rechtfertigung und Entschuldigung: Ein Schlüsselproblem des Verbrechensbegriffes' in R Lahti and K Nuotio (eds), *Criminal Law Theory in Transition: Finnish and Comparative Perspectives* (Finnish Lawyers' Publishing Company 1992) 313–15.

[71] Kai Ambos, 'May a State Torture Suspects to Save the Life of Innocents?' (2008) 6 Journal of International Criminal Justice 278; Ambos, 'Defences in International Criminal Law' (n 14) 300; Bantekas and Nash (n 13) 53; Bantekas (n 13) 266; Antonio Cassese, *International Criminal Law* (2nd edn, Oxford University Press 2008) 255; Cassese, *The Oxford Companion to International Criminal Justice* (n 66) 951–52; George P Fletcher, 'The Right and the Reasonable' (1985) 98 Harvard Law Review 954, 977; Herring (n 69) 712–13; Héctor Olásolo, *Unlawful Attacks in Combat Situations* (Martinus Nijhoff Publishers 2008) 235; Bohlander (n 67) 78; Cryer (n 13) 399; Husak, *The Philosophy of Criminal Law* (n 53) 314; Mousourakis (n 67) 36; Wolswijk (n 53) 329; Shane Darcy, 'Defences to International Crimes' in W B Schabas and N Bernaz (eds), *Routledge Handbook of International Criminal Law* (Routledge 2011) 231.

defendant's action.[72] This does not mean, of course, that it turns the offence (actus reus) fulfilled by the perpetrator into a neutral conduct. The justification justifies this per se illicit or prima facie wrongful conduct[73] but it does not put the justified (permitted) conduct on an equal footing with a per se neutral or irrelevant conduct. The point has famously been made by Hans Welzel[74] when arguing that the law must surely draw a difference between the killing of a mosquito—which is per se, from a legal perspective, neutral—and the killing of a person in self-defence—which is a prima facie unlawful, but permitted conduct.[75] We should thus distinguish between three forms of conduct: legally relevant prohibited conduct, legally relevant permitted conduct, and legally irrelevant conduct.[76] More importantly, the idea of a kind of umbrella codification of wrongfulness ('offence package',[77] *Gesamtunrechtstatbestand*) encompassing the elements of the offence and the substantive defences as its negative elements[78] ('incorporationism'),[79] must be rejected (as regards justifications proper)[80] for it blurs the—normatively important—distinction between the prima facie unlawful conduct expressed by the offence and the (exceptional) permission by the ground of justification.[81]

Despite differences in detail the overall rationale of justificatory defences is 'a balancing of competing interests and a judgment in favour of the superior interest'.[82] In contrast, an *excuse* does not render the act lawful. Rather, the individual wrongdoer is not blamed for

[72] Greenawalt (n 69) 1900; Herring (n 69) 712–13; Knoops (n 7) 22; Lippman (n 52) 212; Robinson, *Criminal Law Defenses* (n 12) 83; Robinson, 'Criminal Law Defenses: A Systematic Analysis' (n 19) 245.

[73] Going even further see Duarte d'Almeida (section 2.3) in this volume (conduct '*is* and *remains* a wrong even in the face of justification' [emphasis in original]). For Ferzan (n 16) 241–42, it is disputed whether justification entails permissible or right conduct.

[74] Hans Welzel, 'Die Regelung von Vorsatz und Irrtum im Strafrecht als legislatorisches Problem' (1955) 67 Zeitschrift für die gesamte Strafrechtswissenschaft 196, 211 (explaining the distinction between the legally permitted as compared to the legally irrelevant: 'Die Tötung einer Mücke ist, weil sie tatbestandslos ist, rechtlich irrelevant. Die Tötung eines Menschen in Notwehr ist eine rechtlich relevante, darum tatbestandsmäßige Handlung, aber erlaubt').

[75] In the same vein see Duarte d'Almeida (section 2.3) in this volume.

[76] Welzel (n 74) 211 ('Es gibt rechtlich relevantes—tatbestandsmäßiges—Verhalten, das verboten (rechtswidrig) ist, es gibt rechtlich relevantes—tatbestandsmäßiges—Verhalten, das erlaubt (rechtmäßig) ist, und es gibt die unübersehbare Fülle des rechtlich irrelevanten, tatbestandslosen Geschehens').

[77] Williams (n 1) 280.

[78] In Anglo-American doctrine this has been most famously defended by Williams (n 1) 262, 277 ('no intrinsic difference between the elements of an offence and an exception ... to that offence'); also previously Glanville Williams, 'Offences and Defences' (1982) 2 Legal Studies 233, 256 ('So what we think of as the definition of an offence and what we call a defence can only be regarded as depending largely upon the accidents of language, the convenience of legal drafting, or the unreasoning force of tradition'); for the civil law doctrine see Adolf Merkel, *Lehrbuch des Deutschen Strafrechts* (Ferdinand Enke 1889) 82 ('Der Handelnde setzt Verhältnisse voraus, deren Nichtvorliegen zum gesetzlichen Thatbestande gehört (negative Thatbestandsmerkmale), also z.B. Verhältnisse, welche, wenn sie vorliegen würden, die That als durch Notwehr ... gerechtfertigt erscheinen lassen'); following this view George P Fletcher and Jens David Ohlin, *Defending Humanity: When Force Is Justified and Why* (Oxford University Press 2008) 30. From a meta level (but *contra*) cf Hage, Waltermann, and Arosemena (section 10) in this volume (negative rule conditions as 'derived rules').

[79] Duarte d'Almeida (section 1.3) in this volume.

[80] It is plausible, however, regarding constitutive, negative elements of an offence, e.g. the (absence of) consent in the sense of an *Einverständnis* in case of trespassing or rape (see thereto Duarte d'Almeida (section 3.4.3) in this volume) or the lack of a licence in the offence of 'driving without a licence' (see thereto Williams (n 1) 274–76).

[81] Welzel (n 74) 211 ('Die Rechtfertigungsgründe sind Erlaubnissätze, deren Vorliegen die Verwirklichung rechtlich relevanten, tatbestandsmäßigen Verhaltens gestattet. Sie sind nicht negative Tatumstände, deren Hinzutritt die Tatbestandsmäßigkeit, z. B. die Tötung eines Menschen, ausschließt und das Verhalten zu einem rechtlich gleichgültigen Geschehen macht, sondern sie sind Gründe, die die rechtliche Relevanz unangetastet lassen und nur das Verbotensein oder die Rechtswidrigkeit der Tatbestandsverwirklichung ausschließen').

[82] George P Fletcher, *Rethinking Criminal Law* (Little, Brown 2000) 769; in the same vein see Mousourakis (n 67) 38; Robinson, 'Criminal Law Defenses: A Systematic Analysis' (n 19) 213; Milhizer (n 19) 844; cf also Eser, 'Die Unterscheidung von Rechtfertigung und Entschuldigung: Ein Schlüsselproblem des Verbrechensbegriffes' (n 70) 308–309.

having carried out the unlawful act since he was unable to recognize the unlawfulness or could not be expected to act lawfully.[83] In a nutshell, justifications relate to the propriety of the act, excuses to the blameworthiness of the actor.[84]

This differentiation is not uncontested. Critics argue that a clear-cut distinction between justifications and excuses is not possible.[85] Even with regard to self-defence, the most important and arguably least contested example of a justification, one can imagine situations in which it seems more appropriate to uphold the unlawfulness of the defendant's conduct and just exempt him from blame. Take, for example, the case where the victim of an attack overreacts and continues to beat the attacker already lying on the ground. In fact, in this case of excessive self-defence some legal systems reject self-defence but provide for a specific excuse.[86]

Be that as it may, it remains nevertheless true that a few individual cases do not make the distinction between justification and excuse meaningless or unreasonable.[87] In dealing with the substantive defences, the underlying differentiation between general wrongfulness and personal blame proves especially helpful in borderline cases, for example, killing under duress.[88] In addition, the distinction has *practical consequences*. Contrary to a view in the literature which focuses too much on the direct outcome for the direct perpetrator (conviction or acquittal),[89] the distinction makes a difference for

[83] Ambos, 'May a State Torture Suspects to Save the Life of Innocents?' (n 71) 285–86; Bantekas and Nash (n 13) 53; Bantekas (n 13) 266; Cassese, *The Oxford Companion to International Criminal Justice* (n 66) 256, 952; Cryer (n 13) 399; Herring (n 69) 716; Olásolo (n 71) 235; Bohlander (n 67) 115; Husak, *The Philosophy of Criminal Law* (n 53) 314; Robinson, 'Criminal Law Defenses: A Systematic Analysis' (n 19) 221; van der Wilt (n 10) 277; Wolswijk (n 53) 329. See also Fletcher, 'The Right and the Reasonable' (n 71) 958; Fletcher, *Rethinking Criminal Law* (n 82) 759; Greenawalt (n 69) 1900; Eser, 'Die Unterscheidung von Rechtfertigung und Entschuldigung: Ein Schlüsselproblem des Verbrechensbegriffes' (n 70) 208; Milhizer (n 19) 816, 846; Roach (n 69) 114; Weigend (n 13) 269; Carlos Gómez-Jara Díez and Luis E Chiesa, 'Spain' in K J Heller and M D Dubber (eds), *The Handbook of Comparative Criminal Law* (Oxford University Press 2011) 507 and Horder (n 56) 9 (stressing the moral component of excuses); Guilfoyle (n 5) 361.

[84] Fletcher, 'The Right and the Reasonable' (n 71) 955; Fletcher, *Rethinking Criminal Law* (n 82) 762; Milhizer (n 19) 726; Catherine Elliott, 'France' in K J Heller and M D Dubber (eds), *The Handbook of Comparative Criminal Law* (Oxford University Press 2011) 223; Guilfoyle (n 5) 361; Lacey, Wells, and Quick (n 65) 121–22. See also Ormerod (n 70) 285; Robinson, 'Criminal Law Defenses: A Systematic Analysis' (n 19) 229; Mousourakis (n 67) 41; critically on this differentiation see Ferzan (n 16) 242.

[85] Ormerod (n 70) 285; Simon Bronitt, 'Australia' in K J Heller and M D Dubber (eds), *The Handbook of Comparative Criminal Law* (Oxford University Press 2011) 64; Ferzan (n 16) 251 (with an overview of the conflicting theories on 244–51); in more detail see Greenawalt (n 69) 1898 (speaking of a 'conceptual fuzziness of the terms "justification" and "excuse"'); Lacey, Wells, and Quick (n 65) 123 ('[T]he neat conceptual frame may be useful as a model, but on close inspection we find that its elements shade into one another in a way that ultimately defies the analytical clarity to which doctrine aspires'). See also Cryer (n 13) 399; Herring (n 69) 725–26; Robinson, 'Criminal Law Defenses: A Systematic Analysis' (n 19) 232–41; Mousourakis (n 67) 55–59. Victor Tadros, *Criminal Responsibility* (Oxford University Press 2005) 116–19 suggests not to categorize defence-types but defence-tokens, ie particular instances of a certain defence.

[86] See e.g. § 33 of the German Criminal Code (Strafgesetzbuch—StGB) ('Excessive self-defence'). According to art 55 of the Italian Codice Penale, the rules on negligence are applicable in this case; for punishability on the basis of negligence in French law see also Juliette Lelieur, Peggy Pfützner, and Sabine Volz, 'Strafbares Verhalten im Vorfeld der Tatvollendung: Frankreich' in U Sieber and K Cornils, *Nationales Strafrecht in rechtsvergleichender Darstellung* (Duncker & Humblot 2010) 117–18. See also Greenawalt (n 69) 1906–1907 (discussing whether a person using physical force in self-defence should be excused if he could have retreated safely); cf also Fletcher, 'The Right and the Reasonable' (n 71) 956; Robert F Schopp, *Justification Defenses and Just Convictions* (Cambridge University Press 1998) 11–15.

[87] In favour also Gabriel J Chin, 'Unjustified: The Practical Irrelevance of the Justification/Excuse Distinction' (2009) 43 University of Michigan Journal of Law Reform 79; see also Fletcher, 'The Right and the Reasonable' (n 71) 954; Fletcher, *Rethinking Criminal Law* (n 82) 759; Husak, *The Philosophy of Criminal Law* (n 53) 314.

[88] See in more detail Ambos (n *) 361 ff.

[89] Greenawalt (n 69) 1907; Horder (n 56) 7; Chin (n 87) 79–80; Bronitt (n 85) 64. See also Herring (n 69) 720–21; Ormerod (n 70) 285; Robinson, 'Criminal Law Defenses: A Systematic Analysis' (n 19) 229.

secondary participants.[90] First of all, in many systems secondary participation is predicated on the existence of an unlawful act, that is, if this act is justified secondary participation is excluded.[91] Secondly, if the actor only benefits from an excuse, he is still acting unlawfully and the victim retains his right to self-defence (which normally requires an unlawful act). In turn, this right does not exist against a lawful (justified) act.[92] Last but not least, an excused but still unlawful (unjustified) act may give rise to compensation claims.[93]

Still more important is the fundamental different *social meaning* of a justification compared to an excuse.[94] If a certain act is justified, this entails a value judgment that this act is approved by the respective legal order and the citizen may even be expected to act accordingly.[95] If, for example, one attributes not only an individual but also a collective meaning to self-defence—in the sense of the defence of the legal order[96]—the person acting in self-defence does not only defend his own interests but also the collective interest that the right prevails over the wrong. In contrast, an excuse has no meaning beyond the concrete case. It neither addresses the public nor does it allow others to act like the defendant whose conduct, after all, remains unlawful.[97] Thus, excuses are individual while justifications are general,[98] or—in the words of Fletcher—'[d]ecisions on justifying circumstances modify the applicable legal norm. Decisions on excuses, in contrast, leave the norm intact, but irreversibly modify the factual background of succeeding claims of excuse.'[99]

In sum, the distinction between justifications and excuses reflects and emphasises the different moral rationales of grounds excluding criminal responsibility. It is therefore not only reasonable, but sometimes even necessary for judging a person's criminal responsibility in a just and fair manner.[100] The fact that the ICC Statute does not

[90] Hans von der Linde, *Rechtfertigung und Entschuldigung im Strafrecht? Überlegungen zu einer funktionalen Straftatsystematik* (Peter Lang 1988) 6; Cryer (n 13) 399; Fletcher, 'The Right and the Reasonable' (n 71) 954; Ohlin (n 66) 319; Jens D Ohlin, 'The Bounds of Necessity' (2008) 6 Journal of International Criminal Justice 295.

[91] Cassese, 'Justification and Excuses in International Criminal Law' (n 66) 952; Robinson, 'Criminal Law Defenses: A Systematic Analysis' (n 19) 761–62; Herring (n 69) 721; Schopp (n 86) 53; Watzek (n 59) 302–10; Mousourakis (n 67) 44. For a different view see Chin (n 87) 109–11, arguing that in the case of a justification the third party may be liable for attempt or perpetration by means. This may be true but does not change the fact that secondary participation as such is excluded.—See generally on the accessorial or derivative character of secondary participation Ambos (n *) 147–48 with n 390.

[92] von der Linde (n 90) 6; Cassese, 'Justification and Excuses in International Criminal Law' (n 66) 952; Fletcher, 'The Right and the Reasonable' (n 71) 954; Fletcher, *Rethinking Criminal Law* (n 82) 760–61; Herring (n 69) 720; Robinson, 'Criminal Law Defenses: A Systematic Analysis' (n 19) 274–75; Knoops (n 7) 23; Mousourakis (n 67) 44–45.

[93] Cassese, 'Justification and Excuses in International Criminal Law' (n 66) 952–53; Mousourakis (n 67) 45.

[94] cf Mousourakis (n 67) 44; Ohlin (n 66) 318; Joshua Dressler, 'Duress' in John Deigh and David Dolinko (eds), *The Oxford Handbook of Philosophy of Criminal Law* (2011) 279; critical thereto see Chin (n 87) 89–108, whose arguments are, however, based on a pure procedural understanding of defences, neglecting their underlying normative meaning.

[95] Fletcher, *Rethinking Criminal Law* (n 82) 810; Greenawalt (n 69) 1900; Schopp (n 86) 8; Ohlin (n 66) 318.

[96] For such a twofold (individual-collective) rationale of self-defence see in particular the traditional German approach, cf Roxin (n 67) § 15 mn. 1–3. This dualist conception can already be found in Rudolf von Jhering, *Der Kampf ums Recht* (Manz 1872) 27: 'Der Widerstand gegen das Unrecht ist Pflicht, Pflicht des Berechtigten gegen sich selber—denn es ist ein Gebot der moralischen Selbsterhaltung—Pflicht gegen das Gemeinwesen—denn er muss, um erfolgreich zu sein, ein allgemeiner sein.'

[97] Greenawalt (n 69) 1900; cf also Fletcher, *Rethinking Criminal Law* (n 82) 811–12; Robinson, 'Criminal Law Defenses: A Systematic Analysis' (n 19) 246.

[98] Greenawalt (n 69) 1915.

[99] Fletcher, *Rethinking Criminal Law* (n 82) 812; cf also Mousourakis (n 67) 36; Milhizer (n 19) 855–57.

[100] Ambos, 'Defences in International Criminal Law' (n 14) 301; Albin Eser, 'Article 31' in O Triffterer and Kai Ambos (eds), *Rome Statute of the International Criminal Court: A Commentary* (CH Beck 2016) mn. 17;

explicitly adopt the distinction[101] should not be overstated. The drafters have been primarily guided by reasons of 'neutrality' vis-à-vis the legal traditions. Apart from that, the ICC Statute only offers some general rules ('general principles') on the general part of international criminal law without pretending definitively to decide the complex doctrinal questions involved. Thus, the rationale of the distinction between justification and excuse should be taken into account in interpreting the grounds excluding criminal responsibility.[102]

2.4 Failure of proof defences and alibi

A so-called failure of proof defence can be invoked if the prosecution has failed to show an *element of the relevant offence.*[103] The defence simply negates this definitional element.[104] Good examples are the defence of consent[105] in case of an offence that explicitly protects the victim's autonomy,[106] or a mistake of fact negating the required mens rea.[107] The classification of these situations as defences can be explained with the process-oriented approach of common law jurisdictions[108] where, as a rule, the state (prosecutor) carries the burden of

Merkel (n 13) 441. See also the detailed analysis on the question of whether a state may torture suspects to save the life of innocents in Ambos, 'May a State Torture Suspects to Save the Life of Innocents?' (n 71) 261.

[101] See also Merkel (n 13) 441; Ambos, *Der Allgemeine Teil des Völkerstrafrechts* (n 69) 826; Mahmoud Cherif Bassiouni, *The Legislative History of the International Criminal Court* (Transnational Publishers 2005), 158; Elies van Sliedregt, *The Criminal Responsibility of Individuals for Violations of International Humanitarian Law* (TMC Asser Press 2003) 242; E van Sliedregt, *Criminal Responsibility* (n 5); Eser, 'Article 31' (n 100) mn. 2, 17; Jens D Ohlin, 'The Bounds of Necessity' (2008) 6 Journal of International Criminal Justice 292; Otto Triffterer and Stefanie Bock, 'Article 33' in O Triffterer and Kai Ambos (eds), *Rome Statute of the International Criminal Court: A Commentary* (CH Beck 2016) mn 11; Robert Kolb, 'Droit international pénal' in Robert Kolb and A Scalia (eds), *Droit international pénal* (2nd edn, Helbing Lichtenhahn 2012) 219; Sabine Gless, *Internationales Strafrecht* (2nd edn, Helbing & Lichtenhahn 2015) mn 713; Kevin Jon Heller, 'The Rome Statute of the International Criminal Court' in K J Heller and M D Dubber (eds), *The Handbook of Comparative Criminal Law* (Oxford University Press 2011) 611; Helmut Satzger, *Internationales Strafrecht* (7th edn, Nomos 2016) § 15 mn 29; Ohlin (n 66) 319; critically therefore George P Fletcher, 'Parochial versus Universal Criminal Law' (2005) 3 Journal of International Criminal Justice 34; Fletcher, *The Grammar of Criminal Law: American, Comparative and International* (Oxford University Press 2007) 107–10; Fletcher, 'The Influence of the Common law and Civil Law Traditions on International Criminal Law' (n 67) 105.

[102] Ambos, *Der Allgemeine Teil des Völkerstrafrechts* (n 69) 828; Ambos, 'Defences in International Criminal Law' (n 14) 301. In the same vein see Cryer (n 13) 399; van der Wilt (n 10) 277; Greenawalt (n 69) 1902; Mousourakis (n 67) 54; more reluctant, however, Valentina Caccamo, 'La Disciplina della Legittima Difesa' in Antonio Cassese, M Chiavario, and G de Francesco (eds), *Problemi attuali della giustizia penale internazionale* (Giappichelli 2005) 134–35; Triffterer and Bock (n 101) mn 11 (arguing that the distinction between justification and excuse 'may be of little practical relevance with regard to the responsibility of the direct perpetrator because both would result in an acquittal' but 'is nevertheless useful as it reflects the different moral rationales of grounds excluding criminal responsibility').

[103] Cryer (n 13) 399; Robinson, *Criminal Law Defenses* (n 12) 72; Robinson, 'Criminal Law Defenses: A Systematic Analysis' (n 19) 204; Milhizer (n 19) 803; Schopp (n 86) 3; Watzek (n 59) 58–59; Law Reform Commission (n 19) mn 1.08; cf also Gómez-Jara Díez and Chiesa (n 83) 507; Michael Bohlander, 'Radbruch Redux: The Need for Revisiting the Conversation between Common and Civil Law at Root Level at the Example of International Criminal Justice' (2011) 24 Leiden Journal of International Law 397.

[104] Robinson, *Criminal Law Defenses* (n 12) 72; Robinson, 'Criminal Law Defenses: A Systematic Analysis' (n 19) 204.

[105] Cryer (n 13) 399; Robinson, *Criminal Law Defenses* (n 12) 75.

[106] cf in more detail Ambos (n *) 387–88.

[107] Robinson, *Criminal Law Defenses* (n 12) 73; Milhizer (n 19) 803; Catherine Elliott and Frances Quinn, *Criminal Law* (Harlow, England: 9th edn, Pearson 2012) 359.

[108] Bohlander (n 103) 397; cf also Andrew P Simester and others, *Simester and Sullivan's Criminal Law* (Hart Publishing 2019) 710 (stating that failure of proof defences are strictly speaking 'no defences at all') and Kai Ambos,

proof (persuasive burden), that is, it has to prove the constituent elements of the offence, and the defendant (defence) carries, at least,[109] the burden of production (evidential burden) regarding the facts excluding criminal responsibility, that is, the defences.[110] Thus, there is, generally, no shift of the burden of proof—the burdens are allocated to the offence and defence side respectively—but only of the burden of production.[111] It must be noted, however, that an equal distribution of the burden (of proof) between prosecution and defence along the lines of the offence-defence distinction[112] is—apart from being predicated upon the rejection of the incorporationist view mentioned above[113]—not at all beyond controversy given that in criminal proceedings the defendant is in a weaker position than in civil proceedings,[114] facing a normally superior prosecution authority, and thus benefits from special protective principles, especially the presumption of innocence, which, as a matter of principle, speak for the imposition of the burden on the prosecution.[115] At any rate, in the more substantive, offence-oriented approach of civil law jurisdictions, the so-called failure of proof situations are not treated as defences but rather as questions of the actus reus (consent) or the mens rea (mistake of fact).[116] The ICC Statute classifies a mistake of fact, at least, as a ground excluding responsibility (Article 32 (1)).[117]

If the concept of 'failure of proof defences' is understood in a broad sense, it may also cover the so called '*alibi* defence',[118] which is frequently raised in international criminal proceedings.[119] In this vein, Rule 67(B)(i)(a) of the ICTY RPE obliges the defence to 'notify the Prosecutor of its intent to offer . . . the *defence of alibi*'.[120] This is a controversial formulation[121]

'The First Judgment of the International Criminal Court (Prosecutor v. Lubanga): A Comprehensive Analysis of the Legal Issus' (2012) 12 International Criminal Law Review 135.

[109] There is, however, a tendency in the (English) statutory law—contrary to the rule for common law offences since *Woolmington* ([1935] AC 481)—to shift the burden of proof to the defendant; see for a critical discussion Williams (n 1) 269 ff.

[110] See also Duarte d'Almeida (section 1.4) in this volume (allocation of burdens of proof according to classification of certain facts as referring to an offence—P-fact—or relating to a defence—D-fact); on a more abstract level see also Hage, Waltermann, and Arosemena (section 11) in this volume (proponent has to adduce reasons in favour of application of the rule, opponent reasons against its application; if reasons are in balance, ie no pro or *contra* reasons outweigh the others, the burden of proof decides who will win the argument); on the burden of production from the perspective of criminal law cf Williams (n 1) 264, 269.

[111] cf Hage, Waltermann, and Arosemena (section 11) in this volume.

[112] Note that, for Williams (n 78) 234, 255 and Williams (n 1) 280, this distinction does not determine the allocation of the burden of proof but his view is certainly influenced by his outright rejection of this distinction in the first place.

[113] ibid.

[114] On both the influence and the difference of civil procedure Williams (n 1) 271, 291–92.

[115] This view is strongly defended by Williams (n 1) 262 ff (emphasizing that the criminal trial is about a 'single issue of guilt' which entails that the burden is on the prosecution).

[116] Cryer (n 13) 399. This is also the approach adopted by Antony Duff, *Answering for Crime: Responsibility and Liability in the Criminal Law* (Hart Publishing 2007) 263; on the German doctrine see Roxin (n 67) § 12 mn 95–150 (mistake of law) and § 13 mn 2–32 (consent); on the German and French account van Verseveld (n 8) 25 ff.

[117] See Guilfoyle (n 5) 376. The mistake of law is also qualified in this sense if it negates the mental element required by the relevant crime; see in more detail Ambos (n *) 366 ff; see also Cryer (n 13) 399; O'Keefe (n 6) 218.

[118] In this vein Law see Reform Commission (n 19) mn 108; Husak, 'The Serial View of Criminal Law Defences' (n 11) 377; William A Schabas, *An Introduction to the International Criminal Court* (5th edn, Cambridge University Press 2017) 225. See also Nill-Theobald (n 10) 57; Robinson, *Criminal Law Defenses* (n 12) 342; Watzek (n 59) 58; Bantekas (n 13) 265.

[119] cf Chile Eboe-Osuji, 'The Plea of Alibi in International Criminal Law as Viewed Through the Prism of the Common Law' (2011) 22 Criminal Law Forum 36; see also the case law quoted in the following notes.

[120] Emphasis added. See also Rule 67(A)(ii)(a) ICTR RPE; Rule 72(B)(i)(a) MICT RPE; Rule 79(1)(a) ICC RPE; Rule 67(A)(ii)(a) SCSL RPE.

[121] Critically see also *Delalić and Others* (n 53) para 580; *Kayishema and Ruzindana v Prosecutor*(Appeal Judgment) ICTR-95-1-A (1 June 2001) para 106; *Prosecutor v Kajelijeli* (Judgment) ICTR-98-44A-T (1 December 2003) para 165.

and, indeed, it should not lead us to ignore the differences between a (real) defence and the plea of alibi. In the former case, the accused has at least in part committed the acts charged but claims that, owing to specific circumstances, he is not criminally responsible.[122] In contrast, in the case of an alibi, he maintains that he was elsewhere at the time of commission and was therefore not physically able to commit the crime charged.[123] This is, in fact, a (qualified) general denial of the incriminating conduct[124] with no impact on the burden of proof.[125] Rather, it remains upon the prosecution 'to eliminate the reasonable possibility that the alibi is true'.[126] Thus, an alibi is not a defence *sensu stricto*.[127] This is also confirmed by Rule 79 ICC RPE which makes a clear distinction between the defence's intent, on the one hand, to raise the existence of an alibi and, on the other hand, a ground for excluding criminal responsibility.

2.5 Hierarchy of defences

Given the existence of different types of defence (substantive and procedural defences, justifications, excuses, failure of proof defences), the questions arises as to how they are interrelated, that is, whether a hierarchy of defences exists or whether they are of equal rank. The ICC Statute itself is silent on this issue, so that any (hierarchical) order may only be inferred from the underlying rationale of the defence types.

According to Paul H. Robinson, defences may be *ranked* as follows: failure of proof defences, justifications, excuses, and non-exculpatory defences. In his view, this hierarchy provides for a logical, serial order, that is '[e]ach successive type of defense need be considered only if those preceding it are unavailable'.[128] However, the proposed subsidiarity of

[122] *Kamuhanda v Prosecutor* (Appeal Judgment) ICTR-99-54A-A (19 September 2005) para 167; concurring *Ndindabahizi v Prosecutor* (Appeal Judgment) ICTR-01-71-A (16 January 2007) para 66; cf also Eboe-Osuji (n 119) 39–40.

[123] *Delalić and Others* (n 53) para 581; *Milošević v Prosecutor* (Appeal Judgment) ICTY IT-98-29/1-A (12 November 2009) para 287; *Prosecutor v Lukić and Lukić* (Judgment) ICTY IT-98-32/1-T (20 July 2009) para 23; *Kayishema and Ruzindana v Prosecutor* (n 121)para 106; *Musema v Prosecutor v* (Appeal Judgment) ICTR-96-13-A (16 November 2001) para 200; *Kajelijeli v Prosecutor*(Appeal Judgment) ICTR-98-44A-A (23 May 2005) para 42; *Prosecutor v Kamuhanda* (n 122) para 167; *Prosecutor v Musema* (Judgment) ICTR-96-13-T (27 January 2000) para 106; *Prosecutor v Ndindabahizi* (Judgment) ICTR-2001-71-I (15 July 2004) para 25; Robinson, *Criminal Law Defenses* (n 12) 342; cf also Eboe-Osuji (n 119) 38 (correctly stating that 'alibi is simply "Latin for elsewhere" ') and Richard Norman Gooderson, *Alibi* (Heinemann 1977) 5–6.

[124] *Prosecutor v Kamuhanda* (n 122) para 167; *Ndindabahizi v Prosecutor* (n 122) para 66; Cryer (n 13) 399 with n 9; Robinson, *Criminal Law Defenses* (n 12) 342; cf also Tadros (n 85) 103.

[125] *Prosecutor v Popović and Others*(Judgment) ICTY IT-05-88-T (10 June 2010) para 56; *Prosecutor v Kamuhanda* (Judgment)ICTR-99-54A-T (22 January 2004) para 84; *Prosecutor v Kayishema and Ruzindana* (Judgment) ICTR-95-1-T (21 May 1999) para 234; *Prosecutor v Kajelijeli* (n 121) para 166; *Prosecutor v Ndindabahizi* (n 123) para 25; Robinson, *Criminal Law Defenses* (n 12) 342–43; cf also *Milošević* (n 123) para 287; *Prosecutor v Musema* (n 123) para 108; *Musema v Prosecutor* (n 123) para 200; in more detail see Eboe-Osuji (n 119) 70–92; Gooderson (n 123) 23–28. As to the standard and burden of proof in case of a real defence see Ambos (n *) 312–13.

[126] *Delalić and Others* (n 53) para 581; *Popović and Others* (n 125) para 57; *Prosecutor v Lukić and Lukić* (n 123) para 23; *Prosecutor v Kayishema and Ruzindana* (n 121) para 106. In the same vein see *Musema v Prosecutor* (n 123) para 201; *Prosecutor v Kajelijeli* (n 121) para 43; *Prosecutor v Kamuhanda* (n 125) para 84; *Prosecutor v Ndindabahizi* (n 123) para 25.

[127] *Prosecutor v Delalić and Others* (n 53) para 581; *Prosecutor v Popović and Others* (n 125) para 56; *Prosecutor v Lukić and Lukić* (n 123) para 23; *Prosecutor v Kayishema and Ruzindana* (n 121) para 106; *Prosecutor v Kajelijeli* (n 121) para 165; *Prosecutor v Kamuhanda* (n 126) para 83; *Prosecutor v Kamuhanda* (n 122) para 167; Robinson, *Criminal Law Defenses* (n 12) 342; Ferzan (n 16) 241; Darcy (n 71) 236; cf also Cryer (n 13) 399 with n 9 and Tadros (n 85) 103 (who calls the 'defence of alibi' an evidential defence).

[128] Robinson, *Criminal Law Defenses* (n 12) 105; Robinson, 'Criminal Law Defenses: A Systematic Analysis' (n 19) 232. Robinson also distinguishes a fifth category of defences called 'offense modification' which ranges between

non-exculpatory defences, that is, essentially procedural objections,[129] is unconvincing. As they operate as obstacles of investigation and prosecution, they should be examined first, in any case before going into the merits of a case. This also makes sense from a practical, resource-driven perspective for it is neither reasonable nor efficient to look for evidence and think about the individual responsibility of a suspect if this suspect must not be investigated and prosecuted anyway.[130] Take the example of a sitting head of state: would a reasonable prosecutor waste time in thinking about his involvement in international crimes if he cannot be prosecuted in the first place *because of* head of state immunity? The answer is clearly no and the problem is partly acknowledged by Robinson himself when he admits that at least some non-exculpatory defences must be raised before the trial starts.[131]

Otherwise, Robinson presents a convincing proposal. Given the close link between failure of proof defences and the (objective or subjective) elements of an offence,[132] they should be considered first. Justifications on their part have—as Greenwalt puts it—'a natural priority over questions of excuse'.[133] As explained above, a person who acts under a justification acts in accordance with the law, that is, there is nothing, from a legal perspective, which he can be blamed for.[134] Fletcher follows Robinson insofar as he sees a hierarchy between justifications and excuses giving the former priority; as an exception to this principle, however, he suggests that the defences of infancy and insanity should have a general priority, since in these cases the actors are not considered subjects of criminal norms.[135] While this argument appears convincing with regard to infants,[136] it is less so with regard to insanity, given that the discussion of the defendant's mental state in open court is a serious invasion of privacy which is only legitimate if he has indeed acted unlawfully.[137]

Husak harshly criticizes any attempt to rank defences since defendants may possess several, differently classified, defences.[138] However, while this is true, it does not mean that all these defences must be treated equally and, above all, fully examined. If, for an example, an act is justified by self-defence, it does not mean that the actor is not insane or that he has not simultaneously acted under duress,[139] but this is plainly irrelevant[140] since the criminal

failure of proof defences and justifications. This type of defence is applicable if 'the actor has apparently satisfied all elements of the offense charged, [but] he has not in fact caused the harm or evil sought to be prevented by the statute defining the offense' (p 77). This comes close to a defence linked to the protected *Rechtsgut* by the offence and the harm sought to be prevented (see Ambos (n *) 60 ff). Such cases may be solved more appropriately by a restrictive interpretation of the relevant offence. Robinson himself points out that 'offense modifications … commonly apply to only one specific offense' (p 79).

129 See section 2.1 above with n 19.

130 In the same vein see Husak, 'The Serial View of Criminal Law Defences' (n 11) 386–87. As to the immunity of heads of third states cf Ambos (n *) 406 ff.

131 Robinson, 'Criminal Law Defenses: A Systematic Analysis' (n 19) 232 with n 124.

132 cf nn 104–16 above and accompanying text.

133 Greenawalt (n 69) 1899. In the same vein see Fletcher, 'The Right and the Reasonable' (n 71) 958, 960; Horder (n 56) 99–103; implicitly also Milhizer (n 19) 726; Ronnie D Mackay, *Mental Condition Defences in the Criminal Law* (Clarendon Press 1995, reprinted 2003) 81.

134 Fletcher, 'The Right and the Reasonable' (n 71) 960. In the same vein see Greenawalt (n 69) 1899 with n 6. Critically Husak, 'The Serial View of Criminal Law Defences' (n 11) 384 who, however, brings in a moral component when he argues that 'bad motives' may make a justified actor blameworthy.

135 Fletcher, 'The Right and the Reasonable' (n 71) 959; as to the underlying differentiation between exemptions and excuses cf also Tadros (n 85) 124–29; Ferzan (n 16) 255–57.

136 As to the qualification of infancy as a procedural defence cf Ambos (n *) 430–32.

137 Critical as to the equal treatment of infancy and insanity also Mackay (n 133) 83–84.

138 Husak, 'The Serial View of Criminal Law Defences' (n 11) 369, 390–91; Husak, *The Philosophy of Criminal Law* (n 53) 287–310 (298–302); against the proposed priority of justifications over excuses also Ferzan (n 16) 243.

139 cf the example by Husak, 'The Serial View of Criminal Law Defences' (n 11) 390.

140 cf also Gardner (n 55) 119; Milhizer (n 19) 726.

justice process is not about the examination of persons who act lawfully. In fact, the mental state of persons is none of the business of criminal justice so long as these persons behave lawfully. Husak further sees the priority of justifications over excuses to be contradicted by ordinary language, in particular by the frequent use of apologies ('sorry', 'excuse me'), which do not normally entail the admission of a wrong.[141] Yet, apart from the highly doubtful importance of the often imprecise ordinary language in interpreting highly normative legal concepts,[142] it is indeed the case that an apology is preceded by a socially or morally, albeit not necessarily legally, wrong behaviour by the person who apologizes.[143] In other words, the apology is indeed a reaction to a socially wrongful act as, in legal terms, the excuse follows the justification.

All in all, there is enough reason to *structure defences* pursuant to their own logic and rationale in the following way: procedural defences, failure of proof defences, justifications, and excuses. This does not deny that practical (economical or strategic) considerations will sometimes prevail and call for a different approach.[144] The system of the ICC Statute may be, following the distinction between justification (wrongfulness) and excuse (culpability), graphically presented in the following way:

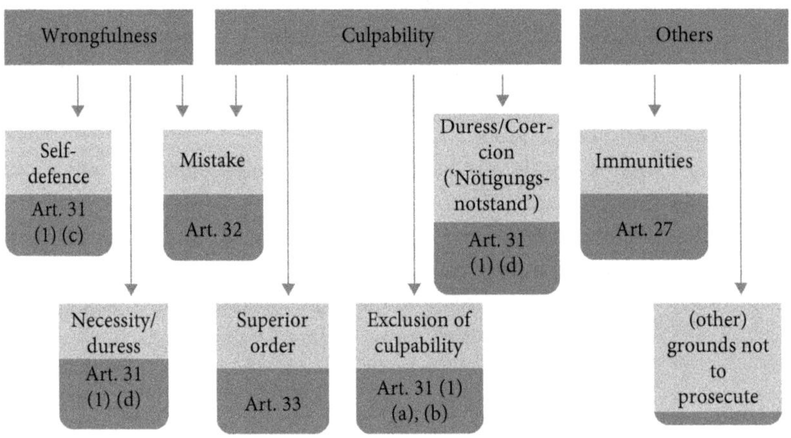

Figure 19.1 'Defences' in the ICC Statute

[141] Husak, 'The Serial View of Criminal Law Defences' (n 11) 381.

[142] Critical to appeals to ordinary language also Fletcher, *Rethinking Criminal Law* (n 82) 702.

[143] This is in line with Lacey's and Pickard's understanding of forgiveness, which is preceded by a wrongdoing; see Nicola Lacey and Hanna Pickard, 'To Blame or to Forgive? Reconciling Punishment and Forgiveness in Criminal Justice' (2015) 35 Oxford Journal of Legal Studies 665, 675 ff.

[144] cf also Robinson, 'Criminal Law Defenses: A Systematic Analysis' (n 19) 232 n 124; Fletcher, 'The Right and the Reasonable' (n 71) 961.

20

Scope Limitation or Affirmative Defence?

The Purpose and Role of Investment Treaty Exception Clauses

*Caroline Henckels**

1 Introduction

Exception clauses (also known as non-precluded measures clauses)[1] permit a treaty party lawfully to take action directed at a particular regulatory objective, industry, or sector of the economy that might otherwise be inconsistent with its substantive treaty obligations towards foreign investors. Parties to investment treaties include exception clauses to preserve their flexibility to respond to future exigencies, whether foreseeable or not. Their increasing popularity is one way in which states have sought to guide and constrain investment tribunals' decision-making, in response to concerns that these tribunals have paid insufficient attention to the need for host states to retain the legal capacity to enact and maintain non-discriminatory public welfare measures. Given that the scope (and, indeed, the normative content) of the substantive investment obligations is not explicit in most treaties, exceptions can play a role in (re)affirming to both adjudicators of disputes and to potential claimants that the objective of the treaty is not solely to protect foreign investments at the expense of other public policy objectives.[2]

This chapter addresses two related questions. First, it discusses whether exceptions should be understood as limiting the scope of the substantive obligations so as to render those obligations inapplicable to measures that come within the exception, or whether such clauses operate as affirmative defences that justify (render lawful) conduct that would otherwise be prohibited.[3] Secondly, the chapter addresses the relationship between security exception clauses and the defence of necessity at customary international law, particularly the question of whether such clauses are *lex specialis* expressions of the defence of necessity between the treaty parties. Section 2 of the chapter surveys the different types of general and security exception clauses appearing in investment treaties, and introduces the two different ways of characterizing them. Section 3 analyses the decided investment cases along with two relevant International Court of Justice (ICJ) decisions, finding a variance in approaches by investment tribunals and annulment committees, and a less than clear approach by the ICJ. Section 4 discusses the symbolic dimensions arising from

* Senior Lecturer, Faculty of Law, Monash University, caroline.henckels@monash.edu. Thank you to many people but especially Lorand Bartels, Jonathan Bonnitcha, Tomer Broude, Federico Ortino, Federica Paddeu, Mona Pinchis, Lauge Poulsen, Ira Ryk-Lakhman, and participants at the Cambridge workshop on exceptions in international law for helpful comments and discussions. All errors are mine.

[1] cf the taxonomy in Jorge Viñuales, 'Seven Ways of Escaping a Rule: Of Exceptions and Their Avatars in International Law' in this volume.

[2] See Jürgen Kurtz, *The WTO and International Investment Law: Converging Systems* (CUP 2015) 169–75, 182.

[3] With respect to the concept of justification see Kent Greenawalt, 'Distinguishing Justifications from Excuses' (1986) 49 Law and Contemporary Problems 89; Federica Paddeu, 'Clarifying the Concept of Circumstances Precluding Wrongfulness (Justifications) in International Law' in this volume.

Caroline Henckels, *Scope Limitation or Affirmative Defence?* In: *Exceptions in International Law*. Edited by: Lorand Bartels and Federica Paddeu, Oxford University Press (2020).
DOI: 10.1093/oso/9780198789321.003.0020

characterizing excpetions, and the practical implications of these different characterizations for the burden of proof and consistency between international investment law and World Trade Organization (WTO) law. The chapter concludes that, subject always to the language of the provision in question, investment treaty exceptions appear to limit the scope of the substantive obligations, meaning that measures falling within the exception are from the coverage of the treaty. By consequence, security exceptions are conceptually separate from the defence of necessity, and are not *lex specialis* manifestations of the defence between the treaty parties.

2 Distinguishing Scope Limitations from Affirmative Defences

General and security exceptions are a type of flexibility device included in investment treaties in order to preserve the parties' freedom to enact and maintain measures to promote public welfare.[4] They typically provide that the treaty does not prevent a party from adopting or maintaining measures that are, for example, 'necessary to',[5] 'related to',[6] 'directed to',[7] 'for',[8] or 'designed and applied to'[9] achieve a permitted objective. For example, Article XI of the US–Argentina BIT provides that '[t]his Treaty shall not preclude the application by either Party of measures necessary for the maintenance of public order, the fulfilment of its obligations with respect to the maintenance or restoration of international peace or security, or the protection of its own essential security interests'. An increasing number of investment treaties also contain general exceptions clauses that incorporate by reference or are modelled upon the general exceptions in the General Agreement on Tariffs and Trade (GATT) and the General Agreement on Trade in Services (GATS),[10] which include exceptions for measures, for example, 'necessary for the protection of human, animal or plant life or health' and contain a separate clause obliging parties not to apply such measures in a discriminatory way or so as to subvert the discipline of the substantive obligations.[11]

One way of describing the role of an exception clause is to say that where the state establishes that it is taking action that comes within the scope of the clause, the treaty obligations *do not apply*.[12] That is, the exception confirms the drafters' intention that such measures will not be captured by the treaty obligations. An exception might therefore be characterized as a treaty-internal limitation on the scope of the substantive obligations[13] or

[4] This chapter does not address other provisions that may operate in the same way as exceptions *stricto sensu*. These include carve-outs, reservations, denial of benefits clauses, exclusion of dispute settlement provisions from most-favoured nation treatment, and express references to police power in expropriation clauses.

[5] See e.g. ASEAN Comprehensive Investment Agreement (2009) art 17(1)(a) (General Exceptions),.

[6] See e.g. Canadian Model BIT (2004) art 10(4) (General Exceptions),.

[7] See e.g. China–New Zealand FTA (2008) art 11,.

[8] See e.g. India–Croatia BIT (2001) art 12(2),.

[9] Common Market for Eastern and Southern Africa Investment Agreement (2007) art 22(1).

[10] See e.g. EU–Canada Comprehensive Economic and Trade Agreement (2016) art 28.3; Japan–India Comprehensive Economic Partnership Agreement (2011) art 11(2); Canada–Latvia BIT (2009) art XVII(3).

[11] See Lorand Bartels, 'The Chapeau of the General Exceptions in the WTO GATT and GATS Agreements: A Reconstruction' (2015) 109 American Journal of International Law 95.

[12] This view is held by Kenneth J Vandevelde, *United States Investment Treaties, Policy and Practice* (Deventer 1992) 222. See also Andrew Newcombe and Lluís Paradell, *Law and Practice of Investment Treaties: Standards of Investment Protection* (Brill 2009) 482; Giorgio Sacerdoti, 'The application of BITs in time of economic crisis: limits to their coverage, necessity and the relevance of WTO law' in Giorgio Sacerdoti (ed), *General Interests of Host States in International Investment Law* (CUP 2014) 3, 11.

[13] Jaap Hage, Antonia Waltermann, and Gustavo Arosemena, 'Logical Tools for International Law' in this volume.

a negative rule-element, to borrow from criminal law.[14] Alternatively, an exception could be regarded as an affirmative defence: the treaty parties agree that conduct coming within its scope should be an overriding consideration to deal with exigent circumstances, and the fact that conduct comes within the scope of the exception serves to negate what would otherwise be the consequences of the conduct. A state relying on the exception would not deny that it had failed to observe its treaty obligations, but would seek to avoid the consequences of its actions by establishing that it was acting to protect interests permitted by the clause. That is to say, action coming within the scope of the exception would justify conduct that would otherwise be prohibited by the treaty.[15]

3 The Decided Cases

Most of the decided investment cases support an interpretation of investment treaty exceptions as limiting the scope of the obligations, although in no case has a tribunal or annulment committee explained how it arrived at this conclusion. This under-theorization reflects a broader trend: while the WTO Appellate Body engages in extensive analysis of the related issue of the burden of proof in terms of scope limitations and affirmative defences, other international courts and tribunals (including, notably, the ICJ) typically devote insufficient attention to the question.[16]

3.1 Exceptions limit the scope of the treaty obligations

3.1.1 Investment decisions

The majority of investment decisions concerning exceptions involve claims by United States investors against emergency measures adopted by Argentina in response to its economic crisis of 2001–2002. In these cases, Argentina invoked the security exception in the US–Argentina BIT as well as the defence of necessity at customary international law, arguing that the measures it took were necessary to deal with the economic crisis and that the fact of the crisis situation could justify the abrogation of its obligations to investors and permit it to escape liability. Six investment tribunals and one annulment committee took the view that the exception operated to *exempt* actions necessary to protect essential security interests from the substantive protections of the treaty, or to *suspend* the treaty obligations during the period that the need to protect essential security interests subsisted. The *CMS v Argentina* annulment committee held that in circumstances where the requirements of the exception were made out, the 'substantive obligations under the Treaty do not apply',[17] and the *Continental v Argentina* tribunal held that the exception 'reserved rights' of state parties under the treaty: where it applied, the substantive obligations would be 'set . . . aside or suspend[ed]' and measures coming within the exception would 'lie outside the scope of the Treaty'.[18]

[14] See e.g. Glanville Williams, 'The Logic of "Exceptions"' (1988) 47 Cambridge Law Journal 261, 276.

[15] See, adopting this approach, Kurtz, *The WTO and International Investment Law* (n 2) 217–18. See also Newcombe and Paradell (n 12) 496.

[16] Joost Pauwelyn, 'Defences and the Burden of Proof in International Law' in this volume.

[17] *CMS Gas Transmission Company v Argentine Republic*, ICSID Case No ARB/01/08, Decision of the Ad Hoc Committee on the Application for Annulment of the Argentine Republic (25 September 2007) [129].

[18] *Continental v Argentina*, ICSID Case No ARB/03/09, Award (5 September 2008) [164], [168].

These adjudicators also found, as a related matter, that the exception had a separate existence and function to the defence of necessity at customary international law. The *CMS* annulment committee observed that although there was 'some analogy' between the two norms, they had 'a different operation and content'—if the exception applied, 'the substantive obligations under the Treaty do not apply', whereas the necessity defence was 'only relevant once it has been decided that there has otherwise been a breach of those substantive obligations'.[19] Similarly, the *Continental* tribunal held that 'the treaty is inapplicable' to measures coming within the exception, whereas the necessity defence regulates the circumstances in which a state can 'escape ... from the responsibility that would otherwise derive from that breach'.[20] And the *Sempra* annulment committee held that 'the terms of the treaty itself exclude the protection to the investor that the treaty would otherwise have provided' and that the treaty 'permits conduct adverse to the investor in specific circumstances'.[21]

In *Mobil v Argentina*,[22] the tribunal referred to the exception as a 'carve-out'[23] and as 'limiting the general investment protection obligations' in the treaty, and as 'exclud[ing] from the scope' of the treaty measures coming within the purview of the provision.[24] One of the arbitrators, writing separately, took the same view: that the exception 'excludes the application' of the treaty obligations and 'defines the operational scope' of those obligations.[25] Curiously, however, the tribunal concluded that the security exception was a *lex specialis* with respect to the defence of necessity (discussed in section 3.2 below).

Two tribunals deciding cases involving security exceptions in Indian BITs also viewed the exception as a scope limitation. In *CC Devas v India*, the tribunal quoted the *CMS* annulment committee decision in relation to its finding that the application of the exception 'excluded the operation' of the BIT's substantive obligations[26] and the *Continental* tribunal's holding that the treaty was 'inapplicable' to measures coming within the purview of the exception.[27] In *Deutsche Telekom v India*, the tribunal cited the *CMS* annulment decision regarding its finding that if the exception applies, 'the substantive obligations of the treaty do not apply'.[28]

In *Copper Mesa Mining v Ecuador*, the tribunal, deciding a claim involving a general exception substantially similar to Article XX of the GATT, referred briefly to an expropriation being established in part by the 'non-application' of the exception.[29] This suggests that the tribunal viewed the provision as a scope limitation in the sense of requiring the claimant to negate the applicability of the exception—although the decision sheds no other light on this issue. The tribunal in *Bear Creek* appeared to view both a general exceptions provision and an annex clarifying states' police powers in the context of indirect expropriation[30] as both

[19] *CMS Gas Transmission Company v Argentine Republic* (n 17) [129], [131].

[20] *Continental v Argentina* (n 18) [164] n 236, [165].

[21] *Sempra Energy International v Argentina*, ICSID Case No ARB/02/16, Decision on the Argentine Republic's Application for Annulment of the Award (29 June 2010) [130]–[131], [208]–[209].

[22] *Mobil Exploration and Development Inc. Suc. Argentina and Mobil Argentina S.A. v. Argentine Republic*, ICSID Case No. ARB/04/16, Decision on Jurisdiction and Liability, 10 April 2013.

[23] Ibid, [1028].

[24] Ibid, Heading XII, p 306; paras [1025], [2016].

[25] *Mobil v Argentina*, Separate Opinion of Professor Antonio Remiro Brotons (27 March 2013), [12].

[26] *CC Devas v India*, PCA Case No. 2013-09, Award on Jurisdiction and Merits (25 July 2016) [293], citing *CMS v Argentina*, Annulment [146].

[27] ibid [293], citing *Continental v Argentina*, n 236.

[28] *Deutsche Telekom v India*, PCA Case No. 2014-10, Interim Award (13 December 2017) [227].

[29] *Copper Mesa Mining Corporation v Republic of Ecuador*, PCA No 2012-2, Award (15 March 2016) [6.58].

[30] Canada–Peru FTA Annex 812.1(c) provides: '[e]xcept in rare circumstances, such as when a measure or series of measures is so severe in the light of its purpose that it cannot be reasonably viewed as having been adopted and applied in good faith, nondiscriminatory measures of a Party that are designed and applied to protect legitimate public welfare objectives, such as health, safety and the environment, do not constitute indirect expropriation.'

limiting the scope of the treaty obligations. The tribunal held (erroneously)[31] that the exception was a *lex specialis* with respect to the police powers doctrine.[32] As one would expect a *lex generalis* and a *lex specialis* to have the same character (ie a scope limitation or affirmative defence), it is possible to deduce from the reasoning that, as the police powers doctrine limits the scope of the doctrine of indirect expropriation, the exception similarly limits its scope.[33] But the tribunal did not make this clear.

3.1.2 ICJ decisions

Although the *CMS* annulment committee cited the ICJ's approach to security exceptions in treaties of friendship, commerce and navigation (FCN treaties)[34] in support of its own view that the exception was a scope limitation,[35] a careful reading of the cases suggests that the position of the ICJ has not been fully articulated.

In both *Nicaragua*[36] and in *Oil Platforms*,[37] the United States invoked a security exception materially similar to the exception in the US–Argentina BIT.[38] The United States claimed that its military actions involving uses of force were lawful acts of self-defence that were 'necessary to protect' its 'essential security interests', in compliance with the exception.

In *Nicaragua*, the ICJ stated that the provision 'defines the instances in which the Treaty itself provides for exceptions' in relation to conduct that would 'otherwise be in conflict with the relevant provisions of the Treaty', but did not elaborate further on how it arrived at this finding or its implications.[39] On the face of it, the ICJ viewed the exception as operating to justify certain conduct that would, but for the exception, be prohibited by the treaty.

In the subsequent case of *Oil Platforms*, the ICJ's view is less clear. The United States had argued in its preliminary objections to jurisdiction that conduct coming within the ambit of the clause was 'outside of scope' of the treaty,[40] but the ICJ ruled that that the clause operated as a 'defence on the merits'.[41] One might argue that rather than determining the status of the exception (a 'defence'), the ICJ was signalling that this question was properly to be determined at the merits stage of the proceedings rather than as a preliminary matter.[42] In some areas of the judgment the ICJ appears to regard the exception as a scope limitation, but in

[31] The police powers doctrine is an internal defeater that limits the scope of the prohibition on indirect exprorpriation. See F Schauer, 'Rules, Defeasibility, and the Psychology of Exceptions' in this volume.

[32] *Bear Creek Mining Corporation v Republic of Peru*, ICSID Case No. ARB/14/2, Award (30 November 2017) [473]–[474].

[33] *Bear Creek v Peru* (n 32) [475], [477].

[34] FCN treaties are the progenitors of modern investment treaties. They typically permit freedom of commerce and navigation between and within the treaty parties, permit nationals of one treaty party to engage in economic activities in the territory of the other party, and contain obligations such as national treatment and most-favoured nation treatment. See Muthucumaraswamy Sornarajah, *The International Law on Foreign Investment* (3rd edn, CUP 2010) 180–82; Kenneth J Vandevelde, 'A Brief History of International Investment Agreements' (2005) 12 UC Davis Journal of International Law and Policy 157, 163–64.

[35] *CMS Gas Transmission Company v Argentine Republic* (n 17) [133]: 'In other terms, and to take the words of the International Court of Justice in a comparable case, if the Tribunal was satisfied by the arguments based on Article XI, it should have held that there had been "no breach" of the BIT', citing *Oil Platforms (Islamic Republic of Iran v United States of America)* (Judgment) [2003] ICJ Rep 161 [34].

[36] *Military and Paramilitary Activities in and against Nicaragua (Nicaragua v United States of America)* (Merits) [1986] ICJ Rep 14.

[37] *Oil Platforms (Islamic Republic of Iran v United States of America)* (Judgment) [2003] ICJ Rep 161.

[38] Treaty of Friendship, Commerce and Navigation between the United States and Nicaragua (1956) art XXI(1)(d); Treaty of Amity, Economic Relations and Consular Rights between the United States and Iran (1955) art XX(1)(d).

[39] *Nicaragua* (n 36) [222], [225].

[40] See *Oil Platforms (Islamic Republic of Iran v United States of America)* (Preliminary Objection submitted by the United States of America) (16 December 1993) [3.36]–[3.42], especially [3.37].

[41] ibid [20].

[42] *Oil Platforms (Islamic Republic of Iran v United States of America)* (Judgment) [1996] ICJ Rep 803, [40].

other areas as an affirmative defence.[43] Perhaps the most that can be said is that greater analytical rigour in this area would be welcome.

3.2 Exceptions are affirmative defences

Cases involving exceptions in this category all involve the security exception in the US–Argentina BIT. The *CMS v Argentina, Enron v Argentina,* and *Sempra v Argentina* awards attracted considerable controversy, particularly in relation to the approaches taken by these tribunals to the question of whether the measures adopted by the government were 'necessary' to arrest the crisis.

These tribunals' characterization of the exception is difficult to untangle from their mistaken characterization of its relationship with the defence of necessity at customary international law. The exception and Article 25 of the International Law Commission's *Articles on the Responsibility of States for Internationally Wrongful Acts* (ARSIWA)—widely regarded as a codification of the necessity defence—are superficially similar, seemingly leading these tribunals to conflate the treaty exception with the defence of necessity.[44] But the necessity defence operates to justify conduct found to be in breach of the state's international obligations, rather than operating as a treaty-internal scope limitation or affirmative defence.[45] These tribunals did not explain or analyse why they adopted this approach,[46] and were heavily criticized by subsequent tribunals and annulment committees[47] and in the literature.[48]

Two other tribunals (*LG&E* and *El Paso*) were more specific in suggesting that the exception was a *lex specialis* expression of the plea of necessity,[49] as did *Mobil v Argentina.*

To characterize an exception as a *lex specialis* is to view it as a modification of the defence of necessity as between the treaty parties. For the *lex specialis* rule to apply, the general and special norms must deal with the same subject matter[50] and there must be actual (although not necessarily explicit) inconsistency between them, or a 'discernible intention' that the special norm would exclude the general norm.[51] The special rule would establish whether and to

[43] See Joost Pauwelyn, 'Defences and the Burden of Proof in International Law' in this volume.

[44] ARSIWA art 25 prohibits invocation of a state of necessity unless the relevant 'essential interest' is threatened by a 'grave and imminent peril'; the measure must be the 'only way' available to protect the interest.

[45] See Federica Paddeu, 'Clarifying the Concept of Circumstances Precluding Wrongfulness (Justifications) in International Law' in this volume.

[46] *CMS Gas Transmission Company v Argentine Republic* (n 17) [320]–[324], [329], [355], [356], [374]; *Enron Corporation Ponderosa Assets LP v Argentine Republic,* ICSID Case No ARB/01/3, Award (22 May 2007) [334[, [339]; *Sempra Energy International v Argentina,* Award (18 September 2007) [376], [388].

[47] See *CMS Gas Transmission Company v Argentine Republic,* Decision of the Ad Hoc Committee on the Application for Annulment of the Argentine Republic, 25 September 2007 [129]; *Enron Corporation Ponderosa Assets LP v Argentine Republic,* ICSID Case No ARB/01/3, Decision on the Application for Annulment of the Argentine Republic (30 July 2010), [355]–[395]; [400]–[407]; *Sempra Energy International v Argentina* ICSID Case No. ARB/02/16, Decision on the Argentine Republic's Application for Annulment of the Award (29 June 2010) [130]–[131]; [208]–[209].

[48] See e.g. Jürgen Kurtz, 'Adjudging the Exceptional at International Investment Law: Security, Public Order and Financial Crisis' (2010) 59 International and Comparative Law Quarterly 325, 341–51.

[49] *LG&E Energy Corp, LG&E Capital Corp and LG&E International Inc v Argentine Republic,* ICSID Case No ARB/02/1, Decision on Liability (3 October 2006); *El Paso Energy International Company v Argentine Republic,* ICSID Case No ARB/03/15, Award (31 October 2011). See also *Oil Platforms* (n 37), where the US argued that the security exception was *lex specialis* in order to exclude from the Court's consideration the law of self-defence: see statements by Prosper Weil and Stephen Mathias on behalf of the US, CR 2003/12, cited by Paddeu, 'Self-Defence as a Circumstance Precluding Wrongfulness' 126.

[50] International Law Commission (ILC), 'Articles on the Responsibility of States for Internationally Wrongful Acts, with Commentaries' UN Doc A/56/10 (2001) Commentary to ARSIWA art 55 [4]–[5].

[51] ibid art 55 [4]; Robert D Sloane, 'On the Use and Abuse of Necessity in the Law of State Responsibility' (2012) 106 American Journal of International Law 447, 499.

what extent other aspects of the necessity defence would continue to apply in a residual way, and the defence would be displaced only to the extent of any inconsistency.[52] Some suggest that the ICJ in *Nicaragua* and *Oil Platforms* viewed the exception as a *lex specialis* expression of the law of self-defence between the treaty parties.[53] The ICJ may have given this impression when it stated that the two categories of law had 'identical content'[54] and that the legality of the United States' conduct in terms of the exception 'overlaps' with its legality in terms of the law of self-defence.[55] But only marginally do the two norms cover the same subject matter, and there is no apparent conflict between them. Rather, these cases were instances where the subject matter of the challenged measure (i.e. a use of force)—rather than the subject matter of the treaty provision—overlapped with the subject matter of a circumstance precluding wrongfulness.

None of the above investment tribunals offer a satisfactory explanation for this interpretation of the exception. Holding that the exception operated 'as a ground for exclusion from wrongfulness of an act of the State,'[56] the *LG&E* tribunal simply purported to read in the 'only way' requirement of the necessity defence. The 'only way' test has, rightly, been applied far more stringently by the ICJ in order to guard against possible abuse.[57] However, the tribunal concluded that 'an economic recovery package was the only means to respond to the crisis', but failed to examine the components of the package in any detail in order to examine potentially available alternatives.[58] The *El Paso* tribunal stated that it would 'dispense to fully analyse and to apply' the necessity defence because the treaty exception was a *lex specialis*.[59] However, it went on to apply the elements of the necessity defence in a residual way, concluding that Argentina could not rely on the exception because it had contributed to endangering its essential security interests.[60] The *Mobil* tribunal took the same approach.[61] This interpretation renders the treaty exception for all intents and purposes unavailable,[62] and would seem to run contrary to the principle of effectiveness, which obliges treaty interpreters to give effect to all treaty terms and to avoid an interpretation that would result in redundancy.[63] The treaty text does not evince an intention to codify the necessity defence[64] and in any event, as the ICJ

[52] ILC (n 50) Commentary to art 55 [2–3]; ILC Study Group on the Fragmentation of International Law, 'Fragmentation of international law: Difficulties arising from the diversification and expansion of international law' (finalized by Martti Koskenniemi), UN Doc A/CN.4/L.682 (13 April 2006) [102].

[53] ibid; Kurtz, 'Adjudging the Exceptional at International Investment Law' (n 36) 353–54.

[54] *Case Concerning Military and Paramilitary Activities in and against Nicaragua (Nicaragua v United States of America)* (Judgment) [1986] ICJ Rep 14 [179].

[55] *Oil Platforms (Islamic Republic of Iran v United States of America)*, Judgment, ICJ Rep 2003, p. 161 [43].

[56] *LG&E* (n 49) [229], [261].

[57] *Gabčíkovo-Nagymaros Project (Hungary v Slovakia)* (Judgment) [1997] ICJ Rep 7 [55]; *Legal Consequences of the Construction of a Wall in the Occupied Palestinian Territory* (Advisory Opinion) [2004] ICJ Rep 144 [140].

[58] *LG&E* (n 49) [257]. See Kurtz, 'Adjudging the Exceptional at International Investment Law' (n 36) 356.

[59] *El Paso Energy International Company v Argentine Republic* (n 49) [552–54]. Although ultimately concluding that the exception was a defence, the tribunal also suggested an alternative interpretation—that measures coming within the exception could be 'excluded from the scope of the BIT' (at [616]–[619]).

[60] ibid [656], [665].

[61] *Mobil v Argentina* (n 21) [1015], [1063]–[1066]. This approach was strongly rejected by the abitrator writing separately: (n 25) [25]–[34].

[62] See Bruno Simma and Dirk Pulkowski, 'Of Planets and Self-Contained Regimes at International Law' (2006) 17 European Journal of International Law 483 (on weak and strong forms of *lex specialis*).

[63] See e.g. Ulf Linderfalk, *On the Interpretation of Treaties: The Modern International Law as Expressed in the 1969 Vienna Convention on the Law of Treaties* (Springer 2007) 393; Richard K Gardiner, *Treaty Interpretation* (OUP 2008) 65, 159–61.

[64] William Burke-White and Andreas von Staden, 'Investment Protection in Extraordinary Times: The Interpretation and Application of Non-Precluded Measures Provisions in Bilateral Investment Treaties' (2008) 48 Virginia Journal of International Law 307, 323. See also Kurtz, 'Adjudging the Exceptional at International Investment Law' (n 48) 344–47.

held in *Nicaragua*, 'even if two norms belonging to two sources of international law appear identical in content, and even if the States in question are bound by these rules both on the level of treaty-law and on that of customary international law, these norms retain a separate existence'.[65]

One way of avoiding ineffectiveness would be for a tribunal to apply the *lex specialis* rule so as to entirely displace the application of the necessity defence in favour of a more flexible test in areas covered by the exception.[66] The ARSIWA provide that the general defences do not apply where and to the extent that special rules govern questions of state responsibility, including circumstances precluding wrongfulness.[67] This would be the case where the treaty provision explicitly excluded the necessity defence[68] or where there was a conflict between the necessity defence and the relevant treaty that was so great as to suggest that both norms could not logically coexist.[69] However, it is difficult to discern an intention to exclude the necessity defence in Article XI of the US–Argentina BIT, and nor does there appear to be an irreconcilable conflict between the exception and the defence.

Other adjudicators discussed the *lex specialis* issue in passing. The *CMS* annulment committee also put forward the view that the exception was a *lex specialis*, but did not develop the point any further except (puzzlingly) to suggest that the necessity defence, like the exception, would exempt actions taken during a state of necessity from the substantive protections of the treaty, rather than justify a prima facie treaty breach.[70] The dissenting arbitrator in *Bear Creek v Peru* also suggested that treaty exceptions functioned as *leges speciales* vis-à-vis Article 25 of the ARSIWA, but opined that unless the treaty otherwise provided, the presence of an exception would not oust the operation of Article 25 of the ARSIWA, 'which continues to function as a "secondary rule of international law" operating even when an exception under the *lex specialis* is not available'.[71]

4 Implications

4.1 Symbolic dimensions

Analysis of the decided cases demonstrates that while it might be argued that a degree of consensus is emerging as to the role of exceptions, the matter is far from settled. Determining whether one approach is preferable requires us to consider the normative and practical

[65] *Nicaragua* (n 36) 95.

[66] The defence would remain available in relation to other circumstances engaging an essential interest of the state that did not come within the subject matter of the exception.

[67] ARSIWA art 55. See Simma and Pulkowski (n 62) 494. See also ARSIWA art 25(2)(a) (discussed above).

[68] See e.g. *Case Concerning Electronica Sicula SpA (US v Italy)* [1989] ICJ Rep 15 [50]: 'the Chamber finds itself unable to accept that an important principle of customary international law should be held to have been tacitly dispensed with, in the absence of any words making clear an intention to do so'; Simma and Pulkowski (n 62) 490–91, 495.

[69] In *Legal Consequences of the Construction of a Wall in the Occupied Palestinian Territory* (Advisory Opinion) [2004] ICJ Rep 136, the ICJ implied that the necessity defence would be excluded pursuant to certain treaty provisions such as the derogation clause contained in art 4 of the International Covenant on Civil and Political Rights (ICCPR), which permits parties to take measures derogating from certain treaty obligations 'to the extent strictly required by the exigencies of the situation' in times of 'public emergency which threatens the life of the nation' (at [136]–[137]). See Sarah Heathcote, 'Circumstances Precluding Wrongfulness in the Articles on State Responsibility: Necessity' in James Crawford and others (eds), *The Law of International Responsibility* (OUP 2010) 491, 498.

[70] *CMS Gas Transmission Company v Argentine Republic* (n 17) [132]–[133].

[71] *Bear Creek Mining Corporation v Republic of Peru* (n 32) Partial Dissenting Opinion of Professor Philippe Sands QC [41].

implications of each approach. Normatively, there is a difference between characterizing conduct as either lawful and outside the scope of the obligations ('a state may act in relation to all matters falling within the clause') or as generally prohibited but justified only in exceptional circumstances ('a state may not act unless specifically permitted by the clause'.)[72] The former approach suggests a default position of regulatory freedom in the areas covered by the exception, whereas the latter paints a picture of a regime of prohibition of state action impacting on foreign investment without specific authorization, granted *ex post facto*, by the adjudicators of the regime.[73] (This might be viewed as especially problematic under current institutional arrangements for investor–state dispute settlement, involving determination of cases by evanescent panels of arbitrators with appeal or review for error of law for all intents and purposes precluded.) Even though a finding that a state has engaged in prohibited conduct is only made as a step in the reasoning process (and therefore defeasible), it is nevertheless symbolically significant from the point of view of the responding state, who might consider it more politically palatable for certain conduct to be outside the scope of the obligations than to be perceived to have acted inconsistently with those obligations in the first place.[74]

Investment treaty preambles, a contextual source of interpretation, appear to signal that exceptions should operate as scope limitations.[75] Preambles, especially those to more recent treaties, often refer to the importance of non-investment objectives by stating the economic objectives of the treaty (the protection and promotion of investment and/or the deepening of economic relations between the signatory states) in instrumental terms—as a means to welfare, development, or prosperity of state parties.[76] More recent treaties also refer to other objectives such as protecting the environment.[77] This suggests, at least in relation to these treaties, that the parties intend that measures coming within an exception should be excluded from the scope of the treaty protections, rather being prohibited (undesirable) conduct that is justifiable in exceptional circumstances. Given recent moves to include exceptions and other flexibility devices in investment treaties so as to more explicitly affirm the right of treaty parties to regulate to promote public welfare, one may speculate that states did not intend that regulatory and other measures directed to legitimate policy objectives were to be regarded as generally prohibited.[78]

4.2 The burden of proof

Perhaps the most important practical implication for the characterization of exceptions relates to the question of which disputing party has (or should have) the burden of proving that

[72] Adapted from Frederick Schauer, 'Review of Luís Duarte d'Almeida, Allowing for Exceptions: A Theory of Defences and Defeasibility in Law' Notre Dame Philosophical Reviews (25 February 2016). See also Caroline Foster, *Science and the Precautionary Principle in International Courts and Tribunals* (CUP 2011) 213.

[73] See Frederick Schauer, 'Exceptions' (1991) 58 University of Chicago Law Review 871, 872–73.

[74] However, framing exceptions as defences can have a useful role in signalling that the conduct, while ultimately lawful in the circumstances, is nevertheless undesirable from the perspective of interfering with the norms protected by the regime. I am grateful to Federica Paddeu for raising this point.

[75] The context of the treaty includes its preamble and 'any agreement relating to the treaty which was made between all the parties in connection with the conclusion of the treaty' (VCLT art 31(2)).

[76] See e.g. the preambles to the US–Argentina BIT (1991) and the UK–Jamaica BIT (1987).

[77] See e.g. the preambles to the Australia–Chile FTA (2008) and the Energy Charter Treaty (1994).

[78] There is a dearth of information available concerning investment treaty parties' intentions as to the intended effect of exception clauses, save perhaps for those modelled on those found in the WTO agreements, which might be said to have been signed on the basis of knowledge of the WTO Appellate Body's interpretation of the effect of the exceptions (namely, as affirmative defences). Section 4.3 discusses these clauses further.

the exception applies. Indeed, as Duarte D'Almeida argues, the decision to characterize an exception as a scope limitation or an affirmative defence is inextricable from the question of which party ought to bear the burden of proof.[79]

The default position in international adjudication is that the party making an assertion must prove that assertion.[80] To view the treaty exception as a limitation on the scope of the treaty obligations means that, where the state raises the exception, the claimant must prove that the challenged measure does not come within its purview (for example, that the measure was not necessary to protect the state's essential security interests). Viewing an exception as an affirmative defence (or as a *lex specialis* manifestation of the necessity defence) would place the burden on the respondent state to prove that the exception applied.[81]

The issue of the burden of proof has rarely been addressed by investment tribunals, reflecting a broader trend on the part of international courts and tribunals including the ICJ, whose allocation can only be deduced by its findings in each case.[82] Investment tribunals are not alone in doing so: for example, the ICJ has allocated the burden of proof in cases concerning use of force to the state raising self-defence, despite the International Law Commission's position that self-defence limits the scope of the prohibition of the use of force (and without the ICJ making it clear whether it viewed self-defence in this way). Only one case addresses the question expressly in relation to exceptions: the *Continental* tribunal placed the burden of proving the applicability of the exception on Argentina, in spite of the fact that the tribunal had found that role of the exception was to limit the scope of the treaty obligations.[83]

One objection to placing the burden of proof on a claimant in relation to an exception clause is that it would be unfair to require a claimant to prove that the exception did not apply. This might arise where discharging the burden would involve the production of evidence that was not on the public record, such as whether it would be feasible for the state to implement an alternative measure to achieve its objective,[84] or where a claimant was obliged to prove a universal proposition (e.g. that a measure was not 'necessary' or was not 'related to' a particular objective).[85] However, in cases where these concerns arise, adjudicators can give consideration to the standard of proof—that is, the amount of evidence required to discharge the burden of proof.[86] Courts and tribunals may employ a prima facie case approach where the evidence that would otherwise satisfy the standard of proof would be difficult to obtain.[87] This approach requires a claimant to make a prima facie case that the exception did not apply by adducing evidence sufficient to prove the proposition in the absence of rebuttal, at which point the burden of production would shift to the responding state. The responding state would be required to rebut those claims or adduce further evidence supporting its position that the exception did apply. It might be argued that even requiring a claimant to make a prima facie case that an exception did not apply would be to place the claimant at an unfair disadvantage due to investors' lack of experience in regulatory policymaking, particularly where the investor is

[79] Luís Duarte d'Almeida, 'Defences in the Law of State Responsibility: A View from Jurisprudence' in this volume.

[80] See e.g. Chester Brown, *A Common Law of International Adjudication* (OUP 2007) 92; Caroline Foster, 'Burden of Proof in International Courts and Tribunals' (2010) 29 Australian Yearbook of International Law 27, 31, 40.

[81] ILC (n 50) Commentary on ch V[8]: 'Where ... a State ... seeks to avoid its responsibility ... the onus lies on that State.'

[82] See Joost Pauwelyn, 'Defences and the Burden of Proof in International Law' in this volume.

[83] *Continental v Argentina* (n 18) [264].

[84] Michelle Grando, *Evidence, Proof and Fact-Finding in WTO Dispute Settlement* (OUP 2010) 196–97.

[85] ibid 194–96.

[86] See Foster, *Science and the Precautionary Principle in International Courts and Tribunals* (n 72) 223–29.

[87] ibid 230.

an individual or a smaller company.[88] Yet, there is no reason why investors should not be able to marshal expert evidence to discharge this burden; a number of the Argentine economic crisis decisions refer extensively to the evidence of economic experts retained by investors in relation to the availability of alternative measures to arrest the crisis.

4.3 Consistency with WTO law

The approach advocated here is inconsistent with the manner in which WTO adjudicators deal with the general exceptions in the WTO agreements. The Appellate Body has long classified the general exceptions as affirmative defences that must be proven by the responding government.[89] Moreover, the presence of the general exceptions in GATT has had a bearing on how the substantive obligations in WTO law have been interpreted. Under GATT Article III (national treatment), for example, WTO tribunals do not analyse the regulatory purpose of a challenged measure in the context of determining whether the obligation was complied with, but only in the context of determining whether the exception applies—an approach that has attracted criticism.[90] More broadly, the approach of the Appellate Body has been criticized for its inconsistent and unprincipled approach to when a provision will be treated as a scope limitation as opposed to an affirmative defence.[91] An argument can be made that a more principled approach would be to require a complaining WTO member to bear the burden of proving that the relevant general exception did not apply.[92]

Unlike WTO case law, the vast majority of investment cases have been decided under treaties that do not contain an exception clause. Due to the fact that until recently exceptions have been a relatively infrequent phenomenon in investment treaties, investment tribunals have not yet had much of an opportunity to grapple with the issues that the presence of an exception gives rise to—and nor does an appellate mechanism guide the development of a jurisprudence at this time. Calls for coherence between these two strands of law seem likely to intensify, given the rise in comprehensive economic agreements containing both trade and investment obligations. It may be that investment treaty exceptions that incorporate or are modelled on the general exceptions in GATT and GATS signal an acquiescence of Appellate Body jurisprudence.[93] Yet, one cannot avoid the impression that WTO exceptions have simply been copied and pasted into investment chapters of preferential trade agreements,

[88] Jürgen Kurtz, 'The Use and Abuse of WTO Law in Investor-State Arbitration: Competition and Its Discontents' (2009) 20 European Journal of International Law 749, 758.

[89] See Appellate Body Report, *Korea—Measures Affecting Imports of Fresh, Chilled and Frozen Beef*, WT/DS161/AB/R, WT/DS169/AB/R (11 December 2000) [157]. See further Viñuales, 'Seven Ways of Escaping a Rule' in this volume.

[90] See Kurtz, *The WTO and International Investment Law* (n 2) 179; Andrew Mitchell, David Heaton, and Caroline Henckels, *Non-Discrimination and the Role of Regulatory Purpose in International Trade and Investment Law* (Edward Elgar Publishing 2016).

[91] Grando, *Evidence, Proof and Fact-Finding in WTO Dispute Settlement* (n 84) 208–209; Tomer Broude, 'Genetically modified rules: the awkward rule exception–right distinction in *EC–Biotech*' (2007) 6 World Trade Review 215, 221–27; Steve Charnovitz and others 'Internet Roundtable: The Appellate Body's *GSP* Decision' (2004) 3 World Trade Review 239, 257.

[92] Grando, *Evidence, Proof and Fact-Finding in WTO Dispute Settlement* (n 84) 208–209; cf also Foster, *Science and the Precautionary Principle in International Courts and Tribunals* (n 72) 191–92.

[93] Some treaty provisions expressly provide that WTO jurisprudence should be followed or taken into account, although—as far as the author aware—such provisions have not been enacted in relation to investment law. In relation to trade obligations, see Korea–Australia FTA art 20.5: 'Where an obligation under [the FTA] is identical or substantially identical to an obligation under the WTO Agreement, the panel shall adopt an interpretation which is consistent with any relevant interpretation established in rulings of the DSB' (in relation to interstate disputes); Trans-Pacific Partnership (2015) art 28.11(3): dispute settlement panels hearing trade and other non-investment disputes should 'consider relevant interpretations in reports of panels and the WTO Appellate Body'.

without a great deal of thought given to the appropriateness of certain phrases in the provisions. For example, the language in the chapeau to Article XX of the GATT, which refers to 'discrimination between countries where the same conditions prevail, or a disguised restriction on international trade', uneasily translates to the context of international investment law.[94] These practical and conceptual difficulties also suggest that rather than incorporating WTO provisions by reference, governments negotiating exception clauses in investment treaties would be wise to adapt treaty language to the investment context, as some other investment treaties have done.[95]

5 Conclusion

Examining the role that exceptions play in the context of investment treaties suggests that, subject always to the language of the particular clause being interpreted, investment treaty exceptions should be characterized not as affirmative defences invoked to justify what would otherwise be unlawful conduct, but as limitations on the scope of the substantive obligations. To characterize an exception as an affirmative defence arguably goes against the very reason for their inclusion in investment treaties: to make it clear to tribunals and prospective claimants that states retain regulatory capacity in the areas covered by the clause.

This interpretation of exceptions has implications for the relationship between exceptions such as the US–Argentina BIT security exception and the customary defence of necessity. As an exception limits the scope of the treaty obligations, no breach of the treaty arises where the elements of the exception are made out, whereas the necessity defence only comes into play to justify conduct in circumstances where that conduct would otherwise be prohibited. Viewing a security exception as a *lex specialis* manifestation of the necessity defence risks the residual application of the defence in such a way as to render the exception all but ineffective through the extremely stringent 'only way' test in Article 25 of the ASR. It is difficult to see why parties to investment treaties would have intended such an approach.

Treating exceptions as scope limitations is, however, inconsistent with the way that the WTO Appellate Body approaches similar provisions in the GATT and the GATS and, it could be argued, with the manner in which the ICJ has approached similar clauses in FCN treaties. It also has practical implications for the burden of proof. To characterize an exception as a scope limitation means that the starting point would be that the claimant must prove (if the issue is before the tribunal) that the exception does not apply. In some cases this might raise potential issues of fairness, such as where a claimant must prove a universal proposition or where information needed to discharge the burden was known only to the responding state. However, adjudicators have some flexibility in dealing with issues of proof and could adjust the standard of proof to deal with any concerns.

[94] See Kurtz, *The WTO and International Investment Law* (n 2) 198.

[95] See e.g. Canada–Latvia BIT (2009) art XVII(3); Canada–Romania BIT (2009) art XVII(3); Canada–Slovakia BIT (2010) art IX(1): '.. … arbitrary or unjustifiable discrimination between investments or between investors, or a disguised restriction on international trade or investment .. …'; Energy Charter Treaty (2004) art 24(2): '… a disguised restriction on Economic Activity in the Energy Sector, or arbitrary or unjustifiable discrimination between … [investors]'.

21

Reasons, Institutions, Authorities

Three Models of Exceptions in World Trade Organization Law

Oisin Suttle

1 Introduction

Some of the most politically contentious disputes managed by the World Trade Organization (WTO) have focused on the interpretation and extent of exceptions. This is perhaps clearest where the law is required to strike a balance between trade liberalization and competing social policies including public health, environmental protection, and animal welfare. It is through the interpretation of exceptions that the Appellate Body has dealt with national measures on the protection of endangered sea turtles, the animal welfare implications of seal-hunting, the health risks of asbestos and air pollution, and the control of gambling and of the media. However, in other cases exceptions or quasi-exceptions are applied to balance competing economic concerns, or competing visions of appropriate economic behaviour. Thus, the trade remedies rules, which began life as limited exceptions to the General Agreement on Tariffs and Trade (GATT) core disciplines on border restrictions, and have since evolved into some of the most litigated WTO agreements, are concerned to balance the undoubted benefits of trade against the costs of economic dislocation, and the perceived dangers of unfair competition and subsidization.[1] The absence of photogenic seals and dolphins from these disputes has not reduced their political significance: indeed, perhaps the longest running and most politically damaging dispute addressed by the WTO concerns zeroing, an apparently minor and technical rule of US anti-dumping practice. Exceptions are tools applied at the margins, where competing concerns overlap or interact, so it is perhaps unsurprising that they should be a regular focus of legal and political controversy.

My goal in this this contribution is to elaborate on the different functions that exceptions play at the margins of WTO law. In particular, I will try to clarify the logic of these exceptions, and the different ways we can understand them, given different images of WTO law. The conclusion towards which I ultimately argue is that thinking about these exceptions not just in terms of the behaviours they license, but in terms of the authority of WTO law and

[1] The origin of the anti-dumping and countervailing duty rules as exceptions to the core disciplines is clear from the terms of GATT art II.2 ('Nothing in this Article shall prevent ...') which mirror the formulation of the general exceptions in art XX ('... nothing in this Agreement shall be construed to prevent ...') and the Security Exceptions in art XXI ('Nothing in this Agreement shall be construed ...'). Further, at least one prominent treatment of WTO law, co-authored by a recently retired Appellate Body member, freely characterizes the safeguards rules as exceptions: Peter van den Bossche and Werner Zdouc, *The Law and Policy of the World Trade Organization* (4th edn, Cambridge University Press 2017) 630–631. However, I readily concede that this contribution adopts a somewhat broader definition of exceptions than might be preferred by many WTO lawyers, reflecting my concern with the underlying structure and justification of the relevant provisions, and their interrelations, rather than, for example, the procedural implications of their classification in particular terms.

Oisin Suttle, *Reasons, Institutions, Authorities* In: *Exceptions in International Law*. Edited by: Lorand Bartels and Federica Paddeu, Oxford University Press (2020). © Lorand Bartels and Federica Paddeu. DOI: 10.1093/oso/9780198789321.003.0021

dispute settlement, can help us to understand both the scope of particular exceptions, and the ways these have been approached by the WTO Appellate Body.

I begin in section 2 by distinguishing two images of law, one normative and one institutional, and two rationales for exceptions that are suggested by the first, normative, image: a reason-tracking and a countervailing rationale. Section 3 shows how these two rationales are invoked in a variety of existing accounts of particular WTO exceptions.

Subsequent sections focus on the institutional image of law, and the ways it might illuminate these exceptions. Section 4 provides an initial sketch of the different ways that thinking about rules in institutional rather than purely normative terms might suggest different rationales for exceptions. These point towards a concern with the authority of rules, which leads me in section 5 to introduce Joseph Raz's service conception of authority. I apply this in sections 6 and 7 to generate an account of the authority of WTO law, and the limits of that authority. The hypothesis motivating this move is that an important function of WTO exceptions might be to police the limits of that authority. Section 8 investigates that hypothesis directly, analysing three prominent examples of exceptions or quasi-exceptions in WTO law to see how far they can be understood in authority-limiting terms. These include the Article XX General Exceptions, the trade remedies rules, and the 'non-exception-exceptions' for domestic regulation deviating from international standards. In each case, I argue that specific features of these exceptions, which appear puzzling given a normative image of law, can be readily understood in institutional, authority-limiting terms.

Section 9 concludes.

2 Two Images of Law and Two Functions of Exceptions

Law can be conceptualized in many ways. Two are relevant for our purposes.

First, law expresses standards of behaviour for its subjects. It prescribes particular acts, policies, and situations as permissible or prohibited, optional, or required.[2] WTO law, for example, prescribes that members should not discriminate in their laws between products originating in different exporting countries, or destined for different importing countries, the Most Favoured Nation or MFN principle.[3] If a member is considering whether to implement a particular policy, the MFN principle is an element that it can be expected to consider in deciding how to proceed. Let us call this *the normative image of law*. This normative image is one that law shares with other normative systems, such as morality, courtesy, prudence, and custom.[4]

However, it is perhaps the first and clearest insight of legal positivism that law is importantly different from other normative schemes, in large part because of its links to institutions, and to intentional human agency. Law is a standard prescribed by some agent or formal or informal institution claiming authority over its subjects, against which subjects' behaviour will be judged by third parties, and compliance with or breach of which may trigger specific responses from those third parties, whether as individuals, or as participants in shared legal

[2] Thus, Hart observes, that '[t]he most prominent general feature of law at all times and places is that its existence means that certain kinds of human conduct are no longer optional, but in *some* sense obligatory': HLA Hart, *The Concept of Law* (Oxford University Press 1961) 6.

[3] GATT art I.

[4] Indeed, this similarity is a common starting point for inquiries about the nature of law, and its distinctiveness from these other systems. See e.g. Hart (n 2) 7–8, 85–91.

and political institutions.[5] WTO law is the conscious product of multilateral negotiations amongst members, promulgated as a treaty with which members are expected to comply. And where a WTO member is concerned about a policy adopted by another, one question they can be expected to consider in determining how to respond is whether that policy complies with WTO law. If it does not, this may trigger a range of responses, from diplomatic protest to international litigation and collectively endorsed retaliation, none of which would otherwise be appropriate. Let us call this *the institutional image of law*.

I start with these two images, normative and institutional, because the choice of which to focus on has significant implications for how we think about exceptions in WTO law. Beginning with the normative image, this suggests two ways that the rule-exception structure of particular provisions might be explained.[6]

In the first, the rule-exception structure is largely an artefact of language and drafting. The reasons motivating the relevant rule do not apply in all of the circumstances that the rule, as drafted, covers, and the exception is simply a convenient way of adjusting the rule's coverage so that it better tracks those reasons. By way of example, imagine a policy to limit the spread of a contagious disease by restricting anyone other than a previous survivor, who has immunity, from entering the area where patients are being treated. In a particular hospital, assume ten staff members are survivors with immunity, while the remaining ninety have no immunity. To facilitate efficient implementation, we might operationalize our proposed policy through one of two rules: either (i) a prohibition on the ninety named persons who have no immunity from entering the relevant area; or (ii) a prohibition on any person entering the relevant area, with an exception for the ten named survivors. These two rules are logically identical. They each define two classes, to one of which a particular reason applies. The choice between them is a matter of convenience in both drafting and implementation. (It is probably easier for hospital security to check a list of ten permitted names than a list of ninety prohibited ones.) The purpose of the exception in this case is to help the rule to better track the underlying reason motivating it. Let us therefore call this *the reason-tracking rationale for exceptions*.

In the second, the rule-exception structure expresses something significant about the underlying reasons. The reasons motivating the relevant rule apply in all cases covered by the rule, including those covered by the exception. However, the exception identifies a subset of cases where some other reason also applies that is sufficient to displace the reasons motivating the rule. So, sticking with the contagious disease example, perhaps not everyone with the required expertise to treat the disease will be immune. We might then want to create a second exception to the general prohibition, this time for staff whose skills are essential for treating the relevant patients. Unlike the first exception, the reason motivating the rule (limiting the spread of the disease) does apply to these individuals: all else being equal, they should be excluded from the relevant areas as they may contract and spread the disease. However, all else is not equal: for medical professionals, being the only person who is capable of treating a particular patient will constitute a very weighty reason to do so, even though

[5] While not all, and perhaps none, of these specific features is a necessary characteristic of law, the relationship between law and formal institutions, the claim of authority, and link between legal obligation and third-party response, are prominent features in a variety of contemporary legal theories, both positivist and anti-positivist. See e.g. on the importance of institutionalization, Hart (n 2) 91–99; on the relations between law and coercion see Ronald Dworkin, *Law's Empire* (Harvard University Press 1986) 93; on law's claim to authority see Joseph Raz, *The Authority of Law* (Oxford University Press 1979) ch 2 'The Claims of Law'.

[6] *The distinction* drawn in the following two paragraphs tracks that drawn between two kinds of suboptimality in Frederick Schauer, 'Rules, Defeasibility and the Psychology of Exceptions' in this volume (section 2).

this exposes them to risk of infection. There are reasons not to enter the relevant area (risk of infection) but also reasons to enter it (ability to treat the sick), and the latter reasons are sufficient to displace the former. This idea is sometimes expressed in terms of outweighing. However, the language of outweighing risks oversimplifying the normative calculus involved, which may not be simply a matter of weighing the importance of the reasons on each side. Where rights are involved, for example, the language of weighing and balancing is less useful. Let us therefore instead call this *the countervailing rationale for exceptions*.[7]

Both the reason-tracking and countervailing rationales for exceptions fit well within the normative image of law. If we think of rules as guiding action, then we will want those rules to reflect the underlying reasons that apply to us. This will include both the requirement that they only apply in cases where the underlying reasons apply (reflecting the reason-tracking rationale) and that they only apply in cases where those underlying reasons are not displaced by other, more weighty, reasons tending in the other direction (reflecting the countervailing rationale).

3 Exceptions in the Normative Image of WTO Law

Both the reason-tracking and countervailing rationales for exceptions are regularly invoked to make sense of exceptions in WTO law. This is perhaps clearest under familiar economic accounts of trade agreements, but is by no means limited to these.

Whether we explain trade agreements as solving the domestic collective action problems that lead to national welfare impairing protectionism, or international terms of trade prisoner's dilemmas, standard economic accounts assume that trade agreements restrain measures adopted with a specific (protectionist or terms-of-trade-manipulating) motivation.[8] Each of the various core disciplines in the GATT, whether addressing tariffs, quantitative restrictions, or discrimination, is explained as targeting measures with the relevant motivation.[9] Yet, in practice, these disciplines apply to broad categories of measures that, while perhaps more likely than others to be motivated by protectionism or trade-manipulation, may also reflect a range of other, non-objectionable, motivations. To the extent this is the case, exceptions can be understood as excluding these latter measures from the core disciplines. WTO exceptions, including most obviously the Article XX General Exceptions, which cover a range of legitimate national policy objectives, are thus understood as exemplifying the reason-tracking rationale for exceptions. Many tariffs, quantitative restrictions, and discriminatory measures are protectionist/trade-manipulative, so—to the extent there are reasons to avoid these motivations—there are reasons to refrain from such measures. However, if there are tariffs, quantitative restrictions, and discriminatory measures that are not protectionist or trade-manipulative, then the reasons for the rule simply do not apply to such measures. The combination of rule and exception better tracks the underlying reasons motivating the rule than would the rule alone.

[7] A similar point is discussed, in the language of prima facie and all-things-considered wrongfulness, in Luís Duarte d'Almeida, 'Defences in the Law of State Responsibility: A View from Jurisprudence' in this volume (section 2.3).

[8] On trade agreements and protectionism see Donald Regan, 'What Are Trade Agreements For? Two Conflicting Stories Told by Economists, with a Lesson for Lawyers' (2006) 9(4) Journal of International Economic Law 951. On terms of trade see Kyle Bagwell and Robert W Staiger, *The Economics of the World Trading System* (MIT Press 2002).

[9] For critical discussion of those explanations see Regan, 'What Are Trade Agreements For?' (n 8) 978–81.

The evolving WTO case law on discrimination can be understood as working through this idea. The 'aims-and-effects' approach adopted by later GATT panels attempted to craft a discrimination rule that fully tracked, without recourse to exceptions, the underlying rationales for these rules.[10] By contrast, the revival of the border tax adjustment criteria in *Japan—Alcohol II*,[11] the progressively more explicit reliance on a competitive conception of likeness in *EC—Asbestos*[12] and *Philippines—Distilled Spirits*,[13] and the firm rejection of any concern with motivation in the identification of less favourable treatment in *EC—Seal Products*[14] have meant that the concept of discrimination in the GATT now captures a wide range of measures that are—at least as regards their motivation, which these views suggest should be our focus—wholly unobjectionable. In these circumstances, we can understand the general exceptions as saving some of those unobjectionable measures, motivated by various other goals, that would otherwise be caught. The combination of a prohibition on discrimination—broadly defined in terms of disparate impact and without regard for regulatory purpose—and a set of specific exceptions for particular policies, means that the combined rule-exception better tracks the underlying concern (protectionism/trade-manipulation) than would the rule alone.[15]

I have elsewhere offered an account of the general exceptions that understands them in countervailing rather than reason-tracking terms.[16] I explain the core disciplines on border measures and non-discrimination as tracking, not protectionism or trade-manipulation, but rather a morally significant category of measures that pursue their goals specifically through the regulation of international economic activity, which I label *external trade measures* or *ETMs*.[17] Adopting a moderate cosmopolitan perspective, I argue that almost all state measures affecting trade require to be justified to outsiders affected by them. However, whereas in the case of many such measures, that justification is relatively straightforward, ETMs require justification in more stringent terms, as pursuing global equality of individual opportunity, subject to a reasonable principle of self-determination (a compound standard that I label *equality in global commerce*, or the *EGC principle*).[18] Because tariffs, quantitative restrictions, and discriminatory taxation and regulation will generally constitute ETMs, they require justification in the terms prescribed by the EGC principle.[19] This is true, regardless of the particular goals that such measures pursue: a regulation that discriminates for *bona*

[10] GATT Panel Report, *US—Malt Beverages*, DS23/R (adopted 19 June 1992) BISD 39S/206, para 5.25; GATT Panel Report, *US—Taxes on Automobiles*, DS31/R (11 October 1994) (unadopted) para 5.5–5.10. For a powerful argument for recovering such an approach see Robert Howse and Donald Regan, 'The Product/Process Distinction: An Illusory Basis for Disciplining "Unilateralism" in Trade Policy' (2000) 11(2) European Journal of International Law 249.

[11] WTO Appellate Body Report, *Japan—Alcohol II*, WT/DS68/AB/R (adopted 4 October 1996) 20.

[12] WTO Appellate Body Report, *EC—Asbestos*, WT/DS135/AB/R (adopted 12 March 2001) para 99.

[13] WTO Appellate Body Report, *Philippines—Distilled Spirits*, WT/DS396/AB/R (adopted 21 December 2011) para 119.

[14] WTO Appellate Body Report, *EC—Seal Products*, WT/DS400/AB/R (adopted 22 May 2014) paras 5.87–5.117.

[15] For this interpretation of the direction of the case law and the limits of this strategy see Robert E Hudec, 'GATT/WTO Constraints on National Regulation: Requiem for an Aim and Effects Test' (1998) 32(3) International Lawyer 619, 636–38. In more economic terms see also Henrik Horn, 'National Treatment in the GATT' (2006) 96(1) American Economic Review 394, 402–403

[16] Oisin Suttle, 'What Sorts of Things Are Public Morals? A Liberal Cosmopolitan Approach to Article XX GATT' (2017) 80(4) Modern Law Review 569, and more generally Oisin Suttle, *Distributive Justice and World Trade Law: A Political Theory of International Trade Regulation* (2017) Cambridge University Press ch 7

[17] Suttle, *Distributive Justice* (n 16) 19–25.

[18] This claim is developed in Oisin Suttle, 'Equality in Global Commerce: Towards a Political Theory of International Economic Law' (2014) 25(4) European Journal of International Law 1043; for more detail see Suttle, *Distributive Justice* (n 16) chs 1–3 and 5.

[19] For this point see Suttle, *Distributive Justice* (n 16) ch 6.

fide environmental purposes is as much in need of justification to outsiders as one motivated by protectionism; and both fall to be judged by the standards set out in the EGC principle. (Obviously, it may be easier to justify the former than the latter, although that will not always be the case.) The general exceptions identify one set of circumstances where measures will be justified by those standards. Specifically, they can be understood as tracking the particular—closely constrained—conception of self-determination that I argue the EGC principle expresses. Article XX is thus understood as exemplifying the countervailing function of exceptions: the reasons motivating the core disciplines (restraining ETMs) do indeed apply to measures falling under Article XX, but they are offset by other reasons (justification in terms of self-determination) that tend in the opposite direction.

However, this is by no means the only account of the general exceptions in countervailing terms. Amongst economic approaches, those that see the WTO as pursuing a broader deregulatory agenda, tackling trade barriers, reducing transaction costs in pursuit of frictionless cross-border trade, or simply stabilizing an incomplete market access contract, are more likely to see measures caught by the core disciplines as *pro tanto* objectionable.[20] However, they may concede that the costs of regulation are sometimes balanced by the need to advance legitimate social goals including public health, environmental protection, law enforcement and so on.[21] The function of the Art XX exceptions, on this view, is to identify those cases where regulation's benefits in terms of non-trade values outweigh its costs in terms of trade restriction, a clear example of a countervailing rationale.[22]

Other exceptions in WTO law can similarly be characterized, with greater or lesser plausibility, in either reason-tracking or countervailing terms. Anti-dumping, for example, constitutes one of the most significant exceptions in practice to the GATT's tariff-binding and non-discrimination rules; where exporters' pricing behaviour can be characterized as dumping, importing states are permitted to impose additional duties, above bound levels, specifically targeting the relevant exports. Some advocates characterize anti-dumping as a *reason-tracking* exception, arguing that such measures are motivated by concerns for fair competition, and as such are not protectionist at all, so that there is no reason to worry about them. Protectionism, on this (somewhat strained) view, is a problem because it distorts trade, whereas anti-dumping duties serve to reduce or eliminate such distortions, serving an analogous role to antitrust rules. Others recognize that the reasons for disciplining tariffs generally apply equally to anti-dumping duties. However, they argue, there are other reasons that also apply in these specific cases, including the need to deter anti-competitive practices and to maintain domestic political support. It is because these other reasons apply to anti-dumping, but not to protectionism generally, that we provide an exception for anti-dumping, an example of the countervailing role of exceptions.[23] Safeguards, similarly, can be explained

[20] Trachtman's regulatory jurisdiction approach points in this direction. See Joel P Trachtman, 'Regulatory Jurisdiction and the WTO' (2007) 10(3) Journal of International Economic Law, 631, 647–48. Despite references to protectionism, this more ambitious deregulatory interpretation of efficiency is also discussed in Jeffrey L Dunoff, 'The Death of the Trade Regime' (1999) 10(4) European Journal of International Law 733, 737.

[21] Dunoff (n 20) 745–46. One significant interpretive upshot of understanding art XX in this was that it suggests an important role for cost-benefit analysis and strict proportionality, which is at odds with the terms of art XX and with the case law thereunder. I take up this point further in section 8.1 below.

[22] See e.g. van den Bossche and Zdouc (n 1) 545: 'Trade liberalisation, market access and non-discrimination rules may conflict with other important societal values and interests. WTO law recognises this and, therefore, provides for a set of rules to reconcile trade liberalisation, market access and non-discrimination rules with the need to protect and promote other societal values and interests'. For a critique of such countervailing interpretations see D Regan, 'The meaning of 'necessary' in GATT Article XX and GATS Article XIV: The Myth of Cost–Benefit Balancing' (2007) 6(3) World Trade Review 347.

[23] For a review of the various arguments and their weaknesses see Petros Mavroidis, *Trade in Goods* (2nd edn, Oxford University Press 2012) 214–22. In making sense of the anti-dumping rules in particular, methodological

in reason-tracking terms, by reference to adjustment costs and temporary downturns, or in countervailing terms, by references to compensating those harmed by trade, or preserving delicate political bargains.[24] Special and differential treatment is explained in terms of the distinctive economic conditions existing in developing countries which make protectionism economically efficient (reason-tracking), or the need for an equitable distribution of obligations and benefits in an unequal international economy (countervailing).[25] Similar points might be made about many other provisions of WTO law. [26]

4 Exceptions in the Institutional Image of Law

It is thus clear that, under the normative image of WTO law, we can make sense of a variety of exceptions in either reason-tracking or countervailing terms. However, this is not the only way we can approach these provisions, and provides an at-best incomplete picture of the roles they play.[27] The remainder of this contribution will therefore examine another way we might think about exceptions in WTO law, emphasizing the institutional rather than the normative image of law. Specifically, I will examine whether we can make sense of WTO exceptions by reference to the legitimate authority of WTO law and dispute settlement. In the next section I introduce Joseph Raz's *service conception of authority*, which I apply in subsequent sections to map the limits of WTO law's authority, and to examine how far prominent exceptions can be understood by reference to those limits. Before doing this, however, let me first sketch some of the ways that thinking about law in institutional rather than purely normative terms suggests different roles that exceptions might play.

To do this, let us return briefly to the hospital quarantine example discussed above. We there identified two plausible exceptions to a quarantine regulation, one for those with immunity, which we characterized as *reason-tracking*, and one for those with skills necessary to treat affected patients, which we characterized as *countervailing*.

Beyond these two cases, we might think that medically trained and experienced personnel have sufficient expertise to decide for themselves whether or not to expose themselves to a contagious disease, and that they therefore need not defer to rules imposed by others on this point, and that those others are not justified in enforcing such rules against them. Importantly, we might think this while still thinking that, all things considered, only those who have immunity or whose skills are necessary have sufficient reasons to expose themselves to such a

problems arise from the fact that many scholars are more concerned to criticize, reform, or repeal these rules, rather than to explain them. Suffice it to note that the explanations sketched here are the most prominent found in the literature or in policy or political practice; we need not regard them as plausible in themselves to recognize their role in motivating or publicly legitimising these rules.

[24] See generally Mavroidis (n 23) 605–14.

[25] For an overview of the many arguments advanced for and against special and differential treatment see Michael Trebilcock, Robert Howse, and Antonia Eliason, *The Regulation of International Trade* (4th edn, Routledge 2013) ch 16.

[26] I have written in depth elsewhere about the ways we can understand anti-dumping, safeguards, and special and differential treatment, advancing a countervailing account of each. See Suttle, *Distributive Justice* (n 16) chs 7, 8.

[27] While the language is different, the move from normative to institutional approaches to exceptions parallels d'Almeida's appeal to integrate primary and secondary rules for a complete understanding of the role of justifications: see d'Almeida (n 7). See also Federica Paddeu, 'Clarifying the Concept of Circumstances Precluding Wrongfulness (Justification) in International Law' in this volume (section 2.3); see also Eleni Methymaki and Antonios Tzanakopoulos, 'Freedom with their Exception: Jurisdiction and Immunity as Rule and Exception' in this volume (*passim*). However, the institutional characteristics on which I focus are somewhat broader than those captured by the primary/secondary distinction there discussed.

disease. It is not that medical professionals *should* enter the quarantine area, but rather that they can be trusted to decide the matter for themselves. Recognizing the institutional character of rules might therefore lead us to include a further exception from the general prohibition on access, covering medical professionals of at least a specified seniority.

Alternatively, given the various agencies that might prescribe rules in these circumstances (national and local health departments, medical professional bodies, hospital management etc), we might think that it was reasonable for decisions in respect of some classes of persons (e.g. the general public) to be made by one agency, while those in respect of others (medical professionals and hospital administrators) should be made by another. The result might be an interlocking system of different rules and exceptions: a general regulation from the government health department prohibiting access to relevant areas, with an exception for hospital staff and medical professionals; a regulation of the medical council prohibiting medical staff from accessing relevant areas, with an exception for those with immunity, with essential skills, or those specifically authorized by hospital authorities; and a hospital regulation prohibiting staff from accessing relevant areas, with an exception for medical staff who, in exercise of their medical judgment, have reason to access these areas.

In none of these cases can the exceptions be entirely understood under the reason-tracking or countervailing rationales for exceptions outlined above; rather, they reflect the respective roles of the various agencies involved, their relations to one another and to various classes of persons, and the capacities of various persons to make particular decisions for themselves. Further, the exceptions mean that each of the relevant rules is incomplete as a guide to action: a medical professional deciding whether to access the relevant areas would need to consult all three rules, and their own professional judgment, before deciding how to proceed.

Different considerations explain each of the exceptions in this example. We will go a little further in later sections in disaggregating rationales for exceptions in the institutional image of rules. For the moment, let us simply describe these collectively as the *institutional rationale for exceptions.*

5 The Service Conception of Authority

What is distinctive about the examples discussed in the previous section is that they are concerned, not with what particular agents should do, but rather with the role that externally mandated rules, imposed by or by reference to particular institutions, should play in their decisions about what to do. This points us towards what, in legal and political theory, is commonly labelled the problem of *political obligation* or *legitimate authority*. When, and in virtue of what facts, do we have an obligation to act, not as we ourselves think best, but as some other, ostensibly legitimate, authority, directs? In domestic law, the question of obligation is at least partly obscured by the fact of coercive enforcement.[28] If we do not obey the law, then in many cases we can expect that some person or persons will require us to do so, on pain of officially sanctioned and socially endorsed penalty. In international law, enforcement is less visible, making the question of authority more prominent.[29]

[28] Recall Austin's efforts to make sense of law's distinctiveness solely in terms of its coercive enforcement: John Austin, *The Province of Jurisprudence Determined* (1832, Wilfrid E. Rumble (ed.) Cambridge University Press 1995).

[29] For two competing views on authority in international law see Allen Buchanan, 'The Legitimacy of International Law' and John Tasioulas, 'The Legitimacy of International Law', both in Samantha Besson and John Tasioulas (eds), *The Philosophy of International Law* (Oxford University Press 2010).

Some observers assume that the question of authority must be answered univocally, whether in the affirmative or the negative. Either we have an obligation to obey the laws that apply to us, whether in virtue of our having consented to them, or their representing the collective judgment of the international community, or because fairness demands that we do our part when others do theirs, or because a law-compliant world is a better, more secure, more prosperous world than one in which the law is regularly flouted; or we have no obligation to obey the law, whether because consent is illusory, or because state consent cannot bind subsequent generations or minorities, or because the international community is itself illusory or procedurally tainted, or because obligations of fair play are parasitic on assumed or implied consent.[30]

However, legal obligation can also be understood in a piecemeal fashion. It may be that some/many/most of us have obligations to obey some/many/most laws some/much/most of the time. If obligation is divisible in this way then we must enquire, in each instance, whether *this* agent has an obligation to obey *this* law, as interpreted by *this* adjudicator, in *these* particular circumstances. Many will find such an answer unsatisfyingly messy. In particular, it precludes our simply deferring, without question, to law or, indeed, to any other ostensibly legitimate authority. Rather, we must continue to exercise our practical reason, if not over the first order question of what to do, then over the second order question of how we should decide what to do, and in particular whether and to what extent our decision should be guided by the ostensible authority of law and legal institutions.[31]

The most prominent such answer to the problem of political obligation in contemporary Anglophone legal theory is Joseph Raz's *service conception of authority*, on which I will draw in the remainder of this chapter.[32] The rest of this section introduces Raz's account. Readers will hopefully forgive this detour, with the promise that these discussions' relevance will become clear in subsequent sections; but those already familiar with Raz's approach may prefer to skip over this exposition, and rejoin us in the next section.

To accept an authority, in Raz's view, is to treat its directives as constituting content-independent, exclusionary reasons for action.[33] Content-independence refers to the fact that we treat the authority's directives as reasons for action *because* they are directives of the relevant authority, and not because of our evaluation of the correctness of their content.[34] Exclusionary refers to the idea that, when we act on authority, we set aside at least some of the reasons that might otherwise guide our action; specifically, we set aside those reasons on the basis of which the authority is assumed to have formulated its directive, labelled *dependent reasons*.[35]

Raz comes to the problem of authority from a liberal perspective that emphasizes autonomy. The problem of authority, from this perspective, is how we could ever be justified in deferring to the directives of others, including in particular those of ostensible legal authorities? How is it possible for an authority, simply by issuing a directive, to constitute new, content-independent, exclusionary reasons for action that apply to autonomous persons?

[30] For an overview of approaches to the problem of authority see A. John Simmons, *Moral Principles and Political Obligations* (Princeton University Press 1981). For a particularly sceptical treatment of the authority of international law see Jack L Goldsmith and Eric Posner, *The Limits of International Law* (Oxford University Press 2005) ch 7.

[31] For an analogous point in developing a Razian account of international law's authority see Samantha Besson, 'The Authority of International Law: Lifting the State Veil' (2009) 31 Sydney Law Review 343, 355.

[32] See generally Joseph Raz, (Oxford University Press 1985); for a more recent presentation see also Joseph Raz, 'The Problem of Authority: Revisiting the Service Conception' (2006) 90 Minnesota Law Review 1003.

[33] Raz, *The Morality of Freedom* (n 32).

[34] ibid 35–37.

[35] ibid 42–48, 57–62.

To answer that question, Raz proposes what he labels the *normal justification thesis*. This holds that:

> the normal way to establish that a person has authority over another person involves showing that the alleged subject is likely better to comply with reasons which apply to him … if he accepts the directives of the alleged authority as authoritatively binding and tries to follow them, rather than by trying to follow the reasons which apply to him directly.[36]

A little explanation may help here. Raz's view builds on the idea that there are objective reasons that apply to each of us. As rational agents, our actions and choices are not simply the expressions of impulse and appetite. Rather, we—at least ideally—act for reasons. These reasons are more than just subjective preferences—they reflect those things that objectively we in fact have reason to want and to do. 'A reason for an action is a consideration that renders its choice intelligible, and counts in its favour.'[37] They include both self-interested reasons (e.g. self-preservation, happiness, personal development) and other-regarding reasons (e.g. charity, patriotism, justice). When we exercise our practical reason, we are engaged in identifying and reconciling the various reasons that apply to us, in order to determine what, all things considered, we have most reason to do.

Raz's suggestion is that, adopting this view of reasons, there need be nothing mysterious or terribly grand about authority; authorities are simply tools that we use to help us better comply with the reasons that apply to us. They are one, but by no means the only, tool that we may use for this purpose. Many cognitive technologies, from mnemonics through writing to calculators and iPhones, serve similar purposes. When we reason, we constantly rely on tools and shortcuts. Reliance on these is not an abdication of reason. Rather, they help us better achieve the goal of practical reasoning, namely to allow us to act fully and faithfully on the reasons that apply to us. Authorities thus provide a valuable service to those autonomous agents subject to them, hence the *service conception* of authority.[38]

But how, we might wonder, can an authority help us to act on reasons that already apply to us? We sometimes distinguish between theoretical authorities, which are authorities in our reasoning about what the world is like, and practical authorities, which are authorities in our reasoning about how we should act.[39] It is straightforward to see how a medical doctor, as an example of a theoretical authority, might help us to identify and act on reasons that apply to us, specifically reasons to keep ourselves healthy. Her years of training and experience mean that she is much more likely than we are to identify anything that is wrong with us, and to select the best course of treatment, so we would do better to follow her prescriptions than to act on our own judgment. Law's authority is sometimes at least in part theoretical in this way: many product safety regulations, for example, purport to be authoritative because they reflect the views of relevant experts or the outcomes of relevant studies, impact, or risk assessments. It is plausible that a public health ministry will have a better idea than I do about which additives I should accept in my food, and that I am likely to remain healthier if I defer to those regulations than if I seek to decide this matter for myself.

36 ibid 53; Raz, 'The Problem of Authority' (n 32) 1022.
37 ibid 1006.
38 For this view of the nature and value of practical reason see ibid 1016–18.
39 ibid 1032–37.

However, in the case of many other laws, there are no such plausible epistemic grounds for their authority. Taking a classic example, rules prescribing which side of the road to drive on cannot be explained by reference to the legislature's greater expertise in determining which side is best. Indeed, it seems likely that the side of the road we drive on is a matter of indifference, provided everyone in a given place drives on the *same* side. We do not, absent a relevant rule, have any reason to drive on either the left or the right side of the road, but we do have a reason to drive on the same side of the road as everyone else, in order to reduce the risk of collisions. Driving therefore presents a pure coordination problem: what matters is not which choice we make, but only that we all make the same choice. Faced with coordination problems, authorities can help us to act on the reasons ('avoiding collisions') that apply to us by providing a coordination point ('In England we drive on the left') around which the behaviour of all those subject to the relevant authority can be expected to converge. Where such an ostensible authority exists, and where we have reason to expect that others will have regard to it, each of us can better conform to the reasons that apply to us by following the authority's directive as to the side of the road to drive on, than by making this choice for ourselves.[40]

Authorities are particularly good at solving coordination problems, and many familiar legal concerns can be explained in this way. Many of us think, for example, that we have reasons of social justice to be concerned about inequalities amongst citizens, and to contribute to the alleviation of those inequalities. However, how much we should contribute, and how our contribution should be directed, is much less clear. Further, realizing any meaningful sense of social justice is likely to require both contributions by a very large proportion of the population, and that those contributions be combined and allocated in a suitably targeted manner. The law, through a system of general taxation and public services and entitlements, provides a mechanism whereby we can each comply with the reasons of social justice that apply to us. It is substantially more effective than if we were each to seek to comply with those reasons on our own.[41] Further, this will be the case, even if the particular answer that the law expresses to the question of how much we should contribute or how our contributions should be used is wrong—we are better off complying with an imperfect shared scheme of taxation and redistribution than seeking, as individuals, to act directly on our own judgment.[42] The reasons constituted by the law are thus content-independent—they apply regardless of whether they are correct—and exclusionary—they replace the reasons we would otherwise have to contribute based on our own judgment.

Aside from coordination problems, we may look to authorities because of the motivational advantages they enjoy over individuals. In renovating my home, I have reasons to limit the impact my works have on my neighbour, for example by restricting the times at which noisy equipment is used, and the amount of dust that is thrown into her garden. However, where acting on these reasons is likely to slow down the completion of my renovation, or to increase its costs, I may be tempted to give less weight to my neighbour's concerns than I should. I may consciously choose to act selfishly, or I may unconsciously give greater weight to my own interests despite doing my best to act fairly. In circumstances like these, where I know I will be tempted to give too much weight to my own interests, I am likely

[40] On authority and coordination see ibid 1031–32.

[41] ibid 1021–22.

[42] Of course, we will in these circumstances have separate reasons to seek to reform the imperfect existing system with a view to making it more just. Recognizing an authority and treating its directives as binding reasons for action does not preclude our questioning the wisdom of those directives.

to better conform to the reasons that apply to me if I defer to authority on the question of how to act; in practice, at least in English law, this is a function that is fulfilled by planning and building regulations, and the laws of private nuisance. Those laws may strike the wrong balance but, we might think, they are more likely to get the balance right than I am acting on my own judgment, given the evident motivational challenges that I face.

Finally, and relatedly, legal authorities can solve assurance problems. Indeed, this is the classic justification that Hobbes offers for the authority of the state.[43] Whereas we may each have reasons to live in peace with one another, to cooperate, and to treat each other fairly, we must also consider the risk that others may choose to act selfishly, aggressively, dishonestly, and so on. We cannot simply trust that, if we act as we should, others will do the same. Legal authorities, by precisely specifying our obligations to one another, and by credibly threatening coercive enforcement against anyone who violates those obligations, allows each of us to act better on the reasons that apply to us, independent of the law's intervention. And again, this will be the case, even if our obligations as specified by the law do not accurately track the reasons that otherwise apply to us; the assurance problems that arise in the state of nature mean that we better comply with reason by following the law's imperfect guide than we would by acting on our own individual views about what reason requires.

These, then, are some of the ways in which an authority might help agents to act on the reasons that apply to them. However, it is important to emphasize that authority on this view is always contingent. It depends on establishing, in a particular case, or for a particular domain, or vis-à-vis a particular agent and a particular ostensible authority, that the agent is indeed likely better to conform to reason by following the directives of the authority than by acting on her own judgment. Sometimes, this will depend on the particular domain or subject matter that the authority purports to govern: is this a domain where the kinds of epistemic, coordination, motivation, or assurance problems that authorities solve are likely to arise? At other times, it may depend on the characteristics or circumstances of the particular agent: government dietary regulations may be authoritative over the population in general, but not over doctors or dieticians; and legal speed limits may be authoritative over all citizens in most circumstances but have no authority over a person driving on a smooth straight desert road with perfect visibility and no other cars for miles around.[44] Finally, the extent of one ostensible authority's legitimate authority may depend in part on whether there are other candidate authorities better placed to help an agent conform to reason:[45] the Royal Automobile Club's *Handbook on Driving Etiquette* might enjoy significant authority in the absence of any legal guidance; but once the government issues its *Rules of the Road*, the authority of the RAC is to that extent diminished. In this last example, the loss of authority is not (or at least not simply) because there is a formal hierarchy of norms that places state laws above private associations' guidelines. Rather, it is because—assuming a significant function of driving rules is to solve coordination and assurance problems—state law is likely to be more effective than private guidelines in solving these problems over a wider class of persons. Once I know, or have reason to think, that others are likely to conform their actions to the government rules instead of the RAC ones, I should do similarly.

Finally, there are matters over which we might think that no authority was possible. These might be matters where there is no 'right answer' that the authority can help us to reach, and where (unlike the driving example) there is no compelling reason for everyone to converge

[43] Thomas Hobbes, *Leviathan* (1651 Richard Tuck (ed), Cambridge University Press 1996) chs 13, 18.

[44] On the agent-relative quality of authority see Raz, *The Morality of Freedom* (n 32) 73–74.

[45] ibid 57.

on the same answer. If we think, for example, that values are plural and incommensurable, such that it is not possible to say which is the better amongst a given pair of possible choices, then we might in turn conclude that there was no scope for authority in determining which of these choices to make. If there is no right answer, then the only respectable answer is the one we choose for ourselves.[46] In other cases, we might recognize that there are better or worse answers, but still think that it is better that we choose for ourselves, even if we choose badly, than that we defer to authority. A common example here is romantic choices: it is better, we might think, to choose our romantic partners for ourselves than to have them chosen for us by a computer, even if we think the computer will do a better job than we will ourselves. There is an intrinsic value in romantic relationships that are freely chosen, that is lost when those relationships are chosen for us.[47] Putting the point at its most general, it is sometimes the case that it is more important for our choices to be our own than it is for our choices to be correct. Where this is the case, there will be no role for authority.

6 Authority and WTO Law

Readers might by now be worrying that we have wandered quite far from either exceptions in general or WTO law in particular. Rest assured, this is as far adrift as we shall go; from here, we will tack back towards these central concerns. It may be useful to sketch here how the rest of the argument develops, if only to tempt any doubters to stick around for a few pages more.

The thought motivating this contribution is that we can generate an account of exceptions in WTO law by focusing not on law's normative image, but rather on its institutional image. Specifically, this thought goes, the normal justification thesis can offer an account of the authority of WTO law. However, that account will—as the service conception is prone to do—support the authority of WTO law in some cases only. It will suggest limits on the WTO's authority, by reference to particular problem structures, subject matter domains, agents, or competing institutions. It is in these limits that I hope to find an explanation for some of the various exceptions that characterize this body of law. We must therefore do two things: first, we must identify the grounds for the authority of WTO law, the ways that it might fulfil the normal justification thesis and thereby enjoy legitimate authority over its subjects. Secondly, we must identify the limits of that authority, and how those limits might be reflected in exceptions.

What, then, are the ways that WTO law might satisfy the normal justification thesis? Two obvious answers suggest themselves, reflecting two economic explanations of trade agreements.

> First, WTO law serves important coordination and assurance functions. We can assume that states have reasons to liberalize international trade, at least to some extent. This need not reflect a free-trader's commitment to eliminating all trade barriers: few economists of any ideological stripe would deny that there are substantial gains to be made from participation in the global economy.[48] However, where a state liberalizes, it is exposed to risks

[46] For this point in an account applying Raz's approach to international human rights see Tasioulas (n 29) 109–12.

[47] For this point, which Raz labels the 'independence condition' see Raz, 'The Problem of Authority' (n 32) 1014–16. And for its application to international law see Tasioulas (n 29) 112–15.

[48] As Dani Rodrik, by no means a cheerleader for unfettered globalization, observes: 'The consensus in favor of the general statement supporting free trade is not a surprise. Economists disagree about a lot of things, but the superiority of free trade over protection is not controversial. The principle of comparative advantage and the case for

of exploitation by others, whether through terms of trade manipulation, predatory competition from behind protectionist barriers, strategic trade under imperfect competition, or otherwise.[49] Addressing these risks requires coordination among affected states, and assurance that each will comply with its commitments. WTO law offers a mechanism through which that coordination can be achieved. States are thus more likely successfully to act on the reasons that apply to them, independent of WTO law, if they seek to participate in the negotiation of, and subsequently comply with, WTO rules, than if they try to act directly on their own judgments of what reason requires.

Secondly, WTO law helps solve an important motivational problem. Political economy teaches that protectionism is a function of domestic collective action problems. Because the benefits of trade liberalization are widely shared among consumers, while the costs are highly concentrated among a small number of producers, policy-makers face incentives to adopt nationally suboptimal protectionist policies in order to appease highly motivated producer lobbies at the expense of the wider population. Trade agreements generally, and WTO law in particular, solve this problem by balancing pro-trade export coalitions against protectionist import-competing interests.[50] A government that aims to select and implement nationally welfare enhancing policies directly is likely to go astray because of lobbying by special interests; binding itself through trade agreements thus allows it to comply with the reasons that all governments have to advance the wellbeing of their citizens.

These first two grounds support the authority of WTO law, as a body of treaty law agreed through multilateral negotiations, but also of the WTO dispute settlement system. Coordination, assurance, and motivational problems are ameliorated when states adopt policies by reference to rules that have been agreed multilaterally; but without ongoing oversight those problems re-emerge at the point of interpretation and implementation. As an impartial and disinterested third party, the dispute settlement system addresses this difficulty.

Beyond these grounds, a number of further explanations support the authority of the WTO Dispute Settlement System in particular. First, WTO dispute settlement helps manage the destabilizing effects of trade disputes. States have, it seems reasonable to assume, reasons to object where others adopt policies that are economically harmful to them, or that defect from existing agreements about acceptable behaviour. However, if states act unilaterally in response to what they perceive to be unacceptable behaviour, there is a risk that misunderstanding and differing interpretations will lead others to respond similarly, undermining the overall scheme of international economic cooperation.[51] States are thus more likely to act faithfully on the various reasons that apply to them, including both their reasons to object

the gains from trade are crown jewels of the economics profession.' See Dani Rodrik, 'What Do Trade Agreements Really Do' (2018) http://j.mp/2EsEOPk.

[49] On exploitation of terms of trade see Bagwell and Staiger (n 8); on strategic trade and imperfect competition see Paul R Krugman, Maurice Obstfeld, and Marc J Melitz, *International Economics: Theory and Policy* (9th edn, Pearson Education 2012) 302–309.

[50] ibid 260–66.

[51] Recall, it is the imperfection of administration of the natural law in the state of nature, and in particular the problems of trust and impartiality in self-judgment, as much as the insecurity deriving from the predation of others, that Locke argues should lead us to give up the freedom of the state of nature: John Locke, *Two Treatises of Government* (1690) Peter Laslett *ed), Second Treatise 1988) ch 9. The idea that WTO dispute settlement is substantially concerned with managing disputes and avoiding escalation reflects its origins in the less formal GATT system, where this focus was more explicit. See on this transition Joseph HH Weiler, 'The Rule of Lawyers and the Ethos of Diplomats: Reflections on the Internal and External Legitimacy of WTO Dispute Settlement' (2001) 35(2) Journal of World Trade 191.

to misbehaviour, and their reasons to preserve international cooperation, if they defer to the judgments of an impartial third party in deciding whether there has been a breach of the rules, whether a response is justified, and, if so, to what extent.

Secondly, the expertise of decision-makers and the use of adversarial, inter-state adjudicative procedures may give WTO dispute settlement epistemic advantages over domestic decisions in certain circumstances. Trade law is not like domestic product safety regulation, where regulators' reliance on scientific experts with specialist knowledge or techniques gives rules an epistemic authority. However, where one member seeks to determine whether another has breached their obligations, a specialized quasi-judicial procedure in which that other member is represented and in which decisions are made by disinterested third parties may be more likely to reach the right conclusion than a unilateral procedure wholly controlled by the complaining state. While by no means infallible, the adversarial process of litigation thus has epistemic advantages that may give it authority in particular circumstances.[52]

Thirdly, the fact that WTO dispute settlement can provide these services for some governments, or in some circumstances, may be a reason for other, or indeed all, governments to regard it as a legitimate authority in a wider set of circumstances. If—as seems plausible—we have reasons to preserve international cooperation, and if—as also seems plausible—disregarding the decisions of WTO adjudicators, even in cases where they do not otherwise enjoy legitimate authority, is likely to undermine the general acceptance of their authority by other states and in other circumstances, then this may be a good reason to accept that authority even in such cases.[53] However, this is clearly—at least from the perspective of the service conception—a deviant case of authority. We recognize that the authority has overreached, but we comply with it nonetheless, to avoid inflicting the reputational damage that would result from publicly disregarding it.[54] This is a second-best solution: the first best solution is that the authority respects its own limits.

While by no means comprehensive, these five explanations together provide a reasonable starting point in thinking about the authority of WTO law under the service conception. They suggest that, in many cases, WTO rules, and the decisions of the dispute settlement system, will indeed meet the standards of the normal justification thesis, and so constitute legitimate authorities. In each case, we can understand the authority of the law, in the first two cases, and of the dispute settlement system, in the last three, as helping WTO members to better act on the reasons that would apply to them anyway, independent of these rules and institutions.

7 The Limits of Authority

It seems, then, that the service conception can make sense of the authority of WTO law on a number of different grounds. We must next ask how far those grounds extend. As noted above, the service conception imports a piecemeal understanding of authority, potentially limited as to subject matter, agents, circumstances, and competing institutions. We

[52] The point here reflects the psychological rationale for impartial adjudication identified in Schauer (n 6) sections 7–8.

[53] The interminable disputes about zeroing, and the consequent undermining of the Appellate Body's social authority in the eyes of the United States and others provides a ready example of the risks.

[54] Rawls' natural duty to support and comply with reasonably just institutions that apply to us seems at least in part to be motivated by this worry: see John Rawls, *A Theory of Justice* (Harvard University Press1999) 99.

cannot understand the extent of WTO law's authority until we have some sense of those limitations.[55]

First, and most obviously, consider limitations as to subject matter. It presumably is not the case that every decision that a state is called upon to make would be better made by reference to WTO rules than by relying on its own judgment. If this were the case, there would be little reason for states to exist at all. Rather, there are particular types of decision, and particular types of regulatory instrument, where the coordination, assurance, and motivational problems noted above are especially evident. It is only in these cases that the normal justification thesis is satisfied. In the goods context, tariffs, quantitative restrictions, and discriminatory domestic regulation and taxation stand out as tools whose use is particularly likely to be tainted by these problems. As noted above, the normative image of WTO law explains the GATT's focus on such measures as reflecting the fact that these measures are necessarily protectionist. The institutional image tells a different story: what is distinctive about these kinds of measures is that—for various reasons—states are especially prone to motivational error when adopting them compared to other types of measure. It is not that they will always be harmful, but that states are less likely to make good choices about the use of these tools, compared with others. It is therefore reasonable to think that decisions about these kinds of measures are best made by reference to quite strict rules of the kind found in the GATT, and carefully policed by the dispute settlement system. In the case of other kinds of measures, including most obviously non-discriminatory environmental or public health regulations, states may be more likely to make good decisions on their own, meaning there is less reason to defer to international rules in relation to such measures.[56]

However, limits on WTO law's authority may also be agent-specific. Consider, for example, the motivational problem underpinning the political economy of protectionism, which it was suggested WTO law helps to solve. This, we might assume, will be stronger or weaker, depending on the domestic institutions and public political culture of a given member. Some policy-making processes are more prone to capture by special interests than others. A state with a robust commitment to cost-benefit analysis and public scrutiny of legislation might, *ceteris paribus*, be more likely to adopt socially optimal policies than one with less transparent processes and a more limited role for economic analysis.[57] Similarly, a state whose electoral laws include both public campaign funding and campaign spending caps to limit the political influence of private donors may be less prone to pressure from import-competing industries than one where politicians depend on such donors for their political survival.[58] Other features that might be relevant here include inter alia the extent of economic literacy among voters, opportunities for domestic judicial review of legislation, and overall economic diversification within an economy. The upshot is that some states may be more likely to select socially optimal policies through their own choices, whereas others will do better by treating relevant WTO rules as authoritative.

[55] For another account of the limits of international legal authority in Razian terms see Andreas Follesdal, 'The Legitimate Authority of International Courts and its Limits' in Patrick Capps, and Henrik P Olsen (eds), *Legal Authority Beyond the State* (Cambridge University Press 2017).

[56] For an analogous point see Regan, 'What Are Trade Agreements For?' (n 8) 963, 967–68, 985–88.

[57] Howse argues that one way to understand the WTO disciplines on domestic regulation, and in particular the WTO Agreement on the Application of Sanitary and Phytosanitary Measures (SPS Agreement), is as tools to maximize the likelihood that states will make these kinds of choices correctly for themselves. See Robert Howse, 'Democracy, Science, and Free Trade: Risk Regulation on Trial at the World Trade Organization' (2000) 98(7) Michigan Law Review 2329.

[58] Although the argument here is less clear, as the motivational problem is not exclusively concerned with industry lobbying, reflecting also the need to respond to the demands of motivated voters in affected industries.

Other limits on WTO law's authority reflect its relationship with other international institutions. These limits highlight the extent to which authority is a function not only of the relative capacities of an agent and an ostensible authority, but may also depend on the capacities of other candidate authorities. Obvious examples here will include subject matter specialized international agencies such as the Codex Alimentarius Commission, and regional arrangements such as the North American Free Trade Agreement (NAFTA) or the European Union. While in the absence of such agencies and arrangements WTO law and adjudication might provide the best guide for states in particular issue areas or in managing their relations with particular other states, once these other institutions come into existence, their greater epistemic capacities (in the case of subject-matter specialized agencies) and political salience (in the case of regional arrangements) mean that they constitute legitimate authorities with respect to the relevant issues, and the WTO's authority is to that extent diminished.

Finally, there will be limits on the WTO's authority reflecting areas where it is more important that states' actions reflect their own judgment about what is best than that they successfully act on the objective reasons that apply to them. Identifying and delineating this category raises fundamental and controversial questions about sovereignty, self-determination, non-intervention and related concepts, the resolution of which is beyond the scope of this contribution. I will simply note that this category is likely to be significantly narrower than many exponents of state sovereignty might assume. In the context of individual action, it depends on identifying some intrinsic value in a particular choice or activity that would be lost if it were made subject to authority, or some instrumental reason why reliance on authority, while it might do better in a particular instance, would ultimately undermine some relevant interest.[59] I have elsewhere sought to map some of the considerations that seem most relevant in the context of state decision-making; key concerns include affording some meaningful space for democratic self-government, ensuring fair equality amongst peoples, and protecting the distinctive cultural and individual goods that are realized through self-determination.[60]

8 From Authority to Exceptions

The Service Conception thus suggests an account of both the authority of WTO law, and the limits on that authority. How does this help us to understand the role of exceptions?

It seems plausible that, *ceteris paribus*, it is better if the authority that the law claims is co-extensive with the legitimate authority that it actually enjoys. Where the law claims authority that it does not legitimately enjoy, the result will be that legal subjects (in the context of the WTO, mostly states) will either: (i) mistakenly act in accordance with legal directives that are not in fact morally binding on them; (ii) act in accordance with legal directives that they know are not in fact morally binding on them because of concerns about reputation, objection or retaliation by others; (iii) act in accordance with legal directives that are only morally binding on them because acting against them would tend to undermine the social legitimacy of an otherwise valuable institution; or (iv) fail to act in accordance with legal directives that are not morally binding on them, and thereby risk undermining the social legitimacy of an otherwise valuable institution. In practice, it is unlikely that WTO law, or any legal system,

[59] Raz, 'The Problem of Authority' (n 32) 1015–16.

[60] Suttle, 'What Sorts of Things' (n 16) and for a more detailed treatment see Suttle, *Distributive Justice* (n 16) ch 5.

can track its own authority with sufficient accuracy to avoid exceeding that authority vis-à-vis at least some agents at least some of the time; and sometimes, it may be that valued goals can only be achieved by doing so.[61] However, all else being equal, a legal system that respects and reflects the limits of its own authority is to be preferred over one that does not.

Assuming authority is piece-meal in the way that the service conception suggests, one important way that a legal system might respect the limits of its own authority is through the use of exceptions. A particular directive, if issued by an ostensible authority, might be morally binding on most agents in most circumstances. However, as regards particular agents or particular circumstances, its authority might fail. The rule-exception structure seems particularly well adapted to capture this phenomenon. The conditions attaching to the exception would, on this view, seek to track those features of the subject matter, agent or relationship, what explain why the institution lacks authority in the particular circumstances. Let us call this the *authority-limiting* rationale for exceptions.[62]

This *authority-limiting* rationale is distinct from the *reason-tracking* and *countervailing* rationales discussed earlier. The assumption underpinning both the *reason-tracking* and *countervailing* rationales is that, where an exception obtains, the balance of reasons applying to a relevant legal subject should lead them to act in the way permitted by the exception, rather than the way required by the rule. Returning to our contagious disease example, if I have immunity then there is no reason for me not to enter the isolation ward, and if I have essential skills, then I am likely to have a weighty all-things-considered reason to do so. The existence of an *authority-limiting exception*, by contrast, tells us nothing about the balance of reasons that applies in cases falling within the exception. It may often be the case that, while there is an exception from a relevant rule, agents falling within that exception still have very weighty reasons to act in the way that the rule would require, if the rule applied to them. An exception from the quarantine rule for experienced medical professionals does not indicate that such persons do not have reason to avoid the quarantine ward, or that they have reasons to enter it. In the case of the vast majority of such persons, the balance of reasons strongly weighs in favour of their doing precisely what the rule requires others to do. Rather, the exception carves out a space in which such persons are left to weigh those reasons for themselves, and to act on their own assessment of the reasons that apply, given their greater expertise and consequent capacity to make such determinations. In the case of reason-tracking and countervailing exceptions, we expect that the conditions applicable to the exception will reflect the extent of the applicable reasons and the balance between them. In the case of authority-limiting exceptions, on the other hand, we can expect that the conditions applicable will track the limits of the relevant institution's authority over particular agents.

We identified in section 3 above various ways that particular WTO exceptions could be understood in reason-tracking and countervailing terms. Let us now turn to consider whether and to what extent the authority-limiting rationale for exceptions can shed light on any of these. In the next three sub-sections I consider three prominent examples of exceptions or quasi-exceptions in WTO law: the general exceptions in Article XX GATT; the trade remedies rules as an exception to the GATT core disciplines on border measures; and the conditions under which states are permitted to depart from international standards under the domestic regulation agreements.

[61] On the likelihood that all legal authorities will overreach in this way see Raz, *The Morality of Freedom* (n 32) 77–79.

[62] This authority-limiting rationale is a subset of the institutional rationale introduced earlier.

8.1 Article XX and the importance of individual choice

As mentioned above, there are accounts of Article XX as both *reason-tracking* and *countervailing*. Can we make sense of it in *authority-limiting* terms? To do this, we need to look a little more closely at the structure of that provision, and the conditions that apply where a state seeks to invoke one of the exceptions thereunder.

At its most general, Article XX comprises a list of ten paragraphs specifying policy objectives in pursuit of which measures may be exempted. These paragraphs also include language specifying the required link or nexus between the measure sought to be exempted and the policy objective pursued. So, for example, in the case of Article XX(a), a measure must be 'necessary' to protect public morals, whereas under Article XX(g) it need only 'relate' to the conservation of natural resources. To these is appended an overarching proviso or *chapeau*, prescribing that measures not be applied so as to constitute 'arbitrary or unjustifiable discrimination ... or a disguised restriction on international trade'.[63]

These three elements—specified policy, nexus, and chapeau—in practice mark the boundaries of Article XX. We must therefore ask how these are to be understood in *authority-limiting* terms.

We might first consider whether the policy areas specified can be understood from this perspective. The most obvious explanation of these is the last considered above: that they describe areas where it is more important that a state should decide matters for itself than that it should act in accordance with reason, such that authority can provide little assistance. Decisions about the protection of the local environment, the public culture, and the health of the population are perhaps more closely linked than any others to the reasons why we value self-determination in the first place. These are matters that require trade-offs amongst different values, and it seems plausible that there are many equally valid trade-offs that might be chosen, so we do best by leaving these choices to individual states, to the extent possible.[64] A state that defers to international legal authority on such matters cedes an important part why it exists in the first place.[65]

However, we can also understand Article XX as in part reflecting the comparative limits on the authority of international law. Recall that an institution's authority may be limited to the extent that there is another institution that can better serve to guide the choices of a relevant agent. In a number of cases adjudicators have, under Article XX, looked to other international law regimes, whether international environmental law or the international law of indigenous rights, for guidance, or reassurance, in interpreting exceptions.[66] Where a member departs from WTO rules, and seeks to invoke Article XX, it will count in its favour if it can explain its measures as giving effect to, or at least being compatible with, the principles of, other, more specialized, international legal regimes. While this is certainly not the most prominent feature of the Article XX jurisprudence, it is one that seems particularly apt for explanation in authority-limiting terms.

[63] On the role of the chapeau see Lorand Bartels, 'The Chapeau of the General Exceptions in the WTO GATT and GATS Agreements: A Reconstruction' (2015) 109(1) American Journal of International Law 95.

[64] The importance of deference to domestic choice under art XX is frequently highlighted by the Appellate Body. See e.g. WTO Appellate Body Report, *EC—Asbestos*, WT/DS135/AB/R (adopted 12 March 2001) paras 168, 172.

[65] Again, these points are canvassed, albeit to a different purpose, in Suttle, 'What Sorts of Things' (n 16) and Suttle, *Distributive Justice* (n 16) chs 5 and 7. Importantly, thinking about art XX in this way implies clear limits on the kinds of policies that can be brought within the individual paragraphs.

[66] See e.g. WTO Appellate Body Report, *US—Shrimp*, WT/DS58/AB/R (adopted 12 October 1998) paras 130–31; WTO Panel Report, *EC—Seals*, WT/DS400/R (adopted 25 November 2013) para 7.292. There are also hints of this approach in WTO Panel Report, *US—Gambling*, WT/DS285/R (adopted 10 November 2004) paras 6.471–6.473.

Finally, aspects of Article XX, and especially the ways it has been interpreted in practice, reflect the agent-specific limits on WTO law's authority. Recall the suggestion above that particular states, by virtue of their domestic characteristics, may be better placed than others to make decisions for themselves, and so have less need of authority. Article XX does not scrutinize the cost-benefit trade-offs involved in measures that are challenged thereunder. However, it does examine the *bona fides* of that legislation, the extent to which it reflects a genuine policy concern of the regulating state, and the extent to which its trade-distorting effects are necessary for (or, a somewhat lower standard, rationally related to) the achievement of that objective.[67] It does not examine whether the correct answer has been reached in the particular circumstances: doing this would require applying the kinds of strong proportionality tests that the AB has consistently rejected.[68] Rather, it examines the measure adopted, and the extent to which that measure is adapted to identify and achieve legitimate policy objectives of the relevant state, whatever these may be. A measure can of course meet that standard and still be suboptimal, whether in economic or other terms. Article XX thus offers no guarantee that a measure is the right one, from either a national or global perspective. It does not guarantee that the measure conforms to the reasons that apply to the regulating member. But a member that can justify its measure by reference to the tests in Article XX does at least give us reasons to trust its domestic policy processes. It may thereby show us that it is more likely to conform to the reasons that apply to it by following its own relevant processes in the particular instance, than if it were simply to apply the strict requirements of the core disciplines. It thus establishes an agent-specific limit on the authority of WTO law.[69]

The overall shape of Article XX is thus comprehensible in authority-limiting terms. Various aspects of that article track the various ways that the authority of WTO law might be limited, whether by virtue of the specific subject-matter of a measure, by the existence of alternative institutions better placed to guide legal subjects, or by the particular capacities of particular states in particular contexts to make the required judgments on their own. Further, the very flexibility of that provision, as it has been interpreted by the Appellate Body, has created space for adjudicators to tailor its impact to track the different ways that these different factors may impact the institution's authority in particular cases.

[67] On *bona fides* and the subjective importance and genuineness of objectives see WTO Appellate Body Report, *EC—Seal Products*, WT/DS400/AB/R (adopted 22 May 2014) paras 5.150–5.167, 5.194–5.203; on policing necessity generally see WTO Appellate Body Report, *Korea—Beef*, WT/DS161/AB/R (adopted 11 December 2000) paras 160–66.

[68] See generally on this point Regan (n 22).

[69] This last point is perhaps clearest in the Appellate Body's treatment of necessity under art XX. While it regularly uses the language of balancing in applying the relevant provisions, the analysis in fact focuses on whether the contribution that a measure makes to the realization of a state's goal could be achieved in a less trade restrictive manner. Despite references to the importance of the goal pursued, there is no effort to second-guess the regulating member's choice to pursue that goal, or the degree to which it is to be realized. Review instead focuses on the extent to which measures contribute to achieving their goals, the alternatives available, and their relative trade restrictiveness. See, for a recent example highlighting the flexibility of this analysis, WTO Appellate Body Report, *Colombia—Textiles*, WT/DS461/AB/R (adopted 7 June 2016) paras 5.61–5.117. It is clear that members can (and presumably often do) accord unreasonable importance to the realization of particular goals, or unreasonably discount the costs associated with a policy, leading them to adopt measures that impair national welfare or otherwise fail to track the reasons that apply to them. However, unlike the specific kinds of regulatory failure policed by the conditions in art XX, there is little reason to think that WTO law or adjudicators are better placed than members to make these judgments. See for this specific point Jan Neumann and Elizabeth Türk, 'Necessity Revisited: Proportionality in World Trade Organization Law after Korea—Beef, EC—Asbestos and EC—Sardines' (2003) 37(1) Journal of World Trade 199, 232–33. Once a member meets the conditions in art XX, it therefore has a good claim to be left to make its own mistakes.

8.2 Trade remedies and the motivational problem

Whereas explaining Article XX draws on a number of different limits on the WTO's authority, the complex exception constituted by the various trade remedies rules is explained more straightforwardly in authority-limiting terms, by reference to the motivational problem and the characteristics of the regulating state.

'Trade remedies' here refers to the WTO rules on subsidies, anti-dumping, and safeguards. While invoking different concerns, each of these provides a mechanism whereby a state can impose duties or other restrictions on imports of particular products, notwithstanding the prohibitions in Articles II and XI of the GATT. Each is subject to its own agreement, within which we find a range of more specific rules and exceptions. This should not, however, obscure the extent to which these regimes as a whole constitute exceptions from the GATT's core disciplines on border measures. [70]

All three have been the subject of recurring criticism from scholars who emphasize the normative image of WTO law and seek to make sense of these rules in either reason-tracking or countervailing terms. The basic difficulty facing these attempts, and especially those adopting a broadly economic approach, is that the conditions for applying anti-dumping and countervailing duties and safeguards do not track any plausible account of the economic benefits and harms from trade. It simply is not the case, on any plausible economic theory, that the conditions for the application of these various measures accurately identify circumstances in which it makes economic sense for them to be imposed. [71]

The authority-limiting account of exceptions offers a way out of this difficulty. Perhaps the most obvious feature of the Anti-Dumping, Subsidies and Safeguards Agreements which distinguishes them from other WTO agreements is the detailed procedural requirements that each applies before trade remedies of the relevant kinds can be imposed. Indeed, the main focus of WTO adjudicators in applying these disciplines is often not whether the substantive requirements under the agreements have been met, but rather whether relevant domestic decision-makers have considered the appropriate evidence and made appropriate determinations prior to the imposition of restrictions.[72] The role of the WTO dispute settlement system here is thus closer to administrative law judicial review than it is to judicial oversight in other areas of WTO law.[73]

How does this procedural focus help us understand trade remedies in *authority-limiting* terms? Recall that a key explanation of WTO law's authority was the recognition that domestic policy processes were subject to capture by special interests, leading them to adopt

[70] See n 1 above. This exceptional quality is perhaps also reflected in the carefully circumscribed nature of the permission to impose such measures (as to which see eg Antidumping Agreement art 18.1 and Subsidies and Countervailing Measures Agreement art 32.1), and adjudicators' willingness to police them strictly, to the point of in one instance resurrecting requirements long thought lapsed: see WTO Appellate Body Report, *Argentina—Footwear (EC)*, WT/DS121/AB/R (adopted 14 December 1999) para 89.

[71] For a detailed review of the arguments see Suttle, *Distributive Justice* (n 16) 244–53. Political economy arguments, emphasizing the need to buy off opposition from import-competing industries and to manage political risk are more successful in explaining the need for these provisions, although they similarly struggle in accounting for the specifics of the relevant disciplines.

[72] While the Anti-Dumping Agreement is the only one of the trade remedies agreements explicitly to address the issue of standard of review, it has also been a prominent concern under the other two agreements. See e.g. WTO Appellate Body Report *US—Lamb*, WT/DS177/AB/R (adopted 1 May 2001) para 97-116.

[73] Although note the rejection of efforts to equate the standard of review under art 17.6 of the Anti-Dumping Agreement with the administrative review standard in US law. WTO Appellate Body Report, *US—Continued Zeroing*, WT/DS350/AB/R (adopted 4 February 2009) paras 267–75. Elements of this kind of quasi-administrative review also appear in eg the SPS Agreement, and in particular its emphasis on scientific evidence and justification, where it is explicable in similar terms to those proposed here. See n 58 above and accompanying text.

collectively sub-optimal protectionist policies. This explanation relies on the fact that decisions about economic policies are in general made by politicians or political appointees who are subject to the kinds of pressures it identifies. Where economic policy is instead made through strictly policed procedures, including quasi-judicial decision-making and oversight, the risk of capture is lower (although admittedly the literature on anti-dumping is by no means reassuring on this point).[74] Given the complexity of economic policy, and its intimate connections with a variety of other politically contested social goals, it is not possible to delegate all economic decision-making to such procedures. However, where it is possible to carve out a discrete set of decisions, and to insulate these partially from politics, then we might conclude that the output of that politically insulated procedure would constitute a more reliable guide to right action for the relevant state than would a strict rule of the kind expressed in the WTO border measure disciplines. Provided the domestic procedure meets the relevant standards, and provided it is faithfully followed in practice, it to that extent limits the authority of WTO law. It is not that such domestic procedures will always do a better job, or that WTO restrictions should yield in circumstances where they in fact do a better job, but rather that they are more likely to do a better job, such that states are likely better to comply with reasons that apply to them by following the outputs of those procedures than by complying with strict prohibitions in WTO law, or by trying through their standard political decision-making processes to follow the reasons which apply to them directly.

This explanation avoids a recurring objection to the trade remedies rules, that they permit the imposition of duties in circumstances where there is no plausible economic rationale for these. Such an objection clearly expresses a *reason-tracking* or *countervailing* view of these rules, which assumes that, where there is an exception, agents will have reasons to act as the exception permits. The *authority-limiting* view makes not such assumption. The existence of an exception on this view indicates not that states have reasons to act as permitted by the exception, but only that the question of how to act should, within the bounds of the exception, be left to states to make for themselves. The recognition of this exception is thus compatible with the view that, in the vast majority of cases, states should refrain from imposing trade remedies.

8.3 Epistemic advantages, international standards, and non-exception exceptions

Article XX of the GATT is the central case of a WTO exception: if anything is an exception, then Article XX is. It takes a moment longer to recognize the exceptional character of trade remedies. However, as a final specific example, let us examine a non-exception, or at least at a pair of provisions to which the Appellate Body has denied the title of exception, notwithstanding their apparent logical structure. These are the provisions governing the relationship between international standards and domestic choice in the Agreement on Technical Barriers to Trade (TBT) and the Agreement on Sanitary and Phytosanitary Measures (SPS Agreement).[75]

[74] Thus Finger memorably describes antidumping as 'ordinary protectionism with a good public relations program': see Michael J Finger, 'Dumping and Antidumping: The Rhetoric and Reality of Protectionism in Industrial Countries' (1992) 7(2) World Bank Research Observer 121.

[75] The Appellate Body's treatment of these provisions as alternate rules, or exemptions, rather than exceptions, and the procedural implications of this move, are discussed in more detail in Joost Pauwelyn, 'Defences and the Burden of Proof in International Law' in this volume (section 4).

Both agreements provide, albeit in different terms, for a similar set of relationships between international standards and domestic regulation. First, where there is a relevant international standard, they require that states use this as a basis for their domestic regulation.[76] The Appellate Body has made clear that the relationship this requires between domestic regulation and international standard is not one of identity; a state can depart somewhat from the international standard while still using it as a basis for its domestic regulation, and thereby complying with this positive requirement.[77] However, where a member goes further, following the international standard particularly closely, they benefit from various presumptions as to compliance with other obligations in the relevant agreements.[78] The agreements thus combine an obligation to be guided by international standard, with an incentive to go further and conform regulation to such standards.

However, in neither agreement is the obligation to base regulation on international standards absolute, or even especially strict. Rather, both agreements provide—again, in different language but with a similar result—that this obligation will not apply where regulation based international standards will not achieve the regulating state's purpose. In the TBT Agreement, this is expressed in terms of the adequacy and appropriateness of the international standard, while the SPS Agreement refers to the level of protection that the member determines to be appropriate.[79]

On their face, these appear to be rule/exception provisions. States are required to regulate based on international standards, except when those standards will not suffice for their purposes. However, the Appellate Body has been firm that the right to depart from international standards is to be regarded not as an exception, but as an autonomous right of regulating states, with consequent effects on the applicable burden of proof.[80]

Setting this point of classification aside for a moment, can we make sense of these rules in *authority-limiting* terms?

The first point to observe is that the requirement to use international standards is at once both a claim to, and a ceding of, authority by WTO law. While the obligation is one expressed by the relevant WTO agreement, the relevant standards are the products of other—non-WTO—international organizations. In the SPS Agreement, these include the Codex Alimentarius Commission, the World Organization for Animal Health, and the Secretariat of the International Plant Protection Convention. Under the TBT Agreement, the list is open, but will prominently include the International Organization for Standardization, as well as specialized agencies producing standards in particular fields.[81] It is thus a recognition, on the part of the WTO system, that it is not itself the best guide for members in determining how they should regulate. This can be readily understood by considering both the epistemic and coordination grounds of authority. On one hand, international standard-setting bodies, relying as they do on cooperation amongst domestic standardising agencies and having access to extensive scientific and technical expertise, have clear epistemic advantages over both the political and dispute settlement arms of the WTO. On the other hand, while international standardizing organizations cannot themselves impose legal obligations or trigger coercive

[76] SPS art 3.1; TBT art 2.4.

[77] WTO Appellate Body Report, *EC—Sardines*, WT/DS231/AB/R (adopted 23 October 2002) paras 242–47; WTO Appellate Body Report, *EC—Hormones*, WT/DS26/AB/R (adopted 16 January 1998) paras 162-166

[78] SPS art 3.2, TBT art 2.5.

[79] TBT art 2.4; SPS art 3.3.

[80] WTO Appellate Body Report, *EC—Hormones*, WT/DS28/AB/R (adopted 16 January 1998) paras 169–72; WTO Appellate Body Report, *EC—Sardines*, WT/DS231/AB/R (adopted 23 October 2002) paras 269–76.

[81] On the identification of such organizations see WTO Appellate Body Report, *US—Tuna II*, WT/DS381/AB/R (adopted 16 May 2012) paras 349–79.

enforcement, their close links to relevant agencies within national bureaucracies may mean that, *ceteris paribus*, their standards are likely to be more readily embraced by national regulators than the prescriptions of the WTO, which although importing hard legal obligation, will generally be less embedded within subject matter-specific domestic policy-making processes. In so far as the goal of disciplines on non-discriminatory domestic regulation is to reduce unnecessary barriers to trade through harmonization while at the same time ensuring appropriate regulation to address legitimate concerns, these two features mean that states will better conform to reason by treating as authoritative the outputs of international standardizing bodies, rather than the WTO itself, and that the best role for WTO law is therefore one that is supportive of those bodies.[82]

So the rule that states should base their domestic regulation on international standards is itself an expression of the relative authority of competing international institutions. But how, from this perspective, might we account for the non-exception exception for domestic regulation deviating from international standards?

One way might be to highlight, as Raz does, the importance of an authority at least purporting to base its directives on reasons (referred to as dependent reasons) that otherwise apply to the relevant agent. Where an international standard does not achieve a member's goal, then we might think that this was evidence that the authority was not basing its decisions on the right reasons. However, this will not suffice: we can assume that the authority is seeking to balance members' concerns for their particular preferred level of protection against the costs of regulatory divergence; the content-independent quality of the reasons constituted by an authority's directives mean the mere fact that the balance chosen in a particular instance is not the one that a particular member would have chosen cannot in itself be enough to undermine that authority.

Instead, the better way to explain this is probably by reference to the subject matter limits on the authority of both the WTO and international standardizing bodies. As noted above, it seems plausible that some regulatory tools, including border measures and discriminatory regulation, are particularly prone to protectionist abuse, and so particularly apt for deferring to international authority. The same is not the case with non-discriminatory regulation. Here, the key advantage establishing the authority of the international standard setting body is one of coordination: to the extent that states have reason to harmonize, and given diverse existing domestic standards, the international standard offers a coordination point, around which others can converge. However, it is not the case that all states will have reason in all cases to coordinate their domestic regulation. Assuming divergent national regulatory preferences, harmonization necessarily involves at least some states adopting a domestic regulation that is locally sub-optimal, in the sense that it is either under- or over-restrictive. Where there are significant benefits from harmonization, this may be sufficient to outweigh the cost of under/over-regulation. However, this will not always be the case, and the outcome of this joint-optimization exercise will vary from state to state and from case to case. While the international standardizing body is an authority on the question of which standard to follow *if* harmonization is preferred, there is no authority that can tell a state whether to choose harmonization or fidelity to domestic preferences. The question of whether harmonization is more important than locally optimal regulation, and hence the question of the authority of international standards, is itself one that requires to be answered by each state for itself.[83]

[82] A similar approach is adopted in recognising and accommodating the authority of the International Monetary Fund at various points in the GATT, most prominently in arts XIV and XV.

[83] For an analogous point see Raz, *The Morality of Freedom* (n 32) 46.

This fact, that the authority of international standards is not simply limited, as in the other examples considered, but contingent on a prior domestic choice, perhaps goes some way to explaining why the Appellate Body has been reluctant to recognize the quality of these provisions as exceptions. In circumstances where WTO law has authority in most cases, it makes sense to put the burden of proof on the party arguing that its authority is limited in particular circumstances. On the other hand, where its authority is contingent on a prior choice falling to be made by the state concerned, it makes sense to think about it in terms not of a rule and an exception, but rather in terms of two alternative solutions, between which neither substantive nor procedural international rules express any preference.

10 Conclusion

This contribution has sought to make sense of exceptions in WTO law by reference to the extent, and the limits, of the authority of WTO law. Building on Raz's service conception of authority, it offered a general account of the grounds of WTO law's authority, and the limits these implied. It suggested that, given the piecemeal nature of both grounds and limits, exceptions might provide a useful tool for tailoring the authority that WTO law claims to the authority it in fact enjoys. Finally, it investigated that hypothesis by reference to three cases of exceptions or quasi-exceptions in WTO law: the general exceptions in Article XX; the trade remedies rules, and the rules on international standards in the domestic regulation agreements.

This is no more than an initial foray into this issue. Much more is required to investigate fully the relationship between authority and exceptions in WTO law. First, much more might be said about the authority of WTO law. In this chapter, I have adopted one particular account of authority, Raz's service conception, but many others have been proposed, and their appropriateness to the specific case of the WTO requires to be considered. Even focusing on the service conception, fully elaborating the authority of the WTO law would require saying much more about the nature of the subjects of that law and the reasons that apply to them, about the kinds of problems WTO law solves, and about the particular features that might expand or restrict its authority in particular cases. Further, a broader doctrinal lens, examining other exceptions and quasi-exceptions, would provide a fuller understanding of the utility of authority as a general perspective on WTO exceptions. However, my hope is that this contribution has at least done enough to suggest that the relationship between the theory of authority and WTO exceptions is worthy of further investigation.

Index

Note: *For the benefit of digital users, indexed terms that span two pages (e.g., 52–53) may, on occasion, appear on only one of those pages.*